FELT IN BRITAIN

PETER WALTER

Copyright © 2013 Peter Walter

All rights reserved.

ISBN-10:1490923837
ISBN-13:978-1490923833

Second Edition

DEDICATION

To my grandchildren
Lisa and Anna, Joseph and Hannah

The future is written in history, a lesson to learn well

CONTENTS

Acknowledgements	vii
Preface	viv
What makes a Felt	11
Early Years and Leeds Feltmakers	29
Rossendale and Other Feltmakers	43
Patents and Innovation	65
The Felt Mills	85
Water and Power	123
Preparing the Fibre	137
Hardening	159
Milling	189
Dyeing and Finishing	211
Block Printing	245
Properties of Felt	261
Products	273
People	317
Glossary of Felt Industry Terms	353
References	367
Index	383

ACKNOWLEDGEMENTS

This book has been thirty years in the making, and it is only now in my retirement that I have been able to complete it, long after the felt industry in Britain has disappeared. There have been many people both within and outside the felt industry who have helped me on my journey. In particular there were thirty or so people who were intimately associated with the felt industry and who provided me with their life histories and valuable insight on what it was like to work in the industry. In particular I am grateful to the contributions of: Mrs. Ashworth, Mr. Barker, H. Clark, N. Clegg, A. Coupe, Mr. Crease, T. Crook, W. Davis, C. Dyson, K. Entwistle, R. Entwistle, D. Fearnley, P. Fuller, F. Haig, D. Hamer, W. Law, J. J. Livesy, Mrs. Lord, J. Lovell, B. Neary, F. W. Nicholls, K. Ritson, J. Roberts, D. Rodgers, J. Rostron, E. Sagar, T. Simpson, S. Smith, W. Suart, E. Townsend. The book would not have been possible without the encouragement, support, and access to archival material that past directors of the major British felt companies have given me while I was in the industry. Amongst those are A. Coupe, A. F. D. Ferguson, P. S. James, L. Notley, and R. J. Ponting who were particularly supportive with material of all sorts. I am indebted to M. Samuelson of Garnett Bywater Limited who allowed access to their daybooks and donated their photographic and engineering drawing archives of felt making machines, when they ceased their manufacture. My thanks also to the Feltmakers Association for information about today's craft felting scene. Although, my purpose for writing this book was to present a detailed picture of commercial felt making, the craft feltmakers also made a deep impression on me and have indirectly helped me in writing this volume. In particular, I am privileged to have known Mary Burkett OBE and to have helped her to found the Feltmakers Association. I would also like to thank Agnete Samdahl for her encouragement to finish my project. My thanks also to Ann Baxendale, who undertook extensive research work on the mills of Rossendale that filled in many gaps in my knowledge. Thanks also to Rawtenstall Library staff who have been very supportive over the years. In addition, it is mostly through the moral support and patience of my wife Liz that I have finally completed this book.

Photograph Acknowledgements

My thanks to the following for use of these photographs:
The Worshipful Company of Feltmakers of London for their Coat of Arms, Melanie Barkley for crimped Wool Fibres, Leanne Buchan of Locate in Leeds for Taylor Wordsworth's Leeds factory at Midland Mill, T. G. Ames for Edward Rostron. Lancashire County Library SE Division Rawtenstall for: Siss Clough Mill with Todd Carr Print Works, Mitchell Brothers letterheads, and Baltic Mill in 1950. Mrs. M. P. Ashworth for Richard Ashworth, Wandle Industrial Museum for Crown Mill at Mitcham, J. Naish for William Naish in 1875 and view of E. V. Naish's Mill, R. Giddins for Albert Mill in 1953, Peter Fisher at smugmug.com for Longholme Mill, Rossendale Free Press for Bridge End waterwheel, Mrs. Hamer for block printing Masonic carpet, Helmshore Mills Textile Museum for the lant cart in the Museum, Ewa Kuniczak for rainbow butterfly felt, Brenda Lees for felt skirts, Mr. E. Bann of Waterfoot for photograph of blockprinters, Northampton Mercury for Kletterschuh, Rozanne Hawksley and Renee Pfister for photograph of embroidered felt clothing, Ashley James and Nick Whitaker for Herbert Smith's Rolls Royce, Winterhur Museum for Ralph Radcliffe Whitehead of Byrdcliffe, Tiffin School Friends for Laurence Notley, Jane Rostron for James Rostron patriarch, Alexander P. Kapp for Christ Church, Friezland, Saddleworth, from Wikipedia, Elmwood Mills courtesy of Leeds Library and Information Service, and West Yorkshire Archive Services.

PREFACE

Of all the textile processes I have experienced in a long career in textiles, felt making was the most magical. Since the moment I joined the felt industry, I was captivated by the whole ethos that felting represented, from its ancient history to the distinctive culture of the feltmakers and their mills.

In direct contrast to the magical atmosphere that felt generated, the attitudes I discovered within the industry were quite depressing. There was an overwhelming feeling from shop floor to management of impending doom due to the perceived inevitable terminal decline of wool felt. True, the sales of wool felt had been declining steadily from the 1950s onwards as the synthetic non-woven industry expanded, but there had been no investment in new wool felt development either. The leading feltmaker had in fact put all its development effort into making all-synthetic non-woven products at the expense of wool.

I was fortunate in being recruited by a far-sighted Managing Director who wanted to breathe new life into the traditional operation and reverse the mood of pessimism about the future. As Technical Manager, I was given a free rein to build both a modern testing laboratory and, more importantly, a new development facility. In this development laboratory, I built a small pilot plant that could explore at great speed any technical aspect of felting and produce new commercial products. With this valuable asset, I was rapidly able to assimilate many years of empirical development of felt making and compare them to all the academic work that had been done in the 1950s and 1960s and later. This was not doing research work for its own sake, but was focused on creating products that could improve sales and profitability. In terms of the underlying remit, the unit was notably successful, increasing annual sales by at least five percent of turnover within two years. Most important of all, it proved that it was possible to increase felt sales at a time when the trend for wool felt was downward.

After several fruitful years of this innovative approach, the company was sold to a major group that was manufacturing textiles for the paper making industry. Unfortunately, their main board directors did not understand the nature of wool felt, nor its manufacture. Worse still, at high level within the organisation, the view was that wool felt was a dying industry and should be treated as a cash generator until the business was unsustainable. Attitudes within the company changed and pessimism returned. The Managing Director who had tried hard to invigorate the business left the company and the development unit was closed down. My position also changed from Technical Manager to Marketing Manager with a remit to generate sales from all the new products I had created. It was then that I realised there was a real danger that the felt industry was shortly going to end in Britain. At that time, there were vast amounts of historical information about the industry that were considered of little value and it struck me that this would shortly be lost forever. During the re-organisations that took place, much of these archival documents, photographs and other materials, were being scrapped in large quantities. With board level approval I collected as much as possible and where I could not save it, I made extensive notes, with the intention of one day publishing it. Many people in the company, directors included, recognised what I was trying to do and volunteered much other material. I also became aware that there were also many people within the Rossendale Valley who had long been retired from the felt industry and who must have had a wealth of knowledge and could tell me what it must have been like to work there. With the help of the local newspaper, The Rossendale Free Press, I interviewed as many people as I could. I recorded their stories and, to be sure that I had interpreted their experiences correctly, I had them verify what I had written to make as accurate a record as I could. I collected them together as Recollections of the Felt Industry, with the intention of publishing them separately. As well as people, I also traced all the mills up and down the country that I knew had manufactured felt and, where they still existed, I photographed them.

A few years later my position as Marketing Manager of the newly re-organised company became untenable and, sadly, I left to continue my career elsewhere in the textile industry. However, my fascination for felt persisted, and as time allowed, I maintained my interest through desk research and trawling the internet, which led me to many surprising new facts about the history of the industry. It was only when I retired and learnt that the British felt industry had collapsed that I realised the importance of the archive I had acquired. Nowhere in the country was there so much previously unknown knowledge and information about felt in the United Kingdom than in my accumulated papers.

I then set out in earnest to write the book that I had intended to do thirty years earlier. I was helped in this by Shire Publications Limited who agreed to publish a monograph written by me entitled "The Felt Industry". This gave a neat overview of the felt industry and included many parts of previously unpublished material that I had researched. The Shire book is aimed at making felt history available to as wide an audience as possible and so there was little room for in-depth treatment of many features of feltmaking. As a complement to this monograph, this book presents the detailed results of all my research and archival efforts into a comprehensive review of the felt industry in Britain. I have tried to be as scientifically rigorous as I can and wherever possible I have included references to qualify statements that I have made. Where no evidence existed, I have drawn on my own experiences. I hope it will satisfy textile historians who are looking for reliable information about commercial feltmaking. I also hope that the technical details I have described will help craft feltmakers to make better felts and be able to take their commercial efforts to the next level. Above all, I hope that it remains as a suitable reference work to acknowledge all the efforts and achievements that have been made by the contributors to this once proud industry.

Peter Walter

September 2013

1 WHAT MAKES A FELT

WHAT IS A FELT

In modern times there are many materials that are described as "felt". The name has become synonymous with any textile that is not woven or knitted and that relies on the entanglement of its constituent fibres for its strength and other properties. Amongst the materials described as felt are: felted woven cloth woollen felt, hat felt, hair felt, carpet underlay felt, needle felt, roofing felt and carbon fibre felt. However, these materials are very different and are manufactured by very different processes. Woollen felt, as the name suggests, is made predominantly from wool fibres and by the processes of wet hardening and milling. Hat felt is made from fine animal fibres such as rabbit and beaver, and which requires a special chemical treatment such as mercury to enable them to matt together like wool. Needle felt is made by a dry process whereby barbed needles are continually punched through synthetic fibres in order to force them to entangle. Hair felt is made from coarse animal fibres such as cow and horse, which is lightly needled with barbed needles and then subjected to a wet hardening process. Underlay felt was made in a similar way to hair felt but the hair used was diluted with waste shoddy fibres to reduce costs. Roofing felt is made by saturating any form of non-woven material with bitumen and forming a semi-rigid sheet from it. Carbon fibre felt is made in a similar way to needle felt but the fibres are exclusively carbon. One other textile also worthy of note is woven woollen cloth that has been felted. Before the advent of woollen felt this fabric was known as baize but because it was milled, the surface looked exactly like a non-woven felt and it too became referred to as "felt".

The fact that all these materials bear the same name indicates that they were all derived from a common ancestral material. This seminal material is woollen felt made exclusively from wool fibres, and, until the industrial revolution, was always known as felt. Its origins are buried somewhere in prehistory and may even have been the first man-made textile since it is so easy to produce by hand. It was well known to the Romans[1] and many ancient peoples revered its magical qualities as can be seen from the discoveries at Pasyryk[2] in Siberia. A Christian slant was given through the apocryphal story of St. Clement who, it is claimed, stuffed his shoes with wool to ease his sore feet whilst on pilgrimage.

St. Clement the patron saint of feltmaking[3]

At the end of his journey, the wool had been magically transformed into felt. St. Clement was therefore adopted as the patron saint of feltmakers[4]. The same traditions of wool felt usage can still be seen in Mongolia where felt is used by nomads there for the outer covering of their circular tent structures known as yurts.

A Yurt or Mongolian tent, showing the construction and the felt covering.

Again, traditional feltmaking is still practiced in Anatolia for producing decorative carpets, and for shepherds' cloaks known as kepeneks[5]. Since the publications of Mary Burkett OBE, these ancient techniques, with their infinite design potential, are being actively explored in Britain by many innovative crafts people and artists, to stunning effect.

Rainbow felt design by Ewa Kuniczac

The content of this book deals exclusively with woollen felt and charts the rise and fall of the commercial industry in Britain that spawned all today's variants of felt. To distinguish it from all the modern versions of felt the feltmakers adopted the designation "pressed felt" to describe their products. In order to make their products stand out against the profusion of other so-called felts they joined together to form The Pressed Felt Manufacturers Association to promote and enhance their industry. They did this even though there had been the Worshipful Company of Feltmakers in London established ever since medieval times. However, this had been set up to protect the interests of felt hat makers since pressed felt had not been invented then. Despite the fact that pressed felt manufacturers did not make hats by the same process, many directors of felt companies also belonged to this illustrious livery.

The coat of arms of the Worshipful Company of Feltmakers

In the last days of the association there was yet more confusion with the advent of the craft felt makers because they were making true woollen felt but not using conventional commercial machinery. Under the leadership of Mary Burkett O.B.E., they too formed their own group known as The Felt Association. With the demise of the British felt industry, the Pressed Felt Manufacturers Association disappeared but the Felt Association went from strength to strength, becoming the International Felt Association.

WHAT MAKES WOOL FELT

THEORIES

There are many theories as to how it is that wool felts, though no theory has satisfactorily explained the mechanism completely. The only agreement between them is that felting is caused by the structure of wool fibres through the peculiar characteristics of their surfaces. Magnifying a woollen fibre shows it to be made up of irregular scales wrapped around a core with the edge of one scale resting on the smooth part of the adjacent scale, giving a structure that looks similar to the trunk of a palm tree.

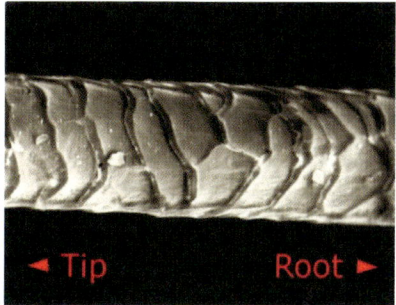

A wool fibre magnified 2250 times showing surface scales, the root is toward the sheep

When the fibre was growing on the sheep one end was anchored to the skin and therefore known as the root and the other end was free on the outer part of the fleece and therefore known as the tip. On each scale, the edge of it is nearest the tip and the smooth end is nearest the root.

This serrated surface structure has a major effect on the frictional properties of wool fibres. Rubbing the fibre against the scales, tip to root, is rougher than stroking in the opposite direction (root to tip). Scientifically, therefore, the coefficient of friction is greater one way than the other, and this is known as the directional frictional effect (DFE). This was first examined as a theory of felting by Monge[6] in 1790. He realised that by placing a wool fibre between finger and thumb and moving them against each other would make the fibre "walk" one way; turning the fibre around and repeating the action makes the fibre walk in the opposite direction. He went one stage further and tied a knot in a single fibre and just by placing it in the fold of his little finger and banging his fist on his knee, the knot mysteriously untied itself. Further research disclosed that the fibres walk in the direction of the root. It is easy to imagine therefore, that if a mass of fibres is rubbed together the fibres will all travel in different directions and should therefore tangle together. It is more difficult to explain how they tangle since it is not just the fibres that wrap around each other but as they do this, the mass of fibres shrinks at the same time. This shrinkage can be explained by considering a single wool fibre as a ratchet that is locked in by other fibres pressing on it.

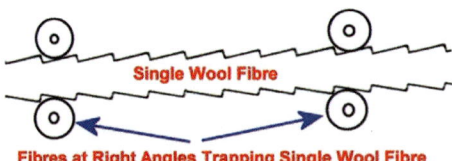

By rubbing the mass, the trapping fibres are moved together and the single fibre kinks causing it to push against one of the places where it is trapped.

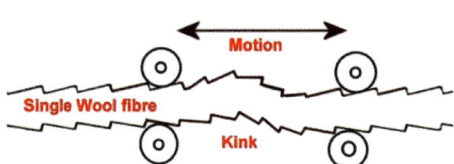

It squeezes through the trap, but when the rubbing stops, the single fibre cannot move back because it is locked in place by the ratchet-like scales. The two places where the single fibre is trapped are not only closer together but are fixed closer together, which means shrinkage has taken place[7].

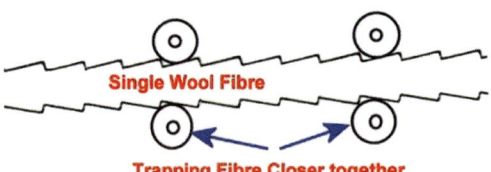

In a mass of fibres, it is also possible for other mechanisms to come into play. In particular there will be fibres that are totally free to move and these can become kinked and form loops that eventually wrap around other fibres giving progressive loop entanglement that amplifies the shrinkage[8]. Microscopic photographs show how these effects can take place in practice; both loops and trapped single fibres can be seen throughout the felt.

WHAT MAKES A FELT

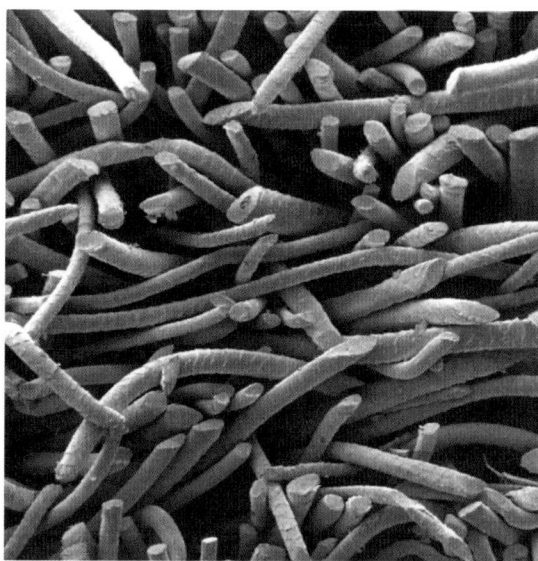

Photomicrograph of a woollen felt at x500 magnification showing trapped fibres and loops after felting

The more pronounced the scales are, the greater should be the ratchet effect and hence those wools with greater differential frictional effect should be better felting wools. Although this holds true for wools at the extremes, high DFE and low DFE, researchers found that there was no significant correlation between scaliness and milling efficiency[9]. It is relatively easy to see that felting needs pressure for it to occur. The fibres need to be pushed together so that some of them can be trapped and therefore provide the right conditions for the ratchet effect to occur: too little pressure and the fibres will not be trapped; too much pressure and none of the fibres will be able to move. It is also clear, that to work, the ratcheting needs some kind of vibration; too little vibration and the fibres will not move far enough to have an effect, too much vibration and the trapping points will be destroyed. In each extreme case felting will not occur properly

EFFECT OF WATER

Although these models give a good idea of how felting takes place and matches in outline what happens in reality, they can only really be used as a basis for a deeper understanding. The actual mechanism is much more complex than this. Significantly, it does not explain how it is difficult to make wool felt when it is dry but when it is wetted felting happens rapidly and with little difficulty. For this to happen the wool must be thoroughly wetted as there is a threshold of relative humidity which must be exceeded before felting is facilitated in this way. To felt properly the wool must be subjected to a relative humidity of greater than seventy-five percent and preferably have the presence of liquid water[9]. In the presence of water, wool fibres undergo profound changes: they swell so that the scales become more pronounced and the directional friction effect increases, the fibres soften to become more pliable and elastic, they can twist more easily, and they lose some of their waviness (known as crimp)[10]. The softening of the fibres allows closer contact with each other to give a better grip and the increase in the frictional properties enhances the ratchet effect. The fact that the fibres become straighter means that it is easier for them to move and migrate, which is aided by the lubrication effect of the presence of liquid water. Some researchers even suggest that forces of attraction take place between the fibres in water, which increases fibre-to-fibre contact and enhances ratcheting. This has been particularly noted in the case of loose wool felting where forces are generally small enough for this attraction to be an important factor[11]. These moisture-related effects could be increased even more by using hot water, but there is a limit of temperature, at around fifty degrees Celsius, above which there is no further benefit[12].

EFFECTS OF ACIDS AND ALKALIS

Marginally more improvements could be made from increasing the lubrication of the fibres with the use of soaps or anionic detergents, which are well known milling agents. Acids are known to increase felting even more than alkali and it has been discovered that this is due to the enlargement of the scales on wool fibres, which increases the directional frictional effect and hence feltability[13]. The diagram below shows how the directional frictional effect depends upon both acids and alkalis. The acidity or alkalinity is measured by the number of hydrogen ions present in the liquid and is given a measure called pH. Ordinary water, which is neutral, has a value of seven, while the less the number the greater the acidity, and the higher the number above seven the greater the alkalinity.

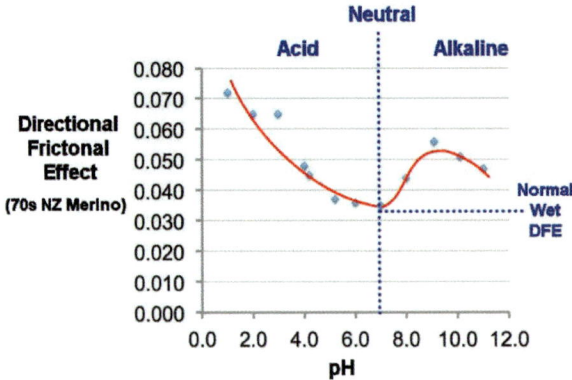

The graph[14] shows that the Directional Frictional Effect increases as the acid becomes stronger and the pH tends to one, and gradually increases as the alkalinity rises towards ten. After this, it declines again.

THE EFFECT OF CRIMP

Theory predicts that the straighter the fibre the easier it can ratchet through other fibres, and this in fact, turns out to be the case. Wool, like Southdown, has a high level of crimp and produces a low-density felt whilst merino, which has a relatively low crimp, gives excellent feltability. However, there is only broad correlation between the crimp and feltability, with some wools that have low levels of crimp being poor felters. Consider the case of kemp fibres, which have no crimp at all and yet do not felt. In support of the theory, though, kemps are extremely mobile during felting and can travel large distances, usually making their way to the surface. The reason why kemps do not felt is that they are so thick that they cannot bend and cannot therefore wrap around other fibres to lock them together. On the other hand, wools that are made up of fine fibres are excellent felters.

The waviness or crimp in a fibre can be difficult to describe but there are three parameters that can give a fair description that is useful in determining how they are likely to felt: crimp frequency, crimp form, and crimp amplitude. The most important of these is the number of waves, or peaks, in the fibre over a given length and is known as the crimp frequency.

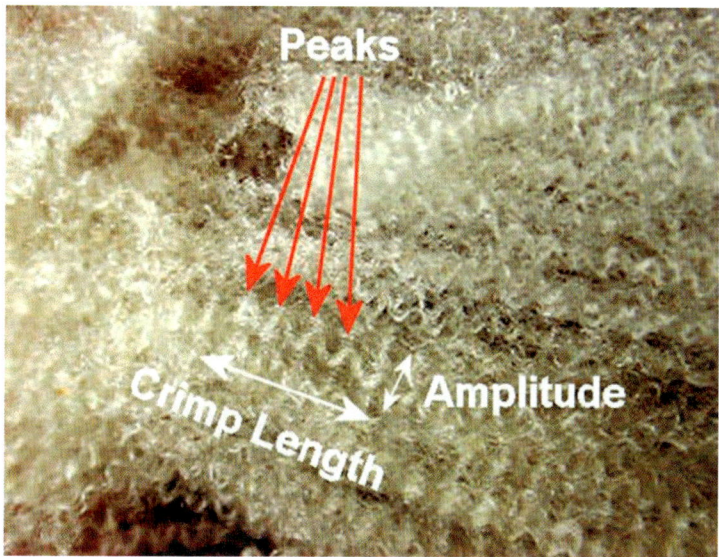

A typical wool fleece showing the crimped fibres and the measurements needed to quantify the degree of waviness

This, however, is essentially a two dimensional description and wool fibres can curl to be like a coiled spring or helix. Measuring how coiled or helical a fibre is, can be somewhat complicated but measurement provides a simple number from 0 to 100, known as the crimp form. This measure indicates how close the coiled wool fibre is to a pure helix. The number 0 refers to completely straight fibre and 100 indicates a pure helix. Lastly, of minor importance, is the height or amplitude of the wave pattern of the fibre, referred to as the crimp amplitude[15]. With these tools it is possible to rank, with greater precision, how different wools will perform during felting.

THE EFFECT OF FIBRE LENGTH

According to the various theories on felting, the length of the wool fibres should have an effect on feltabilty but exactly how, is not clear. Shorter fibres should have more mobility and hence move further by the ratchet effect, and if they are fine enough, should be able to wrap around other fibres. On the other hand, if felting is by tangling, then longer fibres should entangle more than short ones. When producing a felt, unlike yarn spinning, it is not important to have fibres all the same length and in practice, it is beneficial to have a wide range of fibre lengths. The best felting wool for felting is Australian or South African 64s quality merino, which has an average staple length of around sixty-five to one hundred millimetres.

However it is still possible to make an acceptable felt from very short fibres such as the waste fibre left after combing long fibres for worsted yarn spinning, known as noils. These have varying staple lengths with an average around twenty-three millimetres. In fact a felt made from noils can be made into a felt that is denser than one made from first grade merino, though it is not as strong.

FELT IN BRITAIN

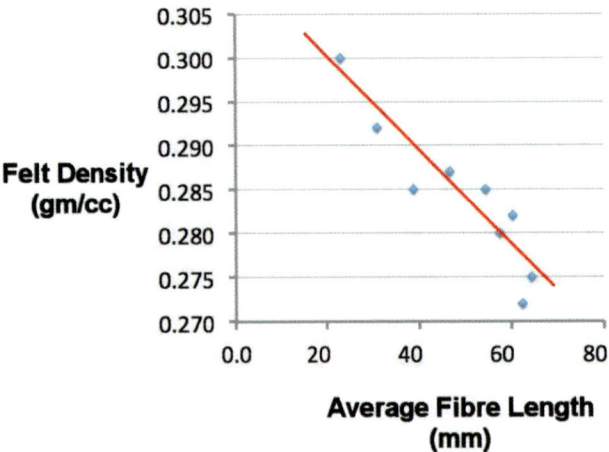

There is a relationship between fibre length and feltability for loose wool felting, where feltability increases with decreasing staple length, as judged by felt density. The effect is relatively small[16] with density going from 0.275 gramme per cubic centimetre (gm/cc) at a staple length of sixty-four millimetres to 0.290 gramme per cubic centimetre at a staple length of twenty-three millimetres. The strength of the felt starts to increase as the average staple length is decreased until it reaches a peak at a length of fifty-four millimetres. After this, the strength of the felt declines as the average staple length is reduced[17].

The feltmakers were quick to exploit this by blending cheaper noils into their first grade wools. Not only did it felt faster and give a firmer product but it also delivered great economic benefit by lowering the cost of the felt. The presence of noils also gave a smoother surface to the felt as the noils filled the surface gaps that would otherwise be present in the felt, hence giving it a higher quality appearance[18]. Feltmakers therefore often added between twenty and forty percent of noils depending on the end use.

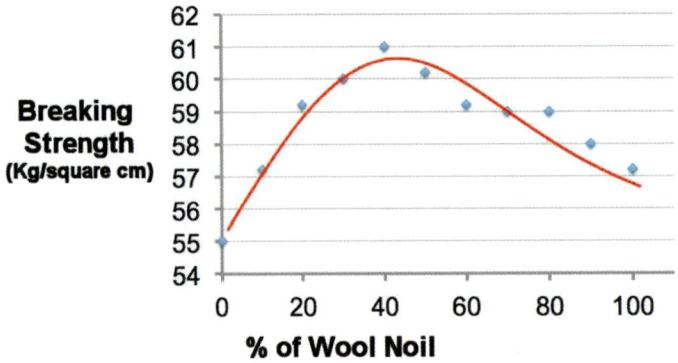

EFFECT OF FIBRE FINENESS

Most scientific studies use the classic reduction approach whereby all the variables except one are held constant and the effects of just the single variable examined. Unfortunately, in the case of woollen fibres, many of the characteristics are interrelated which can lead to either conflicting results or outcomes that are inconsistent. For example, the scale structure of wool is dependent on the diameter of the fibre and the directional frictional effect is in general greater for smaller fibre diameters. However, the quantitative correlation between them and feltability is imperfect[19]. The fineness of wool fibres is easy to gauge visually but measuring it quantitatively is less simple. The main measure of fineness in the woollen industry is the worsted count, which was derived empirically from spinning the wool into a yarn. The fineness of the yarn itself was measured by the length yield of a pound of fibre. This was further complicated because the industry was limited by its spinning machinery and therefore measured yarns in terms of the hanks of yarn that could be wound on the winding frames. For the worsted industry, a hank measured 560 yards. So if one hank of 560 yards length weighed one pound weight the quality would have been designated as 1s quality. However, no wool is this coarse and the finest available wool is ranked as 80s, which means 80 hanks of 560 yards could be spun on the woollen system, or 44,800 yards. In practice, most wools lie within the range 36s (coarsest) to 80s (finest). The beauty of this measurement is that it gives an average thickness for a large number of fibres, but its disadvantage is that it becomes more of a subjective assessment unless a yarn is actually spun from it. It is more scientific to actually measure fibre diameters of a wool type microscopically, and assign a thickness to a wool quality. However, this too is difficult because there is always a spread of thicknesses of fibres in any wool sample and so many measurements have to be taken and an average calculated. The deviation from the mean also has to be calculated to indicate the spread of fibre thickness in the sample, which is + or − the standard deviation. The conversion of wool quality count to microns is shown in the following table[20]

Table showing the conversion of Wool Quality Count to Microns

Wool Quality (Worsted Count)	Mean Diameter (Microns)	Standard Deviation +/- (Microns)
80s	18.42	4.09
70s	19.87	4.59
64s	21.02	5.19
62s	22.77	5.89
60s	24.22	6.49
58s	25.67	7.09
56s	27.12	7.59
54s	28.57	8.19
50s	30.15	8.69
48s	31.85	9.09
46s	33.55	9.59
44s	35.30	10.09
40s	37.15	10.69
36s	39.15	11.19

FELTABILITY TESTS

For felt, it is difficult to draw useful conclusions from the mass of research work because much of this work has been carried out on woven woollen fabrics and yarns, and there has been little attention paid to loose wool felting. As such, many results have not been directly relevant to the felt industry. The most progress in understanding loose wool felting has come from the development of a test method for measuring feltability of wools that consists of shaking a small batt of fibres in a container. The shaking ensures the fibres are agitated in three dimensions and they therefore felt together into a ball. The smaller this ball is, the greater is the felting that has taken place. Since the shaking is standard and the time for felting (one hour) is standard, the size of the ball is a direct measure of feltability[21]. This test is known as the Aachen Felting Test. The felt densities that the test method generated were quite low and are equivalent to that of the first stage of felting on commercial machines, known as hardeners. This simple apparatus opened up the possibility of studying felting holistically. However, few researchers did this, because it involved measuring all the fibre characteristics of different wools before subjecting them to the test. Two researchers who did were Chaudri and Whiteley, who measured all the characteristics of a range of wools and then subjected them to the Aachen test. From this work and for the first time it was possible to construct a holistic relationship between feltability and the main properties of a wool fibre.

Table showing the Characteristics of a Selection of different Wools[22]

Wool Type	Density gm./cc	Crimp Frequency Number per cm	Crimp Form	Anti Scale Tip to Root Friction Coefficient	With Scale Root to Tip Friction Coefficient	DFE (wet)	Fibre Diameter microns
Merino B	0.101	2.0	20.4	0.58	0.24	0.34	23.00
Merino C	0.092	1.6	16.8	0.48	0.26	0.22	26.00
English Leicester	0.089	0.5	18.0	0.46	0.28	0.18	39.90
Romney Marsh	0.089	1.2	22.8	0.55	0.32	0.23	37.50
Merino A	0.088	3.4	18.9	0.45	0.23	0.22	20.90
Lincoln	0.076	0.5	31.3	0.46	0.28	0.18	40.30
Border Leicester	0.073	0.8	12.3	0.52	0.32	0.20	42.00
Scottish Blackface	0.070	1.4	51.4	0.57	0.32	0.25	39.70
Tasmanian Merino	0.056	4.5	43.8	0.53	0.21	0.32	20.20
Dorset Down	0.052	2.0	42.3	0.59	0.35	0.24	34.80
Shropshire Down	0.034	2.1	45.0	0.62	0.40	0.22	31.50
Cheviot	0.036	1.7	61.7	0.49	0.33	0.16	37.90
Hampshire Down	0.029	3.6	56.1	0.44	0.29	0.15	31.00
Dorset Horn	0.028	2.1	57.4	0.44	0.24	0.20	36.90
Ryeland	0.024	2.6	58.9	0.44	0.30	0.14	24.20
Southdown	0.022	4.0	57.3	0.50	0.33	0.17	28.90
Suffolk Down	0.022	4.0	87.4	0.43	0.24	0.19	30.30

Unfortunately, they chose to try to determine correlations between feltability and crimp whilst ignoring the other components that were by no means constant between the different wool types. From the data, it is possible to take an holistic view and determine a close linear correlation between feltability and a mathematical function that uses all the parameters.

Empirically this function is:

$$\text{Feltability} = \frac{\text{A constant x the Directional Frictional Effect}}{\text{Fibre Diameter x square root of (Crimp Frequency x Crimp Form)}}$$

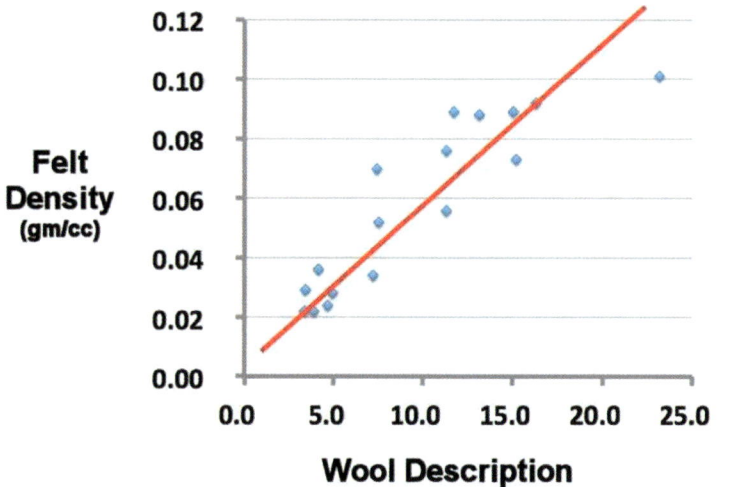

Wool Description = 10000DFE/ Fibre Diameter x √Crimp (frequency x form)

This emphasises the conclusion of most scientists that it is both the Directional Frictional Effect and the fibre diameter that have the greatest influence on the feltability of wools, and crimp is of secondary importance. However, the combination of crimp frequency and crimp form can elevate the importance of the contribution of the wool fibre's shape to feltability. Whilst scientists were labouring to quantify felting and find ways to predict which wools would felt best, the wool buyers for the felt companies had already been evaluating wools by instinctively gauging the properties which had been identified scientifically. Using their experience the wool buyer examined the wool, looking at its fineness, and the nature of the crimp, staple length, colour, and cleanliness. They also conducted their own felting test by taking a bundle of fibres and rolling it between their thumb and forefinger to make a felt ball, almost like an empirical Aachen test. Through wide experience, they could assess the relative feltability of the wool types by feeling and judging the formation of each ball.

WOOL SELECTION

In commercial felt making any scientific evaluation was even more complex because of the use of different wool types in a blend or in the use of multilayered felts, with each layer containing different wools. For example a felt made for slippers had two outside layers of fine wool for the best aesthetics and a coarser wool in the centre to give the felt strength, stiffness and lower cost. Blends may also have included synthetic fibres or even waste fibre such as shoddy in order to reduce costs to compete commercially. These sorts of cost cutting methods inevitably reduced the feltability. Under these circumstances there was no recourse to scientific analysis to determine the outcome and the only way to establish the viability of the resultant felt was through trial and error, using industrial felting methods.

At the height of the industry at around 1950s, the major felt manufacturers, MASCO, Bury Felt Manufacturing Company, Longmeadow Felt Company, R. R. Whitehead and Brothers, and Cooper & Co, together produced over six hundred different felts, which represented ninety percent of the British production. This staggering number of products was a result of the policy to provide customers with bespoke products tailor made to their individual specifications. Even when they all amalgamated to form Bury Cooper Whitehead Limited, they did not rationalise their product range and carried all the ranges of each company. To manufacture such a wide range of products required a vast collection of different wool types because each product had its own unique properties.

This required the use of over a hundred different wools from the finest super white wool to the coarsest reclaimed shoddy fibres. These wools could be ranked into six broad groups: fine white, off-white, grey, noils, dyed fibres, fibres from waste. One type of wool that the feltmakers positively shunned was slipe, which was collected from dead sheep, probably more from distaste than from technical properties. Appendix I gives a description of most of the wools used, with the type identifications used at the time.

Types of wool used in felt making: fine white (centre), off white (upper left), grey (lower right), dyed fibre (upper right)

The best felting wools were 64s to 62s quality merinos from the South African Cape, but Australian merinos of the same count were prized almost as much[23]. These formed the backbone of the industry after around 1930, before which East India wool was most dominant[24]. Because these wool types were superb felters they were used, not only on their own to make high quality felts, but also as the major felt component in blends, where they were the key binding agent that held the structure of the felt together. They were usually mixed with other coarser wools, which were added to lower cost and to provide particular final properties to felts, particularly for technical end uses. Where the product had to be as white as possible, only the best white wools were used and in most instances, this meant the use of carbonised wools that were free of seeds and burr. Much of the wool was also scoured and sometimes bleached to attain the purest white. However, feltmakers believed that carbonised wools did not felt as well as natural wool and some preferred to scour and bleach the finished felt rather than the wool. Until the 1970s, they also preferred to buy the cheaper wools containing vegetable matter and then carbonising the felt after its manufacture in their own carbonising plant. This turned the seeds and burr into carbon, which was then crushed and shaken out as powder. Where final colour was not an issue, off-white wools were used and often the presence of a limited amount of seed and burr was allowable, which enabled cheaper wool to be used. These were mostly New Zealand wools though some Cape and English wools were used. English wools were not favoured by the feltmakers because the fibres tended to be relatively coarse and did not felt well.

Manufacturing grey felts required the use of exotic wools, such as karakul, from such places as Pakistan and Abyssinia, though some also came from the Cape. The term "grey" is a misnomer since most grey felts were actually brown as were the constituent wool fibres. The pre-processing of these wools left a lot to be desired as they arrived at the felt mills in a pitiful state containing a fair amount of sand and detritus that required a thorough breaking up to remove. Although many of these wools consisted of coarse fibres, they could be manufactured into some of the densest felts ever made, with densities similar to those of wood. However, it could take many days to achieve this. In other cases the grey felts were used mainly for their cheapness in say packing and this gave many possibilities to add waste fibres to the blend to achieve the ultimate in low cost. Sometimes garnetted or pulled waste would be added directly to the blend to give a homogeneous mix or it could be laid into the centre of a felt with better quality wools surrounding it, on the face and back of the felt. In many cases, the wool came from areas where anthrax was rife and there was a considerable risk of felt workers contracting the disease. In Baltic Mill even in modern times, there were notices around the factory warning about anthrax and detailing the symptoms. Several cases of anthrax had indeed occurred there.

To produce coloured felts, piece dyeing was the rule, but for some special applications, such as for slipper felt, dyed fibres were used. However, this was not a route favoured by feltmakers because dyed fibres did not felt as well as undyed ones. Most of these coloured blends were used in the mills where grey felts were made since cross contamination of different fibres was not a major problem there. In the mills where white felts were made, contamination of one fibre blend by another was a constant nightmare for the mill managers. This was particularly acute when a carding engine was cleared of one blend and then a second blend run through it. No matter how well the machine was cleared, there were always a few fibres left over from the previous blend. Great care was then taken in selecting the best blends that could follow each other so that the fibres left in the machine did not alter the characteristics of the previous one. For example if a felt was to be dyed the blend was not processed by a machine that had previously run a blend which contained fibres that did not take up dye. Doing so would have left undyed fibres in the dyed felt that would show up as streaks. For this reason, the blending bins and processing machinery were segregated according to the blends that were allowed to run on them. Manufacture of grey felts was therefore carried out in a completely separate mill from those manufacturing white felts.

Noils were the magic ingredients in many felt blends that improved felting, improved quality, and at the same time reduced costs. The type and fineness of the noils were chosen for each specific felt blend and were mostly derived from New Zealand wools between 64s and 56s quality. Often a felt blend contained different noils within it as well as the main wool component. They could also be blended with other white waste fibres, such as botany waste, that were reclaimed from woollen and worsted yarn production processes. Noils were important in producing the very high-density felts since they significantly reduced the effort needed to achieve the ultimate density and surface finish demanded for a technical felt. Most blends contained between twenty and forty percent to give the optimum balance of quality, texture, and felt strength.

SYNTHETIC BLENDS

The first synthetic fibre to be developed was viscose made from cellulose derived from trees, and known as artificial silk. It is not known at what stage viscose was added to a felt blend but the fibre was only available in commercial quantities in 1924 when it was known as rayon. Because of its low cost relative to wool, it was used as a filler fibre to lower the cost of the felt. The characteristics of rayon were similar in many ways to wool, such as its reaction to water and its general physical properties. The dyeing of rayon was also compatible with dyeing wool so that it was relatively easy to match the colour of the viscose fibres to those of wool when dyed together. A dyed felt made from a viscose blend was therefore indistinguishable from an all-wool felt, and visually the presence of viscose was undetectable. However, since the surfaces of rayon fibres were smooth, they did not have the ability to felt and so did not enhance the feltability of the wool in the blend. Neither did it interfere with the felting of the wool so that, in terms of felting, rayon was considered neutral. As a result, the strength of a felt made with rayon depended wholly on the proportion of wool in the mix. This in turn limited the amount of it that could be usefully added to a blend. In practice, the maximum amount of rayon that could be added to a felt was seventy-five percent of the total felt weight. Commercially rayon was only used in such high proportions in superfine felts because the market where these felts were used experienced the greatest competition from other lower cost materials. Eventually this type of felt was replaced entirely by all-viscose needle felts manufactured by needling the fibres rather than through the wool felting route.

The advent of synthetic fibres from the 1930s onwards provided the feltmakers with possibilities for developing completely new types of felt. Most of the oil-based fibres such as nylon, acrylic, polyester, polypropylene, polyvinyl chloride, and triacetate proved disappointing since the surface friction of these were so low that they actually interfered with the felting process[25]. The dyeing of these synthetic fibres was also problematic since it was not possible to dye them in the same process as that used for wool. In a coloured felt, therefore, such fibres could clearly be seen within a felt. Nevertheless, some acrylic fibres were used as a filler on the inside layer of a layered felt in order to soften it and reduce its cost. Great care had to be taken in the mill when using synthetic fibres because of the problem of contamination of all-wool felts. This meant dedicated blending arrangements and processing equipment, which were kept only for the use of synthetic blends. Commercially this was only feasible when the volume of business was great enough to sustain a full utilization of the machinery. One interesting area of development in the 1980s was the use of a special polypropylene heterofilament fibre that had two components: an inner high melting core, and an outer coating of a low melting polymer. When heated to the correct temperature the outer surface melted whilst the inner component retained its physical properties. This enabled these fibres to bond to anything that surrounded it. In this case, although the fibres initially interfered with the felting process, when the felt was heated the polypropylene glued the wool fibres together to form a stronger felt. Although this line of development was curtailed, one major product was manufactured at Bury and Masco Industries for another European company, and this consisted of a three-layer felt with outer layers of two different colours and an inner layer containing a heterofilament blend. On heating, the heterofilaments bonded with the other fibres to give a slightly stiffened felt that was dimensionally stable and shrink proof. This product was used in large quantities as under-collar felts and as such warranted the segregation of a complete production line.

Just after the Second World War, there was considerable interest in manufacturing synthetic protein fibres from milk and peanuts as replacements for wool and eventually commercial quantities of these fibres became available worldwide. The majority of these new fibres were manufactured from casein, which was derived from milk. The trade names for such casein fibres depended on the country of manufacture: Lanital in Belgium and France, Fibrolane BX in Britain, Merinova in Italy, Wipolan in Poland, and Aralac in America. Being a protein fibre, casein had very similar properties to wool. It was soft and pliable, yet resilient, it softened in water and it could be dyed with similar dyes to wool. More remarkable was its ability to enhance the felting process despite it not possessing a scaly surface. Blends containing casein fibre felted faster and reached higher densities than all-wool felts[26]. This is attributed to the way the casein fibre plasticises in the presence of heat and water, not only does it soften but also the surface becomes slightly sticky. This allows the scales on the wool to achieve better traction that amplifies the ratchet effect. The use of casein was particularly important in producing the thick high-density technical felts, which were difficult to achieve profitably by any other means and as an added bonus, the casein gave the felts a desirable stiffer handle. Unfortunately, by the 1980s, most commercial production of casein fibres ceased and the only remaining product available was Wipolan from Poland. The supply route to the production of these technical felts therefore became precarious since it was dependent on a single supplier with a market monopoly. Although protein fibre from peanuts was available through Imperial Chemical Industries under the trade name Ardil, it was not used to any great extent. When production of Ardil ceased in 1957 the feltmakers choice was limited to casein, and despite all the dangers of single source supply, they never found a suitable alternative.

TYPICAL FELT TYPES

The simplest of all felts was one consisting of just one type of wool. A typical example of this was in the manufacture of superfine felt for the hat trade, which was made from hundred percent merino noils, which gave the required smooth fine surface. Such felts were usually manufactured to weigh seventeen ounces per linear yard sixty inches wide. However, felts made from all of one wool type were rarely produced commercially and most were made of blends of different wools. For example surgical felts were made from ultra clean botany waste with a percentage of scoured New Zealand lambs' wool to impart more loft and resilience[27]. Most felts were made by using different layers containing different blends to give specific properties or cost savings. The simplest of this type of felt was the two layered felt where the requirements of the face were different to those of the back. Amongst these were slipper felts where the face was made from 70s Cape or Australian merino and the back from coarser 56s quality. In this way, the face presented a smooth fine surface that was aesthetically pleasing and could be easily printed, whilst the back face gave a more resilient feel to the foot and a greater wear resistance in use. Typically a slipper felt would be twenty-four ounces per linear yard and the face would have a third less weight than the back for commercial reasons[28].

Hard white technical felts were more complex and consisted of three layers: two face layers of similar wool blends and a middle layer that contained a completely different blend. Typically such a technical felt would have face layers of white botany waste or carbonised merino noils and a middle layer of a blend of carbonised merino wool, scoured Cape wool and low cost broken trimmings. Costs could be further reduced using schlumberger noils in place of the scoured Cape wool. Reducing cost by filling the middle layer with cheap filling fibres was a recurring theme in the felt industry and was taken to extremes by Herbert Smith of Longmeadow Felt Company. He used a five layer structure to pack as much waste as possible into a felt to make cheap felt blankets to supply the forces in the First World War. He was so successful that he created a new felt industry in the Kidderminster area. The outer layers contained a blend consisting of fifty percent pulled wool waste and fifty percent wool of 56s quality. The second two layers consisted of two thirds pulled waste wool and one-third 56s quality wool, whilst the inner core layer was all wool. This structure allowed wool fibres to migrate through the waste from face to middle and vice-versa effectively stitching the waste together. In this way Herbert Smith was able to make a felt that contained six times as much waste fibre as there was new wool; a phenomenal technological achievement[29]. Once this was shown to be possible, other low cost felts were made that included jute or cow hair in the middle layers. These low quality felts were used either for packing or as underlay for carpets or linoleum. This technical advantage did not last long, because the development of the needle loom enabled all-hair felts to be made that were considerably cheaper.

APPENDIX I

WOOLS OF THE FELT INDUSTRY c1945 ONWARDS

THE FINEST WOOLS
T1446 Australian 64s Double Picked - very fine white
38L Australian carbonised - fine white
HDC5 Home Carbonised Australian - fine white
7604 Vervier Australian Carbonised - fine white
60s Australian Hore Carbonised - fine white
1486 60s Australian - fine white
Type 7 Carbonised Australian Fleece - fine white
Type 12 Cape Carbonised - fine white
6/9 Cape Carbonised - fine white
474 Cape Carbonised - fine white
T017 Carbonised and bred Cape - fine white.
4065 Cape Carbonised - fine white
865/2 Cape Carbonised - fine white.
B110C Cape Carbonised Lamb - fine white
Type 14 Carbonised Cape piece - fine white
Type 18 Cape - fine white
Type 20 Carbonised Cape piece - fine white
Type 32 Cape Carbonised - fine white
FO25 Scoured Cape Snow White - fine white
KEYN - fine very white
KEDC - fine white
KEYN (v) - fine white
KEYM Snow White - fine white
KEYE - fine white
CEDE - medium off white
17421 Carbonised White - very fine white.
Type 14 - fine white
Type 42 - fine white
Type 71 - fine white
Type 451C - fine white
Type 44 66 Schlumberger
Non Carbonised Schlumberger
Type 471 Super - fine long staple white

OFF-WHITE AND SEEDY WOOLS
B0282 Scoured New Zealand - fine white
196 Scoured New Zealand - fine off-white
T34 New Zealand Carbonised - fine off-white
23103 New Zealand Carbonised - fine off-white
8977 Scoured New Zealand - medium off-white.
Type 34 Scoured New Zealand - medium off-white
471 Cape Carbonised - fine off white
Type 18 Cape Carbonised fleece - fine off-white

Type 21 Scoured Cape Fine and Bred - medium off-white
EAG Cape scoured bulky white - medium dirty white with burrs
EEE Bulky Cape Scoured medium dirty white with staining with burrs
56s 58s English Noble - fine off-white
9083 Discoloured Schlumberger – off-white
CEDY - Medium white with seeds
CEDA Scoured Kemp - coarse off white with low crimp
A077 Scoured Yellow Pakistan - coarse dirty white
T16 Fleece - fine off-white
Type 22 Medium off-white
H3812 - Fine off white with burrs
A039 SGW - Medium off-white
A039 Garnetted and Scoured - medium off-white

GREY WOOLS
G016 Scoured fine Grey - coarse mottled brown and white
B025 Cape Coarse Coloured - very coarse brown and white
Type 479 Coarse Coloured - very coarse brown and white fibres low crimp
Type 471 Fine Grey - very coarse mostly dark brown with white flecks.
B017C8 Coarse Fine Grey - coarse mixed brown and white fibres crimped
Type 481 Coloured Cape - very coarse mixed white and brown fibres low crimp
T481 - Coarse off white with some brown fibres low crimp
C001 Coarse Abyssinian - medium coarse multibrown coloured fibres
B037 Greasy Cape Skin - medium light tan colour
Type 477 - Coarse brown with some white
G055 Karakul - coarse dark brown low crimp
G051 Scoured Cape Grey - coarse dark brown with white kemps
A033 Karakul Noils - coarse brown low crimp

NOILS
N 6040/5 Cart Cape Noble Noil - fine white
061 56s Cart Noil - fine white
Type 43 64s Carbonised Noil - fine white
4 K.C. Cape Carbonised Noil Bier - fine white
Carbonised Schlumberger noil
81XX Carbonised 64/60 Noble Noil
58s Carbonised Noble Noil
14 56s Noil New Zealand - fine off-white
6123500L Carbonised noil - fine white
T6N Wool Noil mix

WASTE FIBRES
Type 51 Botany Waste - fine white
Pulled Blanket Waste - coarse off-white
A045 45924 Garnetted - medium off-white
A045 Scoured and Bred - medium off-white
Type 51 Garnetted White - medium off-white
A077 Willeyed Coarse Waste - very coarse, jute-like low crimp

DYED FIBRES
A031 C.J. Coloured Noils - fine dyed black
A031 Soft Black Waste - medium dyed black
A043 Coloured Waste - medium brown

2 EARLY YEARS AND LEEDS FELTMAKERS

EARLY YEARS - ASPHALT FELT AND LEEDS FELTMAKERS

The commercial woollen felt industry was conceived under strange circumstances. It began with the British navy patrolling in the Caribbean in the eighteenth century. Whilst there, the warships were infested with the toredo novalis worm that burrowed into the timbers of the keel to such an extent that the vessels became virtually un-seaworthy. The solution was to attach copper plates to the hull to cover the external timbers. However, it was found that an asphalt interlayer was required between the copper and the wood to make a good seal and limit corrosion of the copper. The most efficient way of doing this at the time was to impregnate a hat felt with asphalt to make sheets that could be easily handled during shipbuilding. Considering the size of ships and numbers in both naval and commercial terms the market was vast, sufficient to stimulate mass production methods for producing the felt in order to satisfy demand.

The earliest record of a commercial felt manufacturer, other than for hats, was William Wood around 1815[1] and his market was exclusively for covering ships' keels. He made his felt by a batch production process and then impregnated pieces with asphalt. He was followed shortly afterwards by George Borradaile, in around 1821, who rapidly became the acknowledged leader in the field of asphalt felt. As an early pioneer, he opened up the market into other civil engineering applications such as bridge and railway track supports[2], besides ships' keels. He manufactured first under the company name of Wm. and G. Borradaile in 1839[3] and then later traded as Borradaile, Whiting, and Co. in 1840[4]. A short time later William Abbott was manufacturing asphalt felt in his factory in Bermondsey initially by his own batch process and then by a continuous method using T. R. Williams's patent of 1829[5], the rights of which he had purchased. Williams himself set up a rival company in around 1833 under the name Stanbridge, Marshall, Williams, and Co., at a factory at Lamb's Buildings, Bunhill Row, London. This was a partnership to produce mainly roofing felt with a new, patented process. This was a turning point for Williams, for up to this time, he does not seem to have been a manufacturer in his own right as his address in all the publications are from a residential area in the Strand, London[6]. Nevertheless, in 1833 his address changed to 14 Lamb's Buildings, Bunhill Row, London, which was the address of F. McNeill's factory[7].

It seems that Williams' original partnership was dissolved in 1837 after litigation by Abbott[9] and shortly after, Forbes McNeill took over the factory establishing his company, F. McNeill and Company. F. McNeill and Co. had started business in 1833 with the "Lion" Brand of asphalt felt[10] and with T. R. William's support, the company continued until well after McNeill's death in 1845. After McNeill's death in August 1845, T. R. Williams was still communicating from the Asphalte Works at Bunhill Row. At that time, the company was in danger of closure due to McNeill's debts and a potential liability for duty on all goods manufactured.

FELT IN BRITAIN

View of the new Vice-Chancellor's Courts, and the Offices and Passages leading to Westminster Hall, which are Roofed entirely with F. M'Neill and Co.'s Asphalted Felt, under the Direction of Charles Barry, Esq., R.A., by order of Her Majesty's Commissioners of Woods and Forests. Dr. Reid's Offices, and other Buildings, at the New Houses of Parliament, are also roofed with the same Felt.

An advertisement for McNeill's roofing felt[11] showing the elaborate use of roofing felt

The company did survive, or at least its name, since a Mr. E. Nelson filed a patent for reinforced hair felt in 1891[12] as part of the F. McNeill company. In 1918, the company expanded into a disused iron foundry in King Street, London, and remained there until the late 1930s[13] and by then, they also had a manufacturing works in Kirkintilloch, Scotland. They were still using felt making machinery in 1933, as they purchased new parts for a flat hardening machine from William Bywater at that time[14]. The company F. McNeill survived into modern times and was still active up to 1963[15].

> **F. M'NEILL and Co. Patent Felt Works, of Bunhill-row, Finsbury-square, London.**
>
> The patent asphalted felt for roofing houses and every description of farm buildings, for lining damp walls, particularly granaries, as vermin will not touch it) as a light ceiling, to be fixed underneath rafters, as, from its non-conducting qualities, it counteracts the heat of the sun, and totally excludes the frost of winter; weather-boarded roofs which have become imperfect can be made tight with a covering of this felt), improved and manufactured by the exhibitors; a portable rickstand, of a very cheap construction, and an excellent check to vermin, invented by J. F. Williams, Patent Felt Works, Bunhill-row; models and specimen framings, illustrating various cheap constructions of roofs for the application of the felt, also showing its use for ceilings, lining damp walls, covering flats &c.

Advertisement in the British Farmer's Magazine 1852[8]

The period from 1840 to 1850 saw a sharp rise in competition from a number of prominent producers of asphalt felt, initially in 1840 from a company called Pocock's Patent Flexible Roofing, which was using sheets of hat felt and making them into a slate replacement. Then in 1844, both McKibbin's Improved Roofing Felt and Croggon and Co. entered the market. Thomas John Croggon seems to have been very active as he advertised widely in the press of the day, extolling the virtues of his hemp-based product.

Croggon's advertisement in The Merchant's Magazine 1855[16], and Grueber's advertisement in Guide to the Crystal Palace & Park[17]

In 1849, two further companies Grueber and Co. and David Anderson were formed with Anderson expanding rapidly by manufacturing its "Red Hand" brand of flax-based roofing felt made from its factory at Logan Felt works in Belfast. Following them in 1891, Ruberoid introduced a new class of material using wool or hair[18].

All these asphalt felt manufacturers also produced and sold un-impregnated hair felt for use as thermal insulation for boilers, pipe work and the like. No doubt, these products were complementary to the sort of trade and markets that these manufacturers were in and enabled them to extend their sales. As iron-hulled steam ships replaced wooden sailing vessels, the market in asphalt felt for ships cladding shrank, but because of an increasing demand for roofing felt, the total market for asphalt felt actually increased. The expansion of the use of steam increased the need for boiler and pipe insulation, which led to a demand for un-impregnated hair felt; a market that both the asphalt manufacturers and the woollen felt manufacturers competed for. Therefore, even though the asphalt felt industry developed separately from the woollen felt industry they maintained a common interest supplying these insulation felts, up to the time when synthetic products started to replace them in the 1950s. Throughout this tentative relationship, the woollen felt manufacturers considered these products to be the low end of the market and did not recognize hair felt producers as felt manufacturers. For example, the Pressed Felt Manufacturers Association would not allow the Anglo Felt Company, who made hair felt, to join the Association in 1972[19].

THE LEEDS INDUSTRY

It was John Wilkinson of Leeds who had the vision of making woollen cloths without spinning or weaving purely by felting and, being a wealthy woollen cloth merchant, he had the financial resources to fulfil it. It is probable that he was aware of the reported developments in America where it was claimed that non-woven felted cloth had been made of sufficient durability for use as carpeting, floor cloths, rugs, table-covers, blankets, and padding. This was disclosed in patents filed in America in 1829 by William Harrison of West Chester County of New York[20] and a Mr. Raymond of New York[21].

In a further reported development some years prior to 1839, a Mr. Height was using a process for producing continuous lengths of non-woven felted cloth, with a width of thirty-six inches, and capable of an output of six hundred yards per twelve-hour day. This invention was first reported in the Leeds Mercury, with the article subsequently quoted by other publications calling for businessmen to support its development in Britain. The offering was for an initial trial costing £55,000 and, subject to the results, a further £220,000 for the right to use the process[22]. Around 1838 another American, Henry Augustus Wells, was in England claiming to be the inventor of non-woven felted cloth and was in the process of patenting his method of production. He approached John Wilkinson and others to fund his development showing them eight-inch square samples that he had, unbeknown to them, produced using felt hat making techniques. It seems this could have been a forerunner of the flat hardener since a patent by Wells was awarded in 1841[23]. However, he singularly failed to produce a workable machine, at great cost to his investors, who then realised they had been duped. Well's patent agent, John Duncan, also invested in the project and was understandably concerned to gain a return. He knew of T. R. Williams as an American inventor and approached him to find a workable manufacturing method, with the support of John Wilkinson[24].

In 1838, John Wilkinson set up a company, John Wilkinson, Son and Co., with the objective of producing a felt material by a continuous mechanical method that did not require any fibre impregnation. To do this he enlisted the help of T. R. Williams. It was two years later in 1840 that they succeeded in creating a commercial manufacturing process and the company was producing and selling felt. T. R. Williams was declared the inventor and he registered the ground breaking patent[25] that was to define the industry for the next one hundred and fifty years. To fully exploit its potential another new company was formed with John Wilkinson and T. R. Williams as partners, with the company being managed by W. P. Wise. From fire insurance documents of the time the original company name was The Patent Felting Company with John Wilkinson and Williams identified as trustees with Thomas Tolby Laycock, gentleman, and Arthur Lipton, cloth merchant, as mortgagees. In 1841, it was being called The Patent Felted Cloth Company before finally being called The Patent Woollen Cloth Company in 1843[26]. By 1843, the company was manufacturing at two locations, one at Elmwood Mill, Hunslet Leeds and the other in London with the London factory being half the size of that in Leeds. At this time, the company was making a reasonable profit with a return on capital of twenty percent and valued at £60246[27]. Significantly, the accounts show that Wilkinson had a stock account, which indicates he was also trading separately from the company. Around this time there was only one other company advertising in 1841 that it was manufacturing and selling felt carpet, William Hirst[28], and he was known to be active in patenting methods for producing felt, up to 1857[29]. However there is no record of his activities after this.

THE PATENT WOOLLEN CLOTH COMPANY

On 1 January 1844, Williams assigned his patent rights to a new group of entrepreneurs: Charles William Allen, Reverend Humphrey Allen, Henry Morris Kemshead, Stephen Phillips, and Richard Roy John Stewart, who appear to have taken over the company[30]. The company was constituted as a joint stock company by deed of settlement, and the deed dictated that the shares should not be transferable, except with the consent of a board of directors. It also contained the usual provisions for registering the shares in "The Share Registry Book", and provided rights that, "notwithstanding any assignment, the receipt of the registered shareholder should be a good discharge and that the Share Registry Book should be conclusive evidence of the proprietorship of any shares[31]". One major shareholder, James Hay, who was not a patentee and had a hundred and fifty £100 shares took the company to court regarding the transfer of the payment of his dividend to a third party.

The transfer of the original Patent Felting Company to these new owners must also have included some consideration for John Wilkinson's interests as progenitor of the work that led to the felted cloth patent. The evidence for this comes from three distinct agreements with The Patent Woollen Cloth Company one on 27 July 1842, one on 8 June 1843 and one on 24 October 1844[32]. This allowed John Wilkinson to set up his own company making felt using the Williams' patented process. The Patent Woollen Cloth Company controlled very closely what he could and could not produce and he had to pay royalties on every yard of carpet he manufactured. The licence dues were at a rate of 3d per inch or £120 per annum for each eighty-inch wide carding engine, paid quarterly[33]. He may not have been too diligent in paying because in the later stages of their association The Patent Woollen Cloth Company had to go to arbitration in 1858, when the patent had expired, to secure £264 that Wilkinson had not paid[34]. In 1853, the holders of the Williams' patent printed a Jubilee notice in the Leeds Mercury of 1 October 1853 announcing that they were applying for a prolongation of the terms of the patent as it was due to expire on 14 February 1854; but they were unsuccessful.

The takeover of The Patent Woollen Cloth Company in 1843 was far from smooth, as they had to undertake litigation[35] against a competitor using the Williams' process. With affidavits from Williams and a skilled attorney they won the case and prevented the opposition competing with them. If they had lost this case the consequences for them would have been dire, not only would they have lost the investment in Williams' patent but also the license fees from John Wilkinson and it would have exposed them to extensive competition. In the event, their successful action prevented any competitors other than John Wilkinson.

The Patent Woollen Cloth Company became bankrupt in 1845 and the citation in the Law Journal quotes the following as being part of the Company: John McRae, John Steward, James Hay, Henry Morris Kempshead, Thomas Robinson Williams, Francis Norvillar. George Knox, Stephen Phillips, Robert Gardner, Robert Innes Grant, George L. Grant Allan, Michael Rimmington, Robert Roy, Francis Atkinson, Catherine Purvis, Ann Ross, Richard Roy, and Stephen Read Cattley[36]. When the company was reformed under their manager Thomas R. Clarke, the company went from strength to strength, evolving new markets and capitalising on their lead in carpets, winning a gold medal at the British Exhibition of 1851[37] for their carpets, branded as "Royal Victoria Carpets" in 1848[38]. The company went on to win a silver medal for their carpets in the Paris Universal Exhibition of 1867[39] and gold in the International Exhibition at Vienna in 1873. They must have been profitable because they declared two dividends, of £2/10 s/5d per £100 share in April 1849, and April 1850[40].

CARPETS.
ROYAL VICTORIA FELT CARPETTING.

The present period being peculiarly one of economy, the Public should purchase this description of Carpetting, the advantages being, durability, beauty, and novelty of design, imperviousness to dust, brilliancy of colouring, style equal to Brussels, and at a cost of half the price. Purchasers are cautioned against spurious imitations, the Felt Carpetting being always stamped "Royal Victoria Carpetting." It can be procured at all the respectable Carpet Houses in London and its vicinity, and in all the principal Towns of the United Kingdom.

The Patent Woollen Cloth Company also manufacture Table Covers, embossed and printed, of the latest possible designs, and in every variety of style and colour; *thick Felt* for polishing Plate Glass, Steel, Marble, Tortoiseshell, &c., &c.; likewise for Veterinary purposes; Felt Waistcoatings, Cloths for Coach and Railway Carriage Linings, Upholsterers, &c., &c.; Piano Felts.

Manufactories—Elmwood Mills, Leeds; and Borough Road, London. Wholesale Warehouses, only, at 8, Love Lane, Wood Street, Cheapside.

Advertisement for Royal Victoria Felt carpet in New Monthly magazine 1849

In the 1850s, they were expanding their capacity by investing in new carding engines, which they purchased from R. & C. Goldthorp at a cost of £83/9s/1d each in 1853. A few years later, they were contemplating installing a new milling machine from the Leeds textile engineering company of Taylor Wordsworth, and ordering a new hardener from them in 1856[41]. By 1857, their half-year's consumption of wool and tow had risen to 441,834 lbs. weight worth £13,533/1s/8d and in June of that year they were looking for extra drying capacity at the local tenterhouses of Arthington, and Morphet[42].

ROYAL VICTORIA FELT CARPETING.

THE PUBLIC ATTENTION is particularly directed to this manufacture. The Carpeting combines beauty of design, durability, imperviousness to dust, and economy in price—costing half that of Brussels. . It has now been in general use many years, and become well established with the trade and the public, and can be purchased at all respectable Carpet-houses in London, and in nearly every town of the United Kingdom. The PATENT WOOLLEN CLOTH COMPANY, 8, Love-lane, Aldermanbury, also manufacture Printed and Embossed Tablecovers, in the newest designs, Window Curtains, Cloths for Upholsterers, Thick Felt for Polishing, &c. &c.—Manufactories at LEEDS, and BOROUGH-ROAD, LONDON. [I 71.

Advertisement for Royal Victoria Carpets in The Official Descriptive Catalogue of the Great Exhibition of Works of Industry of all Nations 1851

But then disaster struck, and on the night of Sunday October 11 1857, a massive fire broke out in the carding area, destroying carding engines worth £226 with a further six carding engines damaged by water having a value of £250. Including the damage to the buildings and loss of wool and stock, the total damage was valued at £680/15 shillings. It was unfortunate in that the superintendent, Mr. James, of the Leeds Fire Brigade that attended the fire, lost his life through asphyxiation, he being the only casualty[43]. They must have recovered well for the company was building a new mill in 1859.

The new mill expansion was completed in 1860 and was of considerable size[44], involving a requirement for two new steam engines and boilers: one a thirty horsepower double cylinder engine matched by a thirty-five horsepower boiler, and one ten horsepower engine with a fifteen horsepower boiler. The cost of the thirty horsepower engine and boiler was £1145, or £17 per horse, whilst the line shafting to transmit power to the manufacturing equipment was £640 per line. With one engine, they purchased two sets of line shafting both presumably linked to it. Significantly, the cost of the line shafting was greater than the cost of the engine and boiler. The length of the line shaft must have been very extensive and there must have been a considerable number of ancillary pulleys, because these pieces of equipment were simple to produce by low cost engineering techniques. Line shafting certainly did not have the same sophistication of a steam engine and the fact that the company was willing to spend so much on such utilitarian equipment underlines its importance to running the mill. The total equipment that was ordered for this expansion was:

Four cards with batt frames at £190 each with clothing at £130 each.
Four hardeners made by Taylor Wordsworth at £130 each
Eight pairs of 24-inch stocks at £28 each.
Two tentering machines made by William Whiteley, one 60 inch wide, the other seventy-six inches wide capable of holding a hundred and twenty yards of felt, at costs of £640 and £690 respectively.

The cost of the new building was £3439/4s/6d, which included 780,000 bricks, pillars, roofing, slates and flags, making the total investment £5807 for machinery and £3439 for the building, which was around half of the original investment in the Leeds factory in 1843. This investment must have been pure expansion rather than a rationalisation of their manufacturing sites since they were still advertising their other factory in Borough Road, London in 1861[45] and they were still maintaining their wholesale warehouse at 8 Love Lane London. From their entry in the catalogue for the Great Exhibition of 1851, it appears that the printing of their carpets was done in their London factory.

Also, around 1861, they were confident enough to look at the possibility of taking over a rival company, Cornelius Turner based at Airedale Mills Hunslet, but after calculating the potential benefits they concluded that the outlay did not match the return[46]. John Wilkinson, however, had a different view and from the Leeds Directories he must have taken the business over since he was operating at both his Mill at St. Helens and at Airedale Mill in 1872. The company maintained its lead in the 1870's too, winning medals at the World Exhibition in Vienna in 1873 and in 1875 at the Yorkshire Exhibition of Arts and Manufacture, in Leeds, inaugurated by the Duke of Edinburgh[47].

During this time of consolidation for the company, they were active in developing many of the markets for felt that exist today, as witnessed by their advertisements. Clearly they were capable of making thick felts for glass polishing, which indicates they were using flat plate hardeners as well as the roller hardeners and knew how to make dense felt through acid milling. They were also making veterinary felts, which must have been soft for padding, probably of the type that was used as pedicure padding in modern times. Interestingly, they were also making piano felts in 1848, which is well before any other manufacturer in the country, though this may have been for damping rather than piano hammers, as they do not appear to have been prominent in this market[48]. As far as their marketing is concerned, they seem to have adopted a policy of using agents rather than direct selling, at least for their carpets, as they were not prolific in advertising and those adverts that do exist were fairly basic and signposted potential customers to their agents.

After the patent expired late in 1854, the company was faced with mounting competition, initially from other Leeds based companies but none were of sufficient size to challenge their dominance or that of John Wilkinson. However, thirty-six miles away, in Rossendale, a new fledgling industry was taking shape and by 1860 there were mills at Siss Clough and Todd Carr rivalling in size those in

Leeds, though it was not until the 1870's that they were having an impact. Up to this time, the carpet market was sufficiently buoyant to accommodate this increase in capacity and felt still had a significant price advantage over woven carpet. However, from 1890 onwards the felt carpet industry was being pressed hard by the increasing capacity and width of carpets made by power looms, leading to an industry crisis point around 1900. Axminster carpets were becoming ever cheaper and a price war had broken out between woven carpet manufacturers at a time when Axminsters were becoming popular[49]. One company alone, Templeton, increased its sales by four hundred and fifty percent in the period 1893 to 1900. By 1904, The Patent Woollen Cloth Company seems not to have been able to respond to this competition, and was in receivership before being taken over by the Rossendale feltmakers as part of a combine to be known as Mitchells, Ashworth, Stansfield and Company.

JOHN WILKINSON COMPANY

John Wilkinson was a wealthy woollen cloth merchant and mill owner with a warehouse in Woodhouse Lane Leeds and a mill, Elmwood Mill, which he leased to other manufacturers[50]. He was approached, by John Duncan, a London solicitor acting for Augustus Wells who was an American, claiming to be able to make felted cloth by a continuous method that he had patented. Wilkinson built the machine described in Wells' patent but there was no way that it would produce felt like the samples that Wells' had provided as proof of his invention. It transpired that he had produced it through a conventional process used for making hat felts and had effectively duped Duncan and Wilkinson. Not to be outdone Wilkinson, with the help of his machine makers persevered with the equipment endeavouring to manufacture the illusive felted cloth, but without success. Both Duncan and Wilkinson had made a significant outlay in the venture and both stood to lose it all. With every intention of rescuing the situation, Duncan approached T. R. Williams for his help, no doubt because of his work and his patents in the field of asphalt felt. It seems Wilkinson provided the capital and labour for Williams to invent and develop the continuous felting process, though Williams filed the patent[51].

On the formation of The Patent Woollen Cloth Company in 1841, John Wilkinson and Co. remained as a separate independent company and able to work the patent through an initial agreement on 27 July 1842. The future of the two companies seem from then on to be linked, reinforced by the two subsequent agreements of 8 June 1843 before the takeover of The Patent Woollen Cloth Company by Allen and others, and lastly 24 October 1844, after the takeover. The main clauses of the last agreement are as follows:

1st   John Wilkinson is allowed 2 carders and necessary attendant machinery for the manufacture of felt carpets and he shall not be allowed to make any other description of felt.

2nd   John Wilkinson - shall pay to the Patentees Licence dues at the rate of 30/- per inch or £120 per annum for an 80 inch doffer - these dues shall be paid quarterly

3rd   He shall deliver 250 ends of cloth for carpets per month of 27 yards each or 4750 yards

4th   If for 2 consecutive weeks he shall cease to make carpets from one or both cards unless notice have been given in writing to the Patent Cloth Company, he shall not be allowed to make any for the remaining term of the Patent.

5th   His carpets shall weigh not less than 1lb & 2/5th of a pound per yard when perfectly free from seeds and all impurities and shall be 52 inches wide and in all cases equal to sample pieces mutually agreed upon.

6th   H. Brown of Leeds wool stapler shall be the referee in all disputes arising from the fluctuations of wool.

7th   He shall not sell any goods white or printed, although the same may have been refused by the Patent Cloth Company - except with the Company's permission in writing

8th   That anything herein contained shall in any way lessen the monopoly of making or selling felted carpets so far as is at present enjoyed by the said Patent Woollen Cloth Company.

Being so closely controlled, there was not much scope for Wilkinson to be able to challenge the dominance of The Patent Woollen Cloth Company in the carpet market though he advertised his company as a manufacturer of carpets alongside them in the commercial directories of the time[52]. This did not seem to have deterred John Wilkinson as he diversified into many other non-carpet related products such as paddings and medical products[53]. In particular, he developed a range of saddle felts for replacing blankets under horse saddles, known as numnahs, as well as a range of gun waddings for which the company became famous[54].

> 51   WILKINSON, JOHN, *St. Helen's Mills, Leeds*—
> Inventor and Manufacturer.
> New thin ship sheathing, for placing on the ship's side underneath the copper sheathing; thick ship sheathing for placing between the timbers in building.
> Patent padding and wadding for garments; soft white medical cloth, backed with India-rubber, for poultices, or under horse-saddles, &c.; soft white saddle-cloth, without India-rubber.
> Gun wadding of first and second quality; haik felt for steam-pipe and boiler covering, and for deadening sound.
> Indigo blue pilot felt; indigo blue pilot and brown pilot for great coats.

John Wilkinson's entry in the Great Exhibition of 1851[55]

He also seems to have been exploring both the high quality and low cost sections of the felt market at the same time. For example, he was selling hair felts, ship sheathing, and roofing felts that required low cost products, while at the same time he was producing fine quality, heavily milled felts for clothing. His entrepreneurial spirit extended to making composite materials by combining his felts with India rubber, a new material that was undergoing significant development at the time of Hancock's invention of vulcanisation in 1843[56]. Meanwhile at the same time The Patent Woollen Cloth Company was advertising table covers, window curtains, and fine clothing, indicating that they were majoring on thin felts made on roller hardeners whilst Wilkinson was concentrating on thick felts, probably using flat hardeners.

The market for his gun waddings and numnahs must have been good business for the company because it was about this time, 1854/6, that the Crimean war was fought and the demand for ammunition and cavalry supplies must have been high. The union with The Patent Woollen Cloth Company ended in 1852 and by 1854 this company sued Wilkinson for arrears of royalties on the production of carpet, so the separation hardly seems amicable.

As a result of this separation and the expiry of the patent, John Wilkinson and Co. could manufacture felt carpet at will and, by 1861, they were producing 1.6 million square yards of printed carpet a year and the total wool consumption of the factory was 1.6 million pounds weight. This is as much as or greater than the The Patent Woollen Cloth Company was producing in 1857: they used 441,000 pounds weight of wool in the half-year. They also had their own in-house print designer and printing shop consisting of their own block cutter, colour mixing department and block store, so they were completely self-sufficient. As an indication of the size of the company, his St Helens Mill occupied three acres of land with the factory covering 15,745 square yards, and could sustain branches in London, Paris and Manchester[57].

In 1863, Wilkinson's son joined the business and from then on, the firm was known as John Wilkinson and Son Co[58]. By 1878, they were also operating out of Airedale Mill, which was previously the factory from which Cornelius Turner was manufacturing felt, which indicates they had taken him over to increase their capacity, after 1887 there were no longer any entries in the Leeds directories for the company.

CARR AND BUTTERWORTH

Carr and Butterworth first appear as felt manufacturers in 1857[59] some four years after the expiry of the Williams' patent. They set up production in Highfield Mill, an old flax mill, situated on Lady Pit Lane off the Dewsbury Road. They advertised extensively and built up their business sufficiently to be able to open a sales office at number two Marsden Square in Manchester. Their product range was similar to that described in John Wilkinson's advertisements promoting gun waddings, saddle blankets and ship's sheathing with equal emphasis on carpeting. The partnership continued until 1872 when they were described as manufacturing out of St. Helen's Mill with offices in Whitehouse St. and Clarence Road[60]. These were the premises of John Wilkinson, which suggests they were bought out by him or subject to a partnership arrangement. In 1878, George William Carr is recorded as manufacturing at a separate address, 2 Upper Mill, as well as Highfield, whilst his past partner, George Butterworth, is listed separately at St. Helens Mill and Highfield[61]. This suggests that Carr was setting up independently of Wilkinson and Butterworth and from 1878 until 1899, he was manufacturing from Upper Mill with an office at 11 New Station Road[62]. In 1899 the Rossendale felt makers Mitchell Brothers were operating from 11 New Station St. and George Carr from Upper Mill only[63], with his last listing at this address being 1900[64]. This suggests an agreement between Carr and the Mitchell Brothers eventually leading to the moving of Carr's production to Rossendale after 1900.

In the meantime, George Butterworth seems to have parted company with John Wilkinson by 1881 since the listing does not include St. Helens Mill[65]. By 1897, Butterworth had introduced his son into the business being then listed as George Butterworth and Son[66]. At this time, he was also manufacturing hair felt from Beeston Mill as well as wool felt at Highfield Mill. Coincidentally, 1887 was the last time that there was a listing for John Wilkinson who most likely went out of business around this time. The last recorded listing for George Butterworth and Son was in 1905[67] and by 1906 they too must have been out of business. The only entry for felt manufacture in 1906 was the newly formed felt conglomerate, Mitchells, Ashworth, Stansfield and Co. who were operating out of 7 Quebec St[68].

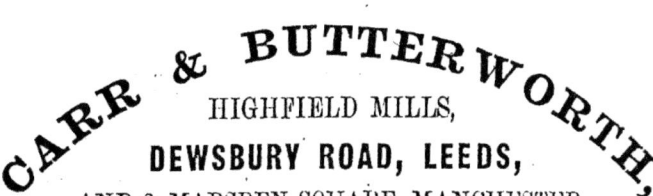

Advertisement for Carr and Butterworth in 1861

OTHER LEEDS FELTMAKERS

The only other carpet felt manufacturer to be listed during the term of Williams' patent from 1840 to 1853 was William Hirst in 1845 whose address was 39 North Street[69], probably using a method he patented in 1840[70]. The method he used, beating wool fibres in a fly press, was hardly competitive and Hirst seems only to have survived in business for a year. Nevertheless he still maintained an interest in felt production obtaining a patent in 1851 that anticipates a flat hardener by felting fibres between two platens, one of which reciprocates[71], then in 1857 a patent for producing a felt by wrapping fibres in a cotton cloth into a roll and beating the roll[72]. However, none of these seems to have developed into a commercial business.

1861 saw two new felt companies start up, Harrop and Mason at Perseverence Mill on the Dewsbury Road, and Cornelius Turner at Airedale Mills on Dock Road[73]. Neither company seems to have survived after 1866.

Advertisement for Harrap and Mason in 1861[74]

Harrop and Mason are not listed after then and in 1875 Perseverence Mill was the felt production site for Matheson and Tavernier[75]. Tavernier was a French inventor, who in 1874 was granted a patent for flat hardening wool fibres between two stone tables[76], and presumably, he went into business with Matheson to exploit the invention. It could not have been very successful as there are no further listings for the company.

Cornelius Turner is listed from 1861 to 1866 and he appears to have offered his company for sale to The Patent Woollen Cloth Company since they assessed his capacity and worth[77]. In 1866, Cornelius Turner was operating from Dennison Street[78] and by 1870, he was in partnership with J. M. Turner at Milgarth Mills, Dyer Street[79]. After this, there are no listings for him and John Wilkinson had taken over Airdale Mill.

Advertisement for Cornelius Turner from the Post Office Directory of the West Riding of Yorkshire part 2 1861

Amongst all the other companies that came and went within a year were: in 1863 Benjamin Waite of Temperence Mill, Staningly [80], in 1870 Rider and Mallett of 2 Basinghall Street[81], 1878 Charles Turner of 7 Lofthouse Terrace. In 1878, there was also Samuel Fillighan of Whitehouse Street, who was operating at the same address as John Wilkinson and so may have had some connection with that company[82]. Other transitory companies were: in 1881, William Roslington of Monk Bridge Mill, Whitehall Road[83], and in 1887, James Hudson and Co. of 76 Mabgate[84].

In 1900, Cockcroft and Marsden set up a felt business at 19 Ventnor Street[85] presumably to exploit Cockcroft's patents for speciality items. In 1894, he was granted a patent for making pouches and in 1897 for making felt bicycle handles[86], which was a growing market at the time. However, this venture lasted only until 1903, which is the last listing, albeit in the name of just Thomas Cockcroft.

After 1903 there were no felt manufacturers left in Leeds. The only legacy of the felt industry was the manufacturer of felting machines, William Bywater, who continued to manufacture there until 1990.

THE LEEDS FELT MACHINE MANUFACTURERS

TAYLOR, WORDSWORTH AND CO.

There was a close relationship between The Patent Woollen Cloth Company and Taylor Wordsworth and Co. of Hunslet Leeds, who built their hardening and milling machines. Thomas Lawson, manager of The Patent Woollen Cloth Company was still ordering hardeners from them and being given special viewings of a new milling machine in 1856[87]. Taylor Wordsworth must therefore have been the leading manufacturer of felt machines at the time, and no doubt were the manufacturers of the original equipment, specified in T. R. Williams' patent.

Taylor Wordsworth and Co. was the leading textile manufacturer of the eighteenth century particularly for flax processing. Joshua Wordsworth and Joseph Taylor established their business in 1812 at Midland Mill in Holbeck Leeds. Their main business was as manufacturers of woollen, worsted, flax, and tow machinery as well as patent axletrees but they also ran a brass and iron foundry in Water Lane. By the time they were involved in felt, the partners were quite elderly. Joshua Wordsworth died in 1846, aged 66, and shortly after Joseph Taylor died in 1848, aged 71, leaving the business to be managed by a Henry Walton Whitehead, a partner in the firm[88]. Felt making machines appear to have been of secondary interest to their flax business, since they never advertised them in any of the directories of the time. This laid the market open to William Bywater to become the leading supplier and innovator of felting machines.

WILLIAM BYWATER

William Bywater established his textile machine company some time before 1861, when at that time his advertising suggests that he had set up to produce machines for the felting industry, from premises in Sweet Street, Holbeck.

Initially he must have rented the property since, in 1868, he purchased it from the executors of the owner, William Sears, in 1868, and prospered until his death around 1885, when the business was conducted by his son William Gaines Bywater[89] until he died in 1930. William Bywater was buried in St John's church Roundhay[90].

SWEET STREET FOUNDRY, HOLBECK, LEEDS.

WM. BYWATER,
MANUFACTURER OF
WORSTED, WOOLLEN, FELT, SILK, HEMP, FLAX, TOW AND TWINE MACHINERY.
SELF-ACTING ENGINEERS' TOOLS, &c.
IRON AND BRASS FOUNDER.

Advertisement for William Bywater from the Post Office Directory of the West Riding of Yorkshire part 2 1861

Since they were situated in Holbeck, they must have been an alternative supplier of machines to The Patent Woollen Cloth Company, though they were closer to the Mitchell Brothers, who were the market leaders in Rossendale. It was as a result of this association that the nemesis of woollen felt making was devised. The Mitchell Brothers were the first company in Britain to explore needle-punching machines to produce felt in 1885, and it was the William Bywater Company that was the first to manufacture a needling machine in England in 1889, branding it the Windsor Loom[91]. From 1900 onwards, Bywater was the exclusive supplier of felting and needling machines to the industry and continued innovating in this area to maintain their market position. Their most significant contribution to the felt industry was the invention of the Bywater-Beanland flat hardener, which was exclusively for making pressed felt, and which subsequently became the workhorse of the industry. The company was also the leading British supplier of roller hardeners with a reputation for making machines that gave the best quality felt, unmatched by other continental suppliers. They had a strong relationship with both the MASCO combine and the Bury Felt Manufacturing Company and by working closely with them, the company was able to continually refine their roller hardeners, particularly the jigging mechanism. Later when the two companies merged to became Bury and Masco Industries, Bywater machines were still predominantly used, though the newly formed company also trialled machines from other manufacturers. For instance, they acquired a Casse roller hardener and compared its performance to a Bywater hardener. The Bywater machine consistently outperformed the Casse. Eventually the manufacture of needling machines became the predominate activity for William Bywater Limited and it was therefore taken over by P & C. Garnett Limited, who had an interest in their needle machine expertise; and the new company became known as Garnett-Bywater Limited. Around 1980, they abandoned manufacturing woollen felt making machinery all together, in preference to needling machines because the demand for felt machines became so low that it was no longer commercially viable to produce them.

3 ROSSENDALE AND OTHER FELTMAKERS

ROSSENDALE FELTMAKERS

Most authorities credit Edward Rostron with being the first to manufacture felt in the Rossendale valley in 1854[1], though at that time the directories were describing him as a woollen agent[2]. In 1865, his business was recorded as baizes, bockings and woollens working out of Myrtle Grove Print Works[3]. This fits neatly with the story that he bought pieces of plain felt carpet from Leeds and had them printed in Rossendale and sold them on. Because of the brighter colours that could be achieved by the Rossendale printers, Edward Rostron's business flourished and he started manufacturing carpet himself, thereby saving carriage costs[4]. However it is unlikely he could have built up sufficient business in 1854 to warrant investment in production machinery, because of The Patent Woollen Cloth Company's monopoly on felt carpets up to that year and he would have had difficulty in securing plain felt for printing. This was the year that the felt manufacturing patent expired and he would have only been able to secure an alternative supply of plain felt when the other new Leeds manufacturers, such as Carr & Butterworth, set up business prior to 1857. The first record of Edward Rostron being a felt carpet maker was in 1876, though he was surely selling, printing or making felt before this time. He was clearly successful, for in 1876, he was manufacturing at both Myrtle Grove and Lumb Mills and by 1879, he had added Tunstead Mills, to his production capacity and had a warehouse in Tipping Street Manchester[5]. In late January 1882 Edward Rostron died and Myrtle Grove Mill was shut until May of that year when his sons tried to continue the business, appointing Thomas Jackson as Managing Director[6]. However by 1886 the business failed and Myrtle Grove Mill lay idle until 1890 when it was acquired by Rowland Rawlinson who transferred his business there[7] from Lumb Mills.

Shortly after Edward Rostron commenced felt making at Myrtle Grove, James Barcroft began the manufacture of felt carpets at Todd Carr, having taken over the mill from John Taylor. He too was successful and built a new mill named Siss Clough next to Todd Carr[8], converting the latter into a print works[9]. He was still producing felt carpet in 1879[10] and on 9 July 1881, the great flood hit his mill, and in 1891, he was still listed as a printer operating out of Siss Clough[11]. Then in 1896, James Barcroft's business was taken over by the Mitchell Brothers[12], and later the mill became the headquarters of the Mitchell, Ashworth, Stansfield combine in 1904.

In the early years of 1857/8, after the Williams' patent had expired, the makers of felt making machinery approached the woollen cloth manufacturers, encouraging them to produce felt by purchasing their machines[13]. One felt maker, Ingham Taylor, manufacturing at Hollin Mill Scoutbottom was even taken over by a machine manufacturer around 1857/8[14]. Many entrepreneurs though, were to find that it was not so easy to secure a profitable business making felt, for it required the use of the correct blends of wool in the final products and selling in the most appropriate markets.

In 1865, Ingham Taylor was recorded as a baize, bocking, and woollen manufacturer[15] rather than a felt maker and it seems his original venture did not succeed because he was later in business with Haworth making felt carpet up to 1871. However, this too was not a success because the "nearly new felt carpet machinery" of Taylor and Haworth was being advertised for auction[16]. A tummer, two carding engines, and two felt hardeners were for sale that had been made by Taylor Wordsworth of Leeds, suggesting that it was this machinery manufacturer that had taken over Ingham Taylor. In addition, of interest, was the sale of a hardener made by S. S. Stott and Co., a manufacturer not readily associated with the felt industry. James Taylor next tried to manufacture felt carpet at Hollin Mill but he died in 1874 and his widow, Elizabeth, petitioned for liquidation on 19 September of that year. From 1875 to 1878, Ingham Taylor and Sons were back at Hollin Mill but this time as woollen printers to John Thomas Barcroft. He was the brother of James Barcroft of Siss Clough, who was making felt carpets, fine felts and skirting felts. Unfortunately, the business failed and J. T. Barcroft was petitioning for liquidation with liabilities of £8,339/6s/3d against assets of £2649/11s[17].

Some of the companies, such as Captain G. W. Law Schofield manufacturing at Baltic Mill, Waterfoot, and John Tattersall at Shawclough Mill in 1857, failed because they concentrated on the lower end of the market by trying to convert wool waste and shoddy into usable felt[18]. In 1876, Henry Rothwell tried to manufacture felt, again at Baltic and at Bridge End Mill, some sixteen years after G. W. Law Schofield, but unfortunately he too failed after only two years[19]. Ironically it was his nephew, J. W. Rothwell, who later went on to found the slipper industry, which revitalised the felt industry by creating a massive new market for felt at a time when the carpet industry was in decline[20]. Although Henry Rothwell made grey felts from hemp, jute and cotton, he still had interests in a wide scope of markets as can be seen from the list of his products submitted for auction after his failure. The fact that he had so much stock of carpets, saddle rugs and costume felts indicates that his problem was in marketing and that he could not sell his products. Soon after this it appears that all the machinery in Baltic Mill was put up for auction and interestingly, it included seven carding engines, a pair of spinning mules, eight hundred and fifty two spindles of worsted spinning machines and twenty-two looms. Therefore, it is difficult to assess the size of Rothwell's felt operation. The most reliable way to determine Rothwell's felt capacity is therefore through the number of felt hardeners used rather than the carding capacity and by this measure Rothwell's must have been a sizeable operation for he had ten tummers, three carding engines, five hardeners, and four pairs of stocks[21]. Rothwell was also manufacturing felt exclusively at Bridge End Mill and his equipment there was auctioned the day after the auction at Baltic Mill. Lawrence Ormerod followed Rothwell making felt at Baltic Mill, trading as Ormerod and Co. and faired little better. He must have rented the mill because, when his creditors met a year later in 1879, he had liabilities of £1,400 and assets of £500[22] so his machinery and equipment were auctioned off "under distraint for rent"[23]. After this Baltic Mill remained empty until 1886[24].

Some time after 1868, Jackson and Whittaker set up a small operation in Lumb Mill to produce felt carpets, rugs, and table cloths; but they too, like many others, failed in 1871 and their machinery was sold by auction[25]. After a disastrous fire in 1872[26], the mill was re-worked as a felt mill by John and Thomas Barcroft, James Barcroft's brothers, with medium sized capacity[27]. It was left to the Mitchell Brothers to utilise the mill successfully after 1890. In 1875 William and James Rothwell started felt manufacture at Lumb Holes Mill with a medium sized felt production capacity of four hardeners and lasted a little longer than most of their contemporaries, though they too failed in 1880 because they could not pay their rent[28].

In 1876 Joseph Stansfield, a wool stapler, was making felt at Higher Hollin Bank Mill[29] with ninety employees, though he probably started felt production in 1873[30]. In 1881, he was in court defending an action brought by Joshua Townsend, Jane Anne Townsend and Henry Frederick Ashworth to recover "a certain mill " because he had defaulted on his contract[31]. He was struck a further blow by a disastrous fire that was the greatest seen in Rossendale and the estimated damage of between £8000 and £9000 was not covered by insurance[32]. He never recovered from this and went out of business.

Other felt makers were simply too small and out of the mainstream to be successful, like John Wadsworth, a Haslingdon mill manager, who was making felt at Plunge Mill, Edenfield, with his partner Joshua Cunliffe, a book-keeper from Helmshore. The company traded as John Wadsworth and Co. and lasted only a year before going into liquidation[33], their equipment going up for auction on 2 December 1870[34]. The equipment included one willow, one devil, one flax trimmer, one woollen trimmer, two carders, two hardeners, three stocks, one patent tentering/drying machine by Whiteley, one washing betty and one squeezer.

MITCHELL BROTHERS

The Mitchell brothers were the most prominent of all the Rossendale felt makers, eventually coming to dominate the felt industry through the creation of the Mitchell, Ashworth, Stansfield combine. The first record of Mitchell Brothers was as woollen manufacturers and merchants in Russell Street in Leeds 1853 as a late entry in the local directory[35]. They were again described as woollen Manufacturers[36] in 1856, and 1857. In 1853 the eldest brother, William, was 15 years old[37] and the next eldest, Thomas, who was only 14 years old, and though this sounds young to be in business, it was reported that they started in business with their father in 1856[38]. There is another intriguing entry in the Leeds Directory of 1854 for a Nathan Mitchell, who was also described as a Woollen Manufacturer[39]. After this time, there are no more entries for any Mitchell in Leeds. Then in 1865 there is an entry in the local directory for Lancashire for John Mitchell and Sons, described as a manufacturer of baizes, bockings, woollens, and spinners, producing out of Carr Lane Mill Stacksteads[40]. John Mitchell was the father of the Mitchell brothers and there is no doubt he provided the capital for the brothers to establish themselves. They must already have been making felt there because in 1861 William Mitchell had a patent granted for alterations to a carding engine and hardener to produce a full width carpet[41]. In 1868, John Mitchell and Sons were making felt carpet in Waterbarn Mill[42]. The turning point for the Mitchell Brothers, as far as felt making was concerned, came when their father, representing the company John Mitchell and Sons bought Albert Works at Whitewell Bottom, Rossendale. In 1860, the mill was erected at a cost of £10,000 by the Rossendale Printing and Dyeing Company[43], but by 1865, they were offering it for rent[44], and in 1866, the company decided to wind up its affairs and put the mill up for auction. John Mitchell put in the winning bid of £3,810, which was a bargain when compared to the original building cost[45]. From 1868 onwards, the company manufactured felt carpet and woollen cloth[46] and the company was known as Mitchell and Sons. They were also printing carpets and woollen cloths as they had their own print works in 1870[47]. By 1876, the three brothers William, Thomas, and Robert were in charge of the business and on 17 April, they were leasing land from William Sutcliffe, James Hargreaves, and William Knowles for expanding the mill and installing filter tanks[48]. The land also enclosed a small mill that drew its water for turning its water wheels from a lodge (reservoir), which ran alongside the river Whitewell. This was known as the "Old Mill" and was still in use in 1882, but was demolished in 1893 to make way for the new two-storey wool warehouse[49].

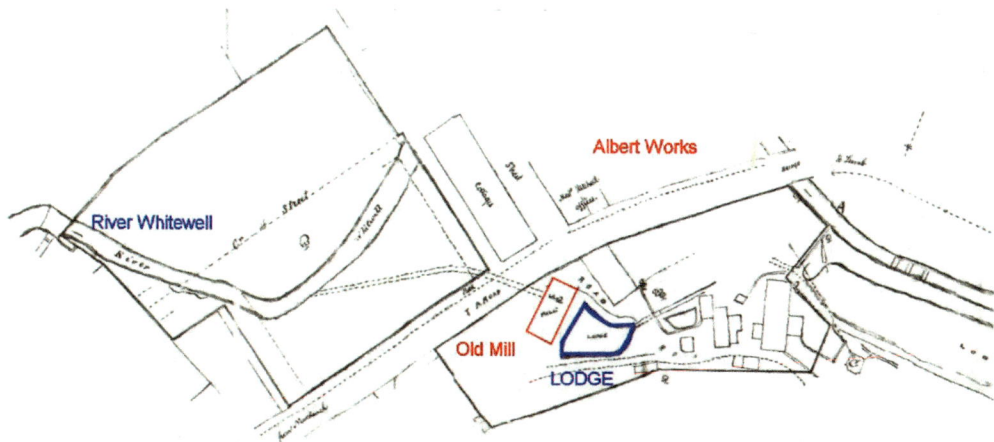

The Old Mill from an agreement dated 1876 between Mitchell Brothers, John Sutcliffe and others

It was not until 1876 that the company became known as Mitchell Brothers and though described as felt carpet manufacturers they were still making baizes and bockings in 1879[50] and they still acquired eight looms and a warp sizing machine at the auction at Baltic Mill following Henry Rothwell's failure[51]. At this time, they also took the opportunity of buying four of the five hardeners for sale as well as six tummers, two carding engines and all the dyestuffs.

The 1880s saw the company continue its expansion, and like the true entrepreneurs that they were, the brothers branched out into other new ventures and manufacturing opportunities at a time when other industries such as cotton were in recession. In 1882, they were quick to capitalise on the rise of the slipper industry, and employed John William Rothwell, the initiator of commercial slipper making, to set up a slipper works at Baltic Mill[52]. He was an inventive and energetic manager and Mitchell Brothers invested heavily in new machinery for the venture on his behalf, eventually employing one hundred people[53]. However, for some reason Mitchell Brothers sold the business in 1890 to James Hill who carried on the business in his own mill at Union Works. At the time of the sale, there were forty-nine males and forty-three females employed making slippers [54]. It may well be that the slipper trade had expanded so much by then, that the Mitchell Brothers were losing more felt sales than they could gain by selling their slippers. The other slipper manufacturers were probably reluctant to buy supplies from a competitor. By 1893, there were ten slipper factories in Rossendale, producing seventy thousand pairs a week and employing one thousand three hundred workers[55], which equates to a considerable quantity of felt. When Mitchells closed their slipper works, they were planning to install tapestry looms in 1889[56]. In 1890, they were enlarging their works to become the largest in Rossendale[57]. As part of their expansion in 1893, they built a new two-storey warehouse on the site of the Old Mill opposite Albert Works and linked the two sets of buildings with a covered walkway bridge over the Burnley Road. For this they had to pay the corporation two shillings and six pence (12.5p) each year for the privilege[58].

As astute businessmen, they were aware of the benefits of new technology and were quick to exploit it. In 1885, they became involved in needle punching, which originated in America as a mechanical method of making felt. The first needle-felting patent was by Hyman Welcome Whipple in 1875 but the Mitchell Brothers seem to have invested in a later American invention by James Broadhead who patented his machine in the United Kingdom in 1885.

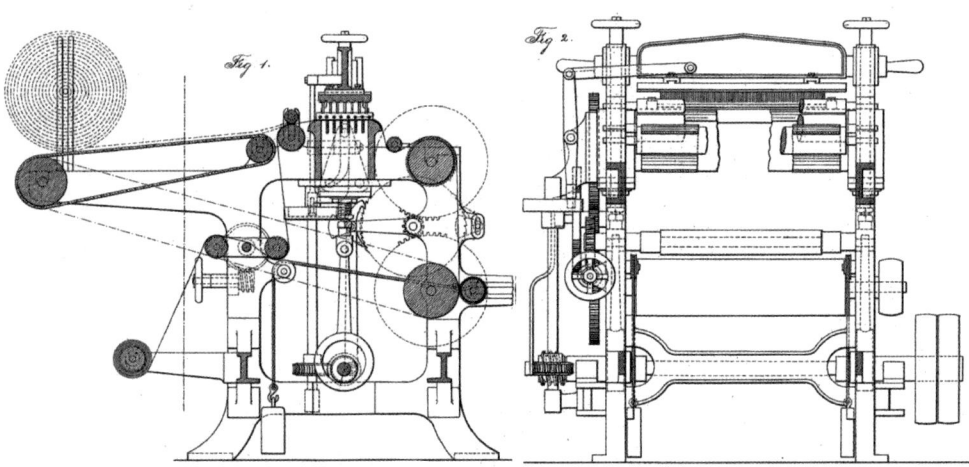

James Broadhead's patent needle loom side and front views

There must have been more than one patent operating in Britain at that time because T. F. Firth at Heckmondwike was also engaged in needle-punching horse clothing. An agreement existed between Mitchell Brothers and Firth in 1885 whereby James Broadhead had set up needle looms for Firth's on Mitchell's behalf, for a fee based on the throughput of Firth's needle loom. However, another patent was involved since Firth's were paying a Mr. Lindsay a royalty on top of a cash payment of £550 for a needling process. Discrepancies seem to have occurred during the discharge of the Mitchell Brothers' agreement since a survey of Firth's daybooks was undertaken on behalf of Colonel Mitchell in 29 June 1892 to resolve the issue[59]. From this correspondence, it is clear that needle punching was used as an alternative to hardening since the resultant felts were milled directly after needling. The Mitchell Brothers were trying to make the needling process replace wool felting, but never quite managed it[60], though they succeeded in "felting" coarse hair or natural fibres like jute and hemp. The experiences gained at this time paved the way for the later evolution of the company when it became involved in the synthetic needle-felt industry. Non-woven production using needle punching became firmly established in the 1950s, and grew to such an extent that a subsidiary company was eventually formed in 1976 called Webron Limited making felts from one hundred percent synthetic fibres.

In the late 1800s, the Mitchell brothers' company continued expanding and they bought Fountain Mill from Alice Ann Rushton, Robert Worswick, and his wife Mary on 1 November 1884 with a copyhold leasehold at a rent of £16 per year for 999 years starting from 4 October 1853. This gave the company valuable space to expand in a position in close proximity to their Albert Works[61]. Then on 29 March 1884, they acquired the Isle of Man Mill on lease from Richard Heyworth and Matthew Hartley including the water rights on a 2000-year lease at an annual rent of £21. Then on 16 April 1889, they bought Whams Farm from Richard Fort on copyhold, and also bought Lower Lumb from George Watkinson in 1896. To complete the expansion they also took Higher Lumb from Alice Barlow and others 31 December 1900 on a 999-year lease at a rent of £14-19s-3d, though it is not clear what the business reason for this was[62]. Lower Lumb was later known as Whitewell Vale Mill and Lumb Mill as Higher Lumb, both mills being separated by just a few hundred yards.

The 1890s, however, was a time of increasing competition and falling quality standards, with increasing inroads being made by woven carpets into the felt market. With this declining demand for felt carpets, the Mitchell brothers reacted with characteristic flair. First, they branded their carpets as "Velveen" and then established a newly patented carpet, "Rockminster", as a superior hygienic product to prevent "the accumulations of dust, too often active agents in the propagation of disease"[63]. They were also active in marketing, not only using their national warehouses and sales offices in London, Leeds, Manchester, and Glasgow but also through distributors in America[64]. Then in the early 1890s when the pressure became too acute they invested in tapestry looms themselves to maintain their markets[65]. However, though they continued to expand, they never challenged the larger woven carpet manufacturers such as James Templeton and Co., or John Crossley and Sons.

Mitchell's letterhead before the formation of The Mitchells Ashworth and Stansfield Combine

On 13 May 1893, the company was registered as a limited company called Mitchell Brothers of Waterfoot Limited, with a capital of £150,000 in £10 shares, and with the remit of carrying on the business of manufacturers, printers and dyers of woollen and other cloths[66]. In addition, from this time on they prospered with an expansion that was truly exceptional so that by 1895 their production of felt and baizes was twenty-five percent more than all of the feltmakers together had produced in the Rossendale Valley in 1867. This must have given them the capital to continue their expansion by a series of company takeovers. After they bought Lower Lumb Mill, known as Whitewell Vale, from George Watkinson in 1896, they went on to acquire the mills of Siss Clough and Todd Carr from James Barcroft on 27 October 1897. Siss Clough was freehold and Todd Carr was copyhold leasehold for a 999-year term running from 3 October 1853 at yearly rent of £38/12s/6d. The brothers' acquisitiveness extended beyond the Rossendale Valley for in 1896 they also took over the Hodgetts Felt Company of Lye near Stourbridge Worcester, and transferred the production to Lumb Mill[67]. Hodgetts manufactured polishing felts after a long history of making felt hats. Therefore, the equipment and markets must have been complementary to the Mitchell Brothers' product and machinery range. By 1895, Mitchell Brothers were employing eight hundred people and producing 1,248,000 yards of felt and baizes[68].

At the turn of the century the company dominated, not only the Rossendale felt industry, but also the United Kingdom with seventy to eighty percent of the country's felt being made by them[69]. However, rather than continue taking over the other companies they became involved in a grand alliance of all the major felt manufacturers and felt merchants of Britain, in particular Richard Ashworth and William Stansfield. Then on 14 September 1904, they completed their agreements and the new felt combine: Mitchells, Ashworth, Stansfield and Company Limited (MASCO) was formed.

The Mitchell brothers had other business interests besides felt. They owned an engineering company, and held other stocks and shares in such companies as "Stockport Works" and "Liverpool & Accrington Property". They also invested in hat manufacture, with William Mitchell being just as prolific in patenting hat-manufacturing techniques as he was in felt making[70]. These other interests were specifically excluded from the MASCO agreements[71].

RICHARD ASHWORTH

Richard Ashworth was born in 1848 and started his career at nine years old, when he worked for the railway as an office boy. He then worked at Baltic Mill as a junior clerk some time after 1857, eventually being promoted to Chief Clerk[72]. At this time the mill was occupied by Captain G. Law Schofield who was manufacturing felt there and no doubt, Richard Ashworth learnt the felt trade there. In 1869, he started his own felt business at Shawclough Mill with twenty employees, probably just after Captain Law Schofield's business had failed. It is said he was financed by his mother Deborah Ashworth who ran a local grocery business and was a well-known local celebrity. Like many other Rossendale felt makers, it was not an easy time for him since he was beset by various disasters at his mill. In November 1874 the embankment of the mill lodge gave way and flooded the lower floor of the mill causing damage to his wool store valued at around £100[73]. In February 1880, the mill was advertised for rent, despite Richard Ashworth still manufacturing felt there[74]. Then in July 1881, before he could move, the mill was severely struck by the Great Rossendale Storm and by the flood that followed. These events completely wrecked the mill and washed away all the machinery and material, causing damage amounting to £4000. Despite this major setback, he managed to restart his business by leasing Bridge End Mill, which was empty after the failure of Henry Rothwell in 1878. By 1895, Richard Ashworth had prospered and grown to employ two hundred people and he was ready to expand again[75]. This time he bought Longholme Mill from William Sutcliffe corn millers, the deal being completed on 4 February 1896.

Richard Ashworth's identity within MASCO

Richard Ashworth, like the Mitchell brothers, was far sighted and struck a deal with the Lancashire and Yorkshire Railway to build sidings by the side of Longholme Mill on land jointly owned by them. This gave him a significant transport advantage in receiving raw materials and coal to fuel the steam engines and the ability to ship his finished felt goods out. Longholme mill also had the advantage of having electric lighting driven by engines, turbines and dynamos[76]. Like the Mitchell brothers, Richard Ashworth had a keen sense of marketing and had a merchanting arm at 4 Warwick Street, London under the name A. V. Humphries. He must have been an exceptional businessman for on 24 December 1900 he re-leased Bridge End Mill and leased Carr Mill from Emily Ann Worrall, Elizabeth Ann Ashworth, and Letitia Jane Bridge[77]. In 1904 he joined the Mitchell Brothers, and William Stansfied in forming Mitchells, Ashworth, Stansfield & Company Limited. In 1905[78], the leases for Bridge End and Carr Mills were re-assigned by Letitia Jane Bridge to the new company, which had its registered office at Siss Clough works.

STANSFIELDS

There were three Stansfields associated with the manufacture of felt, Joseph, William, and John, all from the same family. Joseph Stansfield was first reported as making felt carpets in 1873[79], and in 1876 he was described as a felt carpet maker as well as carrying on a business as a woollen stapler in Hollin Bank Mill, Bridgeclough, and Shawclough Houses[80]. In 1879, he was operating out of Hollin Bank Mill only, still as a medium sized felt manufacturer with a capacity of eight tummers and four carding engines[81]. By mid 1881, his business seems to have been in trouble for he was in court for "non fulfillment of covenant" of a certain mill, the possession of which was being sought by Henry Frederick Ashworth, Joshua Townsend, and Jane Ann Townsend[82]. More trouble was in store for him later that year because on 15 December 1881, his mill at Hollin Bank Mill burnt down in the greatest fire seen in Rossendale, with damage estimated at between £8000 and £9000. Since he was not insured, he lost his business leaving his ninety workers unemployed[83]. This must also have affected his brother William Stansfield who was working for him at the time.

William Stansfield started his career in the woollen trade working for his brother Joseph Stansfield and worked himself up to Manager[84] until the mill burnt down in 1881. In 1881, he began his first business venture into felt manufacture through a partnership with Henry Coupe at Lumb Holes Mill after the failure of W. and J. Rothwell. It is most likely he provided the felt making expertise learned from managing his brother's felt production, whilst Henry Coupe probably provided the capital. His stay at Lumb Holes was fraught with all sorts of disasters that might have deterred a lesser businessman. First, the foundations of the mill were washed away in the Great Flood in Rossendale in 1884[85], and the windows smashed by large hailstones. Then in 1891, the partnership with Henry Coupe was dissolved and William Stansfield continued the business at Lumb Holes. In 1893, a fire broke out in the coal shed and destroyed a quantity of woollen felt causing damage of £200[86]. This forced him to rent Baltic Mill from George William Law Schofield and Annie Louise Law Schofield on 26 August 1893, so that he could continue his production while Lumb Holes Mill was re-built. At that time, Baltic Mill covered an area of seven thousand one hundred and sixty square yards including sheds, dyehouse, stable, outbuildings and a lodge. He held the mill under copyhold leasehold for one shilling for a term of 999 years from 1 July 1893, at a yearly rent of £80, compared to the rent at Lumb Holes of £180. From this time until 1904, he ran both mills. He, like the other successful felt makers, was far sighted in his approach to business adopting innovations that had practical benefit. He was one of the first of three mill owners to install electric lighting in the mill, and even had his house lit by electricity supplied by an overhead cable from the mill to his home. In 1904, he was instrumental in forming the famous Mitchells, Ashworth, Stansfield Combine.

In 1889, William Stansfield's nephew, John Stansfield also took up felt manufacture, renting Hardsough Mill near Haslingdon from Jordon Rostron. He must have only been in business for a short while because it was eventually absorbed by his uncle's company when the mill was sold to Mitchells, Ashworth, Stansfield and Co. Limited, some time after the combine's formation in 1904.

ROWLAND RAWLINSON

It is said that Rowland Rawlinson came to Rossendale from Cumbria with all his equipment on the back of a cart and set up his business dyeing woollen fabrics at a mill on the Whitewell river. At that time, the river was stocked with fish and he was forced to install dye pits to prevent pollution of the river, but had insufficient funds to do this and also keep the mill running. After discussing the position with his workers, they agreed to forego some of their wages to allow him to build the necessary pits. Thereafter he continued to prosper and he never forgot this sacrifice by his workers. He made sure all these early employees were well looked after by him and most of them were promoted to key positions as he expanded[87].

He must have been manufacturing and dyeing woollen cloth sometime before 1878 for he was at the two auctions of Henry Rothwell's machinery buying: a tumming engine, mule bobbins, eight new 15s and 17s reeds, two hundred and ninety pounds weight of woollen warps, loom parts, eight bags of fullers earth and a soaping machine[88]. Compared to the other manufacturers present at the auction Rowland Rawlinson's purchases were very modest and his finances at this stage may have been still limited, though ten years later he had considerable capital with which to expand his business. Around 1888, he was operating from Lumb Mill after the failure of John and Thomas Barcroft in 1887, and at the same time, he had purchased Myrtle Grove Mill for £3,035 when it was put up for auction on the closure of Edward Rostron's felt works. Working from Lumb Mill must have been a temporary situation since he was building a new woollen mill, and printing department and installing one of the most powerful steam engine in the valley, a project that took a year to complete[89]. Whilst at Lumb he faced another disaster, this time from a fire that had broken out in the mill. Once more, he was rescued by his workers who put out the fire using hand buckets[90]. In 1890, the new mill was completed and was the venue for a grand gathering of the Conservative Party, known as the Great Conservative Demonstration, which was attended by the then Prime Minister Lord Salisbury. This must have been the pinnacle of Rowland Rawlinson's career. But just twelve years later he was hit by another fire in 1902 which started in the devilling room and which was far more serious than anything he had experienced, spreading to one half of his mill. All the machines in the area were completely destroyed along with the roof, causing a total of £5000 of damage, more than the mill had cost him in the first place[91]. Nevertheless, he recovered and by 1911, he had expanded again[92].

It is believed that Rowland Rawlinson was friendly with Richard Ashworth and he agreed not to make felt that would compete in Richard Ashworth's markets[93]. However, he was described as making felt in 1891[94] and Richard Ashworth himself cited his friend as being a felt maker then, in an article dated 1921 recalling the growth of the felt industry[95]. It could well be true that such an agreement existed because, in the Bywater daybooks, Roland Rawlinson was only using needle looms and flat hardeners and he was only ordering spare parts for these machines and none for roller hardeners. He therefore did not have a significant capacity for thin felts and was most likely making thicker, coarser felts for insulation and packaging[96]. What is certain is that the main focus of his manufacture was weaving, and his company's business was always described as being a manufacturer of baizes, bockings and woollens. At least until 1924, when the company was producing woollen cloths that went to Paraguay and Uruguay for use as serapes, which were blankets used by the South Americans. They also made a lighter woollen cloth for military and naval officers coat lining, and a khaki woollen cloth. At that time, the company's felt capacity was: two Bywater flat hardeners, four roller hardeners, and six pusher stocks, which made them a medium-sized felt producer[97]. On Rowland Rawlinson's death his sons Herman, Neville, Ernald, and Irwin successfully ran the business until 14 August 1954 when Ernald sold the business to Bury and Masco Industries Limited.

THE FORMATION OF THE MASCO COMBINE

It is intriguing to speculate why in 1904 that three successful felt making companies should combine to form a single company. Reports from companies of the time indicate increasing competition and erosion of prices, but the scale of the amalgamation suggests a much wider strategy. It was not just the market leaders, Mitchells, Ashworth, and Stansfield who were involved in the merger, but also many of the other felt companies outside the Rossendale Valley. These included felt merchanting companies as well as those with manufacturing capability. At the precise time of the merger there were only two other woollen felt manufacturers left: R. R. Whitehead and Brothers, and E. V. Naish, both specialists in piano felts and with little capacity for making other types of felt that could challenge the new combine. The interest of the combine was restricted to woollen pressed felt since there was no attempt to include the hair felt manufacturers such as Rowland Rawlinson, or the asphalt felt makers such as F. McNeill. Strategically this appears as an attempt to monopolise the woollen pressed felt industry in Britain, and as such would have been a brilliant concept. If this were the purpose of the amalgamation, the reality turned out to be quite different.

The companies involved in the merger were: Mitchell brothers, Richard Ashworth, William Stansfield, The Patent Woollen Felt Company, Birtill and Blaikie, Featherweight Pad Company, The Boulinikon Felt Company, The Hardsough Manufacturing Company, and Agar Limited. Although there were elements of opportunism in this merger, in general the formation of the combine was a singularly well planned operation which must have involved considerable time, negotiation, and cost to set up. The legal agreement to amalgamate was dated 18 August 1904[98] and separate agreements that formed the combine indicate that the main driving force behind the project was the Mitchell brothers. In each of the agreements, not only was their limited company named as one of the parties to the agreement, but also each brother was also individually named as a party. The Mitchells certainly stood to gain the most as they were able to convert their stockholding in Mitchell Brothers Limited into a debenture stock in the new company valued at £100,000 and their company was the only one to receive a goodwill payment of £25,000 in respect of twenty-two international patents attributed to the Mitchell brothers[99]. As part of this agreement, the new company was committed to purchasing the Hardsough Manufacturing Company from Richard Ashworth and William Stansfield, who had purchased it for £9,316, a short while before the agreement, probably in anticipation of the formation of the merger. The Hardsough Manufacturing Company was a felt making business carried on by John and Watson Stansfield and the Rostron brothers James and John[100].

At this time, The Patent Woollen Cloth Company was in receivership, which presented an opportunity for the Combine to increase felt making capacity at low cost, widen market penetration, and ensure that there would be no further competition from this source. Consequently, once the head of agreement was signed Thomas Mitchell, Richard Ashworth and William Stansfield purchased The Patent Woollen Cloth Company from the receiver, G. Walter Knox, on their own account for the sum of £20,644/18s/11d in an agreement dated 24 September 1904[101]. Then, the newly formed combine of Mitchells, Ashworth, Stansfield and Company Limited purchased The Patent Woollen Cloth Company from them, for the same price that they paid the receiver[102]. Significantly, the agreement makes special mention of the "Iron Felt" patent licensed by The Patent Woollen Cloth Company from P. Koch. Iron Felt was an impregnated felt for use under rails and bedplates of railways.

Three days after the takeover of The Patent Woollen Cloth Company, on 27 September 1904, they continued their acquisitions by purchasing the Boulinikon Felt Company Limited, which was based in Scotland. The name "Boulinikon" referred to a floor covering made at the time from a waste fibre mix bonded together to make a resilient material similar to linoleum[103]. This is consistent with their interest in in the Iron Felt patent. The purchase was by Thomas Mitchell, Richard Ashworth, and William Stansfield from C. Davidson and Sons Limited, the paper makers, Thomas Griffith, and John Mackie. They arranged to pay in instalments until 31 December 1905, after an initial down payment of £400. They then sold the Boulinikon Felt Company to the newly merged company, Mitchells, Ashworth, Stansfield and Company at its formation on 28 October 1904. The total final purchase price for the Boulinikon Felt Company was £19370/3s/0d for all the trademarks, contracts, patent licenses, other assets, and property[104].

The formation of the new company, Mitchells, Ashworth, Stansfield and Company Limited, in 1904 must have been a momentous time for on that day eight contracts were signed in the presence of no fewer than ten people. Three of the contracts were for the assimilation of the three companies: The Patent Woollen Cloth Company, The Hardsough Felt Manufacturing Company, and the Boulinikon Felt Company, into the new company. Two agreements were for the merging of William Henry Agar's business and William Veitch Blaikie's business into the new company, and the remainder between each of Mitchell Brothers Waterfoot Limited, Richard Ashworth, William Stansfield and the new company.

William Agar was a merchant of six Marsden Square in Manchester carrying on business under the name "Rigby, Agar and Co.". The new company undertook to discharge Agar's company liabilities of £12,075/16s/8d and pay a further £23,138/3s for the business, of which £4000 was for goodwill. This payment consisted of £13,138/3s in cash paid in instalments, 5000 x £1 cumulative preference shares and 5000 x £1 ordinary shares. William Agar also became one of the new company's directors[105]. William Blaikie had a merchanting business called "Birtill and Blaikie" in Manchester, and a manufacturing business making shoulder pads and general padding under the name: "The Featherweight Clothing Pad Company". The agreement undertook to discharge William Blaikie's liabilities of £3,247/17s/2d and pay a further £13,608/11s/9d made up of cash, 5000 x £1 cumulative preference shares and 5000 x £1 ordinary shares. For this company the goodwill was considered to be £5000, which was included in the purchase price[106]. William Blaikie also became a director in the new company.

The remaining agreements for Richard Ashworth and William Stansfield were quite straightforward with payments in cash and shares going to each individual. However, the agreement with Mitchell Brothers Waterfoot Limited is complicated by virtue of the nature of the ownership of this company by the brothers. In the head of agreement, the parties all agreed to an evaluation of their businesses by an independent valuer: Lomax Sons and Mills, and Longrigg and Travis, and the new company apportioned according to the relative worth of each party.

At the time of the merger, William Stansfield had liabilities of £1539/13s/5d and the residue of the evaluated consideration for sale was £54,117. For this he was allotted 27,058 x £1 cumulative preference shares, 27,059 x £1 ordinary shares, and no payments for goodwill. The assets that William Stansfield assigned to the new company was Baltic Mill, its yards, sheds, dye house, dryhouse, stables, offices, outbuildings, and most particularly the water lodge; all occupying 7,160 square yards. He also transferred the lease of the site, which was held in copy leasehold from George William Law Schofield and Annie Louise Law Schofield. Also included in the agreement was the tenancy of the mill known as "Lumb Holes Felt Works" which was rented at £180 per year[107]. Even with the inclusion of three other small plots of land, William Stansfield was the lesser stockholder of the new company.

Richard Ashworth fared much better. He had liabilities of £11,832/10s/3d, but the residue for consideration for sale was £173,363, almost three times the size of William Stansfield. For this Richard Ashworth received 86,682 x £1 cumulative preference shares and 86,681 x £1 ordinary shares. As part of this agreement he transferred the rights and ownership of the three mills he currently occupied namely: Longholme Mill, Bridge End Mill, and Carr Mill. Included in this were outbuildings, stables, sheds reservoirs, watercourses, gas and water pipes, as well as engines, boilers, turbines and significantly electric dynamos, accumulators, wires, globes, and lampshades in and about the mill; indicating that by this time the mill had electrical power. Richard Ashworth also co-owned the railway siding alongside Longholme Mill with the Lancashire and Yorkshire Railway Company, the rights of which he assigned to the new company. Also signed over to the new company were the merchanting operations run by Richard Ashworth, trading under the names of "A. V. Humphries" and "Richard Ashworth", though he received no goodwill payments for the operation or trademarks. Like William Stansfield, he too included other small parcels of land, most having water rights that he owned, in order to maximise his share in the new company. As a consequence of including all these assets, Richard Ashworth became the second largest shareholder in the company[108].

Table showing the distribution of shares and the value of the new company

Masco Stockholders 1904						
Company	Debentures	Cumulative Preference Shares £1	Ordinary Shares £1	Liabilities £	Gross Value £	Net Value £
William Agar		5000	5000	£12,075	£35,213	£23,138
William Blaikie		5000	5000	£3,247	£16,855	£13,608
William Stansfield		27058	27059	£1,539	£55,656	£54,117
Richard Ashworth		86682	86681	£11,832	£185,195	£173,363
Mitchell Brothers	£81,800	113783	113783	48,470	£376,036	£327,566
Boulinikon						£19,369
Hardsough						£9,316
Patent Woollen Cloth						£30,740

MASCO Total Worth   **£651,217**

The agreement for the Mitchell Brothers was slightly more complicated because they were dealing collectively through their limited company in which they had guaranteed debenture stock, and had assigned the rights to various of their patents. As with the others, their liabilities of £48,470/19s/2d were first taken on by the new company and the residue of the consideration of £327,566 accounted for by a cash payment of £100,000 and allocation of shares. They received 113,783 x £1 cumulative preference shares and 113,783 x £1 ordinary shares. The debenture shares were handled separately, the new company made available £200,000 for public subscription of which £100,000 were available to the Mitchell brothers' company. This allowed them to convert their £81,800 debentures into new debentures in the new company before the closing date. Also included in this consideration was the goodwill of £25,000 for the patent rights of the Mitchells' company. The most important aspect of the agreement was the sheer scale of the mills and property that the Mitchell Brothers brought to the new company: Isle of Man Mill, Higher Lumb, Whitewell Vale, Albert Works, Fountain Mill, Siss Clough Mill, and Todd Carr Mill. Adding these to Richard Ashworth's and William Stansfield's mills meant that the new company owned almost every woollen mill in the Rossendale Valley connected to the Rivers Whitewell and Irwell. The Mitchell brothers added other areas of land, including Whams Farm to maximise their interests, making them the largest and controlling stockholder in the new company. On completion of the agreement the company Mitchell Brothers of Waterfoot Limited was to be wound up, but the Mitchell Brothers continued to trade under their own name and even absorbed all the medals and intellectual property of The Patent Woollen Cloth Company.

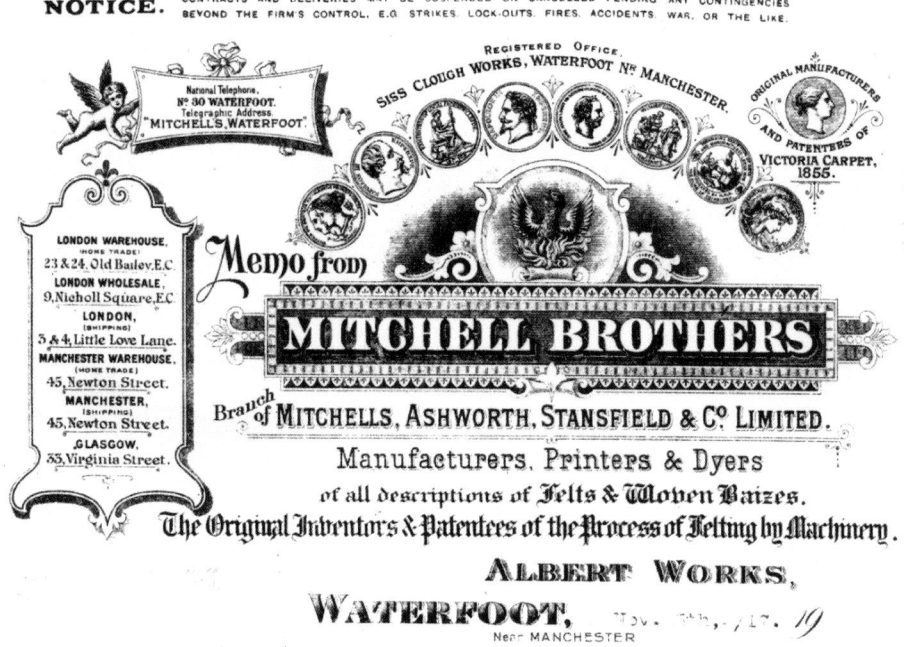

Mitchell Brothers letterhead after the formation of the combine displaying the intellectual property of The Patent Woollen Cloth Company

The most surprising effect of this extensive amalgamation is that each of the manufacturers continued to operate independently with their own individual identities, management, product ranges, and accounting practices. Furthermore, if the plan was to monopolise the felt industry then it fell apart in a seemingly innocuous manner. Hearsay evidence suggests that certain individuals were aggrieved at their treatment as a result of the amalgamation and broke away to form a new felt making company in Bury, Lancashire, which was a most unlikely place to start such a venture

THE BURY FELT INDUSTRY

The breakaway company became known as the Bury Felt Manufacturing Company Limited. It was formed in 1904 by L. H. Clegg, who became the Managing Director, James Byrom JP. the Chairman, and James Preston a Director[109], supported by a consortium of Bury businessmen, including J. Hill, the Mayor of Bury, a builder called J. Turner, and a number of skilled felt makers from Rossendale.

They produced their felt in Hudcar Mill, which was an old historic woollen mill built in 1825, which was once owned by the textile philanthropist William Greg of Quarrybank, Styal. This new company prospered and continued to expand at the expense of the MASCO combine and became a sizeable operation by 1917. By 1928, the company was in difficulty and was rescued by W. O. Street, an exceptional accountant, who turned the company around by engaging in a programme of expansion, acquiring two new mills nearby, one at Bright Street, which was the old Chesham Hat Works, and Springfield Mill next to it. In 1948, it became a public company[110].

As the felt market started to decline in the 1950s, they tried to diversify into other industries, purchasing an engineering company (Lawton Successors), a needle felt company (Coventry Felt in 1953) and establishing a tufted carpet manufacturing plant trademarked Holmbury. In the meantime, MASCO was contracting with the closure of Siss Clough Mill, Bridge End Mill and Albert works in 1952, and Higher Lumb was dismantled piecemeal from 1960 onwards. By 1962, the company rivalled MASCO in size and influence though both companies struggled with the long-term decline in their core markets. Therefore, after over half a century of rivalry, the two companies merged on 25 May 1962 to form Bury and Masco Industries Limited. However, this did not stem the decline and the mill closures continued with Longholme Mill closing in 1973.

When Longholme mill closed, any useful production machinery was moved to Bury along with some of the Rossendale staff. At this point all the Rossendale felt mills with the exception of Baltic Mill had closed down and this mill only survived because it specialised in the production of coarse grey felts for packaging and military uses. This was remarkable since it had the most antiquated manufacturing equipment of all the mills and was the smallest part of the once mighty MASCO combine.

COOPER AND CO[111]

Cooper and Co was a specialist felt maker that developed its own unique collection of thick dense felts as well as techniques for fabricating them into a wide range of products. Its origins were in supplying felt handle bar grips and pedal blocks to the growing bicycle industry in Birmingham. Its fabrication techniques were ideal for making polishing felts for the jewellery industry and this led to its transition into supplying polishing products to the motor, engineering, and metal trades. Because of this, the company became a specialist in supplying all polishing products, which subsequently involved diversifying into other non-felt products such as the manufacture of calico polishing mops and buffs. Even though the company's product profile changed as a result, it always maintained its unique felt production.

Cooper and Company was first registered as a Limited Company on 31 January 1898, with its first directors meeting held on 14 March 1898 in the presence of Josiah Cooper, F. Darling (Secretary Pro Tem), Francis George Bensly (Director), and acting solicitor J. Hargreaves. The Articles of Association were agreed and the shares allocated as: 16,666 fully paid up ordinary shares to Josiah Cooper, 8,344 fully paid up ordinary shares to F. G. Bensly, with the registered office at Little King St., Birmingham.

Cooper and Co. at the 1906 Birmingham Cycle Show

The company specialised in making bicycle handles to a patented process with a licence from the inventor, Mr. H. A. Ollerant, which involved cutting pieces from a solid sheet of felt and turning them into a cylindrical shape on a lathe. In fact Josiah must have been in business before this time because he was writing letters in 1897 about his business[112] and referring to the showing of felt bicycle handles in the 1896 Cycle show. On July 26 1897, he made an offer of £250 to J. M. Cockcroft for his patented method of making handles by felting and milling without the use of a lathe[113], but the offer came to nothing. All the letters at this point were headed "Cooper and Co". At the start of the new company, they were having problems with the inventor, for Josiah Cooper was writing to Ollerant threatening that if he did not re-licence the patent the company would cease production. In the event, he must have complied because the company made sales of £19,541/2s/4d and a profit of £4,390/10s/0d. In the following year 1899, however, the company made a profit of just £189/16s/7d on sales of £14,525/1s/7d, which precipitated the resignation of the company secretary, C. H. Ford, indicating that something dramatic may have happened within the company. In 1900, there was little improvement since the company made a profit of just £771/7s/6d on sales of £14800/14s/7d. On 11 April 1901 an extraordinary director's meeting was held in the presence of J. Cooper, F. G. Bensly, the solicitor F. Darling, and the auditor W. Charlton, at which the company was wound up voluntarily. On the 17 July 1901, a new Director's meeting was held with the same people present, but this time with F. G. Bensly in the chair. At this meeting, it was agreed to form a new company, to be incorporated on 14th August 1901 as Cooper and Co (Birmingham) Limited. The share allocation this time was: Josiah Cooper 5,999 preference shares F. G. Bensly 1,999 preference shares, F. G. Bensly 4,500 ordinary shares, so F. G. Bensly was elected Chairman and now all promissory notes at the bank had to be signed by him only. From now on Cooper took very little part in the company and he is likely to have died between 1907 an 1909 since Mrs. Cooper attended the directors meetings after July 1909.

It was in these formative years that the company started its diversification, adding polishing mops to its production range. In 1907, felt sales accounted for fifty-one percent of the total sales, felt handles six percent and polishing mops and equipment forty-three percent with the total weight of woollen felt produced being 56,936 pounds weight for the year. Compare this to John Wilkinson's output of 1.6 Million pounds in 1857 and it shows just how small the company was in felt terms just some three percent or so of the size of one of the Leeds felters, or Mitchells, Ashworth, Stansfield and Company in 1904.

From the time the company was formed, F. G. Bensly kept tight control of its operation until sometime around 1939 when he passed control of the business to his son Eric Frank Bensly. His son was equally tenacious and continued the company's expansion by moving the company from Birmingham to Brynmawr, South Wales, into a purpose built building, which started production on 20 November 1950. In 1957, they continued their diversification by purchasing the business of James Farrer and Sons Limited, of Sheffield, manufacturers and suppliers of grinding and polishing machines on 18 June. On June 20 1961, a new company was formed called Cooper Plastic Foams Limited with a capital of £40,000 to exploit the growing polyurethane foam industry. Speciality Polishers Limited was also part of the Cooper Group of Companies, advertised as "specialist polishers to the motor industry and allied trades[114].

After all this effort in investment, expansion and diversification, in 1963[115], E. F. Bensly sold the shares in the company to John Crossley of Carpet Trades Holdings Limited, later to become Carpet Trades International. In 1972, the company was then sold to Bury & Masco (Holdings) Limited, and the production moved to Bury from South Wales in 1981 on the formation of a new company named Bury Cooper Whitehead Limited.

R. R. WHITEHEAD AND BROTHERS LIMITED

R. R. Whitehead and Brothers Limited was one of the oldest established textile companies that manufactured felt, its origins being in the wool stapling and clothing market. The company was originally established in 1799 under William Whitehead who was the father of the four brothers: Ralph Radcliffe Whitehead, James Heywood Whitehead, Francis Frederick Whitehead, and John Dicken Whitehead. The family purchased Royal George Mill in 1835 to carry on business as woollen manufacturers and general traders. On 7 Sep 1837, the Articles of Agreement established a partnership of the brothers for carrying out business as woollen manufacturers and general merchants under the name R. R. Whitehead and Brothers. On 9 August 1870, they formed a limited company[116] specialising in the production of woollen felts as well as the manufacture of flags. They were clearly making roll felts in 1863 as James Heywood Whitehead patented a new form of hardener using two sets of jigging rollers[117].

The first general meeting of the limited company was on 21 October 1870 with R. R. Whitehead as chairman and with the rest of the board of directors made up of: Mr. N. W. Turner, Mr. J. F. Tanner, Mr. T. H. Tanner, Mr. J. W. Tanner. The secretary for the meeting was Thomas Hoare Tanner, who was paid £20 per year for the privilege[118]. By this time, James Heywood had died in 1869 and a year after the formation of the company Ralph Radcliffe died on 31 March 1871, leaving the sole brother, John Dicken involved in the running of the company[119]. On 11 March 1871, the Board agreed to purchase the Wandle Felt Company at Mitcham near London, for £20,000, and the minutes refer to a patent by Fortin. To acquire Wandle felt, they increased the capital of their own company by issuing two hundred £100 shares to R. R. Whitehead (just one month before he died), J. D. Whitehead, W. W. Turner, John F. Read, Thomas H. Tanner, and James William Tanner. The latter four members invested a further £500 each on 28 December 1872, which increased the capital by a further twenty £100 shares. The Wandle Felt Company was producing sheet felts for the piano industry and since most pianos were then being made in London, the manufacturing operation was left there under the management of Alfred Rodgers, who was trusted sufficiently to be given power of attorney and authorised to draw cheques on Messrs. Coutts the bankers. The Wandle Felt Company also had a valuable office in Hannover Street in Long Acre, London that R. R. Whitehead Brothers Limited took over and continued its lease. According to Alfred Dolge, the leading Piano innovator of the time, the Whitehead Brothers were the first to make piano felts before Billon and Fortin of Paris, Weickert of Germany (in 1847), and Naish in 1859[120]. It is more likely, that it was the Wandle Felt Company that was the originator since the Whitehead Brothers were then mainly involved in woollen weaving with a relatively minor interest in felt[121]. By 1875, The Wandle Felt Company was renamed R. R. Whitehead Brothers Limited[122] and no doubt the piano felts made there were branded as "Royal George", a name that made Whitehead Brothers' felt famous among piano manufacturers for tone and quality.

Initially the Company seems to have prospered, on 19 July 1872 it declared a profit of £9,957 and issued a dividend of £17/10s/5d per share, and a similar one in 1873 but these were to be the best trading performance in the company's history. From this time onwards, the profits showed a steady decline year on year up to the death of J. D. Whitehead in 1886, when the control of the company went to Wyatt William Turner, John Frederic Tanner (Woollen Manufacturer), Thomas James Reade, Thomas Hoare Tanner, and James William Tanner. After this, the profits declined even steeper ending up at just £53 in 1890, though they declared a dividend of £12 per share. The board minutes reveal the same difficult competitive trading conditions in 1890 and 1891, which the Rossendale felt makers were experiencing. The company problems were compounded by the retirement of Alfred Rodgers, which made it difficult to control the production unit at Wandle with the same confidence. Therefore, in 1905, the company moved the Wandle manufacturing capability to Royal George Mill at Saddleworth[123] and housed it in a special department that was known by the employees there as "the Mitcham".

The performance of Royal George felts was so good that all the top piano manufacturers such as Broadwood, Steinway, Bechstein, and Bosendorfer used it, and its reputation persisted right up to the time of the company's closure in modern times. The mainstays of their piano range were known as wedge and clip felts, which involved cutting and shaping on a band saw, which led the company into fabricating cut felt parts for technical and engineering uses.

In 1924, the company's major income came from woven woollen goods made from coarse yarns, the fabrics being milled so as to produce a woven felt suitable for the paper and filtration industries, specifically for "dry" and "wet" felts for paper making. When the company experienced difficult trading conditions in 1932 and the weaving was cut back to three days per week, it was taken over by Porritt and Spencer Limited; a specialist in supplying woven felts to the paper industry[124]. Under the new Managing Director Mr. C. Phillip Porritt, the woollen felt side of the business prospered and the range increased to include roll felts and superfine felts for handicrafts. The company even negotiated with Mitchells, Ashworth, Stansfield and Company Limited for licensing a process to produce impregnated felt for use as anti-vibration pads, which they marketed as "Regalpak".

R. R. Whitehead letterhead used around 1970

In 1971, Porritt and Spencer joined the Scapa Group, which wanted the company's products to supplement its own range of offerings to the paper making industry. After taking over the company, Scapa moved all the weaving machinery out of Royal George Mill and left it as a purely felt making production operation. As a woollen felt manufacturer, R. R. Whitehead Brothers Limited was then an anomaly within the Scapa Group of companies but was nevertheless allowed to continue as an independent company, under a new managing director, Laurence Notley. Under his leadership, the company prospered and by 1979, the company was producing eighteen percent of the total British felt production[125]. At that time, the Scapa Group was continuing its expansion by taking over Bury and Masco (Holdings) Limited, which had a variety of interests including a needle felt division, felt leaders Bury and Masco Industries Limited, and Cooper and Co. Shortly after the takeover, R. R. Whitehead was merged with these companies to become Bury Cooper Whitehead Limited and effectively ceased to exist. When they were at their peak in 1990, the hammer felt produced at Royal George Mill was enough for over one hundred and sixty thousand pianos in one year, at a time when the total world production of pianos was around nine hundred thousand[126] or eighteen percent of the world production of piano felt. They also received the Queen's Award to Industry for its exceptional increase in export sales, with much of the new output going to Japan.

In 1994, Bury, Cooper & Whitehead closed down, but the Royal George Mill continued making felt until its closure in 1998, when the Chinese company now known as AMBIC Co. Limited, bought the felt making machinery, trademark and know-how. In 2008, this company claimed it was the leading manufacturer of piano hammer felts, and supplied sixty percent of the world market and many of the famous piano manufactures worldwide.

E.V. NAISH

E. V. Naish Limited was one of the two British felt manufacturers with a worldwide reputation for manufacturing high quality piano felts. Like many of the early felt makers, the company's origins were in the woven woollen business founded by William Naish who was making wool corduroy for the local farming community in 1800[127]. He was clearly successful as the family was also processing cloth in Quidhampton Mill, near Salisbury. In 1830, he rented the mill from the Pembroke Estate, using it for fulling the worsted cloths that were being produced by the local cottage industry[128]. Around 1858, William Naish was struggling to find new outlets when he met Joseph Goddard, who was looking for a manufacturer to make superfine felts for pianos. As a result of the meeting, they entered into a sole agency agreement that enabled him to start the production of woollen felt at his mill in Crow Lane, Wilton[129]. By 1859, William Naish was experimenting with techniques for producing tapered hammer felt and was one of the first four European companies to manufacture and sell piano hammer felts[130], probably by 1869. Through William's efforts, the company devised a proprietary process that gained it a reputation for high quality, superior service and unrivalled value for money.

In 1882, William Naish died and the business at Wilton was then run by his widow, Elizabeth Vawdrey Naish, and the company became E. V. Naish Limited, the initials "E.V.", being those of her forenames. The company continued to expand after Elizabeth's death in 1901, adding to their product range. This included: technical felts, products for the foot care market, felts for military applications, and a small amount of cut parts. During the course of the twentieth century, the company continued its development into new markets adding engineering felts, window channelling felt, polishing felts, and packaging felt to its product range. By 1960, the company was employing eighty people at its mill[131], and in 1979, the company's production accounted for just over thirteen percent of all the woollen felt produced in Britain[132]. However, with a declining market in woollen felt the company diversified into an unexpected market making and selling hand-washing equipment, toilets, and wash-basins under the brand name " Wallgate Wilton", through a subsidiary company Wallgate Limited. E.V. Naish was then struck by a series of problems affecting felt production, one was environmental through effluent discharge, and another was an urgent need for reinvestment in key equipment. The money required to address these two issues almost bankrupted the company. It survived, only to be confronted by events in 1989/90 with the aftermath of the Tiananmen Square massacre and the fall of the Iron Curtain, which caused the company's piano felt business to disappear overnight. In 1991, the company ceased felt production altogether, but was kept alive by continuing its cutting and fabrication operation until 1993. At that time, the company entered into a joint venture with a German felt company, Bayerische Wollfilzfabriken (BWF), to form a new company called Naish Limited, dedicated to promoting the felt supplied from Germany. Fortunately, in 2008, the company is still prospering under the leadership and management of the Naish family[133], though it now only imports felt rather than manufacturing it.

WANDLE FELT

At the turn of the eighteenth century, the river Wandle was home to a multitude of mills servicing a host of industries, with the usage of the mills constantly changing. One such mill was Crown Mill, which was one of two located on the same site and known as the Mitcham Mills.

In 1847, the mill was occupied by Richard Jones who was described as a felt maker[134]. Most likely he was a felt hat manufacturer first making felt on a batch process, since felt and silk hats were described as part of his business when he exhibited in the New York Exhibition of 1853. More significant, however, is the fact that he was also exhibiting "piano felt cloth", and "canvas for enveloping pianos"[135]. Then, he was described as manufacturing at Wandle Felt Mills, Surrey with premises also at 27 Bedford Street, Bury, London. In 1855, he is reported to have made boots and other articles for the British troops in the Crimea[136]. By 1859, the name of the company had changed to the Wandle Felt Company and its office in London changed to 13 Hanover Street, Longacre, London. At this stage, the company was involved in medical products, having acquired a patent from Mr. Warwick for a new type of poultice[137]. In 1862, the company was awarded a prize medal at the International Exhibition in London for its felts, at the same event that John Wilkinson Son and Co. received his medal, which implies that the two companies must have known each other[138].

In 1871, R. R. Whitehead and Brothers Limited bought out the company for £20,000 and although it changed its name in keeping with its new owners, it remained in production at Crown Mill under the management of Alfred Rodgers until 1890. In 1905, the mill was closed and the manufacturing capacity moved to the Royal George Mill at Greenfield and the expertise transferred by the Mitcham employees to those at Royal George[139].

HODGETTS FELT

The Hodgetts company was started by Moses Hodgetts Senior, a wool manufacturer, some time before 1820 in the village of Cradely[140]. He was followed by his son, also Moses, and in 1829, they were manufacturing linseys and carpets[141] but by 1845, Moses Junior was reduced to becoming a wool dealer and yarn spinner[142]. By 1854, Moses' son Charles Rubey was in business as a hat manufacturer and woollen spinner working at Park Side, Cradely[143]. In 1860, he was described as having a hat and felt works which by then must have been sizeable since it was mentioned specifically for the first time in the local directory[144]. Between 1864 and 1868 Hodgetts switched production from hats to polishing felts[145], which he maintained until 1873 when he was of sufficient size to employ a manager, William Andrews, to manage his company at his felt works in Park Row[146]. In 1876, the company was listed under Hodgetts, Emily (Mrs.) indicating Charles Hodgetts had died. The business was eventually sold to the Mitchell Brothers in 1897 and the production transferred to Lumb Mill[147].

OTHER LESSER KNOWN FELTMAKERS

E. Edmunds of Berryfield, Bradford, was a director of the West of England Woollen Manufacturing Company (1864-1866) who intended to manufacture felt and to attract investment, published a prospectus of how he intended to achieve this. The venture failed because of insufficient technical knowledge[148]. Another attempt at felt carpet making was by the brothers Thomas & Mark Hutchinson at Barnes Cray in Kent who set up manufacture in a dilapidated saw mill on the river

Cray in 1864. They made felt carpets for about five years before installing Brussels woven power looms but they failed in 1885[149].

William Abbott a feltmaker of Bermondsey Street Southwark Surrey, was responsible for the successful legal challenge to T. R. Williams 1829 patent but he never capitalised on his advantage, making little impression of the mainstream felt industry. He seems to have concentrated on the manufacture of "patent" hair felt suitable for impregnating with tar, asphalt, and he, with his son William the younger, eventually became bankrupt in 1851[150].

Also in London was the London Patent Felt Company, established in 1850, which seemed to offer the full range of woollen felt, hair felts, and even piano felts. The manager, William Marshall, is likely to be the same William Forbes Marshall who was in business with T. R. Williams and Charles Stanbridge[151].

Advertisement for the London Patent Felt Company in the Post Office Directory for 1895

Sometime before 1860, they switched their market to asphalted hair felts for roofing and shipbuilding, and by 1868 they were advertising hair felt and roofing felt with no mention of woollen felt. At this time, their offices were at 94 Leadenhall Street and William Marshall was still the manager[152]. They survived at least until 1895 when they were listed under Woollen Hair Felts in the Board of Trade Journal[153], and their advertisement indicates they were still involved with the manufacture of pressed felts.

In 1855, it was reported that there was a felt manufacturing company in Belfast Northern Ireland[154]. It is most likely that this was McTear and Co., of Cannon Street Works, Belfast who were manufacturing hair felts for boiler insulation and asphalt felt for roofing[155].

The felt industry had very little impact in Scotland or Wales. Apart from F. McNeill's factory in Kirkintilloch the only other felt manufacturers in Scotland was the Boulinikon Felt Company, owned by C. Davidson and Sons Papermakers of Mugiemoss Mills, Bucksburn, Aberdeen. The Boulinikon Felt Company was established around 1883 to manufacture Boulinikon felt[156]. Boulinikon was a floor covering that competed with linoleum and was manufactured by impregnating a mix of animal and vegetable fibres, hair, and wool with a mixture of pigments and oxidised linseed oil, to make a rubber-like material[157]. Boulinikon was first patented by John B. Wood in 1865 as a floor covering and as a material it had a very satisfactory rating, at least the Bolton Town Hall Committee were highly satisfied when they installed it throughout the town hall in 1874[158]. It must have had considerable merit since it was taken over as part of the merger of Mitchells, Ashworth, Stansfield and Co. in 1904, no doubt to supplement the Mitchell Brothers impregnated industrial felts known as "Iron Felt". However, Boulinikon was rapidly superseded by linoleum, which was based on linseed oil and manufactured in Kirkcaldy, in Fife, Scotland.

In modern times, the only new felt manufacturer to emerge was Lancashire Felt Limited, which was established in the mid 1950s, but the company only manufactured felt for a few years before converting its production to tufted carpets[159]. During that time, it employed as its technical manager a recognised felt expert, Ken Foulds, who left the mainstream felt industry to join them. To his credit he wrote a series of articles in the textile magazines of the time describing in unprecedented detail, the technical aspects of felt making.

4 PATENTS AND INNOVATION

EARLY BEGINNINGS

To the casual observer, it would appear that the mechanised pressed felt industry arrived from nowhere in 1840, as a sudden invention by T. R. Williams. The patent record however tells a different story, with the technology building up over a number of years, culminating in the most efficient commercial process for making a woollen felt.

Early in the nineteenth century most interest and activity in felting was in the hat industry, which by then was quite well developed. The process for making the felt for hats was a manual operation with single pieces being made for individual hats. The patents of the time reflect this manual batch production and many of them embody ideas later taken up by the inventors of the continuous process for making felt. For example a patent by James Bennett in 1803[1], discloses felting on a flat stone and rubbing with a polished marble surface until the frictional resistance increases. Although this is clearly a hand operation, it is very similar in operation to the flat hardening felting technique later employed by machines. In this, the hat and woollen felt industries were linked both commercially and technically during the course of their histories. The first patent associated with the founder of the pressed felt industry, Thomas Robinson Williams was for "the manufacture of hats and caps with machinery" on 19 September 1826[2]. This was ground breaking for hat production and was of great interest at the time.

Since Williams was involved in the hat industry he must have been aware of the huge demand for asphalt-impregnated hat felt that had developed for use in copper-bottoming the hulls of sailing ships. It was William Wood who first invented the technique for cladding ships, which he described in his patent of 1815[3], as: "The manufacture of a material or materials, and the application thereof to effectually make water-tight and sea worthy ships, and all other vessels". George Borradaile followed this with a commercial product that became so well used that it was specified in civil engineering publications as Borradaile's Patent Felt[4]. It was even used in the building of the Menai Straits Bridge by Thomas Telford in 1833[5]. Each felt sheet was made individually by covering a board with hair from a devilling machine, covering the fibres with a cloth and felting it by hand over a hotplate. Once the felt had been formed, it was dipped in hot tar or asphalt before finishing it by rolling between two rollers.

In 1829, Williams made a significant improvement in mechanising the manufacture of asphalt felt by inventing a way of making it continuous and without the need for any hand processing. This was his second British patent of 1829[6], which was entitled "Manufacture of Felt for covering Ships' Bottoms, &c." In this patent, a web of fibres was trapped between two endless wire belts that dipped into a bath of molten tar or asphalt. On emerging from this bath the two wire belts separated and the coated web of fibres, now called a felt, was released onto a table for cutting. There is no suggestion of the fibres being consolidated by felting because it discloses the use of cotton and flax, which do not felt. However, it is the first use of endless support bands for transporting a delicate web of fibres, and this is the basis for processing fibres in the pressed felt industry. It must have been a very messy process with tarred and impregnated loose fibres accumulating everywhere in the machine. Clearly there was room for much improvement.

One such improvement was a patent by William Abbott, Junior, on 31 January 1839[7], entitled "Manufacture of Felt." In a curious mix of machinery and manpower, he achieved the felting of a mass of fibres into a manageable fabric. In this invention, the fibres were placed on a heated iron table and covered with a wet cotton cloth. The heat from the metal plate caused the water in the cloth to form steam, which then percolated through the fibres to make them more pliable. A carriage of fluted rollers was then dragged by hand backwards and forwards over the cotton cloth to vibrate the fibrous mass underneath.

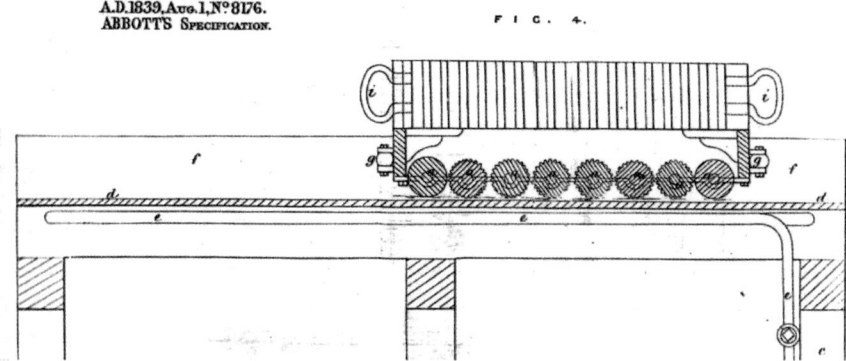

The William Abbott felting machine

The use of a cotton cloth envelope and fibre vibration was similar to Borradaile's method of making patent asphalt felt except that Abbott used rollers. The key claim of the patent was the use of cotton cloths to support a fibre mass, or batt, during initial felting, and fluted rollers for achieving the necessary vibration to cause felting. Both of these elements proved to be vital to the future of commercial felt making and were incorporated into all the felting processes that were later used throughout the felt industry. However, because Abbott's process was still a batch production method, his use of rollers was still inefficient and would never compete with a continuous process. This was probably the reason why William Abbott purchased and worked Williams' patent of 1829, which disclosed a continuous method of manufacture. In 1833, Williams filed a new patent for the continuous "manufacture of a combination of fibrous materials to replace skin, leather, vellum, and parchment", and with a number of partners went into production making patent sheathing in competition with Abbott. This precipitated a celebrated legal action in the Court of Chancery in 1837, when Abbott successfully filed for an injunction to stop the production[8]. Having won the case, Abbott granted Williams, 'assignees, or interested parties, a licence to manufacture, which they operated until 1843[9]. As part of the same arraignment Williams was allowed to re-file his patent, which he did in 1839.

This next patent by Williams was dated 28 September 1839[10], and included many refinements that moved the technology closer to the continuous production of pressed felt. At the same time, he disclosed a process for air laying fibres as a method for producing asphalt felt, which was a concept that was way ahead of its time. For making felt, he expanded the use of two cotton cloths to support a batt of fibres during the felting process, after which they were pealed apart to release the self-supporting felt. The machinery disclosed in the patent was of an altogether different scale than previous processes and was beyond the scope of a single individual to construct. The detail in the patent drawing is so comprehensive it must have been built and operated before the patent was filed, so it was clearly not just an idea submission. This patent does not mention the word "felt" and goes to considerable lengths to avoid confusion with "felted cloth", even though the machine shows all the elements present in continuous pressed felt manufacture. It is the first time that the initial stage of felting of a fibre mass is referred to as "hardening" and it deliberately distinguishes the effect from fulling, which is the vigorous technique for felting woven woollen cloth. This is the defining moment for pressed felt, which separates it from any other material. The machine described is shown below.

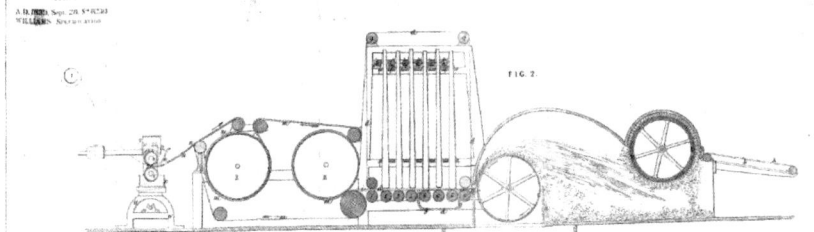

Williams' method for continuous manufacture of Asphalt Felt

There was a devilling machine at one end delivering fibres to the nip between two carrier cloths, a device pioneered in his previous patent. The web of fibres sandwiched between the cloths was passed through a series of rollers and hammered by vertical beaters operated by tappets. Steam was used in the first few rollers to plasticise the fibres to aid hardening, a key feature of the later woollen felt industry. Every roll was individually driven, which was a technique used for every roller machine that followed. In this process, the hardened fibre sheet separated from the carrier sheet and passed unsupported into the bath of tar or asphalt. Now all the fibres were locked into place so that the problem of loose fibres had been solved. The patent gives a clear indication of the shear size and scale of the operation, which considering the complexity of the framework and gear castings, it must have required a large capital investment. Of interest is the title of this patent: "Manufacture of Flexible Fibrous Compositions, Applicable to the Covering of Buildings, &c." which indicates a change in market direction and hints that he had a possible association with a prominent roofing felt manufacturer. In fact T. R. Williams went into partnership first with George Chambers and Leonard Streate Coxe until they became bankrupt in 1835, then with two others, Mr. Sandbridge and Mr. Marshall, forming a company called Stanbridge, Marshall, Williams and Co, based in Lamb's Building, Bunhill Row, London. This last partnership dissolved when Sandbridge and Marshall discovered the existence of the 1829 patent and had to defend themselves against the injunction by William Abbott. The manufacture under Williams' patent was later taken up at the premises in Bunhill Row, London, by Forbes McNeill with Williams joining him around 1845. After Forbes McNeill's death in 1845, his company was faced with the prospect of having to pay duty on the asphalt felt he produced, This followed a challenge by the paper makers, whose tar impregnated board was uncompetitive due to the duty levied on the paper product, but not on a felted product. In 1846, Williams was defending the case and trying to protect the company from potential bankruptcy, and McNeill's family from destitution. He won the case and the company F. McNeill went on to become the leader in the manufacture of roofing felt right up to modern times, long after William Abbott had become bankrupt around 1849[11].

FELT IN BRITAIN

THE DEFINING FELT PATENT

It is claimed that John Wilkinson, a wealthy wool merchant, was the progenitor of the pressed felt industry, for it was he who was specifically looking for a continuous mechanical method of producing felt and who enlisted the help of T. R. Williams to realise his ambition[12]. However it was Williams who filed the patent for the "Manufacture of Felted Fabrics" filed 12th August 1840, British Patent Number 8387, that precipitated the whole of the pressed felt industry as it is known today. The work, bankrolled by John Wilkinson, was so extensive that the patent disclosed all of the manufacturing processes that were used by the industry in a virtually unaltered state right up to the final demise of the industry one hundred and fifty years later. The patent disclosed: the horizontal batt frame, the vertical batt frame, the roller hardener, the use of continuous cotton support bratt cloths, and even the idea of roller milling. The patent is an effective tour de force of the technology of felting. It seems that T. R. Williams was proud of this patent, judging by his choice of title and his confident writing style. It also indicates a new departure from the manufacture of asphalt felt since the patent makes it clear that a new fabric in its own right is being produced, and there is no suggestion of the felt being impregnated in any way. The batt frame was a significant development because, for the first time a web of virtually any length, thickness, or weight could be produced from a fine carding engine. These cards only produce fine webs of fibre too thin and delicate to felt on their own. The batt frame was an endless conveyor belt that went round and round picking up a new web from the carding engines every lap. The more laps the conveyor made, the thicker and heavier the batt of fibres became. In practice, to make a useful length of fabric the conveyor needed to be at least forty yards long. Logistically, a conveyor this length is commercially and technically unviable and this patent provided an innovative solution to the problem. It showed how to bend the conveyor backwards and forwards on itself so that it could be stacked in a convenient practical space. The batt frame consisted of two sets of rollers, as wide as the carding engine, fixed at each end of a wooden or metal framework and separated by a distance of about five yards.

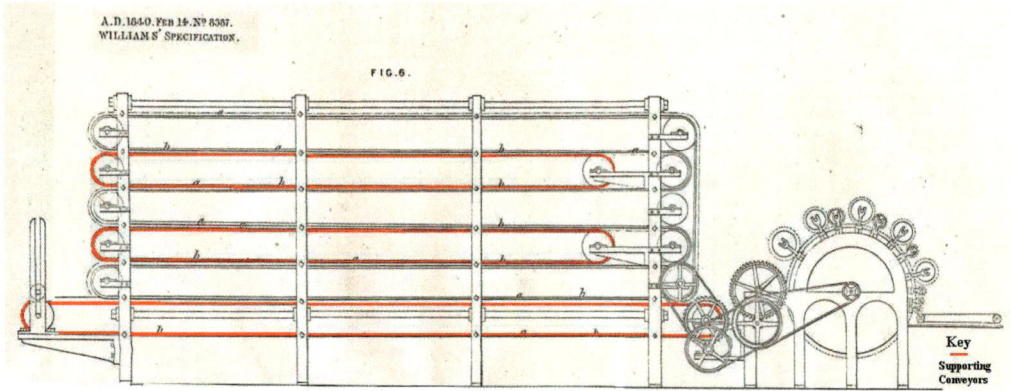

The horizontal batt frame for collecting and accumulating fibres from a carding engine in a long length

The conveying cotton cloth zigzagged between the rollers, the ends being joined to make a continuous loop. The cotton cloth on its own was insufficient to support the web properly since it was prone to wandering on the rolls and subject to creasing. Furthermore, when the cloth doubled back on itself the web was on the under side of the conveying cloth and if unsupported would drop off. Williams solved this problem by having two separate, individual support conveyors stretched between the middle two pairs of rollers, and tensioned by adjustable pulleys. These conveyors were made of material that had a smooth surface so that the fibres did not stick to them leaving the web undisturbed. There was another separate conveyor belt that ran the full length of the lower part of the machine. This not only supported the fibre web, but also acted as a surface drive to wind up the finished lap into a roll. The rollers of the batt frame were driven in synchronisation with the carding engine to ensure a repeatable and even layering of the fibres.

There were considerable problems in controlling a forty-yard long conveyor, particularly with the type of woven cotton cloth used. Over such a distance it was difficult to prevent the cloth from wandering from one side of the frame or the other, no matter how accurately the rollers were aligned. In addition, cloth passing over rollers had a tendency to crease and ruck, which would have produced an unacceptably irregular fabric. Williams solved this by attaching leather strips to the edges of the cotton carrier cloth and special guides fixed to the batt frame, through which the leather strips passed. This type of guide was still in use right up to modern times.

The patent also showed a vertical batt frame, which took up even less floor space, though it required a considerably tall building to house it. Although the vertical frame was used in later times by the industry, it was never popular, because the fibre web had a tendency to fall off the carrier cloth. By the early 1900s, it was largely abandoned and no examples of vertical batt frames existed after 1947.

The patent continued by describing "hardening machines" using rollers for consolidating the fibres by a specific form of felting that made a self-supporting material. The use of the term "hardening" endorses Williams' precise use of the word in his previous patent, which indicates that this new branch of textiles was developing its own terminology. In fact hardening was a unique process that distinguished a pressed felt from any other textile material.

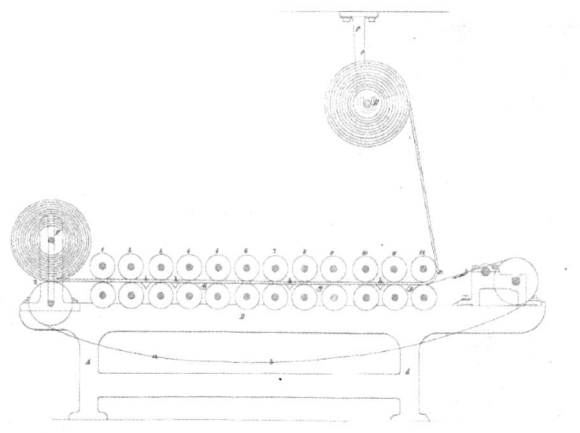

The first roller hardening machine with rollers set one on top of another

In the patent, there were two types of roller hardener described, each distinguished by a different roller configurations. The first machine consisted of pairs of rollers one on top of another acting like a series of mangles. The other machine had the rollers offset so that the top set of rollers nestled in the spaces between the lower set. Williams acknowledged that having the rollers one on top of the other did not give as good hardening as having the top and bottom rollers offset. The industry universally adopted jigging rollers in the offset configuration.

The way these hardening machines worked was truly unique. Both the top and bottom sets of rollers were driven together to give a forward motion, but at the same time, each top roller could move independently from side to side on its axle. No description is given of how the roller could slide over the axle and yet still be positively turned. However, there is a good description of how the lateral movement of the roller was controlled. This was achieved with a unique stirrup shaped arrangement, known from then onwards as a shackle.

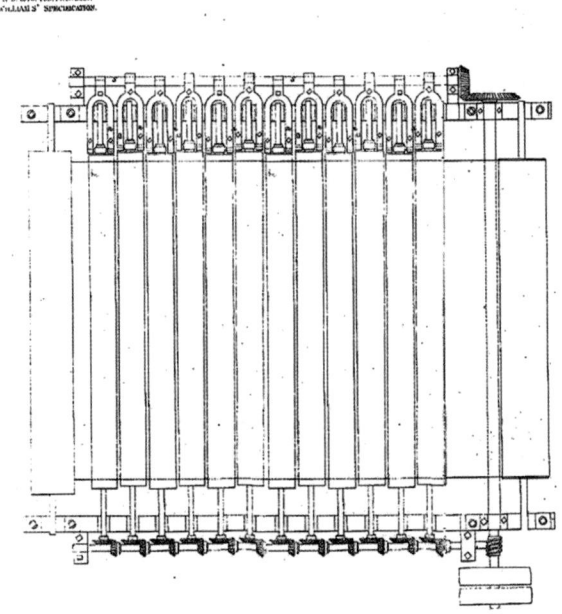

The top view of the T. R. Williams roller hardener showing the shackles at the top of the picture

Later generations referred to this type of hardener as a "Shackle Hardener". The shackle was linked to an eccentric so that it pushed and pulled the roller on the axle. The eccentrics for each shackle were set so that one roller was completely out of phase with the neighbouring one: while one was being pushed, the other was being pulled. The maximum lateral movement was half an inch, and was too large to call a vibration so the action was termed by later felt makers as a "jigging" action. Naturally, these machines were very noisy.

When the lap was taken from the batt frame, it was in the form of a loosely wound roll, which just had sufficient cohesion to be unrolled but insufficient to be handled. When presented to the hardener, therefore, it had to be supported during processing. In the case of the mangle-type hardener, only a bottom cloth was shown in the patent. In the case of the offset roller hardener, which was a more vigorous process, top and bottom carrier cloths were shown. This arrangement was the one that was universally adopted by the industry. In another aspect of the invention the first few rollers had steamers or heated plates between them to plasticise the fibres and increase the felting. Alternatively, the lower cloth could be wetted and allowed to pass over heated plates to generate the necessary steam. In the later years when higher steam pressures were available, this became a common technique.

The patent also included the tappet hammer method of hardening fibre batts as in the patent of 1839, though in this case it disclosed the production of a material in its own right, rather than being part of a line producing asphalt felt. Although Williams claimed this gave a denser felt, it never reached the feltmaking mainstream. Later machine makers like Krafft Goebel of Germany tried to emulate the action in their "Gatterwalker" but it was never commercially successful.

One of the disclosures of the patent was largely ignored until modern times and this was the idea of the roller miller. This is possibly because offsetting the rollers and using a jigging action was more efficient than the roller milling action. Roller milling was more like a kneading action rather than a vibratory one.

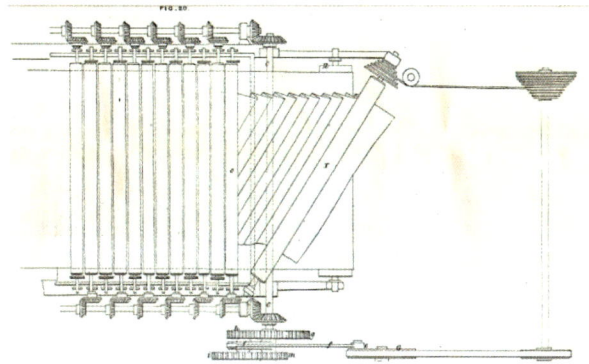

The configuration of the roller miller designed by T.R. Williams, the plaited felt enters the machine at an angle

In this case all the rollers, both top and bottom, were geared together with no lateral movement on their axles, and therefore no shackles. This time the rollers rotated backwards and forwards in a motion best described as "three steps forward, two steps back". In this way, a felt could be inched through the machine whilst kneading it between the rollers. This was achieved by an ingenious set of gears and cranks that could alter the oscillation and throughput speed to any value. This machine worked best with hardened felt and to achieve the maximum effect it had to be bunched up on itself before entering the machine. In the patent, there is a clever way of making forty-five degree folds by having the feed rollers at an angle to the machine and feeding the machine at twice its output speed. In modern times, the roller miller had fewer rollers than the patent and these were of a larger diameter made of wood and fluted. In Williams' patent, the felt was overfed into the machine at an angle but in the modern roller miller the felt was overfed directly into it.

Notwithstanding all these revolutionary processes, Williams claimed a further three, though these had limited, if any, relevance to the later industry. One process was for blowing coarse fibres directly from a devil, probably aimed at the roofing felt market; another was for rolling a lap up in cotton cloth and fulling without hardening, probably an anti-competitive protection disclosure, and finally, a method for raising a nap on a finished felt, which seems quite out of place in the context of the other inventions.

For this patent, T. R. Williams was so sure of the importance of his invention that he patented it separately for "the Colonies"[13]. After this there was only one more patent assigned to him, but this is not concerned with felting and is for the preparation and manufacture of fibrous materials in lieu of horsehair seating.

It is remarkable that Williams' 1840 patent could have specified a complete new industry with processes and ideas that remained virtually unaltered for over one hundred and fifty years. Certainly there were improvements, modifications, and adaptations, but intrinsically the methods remained the same. However, the patent was not without its challenges.

A PATENT CHALLENGE

In 1845, there was a celebrated court case for infringement in a citation by a company led by a Mr. Rawson. The citation was for manufacturing "20,000 yards of cloth, 20,000 yards of woollen cloth, and 10,000 yards of other fabrics, of which wool formed a principal component part, on the said improved plan and principle of Williams, and in imitation of the said invention, in breach of the said letters-patent, and against the privileges granted to Williams and his assigns"[14]. In 1844, Williams had assigned his patent to a group of patentees including Charles William Allen, Reverend Humphrey Allen, Henry Morris Kenishead, Stephen Phillips, and Richard Roy John Stewart, but it was Allen who was the plaintiff in the case, and as originator of the patent Williams gave evidence at the court proceedings[15].

Rawson challenged the patent on the grounds that two workers employed by Williams were the true inventors of significant parts of the patent, and that others had already disclosed other parts, such as the raising machine. He claimed a Mr. Shaw had invented the horizontal batt frame, as a means of creating a long length in a reduced space, this being an extension of Williams' idea of accumulating webs from a carding engine on an endless revolving apron. Rawson also claimed another of Williams' workers, a Mr. Milner, invented the stays for keeping the cotton cloths on the batt frames aligned. Mr. Milner had suggested ropes and grooves, whereas Williams used leather bands and nip, or converging pulleys.

Also challenged was the laying of felts at an angle and testimony was given by a Professor Farey that this had already been done in the hat industry, quoting a patent by Robertson. Even the use of acidulated water and the use of soap and water that was disclosed in Williams' patent, was attacked, in what seems a little like an attempt at discrediting the patent.

Following guidance by the judge the jury found that the patent should stand in its entirety on the grounds that it was not each individual part of the patent that was the issue, more it was the combination of all these things to give a desired result: a commercial length of fabric without the need for spinning or weaving. The plaintiff was awarded forty shillings damages. Rawson was not satisfied and appealed because the judge misled the jury. The later judges deliberations hinged around the relationship between a worker and employer engaged in development and who was entitled to be rightful inventor. In this case, they judged that there was a grand concept of putting all available elements together to give a unique process and product and this belonged to Williams. Shaw's idea was judged to be merely an extension of Williams' initial design whilst Milner's idea of keeping the carrier apron taut was an improvement to the process that Williams was entitled to use to facilitate his invention. The other objections were dismissed as the scope of the patent was limited and did not contravene prior art. Without doubt, this court case ensured the patent's dominance over the industry for its full term.

EFFECTS OF THE PATENT

The first tangible impact was the formation of The Patent Woollen Cloth Company that clearly had control of it, initially for the production of felt carpets and later for technical applications[16]. For the full fifteen years of the patent, they monopolised the industry. The patent was licensed to one other company: J. Wilkinson, who was also allowed to make carpets. In 1854, the company tried to extend the patent but without success. Consequently, there were no other major manufacturers making felt before 1854, the only one described as a felt maker in 1843, was William Hirst of 39 North Street, Leeds[17]. He seems to have been involved mainly in raising and fulling woollen cloth as he had five patents in this area of manufacturing in the period from 1824 to 1840[18]. However, in October 7 1841, he patented in collaboration with Joseph Wright a table felting machine[19] consisting of a flat table with a top platen that vibrated up and down, which is a forerunner of the only major machine that was used by the industry, that was not an invention of T. R. Williams – the flat hardener. With this arrangement it was possible to make lengths of felt by a discontinuous process that would have avoided contravening Williams' patent. In fact, Hirst went on to develop this machine so that the top plate had a reciprocating action[20], which was very similar to the flat hardener adopted by later felt makers to harden thick felts.

However, Hirst does not seem to have had a significant effect on the felt industry as he had no further entries in the Leeds business directories. He was still patenting in 1857, but his patents were of little consequence to the felt industry that followed[21]. Apart from Hirst there was little in the way of innovation during the period that the Williams' patent had to run, excluding Hirst's patents there were just six patents in fifteen years, compared to forty-five in the fifteen years following the patent's expiry (see Appendix). Clearly, the Williams' patent effectively stifled all competition and innovation. However, those patents that were filed during the term show attempts to circumvent the monopoly, and it was during this period that the idea of flat hardeners and table hardeners were being explored[22]. None of these names or their equipment are mentioned in any of the documents or inventories of the later felt makers but their ideas were certainly adopted and modified into efficient machines for batch-wise production. These culminated in the Garside table hardener, the flat plate hardener and the Bywater-Beanland heavy-duty flat hardener, all mainstays of their later respective industries. The Garside hardener was used for the hat industry, the flat plate hardener for the piano felt industry, and the Bywater-Beanland hardener for the production of technical felts.

AFTER THE WILLIAMS PATENT

Once the Williams' patent expired there was an explosion in the number of manufacturers of felt, most of them in the Rossendale Valley. The Williams' patent and the power of its commercial importance must have made a considerable impact on the new generation since all of them at some time, generated their own patents. In particular, those that patented the most, the Mitchell brothers of Rossendale, were the most successful commercially.

The patents following that of T. R. Williams fell into four broad patterns: machine improvements, process improvements, product enhancements, and new product innovations, though none had the same revolutionary impact as his. The new breed of felt makers were very much "hands on" owner managers, as many of the patents bear the names of known business owners and show an intimate knowledge of the technology and machinery. These business entrepreneurs are named either as single inventors or with co-inventors who then disappear from the record. The types of improvements were limited in scale and developed within the business, either through a new production layout of machinery or using their own blacksmith's workshop. For example, W. Mitchell's patent[23] for a carding engine and hardener modification to produce a full width carpet; and Edward Rostron modifying the shackle of a roller hardener with a screw to eliminate slack[24].

The names of owner inventors are sometimes linked with the names of well known machinery manufacturers; indicating an increasing complexity in realising new ideas that were beyond the scope of their own engineers. They also indicate intimate relationships between these companies. For example it appears in 1869 that The Patent Woollen Cloth company was involved in a completely new processing route involving cross laying a web in place of a batt frame and the patent[25] describing this includes William Bywater's name, who was a well known textile machinery manufacturer. Although the felt company is not named the inventors Thomas Robert Clarke, and Thomas Lawson are known to be key personnel in The Patent Woollen Cloth Company. There was also a strong connection between the Mitchell Brothers and the press manufacturer William Bradshaw Leachman and they jointly patented the use of a double daylight press[26]. Leachman presses later became the mainstay of the industry and much of his machinery was still in use in 1980.

Machinery manufacturers themselves appear to have been equally innovative with constant improvements to the operation of their machines, particularly flat hardeners. The form of the roller hardeners seem to have remained basically the same with relatively minor changes, most of which were carried out by the feltmakers rather than the machinery manufacturers, that is until after 1908. Most attention was directed towards alterations to the shackle drives for the jigging motion of the rollers. William Bywater had two patents[27], whilst Thomas Whitehead had an improved coupling[28], and Edward Rostron's attempt has already been mentioned. The drive for roller hardeners has always seemed troublesome since even in the 1980s attempts were being made to improve them.

Many of the patents refer to hardening between flat plates and the patent record highlights the development of the flat hardener from humble origins of James Bennett[29] involving felting between flat stones to the massive Bywater Beanland machine[30] that became the standard in the industry. During the monopoly of Williams' patent, this was the only viable alternative to making felt and was essentially a batch process. From the patents it is clear that this is how William Hirst managed to produce felt during 1840 to 1855 as he had three patents[31] all disclosing the use of platens. Clearly, he had outlets other than carpets, as these methods could not compete with the Williams' process. However, he seems to have left little impact on the felt industry and disappeared after 1857. Judging by the industry that followed, all his processes were too inefficient for commercial success. The result of all this innovative activity was the wide diversity of flat plate hardeners that percolated throughout the industry. The hat industry adopted the Garside hardener, a true tabletop hardener with a wooden top plate and steam chest for the lower plate. The piano felt makers adopted a flat hardener with a floating three feet square top platen loaded with weights, whilst the major feltmakers invested in the huge Bywater Beanland machines with an automatic intermittent drive[32] enabling a continuous process to be achieved economically from a batch operation.

A common attempt to circumvent the Williams' patent was to wrap fibres in a roll of supporting cotton cloth and milling it by various means, for example William Hirst[33], or Henry Augustus Wells[34], and Moses Poole[35] (patent agent). Even in modern times, this has been considered since it represents a tantalisingly rapid and efficient way of felting. Hirst's patent of 1857[36] indicates the main difficulty of this method, which was that uniformity of felting could not be achieved commercially.

He tried to improve felting by constantly turning the roll whilst beating it at the same time, and though this gave uniformity around the circumference of the roll the inside of the roll was less felted than the outside. The industry never adopted this technique.

Felt does not have the same dimensional stability as woven cloth and many patents attempted to solve this perceived problem. These innovations start after the Williams' patent expired, indicating a move towards new markets other than carpets and into products that required more dimensional stability than floor coverings. The first was by Paul Rapsey Hodge, who claimed the laying in of warp threads[37], followed by Cornelius Turner, who also patented a method specifically for introducing weft threads[38]. However, these techniques and products were not adopted by the industry. More successful, in commercial terms, were the attempts to cross lay webs and batts to give transverse as well as lateral strength, though it was more in modern times that this became important. The first disclosure was again by Paul Rapsey Hodge[39], then by Thomas Lucas, and later by William Grimshaw in 1868[40]. At this time, that there was interest in felt for the apparel market as indicated by a patent by William Edward Newton[41] specifically disclosed a cross-lapped felt for "wearing apparel". The Patent Woollen Cloth Company, the leaders of the felt industry of the time, must have been aware of this trend as they patented, with William Bywater[42], a completely new processing route using cross laid webs that was a forerunner of the modern synthetic non-woven industry. Nothing came of this as there is nothing in the records of the later feltmakers that they used this technique, nor is there any indication in Bywater's catalogues that they ever promoted it when the patent expired.

Other variants of stabilising the felt was the inclusion of open weave fabrics, scrims, and knitted fabrics: For example James Heywood Whitehead included linen mesh in a felt to reinforce saddle felt[43] and John Wilkinson used an open woven fabric scrim[44] whilst William Edward Newton disclosed the use of knitted fabric. Another variant was to felt directly on to another woven woollen fabric to make a composite for example William Hirst[45], Louis Ferdinand Tavernier[46], and J. Rousseau[47]. Unfortunately, these techniques led to fabrics that were more expensive and uncompetitive at a time of increasing competition in the textile industry. Consequently, they only found favour in specialist products like saddle felts. The mainstream feltmakers such as the Mitchell Brothers were patenting cheaper methods of manufacture such as three layer felts with low-grade fibres sandwiched between layers of prime grade fibres[48]. This technique proved to be so successful that it was still in use over a hundred years later.

There is little in the patents regarding the drying of felt, other than two specialised approaches for drying and shaping individual saddle felts using standard tenters, which were patented by John Wilkinson in 1855[49] and R. J. C. Mitchell in 1885[50]. Only J. B. Whiteley seems to have been active in the development of machine tenters for felt in the United Kingdom[51] and their machines were in common use in the industry.

There were a number of innovations that appeared to offer an alternative to the batt frame for building a fibre web. The principal of these was the use of air to blow fibres onto a porous surface so that they could accumulate into a thick mass, for example the patent of 1840, by W. L. Wise[52] on behalf of Marthaus and Polster. Their re-discovery disclosed a complete continuous, air laying and felting line. However, this innovative air-laying technique seems to have passed the feltmakers by, even though Williams was clearly aware of it, and it was disclosed in his felt patent. It was only in the 1950s that air-laying became the norm for producing synthetic non-woven fabrics

FELT IN BRITAIN

One innovation allied to felting does however stand out as ground breaking and that is the invention of needle punching. The first sign in Britain of this was in 1875 with a provisional file being granted to Lyman Welcome Whipple from America through an agent: John Henry Johnson[54] as a method of forming a "felt like" product by needling. This was an improvement on the first needle loom invented by Milton Whipple in America in 1872[55]. L. W. Whipple later filed a new modification in a patent submitted through another agent A. J. Boult[56] both being filings from patents having been already published in America. The essence of this invention was to push rough or barbed needles into a batt of fibres.

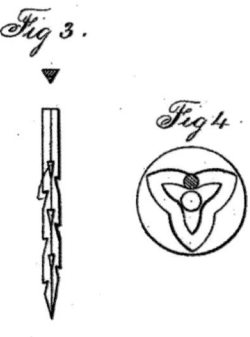

Broadhead's Needle design

The top fibres were pushed through the batt and left there when the needles were pulled out. A fabric much like a felt could be made without the need for steam or vibration. Clearly this was of current interest to the industry as shortly afterwards James Broadhead patented a new design of needle loom in 1885, as well as an improved design of needle to improve the efficiency of needling, a design that has persisted in needle punching to the present day.

The woollen felt makers were quick to adopt this new technique but found it more appropriate for use on jute and coarse horsehairs, which did not felt well by traditional felt making techniques. Often such coarse needle-felts were also hardened to improve their strength and surface appearance. It was not until the 1950s that, with the invention of modern synthetic fibres, needle punched fabrics started to threaten traditional felt and eventually substitute it in most outlets. The Mitchell brothers seem to have acquired a monopoly for this invention as they had an agreement with T. Firth of Heckmondwike in 1885 by which they were due monies for all the amount of needled "horsecloth" that Firth produced[57]. In this agreement, a certain Lindsay also received a royalty from Firth, and perhaps more interesting Firth had to pay James Broadhead a fee for his wages under the terms of the agreement with the Mitchell brothers in 1885. This indicates that Mitchell brothers had acquired the patent rights from Broadhead, and Lindsay had a patent that Firth had licensed and which infringed theirs.

Of later importance is a patent by F. M. Birtill[58], for the manufacture of shoulder pads. This was perhaps one of the few successes for felt in the apparel industry as Birtill went on to co-found the company Birtill and Blaikie that then created the Featherweight Pad Company to exploit the invention. It must have been an influential business at the time since the companies were involved in the formation of the Mitchells, Ashworth, Stansfield Combine that dominated the modern felt industry, Birtill becoming one of its directors.

The Mitchell brothers were prolific inventors with twenty-seven patents to their credit, covering all aspects of felt making as well as extending the usage of felt. Although all three brothers were inventive, it was Robert John Chadwick Mitchell who excelled in new ideas. He not only advanced felt technology but was involved in many other topical areas of interest. For example, he had two patents for the improvements in pneumatic tyres[59] and had significant interests in the hat trade[60] working in conjunction with J. Eaton. This entrepreneurial spirit enabled their company to expand and dominate the market, eventually allowing them to absorb the once powerful Patent Woollen Cloth Company. They certainly knew how to value and exploit their patents, in some cases to gain market leadership such as in double width carpeting and in others in licensing agreements with patents that they had acquired. When they amalgamated with Ashworth, Stansfield and others in 1904, they used seven of their existing patents as capital to increase their stockholding in the new company. A value of £25,000 goodwill was placed on them[61], a great example of the modern concept of intellectual capital.

APPENDIX

FELT PATENTS TO 1803 -1908

Year	Date	British Patent Number	Inventor	Description
1803	10 March	2688	Bennet, James	Felting woven cloth by hot wet treatment on a flat stone, rubbing with a polished marble stone till frictional resistance increases
1815	8 September	3892	Wood, William	The manufacture of materials, and the application thereof to the more effectually make watertight and sea worthy ships, asphalt impregnated felt for ships' bottoms
1825	17 November	5295	Borradaile, W.	Making or setting up hats or hat bodies
1826	19 September	542	Williams, Thomas Robinson	Manufacture of hats and caps with machinery
1829	23 May	5791	Williams, T. R.	Manufacturing felt for covering vessel bottoms
1839	1 August	8176	Abbott, William (Jr)	Improvements in the manufacture of felt. A machine with 7 fluted rollers and 2 plain rollers which travels backwards and forwards on a batt of fibres covered with a cotton cloth and placed on a stone table
1839	28 September	8450	Williams, T. R.	Manufacture of flexible fibrous substances for covering buildings and machinery
1840	14 February	8387	Williams, T. R.	Discloses all the main elements of the felt industry: fine carding, vertical and horizontal batt frames, roller hardening as well as aerodynamic web laying and hammer felting
1840	24 September	8646	Williams, T. R.	Patent 8387 submitted to cover the Colonies
1840	24 September	8642	Hirst, William	Discloses a carding drum for batch batt formation. Felting by winding up a wool batt and applying pressure in a modified fly press, then fulling in the roll on the modified press
1841	17 April	8926	Wells, Henry Augustus	The use of two platens for felting. The top wood or metal the bottom being a steam chest with perforations to release the steam into the batt. The top platen has a reciprocal shuffling motion and is weighted.
1841	6 May	8951	Poole, Moses	Felting by acting on fibres by bars having a curved and alternating motion.
1841	20 September	9090	Newton, William	Machinery for making sheets cross laid then milled and fulled into a felt cloth
1841	7 October	9109	Hirst, William and Weight, Joseph	Felting wool onto faces of a woven cloth in a two-platen press with the top platen moving up and down.
1841	20 October	9122	Smith, Junius	Addition of a carded batt at right angles to the warp direction using a second card. Then hardened between two linen sheets acted on by a "jiggering" plate

Year	Date	Number	Inventor(s)	Description
1846	2 June	11233	Poole, Moses	Felting batts by folding them between woven fabrics and rolling the partly felted cloth
1851	3 June	13651	Parker, Thomas	Machine for preparing fibres for felted fabrics. Discloses a hardening machine with abutting bars of wood. The bottom bars are fixed to end chains and laterally reciprocated, The fibres are supported between a top and bottom sheet
1851	19 December	13862	Hirst, William	Felting wool onto a cloth in a double platen, the lower platen steams by a cloth covered grid. The weighted top platen reciprocates
1855	23 June	1446	Bellfood, A., Loradoux, E.	Introducing flock between layers of wool for felt fabrics
1855	13 November	2553	Wilkinson, J. (Snr), Wilkinson, J. (Jnr)	Forming felt for saddles by moulding during tentering
1856	11 November	2654	Hodge, Paul, Rapsey	Introduction of warp threads during batt manufacture.
1856	12 November	2669	Brookman, Richard, Archibald	Layering of webs to make a wad then pressing between rollers, then stitching together and felting
1856	12 November	2811	Hodge, Paul, Rapsey	Uses a weft batt or sliver to be laid by machinery across a straight lay batt on the travelling apron for a warp/weft strong felt
1857	7 November	363 provisional	Hirst, William	Sliver and wrapper cloth wound up together and the roll rotated in hot water. A second roller is pressed onto the roll and then released continually till the cloth is felted
1857	20 July	2053	Hirst, William	Fibre is wrapped in a roll, with a wrapper. The roll is acted on by a beating lever, a ratchet rotates it to present a fresh surface.
1859	31 May	1341	Carr, Samuel and Butterworth, George	Producing felt thick on the "list" to make it the same as the rest of the piece using a self acting feeder and a suitable eccentric for the hardener aimed at piece uniformity
1861	31 December	3722	Mitchell, W.	Carding engine modification to produce a fleece the full width of a carpet and extending the hardening to suit the width
1862	15 February	408	Turner, Cornelius and Shaw, Jack	The introduction of threads or yarns of wool between layers of fibres either longitudinal or cross wise and felting the whole
1862	21 June	1841 communication	Edmonds, Ezekiel	A flat hardener fitted with rollers, and feeding a sliver transversely from a scribbler, felt is finished with steamed heated rollers
1863	25 June	215	Turner, Cornelius	Laying in weft threads and cutting them at the selvedge for transverse reinforced felt
1863	10 September	2235 provisional	Whitehead, James, Heywood	A sliver is deposited in folds by a roller moving across an endless sheet feeding a roller hardener, both top and bottom roller sets on the hardener jig
1863	31 October	2697	Barlow, Henty, Bernoulli	Fibre is transferred from a picker to a wire cage where it collects, batt is forwarded by two endless aprons between steam heated platens and then vibrated laterally
1864	14 July	1471	Reid, John and Buckley, Thomas	Improved stiffening for backing felt carpets, ornamenting, texturing the surface of felt by passing the felt between engraved blocks

1864	27 June	1612	Clark, William	Claims felting using a perforated or steam permeable cylinder which is made to vibrate using a cam. Also a wire cloth as a felting surface, and a wire guide for felting yarn
1864	23 July	1835	Barcroft, James	Guides of wood or metal put on either side of a fibre web from the card to concentrate the edges to make the felt stronger there
1867	29 May	1588	Mitchell, Thomas	Joining and stitching felt selvedges and then milling them to mask the join
1867	30 May	1609	Newton, William Edward	Napping felted fabrics by teazling, napping, fulling, napping and then shearing
1868	3 August	2255	Wilson, William	Conical rollers for felting hat bodies
1868	4 March	746	Mitchell, William, and Mitchell, Thomas	A seamless felt carpet. To stop edge thinning cards are clothed with coarse wire in the centre and finer at the edges. Alternatively an intermediate roller between two swifts with the pitch regulated to transfer more to the edges. Also disclosed is a cross lapper for a card and the concept of a hardener attached to a card.
1868	6 July	2147	Whitehead, James Heywood	Improvements to saddle pads and numnahs by felting fibre onto a net of linen, and coarse woven horsehair
1868	23 April	1326	Rostron, E and Whittaker, W.W.	Two cam discs acting on pairs of alternate top rollers of a roller hardener to give different throws
1868	5 August	2465	Lake, William, Robert	Stiffening felted fabric by inclusion of horsehair. The horsehair is in the centre of a three-layer sandwich, either as loose weave knitted or openwork fabric
1868	23 September	2917	Lucas, Thomas Grimshaw, W.	Method of laying fibre laps at ninety degrees in a discontinuous operation
1868	8 October	3073	Barcroft, James	Lays narrow laps together with overlapping edges and hardens on a double width hardener, the rollers of which meet in the middle but not directly opposite each other
1868	23 November	3560	Newton, William Edward	Felted fabric for wearing apparel by crosslapping and shrinking by fulling
1868	15 December	3808	William, Bywater	Improvements to a roller hardener using two shafts instead of one eccentric also uses a syphon for the steam rollers.
1868	21 December	7889	Wilkinson, John (Younger)	Saddlecloths, numnahs, felting on opposite sides of an open woven fabric (scrim)
1860		1648	Whiteley, J. B.	Tentering machine with telescopic rollers. Improvements to B.P.s 332 (1854), 382 (1864), 661 (1868)
1869	8 January	57	Tatham, William	Improvements to carding engines and breakers for felt making, quotes Thomas Mitchell BP 746
1869	27 March	874	Bousfield, George Tomlinson	Intermittent carrier cloth on a jiggering machine, horizontal concave machine with intermittent movement of a platen type hardener for uniform felting.
1869	30 April	1328	Spence, William	Felt for pianos, lever and crank for transverse and longitudinal vibration of a table hardener. Also used continually with cotton cloths

Year	Date	No.	Patentee(s)	Description
1869	9 May	1545	Mitchell, William	Three layer felt with the centre having inferior fibres, using three cards and one hardener, Hardener rolls so the end grain is presented to the circumference, and improvements to crosslaying
1869	1 June	1686	Clarke, T.R. Bywater, W., Lawson, T., Lister, L. C.	Cross laying fibres with longitudinal fibres felted together and a method of crosslaying
1869	28 June	1954	Burton, John Watson, Morrell, Robert Wilson	Felting onto a woven fabric from combed wool using ordinary felting machinery
1869	20 August	2492	Fortin, Louis B., Ferrabee, James	Adaptation of a card for producing batts for felts
1869	23 August	2507	Whitehead, Thomas	Improved coupling for shackles of a roller hardener
1869	1 September	2585	Nussey, G. H., Leachman, William B.	Machinery for pressing woollens or felted fabrics using hot and cold rollers
1869	15 September	2697	Newton, William Edward	A batt of fibres is put on a vibrating rubber plate and rubber bed. The plate is lifted to allow the fibre to move
1870	31 December	3404	Newton, William Edward	Felted fabrics with variable thickness by hollowing out rollers to allow more fibres, also the inclusion of knitted or open fabrics
1871	15 August	2145	Mitchell, William	Stretching and tentering felt on a printer's table
1872	4 May	1363	Mitchell, William	Surrounding woven flax with two wool laps and felting round it by hardening
1872	22 August	2460	Rostron, Edward	A screw tapped into the end of an axle of a hardener roller which can be adjusted to bear against the shackle to limit backlash and give a positive drive
1874	5 February	466	Tavernier, Louis Ferdinand Jnr	Fibre batt felted to woven woollen fabric Two flat stone tables, two cotton carrier cloths, top plate oscillating backwards and forwards in the direction of the fibres, steam or soaped water is used to help felting
1875	23 July	2623	Johnson, John Henry for Whipple, Lyman Welcome (USA)	Provisional Patent disclosing needle punching with roughened or barbed needles into a batt of fibres. Claims the method and machinery of manufacture and the product
1875	13 August	2858	Olroyd, John and Blamires, Thomas Howard	Felt from a carding lap is wound onto a drum whilst winding on yarn to make a warp, then from a second card a top lap is wound and the whole felted together to make a cloth
1876	21 July	2972	Schuman, Sigismund	Felting moulded goods by steam hardening in situ using vibration of rods on the mould containing fibres
1877	4 April	1302	Bywater, W. and Berry S.	Laying a batt on a cloth and felting by reciprocating motion
1877	3 November	4089	Westwell, R., Law, R., Rothwell, J.	Revolving steam heated copper rollers replaced by stationary steam chests
1877	16 November	4656	Denison, Slater, Coupland, and Plummer	Making striped felt by feeding beams of different coloured slivers and hardening

Year	Date	No.	Patentee	Description
1880	21 January	259	Mitchell, W.	Intimate mix of wool flax hemp milled in a felting machine, printed or dyed with aniline
1880	23 April	1676	Hunt, B. for Sommer, A.S.H.T.	Flat plate hardener with a bottom carrier cloth and between this and the top platen two "knitted meshes"
1880	2 June	2247	Bywater, W.	Oscillating flat plate table hardener
1880	23 June	2551	Mitchell, W. and Cuttle, M. C.	Tentering carpets using tenter chains and stretching fabric over a roller with pins running at a different speed than the chains
1880	9 July	2825	Ashton R. and Kinder, R. A.	Preparing wool by steam and ammonia gas prior to felting
1881	1 April	1445	Erskine, J.	Table hardener plates for hair felting. The top plate vibrates using a horizontal eccentric and the bottom table is perforated for steam
1881	16 November	5029	Wise, W. L. for Marthaus and Polster	A continuous carding and felting line. A breaker integral with a willey and deposited on an endless belt using an exhaust fan to suck fibre onto a belt to build up a lap feeding into a continuous vertical hardener
1884	26 February	3959	Boult, A. J. for L. W. Whipple	Needle punching machine with intermittent drive as to Johnson's submission
1884	5 July	9772	Bywater W. G. and Beanland, T. B.	Improvements to B.P 2247. This is the flat hardener having shackles and a raising lowering motion and supporting ball sockets
1885	5 March	2922	Broadhead, J.	Design of the modern barbed needle for a needle loom. Also a machine to needle-punch wool to give the appearance of woollen goods
1885	18 April	4791	Mitchell, R. J. C.	Method to make a seamless cover of felt for horses. The bottom and top ends of a tenter seam are shaped to the right profile. The wet felt is draped over it and jacked down.
1886	19 May	6706	Garside, J.	Milling machine
1886	7 July	8862	Anderson, F. S.	Flat plate hardener with horizontal oscillating shaft with vertical rod to give pressure and a perforated steaming plate
1886	8 July	8939	Wise W. L. for Marthaus A.	Details of deposition of fibres in an air lay system for felt (B.P. 5029) also allows water mist into the fibre mix before deposition
1887	8 September	12158	Ingrund, N	Hair is felted between a ribbed plate and a vertical piston rod acting in a cylinder with a base plate perforated to let steam in
1888	21 July	10567	Bywater, W. G., Beanland, T. R.	Stopping motion for flat hardener for hair felt
1888	11 August	11590	Mitchell, W.	Fireproof carpet and underfelt using asbestos or amianthus felted with wool
1888	16 August	11804	Moseley, J.	A four layer fabric an inner one being felt and outer ones fabric for card wire base
1888	4 December	17644	Redman, J.	Felt with design outlines of garments, uppers for slippers, boots, shoes printed on
1889	7 February	2177	Russell, J.	Fulling stock like a double action pusher
1889	12 February	2441	Fisher, C. V. for Dolge, A.	Fulling of felt or cloth in a box miller filled with liquor felting by pleating
1889	21 May	8452	Orlamunder, J	Mangling in a box miller to full cloth
1889	21 August	13173	Holden, J. and Jepson, J. R.	Muslin applied to one side of felt during processing

Year	Date	No.	Patentee	Description
1891	7 April	5934	Bywater, W. G.	Alteration of the drive mechanism for reciprocating the rollers using a drive of a main worm and pinion
1891	10 August	13468	Nelson, E. trading as F. McNeill & Co	Hair felt as a non-conducting covering for steam boilers and pipes strengthened by inserting woven or wire interlayer
1892	24 March	5804	Rousseau, J.	A layer of carded wool interposed between two layers of woven cloth and felted to form a fabric. Fabric weft should be wool
1893	1 April	6883	Chardot, J.	Felt discs for polishing cut from sheets of carded and felted wool enclosed in envelopes and fulled in a special machine, dried and finished in a press
1894	29 May	10414	Coq, V	Top rollers of a hardener replaced by hollow cylinders and the lower set by a concave counterplate. The cylinder and plate reciprocate in opposite directions
1894	1 October	18577	Newton, J	Flat plate hardener with plates given oscillatory motion to make sheets, the top weight is adjusted by levers
1894	6 November	21304	Cockcroft, T. M.	Making pouches and purses by forming a batt around a rubber inflated sphere and felting, then deflating sphere and removing
1895	19 January	1299	Rose, G. D.	Felt for pianoforte hammers by felting layers of silk or woven fabric with wool of different staples, the longest fibres placed outside
1895	5 March	4677	Pilard, A.	Patterned felt by embedding coloured yarns or slivers during carding and felting
1895	26 June	12386	Birtill, F. M.	Shoulder pads from felted material of varying thickness tapered on one side using a table hardener with the lower plate dished to the shape of the pads and perforated to allow steam to penetrate
1895	25 September	16572	Knoch, P.	Felt used under rails or bed plates of a permanent way hardened on the top surface with rubber or resin
1897	16 January	1211	Tippett, U. H. G.	Mats, handles, cycle pedals, rubber backed with felt
1897	1 May	10851	Cockcroft, T. M.	Felt handles by winding on fibre and binding with woollen threads and rotated in a barrel then put in bags and fulled
1897	20 May	12403	Shaw, W. A.	Carpet or floor covering top layer of wool attached to a soft felt layer
1897	14 July	16702	Leachman, W. B. Mitchell, R. J. C.	Double daylight press for steam pressing hardened felt
1897	14 July	16716	Griffith, T.	Felt stair pads treated with essence of cedar, pine, or eucalyptus to protect from moths
1898	18 February	411	Syhre, C. A. E.	Felt for piano hammer head made from leather fibre
1898	13 April	8606	Atherton, G	Felting roller covered with rubber or felt
1899	24 May	10871	Wahl, N.	Felting of carded batt between two carriers. A table with rollers moves backwards and forwards over it, during a steam treatment
1900	4 July	12078	La Brosse, T.A.de	Fabric for boots and shoes made from felt backed with a melton cloth of a different colour and felted together. The backing is teazled and the felt calendered

Year	Date	Number	Name	Description
1900	26 July	13439	Bremner, J. and Warry, J. J.	Thick layer or core of hard-pressed felt has a surface layer of rubber for pump valves or for buffers/ window frame rests, wheel tyres, boot and shoe soles, mats, stair treads
1902	7 February	3097	Mitchell, R. J. C.	Manufacture of seamless felt blankets for calico printing, paper-making, scouring. Endless seamless batt of solid felt is formed on a cylindrical former or endless apron is hardened and fulled. It is made shorter and wider than required then stretched to reduce width and dried
1902	12 July	15545	Reddaway, F.	Woollen felt saturated with oil and cowrie gum as a leather substitute for driving belts
1902	28 July	16648	Cockroft, T. M.	Felt packing ring for bottles, steam pipe joints. Wool wound on a mandrel shaken together, proofed with oils, and cut into rings of the required size on a lathe
1903	19 February	3913	Mitchell, R. J. C.	Rollers for calendering etc. Stringing 1/8th inch thick washers on a metal axle and compressing them together. The metal discs are also interspersed
1903	9 May	10589	Mitchell R. J. C.	Endless sleeves of felt for rollers, A seam is made either at hardening or stitched then milled and ground
1903	9 May	10590	Mitchell R. J. C.	Endless blanket for printing. Ends of roll overlapped, hardened, milled and ground
1904	21 November	25234	Mitchell R. J. C. and Eaton, J.	Nap, raising, dressing to produce a velvet surface effect using an abrading roller
1905	19 April	8403	Wahl, N.	Carded batt divided into small strips and wound on different rollers using a reciprocating traverse to give endless fabric with oppositely wound helical layers
1905	8 September	18167	Mitchell R.J.C. and Brand, H.O.	Felt coucher jackets and dry or wet felts mixing animal fibres with vegetable or sponge after milling, felt is carbonised and the carbon removed as dust by compression to give a porous felt.
1908	16 June	12831	Bywater, W. G. and Beanland, T. B.	Eight roller set reciprocating like Abbotts (1839) over a table but at the end of the travel the rolls lift to allow feeding
1908		17873	Mitchells, Ashworth Stansfield & Co Drummond, A. K.	To prevent endless stretching a non-stretch strip is incorporated on the surface during manufacture. For laundry felts, printers' blankets, dry and wet felt.

5 THE FELT MILLS

THE FELT MILLS OF LEEDS

Locating information on the mills used by the feltmakers of Leeds has been somewhat elusive with data only available to any extent on Elmwood Mill, of The Patent Woollen Cloth Company, and Highfield Mill, of Carr and Butterworth. Pictures of John Wilkinson's St Helens Mill featured in a relatively obscure book about railway journeys[1] and these are reproduced without comment, together with an old map of the St Helens district of Leeds to show its location.

ELMWOOD MILL

The mill and associated fields were originally owned by John Wilkinson who sold them to Lord, Robinson, and Foster, about the year 1824, but when their business failed, Wilkinson again acquired the mill in 1826. The fields went to their creditors in building plots: two plots to Messrs. Watson, dyers, one plot to Ramsden plumbers, and two plots to Robinson, finisher. John Wilkinson then let the mill to a Mr. Hargreaves, who built a new mill and reservoirs. Shortly after Hargreaves gave up the tenancy, it was let to another unnamed person (initials J. P.) and thereafter John Wilkinson went abroad, entrusting the management of the mill to the Northern Capital Banking Company, who later let it out to Robinson and Watson. Later Henry Stack bought the mill for the sum of £4500 and occupied it for about eighteen months before he died and his executors sold the mill to the Patent Felting Company in 1840[2]. At this time, the mill contained one teazer, one willey, seven scribblers, two pair of mules, eight gigs, twelve pair of stocks and one washing machine. In 1853, a new dryhouse was built measuring one hundred and thirty-three feet long by twenty-two feet wide to house the tenters. On 11 October 1857 there was a fire that caused damage assessed at £680/15s/0d (£680/15s/0d). By 1864, a new self-contained felt mill had been built with its own engine and boiler, increasing the capacity by fifty percent.

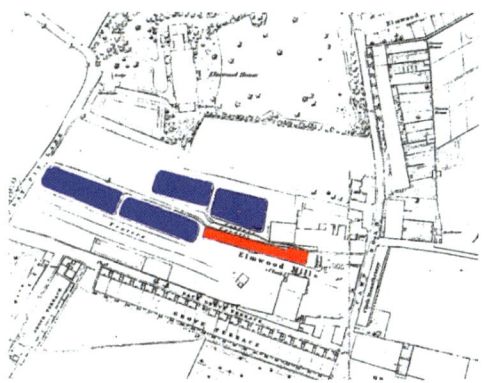

Map showing Elmwood Mill around 1897 and the four reservoirs supplying it with water

FELT IN BRITAIN

The mill was bought by Mitchells, Ashworth, Stansfield and Co in 1904 when The Patent Woollen Cloth Company went into receivership. From their survey in 1914, the area occupied by the mill was 4042 square yards and had a value of £10,500. As a later claim to fame, the mill was occupied, from 1910 to 1914, by Montague Burton as he expanded to become the internationally renowned men's clothing company Burtons.

Glimpses of Elmwood Mill in the background, on the left is Howarth Terrace and on the right the bakery and grocers shop that faced Clay Pit Lane[3].

ST. HELENS MILL

The following are reproductions of John Wilkinson's Mill in St Helens, Leeds

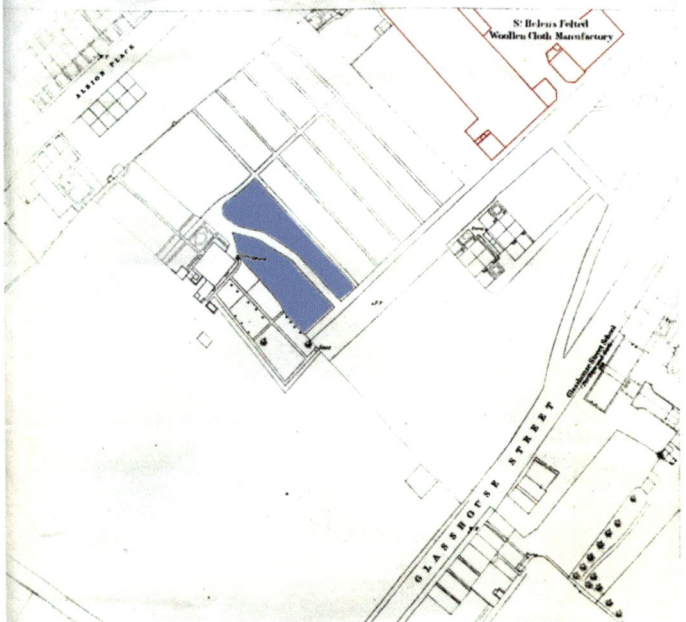

Map of St. Helens Mill circa 1897, showing the mill, tenterfields, and reservoirs, a pump is positioned in the lower lodge

THE FELT MILLS

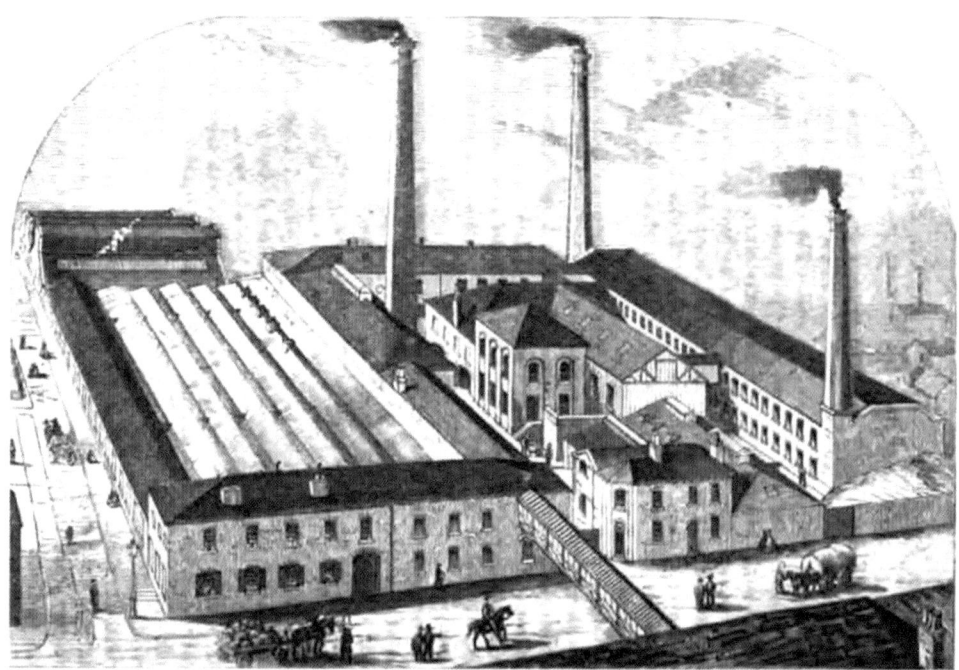

Main Production factory of John Wilkinson's St. Helens Mill 1890, the overhead walkway leads to the factory annex below

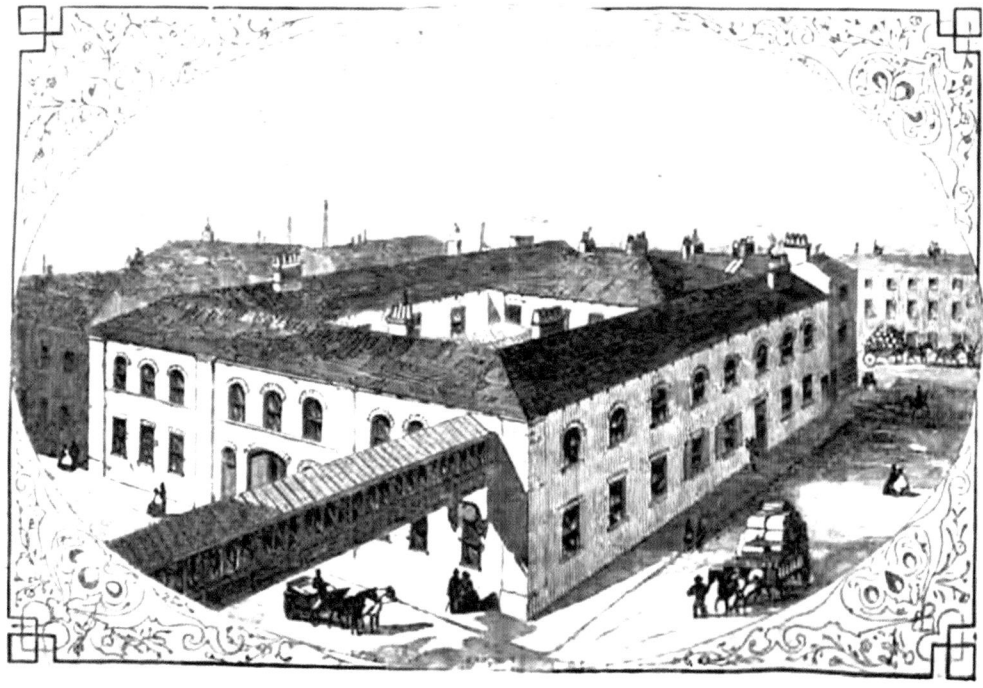

Annex of John Wilkinson's factory St. Helens around 1861, the walkway connected it to the main mill

HIGHFIELD MILL

Carr and Butterworth's Highfield Mill Leeds in 1980 with Lady Pit Lane in the foreground

Highfield Mill, like many early mills, had the owner's house attached to it so he could oversee the day-to-day operations, but at some point in time, the land of Highfield House was sold to West Hunslett Liberal Club who built the present premises on it. The only sign of the presence of the house in 1980 was the dividing wall between the mill and the Liberal Club and this showed signs of much structural alteration. There were the remains of a doorway bricked in and there was evidence that there was a wall running at right angles to the present wall across the length of the yard. In addition, there were once cottages along the length of the yard, long since demolished to make way for a row of garages.

Along the length of one side of the mill, there was a cobbled road that passed a massive square brick chimney, which once served a Lancashire boiler. The large size of the chimney was necessary to give a large up draught for the furnace. At the junction of the road with Lady Pit Lane there was a brick archway and evidence of this was seen in the brickwork of the mill and the remaining wall. There was a similar arch at the other side of the mill, both these arches both leading to cottages on either side of the mill and around it.

The entrance and general office appeared to have been built later than the rest of the mill, though the reception area had gas mountings on the wall similar to those used for gas lighting. There used to be a fireplace in the centre of the office that needed to be cleaned out and the fire lit daily. The mill was single storey with the roof supported by massive wooden beams that were in good condition in 1980. There was also a small cellar. There was no clear evidence of the line shafting necessary to drive old machinery nor was there evidence of a water supply that could have served the heavy demands of the felt trade. However, there was a beck that led from Elland Football Ground through Hunslett and passed underneath the mill but was culverted some time before 1980. From the plans held by Henry Moore, the factory covered an area of six hundred square yards.

The Ground Plan of Highfield Mill, Beeston, Leeds

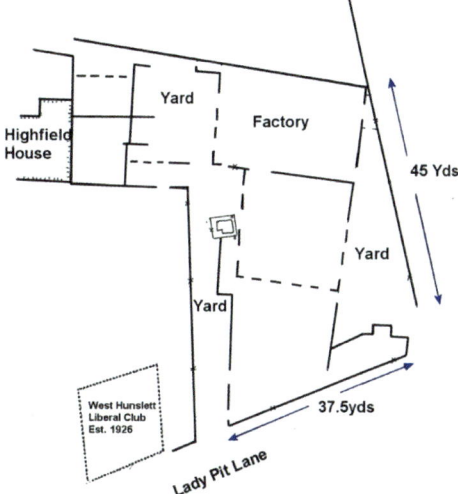

Carr and Butterworth produced felt from Highfield Mill in 1857 until 1870 when Carr and Butterworth were listed separately. In 1881, George Butterworth only was manufacturing felt at Highfield Mill until 1905. Their history can be traced from the list of Securities and Deeds held at Highfield Mill[4] and detailed in the appendix at the end of this chapter.

A list of securities held by the Midland Bank (Leeds), confirmed that the mill was used for felt making, with a mortgage dated 22 October 1868 attributed to G. W. Carr and Geo. Butterworth through the Yorkshire Banking Company. There was a re-conveyance of the Yorkshire Banking Company to G. W. Carr and W. N. Walker on 10 April 1879.

MIDLAND MILL

Midland Mill was the production site of Taylor, Wordsworth and Co, Manufacturer of Felting machinery and was sited in the Holbeck district of Leeds very close to the majority of feltmakers.

Taylor Wordsworth's Midland Mill

FELT IN BRITAIN

THE FELT MILLS OF ROSSENDALE

The felt mills of Rossendale were centred on the rivers Irwell, Whitewell, and Limy Water. The area had a long history of woollen cloth manufacturing with a national reputation for producing high quality block printed fabrics, said to be because of the exceptional properties of the water supply, particularly the Whitewell. When the woven woollen industry experienced a steep decline in the mid 1800s many of the mills were adapted to produce felt, with varying degrees of success. Eventually all the mills succumbed to a changing economic climate and were demolished to make way for modern development. The only exception was the Isle of Man Mill, which in 2009, was still standing, though then used as industrial units.

There is an excellent typescript manuscript entitled "The Mills of Rawtenstall" in Rawtenstall Library written by John Davies that lists the history of the majority of Rossendale mills recording mill news items from the local newspapers of the time. Much of what follows has included his research work, together with information from within the industry itself through records kept by Bury and Masco (Holdings) Limited and other industry documents. The location of the mills is shown in the map below.

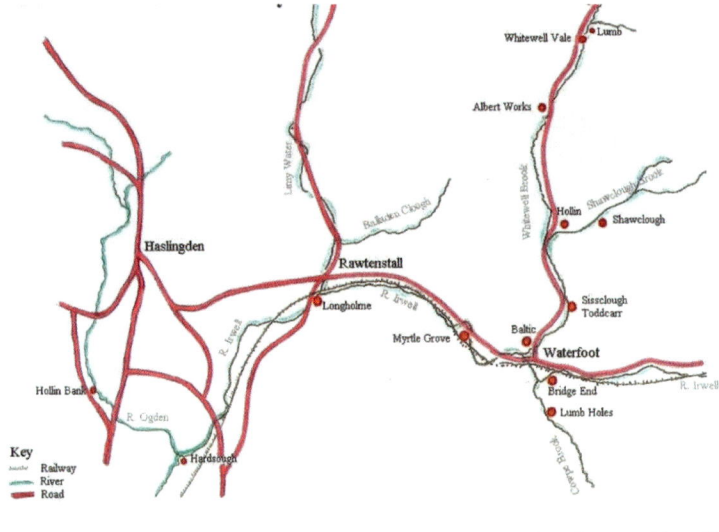

Map showing the location of the felt mills of Rossendale

ALBERT WORKS

The following description of Albert Works has been adapted from John Davies' eyewitness account that gives an evocative picture of what the mill was like.

The mill was typical of the early period of industrial development, having mostly small rooms, some of them holding only one machine. The reason for this was twofold: firstly, additional rooms could be easily constructed as money became available, and secondly, damage by the spread of fire could be minimised. If a fire started and it was caught in time, it would only damage one room, leaving the rest of the mill in tact. Additionally, one of the early fire fighting techniques was to smother the fire with steam, which was ideal when the room was small because the steam could rapidly fill it and dowse the flames.

At one time, it is believed that there were two boiler houses in the mill, but an old engraving shows three chimneys, but this may have been artistic license. In the early days, the boilers served as many as nine steam engines, some of which were directly connected to individual production machines, such as the three large tentering machines, which each had their own engine. Two wuzzers and a printing machine also had their own engines. A large beam engine powered part of the mill through line shafting. Near the dye pits, there was a mortar mill filled with ashes from the boiler house, but the contents were only used when building repairs were made.

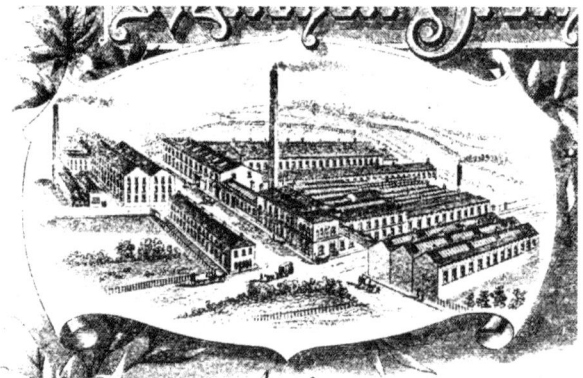

Albert Works c1890 taken from a Mitchell Brothers letterhead.

Albert works plan in 1941 turned through sixty degrees to approximate to the 1890 drawing

In 1882 Mitchells managed another mill known as the "Old Fulling Mill" This was an old mill that was demolished to make way for the new two-storey wool warehouse. The mill lodge by the side of the river Whitewell was probably used originally by this mill for its water wheel

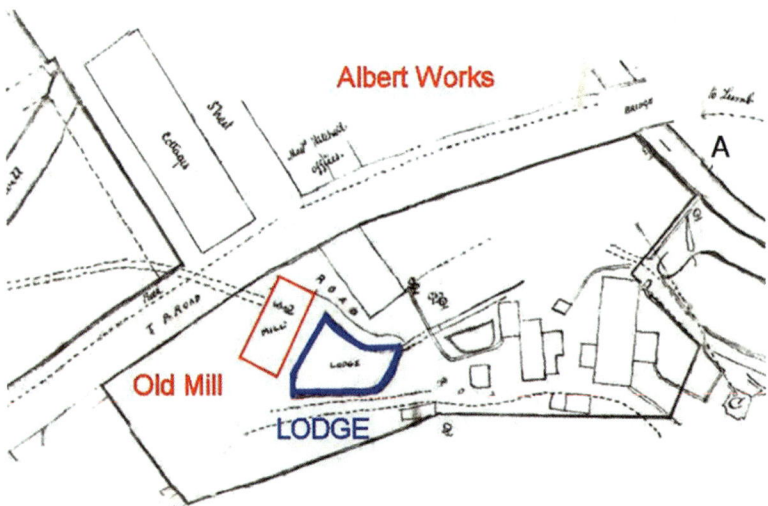

The Map of an agreement dated 1871 showing the old fulling mill acquired by the Mitchell Brothers. The conduit on the left of the diagram that entered the mill diverted water from the river Whitewell to feed the mill. There is also a conduit from the lodge or reservoir back to the Whitewell, on the right below the letter "A"

The old fulling mill was acquired by the Mitchell brothers through an agreement on 17 April 1871 between William John Sutcliffe, James Hargreaves, William Knowles on the one part and Thomas Mitchell, William Mitchell, Robert John Chadwick Mitchell on the other[5].

The Albert Works Mill was built by the Rossendale Printing and Dyeing Company in 1860 at a cost of £10,000, but they only used it until 1866, when they went bankrupt[6]. The mill was bought later that year at auction by John Mitchell and Sons of Fearnes for £3,800[7] where they set up a woollen printing works. By 1882, slippers were being manufactured there until 1889 when tapestry looms were installed in the vacated factory space[8]. From 1890, onwards the mill was extended and a new wool store was built in 1893 as was the wooden bridge connecting it to the main works[9].

The Albert Works wool store lying derelict in 1980, the open space in the foreground is where the mill once stood

In 1953, for the coronation of Queen Elizabeth II, the firm built an archway over Burnley Road East. This was built of canvas on a wooden frame in the joiners shop at the mill[10]."

Decorations being installed at Albert Works for the 1953 coronation

The closure of Albert Works was announced the day before Trinity weekend in 1957 and finally closed two weeks before Christmas. When the mill was demolished, part of the site was occupied by Associated Dairies and the major part of the site landscaped by the County Council.

BALTIC MILL

Baltic Mill was originally known as "Little Baltic" in 1800, when James and William Clegg began to spin cotton yarn[11] there. By 1818, it was a fulling mill that was run by George Schofield[12], and then sometime before 1838, it was occupied by James Schofield, a woollen baize manufacturer, until around 1854. In 1857, Captain G. W. Law Schofield was making baizes and bockings there until at least 1865[13] and must have been making felt during this time because when the mill was being let in 1873 it contained a felt machine[14]. Around 1869, the mill was used by James Law Schofield and Co Limited, listed as a worsted spinner and would not therefore have used the felting machine[15]. In 1876, Henry Rothwell was making felt at Baltic Mill until he failed two years later in 1878[16]. In 1879, the mill was let to Lawrence Ormerod and Co. of Cowpe who manufactured felt there but failed that same year owing £900 and in 1880, the mill was advertised for let and was not occupied until 1886.

Baltic Mill showing the River Irwell flowing past the mill

FELT IN BRITAIN

Baltic was one of the first mills in Rossendale to have electricity installed[17]. Baltic remained a felt mill long after all the other mills had ceased production and in many cases, were demolished. In 1977, when the roof was in danger of collapse, Baltic Mill was on the verge of closure but an investment of £300,000 by Bury and Masco Industries revitalised the mill and gave it another sixteen years of life. It remained under the ownership of MASCO, Bury and Masco Industries Limited, and Bury Cooper Whitehead Limited until they stopped making felt in 1993. The mill was subsequently demolished and replaced by a housing development consisting of fifty-three houses.

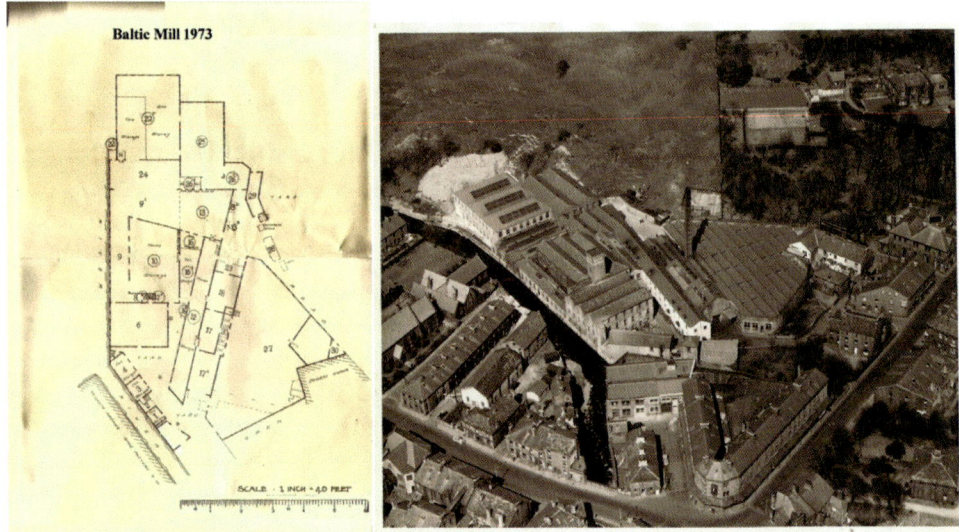

The Plan of Baltic Mill before renovation in 1973 and an aerial view of it in 1977

BRIDGE END MILL, WATERFOOT

One of the first occupiers of Bridge End Mill was George Bridge and Co. and in 1802, it was offered for sale with its contents. The contents consisted of two fulling stocks with six indoor tenter seams and one hundred and twelve field frames, which indicated that this was a woollen cloth mill. Whiteheads, of Rossendale, ran the mill for spinning until 1824, before leaving it and moving production to Higher Mill. In 1832, the mill was occupied by John Pilling and owned by George Ashworth and by 1848, two cotton spinners, John Whittaker and John Ashworth, were resident there. In 1854 they were joined by John Lord, a woollen manufacturer and at that time the mill was small, covering around five hundred and fifty-five square yards[18].

By 1863, the mill was being used by Cunliffe and Bridge, wool-staplers and cotton spinners. Then in 1878, under their occupancy, the mill was severely damaged by fire at six o'clock on the morning of 14 October[19] an event that was to repeat itself many times in the subsequent history of the mill. At that time, the mill was still owned by George Ashworth.

For four years from 1874 to 1878, Henry Rothwell occupied the mill and was the first to make felt there[20], but in 1878, he failed with liabilities of £20,000 and his equipment was auctioned off. The auction of machinery at Bridge End Mill on 28 November 1878 listed carding engines, willeys, tummers, cards, stocks, a tenter machine, and five felt hardeners, which gives a good idea of the size of his business. The Mitchell brothers secured most of the felt making equipment.

In 1879, Richard Ashworth leased the mill[21] for making felt and in 1887, he was described as a felt maker with manufacturing premises in Bridge End Mill[22]. When Richard Ashworth joined the MASCO merger the lease that existed for the Mill between him and by Letitia Jane Bridge was re-assigned to the new company in 1905[23].

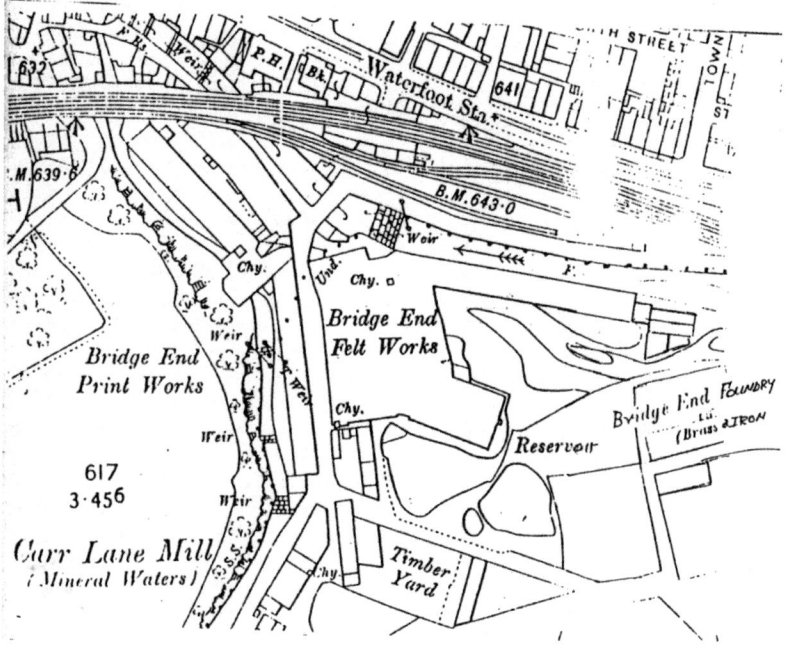

Bridge End Mill from Ordnance Survey Map of 1844 revised 1908

The mill had more than its fair share of bad luck and was plagued with periodic outbreaks of fire, particularly in the summer months. There were fires at the mill in 1902, and in 1903, but the most devastating one occurred on 12 January 1911, when a fire started in the warehouse and gutted the mill resulting in £5000 to £10,000 worth of damage[24]. The mill was rebuilt and a sixty horsepower electric motor was installed to provide an electricity supply. There were subsequent fires in 1927, 1933, and 1949, all in August. The only other time that the mill was closed was when it ran out of coal for one week in 1947[25].

After the Second World War, the fortunes of the felt industry declined and as part of a rationalisation of manufacturing capacity Bridge End Mill was closed in August 1952, with the loss of one hundred and fifty workers[26], the mill later being demolished in February 1956 and the Waterfoot Health Centre built on the site.

Throughout the life of the mill, the power was provided by its water wheel, which was installed before 1877. The wheel, which was twenty-three feet in diameter and fifteen feet in width, was housed in a small room below the lodge, and the speed was regulated by sluice gates, which controlled the quantity of water being fed to the wheel. This, together with one small steam engine, had driven the entire mill.

At the time of its closure, the mill occupied a floor area of some seven thousand four hundred and forty four square yards.

FELT IN BRITAIN

FOUNTAIN MILL

Fountain Mill was a narrow stone building part of which was two-storey and part three-storey with the mill chimney at one end of it but separated from the mill by a flight of steps leading from the mill yard up to Fountain Road[27].

In 1868, the mill was a woollen cloth mill working twenty looms, but the company failed and the equipment went for sale. From 1876 to 1879, the mill was worked by Lord Brothers who were waste cotton manufacturers, failing in 1879 when their equipment was sold by auction[28].

Fountain Mill and Albert Works, the electricity substation supplied power from the National Grid

Fountain Mill was first associated with the felt industry when the Mitchell brothers bought it from Alice Ann Rushton, Robert Worswick, and his wife Mary on 1 November 1884 under copyhold leasehold. The fact that the lease ran from 1853 indicates that they owned the mill as early as 1853[29]. In 1904, the ownership passed to MASCO and in 1957 it was demolished at the same time as Albert works and the site later landscaped.

HARDSOUGH MILL

Hardsough Mill was built around 1800 by John Bowker, a baize and flannel manufacturer, who only occupied it for a short time before he died in 1804. At that time, the mill was sixty-six feet long and fifty-one feet wide and three storeys in height, it was powered by three water wheels each three-foot wide, fed by the nearby River Irwell. From 1816 to 1826, the mill was let to William Hutchinson and Sons, woollen manufacturers, and then to William Sagar, a fulling miller, until the late 1840s. Thereafter, it was occupied by James Hindle who was spinning cotton there as well as fulling cloth until his death in 1857, leaving his sons to run the business for a further four years. In 1861, the Rawtenstall and Hardsough Spinning and Manufacturing Co. took over the mill but when they failed in 1864 the Hardsough Spinning and Weaving Company took their place until 1870, when they too went bankrupt[30].

James Rostron bought the mill on 5 March 1872 from John Moss Kirkman, George Lyon, and Ellen Milne. He bequeathed it to his to his son Jordon, who inherited it in 1890 on James' death[31] and who began making felt there with his brothers Edmund and James, to be joined later by J. and W. Stansfield[32]. During this time the mill was considerably expanded and had two steam engines as well as two water wheels to power the mill, which had six pairs of fulling stocks as well as other felt making equipment[33].

THE FELT MILLS

Hardsough Mill in 1915

On 7 July 1904, the businesses and mill were sold to William Stansfield and Richard Ashworth for the sum of £9,316[34]. The agreement was between James Rostron on the one part, John Woodcock, Henry Tomlinson of the second part, and John Stansfield, Watson Stansfield of the third part, and Richard Ashworth, William Stansfield of the fourth part, and this included an exclusion clause that the Rostrons and John and Watson Stansfield should no longer engage in felt making. Then with the formation of the MASCO combine, this purchase was included in the merger documents as Hardsough Manufacturing Company and used as collateral. The company used the mill for ten years before letting it out to a number of different firms, and in 1938, the mill was demolished.

HOLLIN MILL, SCOUTBOTTOM WATERFOOT

There were three Hollin Mills referred to in the district: Hollin Mill, Hollin Print Works, Higher Hollin Bank Mill, all situated at Scout Bottom in Waterfoot. Hollin Print Works was likely to have been attached to Hollin Mill Waterfoot since it was the norm in Rossendale for a print works to be attached to a woollen mill.

The first reference to Hollin Mill, Waterfoot, was in 1820 when it was a fulling mill owned by John Ashworth, a fulling miller, who probably built it around this time as there were few such mills in Rossendale before 1818[35]. In 1828, Richard Ashworth and Son were making baizes, bockings, and woollens there until 1828, when John Tattersall occupied it. In 1848, George and John Rostron were making woollens there[36] and in 1854, George Rostron alone was manufacturing there[37]. Later the mill was taken over by Ingham Taylor and in 1857, they were the first to manufacture felt there. However, there must have been some difficulties as the business was taken over by a felt machinery maker[38], who at that time was most probably Taylor Wordsworth from Leeds[39]. For a brief period, James Lord was manufacturing there in 1864[40] and in 1865, Ingham Taylor was once more in business there making baize, bockings, and woollens[41]. At the same time, Robert Hoyle was printing woollen cloth in Hollin Print Works, probably in the same premises.

Ingham Taylor then let the mill to Taylor and Haworth for the manufacture of felt carpet but this business had a short history before it went into liquidation and was selling its nearly new equipment at an auction in 1871. The machinery consisted of one forty-eight-inch teazer, three eighty-one-inch tummers, two carders, three hardeners (two made by Taylor Wordsworth and one made by S. S.

Stott, two fulling stocks, and a tentering machine having a chain of one hundred and forty yards in length[42]. It is likely that James Taylor acquired the machinery because felt continued to be made at the mill until 1874 when James Taylor died and his widow petitioned for liquidation of the business[43]. Just before this, the landlord had installed a compound engine, made by S. S. Stott of Haslingden, to power the mill.

In 1876, Ingham Taylor's company was described as woollen printers[44] and in 1879, the printing business was being run by Taylor and Sons[45]. Around 1875, the mill saw its last felt manufacturer in the business of J. T. Barcroft (John Thomas) who seemed to have prospered by 1878 and yet in 1879 he was petitioning for liquidation with liabilities of £8,339/6s/3d and assets of £2,649/11s/0d. His felt capacity on closure was four carders, eighty-one and seventy-two inches wide with batt frames, three ninety-inch wide hardeners, two pairs of stocks and a patent tentering machine[46]. Between 1880 and 1886, the mill was used for woven cloth in a business owned by Joshua Townsend and housed one hundred and twenty looms supplied by seven thousand spindles[47].

From 1873 to 1881, Joseph Stansfield was making felt in Higher Hollin Bank Mill, and he was then recorded as owning it. This is most likely the mill referred to in the court case brought by Joshua Townsend and others for his default. The mill was a block of buildings consisting of three rows of rooms running parallel to the main road at Newchurch. The block was two storeys in height with twelve windows along its length; the top floor was used as a wool store, and the lower floor for preparing the wool for processing. Behind these buildings was a single storey building housing the carding room, which had a timber floor positioned over the River Whitewell. At the rear of this room, there were eight "tummers" and four carders. Unfortunately, the mill was destroyed by fire in December 1881, with damage estimated at £8,000 to £9000, for which Joseph Stansfield had no insurance cover. He subsequently went out of business[48].

For a brief period from 1886 to 1891 the mill was used for slipper manufacture by J. H. Hirst, before being let to John Taylor and Co., manufacturers of belting who manufactured there from 1895 to around 1951[49]. Two other companies, Doric Co. and Woodfield Engineering Co. used the mill before it burnt to the ground in 1979[50].

ISLE OF MAN MILL

In 1848, the mill was used as a cotton-spinning mill first by Henry and John Pilling, then in 1852 by John Wrigley and Co.[51] then later by John Pickup. When John Pickup died around 1865, the mill was offered for let as a spinning and weaving operation and the lease taken by Henry and Thomas Briggs from the owner George Hargreaves until he went bankrupt in 1870[52]. By 1876 the mill was being occupied by two manufacturers: Mathew Hartley, and James & Edward Pickup[53]. James and Edward ran their business until 1888, when their partnership was dissolved and Edward ran the business on his own as James Pickup and Brother[54].

On 29 March 1889, the Mitchell brothers bought the mill from Mathew Hartley and Richard Heyworth in what appears to have been an investment rather than for use in their felt manufacturing business, because Pickup Brothers were still manufacturing there until 1915[55]. However, it is possible that the Mitchells were using another part of the mill because, in 1896, one of their employees was drowned there when he was activating the waterwheel[56]. By 1924 the mill was being worked both by the MASCO combine for felt and by Hargreaves (Lumb) Ltd for cotton goods[57].

THE FELT MILLS

Isle of Man Mill in 2009

From 1936 onwards there was no involvement with the felt industry and the mill was acquired by Excelsior Heels Limited until 1964, when it was let out to local contractors. By 1977, the mill lodge was derelict and renovated by Lumb Valley anglers[58], whilst in 1982 part of the weaving shed was demolished and the rest of the mill used as a garage, and in 2009 was made into industrial units, under the ownership of B. & E. Boys Limited.

LONGHOLME MILL

Thomas Kay bought Longholme Mill in 1812 when it was a dilapidated woollen mill and he rebuilt it as a cotton mill[59]. He installed power looms there in 1824 but suffered from the riots in 1826 when his power looms were smashed[60]. Thomas Kay remained in business at least until 1832 and in 1848 John Robinson Kay, cotton spinner and manufacturer was operating from the mill, with a further entry for him in 1854[61]. By 1876 Peter Halstead Whitehead and Co. were conducting the same business from there but ceased production in 1879, having at that time a capacity of four hundred and sixty-six looms and twenty six thousand spindles[62].

The mill then lay empty for years before being occupied by Messrs. Bracewell of Earby in 1882 and re-equipped with eight hundred and fifty looms employing two hundred and ninety-nine hands[63]. However, this venture was short lived and in 1885 William Sutcliffe, corn millers of Bacup and

Rawtenstall, purchased the property from the executors of the late Mr. Robinson Kay and began a rebuilding programme costing £30,000 to convert Longhome into a corn mill[64].

Longholme Mill in 1844

The new building was two hundred and twenty feet in length, sixty-six feet wide and was five storeys high. It was powered by a fifty horsepower beam engine supplied by Petrie of Rochdale and a ninety horsepower water turbine supplied by Messrs. Kay of Bury. Electricity was also installed for the first time in 1886[65]. The mill also had its own fresh water supply from a well, the water being pumped by a submersible pump up to towers, which were used to supply the factory's sprinklers[66].

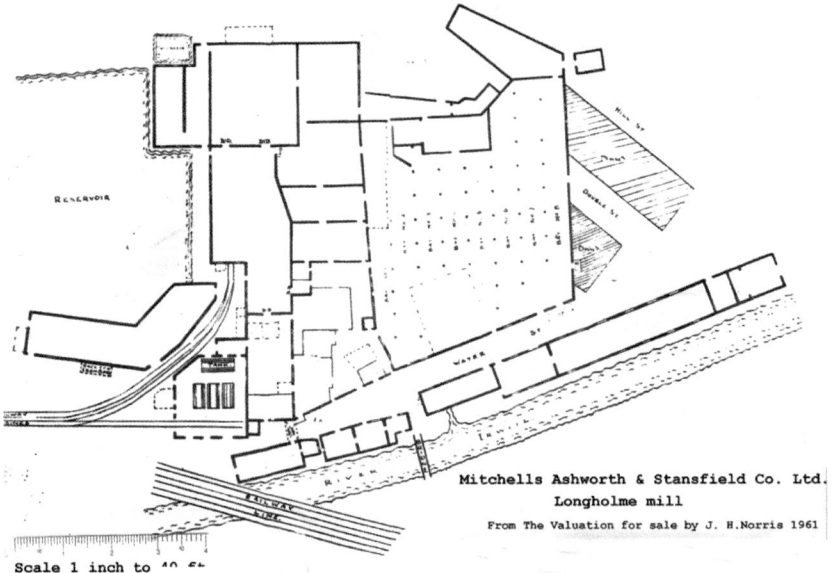

Plan of Longhome Mill in 1961 prior to the formation of Bury and Masco Limited

In 1895, William Sutcliffe and Sons sold the mill to Richard Ashworth, who then converted it into a felt mill[67], building a new section that connected the five-storey building to the buildings at the rear of the site in 1896[68].

THE FELT MILLS

After the merger of Mitchells, Ashworth, Stansfield & Co. the ownership of the mill transferred to the new company and life in the mill was relatively uneventful with just a minor fire occurring in 1935[69], a stable situation that continued until 1962 when MASCO merged with Bury Felt Manufacturing Company to form Bury and Masco Industries Limited. As the felt industry declined further in the late 1960's, the closure of Longholme was announced in 1971[70] and the mill was shut in July 1972 with the loss of thirty-three jobs out of a total of eighty-six. A year later, the mill was demolished and the site cleared to make way for a new supermarket, which was built there in 1977.

Longholme Mill in 1972

LUMB HOLES

In 1810, Lumb Holes Mill was owned by George Ashworth and occupied by Samuel Whittaker[71] and by 1828, James Ashworth was working the mill for the manufacture of woollen cloth and baizes. By 1854, Robert Cunliffe and Sons were making woollen cloth there and in 1863, Emanuel Nutall was renting the mill from the executors of another Richard Ashworth of Bridge End House[72]. At that time, the building was described as an ancient two-storey mill that had been burnt out by a dramatic fire. Fortunately, the building was insured and the mill rebuilt, and then in 1869, it was occupied by Hindle, Gaskell and Hargreaves, who were described as felt manufacturers[73]. The firm did not last long because in 1870, there was a sale by auction of woollen and woollen felt manufacturing equipment[74]. In 1872 John Hargreaves and Co. were using the mill for block printing woollen cloth, but their business too, was liquidated that year and the equipment sold by auction[75].

The remains of Lumb Holes Mill in 1979

FELT IN BRITAIN

Lumb Holes and Carr Mills on Cowpe Brook in 1820

In 1875 the mill was again manufacturing felt, this time for carpeting, by W. and J. Rothwell (William and James), but again this was a short lived enterprise because they were selling their equipment at auction in 1880[76]. Around this time, William Stansfield formed a partnership with Henry Coupe to produce felt at the mill, a partnership that lasted until 1891, when William Stansfield continued to manufacture felt there as well as at Baltic Mill. By 1893, William Stansfield owned the mill and used it as collateral in the merger between his company and those of the Mitchell brothers, Richard Ashworth, and others when they merged to form MASCO in 1904.

Like the majority of mills in the area Lumb Holes suffered from a series of disasters: a great flood in 1884 washed away the foundations and hailstones broke the windows, a fire in 1893, another major flood in 1894 that also washed away part of the foundations, and finally a major fire in 1906 that brought the roof down. However, the mill remained in use in the felt industry until 1929 when it was put up for sale by MASCO[77]. A portion of the mill was demolished in 1937 but the remainder of the mill was still in use in 1943 when tallow was being made there by Everitt Brothers[78]. In 1979, it was a romantic but derelict ruin.

MYRTLE GROVE MILL

Myrtle Grove mill was built by Edward Rostron in 1854 specifically for making and printing felt. He ran the business until his death in 1882, when the mill closed[79]. It was reopened briefly by his sons who ran it until 1886, when the business failed[80] and the mill with its contents was put up for sale in 1887 and for auction in 1888.

At that time, the mill comprised of three main buildings, one of one-storey, one of two-storeys, and one of three-storeys. The one storey building consisted of a warehouse, scribbling room, card room, and hardening house. The two-storey building housed a dry house, washing room, and pattern room. The three-storey building contained the mechanics shop, printing block store, dye house, joiners shop, print room, colour shop, and drugs room. The mill was serviced by two steam boilers twenty feet long and seven feet in diameter powering five steam engines, four of them vertically aligned and one horizontal. There were two vertical engines with a cylinder diameter of twenty inches and forty-inch stroke, one vertical engine with a fourteen-inch diameter cylinder and twenty-eight inch stroke, another with a ten-inch diameter cylinder and twenty-eight inch stroke. The horizontal engine was new and had an eight-inch diameter cylinder and a twelve-inch stroke[81].

THE FELT MILLS

The mill was bought by Roland Rawlinson in March 1888 for the sum of £3,035[82] and he installed equipment for producing woven cloth, concentrating on the manufacture of baizes, bockings, and woollen fabric. In 1889, he built a new weaving shed and printing department[83], and in 1890, the new buildings were visited by Lord Salisbury, the Conservative Prime Minister of the time, who addressed a great Conservative rally there[84]. The mill was further expanded in 1896 with an extension to the new weaving shed and by 1902 it had a five hundred horsepower cross-compound engine built by S. S. Stott and, as well as driving machinery it also pumped water from the River Irwell to the steam boilers[85] to supplement the water from its two lodges.

In 1902, the mill was made up of two separate two-storey buildings. The one nearest Waterfoot was used for storing wool and other manufacturing materials and said at the time to be "fourteen windows in length". The other building was destroyed by fire and was eighty-five yards long and twenty yards in breadth. It was used for wool washing, teazing (skutching) and as a wool warehouse. In February of that year, a massive fire broke out causing £5000 worth of damage, mostly in the wool-teazing department, for which the company was not insured[86].

Myrtle Grove Mill c 1970

In 1904, when the MASCO combine was formed, felt was again manufactured at the mill. When Roland Rawlinson died, the business was run by his sons Herman, Neville, Ernald and Irwin, though it was Herman who took charge[87]. By 1954, only Ernald was left alive and he sold the business to MASCO Limited in August of that year. In 1962 when MASCO merged with the Bury Felt Manufacturing Company Limited, the mill became the property of Bury and Masco Limited, who adopted it as the headquarters for the new company and holding group, Bury and Masco (Holdings) Limited. It was then being used for the manufacture of coarse felts both needled and felted using jute and hair fibres. Part of the mill on the left of Lench road, known as little Siberia because it was so cold, was converted into a facility that the company used as a felt fabrication unit.

FELT IN BRITAIN

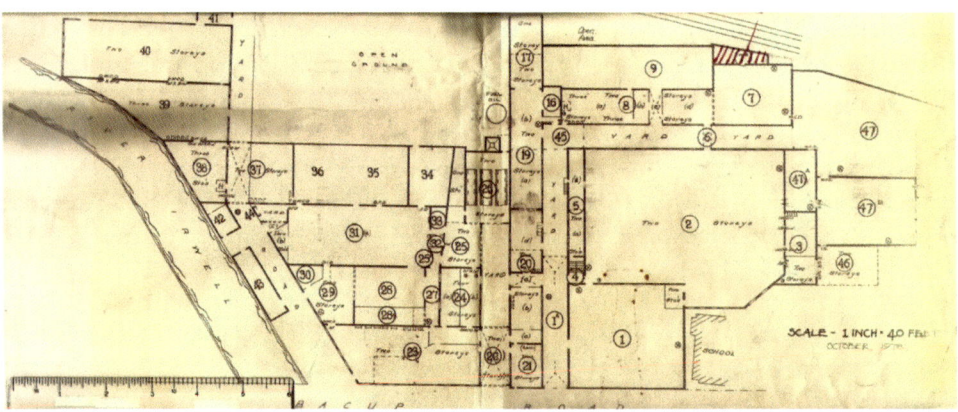

Plan of Myrtle Grove Mill in 1973

By 1976, the mill was making purely needle-felts using only synthetic fibre, mostly for filtration cloths, under the name of Webron Products Limited. This company was wholly owned by Bury and Masco (Holdings) Limited, which in turn was owned by the Scapa Group plc. In 1981 Webron Products Limited closed the needle loom division in Myrtle Grove and the mill was demolished in 1982[88].

PLUNGE MILL

The mill was built in 1801 by Giles Hoyle, a clothier, for fulling woollen cloth, under leasehold from the New Hall Estate, but he went bankrupt in 1812. John Wallwork took over the lease and on his death in 1836, his son Thomas worked the mill for fulling and cotton spinning, and bought it in 1844. When he died in 1862, his daughters ran the business for five years before renting the mill out to Robert Heyworth and John Wrigley. In 1869, the mill was producing felt under the management of John Wadsworth and Joshua Cunliffe, trading as John Wadsworth and Co. but they failed in 1870.

All that remains of Plunge Mill in 1980

The last tenants to occupy the mill, before it was sold to Alexander Barlow and Sons in 1904, were Walter and John Rushton, cotton manufacturers, the latter going bankrupt in 1879. For almost fifty years, the mill was neglected and it fell into ruin until it was demolished around 1950[89]. By 1980, little of the mill remained, though the waterfall that once powered the water wheel was still prominent.

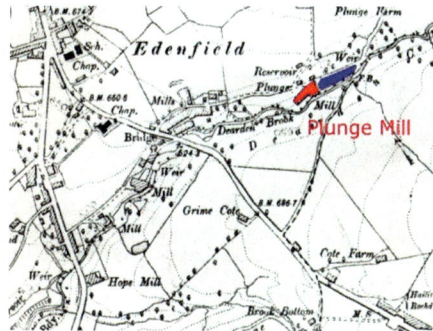

Map showing the position of Plunge Mill

SHAWCLOUGH MILL

The mill was known as Lower Mill Shawclough, and was situated on the Burnley Turnpike Road, near Hollin, Newchurch in the district of Scout. The mill was built before 1818[90]. At the rear of the mill was a narrow gauge railway, which was two feet between rails, and which carried the mill waste to the Shawclough Road where it was tipped into horse drawn carts and taken for disposal.

Up to 1869, the mill was occupied by G. & J. Sandham who were cotton spinners and manufacturers and who became bankrupt that year. That same year, Richard Ashworth rented the mill and started making felt there. In 1874, the lodge of the mill collapsed and flooded the lower floors but caused little damage, valued at £100[91]. In 1880, Richard Ashworth vacated the mill and moved to Bridge End mill and the mill was up for rent. In 1895, the mill was occupied by Whitehead and Pilling, dyers, and up for sale in 1900. In 1910, the mill was bought by Mr. Mercer and Mr. Holland who made soft drinks there as Bowness Limited, and later, as Whitefield Soft Drinks Limited. Drinks continued to be made there until 1974 when a fire severely damaged the mill and the company went out of business[92]. During this period, the mill seems to have been divided and let to different companies. Amongst them was The Rossendale Rubber Company, making crepe soles for shoes (1932), the Doric Unit Company, making spring interior mattresses (1952), H. Hurst Limited, jute manufacturers. All of them had disastrous fires that gutted their buildings. In 1982, the mill was occupied by a two-man firm: Electro Supplies Limited[93].

SISS CLOUGH AND TODD CARR MILLS

Before it was a felt mill, Robert Holt was manufacturing woollen cloth at Todd Carr in 1854[94], then in 1876 by John Barcroft[95]. It was some years later when James Barcroft began the manufacture of felt carpets at Todd Carr, having taken over the mill from John Taylor. He built a new mill named Siss Clough next to Todd Carr[96], and then converted the latter into a print works[97]. He was still producing felt carpet in 1879[98] and on 9 July 1881, the great flood hit the mill, though it did little damage. In 1891, James Barcroft was still listed as a printer operating out of Siss Clough[99], but in 1893, part of the mill was idle and another part was manufacturing felt slippers[100], indicating that the business may have been in difficulty.

FELT IN BRITAIN

Siss Clough Mill with Todd Carr Mill in the background on the right

In 1896, the Mitchell brothers, bought out the mill and business[101] and when they merged with Richard Ashworth, William Stansfield and others in 1904, the mill became the headquarters of the combine. The mill was run by MASCO as a felt mill until 1952, when it was shut due to a fall in the felt trade[102]. Thereafter from 1960, onwards the mill was demolished piecemeal, the destruction being completed when the circular chimney was dropped in 1965. The engine beds were so massive and secured with such huge iron bolts that they could not be removed from the site, so they were left in the ground and covered over to remove all evidence of them[103].

WATERBARN MILL

There was a mill in Waterbarn, Brandwood, in 1700 but it burnt down. The mill was later rebuilt as a two-storey building, and was owned from 1751 to 1814 by Lawrence Ormerod. From then until 1816, John Ormerod and Sons were making baizes and bockings there[104], until at least 1845. During this time, sometime around 1830, it was reported that Richard Rostron, brother to Edward Rostron, took over the ownership of the mill[105], while the Ormerod family were still manufacturing there until 1863, when Ormerod and Brother and Co. auctioned their cotton and spinning machinery[106].

Up to 1838, John Ormerod and Sons were manufacturing baizes and bocking converting to cotton as well as woollens shortly before this[107]. This coincided with the building of a chimney in 1837 signifying a change in the power supply to the mill from waterwheel to steam engine. Before 1838, there was a waterwheel twelve feet wide and thirty-four feet in diameter providing twenty horsepower; thereafter the mill was supplied by a steam engine delivering thirty horsepower and a Petrie condensing beam-type steam engine with a capacity of fifty horsepower[108]. In 1865, the mill was being advertised for sale or let as a four-storey building, which is probably when it was let to John Mitchell and Sons because they were recorded as making felt carpets there in 1868[109].

Eventually the mill came to Richard Rostron and after his death in 1886, the mill was bought by Alderman Disley[110] when it was again being used to manufacture woven woollen and worsted cloths, having three hundred and eighteen looms[111]. The mill continued manufacturing under the name of Richard Rostron Limited until 1924, when it was purchased by Thomas Hill, Henry Atkinson, and a Mr. Halliday with a view to making felt as well as woven woollen cloth[112] but they did not survive a year. Thereafter the mill passed through a succession of companies until 1953, when George

THE FELT MILLS

Cormack and Sons (Waterbarn) Limited began manufacturing hair felt and needle felts there until the 1970's when the mill was owned by Antrobus Plastics. Following a number of fires the mill and chimney were demolished in 1983.

LUMB MILLS

There were two mills at Lumb separated by only a short distance; the smaller of them was positioned in the village of Lumb and the larger one, and probably of later construction, was south of it. Consequently, it is difficult to distinguish from the written accounts which mill is being referred to. The mills were sometimes identified as Higher Lumb for the smaller mill and Lower Lumb for the larger southern mill. Later, to simplify identification, the lower mill was named Whitewell Vale Mill and the higher mill called Lumb, or still Higher Lumb. This identification was equally confusing since there was another mill much lower down the river Whitewell that was called Whitewell Bottom Mill that was a spinning mill with no association with felt making.

The water supply at Higher Lumb Mill situated above Whitewell Vale Mill

John Davies records that Lumb Mill was built in 1751, and this is likely to be Higher Mill since this was built directly by the river, and therefore most likely to be powered by a water wheel, because steam engines were not in use then. In 1828, the mill was a cotton-spinning mill owned and operated by George Howarth, who continued there until 1848 when Edmund Howarth and Brothers took over the manufacture. In 1854, there were two businesses at Lumb: Edmund Howarth, processing cotton, and Samuel Lord and Co. manufacturing woollen goods. This implies that two mills were operating at this time and it is probable that Samuel Lord was working out of the lower mill because his initials SAL and the date 1859 were carved in the archway stone to the water tower at Whitewell Vale Mill[113].

By 1865, Lumb Mill was being worked by James Howarth, though he died in that year and the mill was put up for auction[114]. At that time, the mill had two steam engines, one sixteen horsepower and the other twenty-four, which powered the mill alongside a waterwheel. Interestingly, the mill had its

FELT IN BRITAIN

own gasometer that fed the mill with gas[115]. In 1868, Edmund Ashworth went bankrupt and his cotton spinning equipment was for sale by auction[116]. The mill seems to have then been rented by Jackson and Whittaker for making felt carpets and rugs, though they were out of business by 1871. Their business consisted of one willow, one devil, one tentering machine, one carder with batt frame, two hardeners, two stocks and a washing betty[117]. In 1872, Lumb Mill was described as a woollen felting mill when it burnt to the ground. At that time, it was being rented by Edward Rostron from the actual owner of the mill, John Tattersall. Edward Rostron must have rebuilt the mill because he was operating from there as a felt manufacturer in 1876[118]. Thereafter the mill was worked by John and Thomas Barcroft from 1878 until 1887, when their machinery was for sale by auction. The business production capacity consisted of two willows, six scribblers, five carders with batt frames, five hardeners, five stocks, and a patent tentering machine[119]. Then, the mill was powered by a waterwheel and a vertical steam engine with a nine-inch diameter cylinder and twelve inch stroke.

Whitewell Vale Mill c 1950, the small chimney is Higher Lumb Mill

Roland Rawlinson occupied the "woollen mill" briefly in 1889[120] before the Mitchell brothers took over the running of both mills in 1890[121]. However, they did not own the mills until much later. In 1896, they bought Lower Lumb Mill in March from George Watkinson, and in 1900 they bought Higher Lumb Mill from William Barlow in December 1900. They later used these mills as collateral in the formation of the combine Mitchells, Ashworth, Stansfield and Company Limited in 1904[122]. Felt was made there continuously until the 1950s and some time around 1957, the mills were closed as part of a rationalisation process due to falling trade. The mills inevitably declined and were demolished piecemeal in the 1960s with the main water tower of Whitewell Vale mill being spectacularly demolished in 1966.

Plan of Whitewell Vale Mill in 1961

THE MILLS OF BURY LANCASHIRE

The felt mills of Bury were all located in the same area of Freetown. This was due to the Bury Felt Manufacturing Company Limited, that was located there, and which expanded by buying out the mills surrounding their main site at Hudcar Mill.

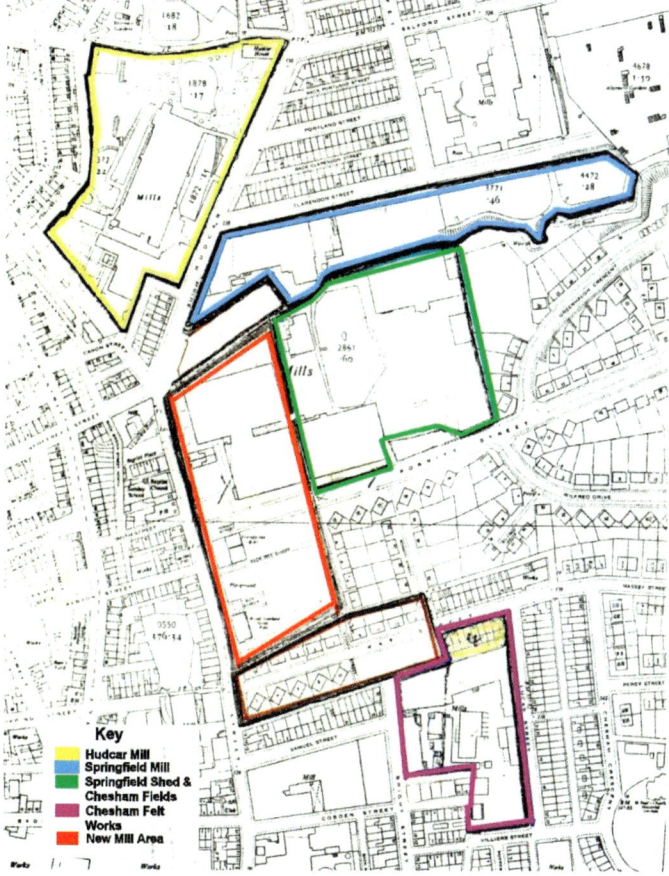

Map showing the location of the Felt Mills in Bury

HUDCAR MILL

Hudcar Mill was probably built in 1822 because the cast iron stanchions supporting the building had "1822" embossed in them[123]. It was probably built by Thomas Haslam and Son who were spinning cotton there in 1824, when the mill was known as Hudcar[124], and at the time, it was the first fireproof mill in the country. In 1827, Samuel Greg and Co, the pioneering philanthropic company based at Quarry Bank Mill in Styal, purchased Hudcar Mill, together with spinning, weaving machinery, and mill cottages for the sum of £30,000. The mill was managed by the youngest of the Greg brothers, William Rathbone Greg, when he became a partner in the business in 1828[125]. By 1832, William Greg was reported to have gone into business on his own[126], although up to 1844 Hudcar Mill was still operating under the name of Samuel Greg and Co[127]. However, by 1850 the mill was being operated by William Greg and Co[128].

The rear of Hudcar Mill in 1950 showing one of the lodges in the foreground.

There was no sign of any suitable water course nearby that could power the mill nor was there any recorded mention of a water wheel for the mill, or any signs of a wheel pit. The mill must therefore have always been powered by steam engines and in 1833, it used two engines delivering seventy horsepower[129]. The mill had an ample supply of water from three reservoirs or lodges, one at the front of the mill, one at the rear, and a small one at the west end, each were connected and fed by a brook called Green Brook. There were also two artesian wells situated within the mill grounds from which water was pumped into storage tanks[130].

By 1870, the mill was owned by R. H. Alcock and Co., who maintained the tradition of cotton spinning and manufacture there[131]. Randal Herbert Alcock lived in the mill owner's house, Hudcar West House, which was at one end of the mill and separated from it by a small round mill lodge. Running alongside the back of the house was a small lane that became known as Alcock's 'ollow (hollow). Legend has it that Alcock committed suicide by hanging himself in the mill and his ghost was said to haunt the hollow[132]. It remained in the Alcock family as cotton spinners and manufacturers until at least 1889, though by then they were trading as R. and S. Alcock and Co., the "S" being Samuel Henry.

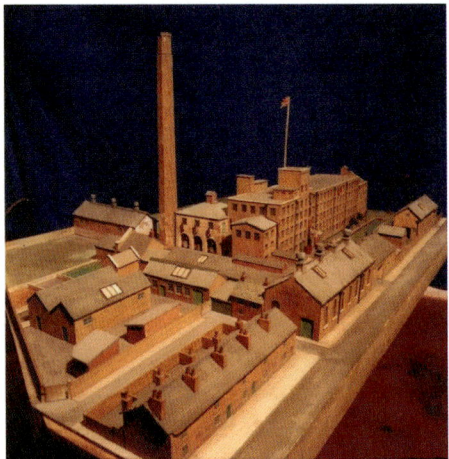

Model of Hudcar mill c1950, showing the front view

THE FELT MILLS

By 1904, the mill was owned by Charles Williams, James Preston and Charles Robert Scholes, who sold it to the Bury Felt Manufacturing Company on 31 December 1904, and from that time on it became a felt mill[133]. When the Bury Felt Manufacturing Company Limited merged with Mitchells, Ashworth, Stansfield and Co. Limited Hudcar Mill was conveyed to the new company, Bury and Masco Limited on 31 December 1965. This new company changed its name to Bury and Masco (Holdings) Limited, and another company devoted exclusively to felt making was formed and called Bury and Masco Industries Limited and the mill was conveyed from the holding company to the felt company on 15 September 1966[134]. From then until the late 1970s the fabric of the mill gradually deteriorated and in 1978 it was demolished along with the chimney.

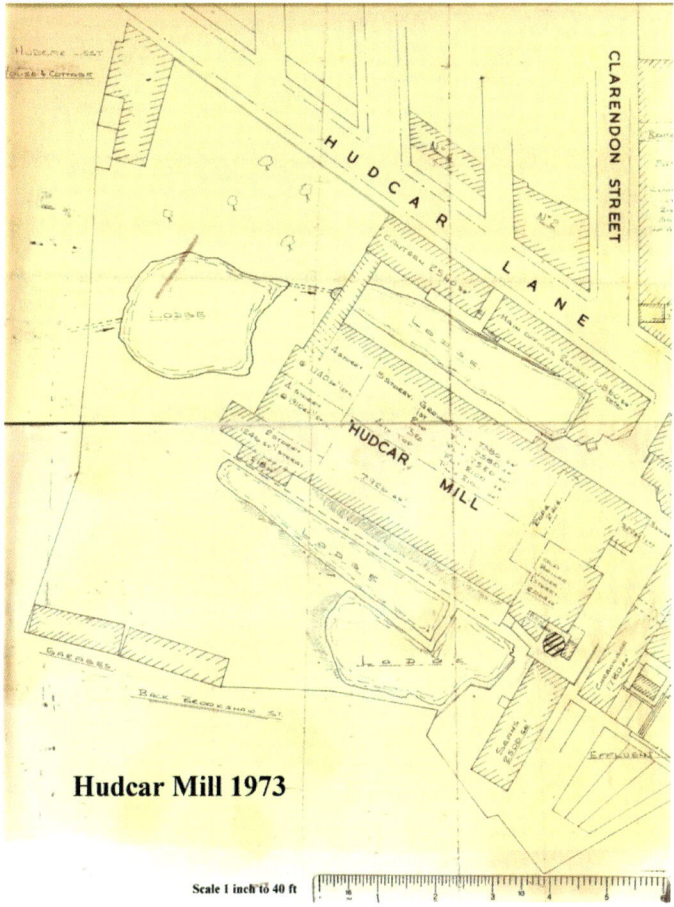

Plan of Hudcar Mill in 1973

SPRINGFIELD MILL

Springfield Mill was part of a complex of mills in the Freetown area of Bury in Lancashire that included Springfield Shed and Chesham Fields works. The first recorded use of Chesham Fields Mill was in 1824 when it was occupied by Thomas Greenhalgh, who was a cotton spinner[135]. He appears to have worked this mill until at least 1850[136]. The first time Springfield Mill appears on record was in 1871 when it was being worked by William and Joseph Schofield, cotton spinners[137] becoming J. K. Schofield by 1880 and continuing until the turn of the century[138].

Springfield Mill with Hudcar mill in the background c 1940's

Springfield Mill was later owned by Shepherd and Co. (Slippers) Limited, who manufactured slippers there until 1940, when they sold the mill to the Bury Felt Manufacturing Company Limited and from this date onwards it was used to process woollen felt. In 1962, ownership was then transferred to a new company, Bury and Masco Limited when Bury Felt merged with Mitchells, Ashworth, Stansfield, and Co. Limited[139]. In the early 1970s, a new mill was built opposite Springfield Mill and the carding, hardening and dyeing machinery was transferred there from Hudcar Mill, which was later demolished. Other equipment was transferred to Springfield Mill, which then accommodated the felt finishing processes and the upper floors were used for storage of finished goods. By then, the company had diversified into the manufacture of loop pile tufted products, the production of which was located in the Chesham Fields Mill. In 1978, this mill housed two main product lines; simulated fur fabric trademarked "Dawnbury" and moulded carpets for the automotive trade. As the company rationalised, the fur fabric was segregated from the automotive carpets and transferred to Springfield Mill leaving the carpets in the Chesham Fields Mill to be operated as a separate going concern.

BRIGHT STREET MILL

The original name of the mill was Chesham Felt Works and was built in 1871 and occupied by Walter Lucas, a felt hat manufacturer, when he was recorded as manufacturing hats as T. and W. Lucas, in Samuel Street, which was the street opposite the mill, in the Freetown district of Bury in 1871[140].

In 1878, when he leased the land from Daniel Standring[141], he was recorded as manufacturing hats up until at least 1883, though in 1910 the company was reformed as Walter Lucas and Sons (1910) Limited.

THE FELT MILLS

Bright Street Mill. The inscription on the front of the mill on the right reads "Chesham Mill 1871"

He continued the manufacture of felt hats at Chesham Felt Works until 1939 when the mill was taken over by the Bury Felt Manufacturing Company Limited who commenced the manufacture of woollen felt there. The company renamed the mill after the name of the street on which the mill was situated. The mill was re-conveyanced to Bury and Masco Industries Limited in 1965 and felt continued to be made there until the early 1970s.

Bright Street Mill showing the structure of the mill c1948

Bright Street Mill made surgical felts and superfine felts. The front half of the ground floor nearest Hudcar Lane was the mill bottom where hardening and milling was done, as well as bleaching and dyeing. There was also some carding done at the back of the mill on the ground floor but most of the carding was done on the second floor where there was also a sewing room and canteen. The offices were under the sign saying Chesham Felt Works. During the war, there was also a nursery at the mill to take care of the children of the women workers.

OTHER FELT MILLS
ROYAL GEORGE MILL

Royal George Mill, situated in Saddleworth Yorkshire, was the headquarters for R. R. Whitehead and Brothers Limited, which was the company famous for producing Royal George piano felts. Within the vault at the mill was a large collection of old documents pertaining to all aspects of its history. In the early 1980s, it was partially analysed by an unnamed archivist in order to determine the origins of the site. The following is taken from a transcript of the initial findings.

Aerial view of Royal George Mill, Saddleworth.

The first reference to a mill on the site was in 1785, when James Harrop of Grasscroft, a clothier, John Smith, and James Schofield, acquired the rights to build a mill, dam, and goits for "the purposes of fulling woollen cloth and for scribbling, or separating sheep's wool for spinning". By 1788, the mill was completed and known as Gibbs Mill, powered by two water wheels and several engines, and it was then that James Schofield assigned his share of the mill to John and James Schofield. In 1801, James Schofield and his wife Mattie sold their share in the mill to John and James Harrop for £650. Sometime between 1804 and 1806, the mill became known as Royal George Mill rather than Gibbs Mill or alternatively New Mill. In 1826, James Harrop went bankrupt but the mill seems to have been managed by a relative, Joseph Harrop, who also went bankrupt in 1835 and the mill was managed by the trustees. In 1835, the Whitehead brothers agreed to buy the mill from the Harrop estate for £7,500, but the purchase was not completed until 1838.

There were also two other mills on the same site, Throstle Mill, a scribbling mill, and Charlotte Mill, a cotton mill, both of which were operating in 1770. These mills were assigned to Thomas Cresswell for one thousand years, and he later sold his title in 1797 to James Kershaw with James Harrop as trustee. The mills were later owned by James Wright who went bankrupt in 1827 and they were acquired by George Bramall, who manufactured woollen and worsted woven cloths there in 1833.[142] He sold the mills to the Whitehead brothers in 1845. Charlotte Mill was a sizable mill, being four-storeys high and measuring thirty-one yards long and thirteen yards in breadth and was powered by a twenty horsepower engine as well as a waterwheel thirty-six feet in diameter and four feet six inches in breadth. It is possible that this mill was the large multi-storied building in the centre of the photograph above. A prominent feature of the mill was the presence of the Huddersfield canal that went directly past it and the entrance to the mill was over a hump-backed bridge that spanned the canal. The mill owners clearly gave greater emphasis to transporting raw materials into the mill, and finished product out of the mill, by canal rather than by road.

Under the Whitehead brothers the mill prospered, manufacturing woven woollen fabrics that were milled to make cloths suitable for industrial uses such as filtration, an activity that was maintained up to modern times. It is uncertain when they started making felt but one source maintains they were manufacturing felts for pianos as early as 1847[143]. In 1871, they bought out the Wandle Felt Company, which also made piano felts and transferred this production facility to Royal George Mill in 1905[144]. Thereafter, a wide variety of felts was made there, but the mill was still predominantly a woven woollen manufacturing mill up to 1979. In 1981, the mill was manufacturing felt exclusively within a new company ownership of Bury Cooper Whitehead Limited, but ceased manufacture entirely in 1998. In 2008, some parts of the mill were demolished to make way for a housing complex, and others were redeveloped as luxury flats.

Royal George Mill. The Huddersfield Canal runs underneath the bridge, the wall of which is on the left. One of the Mill Manager's daily duties was to wind up the clock shown on the tower.

CROW LANE MILL

Crow Mill, situated near Wilton, was the manufacturing headquarters of E. V. Naish Limited, the company famous for its piano felts. The following history of the mill is adapted from the history of the company written by John R. Naish[145].

Crow Mill was in existence before 1830 and rented by Wood and Ogilvie until around 1839, when William Naish took on the lease at an annual rent of £40, despite the mill being in a considerably dilapidated state. In 1840, repairs were made and the water wheel renovated in order to power the spinning machines that William Naish had installed. He ran the mill until 1852 when he died, and his son William took over the business and started to make piano felts there about 1859. Around 1867, a new brick built mill was constructed consisting of a two-storey carding shed and a single-storey building to house the wet processes. Both parts of the mill were powered by a steam engine rather than a waterwheel. At this time, the chimney was constructed to service the boilers, and by 1880, it was a hundred and twenty feet tall. The new mill accommodated five sheet-carding machines on the lower floor and one roll felt carding machine on the upper floor.

E.V. Naish's Mill at Crow Lane, Wilton c. 1959

In 1906, a new production office was built to quality control the finished felt sheets. This was followed by the construction of a new three-storey brick building that was started in 1922 and completed in 1935, in order to increase capacity. Five new carding machines with batt frames, indicated that the company had expanded into roll-felt production. In 1945, a new steam engine was installed and supplied with steam from a Lancashire boiler, the power being transmitted via the considerably inefficient line shafting. It also powered a direct current generator to supply electricity, which was contrary to the normal practice of using alternating current.

The 1950s saw many changes to the mill complex. A new twelve thousand square feet "washery" to house the dyeing equipment, hardening machines, and fulling stocks, was started in 1958 and completed in 1961. The mill was completely rewired for an alternating current supply and motors fitted directly to machines in place of line shafting. At the same time, many older buildings were demolished. By 1975, felt manufacture at Crow Lane declined and the company began making hand driers and water heaters there under the name of C. and A. Wallgate Limited. When the piano felt market was decimated around 1990, the company ceased production of felt and by 2009, it was importing felt from Germany and fabricating it at the mill.

THE FELT MILLS

CROWN MILL

Crown Mill was one of three mills situated on the river Wandle in Mitcham Surrey. It was built as a corn mill by Edward Nash sometime between 1741 and 1765 on land then owned by Charles Parry. When Edward Nash died in 1786, Richard Glover took over Crown mill and converted it into a snuff-grinding mill. At that time, the property was owned by William Frye, but by 1792 Henry Hoare, a Fleet Street banker and associate of Richard Glover, acquired the head leases of the three mills.

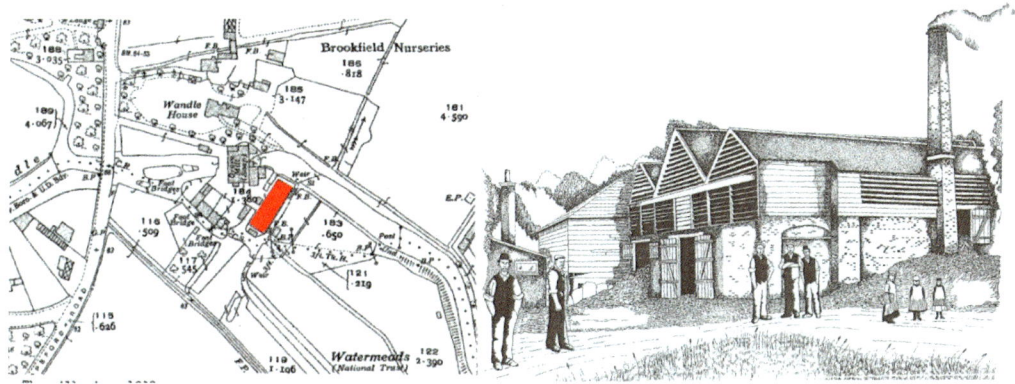

Map of Crown Mill, the home of the Wandle Felt Company, and a reconstruction of Crown Mill [146]

Richard Glover continued in business with his sons until 1824, when he died and his son, also called Richard, took over the snuff business at Crown Mill. He maintained the lease at a rent of £150 per annum for the term of seventy-six-and-a-half-year lease dated from Christmas 1787. The head lease was sold at auction when Henry Hoare died in 1828. The land itself was owned by Henry Leigh Spencer who had inherited it through family connections with William Frye on his death in 1829 and it reverted to his wife, Elizabeth Frances Spencer. The younger Richard Glover continued in business until 1835, when he was insolvent, but he managed to recover and continued manufacturing until 1846 when he was declared bankrupt. The mill then stood vacant until around 1848 when it was advertised for sale, and presumably bought by Richard Jones who started the manufacture of felt there around 1851. At that time, the mill had recently had a new sixteen feet diameter water wheel installed, capable of delivering twenty-four horsepower.

Richard Jones was making piano felts and surgical felts there, changing the company name to the Wandle Felt Company sometime before 1859. In 1871, R. R. Whitehead and Brothers Limited bought out the mill when they took over the Wandle Felt Company, changing its name to R. R. Whitehead and Brothers Limited in 1875. Piano felts continued to be made there until 1905 when the mill was shut and production moved to Saddleworth in Yorkshire.

The mill was unused until 1910 when Lyxhayr Manufacturers Limited took it over to process vegetable fibres for mattress stuffing. In 1919, they bought out the freehold from the then landowner Sir Frederick Fowke and changed their name to Mitcham Fibre Mills Limited, and later in 1948 to Mitcham Hair and Fibre Mills Limited. They continued trading at Crown Mill until 1959, at which time the mill was taken over by C. S. Walker (Sacks) Limited, and the Associated Jute Company Limited. Unfortunately under their tenure the mill burnt down on 9 August 1964 and was never re-built.

LONGMEADOW MILL

From 1855 to 1894, Henry Jecks Dixon and Sons made Brussels and Wilton carpets at Longmeadow Mill, under the trade name Longmeadow Carpets, using the Bigelow Collier weaving looms[147]. After the firm went into liquidation in 1894, the mill was idle until 1897[148] and the mill was then taken over by Charles Harrison and Co. By 1909, the company was struggling to survive and Herbert Smith was invited to run the business, which he successfully turned around and bought out by 1914. As there was a large demand for blankets in the First World War, Herbert Smith converted carpet looms in the mill to manufacture woven woollen blankets and also produced felt blankets by doubling the size of Longmeadow Mill[149]. After the war, when the demand for blankets receded Herbert Smith, against all the odds, converted the mill again to produce non-woven woollen felt exclusively trading as the Longmeadow Felt Company Limited, which became part of his newly created conglomerate Carpet Trades Limited. By 1943, the output from the mill was a serious threat to the Bury and Rossendale feltmakers.

Longmeadow Mill in 1978 after the mill was shut.

In 1972, Longmeadow Felt company was sold to Bury and Masco (holdings) Limited, who moved production to Bury and closed the mill. In 2013, the mill no longer existed and the area has become an industrial estate.

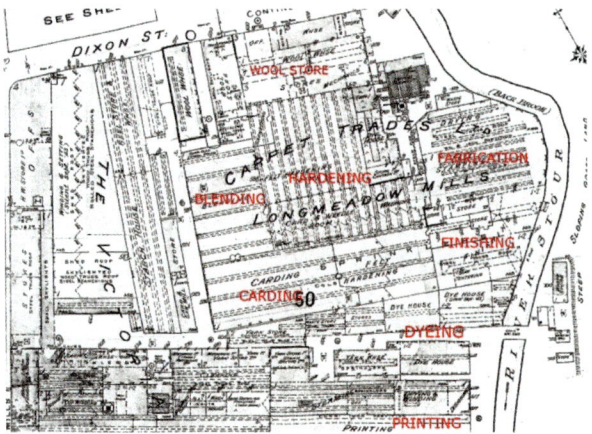

The layout of felt production in Longmeadow Mill in 1943

THE FELT MILLS

COOPER'S BRYNMAWR FACTORY

This was a modern purpose built factory, rather than a mill, built in South Wales and completed in 1950 by Cooper and Co (Birmingham) Limited to house their felt and polishing products.

Aerial view of Cooper and Co.'s factory in Brynmawr South Wales

It was expanded in 1972 when the company was taken over by Bury and Masco (Holdings) Limited with an investment of £500,000 to create a new production facility, called the Horton Factory, for manufacturing impregnated bonded felt. The new building was named after the company's works director, John Horton, and is visible as the building with the white roof in the aerial photograph[150]. In 1981, Cooper and Co. ceased production there and moved all the equipment to the Bury facility in Springfield Mill when the company was integrated into Bury Cooper Whitehead Limited.

COMPARISON OF MILL CAPACITIES

Some idea of the relative sizes of different felt making companies can be gauged qualitatively by studying the visual evidence of photographs, plans, and numbers of sites, but quantitative evaluation is somewhat more difficult. This is because of the secretive nature of the industry and the need for companies to prevent competitors from knowing their capacities in order to keep ahead of the competition. The most revealing information was in the internal archives of each company. Not only was the data inaccessible but also in most cases it was lost when felt companies closed or merged. The only time the production capabilities came into the public domain was in 1917, during the First World War, when the imports of wool were severely rationed, and the Committee for Wool Rationing carried out a census of felt machines[151]. Another source of information on the machine capability was in the lists that had to be drawn up for insurance purposes and these were usually undertaken by an independent consultant. These too only existed in company archives but because they were usually in the form of books tended to survive. Exclusive access to Bury and Masco Industries has revealed the total machine inventories for the Bury Manufacturing Company for 1913 and 1944, which together with the census of 1917 gives a clear picture of how this company expanded. Fortunately, The Patent Woollen Cloth Company lodged their insurance inventory in Leeds library and this has given a benchmark to judge the evolving felt industry, particularly since it also gives snippets of information for John Wilkinson and Cornelius Turner.

FELT IN BRITAIN

MILL CAPACITIES

Company	Date	Willeys	Scribblers	Cards	Hardeners	Stocks	Betties	Tenters	Croppers	Presses
C. Turner [152]	1860	1		2	2	4*		1		
John Wilkinsons [153]	1857			20						
Patent Woollen Cloth [154]	1861	6		25	19	38*		3		
W.G.R.Fox (Batley)	1917			5	1	4	2	1	2	1
R.Rawlinson	1917		6	6	6	4	1	1	2	1
R.R.Whitehead & Bros.	1917			11	9	6	1	1		2
H.Smith	1917		16	12	10	7	2	2	2	2
Cooper & Co., Ltd.	1917			4	10	9	2			
Stansfield & Co.	1917	8	8	18	13	5		2	4	2
R. Ashworth	1917		19	18	32	16	5		7	9	3
Mitchell Brothers [155]	1917		63	27	50	36	13	5	14	7
Bury Felt Mfg. Co.Ltd. [156]	1913	7	5	6	7	5	3	1	3	1
Bury Felt Mfg. Co. Ltd [157]	1917		6	7	8	7	3	1	2	2
Bury Felt Mfg. Co Ltd. [158]	1944	10	13	19	15	21	12	2	3	2

* Pairs of 24 inch wide stocks

Total Carding Capacity 1917   98

A 52 inch card gave 1400 lbs per week

Total Carded Output 1917 (lbs)/yr   7134400

Even knowing the number of machines recorded for a company still gives difficulties in interpreting what the relative felt making size was, because some machines may not have been in full use and other companies, such as Roland Rawlinson, may not have been using all their capacity for felt making alone. In the early days The Patent Woollen Cloth Company judged the carded weight as being their measure of felt production capacity because at that time all the wool went directly into felt. On this basis the number of carding engines was a measure of felt production, and this makes John Wilkinson almost as large a producer of felt as The Patent Woollen Cloth Company with twenty carding engines against their twenty five. On the same grounds, Cornelius Turner was a minor feltmaker with just a tenth of their capacity.

As the industry developed and became more sophisticated, comparing the modern feltmakers with the early pioneers becomes more difficult when considering carding engines alone. The most reliable way of comparing felt production is through the number of hardeners that a company possessed because this was the only piece of machinery that was used exclusively for making felt. Furthermore these machines were always operational, unless they were stopped for maintenance or repair. On this basis The Patent Woollen Cloth Company, and John Wilkinson, were almost the size of the Stansfield operation in 1917 and less than half the size of Mitchell Brothers in that same year. Cooper and Co., R. R. Whitehead, and Herbert Smith were all of comparative size in terms of felt output and just over half the capacity of Stansfield, the smallest company in the MASCO combine. By 1917, Richard Ashworth had built his felt output to be almost two thirds that of the Mitchell brothers, which was a phenomenal achievement for a single-handed operation.

Bury Manufacturing Company was one of the smallest felt making companies in 1917 but by 1944 it had doubled its output, at a time when both the Mitchell Brothers and the Richard Ashworth operations had halved in size. Only Stansfield seems to have prospered by increasing its output in 1939.

MASCO Combine Companies Output[159]

Year		Mitchell	Ashworth	Stansfield
1917	Sales (£)	432863	228827	102529
	Profit (£)	50138	26622	12205
	Wages (£)	28265	12718	5854
	Salaries (£)	12979	4111	710
	Wool (lbs)	198264	125331	24041
	Hair (lbs)	0	0	5781
1939	Sales UK (£)	238551	156615	88875
	Sales Export	126610	92553	54497
	Profit (£)	31785	28485	21308
	Wages (£)	30071	17037	8622
	Salaries (£)	11214	8556	2767
	Wool (lbs)	82190	55744	33624
	Hair (lbs)	0	0	0

Not only did Mitchells' and Ashworth's sales halve but the volume of wool used also halved. However, their profit levels remained constant at ten percent, which is due to the constraint in the wages and salary levels, which hardly rose between 1917 and 1939 despite inflation. By contrast, Stansfield's profit increased from ten to fifteen percent, which was due to increased sales, volume usage, and modest employee costs. Nevertheless even the comparative figures show the steady decline of the industry.

APPENDIX

HIGHFIELD MILL DEEDS RELATING TO HIGHFIED MILLS LADY PIT LANE LEEDS

Securities held by Midland Bank Limited, of City Square Leeds and dated 27 February 1963 being an account of Hy. Moore and Co Limited, taken over by J.B. Hoyle of Hebden Bridge.

16 May 1844   Conveyance Burton and Cash and Trustee to Mr. Samuel Carr.

1844   Abstract of title of the mortgages of Mr. John Carter.

1852   Suplemental abstract of title of Mr. J. Carr.

3 August 1857, Attested copy of mortgage Mr. Josiah Carr to Messrs Nelson, Ikin , Wilson,

22 October 1857, Mortgage Messrs G.W. Carr and Geo. Butterworth and others to Yorkshire Banking Company.

30 October 1868, Probate of the will of Samuel Carr.

15 February 1869, Attested copy of conveyance Messrs Nelson, Ikin, Wilson and Nelson to Mr. Josiah Carr.

10 April 1879, Reconveyance Makin Durham and James Kitson Esqrs (Trustees for the Yorkshire Banking Company) and the said company to Messrs G.W. Carr and W.N. Walker.

1 October 1881, Mortgage Mr. Geo. Wm. Carr and others to Mr. J.G. Turner.

2 December 1882, Further charge G.W. Carr and others to J.G. Turner (endorsed)

16 September 1884, Reconveyance John G. Turner Esq to Messrs Carr and Walker.

19 October 1896, Conveyance of the trustees of the late Samuel Carr to Herbert Carr Walker Esq. and Miss Eleanor Carr Walker.

27 November 1897, Mortgage H.C. Walker Esq. And another to John Kitchen Esq and others.

5 July l898, Reconveyance endorsed.

11 July 1890, Conveyance Miss Eleanor Carr Walker to Herbert Carr Walker.

19 July 1898, Transfer of mortgage Miss Ealeanor Carr Walker to Messrs Walter Nathanial Walker, Charles Doughty and John Bouchier Winibush

31 October 1904, Conveyance H. Carr Walker Esq. And his mortgages to Messrs Moore and Mallinson (Trading as Henry Moore and Co).

19 December 1904, Acknowledgement Messrs C. Doughty and H. Carr Walker to Messrs H. Moore and Thos Mallinson

15 December 1904, Security over Real Estate (First charge)

26 April 1918, Receipt endorsed

26 April 1904, Abstract of title of H. Carr Walker Esq. And mortgagees.

20 May1909, In the matter of title Samuel Carr.

4 March 1924, Copy acknowledgement H. Moore and Co.

1926, Abstract of the title Thomas Mallinson

15 November 1926, Conveyance Mr. Thomas Mallinson to Messrs David Little, James Lincoln Little, Basil Lincoln Little, and David Dewsbury Little. Agreement 8 October 1926

1953, Abstract of title

2 November 1953, Conveyance Personal Representatives of Basil Lincoln Little deceased and others to Hy Moore and Co Ltd.

27 November 1962, Conveyance Bramston Clothing Co Ltd to Hy. Moore and Co Ltd. 3 search certificates. This schedule is attached and forms part of receipt no F635483

6 WATER AND POWER

WATER

The two major production requirements of the felt makers were: water for processing into felt, and power to drive the machinery, both of which were inextricably linked. Most of the felt processes, such as hardening, dyeing, and washing, required treatments that used considerable amounts of hot water and steam. Because wet processing was carried out in different parts of the mill, an intricate network of pipes was needed to deliver the steam and cold water throughout the works. Central to this delivery network was the need for a constant and sustainable water supply. Early textile mills were powered by waterwheels and consequently they had to be built near a reliable water source, which made them ideal for conversion into felt mills. The majority of felt mills were therefore close to rivers or reservoirs, with the most successful feltmakers supplementing these by building and maintaining their own local reservoirs, known as lodges, directly alongside their mill. Even when steam engines were introduced to run the mills, the need for water was just as great, because water was needed to feed the boilers to generate the steam that powered the engines.

The need for water, therefore, dictated not only the size of the lodges that were needed close to the mill, but also ultimately determined the size of the business that the mill could sustain. To the feltmakers, the rights to water supplies were of paramount importance, equal in value to land and property; and they went to extraordinary lengths to secure a sufficient quantity of the right quality of water to their mills. Eventually through the Land Drainage Act 1930 and the Water Resources Act 1964 the water supplies came under control of twenty-seven river authorities of which the Mersey and Weaver River Authority took charge of the water supplying the Rossendale and Bury felt companies. Thereafter, the felt companies had to apply for a licence to abstract water and specify the maximum usage.

WATER CAPACITY

Even though the greatest amount of water was needed for the wet felt treatments, the advent of the steam engine had a significant impact on the water supply, not only in terms of the extra capacity required but also in dealing with the cooling water needed to keep the engine running efficiently. The amount of water needed to condense the steam required was twenty-five to thirty times greater than the amount of water needed to generate the steam feed, since it also had to be cooled before it could be used again[1]. In 1853, at Elmwood mill, it took two hundred and fifty cubic feet of water (almost two thousand gallons) a day to feed a twenty-five horsepower engine at low pressure, which was the common engine of the day. However, if the then newer high-pressure engines were used, correspondingly less water was needed[2]. Therefore, just to service the power of the mill alone, reservoirs needed to have the capacity to handle at least seven thousand five hundred cubic feet (fifty-six thousand gallons) per day per engine.

Besides powering the engines, steam was also needed to provide heat for the various processes, and this generally meant that the rating of the boilers that generated the steam were always at least five horsepower greater than the engine. For example, Airedale mill had a twenty horsepower engine and a thirty-five horsepower boiler and Elmwood Mill had a thirty horsepower engine and a thirty-five horsepower boiler, as well as a ten horsepower engine with a fifteen horsepower boiler[3]. The quantity of water needed to produce the necessary steam for heating was between six and ten percent of the water needed for processing. In 1974, Bury and Masco Industries Limited was averaging a hundred thousand gallons a day of which six thousand gallons was for boiler feed, and eighty-eight gallons was used for processing and then discharged after suitable filtering and treatment[4].

By the early 1900s, there was yet another demand on the mill's water supply. After the major fire at Myrtle Grove Mill in 1902, it was imperative that measures were needed to minimise or eliminate the perennial fires that most mills suffered in their time. From 1913, Bury and Masco Industries Limited protected their mills with a water sprinkler system connected to another separate system of water pipes. Although these were only used in an emergency, and therefore had no intrinsic flow rate, the water capacity still had to be factored in when accounting for water capacity. To guarantee supply in the event of a fire most of the sprinkler systems were supplied from tanks situated either on top of the building or in a purpose-built water tower. Sprinkler systems were also connected to the town water main to supplement the gravity fed system or were operated directly without the need for auxiliary tanks.

An indication of the scale of the water requirement of the largest feltmaker can be gauged from an application in 1973, for an increase in abstraction rate to the Mersey and Weaver River Authority. Any application had to show the total water usage for the mill, and the table below is for the production of Bury and Masco Industries Limited[5], which was the largest British felt producer.

Table showing the Water Usage of Bury and Masco Industries Limited's Felt Production Prior to 1973

Mill	Licence Number	Authorised Abstraction Millions of Gallons Per Year
Baltic	25/69/1/73 &74	17
Longholme*	25/69/70 & 78	117
Bury Mills	25/69/1/107 &116 & 211 & 212	27

* Longholme Mill closed in 1973 and production absorbed into the Bury Mills

In 1974, the total weight of felt produced was 4.3 million pounds of which Bury and Masco had sixty-five percent of the total[6] and their maximum water abstraction was forty-four million gallons indicating that the water requirement to produce one pound of felt was around sixteen gallons.

An idea of the capacity of a typical lodge can be gained from data on Hudcar and Springfield Mills. Throughout its history, Hudcar Mill operated from three reservoirs and a lodge attached to the mill owner's house. These have known capacities: the two lodges at the back of Hudcar Mill held two hundred and twenty thousand gallons, the one at the front of the mill known as Hudcar Bottom held one hundred and fifty thousand gallons, and the remaining Hudcar West lodge held two hundred and forty gallons. By comparison, the Springfield Mill lodge had a capacity of eight hundred thousand gallons and being much deeper than those of Hudcar, it had a much smaller surface area[7]. In general, therefore, mill lodges of the felt industry probably had an average capacity of around three hundred thousand gallons, which would have been sufficient to keep the mills running for just fourteen days.

Keeping a mill adequately supplied with water was a constant balancing act since the water usage had to be matched to the rate at which the lodges could be re-supplied from other sources such as feeder streams or adjacent rivers. The flow of these in turn depended heavily on the local rainfall, so the mill engineers closely monitored the monthly rainfall to ensure that there was an adequate supply of water. Two weeks of drought would seriously deplete the lodges and after a month, emergency measures would have been taken utilising supplies from special reservoirs reserved for such occasions. In exceptional times, production may even have had to be curtailed. The rate of flow of water to a mill was as important to the efficient running of the works as was the total capacity needed. For example, Bright Street Mill owned by Bury Felt Manufacturing Company in 1960 required a flow of two thousand four hundred gallons per hour and Hudcar needed between four thousand and five thousand gallons per hour to operate satisfactorily. To gain extra capacity, recycling of the effluent water was considered as a possible source

SOURCES OF WATER

Unusually, the felt mills of Leeds did not lie directly on a recognised watercourse. Elmwood Mill, St. Helens Mill, and Highfield Mill were some way away from the river Aire, so their water supplies must have been delivered through conduits to their buildings, and in fact, a map of Elmwood around 1890 shows three very large mill reservoirs that are connected to three such conduits. Elmwood House, which would originally have been the home of the mill owner, had its own lodge, indicating that there may well have been a small stream that once fed all four of the mill's reservoirs. St. Helens Mill is closer to the river Aire and it is feasible that this could have been connected directly to the mill through some sort of underground conduit or goit. Butterworth's Highfield Mill, too was a similar distance from the river Aire as Elmwood, and was known to have a stream flowing directly through it that was later conduited, though there were no indications that there had ever been a water wheel there[8]. In the 1800s the area of Leeds in which the felt mills were situated was heavily industrialised and there must have been many steam engines operating in the district, so it is likely the city had organised a communal water supply to service industry.

The mills in Rossendale conformed more to the recognised typical textile mill where all of them were connected directly to a river, stream or beck, though it was only the oldest mills that were at one time powered by water wheels. Amongst these were Baltic, Lumb Mills, Lumb Holes, Bridge End, Hardsough and Plunge mills, though it was only Bridge End and Hardsough that maintained their water wheel for the whole life of the mill, using them to supplement their steam engines when they were installed. Lumb Holes and Plunge mills never made the transition from water to steam power and consequently they were abandoned as production units. The majority of the felt mills had their own lodges but a few like Baltic Mill and Longholme Mill drew their water directly from adjacent rivers and from bore holes. Since many mills shared the same river as a key water source, there was much rivalry between companies to obtain the best and cleanest water supply. All mills discharged their effluent into the very river that supplied them with their water, which meant that the further downstream a mill was, the less pure was the water supply. In the earliest days of untreated effluent, this was also the cause for animosity and disagreement between mills, and companies went to extraordinary lengths to secure a water supply from higher up the river than the geographic location of the mill. For example, Richard Ashworth records a major engineering achievement in the construction of a goit that was three quarters of a mile long running from Waterbarn Mill to the lodge at Bridge End Mill[9]. This need for the control of the best water supply must have ranked highly with the Mitchell brothers when they expanded their company as they systematically took over all the mills on the River Whitewell, specifically north of their main operation at Albert Works. When they took over Whitewell Vale Mill and built the settling pits there, they built a conduit from the outlet of these pits to a position further downstream, so that it by-passed the water intake of Albert Works. The intake was at the head of a reservoir from which the mill abstracted its water, and the effluent was discharged into the river Whitewell below it. The water in the reservoir, and hence the supply to Albert Works, was pure and free of contamination.

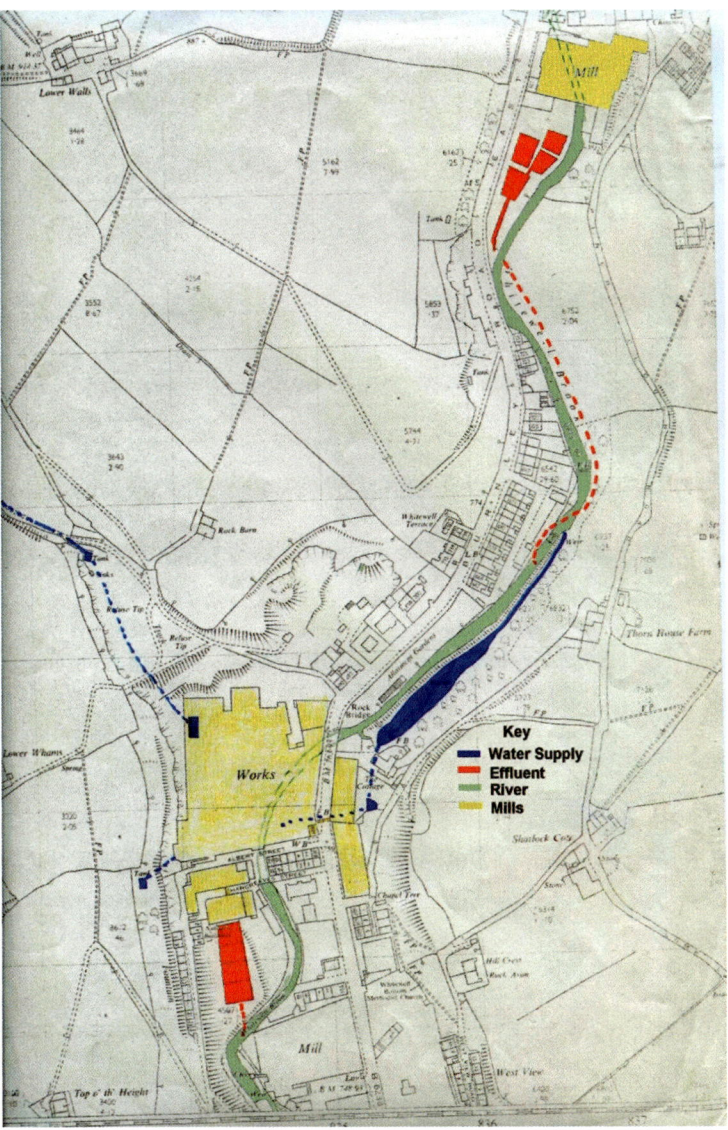

Effluent outfall of Whitewell Vale Mill (top mill) discharging into the river Whitewell just below the intake of the reservoir supplying Albert Works

The water supply for Whitewell Vale came out of mine workings. At one stage the supply was separated, one half going to Barley lodge to service the mill, and the other half going to Jack lodge to supply another mill (still extant) up at Shawclough. There was also a water supply from the Higher Lumb lodges and water was taken from the river Whitewell itself. It was thought that Barley lodge gave the best water for felting, but analysis showed that the water direct from the Whitewell was superior. Below the water tower at Whitewell Vale was a water wheel, but the wheel itself had been removed before the 1930s[10].

Another water feature of some of the mills was the use of a water tower, of which the two notable ones were Baltic and Whitewell Vale. The water towers were important for delivering the correct flow of water to service the whole of a mill's needs. There was also a close connection between the height of the water towers and the diameter of the water supply pipes. A typical dye house would require a flow of at least thirty gallons per minute, which would fill one dye vessel in fifteen minutes. Using a four-inch diameter pipe as a feed from a water tower, it was possible to deliver a flow of one hundred and sixty to two hundred gallons of water per minute, which could fill two vessels in three minutes. Since Baltic did not have its own lodge, the water tower was vital to store the water, and provide good pressure, and adequate flow to the processing equipment. The storage tanks were supplied continuously by pumping water from the river Irwell and from a spring that belonged to the mill. The capacity of the tank acted as a reservoir that ensured that there was always sufficient water to supply the mill despite the low rate of delivery of the pumps. Whitewell Vale had both a lodge and a water tower but the positioning of the tower indicates it was used to generate the necessary pressure and water flow to service the three-storey building that it was attached to, a situation reflected in the mills of Bury, and of Longholme Mill, which had five storeys.

Bury is not blessed with an abundant river system such as exists in the Rossendale Valley. The nearest river of note is the river Roche some four miles away from the Bury felt mills. However, the area is served by a number of small brooks or streams, which individually had a small fraction of the volume flow of the Rossendale rivers, but collectively they could be harnessed to supply a mill's needs. Because these flows are so low, there was no way that a mill in Bury could have been powered by water, so without the invention of the steam engine there would never have been any mills in the area. When the Bury Mills were built, the meagre water supply was augmented by local boreholes, two of which were drilled in the grounds of Hudcar Mill behind the back lodge, and one was drilled close to Chesham Works. The water from the wells at Hudcar was pumped up to two storage tanks on top of the mill using pumps located in a pump house in Villiers Street. Of Hudcar's wells, one was under the Personnel Manager's Office below the Managing Director's Office and another was in the mill grounds opposite the Technical Department. This borehole went down one hundred and twenty feet but by 1980, it was silted up and needed re-boring and the only evidence of its existence was marked by a sealed pipe. The borehole in Bright Street served Chesham Mill and the water rights to this were owned by Bury Felt Manufacturing Company and were still valid and owned by Bury and Masco Industries Limited in 1980[11]. With these resources there was just sufficient to generate the necessary steam power and water for processing.

The use of boreholes was a significant method by which other feltmakers, besides Bury Felt Manufacturing Company, supplemented their water supplies. There were boreholes at Longholme Mill capable of delivering thirty-six million gallons a year, at Baltic Mill delivering two million gallons a year, and the Chesham borehole in Bridge Street supplied two million gallons[12]. The well at Longholme is now under the current Asda Supermarket and when it was operational, water from it was pumped by a submersible pump to towers on the top of the mill to provide the necessary flow into the mill and to provide a suitable pressure head for the factory's sprinklers, in case of fire[13]. Even E. V. Naish resorted to sinking a two-hundred-foot borehole in 1962 to supplement its ready supply of water from a tributary of the river Wylye, because the river was becoming polluted and using mains water was too expensive. At that time, their water usage was twenty-two thousand gallons per day. Like all the other felt producers, they too discharged their effluent into the river via settling tanks that had to be cleaned of sediment every month[14].

WATER QUALITY

Water never occurs in its pure state in nature. It always contains impurities in suspension, often in the form of calcium and magnesium salts, mostly as bicarbonates, sulphates, or chlorides, which are particularly common in well water. By comparison, surface water has fewer concentrations of these chemicals but more bacteria. For felting, soft water is preferred over hard water that contain high concentrations of calcium and magnesium salts. These salts react with soaps used in felting to form unwanted insoluble scum and limit the effectiveness of soaps as agents for felting. The hardness of water is measured by the grains of calcium carbonate per gallon of water and on this scale a number of four or less is considered as soft, whilst four to eight is medium hard, and eight to sixteen as very hard. For the purposes of felting the hardness needed to be less than eight. Careful monitoring of the quality of water was a constant necessity for most mills and water samples were analysed by the companies' laboratories on a regular basis, usually around once every week.

When the Bright Street Mill was operational its main water supply came from wells that gave very hard water, having a hardness of twenty three degrees and had to be controlled using a lime-soda treatment to give a degree of hardness between three and five. The components had to be carefully added at rates to match the flow of the water or the result would be a turbid water supply to the mill. Unfortunately, this gave water of a high alkalinity that was detrimental to the well-being of the mill operatives as well as having an adverse effect on the water pipe lines, depositing chalk on the inner surfaces of the pipework causing a restricted flow. Adding traces of sodium hexameta phosphate to the storage tanks cured this problem.

Hudcar Mill was served by both springs and surface water and so had a mix of hard and soft water, with the hardness of the lodge being less than eight. Lime-soda was therefore not used; rather a base exchange method was used to precipitate the calcium carbonate, changing the calcium carbonate to sodium carbonate.

The nature of the water was also important from the point of view of the boilers, economisers and pipes that supplied the heat and power needs of the factory. Very soft water was known to attack and corrode iron and steel pipes very rapidly, though slightly alkaline water of one degree of hardness had little corrosive effect. When the water was softened by the base-exchange process the water was too soft to be used for the boilers and even after treatment with soda and sodium hexameta phosphate it was unsuitable because of the high bicarbonate content led to the deposit of chalk. The only way to rectify this was to add high concentrations of caustic soda that was also unacceptable. Mills therefore opted to use the soft water and accept the resultant corrosion.

EFFLUENT

As well as managing water sources, arranging the treatment and disposal of effluent was equally important. In the early days of textile manufacture, untreated effluent was discharged directly into the source rivers but downstream of the mill. This was a major cause of disputes between mills located in the lower reaches of the river, since each subsequent mill added to the pollution. However, around 1860, effluent treatment was taken very seriously and costly steps were taken to reduce river pollution, with pits or settling tanks being built to contain and treat the effluent before it was put into the river. For most companies at the time it was a major undertaking and cost. For Roland Rawlinson it almost bankrupted him and it was only the support of his workers, who worked for nothing for a period, that he could afford to finance it[15]. In the case of the Mitchell brothers, in 1871, they bought out an old fulling mill and its land, on which to build their pits (see the map under Lumb Mills in Chapter 5) and these were used right up until the mill closed in 1952. These settling tanks became key but unsung features of the felt mills, increasing in importance as environmental legislation became increasingly tougher during the 1970s, 1980s, and 1990s. A consequence of this was the need to employ a works chemist who was given the responsibility for measuring the chemical composition of the incoming and outgoing water supplies and advising on necessary treatments. The statistics for Bury and Masco Industries in 1974 indicate the scale of the problem, recording that eighty-eight percent of the total usage of water actually went to waste, equating to eighty-eight thousand gallons a day for just one mill.

The basic requirements for effluent treatment were to neutralise the acids used in felt manufacture, to remove the colour and suspended solids, and to prevent bacterial growth. This was done in specially constructed effluent pits where suitable chemical treatments could be applied. Neutralisation was done by adding lime to form calcium sulphate, which remained in solution. Soda and aluminate were then added to precipitate the chalk and deposit any flock as a sediment. The resultant alkaline solution was sufficient to eliminate bacterial growth. All that was then required was to remove the sludge that collected at the bottom of the pits and dispose of it. The frequency of removal of the sludge was once a month for the primary pits and two to three months for the secondary pits.

WATER MANAGEMENT

The importance of water management should not be underestimated despite the fact that there is little in the records of the feltmakers about how this was done. Some idea of the scope of organising the water supply can be gleaned from a survey carried out by Bury and Masco in 1974 when the company centralised all its felt making in Bury.

All the feltmakers managed their water supplies using reservoirs, even when they had adequate volumes of water available from the rivers that fed them. Usually this was an insurance against drought and therefore was just a single local reservoir and positioned most commonly alongside the mill. In Bury, Hudcar Mill itself was well served by reservoirs, having three local ones and three at strategic distances from the mill, the furthest being one and a half miles away. The three distant reservoirs were fed and connected by a single stream known as Pigs Lea Brook. The most northerly reservoir was Leaks Water that fed into Mather Road Reservoir, with the water rights of both being owned by Bury and Masco Industries. The third reservoir, known as the Clarence Lido, was however owned by Bury Council. This gave rise to an interesting situation, because the company controlled water flow into the Lido and could technically have prevented it from filling, because there was a culvert that diverted the water flow around the reservoir, effectively by-passing it. In the event, an arrangement was made whereby the company allowed water to flow into the Lido provided it could draw water from it in an emergency. This was fine until the Council wanted to chlorinate the water, which would have rendered it useless for felt production. Fortunately by this time the Bury Mill was less dependent on this supply route since it had two alternative sources: Green Brook and Gipsy Brook. Green Brook ran north of the Chesham district and filled the three lodges of Hudcar Mill, whilst Gipsy Brook flowed south of Chesham, filling Clarendon reservoir and the Springfield Mill lodge. Historically the water rights to these streams were owned by different companies to service their own mills and the Bury Manufacturing Company had the foresight to buy out these mills and establish common ownership of these rights. This later enabled felt making to expand in Bury at the expense of Rossendale when the company merged with MASCO, and the new company, Bury and Masco Industries, concentrated all its felt making there in the early 1970s.

The water supply for Hudcar and Springfield Mills in 1973

When the M66 motorway was proposed, it cut across all of the streams supplying the mills, and posed a potential threat to the water supply. In itself, the physical aspect was not a major problem as it was a relatively simple engineering solution to construct culverts to contain the streams. However, of greater concern was the run-off from rainwater falling on the motorway itself. The main concern here was the contamination of the water supply by the run-off, which could ultimately affect the felting process. The main difficulty was in winter when tons of salt and grit could be spread on the road to prevent icing and dealing with snow, and this salt would inevitably find its way into the local water streams. In fact, all three of the feeder streams supplying the Bury Mills were crossed by the motorway, so potential pollution was a major concern. Since the streams also passed through built up residential areas, there were other threats to the purity of the water from domestic contaminants. In the case of Gypsy Brook, the surface water outfall from a housing estate discharged directly into it. In the event, any effects were minor.

Matching the water content of the reservoirs to the needs of the mills was a considerable balancing act, particularly at times of low rainfall. The capacities of the reservoirs are shown below.

Water capacity of Bury and Masco's Bury Mill 1974

Reservoir	Capacity (Gallons)
Leaks	3,000,000
Mather Road	4,900,000
Hudcar Bottom	150,000
Hudcar Back	200,000
Hudcar West	240,000
Springfield	800,000
Clarendon	530,000

These reserves had to be balanced against the abstraction rates needed to run the mills. The daily demand from Springfield reservoir was one hundred thousand gallons and from Hudcar six thousand, so even though the reservoirs appear to contain vast amounts of water, each could only sustain between four and seven days of production at the mills. If all the reservoirs were used without being recharged, the mills could only operate for two and a half weeks. To give an idea of how precarious the situation could become Bury and Masco Industries was considering creating a new reservoir during a drought of 1974 that threatened to curtail production.

Apart from preserving water sources and supplying the mills, the felt companies were also legally restricted as to how much water a company could abstract from water sources. For this a company had to apply for a licence from the local water authority. In the case of Bury and Rossendale, licences were issued by the Mersey and Weaver River Authority. Generally, the licence fee was a nominal amount and based on the maximum quantity of water allowed for abstraction. In addition to the licence fee was an abstraction charge also based on the allowable water usage.

POWER

By the time the felt industry started in 1840, the condensing steam engine pioneered by James Watt was well established in textile mills and must therefore have been the preferred method of driving the felting processes, with only a few mills being driven by water wheels. By around 1850, compound engines were being introduced, which used high-pressure steam for the first cylinder and then using the exhaust to drive a second low-pressure cylinder[16]. So by the time the industry expanded in 1854, there would have been a mix of condensing and compound engines in use, with companies re-investing as the steam engine and boiler technology developed. By 1860, all mills were likely to have been using compound engines as the primary power source. By the turn of the nineteenth century, feltmakers in Rossendale made their first tentative steps in adopting electricity by lighting their mills with electric lights powered by dynamos driven by their steam engines and by 1926, most textile mills had abandoned steam engines in favour of alternating current motors[17].

THE LEEDS MILLS

In 1840, the original Patent Cloth Company was known to have had a steam engine, boiler and chimney. The engine was probably a single cylinder condensing engine since the company was most concerned about the water usage for such an engine in 1853, consulting the Scientific American periodical dated December 17 1853[18]. By 1857, the company had invested in a twenty horsepower high pressure engine to supplement its thirty horsepower condensing engine, both fed by two forty horsepower boilers. Of interest too, in this inventory, was the fact that to deliver the power to the various machines in the mill required two hundred and thirty-four yards of line shafting of diameters varying from one and three-quarters of an inch to seven inches in diameter, with the average being around two and a half inches. By 1860, the company had replaced its thirty horsepower condensing engine with a double cylinder compound engine fed by a thirty-five horsepower boiler.

From the existing pictures of John Wilkinson's mill at St. Helens there must have been at least three boilers and engines as judged by the number of chimneys, though he is known to have had at least two forty horsepower engines made by J. Whitham at a cost of £1500[19]. From the layout of the premises there is no possibility for there to have been a waterwheel there. By contrast Cornelius Turner had only one engine rated at twenty horsepower and a boiler of thirty-five horsepower, whilst at Butterworth's Highfield Mill there was only one extant chimney and since it was a relatively small site it is likely to have had only one engine, and in 1980, there were no longer any signs of old line shafting there.

WATER-POWERED MILLS

It is surprising that the early Leeds feltmakers seemed to have used only steam engines to power their mills whilst many of those who set up after 1854, when the felt patent expired, used water power as their primary source supplemented by steam. Possibly this was a low cost alternative that gave them a competitive edge, since the water was free while steam engines required considerable quantities of coal. However, the power output of water wheels seem to have been limited to around twenty to thirty horsepower so that as the businesses expanded the need for more power could only be met by using steam engines. Some feltmakers persevered with waterpower right up to the twentieth century and Bridge End Mill in particular was using its water wheel right up until 1955, when it was dismantled. This water wheel, which was installed before 1877, was twenty-three feet in diameter and fifteen feet in width, and was housed in small room below the lodge. It ran continuously throughout the life of the mill, being supplemented by one small steam engine.

Hardsough Mill, too, relied heavily on its three, three foot wide, water wheels up to 1890 and even then production continued with two wheels supported by two steam engines. Evidence from Waterbarn Mill gives a good indication of the balance between waterpower and steam power at a time when mills were converting to steam. Before 1838, the mill was driven by a waterwheel twelve feet wide and thirty-four feet in diameter providing twenty horsepower and a steam engine delivering thirty horsepower to be replaced after 1865, by a single Petrie condensing beam type steam engine delivering fifty horsepower. Similarly, Lumb Mill in 1865, was being powered by a waterwheel and two steam engines, one sixteen horsepower and the other twenty-four, and after 1887, the mill was using the waterwheel and a single vertical steam engine with a nine-inch diameter cylinder and a twelve-inch stroke. This pattern was not restricted just to the Rossendale feltmakers but was repeated elsewhere. In 1788, the Royal George Mill in Saddleworth was powered by two waterwheels and several engines when it was known as Gibbs Mill, whilst its sister mill, known as Charlotte Mill, had a waterwheel thirty-six feet in diameter and four feet six inches in breadth as well as a twenty horsepower engine. At E. V. Naish's Mill in Crow lane, a waterwheel was used up until 1867, when a new steam engine was installed and uniquely the company persevered with steam engines even as late as 1945, when a new engine was installed together with two Lancashire boilers. Unusually the company opted to use direct current power for its electricity supply, which was generated using the steam engine. It was only in 1959 that the company dispensed with its line-shafting and installed individual motors powered by an alternating current supply. Finally, in 1973, they converted from coal to oil as their primary fuel.

The waterwheel of Bridge End Mill in 1955 before it was dismantled

Other mills having past evidence of water wheels are Lumb Mills, Isle of Man Mill in Rossendale, and Crown Mill in Mitcham Surrey. Unusually, the Isle of Man Mill had a water turbine[20]. In 1896, Lumb Mills was still using waterpower because an employee there was drowned by being caught in a waterwheel. Crown Mill was still investing in waterpower in 1851, when a new sixteen feet diameter water wheel was installed that was capable of delivering twenty-three horsepower. However, all of these mills had chimneys built that indicated that they were also powered by steam engines. Of particular note is Longholme Mill, which was rebuilt in 1886 and was both water and steam powered. However, rather than a waterwheel the mill was fitted with a ninety horsepower water turbine supplied by Messrs Kay of Bury as well as a fifty horsepower beam engine supplied by Petrie of Rochdale. Electricity was also installed for the first time in 1886, but this is likely to have been for lighting as the alternating current motor capable of driving machinery was only invented by Nicola Tesla around 1887.

Although there is no direct evidence that Baltic Mill was ever water powered, its positioning on the river Irwell and the fact that it was one of the oldest mills in Rossendale suggests that it must have once have had a water wheel. The mill was built right alongside the river Irwell and there were deep pits built beside the mill on the riverside that could have contained a waterwheel pit. By 1980, these were used as effluent pits and covered over with flagstones. Since it was primarily a single-storey mill, any steam engine employed was most likely to have been a single engine used to power the machinery through line shafting. Since the mill had only one chimney in the centre of the mill it is probable that it only had a single steam engine, and there was plenty of evidence of line shafting around the mill to confirm this, and some of the shafts were still in use in 1980.

It is likely too, that Albert Works was powered by water since a stream from the river Whitewell ran right through the middle of it. By 1890, it was powered by engines fed by three separate boiler houses, as indicated by an old letterhead showing three chimneys.

The side of Baltic mill next to the river Irwell showing the pits, covered over with flagstones.

It seems that the Mitchell brothers were innovative in the deployment of their engines as there were as many as nine steam engines in use at the mill in the early days. Some of these engines were used to power individual machines, each of the three large tentering machines had their own engines, as did the two hydro-extractors and the printing machine. As well as these small engines, there was a large beam engine that powered part of the mill through conventional line shafting. They too embraced electric power when it became available

Some mills like Lumb Holes and Plunge Mill never made the transition to steam power and were eventually abandoned as felt manufacturing operations. Plunge mill is situated in open country with only a path leading to it, so it is difficult to see how adequate coal supplies could have been transported there without a substantial investment in infrastructure.

The two major feltmakers, Edward Rostron and James Barcroft built their own mills and dispensed entirely with waterpower, relying only on steam to drive their machinery. When Edward Rostron built his mill at Myrtle Grove, he equipped it with two vertical engines with a cylinder diameter of twenty inches and forty-inch stroke, another two vertical engines one of fourteen-inch diameter and twenty-eight inch stroke, one of ten-inch diameter and twenty-eight inch stroke. He also installed a new horizontal engine with an eight-inch cylinder and twelve inch stroke, supplied with steam from two steam boilers twenty-six feet long and seven feet in diameter. In 1902, these were replaced with a cross compound engine built by S. S. Stott, the same engineer who installed one in Higher Hollin Bank. When James Barcroft built Siss Clough and Todd Carr mills he powered each of them with steam engines, and the chimney and engine houses can clearly be seen integrated into the factories' structure. When the mills were demolished, the engine beds were so massive they could not be dismantled.

There were other mills that had never been powered by water and were too far from a watercourse to entertain a waterwheel. Fountain mill for example in Rossendale was situated well away from any water source but had a single chimney and boiler house at one end of the mill, probably delivering the power though shafting. In Bury, although there were watercourses these had too low a flow to be able to deliver the horsepower necessary to drive a mill through a water wheel. The earliest Bury mill, Hudcar, shows no signs of a wheel pit or suitable waterway infrastructure and must therefore have been powered by steam engine from its construction in 1827 and in 1833, it was known to have used two engines delivering seventy horsepower. The next oldest mill, Springfield, boasts a splendid engine house and chimney that most likely housed a vertical beam engine as well as boilers. The other mill in Bury, Chesham Felt Works had a single chimney and boiler house sited centrally in the factory indicating the likelihood of a horizontal steam engine in the far building.

Springfield Mill in 1940's showing the engine house and chimney on the right

Model of Chesham Felt Works, Bright Street, the chimney and boiler house are in the centre

Chimneys were the defining feature of steam power in the mills and were often elegant structures that towered above the buildings. This was necessary because of the low-grade coal that was used, which led to large volumes of smoke when it burnt. This had to be discharged well above the surrounding land so that people living nearby would not be subjected to the soot and the noxious gases that were released. Most chimneys had to be over one hundred and twenty feet tall to achieve this, which gave architects and builders considerable difficulties. They had to be narrow in diameter compared to their height giving a slender construction that resulted in considerable pressure on the base area, which was relatively small. The chimney had to be built with extreme accuracy since a small lean could cause it to topple over. As well as this, the structure was subject to extremes of fluctuating temperatures that over time affected the brickwork and mortar. It is no surprise therefore, that many mills at some time, experienced problems with their chimneys and some of these had devastating consequences. On 10 August 1864, the chimney at Royal George Mill collapsed and killed several people. The chimney had been built on gravel near spring water and when it was seventy-five feet high it started to lean, the builder tried to correct it and at one hundred and fifty feet tall, it leaned even more and then catastrophically collapsed[21]. For E. V. Naish their one hundred and twenty feet chimney survived from 1880 to 1950 through careful maintenance but it too eventually started to lean and on three occasions the top fifteen feet had to be taken down to stabilise it. The same situation arose at Bury Manufacturing Company's chimney at Hudcar Mill when the top part of its chimney had to be dismantled.

The problems with power supply in the mills were eventually resolved with the advent of electricity as a power source. At first, the mills had their own generators to supply just the lighting but as the national electricity grid developed and powerful electric motors became available, all the machinery became electrically powered. This gave the feltmakers total freedom to be able to site their machines anywhere in the mill rather than the position dictated by the presence of the line shaft. This led to a more efficient, ergonomic operation with improved safety as it dispensed with the need for belt drives. The mills still needed to have boilers to generate the steam for processing but as the oil industry developed the mills converted to oil-fired boilers that removed the need for chimneys. By 1970, most chimneys had been demolished and the mills operated at peak power efficiency

7 PREPARING THE FIBRE

RAW MATERIAL

The wool, when it arrived at the mill, was delivered in compact, hessian-covered bales. Once in the wool store, small slits were cut in the side of the bales and a small sample of wool was extracted to assess the quality and conformance to the order.

Delivery of bales to the wool store, the tears in the bales are where samples have been taken

Each wool type was segregated and allocated its own area in the warehouse, to facilitate later selection when preparing the appropriate blend. Unlike the woollen and worsted industries, felt production needed a vast array of different wool types, as well as other natural and synthetic fibres. Therefore, there was a high potential risk for making a mistake when preparing a blend, and there was a danger of cross contamination of the different fibre types. The wool store covered a large area compared to the rest of the mill and was invariably based in a cool dry building well away from the main production area. This was a legacy of the early days of felt making when many mills were almost destroyed by fires, which nearly always started in the wool store.

Felts rarely consisted of one type of wool only, so blending different wools together was a major part of the production process. In addition, it was common for a felt to be made in a layered construction with different blends in each layer. This made for a complicated blending regime and a need for tight control. To make a prescribed blend the constituent wool types were identified in the warehouse and the bales broken open and amounts from each wool or fibre type were carried manually in a cart or wicker basket to the weighing area.

Weights of each of the fibre types were measured out according to the felt specification and the length of felt to be made. This blending was either done on the run in the weighing bin or by spreading each weighed element on the floor one on top of the other in three or more discrete layers, as a form of pre-blending.

FELT IN BRITAIN

Using a weighing bin for blending a white felt, wicker baskets were also used for organising wool blends

WILLOWING

The weighed blend was carried by basket to the feeding hopper of a machine to open out the fibres and begin the blending process. This machine had a fierce tearing action that thrashed and scraped the fibre to break up the matted clumps of raw wool and shake out the grit, burr and seeds that were tangled in the wool. Historically in the days before industrialisation, this was done by beating the wool with willow rods so that when machines superseded the manual process the operation became known as willowing. These machines were therefore called willows, though over time they acquired a variety of other endearing names that were synonymous with its action, such as willey, shaker willey, picker, and breaker. The whole process of separating the wool fibres became known as teazing and this machine was then referred to as a teazer.

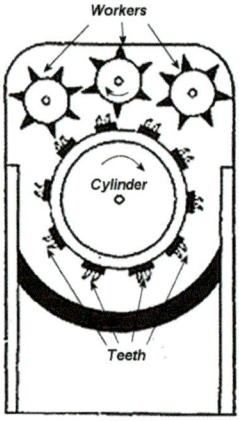

The action of a willow

The operation of this machine was derived from the traditional hand method for preparing wool for spinning into thread. In this technique, wool fibres were separated and straightened by pulling them across the dried head of the teazel plant. Later several teazels were mounted on a pair of small rectangular frames with handles. Wool was placed between them and the two frames moved in opposite direction to give a combing effect, which became known as "carding". The name is derived from "cardus", the Latin word for teazel or thistle. This method of sliding one set of spikes passed another to open up the wool was the principle used in every mechanical process for separating wool fibres.

All mechanical carding processes therefore looked alike because the teazing action is provided by the interaction of a rotating spiked roller and a fast moving drum, which contained rows of spikes, or teeth. The drum or cylinder rotated one way whilst the smaller roller, called a worker, rotated in the opposite direction, usually at a tenth of the speed of the cylinder. The main difference between all these machines was the type of spikes that were used. For pulling matted wool, spikes had to be used whilst later opening processes needed gentler treatment and hooked wires were used.

For the willow, spikes were used on both the worker and the drum. The spikes of the two surfaces did not touch but each spike of the worker was positioned so that it fitted between the gaps between two adjacent teeth on the cylinder. This gave a tearing action to the wool fibres that travelled between the worker and the drum. In practice, more than one worker roller was needed to open the matted wool efficiently and sometimes the first roller was replaced by a static row of spikes.

Beaumont[1] gives a good description of the action of a commercial willow as in the following précis. The diagram shows a side view of a typical self-acting teazer that was commonly used in the felt industry, shown with all the requisite drive belts.

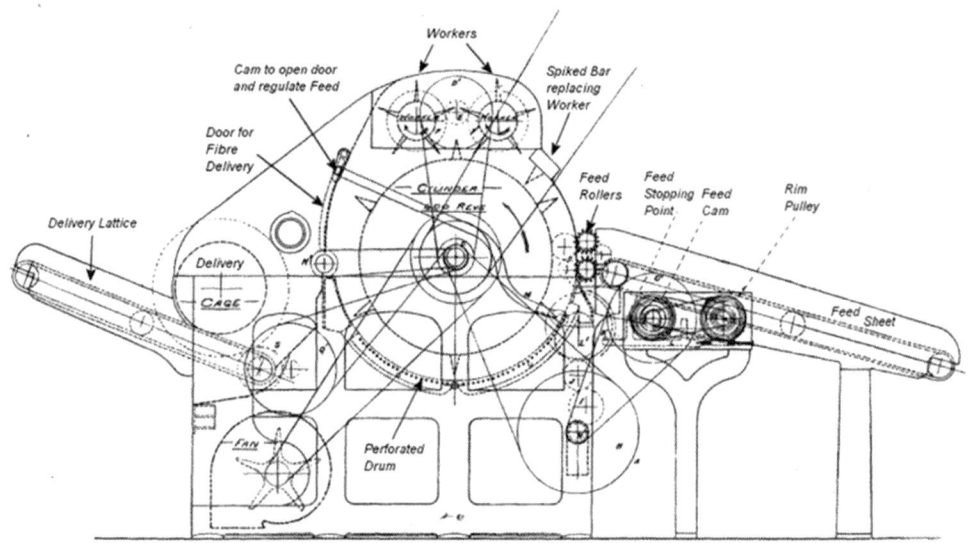

A self-acting teazer or willow made by Platt Brothers & Co Ltd

The raw wool was loaded onto the wooden lattice feed sheet, on the right, which moved it progressively to the feed rollers. These gripped the wool and forwarded it onto the teeth of the main cylinder rotating at around four hundred to five hundred revolutions per minute (rpm). In the diagram, it is shown rotating in an anticlockwise direction. This dragged the wool into the machine and onto the first spiked bar. This gave the first teazing action and prepared the fibres before it reached the first rotating worker roller, which rotated at thirty to forty revolutions per minute in the opposite direction to the cylinder. In the diagram, this is shown as a clockwise direction. At the point of contact of the roller and the drum, the surfaces were therefore travelling at very different surface speeds giving a shearing action that tore the matted wool apart. The first worker was geared to the second and together they vigorously separated out the fibres and shook the burrs and other debris out of the wool. This detritus fell to the bottom of the machine and through the perforated mesh

FELT IN BRITAIN

drum to be removed by the fan, shown on the right of the diagram. When the wool had been sufficiently worked and there were enough fibres circulating in the machine, a cam was activated that stopped the feed and opened a door on the side of the machine. This had the effect of throwing the wool out onto a cage, which deposited it onto the delivery lattice.

A willow in practice at Bury Felt Manufacturing Ltd Mill c1948

For continuous processes, the feltmakers collected the wool from the delivery end of the willow by means of a suction fan, which then blew it through wide ducting to other parts of the mill for further processing. The ducting can be seen in the above photograph of a teazer in Hudcar Mill of the Bury Felt Manufacturing Company Limited. In the early days of feltmaking, willeys were an important part of the process, as witnessed by the machine inventories of felt companies. In modern times, around the 1980s, willeys were hardly used for making white technical and superfine felts, the blending being done only by the use of fearnoughts or devils. Nevertheless, willeys were used extensively in the manufacture of grey felts since the raw wools such as karakuls came in directly from eastern countries with lower quality control than mainstream wool-producing countries such as Australia and South Africa, and consequently were full of sand, grit and seeds. These wools therefore needed considerable cleaning, to a degree that made the use of a willow a necessity.

DEVILLING

Having partially opened the fibres and removed much of the debris, the wool was then sent via the ducting to the next process to continue the opening process, to blend together different fibres, and to start to align the fibres ready for the fine carding operation. The mainstay of this process was the fearnought, also known as a devil or tenterhook willey as shown next.

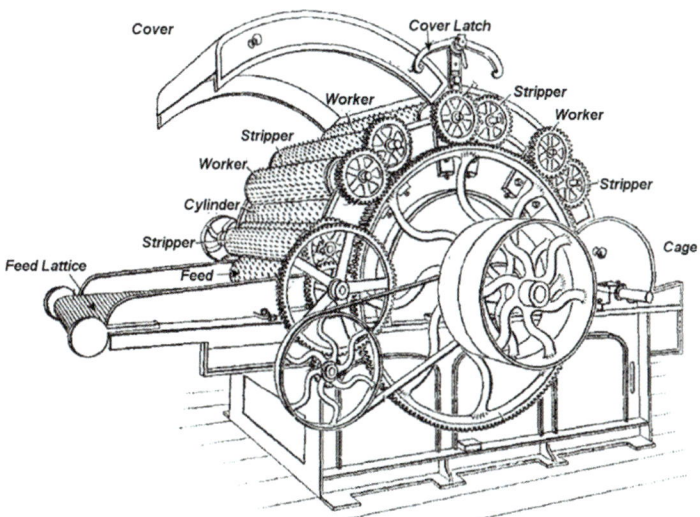

The fearnought, showing its construction

The following explanation of the action of the fearnought is based on Beaumont's description, which gives a good view of how a fearnought works, something that has changed little over the course of the years. The only main changes that have been made are the use of materials in the machine's construction, and the design of the teeth that enclosed the rollers.

The devil or fearnought at Bury and Masco Industries in 1980

As in the willow, the main component was a rotating drum studded with rows of teeth or spikes, which were raked at an angle and resembled the hooks on a cloth drying tenter: hence its other name "tenterhook willey".

Later, teeth that resembled those of a circular saw, called cockspur teeth, superseded the spikes. The fearnought, like the willow, made use of workers rotating in the opposite direction to the cylinder to open the fibres, but in this machine a new set of rollers called strippers were introduced. A stripper worked in conjunction with a worker to help align the fibres, improve the opening, and blend the different wools together.

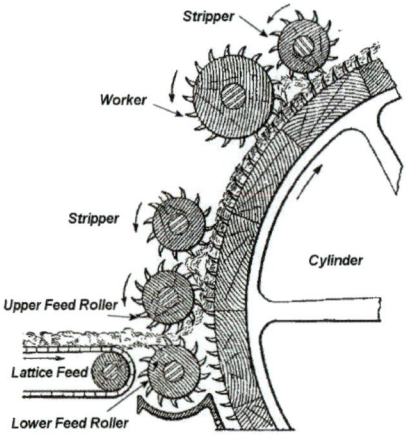

The configuration of the workers and strippers, note the directions of the teeth of the various rollers relative to the cylinder

Feeding the blend into the fearnought at Cooper & Co. (Birmingham) Ltd in 1980, dust extraction is on the left, the ducting on the right transported the wool to the carding room

The wool blend was fed into the machine by the wooden lattice feed that took it into the feed rollers, and pushed the fibres onto the teeth of the rapidly rotating cylinder. The interaction between the feed rollers and the cylinder started the opening action helped by the first stripper. This lifted the fibres off the teeth of the cylinder and deposited them back onto the upper feed roller to be fed back to the cylinder again. The looser fibres were then carried round to the first worker roll. This had its teeth and rotation in opposition to those on the cylinder, creating a vigorous tearing action that further opened the fibres. The stripper, which was positioned just above the worker, had its teeth pointing in the same direction as the cylinder and opposite to that of the worker. This created an action that stopped the build up of fibres on the worker, lifted some of the fibres off the cylinder, and deposited them back onto the worker. The workers and strippers therefore were designed to work in pairs. To ensure the optimum separation of the fibres, there were three of these sets distributed around the circumference of the cylinder. Where manual doffing of the fearnought was required the fibre was drawn onto a cage that collected the blend and deposited it onto a delivery lattice that moved it forward ready for manual collection. Alternatively, a fan was fitted to the exit of the machine that drew the blend off the machine and blew it, via ducting, to special blend bins ready for the next carding stage in preparing the fibres.

View of a blending bin taken from inside another blending bin

In some cases, the fibres were blown over considerable distances to the bins, which had the added effect of making the blending more effective. Some manufacturers (e.g. Bury and Masco Industries) even added a cyclone at the end of the blowing line so that the fibres were churned up in a vortex in order to increase the efficiency of the mixing. The bins were situated, wherever possible, directly behind the carding machines so that there was a minimum of manual effort required to feed the woollen mix directly into the hopper of the card.

Technically fearnoughts varied in size, having cylinder diameters of thirty-six, forty-two, and forty-five inches, with a thirty-six-inch diameter rotating at two hundred revolutions per minute, and a forty-eight-inch diameter rotating at one hundred and fifty. These gave outputs of between eight hundred and one thousand pounds per hour. The standard size of a worker was six inches and rotated at twenty-five revolutions per minute, whilst the strippers were four inches in diameter and rotated at thirty. The teeth of the rollers and cylinder were offset, otherwise known as staggered, so that the teeth of the workers passed between adjacent teeth in the cylinder, and so that the tips could be set to penetrate the teeth on the cylinder just below their tips.

FELT IN BRITAIN

FINAL CARDING

From the point of view of the feltmakers, the objective of carding was to open up the fibres as much as possible and collect them in a form that was suitable for the first stage in felting known as hardening. Different felt companies had many different ways of doing this either through preference or through limits of space in the mill[2]. However, most manufacturers used a three-stage process using three carding engines each having different configurations. The first stage was a breaker card known as a scribbler, the second was an intermediate card and the final one was the finishing card, all three being referred to as a carding set. The designs of the carding engines were superficially similar in construction and operation and superficially similar to the fearnought, though far more sophisticated. In some cases, all three stages of carding were done in one continuous process but this made for a very long machine. Since the majority of British felt mills were adapted from old woollen mills, which had considerable space limitations, it was usual to separate the scribbling from the other two processes.

THE CARDING ACTION

Unlike the willows and devils, the surfaces of the rollers and cylinders of the scribblers and cards were covered with wire rather than teeth or spikes. The wires were set in leather or felt, known as card clothing, so that the wires pointed vertically outwards when wrapped around the rollers and cylinders. The thickness of the card clothing was around half an inch and the wire itself protruded a further half an inch above it. The end of each wire was bent over to form a lazy "L" shape, the actual angle of bend being known as the knee.

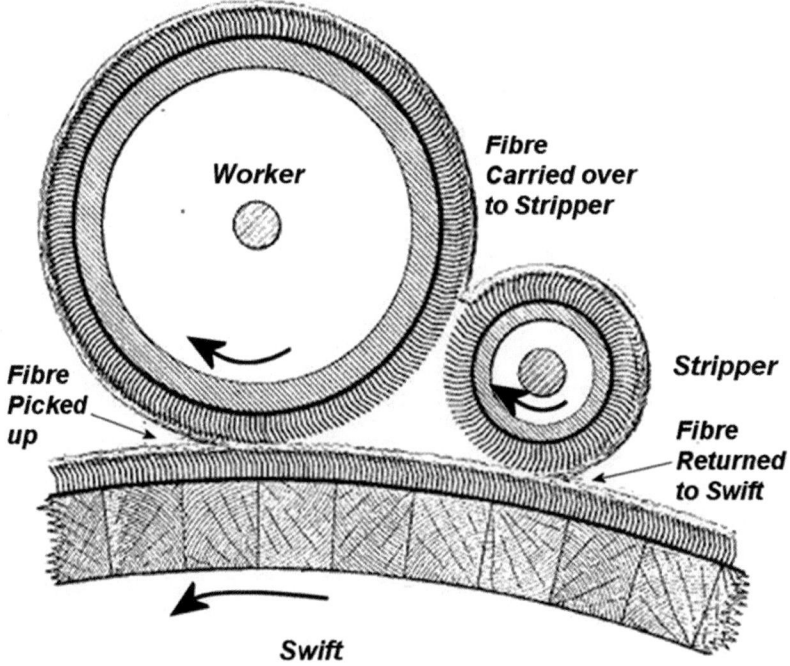

The essential elements of carding showing the interaction of worker, stripper and swift

The wires were mounted on the worker roller so that the points of the wires were opposed to the points of the wires on the cylinder, also known as a swift. In contrast to this, the points of the stripper were aligned in the same direction as those on the worker and cylinder. The points on one roller did not touch those of another or those on the swift; all the action therefore took place in the gaps between them. The width of these gaps was therefore crucial to creating the best fibre distribution for felting. The gaps between the rollers were adjusted meticulously using feeler gauges using Imperial Standard Wire Numbers and these varied in thickness from 0.2 millimetres to two millimetres. This was known as setting the card.

For carding, the cylinder had a rotation speed of between sixty to one hundred revolutions per minute, equating to a surface speed of between seven hundred and one thousand two hundred feet per minute, depending on its diameter. This was considerably faster than that of the workers or strippers, which rotated at three to five revolutions per minute and had a surface speed of around three hundred and fifty feet per minute[3]. Any fibres passing between the worker and swift were effectively combed, and at this point, some fibres adhered to the swift and some were caught by the worker. The fibres caught on the worker rotated with it until it came to the stripper, which had a slightly slower surface speed than the worker did. As the points of the two rollers were pointing in the same direction this slower speed had the effect of gently lifting the fibres off the worker and carrying them round to the swift. Since the points of the stripper and swift were also pointing in the same direction, the fibres were transferred from the stripper to the faster moving swift. The fibres then made their way to the worker again, at which point some went past it on the swift, though some were caught again by the worker and the cycle repeated. In practice, each carding engine needed at least six pairs of workers and strippers to give a satisfactory web of fibres. The resultant effect can be seen in the following photograph of workers and strippers in action in a working carder.

Carding wool in practice, the worker is the larger roller, the stripper is the small roller underneath it

FELT IN BRITAIN

The full configuration of the workers and strippers on a typical carder is shown in the diagram below.

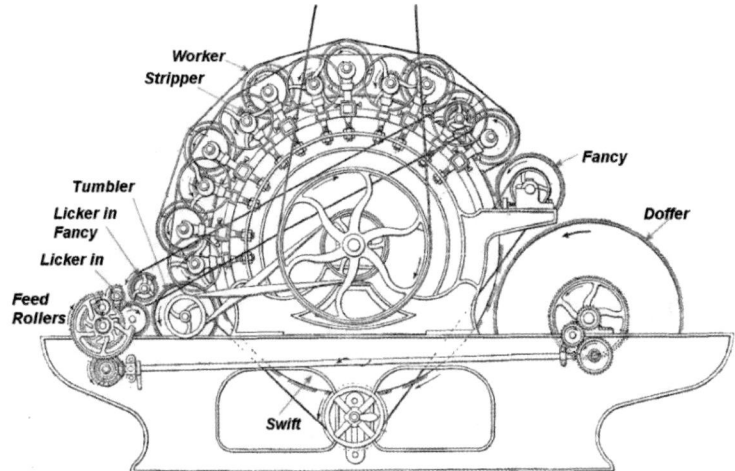

A single carding engine showing the workers and strippers arranged around the swift

The wool fibres entered the card on the left through the feed rollers and were fed onto the swift by the action of the licker-in and licker-in fancy. Thereafter, they were worked through the machine via the six workers and strippers until it came to the roller called a "fancy". This roller was clothed in very long wires, the points of which pointed in the same direction as those on the swift. They penetrated one to two millimetres into the gaps between the wires of the swift, the only roller to do so. The surface speed of this roller was thirty percent faster than the swift, which had the effect of lifting the fibres off the wires on the swift and depositing them on the doffer from which the fibres emerged.

CONFIGURING THE SCRIBBLER

The scribbler was in effect a coarse carder, generally having thicker wire and wider wire spacing than the later processing cards, and as such continued the work of the fearnought. Over the years, the felt industry used several different configurations of scribbler sometimes using just one carding engine and at other times, combining two carding engines in one scribbling machine. The preferred combination was to have three engines combined with the first engine being a "mini card", known as a breast[4].

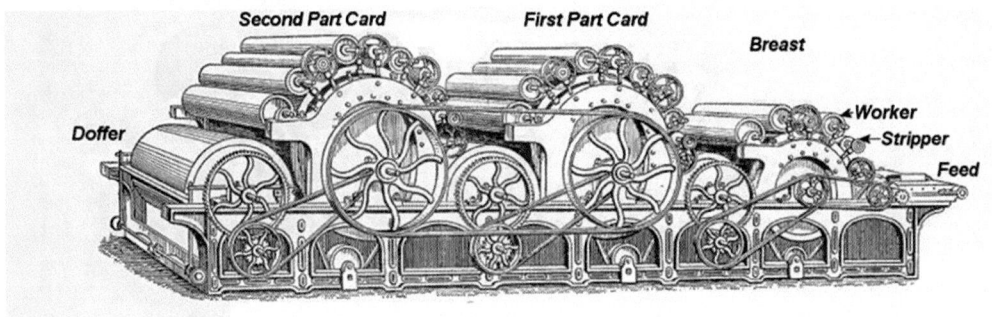

Plan of a two-part Scribbler with a breast

The breast continued the work of the fearnought in separating out any matted fibres. Consequently, the card wire used in this section was much coarser than the rest of the machine and some feltmakers even preferred to use garnett wire instead of card wire[5]. Garnett wire was not really a wire but a thin continuous band of metal teeth that could be wound around cylinders and rollers. Because of the robustness and resistance to bending of the teeth, garnetting gave a superior tearing action to ordinary card wire.

Sometimes, the scribbler also contained a set of "peralta" rollers to help disperse the burrs and seeds in the blend by crushing them. The two peralta rollers were made of steel and acted like a mangle, exerting considerable pressure on the fibre web to crush the burr and seeds into tiny fragments that were then carded out later in the scribbler. This was mainly used where non-carbonised wools were used or when making superfine felts.

Banks of scribblers at Bury Felt Manufacturing company c1948

As the wool progressed through the scribbler, it became more open and easier to card, so to compensate for this, each subsequent carding engine had finer wires set closer together. In addition, because the web of fibres going through the machine became finer the gaps between the swift and the workers and strippers were set progressively narrower. When the fibres reached the doffer they came off the machine as a coherent web, though still not consistently uniform, with some fibres still matted together. At the end of the doffer was a metal comb, known as a fly-comb, which ran the full width of the machine and vibrated up and down very close to the doffer wires. This had the effect of peeling the web off the doffer ready to be collected for the next carding stage.

FELT IN BRITAIN

Doffing a web off a card, the oscillating comb is the black bar on the top right, next to the swift, and ridges of the web show where the teeth of the comb are

CONFIGURING THE FINAL CARDS

The object of the final stage of carding was to align the fibres and create a consistent uniform web in terms of weight per unit area and fibre distribution, as well as having no matted fibres or neps. In order to do this most efficiently the intermediate card and the fine card were linked together in a continuous process.

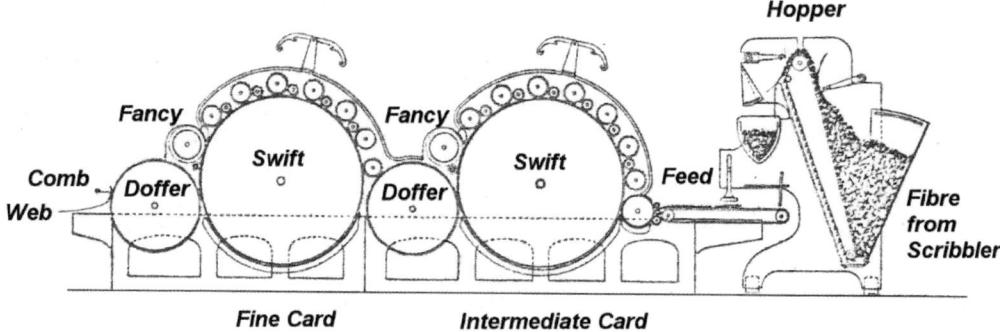

The final two stages in carding showing the take off from the intermediate card feeding directly into the final fine card, the hopper feeds weighed amounts of fibre onto the feed lattice

The wool from the scribbler was loaded into the hopper making sure that it was spread evenly across the width. This ensured the best distribution of fibres across the cards. The hopper contained a wooden lattice studded with spikes pointing upwards, which dragged an appropriate amount of fibres over the top and into a weigh pan. When the weight in the pan reached a pre-determined level, the sides of the pan opened and dropped the fibres onto the lattice feed into the feed rollers of the intermediate card. Once this intermediate carding was complete, the fancy roller lifted the web off the first swift and onto the first doffer, which then fed the web to the next fine card. At this point, the licker-in roller transferred the fibres onto the swift of the fine card. After passing through this second card, the fibres were transferred from the swift to the second doffer and the final web stripped from the doffer by the vibrating comb. This web was now in a suitable state for it to be formed into a carded batt of fibres, by a process that was unique to the felt industry.

Intermediate and fine cards in operation, the hopper is on the right, the finished web exits at the left

In setting the actual cards, great attention was paid to the types of wire used on the two different cards. This also extended to each set of workers and strippers, which were all treated differently. The closer a set was to the final doffing end of the machine the finer was the gauge wires of the card clothing used to cover the rollers. In addition, the rotational speed of the workers was progressively increased from four revolutions per minute for the first worker to six for the last[6].

Although this was the most commonly used configuration of cards used in the felt industry, feltmakers also used different configurations, chief amongst these was the introduction of a cross-lapper between the two cards. The object of this was to align the fibres passing to the second card to lie at ninety degrees to the direction of travel through the machine. This ensured better distribution of the fibres in the web and more efficient fine carding. Several different types of crossers were employed, such as Scotch feeds, Blamire, Apperley, and crosser cards[7]. These feeds adopted one of two different techniques. The first and most popular was the Scotch feed, where the web was collected together to form a thick roving, like a very thick rope, which was then laid backwards and forwards on a lattice conveyor feeding into the second card.

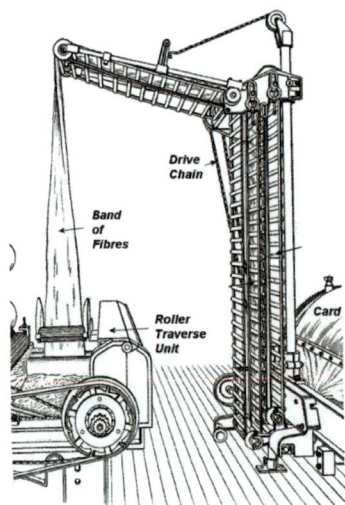

A typical scotch feed that takes the web from the carding engine on the right and cross lays it on the second card on the left.

In the second type, the web of the intermediate card was collected together into a band of fibres, fed between two vertical lattice conveyors or aprons, and positioned over the feed of the final card. Mounted on this card was a roller traverse mechanism that had two rollers to guide the fibres back and forth across the final card's feed lattice.

Feeding a fine carding engine via a Scotch Feed, cross-lapper at Bury Manufacturing Company Ltd. c1948

The height of the lattice aprons facilitated the cross laying of the fibres which gave the mechanism a distinct hump-like appearance. Hence, it was also known as a camelback feed. There were several arrangements of the Scotch feed because once the band of fibres was constrained in the lattice aprons it could be transported virtually anywhere. This made it possible to make the maximum use of the limited space available in felt mills. For example, Bury Felt Manufacturing Company Limited

PREPARING THE FIBRE

was able to squeeze in back-to-back carding engines so that there was virtually no space between them. The Apperley cross lapper laid a roving in a similar way to the Scotch feed but with a more complicated mechanism and was very rarely used.

The second technique was to lay down a web, rather than a roving, in a zigzag pattern that was somewhat more complicated. This necessitated a lattice conveyor the same width of the card and two feed rollers that were mounted on a carriage, in such a way that the emerging web could pass between them.

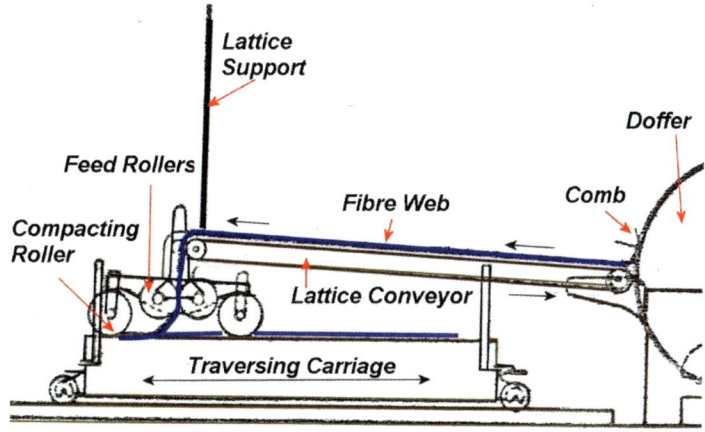

Diagram of a web cross-laying mechanism

The carriage with the rollers was made to travel backwards and forwards in order to deposit the web onto a second lattice conveyor that was oriented at right angles to the first. This formed a crisscrossed lap on the feed conveyor. The thickness of the web was controlled by the speed of the second conveyor[8].

A Befama Blamire cross laying machine in action.

Because of the way that the cross laying worked, it meant that the two cards needed to be at right angles to each other and this took up an inordinate amount of space. Consequently, in Britain, where space was at a premium, this configuration was not popular. In the United Kingdom, William Tatham Limited specialised in carding engines and especially these types of feeds, and they managed to redesign the cross lapper to take up fifty percent less space, but it still did not gain wide acceptance. Blamire feeds were also made on the Continent notably by Befama.

FETTLING

Considering the forces and actions, taking place within a carding engine it is clear that considerable maintenance was needed to keep them running at optimum efficiency. After a period of running the spaces between the wires of the card became filled with fibres and other debris, which affected the ability of the card to provide a good web. This filling had to be cleaned out on a regular basis, depending on the type of wool that was being carded, coarse or fine, clean or dirty. This may have been once a day for dirty wools and over a week for clean wools[9]. This cleaning of the carding engines was called fettling and had to be done by hand. Sometimes the carding engines were dismantled but most times the carder had to complete the fettling by standing on various parts of the machine and lean over the swift. This had to be done very carefully so as not to damage the carding wires. Consequently, in the early days the carders took off their shoes and wrapped their feet in thick felt. It was from this that the slipper industry and later the shoe industry was born. To clear out the debris from between the wire the carders used fettling combs that were about six inches long and equipped with a wooden handle, the teeth of the comb being matched to the pitch of the spacing between the wires.

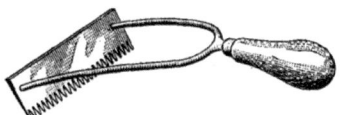

A fly-comb for fettling or cleaning between the wires of a card

The fettling consisted of fitting the teeth between the wires and combing out the detritus; making sure that the combing was done in the direction of the wire point and not against it.

GRINDING

Inevitably wear took place on the wires themselves and this usually occurred with the ends of the point becoming rounded, which led to a deterioration in carding and poor web formation. When this happened the card had to be dismantled and all the rollers removed for the wires to be reground, though the swift was usually ground in place. Because of the investment feltmakers had in their cards, all the maintenance was done in-house and was the responsibility of the mill engineer. The mill engineering shop had all the specialised equipment it needed to grind the cards and the skill to produce exactly the right profile on the points of the wires that best suited felt making. The grinding process was done by turning the roller against a rotating grindstone or an emery coated roller, taking care not to over grind the wire and leave burrs on the ends. The preferred shape of the point was similar to a needle, though other shapes such as a chisel shape were also considered. Typically regrinding was only done once a year or sometimes twice.

COLLECTING THE FIBRES

All the carding processes up to this stage were similar to those of the woollen and worsted industries, but from this point on, the techniques for handling the carded fibres were specific to the felt industry. It was the collection of the web and its transformation into a long, thick batt of fibres that helped to make the production of felt unique. The web was collected on a forty-yard long cotton or flax conveyor that was mounted on a special wooden or steel framework. The whole assembly was known as a batt frame dating from the original Williams' felt patent of 1840, and its design remained constant throughout the history of felt making.

Rolling up a finished batt on a horizontal batt frame c 1948 at Hudcar Mill, the black PVC coated fabric of the supporting conveyors can be seen on the rollers at the end of the machine

At the ends of this frame, there were large diameter rollers over which the conveyor passed so that it looped backwards and forwards across the frame in order to minimise the space required. It was usual to have three of these loops so that the batt frame was only about thirty feet long and seven feet high. The conveyor drive was linked to the last carding engine so that its surface speed matched that of the doffer and the web was laid without tension onto the carrier.

After the conveyor had travelled forty yards, exactly one web was laid down and the conveyor was back in its original position to take up a second web layer, which was laid on top of the first. Each one of these circuits was called a "lap" and these were counted as the web accumulated on the conveyor to give a thick layer. Counting the laps established the weight of fibre that had been collected and this was matched to the final felt specification.

There was a major problem in having the conveyor travelling backwards and forwards. As the conveyor went forwards the fibres were resting on top of it, but on the return journey, the carrier and batt were upside down with the fibres hanging below the conveyor surface. Therefore, without support from underneath the fibres would have dropped off. The solution was to put in other special support conveyors where the carrier and fibre batt were upside down. The material for these needed to be stiff coated fabrics so that the fibres of the web did not stick to them.

After the appropriate number of "laps" was achieved for the felt specification, the batt frame and card were stopped and the batt cut across the width. The frame drive was disconnected from the card and one edge of the batt threaded onto the wind up. Because the batt frame could now be driven independently of the carding engine, it could be activated to roll up all forty yards of the accumulated batt of fibres. Once this had been completed the roll was removed, the frame reconnected to the card and the whole process repeated. In this fibrous form, the roll was also known as a lap, which was cause for confusion. However, there was a certain logic to the nomenclature because a felt could be made of several of these rolls and it was necessary to identify them when loading a felting machine.

It proved to be difficult to keep the long continuous carrier cloth straight and free from wrinkles as it continually progressed around the frame. Therefore, the end rollers had adjustments on each side of them in order that each side could be moved forwards or backwards to adjust the tension. Even so there was still a tendency for the cloths to wander to one side of the frame or the other. This problem was solved by stitching narrow leather belts on the edges of the carrier cloth and leading them between horseshoe guiders bolted to the frame. The only weakness in this system was the increased frictional drag caused by constant rubbing on the leather belts. This was resolved with the use of rollers to replace the static horseshoe restrainers.

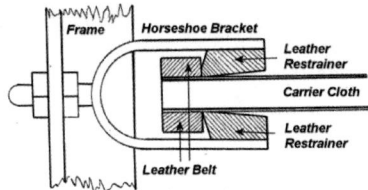

Restrainer for keeping the carrier cloth
straight and crease free on the batt frame

This second solution, though more elegant and efficient, was costly to produce. It consisted of forming a long leather loop and riveting it to the carrier cloth, in a similar way to upholstery beading. This loop was then fed between two angled wheels that pressed either side of the neck of the leather loop. As the carrier pulled through the guide the rollers turned rather than dragging on the carrier cloth, and hence minimised the friction.

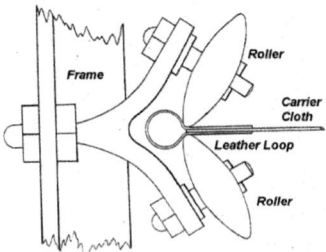

Roller guide used to keep the carrier
cloth under tension preventing it
from wandering or creasing

Even with these controls in place, the carder needed considerable skill to keep the batt frame tuned to give trouble free running. The woven carrier cloth, being of cotton or flax, was sensitive to moisture and therefore varied in length depending on the humidity of the atmosphere. When it was damp, the length increased so that the tension in the system dropped, and when it was dry the cloth tightened up. To keep the carrier running true at the correct tension, the carder had to continually adjust the rollers at the ends of the batt frame according to the conditions in the carding shed.

The width of a batt frame matched the width of the card and was either sixty or eighty-four inches wide so that acquiring woven cloths or coated fabrics at these widths was a perennial problem as only specialised weavers were capable of manufacturing to these dimensions. Another limitation was the thickness of fibres that a batt frame could accommodate because the geometry of supporting the batt with two carriers restricted the amount of fibre that could be accommodated between them. The weight of the batt at any time was derived by knowing the output of the card in terms of the weight of the web produced. Each time the carrier cloth completed one revolution of the batt frame this weight was added to the batt of fibres collected. By counting the number of times the carrier cloth went round the frame, the weight of the batt could be estimated. In general, the maximum amount of fibre that could be collected equated to around thirty cycles of the carrier cloth, which equated to producing a lap weighing around one hundred and twenty pounds. To gauge the number of cycles of the carrier, a mark was made on the side of it and each time it passed a fixed point it was counted as a "lap" (beware confusion of terms). Either this could be counted manually by making a chalk mark on the frame, or mechanically with a lap counter and sometimes by setting a bell that rang when the necessary number of "laps" had been made.

For technical felts, only lengths of ten, twenty, and thirty yards were needed. To do this marks were made on the side of the carrier cloth at ¼, ½, and ¾ lengths of the cloth. The machine was run until the full length of batt had been collected, it was then stopped, disengaged from the carder, and the batt doffed as usual. If a ten yard length was needed the batt was wound up until the ¼ mark reached the doffing end. The batt was then separated across the width and the first ten-yard roll removed from the wind up. The machine was restarted until the ½ mark reached and the second ten-yard roll doffed. This was repeated for the ¾ mark and for the final doff, which in total gave four ten-yard rolls. For twenty-yard laps, the rolls were doffed at the ½ mark and at the end.

The use of a batt frame gave considerable versatility to the construction of the finished felt in terms of the different layers that could be created in combination with the carding engine attached to it. The most common type of felt was a three-layered felt having a different fibre blend in the middle relative to the outside two faces. This was done by weighing out the necessary weights of the fibres required for the different layers of a forty-yard felt. Then each was fed in turn into the hopper of the card, the face layer weight first, then the middle layer weight second, and then finally the back layer weight. While the batt frame was kept in motion it accumulated all these layers as the web of fibres arrived from the card. A typical construction of such a felt was fifteen pounds of wool for the face, then forty pounds of other fibres for the middle, and then a repeat of the fifteen pounds for the back: making a total weight for the lap of seventy pounds and a length of forty yards[10].

To reduce the space taken up by the batt frame feltmakers tried using a vertical version where the carrier cloth moved up and down over rollers instead of horizontally. Most vertical batt frames produced laps of forty yards but some were capable of sixty-six yards. They were never popular in Britain because they could not carry as much weight of fibres as horizontal batt frames. Consequently, it was less efficient commercially, and also proved to be more troublesome.

FELT IN BRITAIN

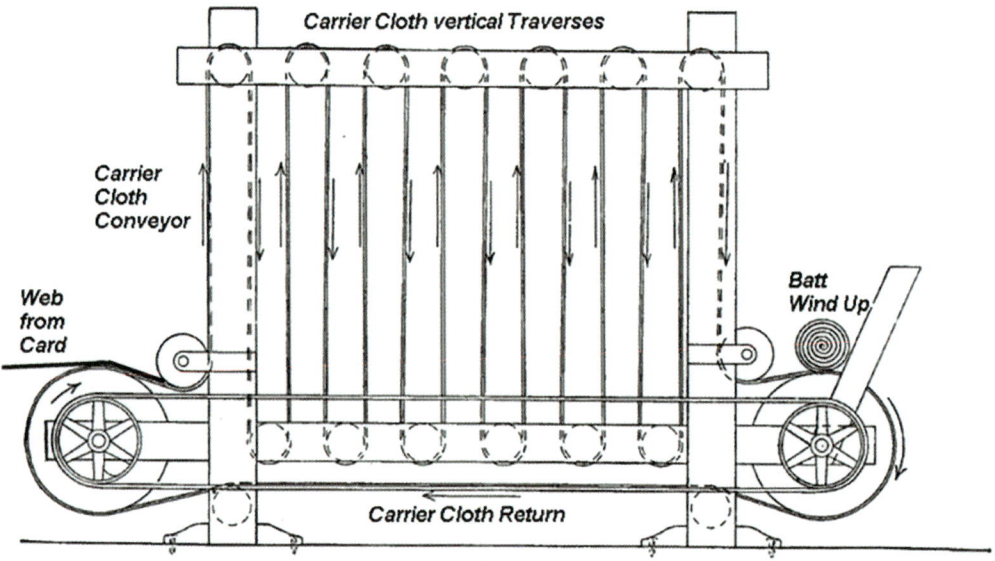

The vertical batt frame[11]

For very thick felts, such as technical sheet felts or felt stock for polishing wheels, a different technique was used. For this the batt frame was replaced by a wooden cylinder, six feet in diameter and the width of the card. This was placed at the end of the card and the web wound up continuously on its surface. This gave a batt of around six yards long and of virtually any weight. Once the specified weight had been reached, the machine was doffed in a similar way to the standard batt frame. The card was stopped, the drive of the cylinder disengaged, and fibre batt was broken across the width. This time, however, because the layer of fibres was so thick it was rolled up by hand rather than using an automatic wind up.

The cylinder frame for winding a heavy batt   Doffing a cylinder lap frame.

At the height of the felt industry, this form of lap formation was done on a considerable scale as technical felts were used in virtually every type of engineered product and demand was high. The photograph overleaf shows the carding shed of Bury Felt Manufacturing Limited dedicated to producing batts on cylinder frames.

PREPARING THE FIBRE

The carding shed at Bury Felt Manufacturing Company Ltd. making technical felts on cylinder frames.

A row of cylinders can be seen on the top right and centre of the picture. Identifiable by the long vertical stanchions attached to them. These stanchions housed a roller that rested on the accumulated web keeping it compact and free from folds. The height of these roller guides could be up to six feet, which gives an indication of how thick a felt could be made by this technique.

Cylinder frames for creating thick batts, on the left is
a web being wound, on the right is an empty frame

It has long been known that batts could be made by putting a cross lapper at the end of the card, and this technique had the versatility to produce thick laps as well as thin ones. In a cross-laid web the fibres were aligned across the piece, which meant that, though the web was strong laterally, it was weak along its length. All handling and processing was done by pulling along the length and so cross laid webs had a tendency to distort easily and narrow along the width; similar to opening a concertina. By contrast, straight laid webs were strong in the length and weak in the width and therefore were less prone to narrowing or distortion. The act of cross-laying fibres meant that this technique could not satisfactorily produce a layered felt, which limited its commercial possibilities. Historically, therefore, cross laying was not popular amongst the felt makers in Britain. With the introduction of high-speed cards with improved cross-laying capability, this technique found good use in the manufacture of very thin superfine felts, particularly where the blend used had a high proportion of synthetic fibres.

High speed Krupp cross laying machine producing a wool-viscose batt for producing superfine felt

The photograph above shows a cross laying line in 1980. The two-part card can be seen at the top of the picture and the mechanism for cross laying at the top right, whilst the right-angled lap conveyor is just visible underneath it. Since the card delivered a web at a constant rate, the speed of the conveyor dictated the number of layers and the ultimate felt weight. The conveyor fed the batt of fibres into a set of rollers, which lifted it and stretched it lengthways to even out any winrows that might have developed during cross laying, and so produce a more uniform felt. The batt was then lightly needled to impart some strength in the web to improve the handling and finally it was rolled up ready for felting. The equipment was ideally suited to producing superfine felts with high synthetic fibre content and felts could be made containing just thirty percent by weight of wool and seventy percent of synthetic fibres. The preferred synthetic fibre was viscose rayon because it had similar physical properties, and was significantly cheaper than wool. It was only after this process was established, that it became possible to produce an all-synthetic felt by replacing the tacking machine at the end of the line with a heavy-duty needle punching machine. Although the resultant all-synthetic felt did not have the same strength and aesthetics of a pressed wool felt it was much cheaper to produce, because it did not require additional felting. Therefore, synthetic superfine felt eclipsed its woollen counterpart and by 2013, all craft and felt for soft toys was synthetic.

8 HARDENING

CONDITIONS FOR HARDENING

Hardening is a process unique to the felt Industry. It converts a loose mass of wool fibres into a non-woven fabric with the strength to be handled and processed further. Before hardening, the wool is a fragile mass of virtually unconnected fibres and after hardening, the fibres are firmly entangled and locked into a robust cohesive structure. This intermingling is induced by a special process, which vibrates the wool fibres between two surfaces, while simultaneously applying pressure, moisture and heat. Since no other textile is formed in this way, only felts produced by this process are "true felts". However, in defining a true felt, the felt manufacturers chose to distinguish their products as "pressed felt" because of the importance of pressure in the hardening process.

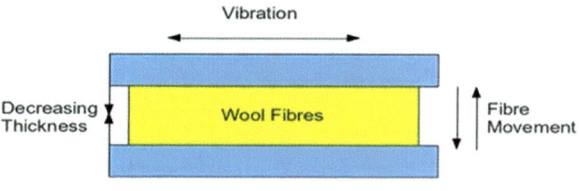

The Dynamics of Hardening

The simplest hardening process traps fibres between two plates and then vibrates one of the plates from side to side. The plates constrain the fibres closest to their surface, and stop any shrinkage in length or width from taking place. Therefore, during the vibration, the fibres are forced to move vertically, so that the only shrinkage that takes place is in the thickness. Only a few percent of the fibres actively respond to the vibration and these twist, turn, move up and down, and tangle with other fibres, stitching the fibre mass together. When the wool is fully hardened, there are no longer any more active fibres on the surfaces. This is important from the point of view of future processing, because it means that once a felt has been hardened it can be safely rolled without the surfaces felting together.

To induce the fibres to felt during hardening, conditions other than just vibration are necessary. The main factors conventionally considered by the industry were heat, moisture, and pressure. The heat and moisture were provided industrially by steam, and the pressure either by a heavy plate or by offset rollers both of which will be described later. In recent times, (from the 1970s onwards) the craft felters have shown that felt hardened with just water can be as good as felt that is felted with steam. This has been confirmed by a full-scale trial on production machinery at Bury and Masco Industries Limited, though this was not adopted because of the difficulties of water spraying compared to the convenience of using steam. From a quality point of view, it was important that all the fibres were equally wetted, as a dry patch will not felt during hardening. Such patches created problems throughout further processing, leading to a fault in the finished felt. Commercially this problem was minimised by careful steaming of the fibres prior to hardening.

Given well-moistened fibres, the other two important factors in the hardening process were: the amplitude of vibration, and the pressure. For any given felt thickness, there is an optimum amplitude of vibration that fully hardens a felt. If the amplitude is too small there is not enough vibration to move the fibres, too much vibration and they are pulled back and prevented from penetrating through the thickness of the felt. During hardening, the area of the felt remains constant so the weight of the fibres is the same as the hardened felt weight, which is reflected in the diagram by the term "felt lap weight". Commercially a felt was generally defined by its weight for a given area (grammes per square metre, or ounces per square yard) as well as its thickness.

Optimum Vibration Displacement for Different Felt Weights

[Graph: x-axis "Felt Lap Weight (gm/sq m)" from 0 to 1000; y-axis "Vibration Displacement (mm)" from 0 to 14. Data points approximately at (0,0), (250,6), (450,8), (950,12).]

Technically, amplitude is the convention for describing the size of a vibration, but this is only half of the actual displacement that a felt undergoes when it is hardened. Feltmakers used the term "throw" in place of amplitude because it was a direct measure of how far an eccentric shaft was offset from the driving shaft. To describe what actually happened during hardening the graph above shows the total displacement that a felt requires to harden it, and this is twice the conventional amplitude measurement and twice the throw. The graph shows clearly that the heavier a felt is the greater the displacement it has to undergo if it is to harden properly. Surprisingly, the optimum displacement is independent of the speed of vibration and independent of the pressure applied during hardening.

There is also an optimum pressure for hardening: if the pressure is too low there is not enough force to move the fibres whilst too much pressure and the fibres are prevented from moving. The optimum pressure also depends on the felt weight.

At the optimum pressure and amplitude of vibration, the time to harden a felt is the same for all felt lap weights when submitted to the same speed of vibration. At nine hundred and fifty revolutions per minute, the time to harden felt weights from 250 gm/sq.cm to 950 gm/sq.cm is sixty seconds[1]. This means that full hardening of any felt takes place after nine hundred and fifty vibrations. Hardening at different speeds does not alter the optimum pressure or the amplitude of vibration. The final density of hardened felt is around 0.14 gm/cc, independent of the felt lap weight.

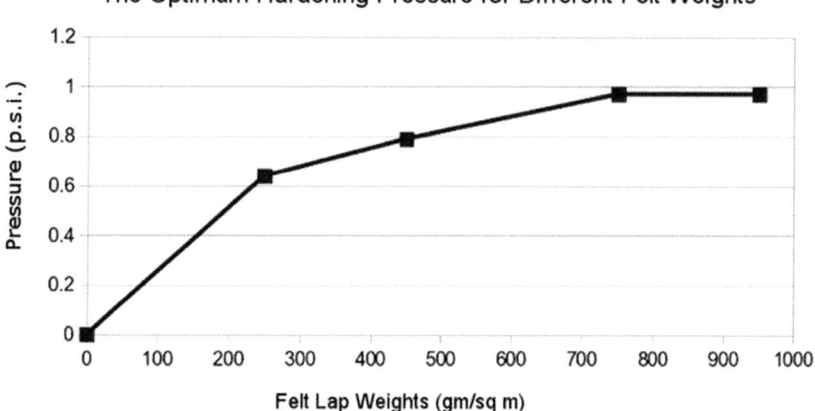

OTHER FACTORS

TEMPERATURE

Much work has been done on the effect of temperature on the milling of wool fabrics but very little on the felting of loose wool. Information on the temperature effects on hardening is scarce though all feltmakers agreed that heat has a beneficial effect on the commercial process. The actual temperature is not considered critical and is constrained mostly by the economic use of steam. For milling a temperature of over thirty-five degrees Celsius improves milling but at high temperatures milling efficiency drops[2]. From the limited scientific work undertaken, the same temperature relationship seems to hold true for hardening as well[3]. The following graph shows how the felt thickness changed with temperature during hardening on a commercial hardener, the thickness being a measure of the degree of felting.

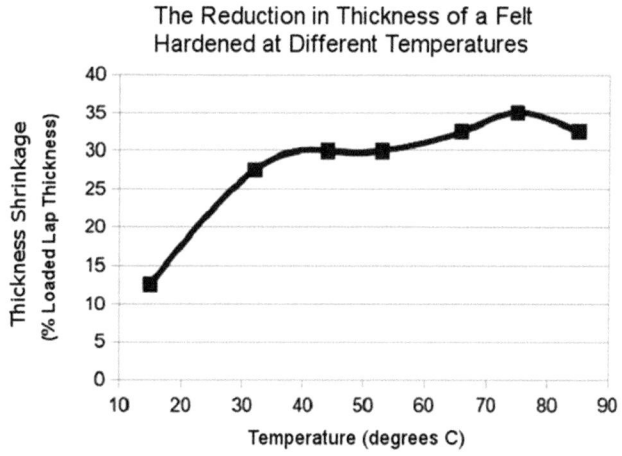

In practice, wool was steamed before hardening took place, which had the dual effect of providing the optimum moisture throughout the lap and also heating it above thirty-five degrees Celsius, thereafter the wool was kept hot indirectly through the heating elements of the hardening machine.

THE EFFECT OF ACIDS AND ALKALIS

There are some factors that affect felting but these do not have much significance in commercial hardening mainly because it is difficult to implement practically on industrial hardening machines, so these treatments were usually reserved for the milling of felt.

Of these factors, the presence of acid or alkali is the most important. Wool is acid resistant and begins to absorb acid when the pH level is about 4.8[4]. As the acid level becomes higher and the pH level falls, there is a rise in the degree of felting that takes place, rising to a maximum when the pH level is 2, and this is independent of the type of acid used. The acid of choice in the felt industry was sulphuric acid but acetic, formic, and phosphoric acids worked equally well. As the pH rises from two towards the alkaline levels feltability falls sharply reaching a minimum at a pH of 12-13. Since wool is not resistant to alkalis the wool fibres become increasingly damaged and for the most alkaline treatments, this becomes visible as the wool shows clear signs of yellowing.

EFFECTS OF SOAPS AND DETERGENTS

The use of soap to enhance the felting of wool has been known for so long as to be regarded as traditional and even the pioneer of the felt industry, T. R. Williams considered it worthy enough to patent it. Although not widely used in commercial hardening, it is of particular importance to craft felt workers who tend to use wet hardening rather than steaming. In this case, detergents such as washing-up liquids are the chemicals of choice. Soaps and detergents enable better wetting of wool fibres by overcoming the natural oils and grease of the wool, ensuring that the wool is uniformly wetted and that water can penetrate into the fibre structure. In the presence of water, soaps, and detergents become slippery and therefore act as a lubricant allowing fibres to slip past each other more easily, thereby allowing greater and faster movement of the fibre[5]. The effects of different types of washing soaps and powders are not so clear as different brands have different and complex recipes that can inhibit as well as enhance felting. The common factor of those that improve feltability are those that generate a good lather, foaming being a key feature that correlates with good felting.

FLAT HARDENERS IN PRACTICE

Although roller hardeners were the first machines to manufacture felt on a commercial scale, flat hardeners became the workhorses of the industry. Over the years, they were redesigned, modified, and engineered into a variety of different shapes and sizes so that they could produce a multitude of products such as hats, polishing wheels, and sheet felts over three inches thick. The smallest flat hardener was eighteen inches square with a top platen made of wood, and the largest had steel platens measuring over ninety inches square, were six inches deep, and weighed over a ton.

A flat hardener consisted of two perfectly flat plates that sandwiched the wool fibres to be hardened between them. Then, either one or both plates were vibrated horizontally with a motion that was either rotary or reciprocal and some machines were even capable of an elliptical motion. For some specialist uses, three or more platens could have been used so that several felts could be made at the same time. These were consequently known as multi-plate hardeners. Since flat plate hardeners could only felt a section of a wool batt at a time, the process was discontinuous and therefore ideally suited for batch operations such as the manufacture of hat bodies. They were modified to simulate a continuous process by moving a long length lap a section at a time through the machine and hardening each section in turn. This method was well suited for the manufacture of thick felts.

FLAT HARDENERS FOR BATCH PRODUCTION

The simplest hardeners were also generally the smallest and were used predominantly in the hat industry. Mainstream bulk felt manufacturers tended to use small hardeners for specialist applications where a batch process was required, such as the manufacture of felt boots. The most elemental machine was one manufactured by Thomas Garside and Son of Ashton-under-Lyme and appropriately called a Garside hardener.

 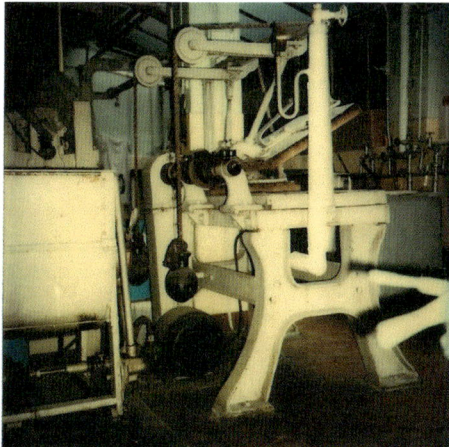

Front and rear views of a two-position Garside Hardener

This consisted of a sturdy cast iron frame housing a steam chest measuring approximately two feet square and having a perforated steel plate on top, the whole assembly acting as the lower platen. The upper platen was made of wood, approximately two inches thick and connected by a substantial bracket to an eccentric mounted on a horizontal shaft. This mounting gave a back and forth motion to the top platen whilst at the same time acting as a hinge to allow the platen to be tilted open or closed. Both the perforated plate and the wooden platen were covered with a heavy cotton cloth to give good frictional surfaces to ensure that the maximum amount of vibration could be transferred to the wool fibre during hardening. The top wooden platen also had a large metal leaf spring mounted on it that could engage with a lever mounted on the machine frame. This facilitated the adjustment of the pressure to create the right conditions for hardening. To raise the platen the lever was swung out of the way and the platen tilted open in a similar way to that of a hinged box. The wool batt was then laid on the lower platen and steam was allowed to percolate through the perforated plate and cotton cloth and through fibre mass. After a suitable steaming time, the lid was closed and the lever was swung down to engage with the U-shaped leaf spring. The pressure was crudely adjusted by pulling the lever further up the spring to compress it further, causing it to press further down upon the top platen and increasing the pressure on the wool. The top plate was then vibrated for the appropriate time with steam still being fed into the lower chest so that the fibres were kept warm during hardening. Finally, the pressure lever was then swung out of the way, the lid lifted and the hardened felt retrieved.

Bury Felt Manufacturing Company Limited had a number of these machines as they had taken over a hat manufacturing mill in Bright Street Bury. They put these to good use for making felt boots. Initially they were made to supply to Russia during the war. Known as Valenki boots, they were excellent for arctic climates and had superb wear characteristics because the more they were walked on, the tougher the soles became. They also had natural thermal and waterproofing properties, with a superior performance at sub-zero temperatures.

They continued to make a variety of different boots, some were sprayed with green rubber dissolved in a highly inflammable solvent to make them waterproof, and some were special boots made for the Korean War. These had wire stuck to the soles and were ideal for jungle warfare because they were tough and silent, though walking on them was like walking on springs. They also manufactured boots dyed in different colours and fitted with rubber soles[6].

The manufacture of Valenki boots using Garside hardeners, on the left the sleeves are being hardened and on the right the hardened sleeves are being cut and sewn into a boot shape

The boots were made by carding wool into a tube that was rounded at one end and a former placed inside. Each tube was hardened on a Garside hardener in sections until the full length of the tube was hardened. The former was then removed and the hardened tubes sent to the cutting shop. The rounded end was cut at a forty-five-degree angle turned through one hundred and eighty degrees and sewn back onto the tube. The rounded end was now at a right angle to the tube, giving a recognizable boot shape but about twice the size. The hardened boots were then sent for milling where they thickened, shrank to size and became both dense and tough, and after drying, ready to wear[7]. A similar machine to the Garside was made by Reinits of Recklinghausen Germany.

Double position flat top hardening machine by Reinits [8]

HARDENING

Another type of table hardener also existed in Leeds University in 1987, which was an all-metal machine measuring approximately three foot square with a sunken lower platen and a weighted steel upper platen, which was raised and lowered with a chain mechanism.

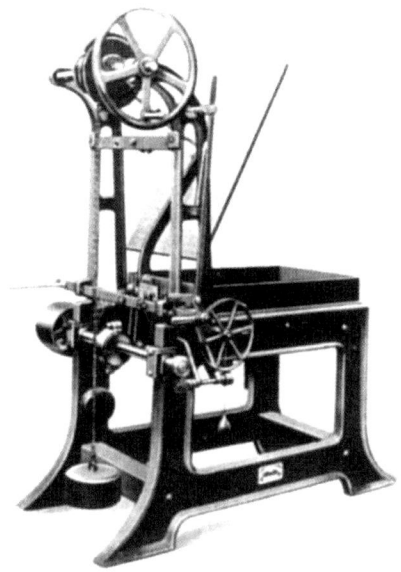

The Leeds Hardener 1981

Early full-scale flat hardeners were similar in action to the Garside hardener in that they used a linear vibration and had a hinged top plate. They were comparatively massive with a plate area measuring ninety inches by thirty-two inches, the pressure being generated by the sheer weight of the plate.

An American single plate flat hardener in 1907[9]

With this sort of vibration and linkage, it was simple to modify the machine to make both the top and bottom plates vibrate in opposite directions. Although this had the effect of increasing the amplitude of vibration, it offered no other advantages than could have been achieved by just vibrating one plate on its own. Consequently, this form of hardener was later abandoned by the industry.

A flat hardener in 1907 with top and bottom vibration plates[10]

The great advance in flat hardeners came with the inventions of the William Bywater Company. Bywater was an engineering company based in Leeds that specialised in manufacturing machines for the felting industry, especially roller hardeners, and came to prominence when they started to manufacture flat table hardeners.

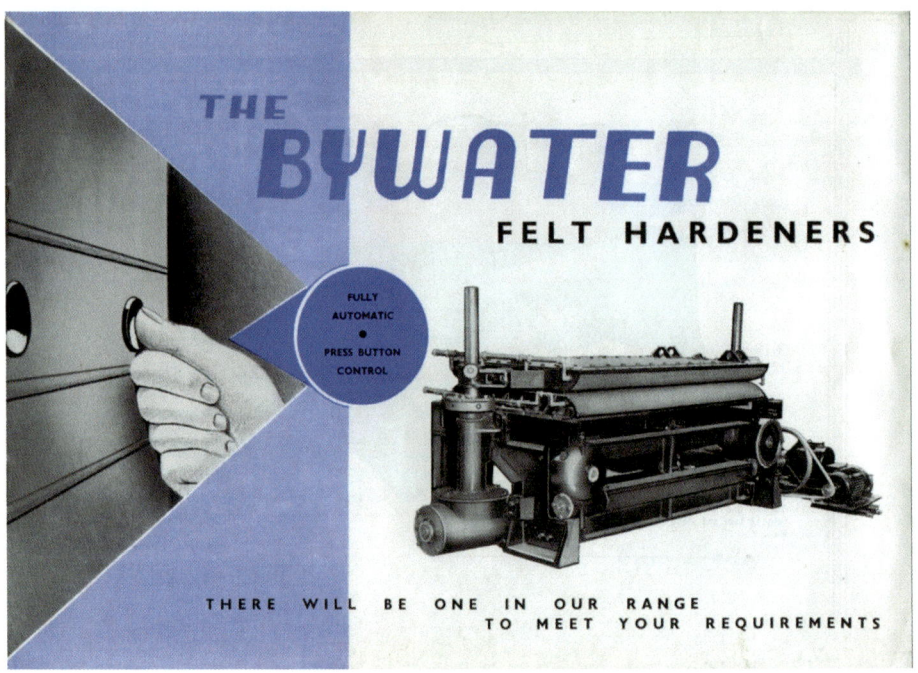

Bywater leaflet circa 1970 highlighting their table flat hardener

William Bywater was making roller hardeners before 1868 and the company was making flat hardeners around 1880 when a patent was granted to William Bywater for an oscillating flat plate table hardener[11]. This was the forerunner of the flat hardeners that were capable of rotational oscillation rather than the early machines that only had a side-to-side vibration.

HARDENING

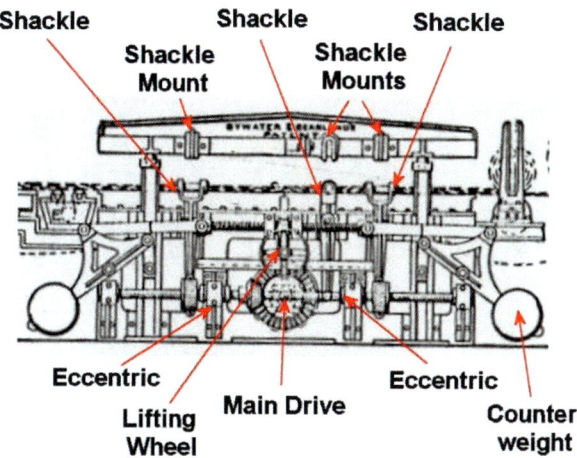

The Bywater Beanland Flat hardener

The Bywater Beanland patent of 1884[12] revolutionised flat hardening. It was an improvement on the table hardener of 1868 in that it had shackles, a raising and lowering motion, and ball sockets as supports. The machine was constantly developed through the inventiveness of its leading engineer, T. R. Beanland, so that it became the industry standard for the next hundred years or so. The shackles that provide the oscillatory motions, each of which were driven via an eccentric mounted on a rotating shaft connected to the main drive. There were two shackles at the front of the machine that looked like stirrups and moved from side-to-side, and another one that oscillated backwards and forwards. The shackles fitted into mounts located on the top plate. Working all these shackles in combination could produce any oscillation from a circular motion to a linear motion. The top plate rested on ball sockets on top of pistons that were raised or lowered mechanically by turning the wheel located in the centre of the machine. This rotated two opposing screws that pulled a lever mechanism that acted like a car scissor jack to raise the platen. The arrangement can be identified by the spherical counterweights on either side of the machine. In later developments, the shackles were replaced by eccentric shafts that gave greater control over the vibration and were significantly quieter in operation.

Modern table four-shaft hardener of 1970 manufactured by William Bywater Limited

The first and most obvious difference between this machine and the shackle-type hardener was the massive vertical shafts that passed through bearings attached to the top plate. The synchronisation of these shafts imparted any required type of vibration to the top plate. Each shaft was connected to a five horsepower motorised drive that rotated them at a pre-determined speed, typically at two hundred to two hundred and twenty-five revolutions per minute. However, each shaft was not one continuous piece but was split near the base and the two parts offset to provide an eccentric that transmitted a vibration to the top plate. The two parts of each shaft were connected by a substantial flange arrangement that allowed the top shaft to be adjusted through a slider so that the amplitude of vibration could be changed to the required value.

A Bywater hardener showing the split between the two shafts and the slider arrangement that creates the eccentric.

The raising and lowering mechanism was simplified in the case of the table hardeners by the use of two vertical toothed racks. A gear wheel or pinion engaged with the teeth in the rack and as it turned it moved the rack up or down and since this was connected directly to the top plate this too was raised or lowered. The two mechanisms clearly had to be synchronised to lift the top plate smoothly. This simple arrangement altered the gap between the plates precisely, which was measured by the dial situated on the right hand side of the machine. For larger felt machines, there were four such racks one at each corner of the top plate. The time to raise and lower the top plate was critical for efficient performance and the mechanisms to do this were constantly improved so that it took between twenty and thirty seconds to lift or lower a seven ton plate. By the 1970s, Bywater boasted of a time of five seconds to lift the plate.

Other felt machine manufactures such as Nik Wahl, Dzulke, Schuko, and Zahl, in Germany followed this pattern but Bywater machines remained the dominant force in the British felt industry. However, none of these companies recaptured the early pioneering work of Bywater and Beanland and all were modifications of existing flat hardener types.

HARDENING

A flat hardener made by Nik Wahl in Germany

FLAT HARDENER CONFIGURATIONS

The flat hardener was one of the most versatile machines used in the felt manufacturing process. This versatility came from the number of different configurations that became available, and the way it could be used in conjunction with other equipment.

In its simplest form, the flat hardener was used on its own without any attachments, carrier cloths or feed mechanism. This configuration was used in batch production where it was used for making single sheets of felt or for other felt components like polishing wheels.

A simple flat Hardener loaded with individual woollen batts shaped to make polishing wheels

By attaching a feed mechanism at one end of the hardener and a wind up system at the other, it was possible to convert the batch process to produce continuous rolls of felt. This was done by hardening a section of felt equal to the length of hardener plates. On completion of the hardening, the plates were lifted and the finished section pulled out of the machine dragging the next section of the woollen batt into position between the plates. The plates were then lowered and this new section hardened. This process was repeated until all of the batt was felted.

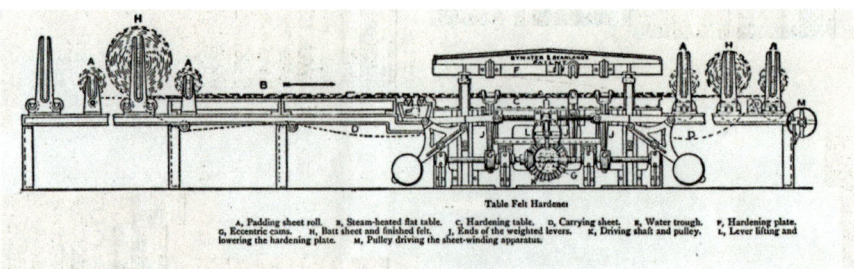

An early Bywater Flat hardener, hardening a felt between two cotton cloths

In order to make the transformation of the flat hardener from a batch production to a continuous process it was necessary to use carrier cloths, in order to convey and protect the delicate wool lap into and out of the hardening zone. Because of the forces involved and the general scuffing involved in the hardening process these cloths were usually thick cotton duck cloths with a tight weave. Cotton was preferred because of its exceptional frictional properties when wet, though flax was a good alternative. The thickness of the fabric prevented it from rucking and creasing during the vibration and the high coefficient of friction minimised slippage, ensuring the maximum transmission of the vibration into the felt. This was particularly important when producing thick felts. In the oldest form of this configuration it was the lower carrier cloth that provided all the traction to convey the batt into the hardener, pull the hardened felt to the other side of the machine, and finally wind up the felt.

The wind up end of a flat hardener at Baltic Mill in 1980
showing the lower main carrier and upper carrier cloths

The top carrier cloth also had to be wound up, ready to be re-used for the next length of felt. In later manifestations of this technique, rolling up the top carrier cloth was replaced by a continuous loop of cloth that went through the machine, up and over the top plate, and then returning to the input of the hardener. Rollers situated at suitable places around the machine controlled this loop, and these guided it so that it continuously ran straight. Because the cloth was in a continuous loop there was no need to handle rolls of cotton fabric from one side of the machine to the other, after a run.

There was also a major advantage in this configuration, because of the way that the felt was released from the carrier cloth. During the hardening process there were inevitably some wool fibres that penetrated the cotton cloth weave imparting a virtual tackiness between cloth and felt. When the hardened felt was separated from the cloth, the stray fibres between them would either be snapped or pulled out. By having the upper cloth as a loop, a roller could be positioned at the point of separation. This provided an action whereby the cotton cloth was peeled away from the felt in a controlled way and with the minimum effort. When the cotton cloths were new more of the wool fibres migrated into the weave and gave problems both in terms of release of the felt from the carrier cloth and in the degree of hardening. Fibres that should have gone into the felt were lost to the cotton cloth. Feltmakers therefore always made allowances and adjustments to the process until the cloth had bedded in and most of the available gaps in the weave were filled with stray wool fibres. Once this had been achieved little if any wool fibre could migrate into the cotton, and the cloth operated at optimal efficiency.

The lower carrier was also made into an endless loop but in this case it spanned the whole of the machine and therefore acted as a primary conveyor. Because all the forward driving forces were dependent on this, the cloth was usually more substantial than the top cloth. Furthermore, it was a vehicle for additional pre-treatments of the woollen lap before hardening. It was common for this lower carrier cloth to pass through a trough of water at the front of the machine, to make sure it was fully wet before it reached the hardener plates. The heat from the plates ensured that the water in the cloth turned to steam and penetrated the wool whilst it was hardening. The trough could also contain other chemicals, such as soaps or acids, to further facilitate felting. Another addition to the machine was a steaming chamber positioned just in front of the hardening plates to allow steam to percolate through the lap whilst the previous section was being hardened. This meant that the lower carrier cloth had to be woven in such a way as to allow the steam to pass through it.

A flat hardener viewed from the output side, the top plate has been lowered onto the lower plate and is in the process of hardening, the steaming chamber is on the right, steam is percolating through the wool fibre lap waiting to enter the hardening zone.

On the input side of the hardener there had to be sufficient space to accommodate up to six laps in order to make thick felts. Each lap had sufficient integrity to enable it to be unrolled as a continuous sheet of fibres. The lower carrier cloth facilitated the gentle forces necessary to unroll the first lap, which rested by gravity on the carrier. The second lap now rested on the fibres of the first lap and the forward force of these was sufficient to unwind the second roll, and so on for the other rolls. By the time the fibres reached the plates at the hardener, the total lap could be several feet thick.

The output side of the machine could be much shorter since only one finished hardened felt needed to be wound up, and this had undergone a huge reduction in thickness, which produced a significantly smaller roll. Older machines used a roll of cotton as the top sheet instead of a fabric loop, and this had to be accommodated by unrolling it at the input side of the machine and then rolling it up at the exit. On the output side of a flat hardener, the lower carrier cloth provided a constant speed drive that wound up the felt and other auxiliary cloths into suitable rolls. All these logistics of unwinding and winding meant these types of hardening machines were very long indeed.

The input side of a flat hardener at Baltic Mill 1980, four laps are being unwound onto the continuous lower cotton carrier cloth, the laps are of different diameters and the axles are at different heights on their individual stanchions. This machine could process up to eleven laps

All the rolls had to be surface driven because they could not be secured on fixed axles without a programmed variable speed drive. This was because the diameter of the roll of felt varied as it was unrolled or rolled. For example a lap may have started out as a roll at around five feet in diameter, but at the end of process, as the last sections of wool were being felted, it would have been just a few inches in diameter. With a fixed axle rotating at a constant speed, the tension in a lap would be considerably different at the start of the process compared to the end. Because a lap, or the hardened felt, was very sensitive to tension, using a fixed axle would have induced significant differences in properties from one end of the felt to the other. The felt makers solved this problem by using pairs of upright stanchions. Each of these had a vertical slot cut into them, which allowed the ends of the axles to fit into them and move up or down as the diameter of the roll changed. This provided a constant tension, constant speed operation.

HARDENING

Two stanchions showing the vertical slot for one end of an axle, the right stanchion allowed the top carrier cloth to adjust for different felt thicknesses

FELT SLEEVE PRODUCTION

Flat hardeners that were fitted with the top carrier as a continuous loop, were important machines for creating both very thick felts and felts in the form of seamless, endless belts. They used the same conventional configuration of an endless top cotton carrier cloth passing through the plates and over the machine. However, on the output side of the machine, instead of winding up the hardened felt, it was separated from the bottom sheet and allowed to remain attached to the top sheet. As hardening progressed the initial end of the hardened felt reached the input side of the machine and was allowed to pass back between the vibration plates with a new section of the fibre lap. The new fibres were then hardened on top of the previously hardened felt. By repeatedly doing this, hardened felt of virtually any thickness was constructed. For a sheet felt, hardening would continue until the appropriate thickness had been reached, the machine was stopped, the felt cut across the width, and then rolled or plaited on the output side of the machine. If an endless belt was required both the upper carrier cloth the hardened felt attached to it, had to be removed from the hardener.

The technique for removing the endless felted sleeve was itself ingenious. It involved using a separate metal A-frame made of tubular steel that could engage with sturdy metal eyelets welded to the top of the upper vibration plate. The length of the arms of this A-frame was the same as the width of the felted sleeve. The eyelets can be clearly seen in the photograph below.

Bywater flat table hardener used for manufacturing endless felt belts, the eyelets on the right are for lifting off the top plate

FELT IN BRITAIN

Removing the sleeve involved the use of three hoists: two to lift the top plate and the third to lift the A-frame. When it was time to remove the felted sleeve, two of the hoists were attached to the top plate, one at each end, and then activated in synchronisation to lift the plate completely clear of the upright eccentric shafts. The two arms of the A-frame were then located into the eyelets in the plate and the weight of that end taken by the hoist that supported the frame. At this stage there were three hoists supporting the weight of the plate.

The middle hoist was then lowered and removed leaving the plate supported by the A-frame and the hoist at the far end. The felt sleeve could then be slipped off the plate and onto the arms of the frame. The middle hoist could then be reattached to the plate and raised to take the strain off the A-frame, which was then detached from the hardener. The top plate was then repositioned onto the upright eccentric posts and re-engaged with the ratchet mechanism of the hardener that bore the plate's weight. The hoists were removed and the hardener was ready for the next operation. The hardened sleeve was then pulled off the arms of the A-frame ready for the next processing stage.

Unloading an endless hardened felt sleeve from a table hardener, the frame on the left is attached to the top plate as the middle hoist is being removed, the sleeve is ready for sliding over the frame

MULTI-FELT MANUFACTURE

Perhaps the most innovative technique that felt makers devised for using the flat hardener was one that enabled the production of thin felts. Flat hardeners were neither efficient at producing single thin felts, nor is the action conducive to making good thin felt. A roller hardener was both a faster and more efficient machine for manufacturing superfine felts. However, feltmakers developed a method of hardening multiple thin felts at once in a flat hardener, which was able to compete commercially with a roller hardener.

In practice, up to six felts at a time could be produced. This was done by sandwiching each lap, which made up the finished felt, between two cotton cloths so that there was one cotton separator between each lap. A roll of cotton cloth was positioned before and after each rolled lap of wool, on the input side of the machine. As the rolls unwound they produced a thick, layered sheet consisting of cloth, wool, cloth, wool, cloth, etc., which was pulled between the hardener plates. So to all intents and purposes it presented the equivalent of a thick felt to the plates. The hardener could then process the multiple felts with maximum efficiency. If six felts were being produced it meant that the process was effectively operating at six times the speed of hardening a single felt. However, in practice this was not quite the case; firstly time and effort were needed to mount so many rolls of cloth and woollen laps on the input side of the machine; secondly on the output side of the machine each hardened felt had to be separated from its supporting cloths and both felt and cotton cloths had to be independently rolled up. This of course required more labour as well as making the overall machine extremely long.

FLAT PLATE FELT HARDENER.

Flat plate hardener, in side and plan views, it is configured to harden four thin felts at a time, the small rolls are the cotton cloths on the left and are rewound on the right, the four large rolls on the left that are the woollen laps and on the right they are thin hardened felts

Innovative though this technique was, it did not prove to be a replacement for a roller hardener. The method was cumbersome, and with so many sheets to control it was difficult to prevent them from creasing. Of greater concern, was that felts in the middle of the stack were less felted than the outer ones. This is a characteristic of the vibration of the two plates because the plane midway between them receives virtually no displacement. This effect has been observed in hardening a thick felt because the inside layers were not as strong as the outer layers, as measured by the tear strength of the felt at different positions within the felt. Fortunately, in practice, subsequent milling ensures that the felt becomes more homogeneous.

With multiple felt hardening, feltmakers hardened only even numbers of felts so that the place where the displacement was zero came between felts rather than through the middle of one. With an odd number of felts, one felt would lie exactly on the null plane and would therefore not be hardened properly. Because this technique generally led to felts of slightly different properties this method of hardening did not become mainstream and was only used to supplement the roller hardeners when the demand exceeded their capacity.

FELT IN BRITAIN

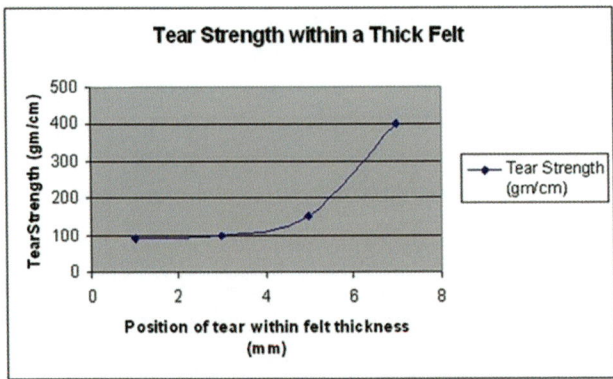

The tear strength at different positions in a thick felt, 0 represents the centre of the felt[13]

HARDENING PIANO HAMMER FELTS

Producing piano felts was the most sophisticated of all the felt manufacturing techniques because a single sheet of finished felt had to contain felt at different thicknesses and densities. This meant that the hardening stage was the most critical part of the operation since this process defined the future properties of the felt. Hardening felt for piano hammers was therefore shrouded in a high level of secrecy. So much so that some companies manufactured their own hardeners rather than having them commissioned by external engineers such as William Bywater.

Piano felt production was a batch technique and consisted of making a single one metre square sheet at a time. These sheets were wedge-shaped with the thin edge being between two millimetres and eight millimetres thick and the opposite thicker edge being ten to thirty millimetres thick.

Finished milled piano felt sheets drying, showing the taper of the sheets, the thicker part at the top and thinner part at the bottom

The density of the felt also varied across the sheet, being lower where the felt was thickest and of high density where the felt was thinnest. A strip from one of these sheets, cut from the thin to the thick end provided the appropriate felt for all the hammers in a piano. The thin hard part of the felt strip was for the small treble piano hammers to produce the highest tone, and the soft thicker parts were for the bass hammers to produce the lower notes.

Because of the secrecy involved in the hardening of hammer felts, photographs or engineering drawings for these hardeners are rare. The schematic diagram below represents an approximation of the construction of the machine based on a cursory visual observation. In one photograph in a brochure by E. V. Naish a piano hammer felt hardener could just be seen in the background.

Schematic diagram of a table hardener for producing a wedge shaped piano hammer felt, compared to the production at E. V. Naish[14]. The top plate profile was adjusted by hoists fixed to the ceiling and suitable weights were placed in the appropriate honeycomb cells, two vibration shackles positioned at a right angle to each other could gave any type of motion from linear to circular

The actual framework was unremarkable, consisting of a simple but robust table-like framework one metre high, just over one metre wide and just over one metre long. This supported a substantially built steam-heated chest that served as the bottom platen of the hardener. Below the chest the framework supported the drive mechanism for vibrating the top plate. The top plate was a flat steel sheet reinforced by ribs running both along its length and its width. This enabled suitable weights to be placed securely in the interstices of these ribs. The top plate was secured at each corner by a chain that was connected to the ceiling via a pulley, which allowed the plate to be tilted in any configuration during hardening. It also gave the means of lifting the top plate when hardening had been completed. In practice, during hardening, one side of the plate was lowered to make the thin edge of the wedge-shaped felt and the opposite side was raised to make the thick side. Independent weights were placed on the top of the plate at different parts corresponding to the pressure needed to create the correct density distribution through the felt sheet. The top plate was vibrated through shackles on two of its sides and driven by the motors situated in the frame underneath. These could be synchronised to provide any form of vibration from linear to elliptical to circular. The use of open-ended shackles enabled the top plate to be easily lifted off the machine when removing the hardened felt, and facilitated re-engaging them when recharging the machine with a new woollen batt.

FELT IN BRITAIN

ROLLER HARDENING

Roller hardening was the first process specifically developed for hardening felt and yet little is known about how felting takes place in this process. The concept of a roller hardener was relatively simple but its implementation in practical terms was somewhat more complicated. It has always been known that pressure and vibration were necessary to produce a felt, but the problem in commercial terms was how to do this in a continuous production process. T. R. Williams' solution was to use two rollers pressing together and make one of the rollers vibrate from side to side. Two rollers, proved insufficient to felt the fibres together, so he employed a large number of them acting in pairs. This in turn created other problems, because the top rollers could not be vibrated collectively at the same time or the machine would have shaken itself to pieces. Therefore, each roller had to be vibrated individually and had to be out of phase with its neighbour. Then as one roller vibrated one way its neighbours moved in the opposite direction, so that the forces on the machine were balanced.

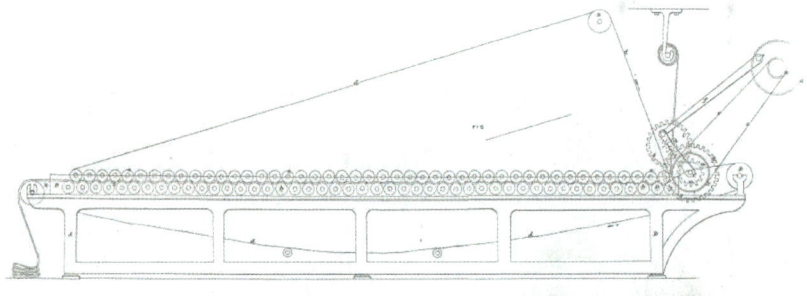

T R Williams' preferred roller hardener, using endless top and bottom carrier cloths

The next problem was how to allow the vibrating roller to turn whilst it was jigging. This was achieved with the invention of the shackle that enabled a loose connection between the vibration mechanism and the roller. This consisted of a wishbone bracket connected to an eccentric on a rotating shaft. The open end of the wishbone had holes drilled through the ends of the arms to accommodate a shaft fixed to a bearing located on the axle of the vibration roller. These small rods transmitted the vibration from the shackle to the roller via the bearing, which was fixed on the roller's axle.

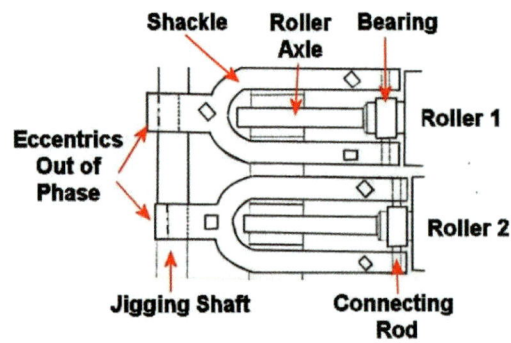

Two adjacent shackles of a roller hardener   The jiggers of a modern roller hardener c 1970s

In operation, therefore, the roller was pushed and pulled to give the required vibration. The loads on these shackle components were colossal and it is no surprise that there were frequent failures in them. Because the shackles were loosely fitting, they tended to clatter and with up to twenty rollers in a machine, the cumulative noise was deafening. Consequently the industry was continually developing new types of shackles, later to be known as "jiggers".

A further complication arose because the woollen lap had to be supported between two carrier cloths (known as bratt cloths), so that any vibration had to be transmitted through these and into the fibres. It transpired that a set of nip rollers was insufficient to harden the felt, at a commercial speed. A redesign of the machine made use of the carrier cloths to create more sustained pressure than could be generated by having rollers positioned directly one above the other. This was done by offsetting the rollers and moving them together so that the top rollers almost touched those at the bottom. The carrier cloths and felt therefore had to bend around the rollers. This not only increased the contact with each vibrating roller but also forced the cloths against the roller to create a more controllable pressure. The greater the tension in these cloths the greater pressure that could be generated.

The very first roller hardener of this type had forty-four top rollers and forty-five bottom rollers so, even with this improvement, the technique was not very efficient. Nevertheless, this configuration set the standard for the foreseeable future, and over the years, considerable improvements were made to the efficiency so that by the 1940s, only eighteen top rollers and nineteen bottom rollers were needed. In the 1980s, experiments were undertaken to create an efficient roller hardener with only nine top rollers and ten bottom rollers though this met with somewhat mixed results in terms of hardening performance.

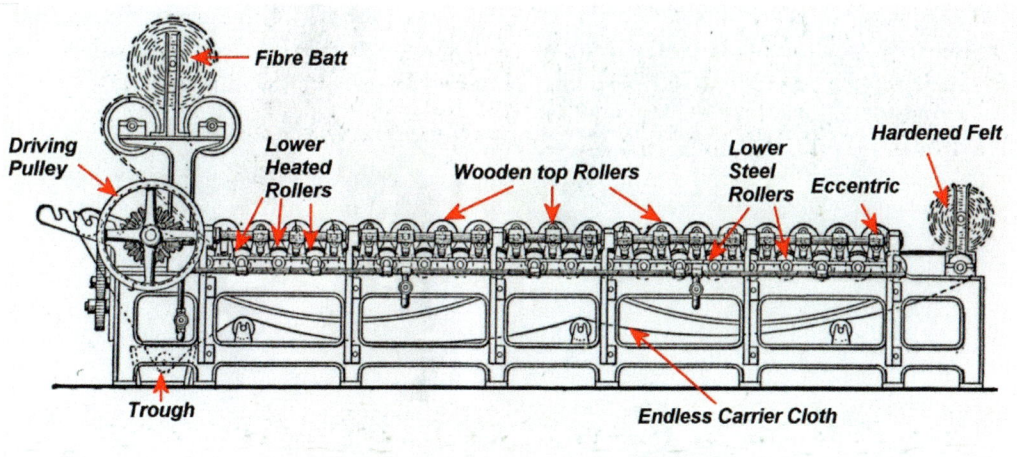

An early commercial roller hardener made by William Bywater

From the descriptions of the hardeners in T. R. Williams' patent it seems that the early roller hardeners had the vibrating rollers positively driven as well as jigging and this must have made their construction complicated in that the roller would have had to slide over the driven axle. By contrast, modern hardeners only drive the bottom rollers, relying on the cloths to give the traction to the top rollers.

In addition, compared to the early hardeners, the modern versions had much larger diameter rollers and the lower bank of rollers could be steam heated and this dictated the materials used for the roller surfaces. The top rollers were until recent times almost exclusively made from wood, which had to be a fine-grained hard wood such as mahogany or sycamore that was resistant to water, steam, and abrasion. Soft woods were avoided because they had a short life being easily worn away by the constant rubbing of the carrier cloths. In recent times, synthetic rubber coverings were tried but these tended to lose grip due to the constant presence of water and steam.

Bywater roller hardener showing the vibration mechanism of the top rollers and the chain drive of the bottom rollers

Since the top rollers were no longer directly driven it was possible to improve their vibration by having shackles at each end of the roller so that one pushed whilst the other pulled giving a synchronized vibration, which minimized the wear on the shackles. The design of the shackles was therefore much different from the early wishbone types. They were also provided with adjusting nuts that could fine tune the vibration and minimize the noise associated with the vibrating roller.

The roller hardener at Bury & Masco Industries showing the finished hardened felt being plaited at the end of the machine, the extraction system was via a polythene shroud, the vibration mechanism was covered by wooden box sections to protect the operatives

The purpose of the heated rollers was to provide the necessary heat and steam to the felt during the hardening process. Since the rollers were separated from the wool fibres by the carrier cloth, this acted as the transfer medium. This was done by passing the lower carrier cloth into a trough containing water. The soaked cloth then passed over the heated rollers causing the water in the cloth to steam. Usually the water in the trough was itself heated to maximise the efficiency. Other felting agents such as soap or sulphuric acid could be put into the trough, but in the main, it was ordinary water.

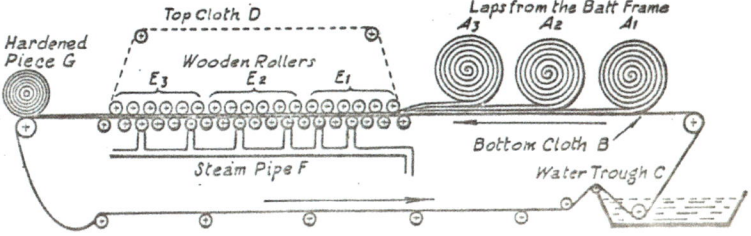

Roller hardener configured for producing felt from three laps of woollen fibres, the water trough is on the right, there are three roller sets with steam heating[15]

It was usually the first three or four rollers of the lower set that were heated, though others could also be used to maintain heat in the system. It usually took some time for the machine to stabilise its heat profile, so that the first pieces through an idle machine would not be as well felted as those when the machine had reached equilibrium. Atmospheric conditions also played a major role in determining felt properties. Felt made on a cold winter's day was less felted by the same machine working on a hot summer's day. Similarly on a dry day with low humidity, the machine was not as efficient as on a humid day. On cold days, the steam from the machines could not evaporate and caused a localised fog in the factory and on these days, it was impossible to see from one end of the machine to the other. Even shrouding the machine in polythene and having an extraction system was insufficient to stop mists forming.

Three roller hardeners in Hudcar Mill circa 1948, in the foreground a lap is waiting to be hardened, on the right a lap is being fed into the machine

The construction of the carrier cloths was of fundamental importance to the production of properly hardened felt. If the cloth was too thin it had a tendency to crease and therefore cause a ridge in the hardened felt. Thin cloths also had a tendency to tear and had a short working life due to the wear caused by the vibration. A cloth that was too coarse left indentations in the felt that could not be removed by further processing. A cloth that was too thick or stiff did not transfer the vibration easily from the rollers to the fibres and could slip rather than transmit the vibration. Because of these constraints, the top carrier cloth was of a different construction and weave than the bottom sheet. The top sheet was much thinner than the lower one and a much finer weave. Nevertheless, by textile standards it was still coarse and akin to tent and awning fabric. It was usually made of cotton, though flax and flax-cotton mixtures were used. The sheet was made endless and it looped over the top of the machine and over a number of free running rollers positioned above the hardener. Some of these rollers were bowed, in order to ensure that no folds or wrinkles developed as the cloth moved round, and that the cloth ran true. Because of their shape they were called "banana rollers". The lower cloth had to perform many functions, from acting as a friction drive belt for the top rollers to carefully transport the delicate fibre mass, to providing the steam medium necessary for hardening. This too was made endless but it had to traverse the full length of the machine and back under considerable tension. Consequently, the fabric was much thicker, around three times as thick as the top sheet and woven from much thicker yarns, but it also had to be very tightly woven to give the minimum of patterning on the hardened felt surface. Since the lower rollers did not vibrate, stiff cloth was used to give stability over the necessary long length. It was also strong enough to provide the force to drive the top rollers and to control the unrolling of the laps and the wind up of the finished hardened felt.

During the felting process wool fibres tended to work their way into the interstices of the weave, so it was vital to have densely woven cloths. The top cloth always seemed to be more prone to this than the bottom sheet and as the hardened felt emerged from the hardener, it had a tendency to pull up off the bottom cloth and stick to the top cloth. As the felt was wound up, it pulled away from the top sheet and fibres could be seen being pulled out of the cloth. This gave the felt a fuzzy surface that could persist through the subsequent processing. In these cases, the felt had to be cropped to remove the fibres that were outstanding. Alternatively, the felt could be pressed to flatten them and give a smooth matt surface.

ROLLER HARDENER OPERATION

Because the upper set of rollers were a fixed distance away from the lower set there was only a limited range of felt thicknesses that could be produced on a roller hardener. Furthermore, whilst the felt was being hardened there was very little control over the pressure on it, and this further limited the versatility of the machine. In fact, setting up a roller hardener was more art than science and it was usual to have similar machines all performing differently. Once a roller hardener was installed and set up, there was little facility to alter the conditions, other than the speed of the machine. This made the machine virtually independent of the abilities of operator, which made it ideal for the mass production. This is hardly surprising since the roller hardener was invented specifically to produce carpet felt at the highest output and lowest cost. In practical terms, the machine limitations meant that the machine could only handle between one and three laps at a time. If more than three laps were used, the pressure would be too high and the vibration too low for hardening to take place. If one lap was used it had to be of a minimum weight. With a very low lap weight there would be insufficient active fibres to bind the felt together so that resultant felt was too weak to be able to pull away from the carrier cloths and was therefore torn apart at the exit of the machine. In practice, a felt weight of around two hundred grammes per square metre was the minimum weight that could be hardened on a roller hardener, and the machine was optimised to make felts around two millimetres thick.

Due to the construction of the machine, it was very difficult to measure the pressure or the magnitude of the forces involved through the roller hardener. All that was known was that the pressure varied from a high when in contact with a roller, to low in the small space between rollers. An attempt was made to measure these pressures using a specially made pressure sensor during an undergraduate project at Sheffield University in 1980. The transducer consisted of two thin copper films separated by a one-millimetre layer of conductive fibre that changed resistance when under pressure. Because of its construction, it had similar compression characteristics to the fibre lap, which enabled it to be embedded in the wool without disturbing the conditions of hardening. Six different roller hardeners were examined and all gave different pressure readings when making the same felt. Significantly the pressure on the fibres induced by the top rollers was considerably higher than on the bottom rollers, probably due to the fact that the pressure on the top rollers is created by the stiff, heavy bottom sheet while the pressure on the lower rollers is created by the softer, thinner top sheet. All the pressures were in the range ten to thirty pounds per square inch. By contrast, the pressure in the gap between the top and bottom rollers was in the range two to six pounds per square inch. The presence of the transducer itself could have affected these results by giving higher readings than would normally have existed. The inescapable conclusion is that the hardening of the wool fibres took place between the rollers rather than when the carrier cloths were in contact with either the top or the bottom rollers, since these pressures were far too high to allow fibre movement.

Because of the dynamic nature of the roller hardener, it was even difficult to determine exactly what vibration was being transmitted to the wool fibres. It was relatively easy to determine the speed and amplitude of vibration of the top rollers because these were fixed by the design of the machine. The carrier cloths did not necessarily transmit these vibrations to the fibres, due to slippage between the fabric and roller surface. Furthermore, as these carrier cloths aged and wore down, the surface became polished and the friction between it and the rollers decreased so that slippage increased. Most hardener rollers had fixed displacements of around four to six millimetres, but it was possible for cloths to slip on the rollers and only transmit vibrations with an amplitude of one and a half millimetres. This is unsurprising, considering that the rollers were vibrating at a rate of eight hundred and fifty to one thousand two hundred revolutions per minute. This slippage could be compensated for, by increasing the tension in the cloths, but this also increased the pressure on the felt, which then had an adverse effect on the ability of the machine to harden the wool. All these adjustments were further complicated by the fact that the nature of the hardened felt changed as it passed along the machine with the matting of the wool fibres continually increasing, and becoming harder to vibrate. Therefore, the rollers of a hardener were arranged in up to three banks, each bank having its own amplitude of vibration, with the first set having an amplitude of around three millimetres, the next four millimetres, and the final set six millimetres. To prevent the machine from shaking itself to pieces each roller vibration was out of phase with its neighbouring roller so that looking along the length of the machine the rollers gave the appearance of a rippling motion.

The only variable that an operator could control once the machine was set up was the linear speed of the machine. This gave the operative the ability to increase or decrease the amount of felting that took place because the speed controlled the length of time the wool fibres were vibrated. A roller hardener typically operated at a speed of around nine feet per minute and for a hardener with eighteen top and nineteen bottom rollers the effective length of machine where felting could take place was around twelve feet. To give a well-hardened felt at this speed the rollers vibrated at nine hundred revolutions per minute, so that the hardening process took eighty seconds in total. This correlates well with the flat hardener results that showed that hardening could be completed after one thousand vibrations. Slowing down the machine increased the amount of felting and increasing the speed decreased the felting. Care had to be taken in slowing down the machine or the felt would be over hardened. This showed up as longitudinal ridges in the surface of the felt commonly known as "lashing" where surface fibres had started to matt together into a long ridge by pulling fibres out of the body of the felt. Conversely, too high a speed caused the felt to be soft and fluffy, which later caused difficulty in achieving the correct density and toughness when the felt was milled.

In the early days, the length of a hardened felt was dictated by the length of the lap that could be carded and accumulated on a batt frame, usually forty yards. However, around 1960 feltmakers were developing laps formed by cross-laying the carded web, and this gave the opportunity to manufacture felts of any length and this gave the possibility of creating a continuous hardening process. Unfortunately, the output of the carding engine did not match the speed of the hardener and the atmospheric conditions of the two processes were not compatible. Nevertheless, cross-laid carding enabled long lengths of thin felts to be produced that were in excess of the traditional forty-yard pieces. Rolling up hardened felt therefore became untenable, as the roll would have been far too large to handle. The lengths became so long that it was not tenable to roll them up for transporting to the milling department. Instead, a plaiting mechanism was fitted at the end of the hardener, which folded it gently onto a truck known as a scray, which could then be conveniently wheeled away.

ROLLER HARDENERS MAKING FELT SLEEVES

During the two World Wars and the years in between, rubber was scarce and heavily milled felt was considered as a suitable replacement, because the properties of the two materials were very similar. Although felt never managed to replace rubber for vehicle tyres, there was a considerable move towards coating rollers in industrial processes with felt rather than rubber. Richard Ashworth and later the MASCO combine therefore expanded production developing specially made roller hardeners at Longholme Mill to produce endless sleeves. At the height of activity, there were four of these hardeners, two large machines, one medium machine, and one small machine.

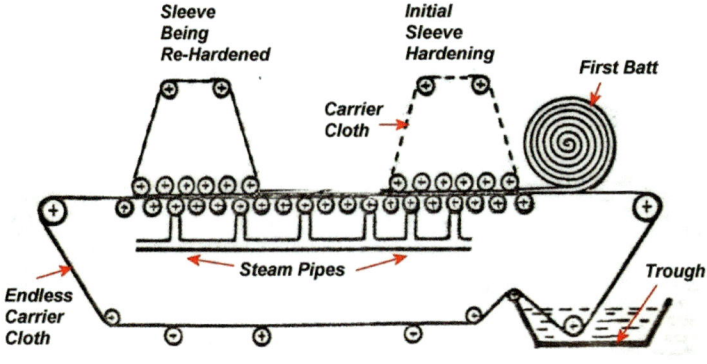

A Roller hardener specially adapted to harden sleeves

For maximum utilisation of the hardener two sleeves were manufactured at once. The hardener was divided into two sections, each having an endless cotton cloth as a top carrier that fitted over six of the top vibrating rollers of the hardener. To make the first sleeve, a carded lap was loaded onto the hardener and fed between the main bratt cloth and the top carrier cloth on the second set of rollers. As it emerged from between the cloths the operator ensured that the semi-hardened felt adhered to the top carrier cloth and went around with it to the starting point. There it met the new lap just entering the machine and they were then both hardened together. This was then repeated up to fourteen times until the sleeve of the right dimensions was formed. For each completed circuit a peg was put in a board on the side of the machine that acted as a counter. When the required number of circuits was made the remaining carded lap was removed from the machine. The thickness of the sleeve at this stage depended on the specification required, and for fourteen times round would have been about five eighths of an inch and for seven times as low as one eighth of an inch. To ensure that the hardening was uniform the endless sleeve then had to be removed from the hardener, turned inside out and hardened again. This second hardening was done at the same time as forming a second sleeve on the first roller set, so that the hardener was fully utilised.

For removing the hardened sleeves, the six rollers of the set had to be lifted out in order to slip the sleeve off them. At Longholme, the two largest hardeners had two blocks and tackle to do this, and they were mounted on an overhead I-section girder that allowed them to be located wherever required. The two blocks and tackle were positioned on one side of the roller set and an iron lifting bar was fitted underneath the shafts of the six rollers. Each tackle was connected to each end of the bar and by raising the iron bar the rollers were lifted out of the jigging shackles. The hardened sleeve and the upper bratt cloth were then pulled and ruched towards the free end of the rollers so that it passed the half way position on the rollers. A long plank was placed underneath the rollers where the sleeve had just been removed. The iron bar held by the block and tackle was then lowered so that the plank took the weight of the rollers without disturbing the hardened sleeve. The chains from the block and tackle were then detached from the bar, and the bar taken away to leave the sleeve and carrier free to be removed. The sleeve was then turned inside out and the carrier cloth separated from it. The sleeve was put to one side and the carrier cloth threaded onto the roller set to be ready for hardening the next sleeve. Again the rollers were lifted with the iron bar, the plank was removed, the axles re-seated in the shackles, and the carrier cloth repositioned on the rollers. Then the hardened sleeve was fitted onto the second roller set, following a similar method, but this time no carrier cloth was used. The sleeve was positioned on the rollers so that it would run true and any wrinkles were straightened out. The machine was then switched on and hardening re-commenced[16], so that, while one sleeve was hardening the other was being formed.

The other two smaller hardeners were served by moveable hydraulic jacks that performed the same function as the block, but these raised and lowered the iron bar by pushing up from underneath.

ROLLER HARDENER MACHINE MANUFACTURE

The earliest recorded manufacturer of roller hardeners was Taylor Wordsworth, followed by William Bywater Limited, the company that became pre-eminent in the manufacture of roller hardeners. They were by no means the only company manufacturing roller hardeners, because, historically, German manufacturers had been very active from the late nineteenth century[17], and production also continued in France mainly through Casse. Even in the 1960s, when the felt industry was declining, one of Bywater's main competitors, Krafft Goebel, was still developing roller hardeners, as was a company called HEH (Hans Ernde Horimontal?). Roller hardeners were then a commodity product and machines were mainly made to order, therefore no promotional literature existed. Some idea of the technical specification for a roller hardener can be gauged from the description in Bywater's Sales Day book in Appendix II. By 1985, machine manufacturers were concentrating more on needle-punching machines than felting, so companies like Bywater stopped producing felting machines and scrapped all the wooden formers that were used for casting the machine components. Felt manufacturers such as Bury and Masco Industries had roller hardeners made to their own specifications and had considered manufacturing themselves. They salvaged the wooden formers from William Bywater and stored them for quite some time before realising that they did not have the capability to manufacture machines themselves. The formers were eventually scrapped without ever having been used.

Most hardeners manufactured were ninety-four inches wide but there was one at Longholme mill that was one hundred and fifty inches wide. Mitchell Brothers were known to have a card one hundred and sixty-six inches wide with a hardener to match, whilst there was also a hardener that was one hundred and forty-four inches wide that was used to manufacture grey felts for making carpets and paper makers felt.

APPENDIX I

FLAT HARDENER SPECIFICATION 1924 FROM WILLIAM BYWATER'S DAY BOOK

Extract from William Bywater Sales Day Book July 8 1924

The Bury Felt Manufacturing Co. Ltd Bury

One latest improved Patent Flat Plate or Table Felt Hardening Machine constructed very strong, with feed end arranged for one Piece or Batt the winding up end to wind one Piece or Batt Machine has Top and Bottom Hardening Plates. These Plates are planed corrugated on each face; these are made 96" square. Bottom Plates made Steam heated, with copper Steam pipes fitted in same for heating same evenly over the Surface. Top Plates having 4 Side ribs and Centre Cross made specially strong. These are for adjusting the Plate keeping it straight, so giving even and level Felting. Double oscillating motion on the longitudinal & Transverse Principle for giving movement to the Top Plate Driving Shaft. Also Fast Motion side Eccentric Shaft each made 2 1/4" diam and running in self ring oiling Brass Bearings. Eccentrics made from improved Strong patterns to give from 1/8" to 3/8" of an inch Oscillation Fast Motion Eccentrics made 4" wide on Brass straps, slow motion Eccentrics are 2 3/4" wide on Brass Straps, all these Eccentrics have lubricating oil Boxes fitted on same 2 inch Traverse Screw Motion for Rising and Lowering Top Plate and for feed and winding up ends. This end has one 10" diam Surface wood Roller having strong 1 5/8" square shaft with all the necessary Stand and Brackets to carry all the wood Rollers. Machine provided with 4 Cast Iron Steamng Chests or Heaters each 8 feet long × 2 feet wide to form a Steaming Table 96" Square each Chest fitted with Copper Perforated Sheet these are not fastened down to the Chests made to lap over at the Side and ends so that they can readily be removed when desired one Strong wood water Trough for endless bottom Sheet to pass through this Trough is fitted with one Solid Roller 3" diam working In suitable brackets bolted to Trough. All Steaming Chests and the bottom Tables or Plates having the necessary Steam piping valves and fittings ready for you coupling up to steam Supply and waste outlet at your Mill. The outlet of the 4 Steaming Chests arranged to exhaust into Two Cast Iron Spouts fastened under the Chests. Main drawing Pulleys 18" diem x 5 1/4" wide face to make 225Rev per Minute with Belt motion complete one Set of Screw keys, 8 Foundation Bolts each fitted with Strong Cast Iron Plates. Washer Nut
Net £950

NB The transcription includes all the strange use of capital letters and punctuation.

APPENDIX II

A ROLLER HARDENER SPECIFICATION IN 1928

The following specification is a transcription of the William Bywater Daybook for July 8 1928 concerning a roller hardener for delivery to the Bury Felt Manufacturing Company Ltd, it includes all the strange use of grammar, punctuation and capital lettering as in the original

To one Fine Felt Roller Felting and Hardening Machine suitable for Fine and Medium Shoe Felts constructed with 16 Cast Iron Rollers and 10 Solid Drawn Copper Steam Heated Rollers all fitted at the bottom of the frame all these Rollers made 90 inches long x 4 inches diam outside No Steam Glands or Piping for heating Copper Rollers supplied. These Copper Rollers arranged with 5 Rollers having Steam outlet Syphons or Brackets on one side of machine, the other 5 Rollers arranged for steam outlet on the other side of Machine. No top Wood Rollers supplied, Machine has Two Steel Eccentric Shafts viz. one for each side 1¾ " diam. each having 24 Eccentric Necks turned in same viz. first 6 Necks 3/16" throw reset 12 Necks ¼" throw Final 6 Necks 5/16" throw. These Shafts arranged to work in Square. Bushed Gun Metal Bearing all the Cast Iron Side bearing brackets made square shape in part where gun Metal Bushes are fitted suitable for the Bushes. The Caps made of wraught Iron. The Cross driving shaft made 1¾" diam with Gun Metal bearings made square in shape. This Shaft turned down to 1¾" diam for bearings, Feed End of Machine arranged to carry Batts to take up and made with additional bearing pedestals and brackets for endless sheet with additional extension frame piece or the cast iron side bearing brackets made square shape in part where can metal bushes are fitted suitable for the pushes the caps made of cast iron across driving shaft made 1¾ inch diameter with gunmetal bearings made square in shape this shaft turn down to 1¾ inch diameter for bearings feeder end of machine arrange to carry Batt Take up End made with additional wood roller and a bearing Pedestals on Brackets for Endless Sheet. with additional Extension Frame Piece fitted on each Frame Side at Take up end so as to arrange for the usual stand brackets to be fitted. 2 wood gear driven rollers Set 7" pitch, All the 3 Rollers viz Sheet Rollers and Take up Rollers Set 7" pitch a complete set of change gearwheels viz 15, 20, 25, 30, 35 teeth driving Pulleys 12" diam x 4¼ " wide face with single Flange on each side. Stays Stand for driving Shaft bushes with gun metal bearing. 5 Round Wood sheet carrier Rollers underneath the Frame Set at equal distances. Strong Wood water Trough for damping Endless sheet as it passes through the Machine

Delivered Free your Mills by Motor   Net £280

NB The transcription includes all the strange use of capital letters and punctuation.

9 MILLING

THE DYNAMICS OF MILLING

After hardening, the felt has a low density and is still not strong enough for most purposes. For it to be a useful fabric, it needs to be strengthened by making the fibres knit together more. However, after hardening, the fibres are restricted in their movement because the process exhausts their ability to move in the thickness direction. The only way to consolidate the felt is therefore by moving fibres either along the length of the felt or across its width. This requires a method that can push the fibres together from the sides of the felt. This process is known as milling.

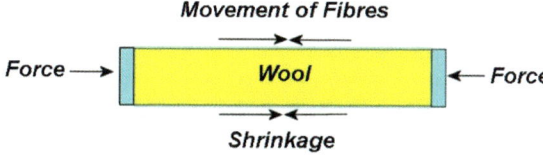

The Dynamics of Milling

In practice, this was first achieved by rolling up or plaiting the felt and striking it with a heavy hammer, a process that was known as fulling. Milling and fulling are both names synonymous with increasing felting, but with the advent of new machinery, which did not use hammers to compact the felt, "milling" became the favoured generic term. Thereafter, "fulling" was relegated for use only when felting by hammers was used[1].

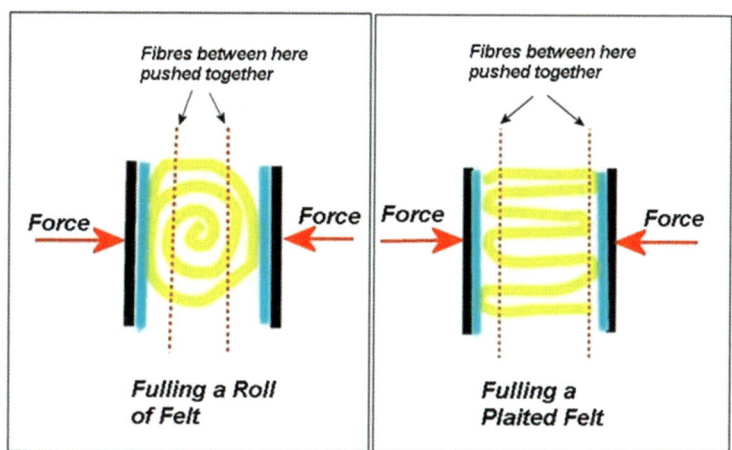

How fulling works for rolled and plaited felt: the hammer strikes on the sides and the fibres of the felt are pushed together between the red lines, outside the lines the fibre alignment is in the wrong direction and are only squashed

FELT IN BRITAIN

FULLING

In order for fibres to be pushed together along the length, the felt has to be presented to the force of the hammer either as a roll or in a plaited form. Those fibres in the parts of the felt that are parallel to the direction of strike felt together but those at right angles to the blow do not. Therefore, to ensure that the felting is even throughout the felt, the felt must be constantly moved to present a different aspect every time the hammer strikes.

Fulling woollen and worsted cloths by using hammers was a well established practice long before the advent of the felt industry, and indeed many of the early feltmakers established their manufacturing business in old fulling or woollen mills. At that time, the equipment for fulling used a falling hammer powered by a waterwheel, which pounded the cloth in a specially shaped container. The machine was referred to as a "stock", and therefore fulling also became known as "stock milling".

The diagram shows a schematic view of a typical falling hammer fulling machine

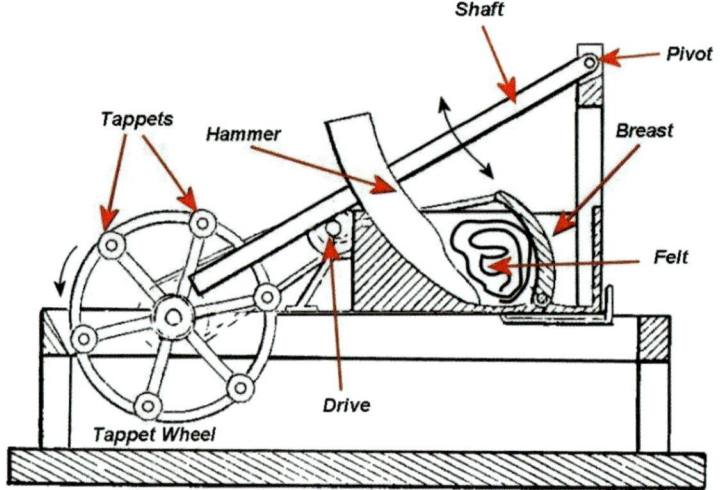

A typical falling hammer fulling machine, showing only one hammer of a pair.

The hammer was fixed to a shaft that was pivoted at the front of the machine and raised by wooden tappets (sometimes spelled as tappits) fixed to a rotating tappet wheel. As the wheel turned, the tappet lifted the free end of the shaft upwards sliding along it until the tappet reached the end of the shaft. The shaft then slid off the tappet and the hammer went into free-fall to strike the felt and push it against the cast iron front of the machine, called the breast. The forces on the felt were controlled by the weight of the hammer, the height from which the hammer fell, and the quantity of felt being fulled. There were plates bolted to the sides of the breast to prevent the felt from squeezing out and to ensure that the width of the felt was maintained. There were usually two hammers in each stock and phased so that as one struck the felt as the other was being raised ready to fall. To deliver the necessary forces the hammers had to be massive, usually made from oak with a beech shaft (also known as a stock). These woods were used because of their resistance to the acid and other chemicals used to promote felting. The hammer weight depended on the size of the fulling stock being around fifty kilogrammes each hammer for milling a thin felt[2] and eighty to one hundred kilogrammes for heavy felts. Early hammers heads measured around four feet long, by twenty-one inches wide and eight inches thick, and, being made of oak, weighed one hundred and seventy-four pounds. This excludes the weight of the shaft, which measured eight feet long by twenty inches wide by three inches thick[3]. In order to ensure that all the felt was evenly felted it needed to be turned in the machine. This was done by shaping the end of the hammer in a roughly pyramid shape so that it forced its way under the felt and lifted it up. In addition, the breast was specially curved so that as the felt was lifted by the hammer blow it was also forced to turn over. The mass of felt in the trough of the stock was therefore continually turned automatically throughout the fulling process.

There were many different variants of the falling hammer stock in terms of size, configuration, and construction but all operated the same way. All were designed to be compatible with waterpower and were driven either directly through the waterwheel or indirectly through the line shafting. Even as steam gradually replaced water as the driving force, falling hammer stocks remained the mainstay of the felt industry. In the early days of the felt industry the stocks were narrow and only twenty-eight inches wide[4] and an example of stocks made by William Kilburn dated to this period can be seen at Leeds Industrial Museum[5]. They were also slow and cumbersome, each hammer working at the rate of thirty to thirty-nine knocks per minute, though it was usual to have two hammers in each stock giving a total of up to seventy-six knocks a minute[6]. Milling was therefore a slow process and it was common for pieces to be fulled for over seven hours for a finished piece[7].

A sketch of how a fulling department looked in the mid 1880s is shown in the diagram below, with the stocks being similar in design to those of William Kilburn. Each stock has two hammers and it is noticeable that they are arranged in pairs. Coincidentally, both William Kilburn, the manufacturer of fulling stocks, and the first felt maker, The Patent Woollen Cloth Company Limited, were both located in Leeds within a mile of each other. It is likely therefore, that Kilburn supplied the first felt fulling stocks. However there is nothing in the insurance records of The Patent Woollen Cloth Company to confirm that Kilburn's stocks were employed at their Elmwood Mill. What the record does show is that the stocks were worked in pairs up to 1864 and this system was used in at least one other mill in Leeds (Airedale Mill).

The stocks here are similar to those manufactured by William Kilburn of Leeds; this may have been how the fulling area of The Patent Woollen Cloth Company Limited may have looked

Unlike the woollen and worsted industries, the felt industry never abandoned fulling when other techniques like rotary milling, invented by John Dyer in 1833, were introduced commercially. In fact, they continued to invest in ever improving hammer stocks right up to 1981. The most significant change was to move away from heavy gravity powered hammers to lightweight pendulums with stepped hammerheads that were positively driven through eccentrics and crankshafts. By that time, stocks were driven by line shafting, which was powered by a central steam engine, rather than by waterwheels.

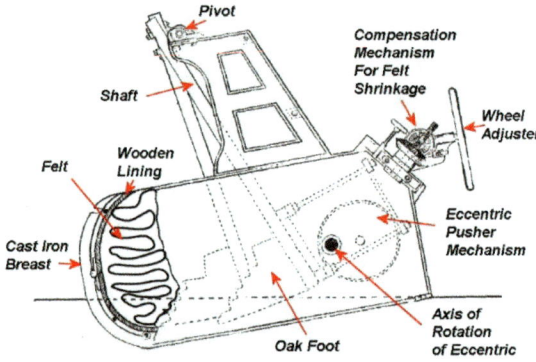

A pendulum stock showing the eccentric that pushed the hammer head against the felt.

The pendulum stock looked superficially like a falling hammer stock in that there was a stepped foot connected to a shaft pivoted at one end like a pendulum. Both the shaft and the foot were much lighter than the old hammers because the force no longer depended on weight and gravity but on the force that the driving mechanism could deliver. An eccentric wheel contacted the stepped foot directly, being guided by a metal cage attached to it. As the eccentric rotated it pushed the foot onto the felt giving a positive force that increased as the foot progressively squeezed the felt and then the eccentric pushed the other side of the cage to move the hammer away. This positive driving system enabled far faster knock rates on the felt up to around one hundred and twenty knocks per minute

Conventional pendulum fulling stocks in Cooper and Co.

The effect of the pendulum stock was the opposite of a falling hammer. A falling hammer impacted the felt with the greatest force at the beginning of the strike and had no energy or force left at the end of its stroke. In a pendulum stock, the force started at zero and built up as it compressed the felt. In addition, when a falling hammer struck the felt the shaft had to absorb the impact of the strike, but for the pendulum stock, all the energy was transferred through the eccentric drive rather than the shaft. The purpose of having a shaft in a pendulum stock was therefore to guide the hammer to give a clean strike on the felt. This opened the possibility for other designs of shaft and hammer to accommodate a wide range of different felts. For lighter felts, the shafts were replaced by boards and relatively small stock feet. These were known as paddle stocks, both from the point of view of their shape and the high frequency of strike of one hundred and twenty knocks per minute, which gave the distinct impression of paddling. In the Bury Felt Manufacturing Company's fire insurance list, they were also referred to as cradle stocks and were made by J. Downham.

A modern pendulum stock built in 1980

Later versions of pendulum stocks had two shafts for each stepped hammer foot instead of one to give greater stability to handle dense felts without twisting. These fulling stocks were much favoured for the fulling of felt polishing wheels.

Modern pendulum stock built by William Bywater Ltd for R. R. Whitehead Brothers in 1970s. There were three hammers with eccentrics driven by an electric motor

Although most stock mills used two hammers, some designs had three and even four hammers, though there was no evidence that they were superior to the conventional ones. Bury Felt Manufacturing Company had a pendulum stock that had three hammers each of a different width: nine and a half inches, fourteen inches and eight and a half inches.

The main disadvantage of a driven hammer compared to a falling hammer arose from the fact that the volume of the felt in the stock decreased as fulling continued. A falling hammer could accommodate this because it was free to move and take up any slack in the system. It therefore maintained its efficiency throughout the fulling process. However, a driven hammer had a fixed stroke independent of the volume of the felt. Consequently, as the felt shrank the hammer could not deliver its full force at the end of its stroke[8]. It therefore became less efficient as fulling proceeded and, in the ultimate, did not deliver a fulled felt with the required specifications. This was remedied, to some extent, with a hand-operated mechanism to move the eccentric forward mechanically. Alternatively, the front of the stock was adjusted to make it into a smaller vessel, to compensate for the shrinkage. As each stock had its own characteristics, it was important to match the felt to be fulled to the stock that could give the best properties. This involved gauging the thickness of the felt, the volume that it was likely to take up after fulling, and the maximum weight that could be loaded into the machine.

Another innovation was the introduction of a crank to drive the foot directly with a more positive piston-like action that dispensed with the need for a shaft. These were first developed in the United States of America and became known as American stocks, though they were also known as bumper stocks, since each knock against the felt was referred to as a bump. They were also developed in Germany notably by Nik Wahl.

Horizontal fulling machine of the American pattern made by Nik Wahl

These bumper stocks were the fastest and most powerful stocks built, so much so, that if the trough was overloaded the hammer could break the cast iron breast. Being seventy eight to eighty-four inches across they were most suited to wide-width fulling of thin technical felts and at one hundred and thirty knocks or bumps per minute[9] outperformed pendulum stocks. Having a single hammer the machine milled the felt more evenly across the width of the felt than the double hammer stocks.

Since felt makers were manufacturing a considerable range of felts, it was necessary for them to have as wide a range of stock types and widths as commercially viable. Because of the methods they employed in fulling their felts, they had stocks varying in widths, most usually, twenty-one, twenty-five, twenty-eight, thirty-four, thirty-six, sixty, sixty-four, seventy-eight, and eighty-four inches.

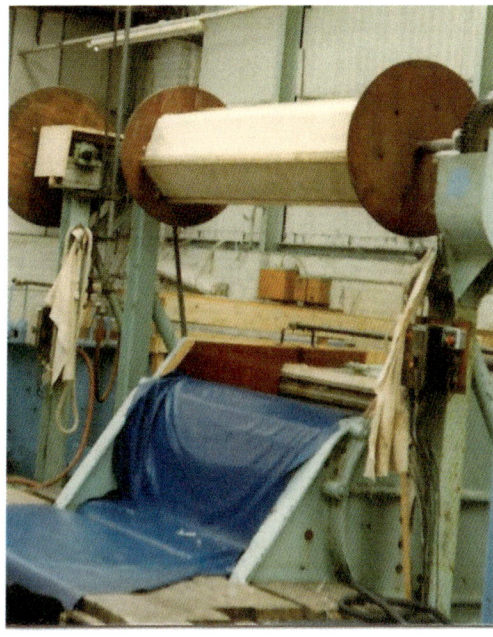

An American style bumper stock at Bury Mill with a plastic sheet to prevent contamination of the felt

OPERATION OF A FULLING STOCK

The mechanics of operating a stock milling were intrinsically very simple; involving short periods of strenuous activity followed by long periods of light maintenance duties. The felt, still wet from hardening, was delivered in plaited form to the milling room on pallets known as scrays. Over each stock was a winch, shaped like a huge bobbin. A rope was thrown over the winch and one end tied to the uppermost end of the felt. By pulling on the rope, the felt was pulled over the winch, which fed the felt into the stock. At this stage, the miller had to make sure that the felt plaited properly into the stock so that it would turn in a controlled way during fulling. Once all the felt was in the stock either a soap solution using soda ash, or a weak acid solution was added and the hammers set in motion. After thirty minutes, the felt was hauled out of the stock and over the winch using the same rope technique. At the same time as it was being pulled out of the stock the miller had to measure the length using a yardstick, which had to be one-handed because one hand had to pull the felt while the other had to measure. The miller did this by holding one end in a fist like grip with one thumb over the end of the yardstick. Having measured the first yard, he flipped the stick over to measure the second yard and then lightly dug the free end into the felt in order to flip his fist over to measure the third. By this constant flipping of the yardstick the miller was able to measure the length of the felt both speedily and accurately. To maintain accuracy the miller chopped a small piece off the end of the yardstick equivalent to the thickness of his thumb, so that the distance from the free end of the stick to the end of his thumb measured exactly a yard.

Having noted the new length of felt, the miller returned it to the stock over the winch and milled for a further ten minutes. Each felt had its own specification of density and final dimensions, which were controlled by the degree of shrinkage that took place. Usually the width of the felt corresponded to the width of the stock mill since the sidepieces of the stock prevented it from widening. There was little alteration in the thickness of the felt, therefore only the length changed. So setting the length defined the ultimate felt properties. As the shrinkage became closer to the specification, the miller took measurements at shorter intervals, ten minutes or less only stopping the milling when the felt was exactly the right length. Shrinkage was commonly up to fifty percent. In practical terms this meant, for example, that a hardened felt of density 0.14 gm/cc would be milled to a density of 0.28 gm/cc, which was the average for a technical felt.

Up until the 1930s, the favoured milling agent was urine, also known as lant, with the most prized milling solution being mare's urine. Since urine is slightly acidic and contained a variety of enzymes, it was the perfect medium for felting. Regular collections were made from the local community using a barrel on wheels called a lant cart and at a time when toilet arrangements were rudimentary at best, there was a ready supply.

A lant cart used for collecting urine for use as a milling agent (courtesy of Helmshore Museum)

Baltic Mill also had trough urinals situated at various places in the mill and the urine was piped into a central tank to be drawn off by the miller as required. This had the added benefit of being able to monitor the operatives at all times, because they never left their place of work. Soda ash and soap were also used, as it was well known that alkalis aided felting and they combined well with the lanolin on the wool. With soap, there was also an added effect from the foam generated during the milling process. Dilute sulphuric acid was preferred as it had a good milling effect and did not need to be washed off before dyeing as most dyeing was by acid dyes. The milling solution that was actually used depended on the specification of the final felt type and what the eventual end use was.

FULLING POLISHING WHEELS

A polishing wheel, colloquially referred to as a bob, originated as a hardened disc of felt which was milled to an ultra high density. Each bob was produced from a specially shaped cylinder of carded wool fibres. Many of these were loaded into a flat plate hardener and hardened all at the same time. A batch of these discs, weighing a total of two hundred pounds, was loaded into a two-hammer pendulum stock with specially strengthened pillar bolts. This strengthening was necessary because of the sustained heavy loading on the machine.

Checking the shrinkage of a polishing wheel bob during milling, in a pendulum stock at Cooper and Co. (Birmingham) Limited

A batch typically consisted of a hundred and thirty discs that that would eventually make bobs eight inches in diameter and a further hundred and thirty that would make ten-inch diameter bobs. The stock was also pre-loaded with a number of rejected bobs that had already been milled, which enhanced the milling action by distributing the hammer blow to all the individual hardened discs. These drone bobs, over time, acquired an irregular shape, much like a smooth stone about seven inches across, with a density of around 0.7 gm/cc.

The batch was milled, first for ten minutes, then for twenty minutes, then for a further thirty minutes. At each interval, the batch was examined and any bob that was being distorted was manually knocked back into shape. Milling was then continued for eight hours. By the end of the fulling process, the hardened discs had shrunk in diameter by around fifty percent[10].

The milled bobs were then treated to a special after-milling process that increased the density and removed any distortions to ensure that they were homogeneous and exactly circular in shape. This was done on a rollering machine made by Nik Wahl, the German Manufacturer who specialised in felt making machinery.

The main element of the machine was a heavy steel roller, with a slight convex curvature, which was pressed by strong springs onto the circular table holding the felt. The table ran on tracks, and was pushed backwards and forwards under the roller.

FELT IN BRITAIN

The after-milling process for a polishing wheel bob at Cooper and Co. (Birmingham) Ltd

The felt was held in a brass ring three inches thick that was bolted to the table bed. The felt was forced into this fitting and then rolled for six minutes. The bob was then chiselled out of the brass ring. During the process, a lip developed on the trim of the bob, and had to be trimmed off before the bob was turned upside down and knocked back into the ring for a further six minutes of rolling. Bury Felt Manufacturing Company Limited had a system that could roller three bobs at a time, where the single brass retaining ring for the bob was replaced by three rings which were specially arranged to facilitate the removal of the bobs.

The bobs were then dried vertically in a special rack, containing wooden dividers that kept the bobs upright. The rack was mounted on a wooden roller on which the lower edge of each bob rested. Attached to the roller was a handle which was turned from time to time in order to rotate the roller and move the bobs so that they dried uniformly. The drying time varied from one day to two weeks for a two-inch thick felt[11], after which they were sent for final finishing.

MILLING MACHINES

ROTARY MILL

The invention of the rotary milling machine in 1833 by John Dyer revolutionised the milling process for woollen and worsted fabrics by dispensing with hammers altogether. Instead, a woollen fabric was fed between the nip of two narrow-width rollers that gripped it and pushed it between two boards set at an angle to one another.

There were also two adjustable vertical rollers set in front of the nip rollers to control the width of the felt, known as "stanging". The gap between the boards at the end nearest the rollers was wider than that at the far end where the fabric exited. This caused the fabric to buckle and fold between the plates. Meanwhile the rollers kept feeding more and more fabric into the gap causing the pressure on the folded fabric to build up, until eventually the fabric was pushed out of the gap.

MILLING

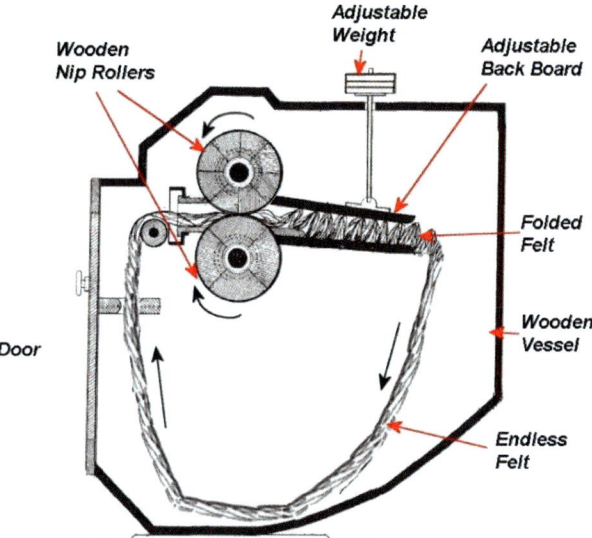

A rotary miller as invented by John Dyer of Trowbridge in 1833

The lower board was fixed but the upper board could move up and down to make the gap wider or narrower. A weight was attached to the top board so that the weight pressing down on it controlled the distance between the boards. This in turn altered the pressure experienced by the fabric as it passed between the gap, the greater the weight the smaller the gap and the greater the pressure. As the fabric exited the boards, it fell to the bottom of the machine and into hot water, soap or other suitable milling agents as required. The heat and moisture in the machine was maintained by making it totally enclosed, with only a door to gain access to the fabric or felt. Lengths of fabrics were sewn together to make one endless loop through the machine, so the fabric was lifted upwards again by the nip rollers and the whole process repeated. The folding action and pressure had the effect of pushing the fibres together, but this had to be done many times to generate the necessary shrinkage. However, the use of rollers meant that the process could run at high speed, between one hundred and fifty to two hundred feet per minute[12], and milling was therefore very efficient compared to hammer fulling. The degree of felting was controlled by measuring the felt length, but since this was in an endless loop, it had to be done whilst the machine was running. This was done by timing the successive appearance at the front of the machine of the stitches where the two ends of the felt were joined together. To make sure that the felt did not become too bunched up, the machine was stopped and the felt accessed through a door at the back of the machine and the felt disentangled. Despite this, the biggest fault of the rotary millers experienced by the feltmakers was the wide variation in the degree of felting along the length of the felt that occurred. This had to be remedied by extra milling in the hammer stocks.

Although this was a revolution for the woollen worsted industry, it had little impact on the felt industry, since only lightweight felts could be milled on this machine. Furthermore, there was no control over the width of the felt, which unlike woven fabrics could not resist the pull exerted by the nip rollers and so tended to stretch in the length and shrink in width. The rotary mill or box mill, as the feltmakers referred to them, were used only for very specialised thin felts. Some indication of this can be gained from the photograph overleaf where the box mill sits in isolation to the rest of the fulling machines.

A rotary miller or box mill surrounded by stock mills in Hudcar felt mill in 1948, they were unpopular with felt makers who preferred hammer stocks

The main application for box millers, apart from thin felts, was the milling of sleeves, which were long tubes of felt. The end of one sleeve was carefully sewn onto another to make a long length of tubular felt. Twists were deliberately introduced between the sewing of one sleeve and the next in order to aid the milling process. After feeding the long length tubular assembly into the box miller, the free ends were sewn together to make it into an endless loop and the milling commenced.

The milling action on the sleeves was largely due to the air that was trapped inside the sleeves and to enhance this effect the sleeves were milled in soap solution. The foam from the soap provided a film on the surface of the felt that made the air work as it was forced through the felt. As the felt sleeve moved towards the nip of the mangle much of the air trapped in the tube was driven backwards through the hollow sleeve but some was forced through the felt, and the balance of these two effects was important. This was the reason behind twisting the sleeves during the stitching operation. Because the sleeve was slightly twisted the air pushing backwards from the nip rollers in the box mill tried to straighten the sleeve up. This had the effect of turning the sleeve round a small amount for each passage through the mangle rollers. In this way, milling was even all the way round the sleeves. If the stitching between the sleeves was too slack the trapped air escaped through the joint and the sleeves were effectively milled flat. The turning action on the sleeves did not then occur so that the same area of felt was milled on the same part of the mangle at each pass of the sleeves. This caused uneven milling of the middle preferentially to the edges giving a distorted sleeve which later required edge trimming.

The control of the milling process was done by "clock, yardstick, and commonsense". The sleeves were left milling for fixed periods that were known as "shakes". The first shake was usually thirty minutes. The doors were opened and the length and circumference of the sleeves measured. Dependent on these values the time of the next shake would be estimated and the stretch and stanging adjusted. The process was repeated until the measurements met the standard.

MULTI-ROLLER MILLING MACHINE

The multi-roller milling machine was very similar to the roller hardener but without the carrier cloths, and it was first mentioned under the original felt patent of 1840 by T. R. Williams where a felt was plaited and taken through a set of rollers.

The actual roller-milling machines that were in use up to the 1950s had two sets of rollers, nine upper rollers and ten lower rollers, the upper rollers being offset to the lower rollers in a precise relationship[13]. Both sets of rollers could vibrate or jig along their axles with the upper set out of phase with the lower set so as to cause a shear on the felt as it passed through the machine, the jig rate was usually between three hundred and four hundred oscillations per minute, at an amplitude of around one millimetre. At the same time, the rollers were driven in order to rotate and forward the felt at a speed of around eight feet per minute giving a transfer time of the felt in the machine of some twenty to thirty seconds. Because of all these motions, the felt experienced three distinct actions that varied as it passed from one roller to the next. The first was pressure, the second flexure as it bent around each roller, and thirdly a shearing action caused by the jigging of the rollers.

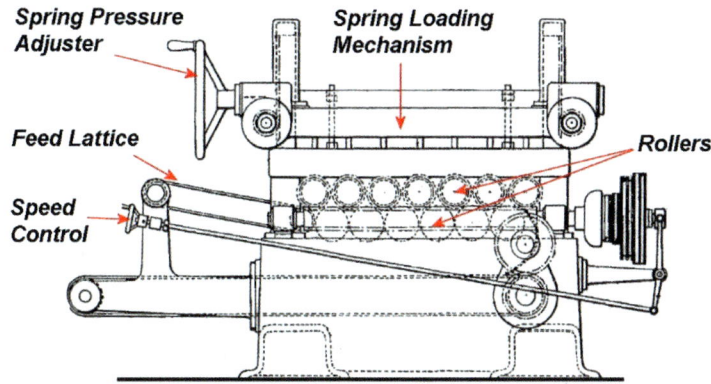

The Casse multi-roller milling machine

For greater control, the top set of rollers were mounted in such a way that they could be pushed closer to the lower set in order to generate more pressure on the felt. Increasing pressure could also be done by putting extra weights on the top rollers or with the use of adjustable springs[14]. Solutions of milling agents or plain hot water could be sprayed on the felt to aid the felting process through the machine. As the felt went between the rollers, excess liquid was forced out and caught in a drip tray below the rollers, after passing through a fine gauze filter on top of it. The liquid was collected ready for re-spraying onto the felt. As they became more efficient, roller millers could use fewer rollers to provide the same milling ability, such as the Casse multi-roller milling machine, though other machine manufacturers preferred to keep an extended roller configuration.

The pressure profile for milling was the opposite of that for hardening. In milling, the pressure was greatest at the nip of the upper and lower rollers, whilst for hardening it was at a minimum. For milling, the pressure fell rapidly to zero as the felt passed directly over each roller but in hardening, the pressure was at a maximum here as the carrier cloths pressed the fibres against the roller. In milling, the flexure over the rollers was important since the felt was effectively compressed on the inside where it contacted the roller surface and stretched on the side of the felt away from the rollers. This had the effect of shuffling the fibres of the felt together. Because of the closeness of the rollers, the shearing action due to the jigging showed little variation passing through the machine.

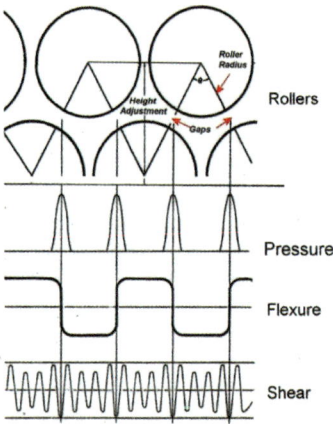

The relationship of pressure, flexure and shear on a felt compared to the configuration of a roller miller

One pass of the felt through the machine was rarely sufficient to mill it to the required density and it required several prescribed passes to meet the technical specification. Other methods of loading the machines were therefore devised to increase the efficiency. In some instances, more efficient milling could be obtained by plaiting the felt before it reached the first nip of the rollers, which increased the pressure on the felt and enhanced the milling action. A more favoured way to improve operational efficiency was to pass the felt through the machine, then take it over the top, and sew the leading edge to the trailing edge, to make an endless loop. This loop could then be run continuously through the machine with the minimum of handling, and the felt could then make any number of passes until the specification was reached.

A technical felt being milled in a multi-roller miller in a continuous loop

ROLLER MILLING SUPERFINE FELTS

Before the advent of roller milling machines, superfine thin felts of less than two hundred and fifty grammes per square metre were stock milled, which was a relatively inefficient process. As the demand for superfine felts increased, there was a need for a more efficient way of milling them and roller milling appeared to offer a suitable solution. However, roller milling was more suited to thick felts and was inefficient in milling thin felts. It was Welker, a company based in Germany that solved the problem by producing a high-speed roller machine called a roller conditioner.

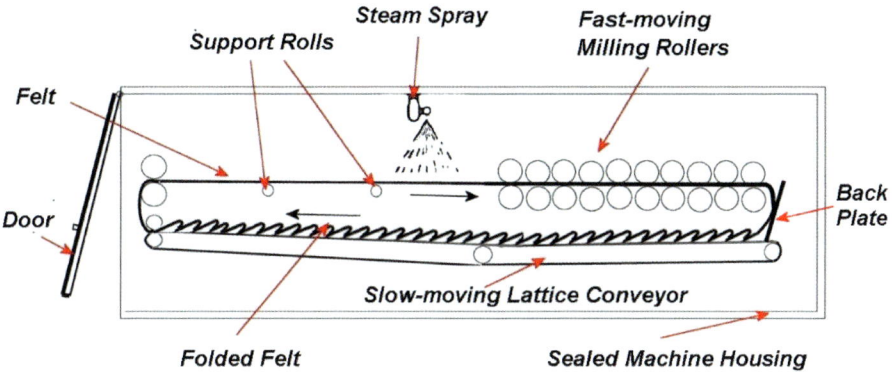

Diagram showing the elements of a roller conditioner for milling superfine felts

This machine again had an upper set of ten rollers and a lower set of rollers, but instead of being staggered, the top rollers were positioned directly over the bottom rollers. Instead of the relatively slow speed of roller millers, these small diameter rollers operated at high speeds around two hundred and fifty metres per minute[15]. These projected the felt onto a spring loaded back plate that guided the felt onto a slow moving lattice conveyor belt, causing an overfeed that plaited the felt. The conveyor fed the plaited felt towards the front of the machine, through two cylindrical guides and over a roller. At that stage, the felt was rapidly accelerated back to the milling rollers to repeat the process. In practice, the acceleration was so rapid that the felt became airborne. The plaiting on the lattice conveyor acted as a reservoir for felt so up to six forty-yard felt pieces could be joined together and formed into a two-hundred-and-forty-yard loop. Being able to mill six pieces of felt at once made this machine highly efficient. The machine was run for around thirty minutes, which theoretically meant that each piece made thirty passes through the machine. In practice, it was much more because when the felt arrived at the milling rollers it bunched up causing folds in the felt and these passed right through the milling rollers. The top set of rollers could move up or down depending on the load arriving between the nip so when a fold arrived the rollers would bump up and down, which helped the milling process. This bunching up of the felt could be encouraged by having the later rollers working slightly slower than the earlier ones. The folds were never in the same place twice because when the felt left the conveyor the rapid acceleration pulled all the creases out. Keeping the felt aligned through the machine was important and in practice, makeshift guides were employed to keep the felt on track. The machine itself was totally enclosed and heated with live steam to keep the humidity high and the temperature at around twenty-eight degrees Celsius. Once the milling was complete, the felt was unloaded on a pallet or scray ready for dyeing.

FELT IN BRITAIN

The two Welker roller conditioners used by Bury and Masco Industries at Bury Mill for milling their superfine felts. The milled felts in the photograph are just being unloaded from the machines, the pieces of felt tied around the guide rollers, prevented the felt from wandering

THE GATTERWALKE

The feltmakers were always sympathetic to inventions and new techniques that became available and in many ways the machines they kept in their mills was testament to this. One such experiment was the grate planker or Gatterwalke manufactured by Krafft Goebel that promised considerable improvements in milling.

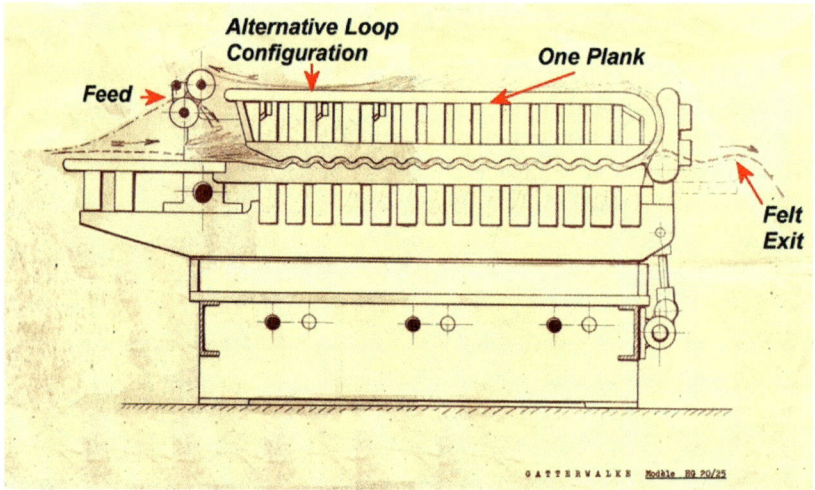

Side view of the Gatterwalke for milling felt

It turned out to have limited use for felt makers since it had too many moving parts that needed constant maintenance, though MASCO persevered with it to make specialised grey felts. It was kept in working order right up until the 1980s, despite its unpopularity within the company.

Back and front views of the Gatterwalke made by Krafft Goebel in 1952 for milling felt

The Gatterwalker was made up of around forty-eight independently operating shaped wooden frames that pounded the felt and at the same time shuffled it through the machine. This machine was quite remarkable in that the motion, operation, and design were completely different from any other milling machine that had gone before it and indeed has since never been matched.

THE PILGRIM STEP MILLER

The most significant advancement in the development of milling machines for felt was the introduction of the Pilgrim Step by Krafft Goebel in the late 1950s. Since it was capable of milling either roll felts or thick sheets, it rapidly became a mainstay of feltmakers as a more efficient alternative to stock milling. In particular, the machine was ideal for the manufacture of piano sheet felts

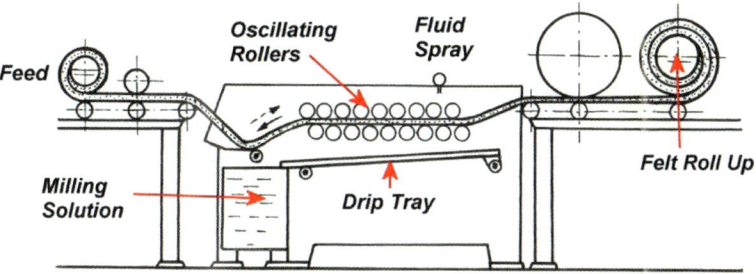

A Krafft Goebel Pilgrim Step milling machine set up for milling roll felts

As with a conventional multi roller miller there were two sets of rollers, with the upper set offset from those in the lower set. The six-inch diameter rollers were made of a thermoset resin like phenol formaldehyde and profiled with small squares to give good grip to the felt, though dimpled stainless steel rollers were also used. The rollers oscillated on their axes, turning more in one direction than another, equivalent to moving two steps forward one step back. Consequently, the felt was subjected to a kneading action by the rollers and at the same time, it was inched through the machine. The true versatility of the machine was that this action could be varied so that the oscillation rate, displacement, and speed through the machine could all be altered to provide any desired milling conditions. The linear machine speed could be varied from 0.36 to 3.6 metres per minute, but it was also possible to alter the speeds of the rollers individually so that the later rollers had a slightly lower speed than those at the front. This was a clever way to generate extra shrinkage in the felt.

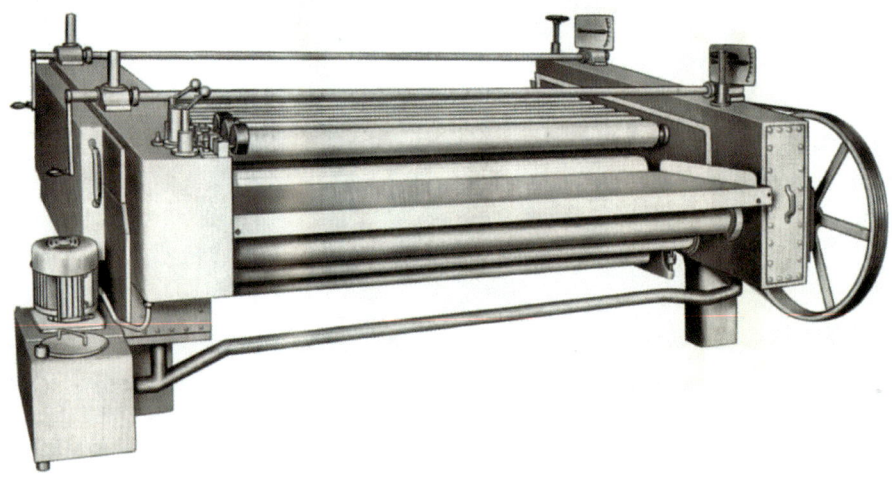

The basic Pilgrim Step roller miller made by Krafft Goebel

The machine could even be put into reverse so that the rolled felt could be returned through the machine and be milled again without any handling. As well as oscillating around their axes the rollers could also vibrate, or jig, along their length as in a roller hardener. This provided a shearing action to the felt at the same time as kneading it. The gap between the upper and lower rollers could also be adjusted to accommodate felts up to one hundred millimetres thick, and the pressure between them adjusted as necessary. There was also provision for spraying the felt with milling solutions together with effective means for collecting the surplus through a drip tray and tank, and recycling it.

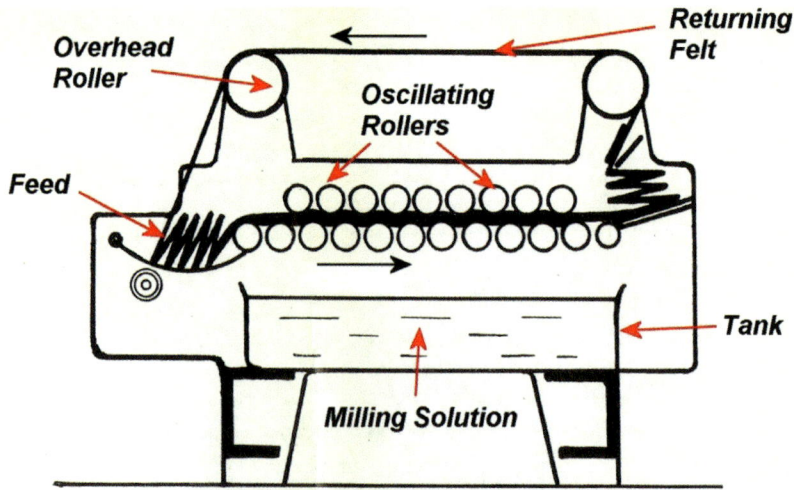

The Pilgrim Step set-up for milling endless lengths of felt

For a thin felt that needed multiple passes through the machine, an alternative arrangement was employed, whereby the exiting felt was guided over the machine and back into the feed. One end of the felt was then sewn to the other end to form an endless loop. The felt was then passed through the machine in as many passes as was necessary to attain the required shrinkage and density.

Pilgrim Step with dimpled stainless steel rollers at Bury Mill in 1980, set up for multiple passes through the machine, the felt has just been doffed onto the pallet at the lower left of the picture

The Pilgrim Step machine was ideally suited for milling sheet felts since they could remain flat throughout the milling process. Previously, sheet felts had to be milled in hammer stocks that tended to distort the shape of the sheets. The move to use the Pilgrim Step was ideal for the manufacture of piano hammers because it guaranteed uniformity in the sheet as it milled, giving a high quality well milled felt. Direct milling of a sheet felt was the simplest way of using the Pilgrim Step because it required only the basic machine, without extra attachments

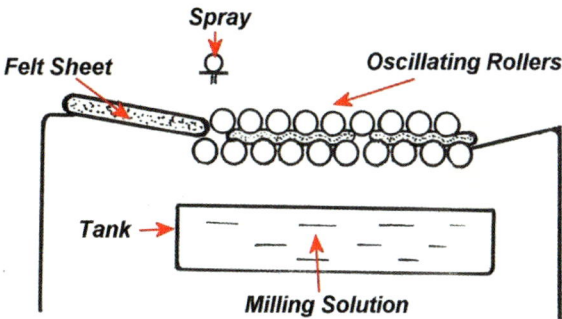

The arrangement of the Pilgrim Step for milling sheet felts

Milling a sheet of piano hammer felt at Royal George Mills

ACID MILLING

Most milling and fulling processes could compact the felt to densities of up to 0.4 gm/cc, and although this was suitable for the majority of end uses, it was insufficiently dense for many technical applications, such as oil lubrication. For such applications, felt densities were required up to 0.7 gm/cc[16]. In order to achieve these high densities a further special milling treatment was needed known as acid milling. This consisted of running a previously milled felt, configured as an endless loop, through a roller mangle and into a bath of hot dilute sulphuric acid. Such "After Millers" had a variety of different designs but the simplest machine configuration of this type was that used by the Mitchells, Ashworth, Stansfield, and Company Limited in their Baltic Mill. This versatile machine consisted of three rollers mounted on a square oak wooden trough. The rollers were configured as a three-roll mangle with one roll pressing on the other two.

An acid mill processing a grey felt at Baltic Mill in 1980, the pressure adjustment wheel is at the top right, two live steam pipes heated the wooden tank, the diagonal wooden pole is a stang for maintaining the width of the felt

The position of the upper roller could be manually adjusted to create any desired pressure on the other two lower rollers. The felt was fed between the nips of the three rollers, into the trough, which contained dilute sulphuric acid. The free ends were sewn together to form an endless loop so that the felt could be continuously circulated round the machine by the powered mangle rollers. Every time a piece of the felt passed through the mangle and over the rollers, it was compressed and flexed twice. For thick felts, this flexing and pressing action was sufficient to cause further, more intense, felting to take place though it needed many such flexings to increase the density sufficiently. The process was therefore a lengthy one exceeding even the time taken for fulling in hammer stocks. The shortest time for a felt to be milled in these acid millers was seven hours, and for some of the densest felts processing could take several days. Controlling the running of felts for such a long time meant that there had to be a way of making sure that the felt did not wander to one side or the other of the rollers. To cure this, two wooden beams, called stangs, were placed across the acid trough on either side of the felt, which pushed against the edges. These stangs had the added effect of preventing the felt from increasing in width. This was because the mangling action, as well as causing length shrinkage, also caused the felt to spread out sideways. Once the felt had reached the required milled length, the stitching connecting the ends was cut and the felt was run out of the machine.

Acid milling was used extensively for the consolidation of felt sleeves in order to produce the high densities that were needed to compete with rubber. Because these sleeves were endless the mangle rollers had to be dismantled from the machine, the sleeve threaded onto them, and the rollers re-assembled back into the machine. This is where the simplicity of the machine demonstrated its versatility. The rollers were gear driven at one end and in loose bearings at the other. The geared ends were lifted out of the drive using a block and tackle arrangement and were propped up by wooden beams at the centre of the rollers. The tackle was released leaving half of the rollers free to slip the sleeve over them. The tackle was then reattached, the props removed, and the rollers lowered back into their gear trains. To simplify the process the top roller could be removed altogether and replaced as the last operation before milling.

The acid mill at Baltic mill with the rollers removed in order to fit an endless sleeve

Widths of acid mills varied from thirty-six inches to forty-eight inches, but all were of the same design. In 1939, there were thirteen such machines at MASCO's Higher Lumb Works and there were a variety of them in Baltic Mill. For special felts there were machines that had extended length tanks measuring about ten to fifteen feet long and ninety inches wide; one was for milling white felt and the other for grey.

Acid milling a white felt sleeve at Cooper Co. (Brimingham) Ltd., showing the stangs being adjusted to control the width of the felt

Oak was chosen as the container material because of its resistance to acid and, considering the age of the milling machines that were still operating in 1984, it is a testament to this astonishing property of oak. Of interest, is the fact that a new trough of oak always leaked but after twelve hours, the wood had absorbed sufficient water to swell up and seal the joints making it watertight. This happened wherever wooden vessels, like stock mills, were used, and because of this, any piece of equipment that used wood was never allowed to dry out.

The temperature and acidity of the milling solution in the trough was monitored constantly, the temperature was kept at around thirty-eight degrees Celsius. The acidity was controlled by the specific gravity of the acid using a Twaddell hydrometer and maintained at a level of two, which was approximately a one and a half percent solution. All adjustments were made manually either through turning on the steam valve to increase the temperature, or by adding more sulphuric acid to the bath to increase the acidity. Before the 1950s, setting the acidity was largely subjective and the miller added concentrated sulphuric acid into the tank of water from carboys wrapped in straw. He added enough until he thought there was sufficient and then dipped his finger in and licked it and if it tasted right, he judged that the acidity was right. Later, more scientific equipment was installed to measure the pH of the acid using acid indicators. When the indicator turned green the acidity was judged correct. This equated to a pH of five and a half to six, about the same level of acidity as urine but less acidic than vinegar[17].

After milling, the acid had to be washed out and this could not be done effectively by normal processing. The felt had to be removed from the milling machine containing the acid and transferred to another tank fitted with squeeze rollers and filled with just water rather than acid. This time the continuous mangling process squeezed out the acid so that it was replaced with clean water as the felt dipped into the tank. To ensure that this tank remained acid-neutral, fresh water was constantly trickled in while at the same rate as fluid in the tank was drained away. In the acid milling department there was always one tank that was used exclusively for washing off the acid[18]. Once the felt had been deemed neutral, it was given a final mangle to express all the water and the felt was sent for drying.

With simple machines such as these, felts from one eighth of an inch to four inches thick could be made into felts with a density of 0.7 gm/cc, which was equivalent to the density of many hard woods. The majority of felts that were acid milled were grey felts with a thickness of one and a half inches.

10 DYEING AND FINISHING

TECHNIQUES

In order to fulfil the varied requirements and specifications of many different customers, the feltmakers had to employ a myriad of different dyeing and finishing processes. Felts for domestic use were usually coloured and went for dyeing or for printing, whilst the technical felts were given various proofing treatments and were only occasionally dyed. After these wet treatments the felts were dried and then subjected to other processes such as pressing, cropping, and sanding to improve the quality, surface characteristics, or to meet stringent technical specifications.

DYEING

Dyeing of felt used the same techniques that were employed in the woollen and worsted industries and, like them, modified the process as the development of dyestuffs progressed from natural to synthetic dyes. Dyeing was the most important part of the production of a felt since if a mistake was made at this stage the whole of the felt could be scrapped and all the prior production effort wasted. For some, the responsibility was so great that it could be life threatening and at least one dyer was known to have committed suicide by drowning in his dye vat, because of a major error.

Dyeing took place in a vat that had a winch, shaped like a large bobbin, positioned overhead for hauling the felt in and out of the vessel. Dye vessels for felt were usually shallower than in other industries and the winch was nearer the vat. This was because the weight of the waterlogged felt caused a heavy drag on it that tended to pull the felt out of shape making it longer in length and narrower in width. A typical dye vessel was constructed largely of oak and measured seven feet square, four feet six inches deep with the winch two feet from the vat, and was capable of holding around four hundred gallons of dye liquor[1].

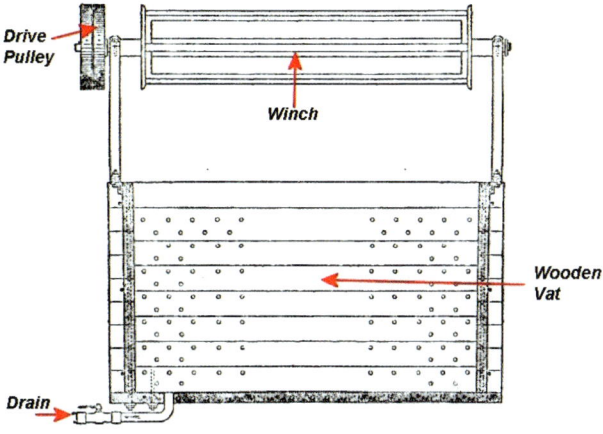

Front view of a dye vessel or vat showing the winch and drive

The dyestuff in the vat was heated with an open steam pipe that was separated from the felt by a wooden partition so that no fibres came into direct contact with the pipe. To load the machine, a rope was thrown over the winch and tied to one end of the felt. The felt was then threaded over the winch with the aid of the rotation of the winch and by pulling on the rope. The rope was then detached from the felt and the one end of the felt sewn to its other end to form a continuous loop. On activating the machine, the winch hauled the felt from the scray and into the vat of dye, where the felt became plaited as it entered the dye bath. Thereafter it was a continuous process with the felt being hauled up out of the bath, over the winch and back into the vat. When the dye vat was full of the appropriate dye liquor, the temperature of the solution was gradually raised by controlling the steam pipe until the liquor reached boiling point, and this normally took forty-five minutes to one hour. The felt was kept moving through the dye for a further hour at the boil, after which the dyeing was complete and the dye exhausted. The felt was then rinsed two or three times to ensure that all the excess dye was removed[2].

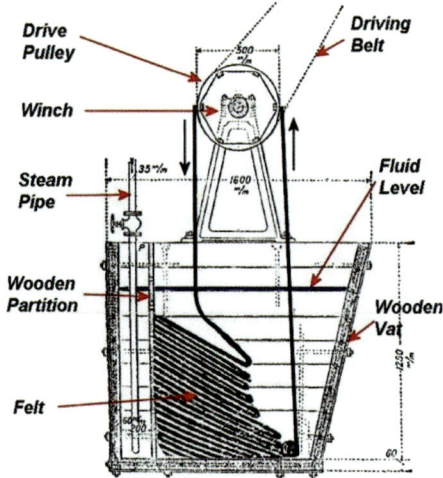

The circulation of felt in a standard winch dye vessel,
the partition prevented the steam pipe touching the felt.

In practice three felts were sewn together in an endless loop and two of these were dyed making a total of six felts per dyeing with the total weight capacity of a vat being around two hundred and twenty pounds weight[3]. To conserve space the felts were usually dyed in rope form rather than spreading them out full width. One man worked one vessel and he had to continually open out the pieces with a pole to ensure even dyeing and avoid crease marks. Penetration of dye into the felt, particularly thick or oily felts, was a constant difficulty that had to be dealt with, and in extreme cases even restricted the use of some dyestuffs. To alleviate this, the percentage of the natural oils in the wool had to be limited to less than 0.3%[4] and if this was exceeded the felt had to be scoured before dyeing. Another alternative was to add a detergent to the dye bath. In some mills, notably in the MASCO combine, longer dyeing cycles were used, which allowed a longer levelling out period and better wetting out. Consequently, the operator did not have to open the felt out, which allowed one man to look after two vessels. For some high quality felts such as carpet felt, slipper felt, hat felt, the pieces were dyed open width rather than in rope form, and were dyed four pieces at a time. These dye vessels were therefore unusually wide compared to the woollen worsted industry. Dyeing full width was a well-behaved process, because the operator only had to smooth the felt out initially, and then it ran smoothly on its own.

Transporting the felt to and from the dye house was a fairly crude operation. The felt was transferred by truck from the mill bottom, where the felt was milled, to the dye house. Because the felt was so wet and to minimise the number of journeys, each truck was so heavily laden that it required two operators at the front pulling with a rope and three men at the back pushing to move it. At Hudcar Mill, to facilitate the transport, the truck was located on three iron-rail tramlines that ran from the mill bottom to the dye house. The truck had two fixed main wheels on either side of the truck and a wheel centred at the front and one at the back that moved on their axles, which enabled the truck to turn. When the truck reached the dye house the pieces were thrown out of the truck and stacked outside against the factory wall. These pieces stayed there overnight and sometimes in all weathers. When the pieces were required, two men went outside with a dye house truck and picked up just enough for a vessel, usually four to six pieces.

The dye house in Baltic Mill in 1977 showing wide-width vessels dyeing full width pieces

The head dyer maintained an air of secrecy around the recipes used for the dyeing of each coloured felt, and kept a notebook with them all written down. In the early days, the dyes were natural dyestuffs such as Logwood, Fustic, and Indigo. A typical recipe used by The Patent Woollen Cloth Company around 1850 was: sixteen parts Alum, four parts Argol, six parts Picric, two parts Tumeric, fourteen parts Cudbear, twenty-four parts Barwood, one and a half parts Indigo, and a mordant; all to make the colour "Olive"[5]. For a full description of these natural dyes and their use, refer to Manual of Dyeing by Knecht and Rawson[6]. By the turn of the nineteenth century, synthetic dyes had replaced natural dyestuffs and the use of acid dyes were readily taken up by the felt industry. By 1957, the recipe for Sage was: equal parts of acid yellow, acid orange, disulphine blue and a third part of coomassic blue. Joseph Spencer recorded the changes in the dyes used for one felt colour dated from before the invention of synthetic dyes by Sir Robert Perkins to 1948[7]. There was a further change in dye recipes when the woollen felts were diluted with other synthetic fibre components such as viscose rayon. In this case union dyes had to be used to ensure that the synthetic component was dyed the same colour as the wool. Unlike acid dyeing, union colours had to be dyed in neutral liquor so it was essential to ensure that there was no residual acid in the felt before dyeing. Often this meant the felt had to be washed first to remove all traces of any acid.

Because of all the variables in wool quality, hardening, and milling, the job of the dyer was more an art than a science and it meant constant vigilance on the pieces as they dyed in order to develop the correct shade. The dyer also had to judge a colour when it was wet, which was a very different shade to when it was dry. When the colour was assessed as correct, the dyer snipped a small piece off the end of a felt and dried it on a hot air blower. It was then compared for colour against a standard sample that was kept in the head dyer's office. This technique had to be done a few times to ensure a commercially acceptable match and to avoid over-dyeing the pieces. When dyeing was judged complete, the dye vessel was drained, filled with water, and the excess dye washed off. The pieces then had to be hauled out onto a scray and transferred to the drying department to be mangled or spun dried before final drying and tentering.

Until the 1960s, conditions in the dye house were fearsome with the floors continually wet with water and acid and the air filled with steam. An ordinary pair of shoes in this environment would last about a fortnight before they disintegrated. Clogs and wellington boots were the order of the day in the dye house and of these clogs were the most durable. Even as late as 1984, the assistant head dyer always wore clogs.

With the advent of the large scale production of superfine felts it became possible to invest in other forms of dyeing that held the promise of economies of scale. Most important of these was beam dyeing which had the potential for automatic control of the dyeing process, reducing the dyeing cycle by half, and cutting water and steam consumption by half. As an added benefit, beam-dyed felt became resistant to temperature and boiling water shrinkage because it had been held to width during the hot, wet process. In terms of output, these machines far outweighed conventional winch dyeing with three beam dyeing machines capable of dyeing five thousand pounds weight of felt per day[8].

The beam dyeing process consisted of winding felt onto a perforated drum, known as a beam, and pumping dye from the inside of the drum to the outside of the felt wound upon it. The machine for winding the felt onto the beam used two endless tenter chains with pins attached to them on which the felt edges were attached. As the chains moved forward, the distance between them increased to stretch the felt across the width, remove any creases, and set the felt to the correct width of the beam. As the felt moved onto the beam to be wound up, it was lifted off the pins and the chains looped back to the beginning to continue to pick up more felt. When the wind-up was complete, the beam was loaded by crane onto a special cradle that was then slid into the beam dyeing autoclave. The autoclave was an airtight enclosure accessible through a substantial hinged door capable of resisting the high pressures needed to force the dye through the drum and felt.

Because everything was sealed during dyeing, the dyer was effectively blind to the change of colour that was taking place in the felt and he was completely dependent on the automatic operation of the machine. However there was a facility for sampling the dyed felt. As the pieces were being wound upon the perforated drum, small squares of felt were interleaved at different positions at the edge of the roll. These were all connected together with a ribbon so that by pulling the ribbon each of the squares could be pulled out in turn. When the drum and felt were loaded into the autoclave the free end of the ribbon was threaded through a small outlet in the casing that acted as a sort of miniature air lock. When the machine indicated that dyeing was complete, the dyer opened the "airlock" and pulled out the first small square by the ribbon. This was dried and compared to the standard sample. If it did not match, dyeing was resumed and the next square examined and so on until the last sample was extracted. After successful dyeing, the felt was mangled and finally dried on a tenter.

DYEING AND FINISHING

The beam dyeing installation at Bury Mill in 1984 showing two autoclaves, on the left is a beam of red felt on a perforated drum, on the right the control panel, the spider-like projection on the autoclave is for dye sampling

The whole process was fraught with difficulties for the dyer since the risks were high because of the scale of the dyeing. One mistake meant a huge amount of felt designated as scrap. In practice, the process turned out to be anything but efficient since large quantities did not meet the standard colour and were unable to be reworked in the normal dye vessels. As much of this felt as possible was dyed black but there was a limited market for black felt, because demand usually only followed the death of a famous public figure. Felt that could not be re-dyed was stored in the hope that it could be sold at a later stage. This gave a major problem in rising stock values since, for accountancy purposes, off-colour felt was valued the same as first grade material but could only be sold at a clearance price. Eventually for Bury and Masco Industries Limited, the second grade stock was so large it could not be sold at clearance prices because it would have upset the market price for first grade felt.

WASHING, SCOURING, PROOFING

Whatever finishing process was used on a felt, it was always followed by a washing off process to bring the felt back to a neutral position and although it was a simple and mundane operation, it was fundamental to successful felt production. Among the other wet finishing processes for felt that required washing off were: scouring, carbonising, proofing, and bleaching.

WASHING

The washing vessel was a simple affair consisting of a rectangular tank on which was mounted a two roll mangle, equipped with large diameter rollers usually covered in rubber. The mangle was mounted as close to the tank as possible to minimise the drag on the felt and the width of the rollers was just slightly greater than the width of the felt in order to process it at full width. After threading through the mangle the felt was made endless by stitching the ends together.

The tank was supplied with cold water, a steam pipe, and sometimes a spray bar was fixed across it positioned just before the mangle nip to give a greater flow of clean water through the felt. The action of the mangle squashed the felt so that most of the unwanted fluids were squeezed out, and when the felt emerged from the rollers, it expanded again to suck in fresh water as it re-entered the wash tank. The time spent in washing-off, depended very much on the prior treatment and the thickness of the felt. At the end of the washing off process, the felt was passed through the mangle one more time and onto a pallet or scray, which gave a modicum of drying to the felt. After this, the felt was pre-dried in a spin drier known as an hydro extractor, affectionately called a "wuzzer".

In the felt industry, the washing vessel was always referred to as a "betty" or "dolly". These vessels were universal pieces of equipment, which were used for all kinds of felt treatments other than washing off, such as stiffening or moth proofing.

A washing betty with a two roll mangle in the wet treatment room in Hudcar Mill c1948, the scray is on rails to maximize the load of wet felt that it could be carry

SCOURING

Scouring was necessary for felts because the oils and fats connected with wool fibres interfered with milling and dyeing, giving felts with uneven properties and colour. In the early days and up to 1930, urine or lant was used because it removed the greases and left the wool soft and pliable[9]. Soda ash (sodium carbonate), potash (potassium carbonate) and soap were also used but these tended to make the felt stiff. Scouring was usually done at a temperature of sixty degrees Celsius, which was just hot enough for the operator to test it by putting his hand in it. The performance of the scouring solution depended a great deal on the geographic location of the felt mill and where its source of water came from. At Longmeadow Mill in Kidderminster, the water was so hard that using soap became impossible[10] and the mill had to buy in scoured wool for its production. This is another reason why the felt industry was centred on Rossendale because it had a copious supply of soft water that aided soap based processes such as scouring, milling and printing. As the wool industry developed, scoured wool became more available at commercial prices, which enabled the felt industry to use scoured raw materials rather than having to undertake its own expensive scouring process. This was important for the superfine, and white technical felts.

CARBONISING[11]

Up to the 1950s, non-carbonised wool was the main raw material for making felt even though it contained undesired amounts of natural contaminants, and even after thorough devilling and carding, there were always seeds and burrs trapped in the felt. To remove these, the felt was treated with sulphuric acid and then hot air dried, which left the felt unscathed but turned the seeds and burr to carbon. By passing the felt through steel rollers at high pressure the carbon was broken up into a powder that fell out of the felt, leaving it in a more pristine state. To enable the felt to be processed further it had to be made as neutral as possible, so the sulphuric acid had to be washed out. This whole process was referred to as carbonising.

Carbonising was a messy and unhealthy process demanding a huge piece of equipment occupying a large area, all of it awash with dilute sulphuric acid. Bury Felt Manufacturing Company Limited had a carboniser that occupied a complete shed that was kept well away from the other processes. Because of the difficulties involved, carbonising felt was abandoned around 1970 and where the specification demanded it, carbonised wool was used instead. The carboniser at Bury was dismantled in 1982.

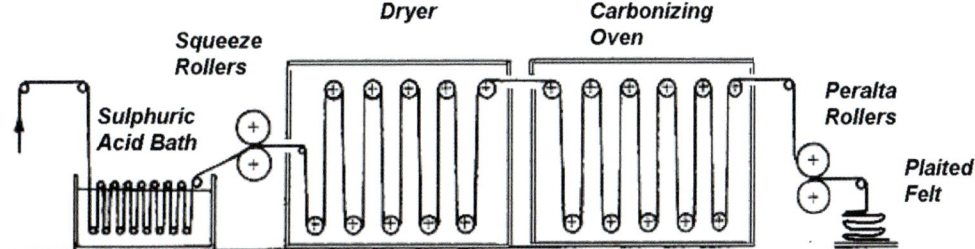

Carbonising felt, the peralta rollers at the end of the line crushed the carbonised seed and burr to powder

The last carbonising plant of the felt industry at Hudcar Mill showing the acid bath and squeeze mangle, and in the second photograph, the drying and carbonising oven

The major products carbonised were carpet felt, black felts and some superfines. The greatest use of the carboniser was in the 1950s, when up to forty pieces of felt each forty yards long were carbonised every week. By the 1970s, demand dropped to just a few pieces a month, and in 1980, there were none.

1. THE ACID TROUGH

The main acid tank was a pitch lined cast iron trough, which contained eight rollers, four on the top and four submerged in the acid. Originally, there were fourteen. The felt was delivered by trolley from the milling department in a plaited form directly after milling and therefore had to be pre-tensioned before being processed. It also had to be spread out so that it could be treated full-width, which was done using a simple fabric spreader consisting of a wooden beam with a curved edge. The felt was threaded between the top rollers and the submerged rollers until it emerged out of the acid bath and arrived at the nip of the first mangle. There was a spreader beam in front of the mangle to ensure that the felt remained spread out and that it contained no creases as it was mangled to remove the excess acid. The pressure on the rollers was adjusted by a screw handle to give the maximum amount of acid removal without damaging the felt. The excess acid was channelled back into the acid bath. Originally, the acid bath was fed with fresh acid from a side tank through a manifold in order to ensure uniformity of acidity, but this was later abandoned as just pouring buckets over the side proved to be just as effective[12].

2. MANGLING

After the first coarse mangling the felt was again pre-tensioned before entering a second high-pressure mangle that was hydraulically operated, with a normal operating pressure of two hundred pounds per square inch. The rollers were steel covered with half-inch thick rubber and positioned so that the excess acid was again channelled back into the trough. This mangle was driven electrically and independently of the acid rollers and the rollers in the oven, which were driven by line shafting and leather belts. The speed of this second mangle had to be continually adjusted manually during processing to generate a slack loop between the mangle and the oven. The purpose of this was to control the loop and keep it at a constant length.

3. THE OVEN

The oven was divided into two distinct sections or chambers, each being five feet long and fed by two fans. One fan was positioned at the top of the oven and the other at the lower part of the oven. Hot air from the fans was directed through slots onto rollers situated inside the oven with each roller having one slot directed onto it. There were ten lower rollers and ten upper rollers in each chamber, each being covered with dense half-inch thick felt. This protected the steel rollers from acid attack and gave resilience to take up tension fluctuations in the felt. All the rollers were geared and driven together. The felt passed over the top rollers and under the bottom rollers like a conventional fabric accumulator, to eventually pass over the final top roller and down to one outside the oven. The felt was then crushed between two special steel rolls called peralta rolls that could exert considerable pressure in order to pulverise the carbonised burr and seed. As the felt emerged from the peralta rolls, it was fed into a plaiting mechanism and allowed to accumulate onto a wooden trestle or stillage in preparation for transportation to the breakers to remove all the carbon dust.

The oven heaters were supplied by a seventy-five pounds per square inch steam line, and the temperature of the two chambers was set at two hundred and twenty degrees Fahrenheit[13]. The line speed of the machine was about nine to twelve feet per minute. The effluent from the acid tank was pumped to settling tanks behind the dye house and treated before disposal.

4. THE BREAKER

The breaker was similar in design to a box miller consisting of two twelve-inch diameter horizontal and two vertical steel rollers through which the felt, in a continuous rope form, was passed. The felt then passed over a wooden idler roll and then into the body of the breaker where it was forced towards the back of machine The felt was then dragged back towards the rollers after passing through a wooden chute three feet long and about eighteen inches wide. This chute had a foot-square wooden plate positioned above it to control the drag, by adjusting the height of the drag plate using an outside control wheel. By continually circulating the felt through the mangle rollers, the carbonised matter was shaken out. Each felt piece of forty yards took forty-five minutes in the breaker for a satisfactory felt. Two breakers were used to service the carboniser.

5. GENERAL

The carboniser plant ran on a twenty-four-hour basis until around 1950, when the workload gradually eased off. The operation was run by a chargehand and three operatives. One man controlled the piece input and the acid bath, another controlled the main mangle drive, another looked after the oven and plaiting setup, and the last man looked after the breakers. Occasionally dyed pieces were carbonised and surprisingly in these cases, the dye did not leach out and contaminate the acid bath. The acid in the tank was changed every month and the concentration checked daily using a Twaddell hydrometer, and if the density were not correct, sulphuric acid was added.

6. MEASUREMENTS OF THE CARBONISER

The acid tank was thirty inches deep. The bearing flanges on the side of the tank were eight inches in diameter secured with eight nuts. The tank was rubber lined with two layers totalling four millimetres thick. The internal bearing shaft was four inches in diameter. The tank was ninety inches long by eighty-eight inches wide. The mangle was eighty-four inches wide with eleven and a half inch diameter rollers. The oven was ninety inches long, twenty feet long, and twelve feet high. In those days, there was little regard for the nature of the fumes coming from the oven and these were vented to the atmosphere through a chimney in the roof.

MOTHPROOFING

Many grubs, insects and beetles, such as moth larvae and carpet beetles find wool an attractive source of food and yet others prefer to shelter in the interstices of felt. Thankfully, a simple mothproofing treatment was all that was needed both to discourage beetles and insects from penetrating the felt and to kill them or their grubs. Two treatments were used, one non-substantive that left a surface deposit on the wool, and the other that formed a permanent bond with the fibres. The oldest treatment was the use of sodium silicofluoride, which was applied as a solution to the felt in a washing betty. After hydro extraction and drying, the level of sodium silicofluoride needed to be in excess of 0.25% of the dry weight of the felt, and since this was a non-substantive treatment, it meant that the chemical just lay on the surface of the fibres and could be washed off easily. As well as giving a harsh feel to the felt, the surface crystals could be dislodged if the felt was shaken, which reduced its effectiveness against moths. The other non-substantive treatment commonly used was pentachlorophenol that was applied in a similar way to sodium silicofluoride but it had the same deficiencies of solubility in water and a tendency to be shaken out with use. One other such treatment was dinitroalphanaphthol (known as DAN), which was favoured by the military for packing armaments, because it did not corrode the metal casings, but it was not often used.

Substantive treatments that were chemically locked on to the wool were preferred because they provided a permanent protection. The chemicals used were mostly halogenated organic compounds that possessed a sulphuric group in them to lock into the chemical structure of wool. The first of these compounds to be used was Eulan N developed by I. G. Farben (later Bayer), which had cyfluthrin as its active ingredient. This was later superseded by Mitin FF, consisting of sulcofuron, when it was introduced by Ciba Geigy around 1948[14] and which became the standard for the industry.

Both these chemicals were applied during dyeing when using acid dyes. Mitin FF was applied at a dry level of three percent of the felt weight. Since they were chemically attached to the woollen fibres, these agents were resistant to washing and dry cleaning. They were also completely fast to light and could not be rubbed off once applied. Felts could even be milled without affecting the efficacy of the mothproofing. The successful use of these mothproofing agents is highlighted by the fact that, in 1978, the military accepted Mitin FF and Eulan WA as satisfactory replacements for DAN[15]. However, the one moth that was resistant to Mitin FF was the common brown moth, which unfortunately, is the one most often found in domestic circumstances. Mitin FF was therefore mostly used in commercial applications. In 1989, the UK Department of the Environment regulated the effluent arising from the use of mothproofing agents and classed these chemicals as dangerous, and so restricted their use. Coincidentally, the felt industry in Britain ceased shortly after this.

Care had to be taken with all of these treatments to ensure that the mothproofing agents were distributed evenly throughout the felt. If for any reason any area was not covered by the agents or had too little on, the felt was open to attack by moths or beetles.

ROT PROOFING

Under warm and humid conditions, wool is susceptible to attack by moulds and bacteria that cause the felt to rot and disintegrate. Since much felt was exported and used in hot wet climates, it was important to introduce a treatment to prevent rotting. Some of the mothproofing chemicals could provide a degree of rot proofing, such as dinitroalphanaphthol that could double the life of normal untreated felt, and pentachlorophenol that could treble the life. Zinc naphthenate improved on these by providing four times the life and at the same time imparting insect repelling properties. Copper naphthenate was the most effective treatment against rotting, because it increased the life tenfold and at the same time proved to be an effective repellant against insects and moths. Unfortunately, naphthenates are insoluble in water and had to be applied to a felt in oil-water emulsions that left an oil coating on the fibres, and this was a distinct fire risk when the final felt was dried at high temperature. Cuprammonium hydroxide was a very effective rot-proofing agent, though not as good as copper naphthenate, but its ease of use and low cost made it an attractive treatment. These treatments were applied to the felt at one percent of the felt weight.

Pentachlorophenol (PCPL) was also used from around 1930 onwards and was particularly favoured by the military because of its compatibility with munitions and armaments. In 2001, The Convention for the Protection of the Marine Environment of the North East Atlantic declared PCPL a hazardous material being toxic, persistent and liable to bioaccumulate[16].

BLEACHING

Natural wool is a delicate shade of yellow, which for most technical end uses is perfectly acceptable, but for the domestic market, there was a demand for good white felt or for pale and bright shades. For these markets, the felt had to be bleached. Early bleaching was done with sodium sulphite, but this was readily superseded by the use of hydrogen peroxide. Felt was bleached in dye vessels filled with a solution of hydrogen peroxide that was made slightly alkaline to increase the rate of bleaching. The liquor in the dye vat was a 0.75% solution of hydrogen peroxide adjusted with alkali to give a pH 8–9, and kept at a temperature of sixty degrees Celsius. The felt was plaited into the dye vessel and steeped in the liquor for several hours. It was then removed and transferred to a separate dye vessel where the bleach was washed off. Sometimes a dye house could become short of dyeing capacity and it was more important to dye felts rather than bleach them. Therefore, as an expedient, felts to be bleached were just run through the bath once and then allowed to stand on stillages for a few days, which allowed the bleaching to continue, until a dyeing vessel became available to wash them.

STIFFENING

Stiffening was mostly used on technical felts, either to meet a specification or for aesthetic purposes to give a firmer handle, particularly for the coarse low qualities of felt. The process was simple and used a wide-width washing betty fitted with a mangle, and a roller positioned at the bottom of the fluid trough that was filled with the stiffening solution The felt was threaded, full width, underneath the roller and led into the mangle, which was then set in motion. The felt became saturated with the stiffening solution as it was dragged through the trough and the excess liquor was squeezed out by the mangle. The felt was then plaited on a scray and taken for drying,

Most stiffening treatments used a starch solution at a concentration that depended on the degree of stiffening that was required. The starch solution needed to be very fluid in order to fully penetrate the felt and the mangle had to be carefully adjusted to give an even expression of fluid across the felt. If good penetration was not achieved, the outer layers of the felt would be stiff after drying, while the inside of the felt would be soft. Consequently, when an imperfectly stiffened felt was bent, it buckled and created ridges across the surface. To overcome such penetration problems, the starch solution in the trough was kept at a temperature of sixty degrees Celsius. This lowered the viscosity of the solution and helped to reduce the resistance to wetting, caused by the natural oil on the wool.

Urea Formaldehyde was also used to give a stiffening that was more permanent and being white it made an ideal substrate for a felt for use as marker-pen nibs. Phenol formaldehyde was preferred in the manufacture of industrial anti-vibration pads and products for the construction industry, because it also rendered the felt both mothproof and rot proof. These stiffened felts were designed to compete with rubber and were marketed extensively, by MASCO under the trade name of Mascolite and by R. R. Whitehead and Brothers under their brand, Regalpak. Both these formaldehydes posed significant health risks in the liquid state, not the least being dermatitis, so great care had to be taken in handling the solutions and the wet felt.

DRYING

In drying a felt, the simple processing of mangling should not be overlooked and in fact, it was the mainstay of the industry. Simple though it was, the process had hidden complexities that needed careful engineering of the mangle's construction. The most common mangle had two large-diameter rollers, one of them fixed and the other able to move vertically. The moveable roller was connected to a device that could push it down on the other roller to create any required pressure in the nip. Most mangles had a screw device at each the end of the roller, and by turning the screw, the pressure at each end could be adjusted. Care had to be taken to ensure that the pressures at both ends were the same or the felt would receive a different treatment across its width. For greater uniformity, pneumatic cylinders replaced the screw mechanism, so that equal forces were guaranteed at each end of the roller

The mangle squeezed out, or "expressed", the water from the felt by pushing the fibres together and making less space for the water to occupy, and the excess was therefore forced out. This has implications as to the maximum amount of water that can be extracted by using pressure alone. No matter how hard the fibres were pressed together there would always be spaces that could be filled with water therefore mangling could only achieve a limited amount of drying.

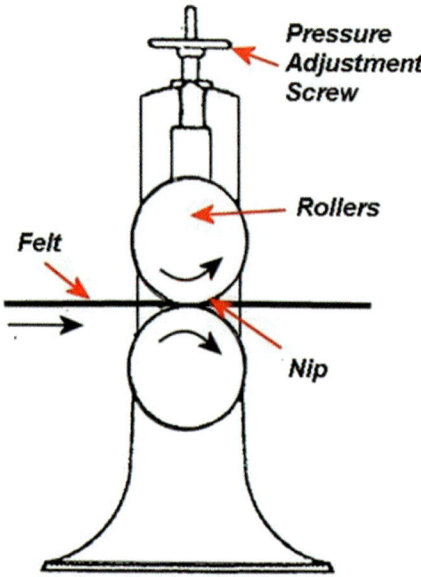

A simple two-bowl mangle used for expressing water from a felt

The amount of water left in the felt was usually measured as a percentage of the dry weight of the felt. A mangle could easily reduce the moisture content to around seventy to eighty percent and even using the ultimate high pressure mangle with a force of twelve-ton at the nip it was only possible to achieve sixty percent[17]. This is almost the theoretical limit achievable by pressing. Unfortunately, at high pressures, mangle rollers tended to bow in such a way that they pressed more on the edges than at the centre producing different drying characteristics across the felt. This was minimised by using rollers of as large a diameter as commercially feasible. Despite this difficulty, mangles were used extensively because of their simplicity, ruggedness and high speed of operation, which at a running speed of eighty yards a minute made it the most economical method of reducing moisture content.

The most effective method of extracting water was by spin-drying a felt which could reduce water content to as little as thirty percent. However, the process was a more expensive process than mangling, and was therefore reserved for use with thick felts that held large quantities of water. The industrial version of the spin drier was called an hydro-extractor, or more commonly a wuzzer, and consisted of a copper or steel perforated drum, seventy two inches in diameter, housed inside a solid steel container and spinning at six hundred revolutions per minute. The machine was loaded by carefully laying the felt round the inside of the drum and winding it loosely so that it was as well balanced as possible when the spinning started. The machine acted on the felt in two ways, firstly the huge centrifugal force that was generated pressed the felt against the drum squeezing the water out, and secondly it acted directly on the water spinning it out. All the water extracted flowed outwards and through the perforations in the drum to be collected in the outer casing and discharged through a water outlet at the base of the machine. The cycle time for spinning ranged from two to ten minutes depending on the density of the felt, with the lower densities needing less time in the extractor than denser felts.

DYEING AND FINISHING

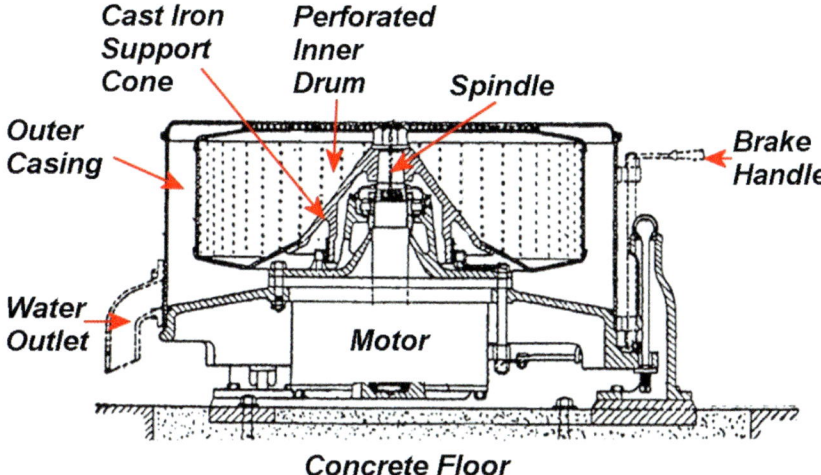

An hydro-extractor used to spin dry felt

Although the hydro-extractor was capable of reducing the moisture content to as low as thirty percent, in practice it was usual to achieve fifty percent with an acceptable commercial spin time. Nevertheless, on a heavy felt this gave significant cost benefits in reducing the later air-drying time. The minor disadvantage of using the hydro-extractor was the crumpled state that the felt was in when it was removed from the machine. In addition the felt was often left with an imprint of the perforations of the drum due to the high centrifugal force that pushed it against the inner wall of the hydro-extractor These were not serious issues since the later tentering process and final finishing removed most of the imperfections.

An hydro-extractor, the braking lever is on the right, the water outlet on the left. These machines remained the same from 1940s to 1980s

TENTERING

Before the advent of drying machines, felt was hung out to dry in the open air on specially made stretching frames known as tenters.

Tentering in the woollen district of Vicenza in 1836[18], the tenter frame is wooden with the top beam fixed and the lower beam adjustable, the winch the left of the picture is used for stretching the cloth to length.

However, the changeable British weather made this an unsatisfactory form of drying. Therefore, heated indoor corridor-like rooms over forty yards long were constructed to house the tenter frames. These rooms were known as seams. The air in the room was heated by a network of six-inch diameter steam pipes, which were positioned just below each tenter frame so that the convection currents drew the moisture away from the felt. No doubt, indoor and outdoor frames were used at the same time with drying outside only taking place when the weather was fine. The whole output of the mill depended on the drying capacity and there were times when extra capacity had to be found. For example, The Patent Woollen Cloth Company rented indoor tenter seams from other Leeds manufacturers to supplement their capacity when they were busy. In Albert Works, MASCO had six hand tenters on the ground floor, six hand tenters on the first floor, and two hand tenters on the top floor, and at Siss Clough, they had hand tenters that were eighty yards long. Originally, wooden tenter frames were used as the felts were relatively thin, but later iron frames were used as the technical felts became thicker and required more force to stretch and dry them. The construction of all tenter frames was the same except that the crossbeam supporting the top of the felt was fixed for a wooden frame and for a metal frame, the beam could be bolted at different heights from the ground. Both the top and bottom beams had a row of hooks mounted on them which were raked at an angle, the top pins pointing upwards and the ones on the lower beam pointing downwards. This ensured that the more the felt was stretched the firmer it was gripped. Stretching and drying lightweight felts on a tenter was relatively easy and could be done by hand, but thicker denser felts needed special tools in order to generate sufficient leverage to stretch them.

DYEING AND FINISHING

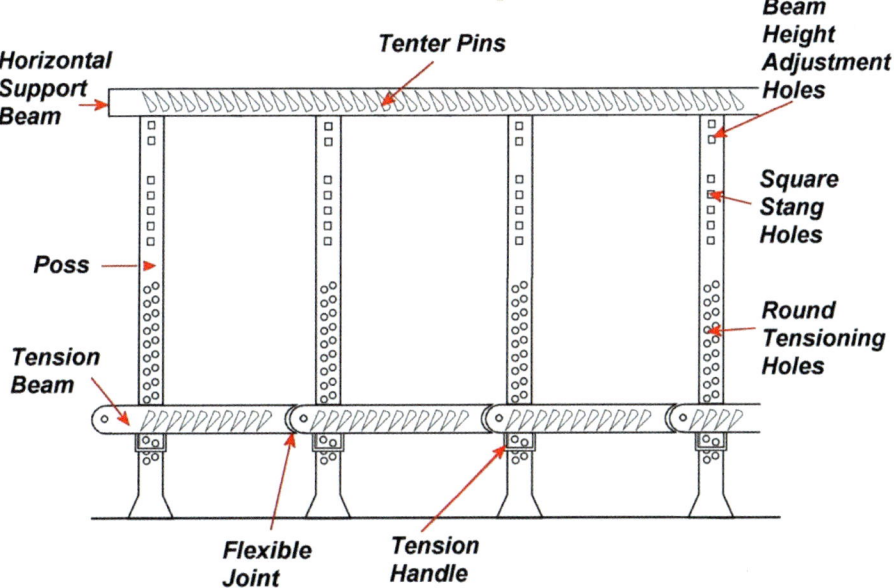

The construction of a metal tenter frame for stretching and drying felt.

The upright support posts of the tenter were known as "posses" and had three series of holes machined in them, the first upper holes were one inch square, spaced one foot apart, to which the crossbeam was bolted, to allow for different heights. The holes of the second set were rectangular one inch wide and two inches long into which the two ends of the support stangs were slotted. These stangs were three quarters of an inch thick made of cast iron in the form of a shallow U-shape supported by one or two brackets with square ends. These stangs were important because they made it possible for two rather than three men to tenter a felt.

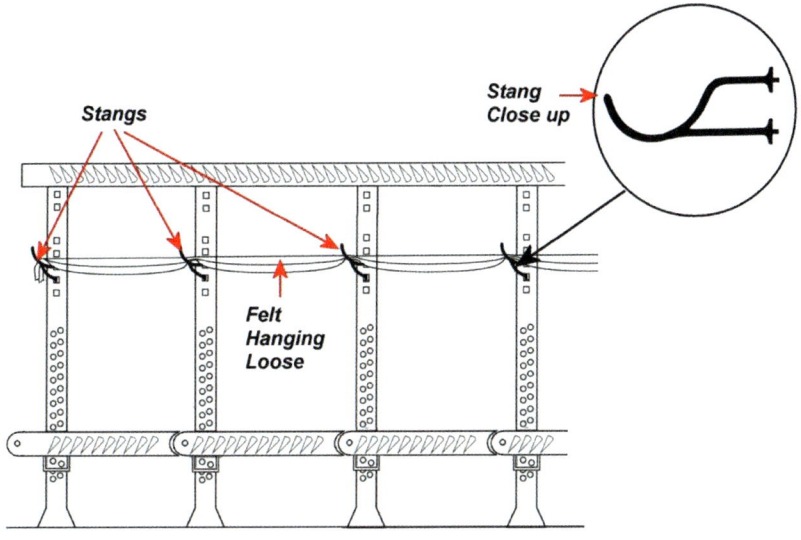

A metal tenter fitted with stangs supporting wet felt before hanging on the top tenterhooks

225

When in use, the square ends of the stangs were pushed into the square holes in the tenter frame to provide a stable support for wet felt. The felt was draped over the stangs to bring it closer to the top row of tenterhooks, to make it easier to hang. The edge of the felt was then securely fastened to the tenterhooks on the top beam and each stang removed one at a time to allow the felt to hang freely, ready to be fixed to the lower beam. The lower holes were round, half inch in diameter, and were in two offset columns in each poss, with thirty-nine in one column and thirty-seven in the other. These were for tensioning the felt and holding the lower beam in place while the felt dried. The lower beam was divided into segments each connected to the adjacent one by a flexible joint. In this way, the felt could be stretched one segment at a time with the maximum force applied to the minimum section of felt.

A view of a typical felt indoor tenter seam shown without felt

It was usual for each forty-yard seam to have two such tenter frames joined back to back to maximise the space in the drying room, and to fix the two upper beams either side of the poss so that their height above the ground could be adjusted without them falling off. However using two back-to-back tenter frames at once was very difficult because the tensioning of the felt on one side then affected the tension on the felt on the other.

The process of tentering started with the plaited felt being brought to the drying room on a special, tall trolley that was three feet high. This made it easier to attach the felt to the tenter because it substantially reduced the height needed to lift the felt into place. Ideally it needed three men to hang a felt, one man feeding it off the trolley, one to locate the edge of the felt on the top tenter hooks and one to hammer the felt firmly onto the pins using a rubber mallet. Thin felts less than three quarters of an inch in thickness could be easily manhandled but for felts over this thickness, the services of a winch and crane were needed. For thin felts, the use of stangs could reduce the manpower needed to two men, one feeding, the other positioning the felt over the stangs. The felt was arranged so that one edge was uppermost so that, once on the stangs, it only needed one man to hang the felt on the pins and secure it with a hammer. Even though there were no moving parts in a tenter, it was still a dangerous piece of equipment to be around since accidents could easily happen. For the sake of safety, there always had to be a second operative present or the consequence could be tragic. In one recorded case, an operator, working by himself, slipped whilst hanging a felt and caught his hands on the tenterhooks, which pierced his palms and he was left helplessly suspended. Since there was no one there to assist him, it was not until the following morning he was discovered and could be lifted off. He was lucky and survived.

DYEING AND FINISHING

The last felt tenter seam in the UK at Baltic Mill c1980, a thick felt is drying on the left, note also the high trolley, steam pipes, and the set of tools

For thick felt the first part of the felt was hung inch by inch off the trolley until a good length was secured and then a bar was fixed to the other free end and the bar attached to a block and tackle. The end was then hauled up towards the ceiling to form a long loop, tangential to the upper tenterhooks. As the hanger called for more felt the end was lowered to give him more slack to locate it on the hooks and also allowed the fixer to hammer the felt firmly onto the pins. It therefore required four men to tenter thick felts, one to hang, one to hammer, one to feed the felt, and one to operate the block and tackle.

Once the felt had been securely fastened to the upper tenterhooks, it hung vertically over the lower set of hooks ready to be fastened onto them. At this stage, the lower beam was resting on rods positioned in the tension holes in each of the upright posses. The felt was located on the lower tenterhooks and hammered home until all of the felt was secured along the full length of the frame. The rods were removed from each of the posses and the lower beam was allowed to hang from the felt by its own weight. Tensioning was started at one end of the seam using a purpose built jack called a "handy".

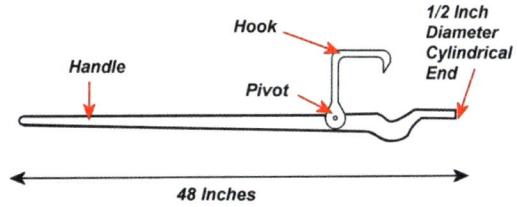

The "handy" tool for stretching felt on a tenter

FELT IN BRITAIN

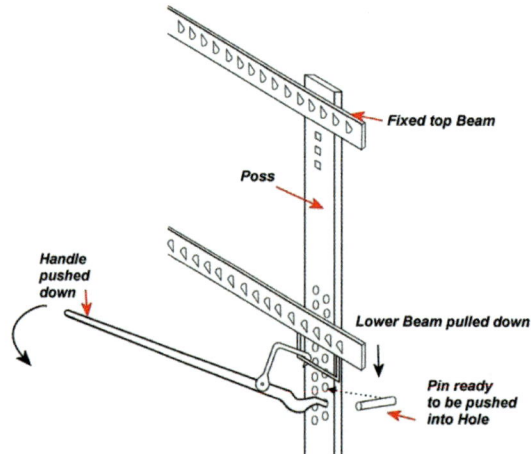

Using the "handy" to stretch the width of the felt, shown without felt for clarity

The handy was a long steel pole over forty eight inches in length, with one end rod-shaped of a diameter that enabled it to fit into the tensioning holes in the lower part of the poss. Just behind the rod section was a hinged hook that was designed to engage with a square-shaped tensioning loop fixed to the lower beam. To use the tool, the hook was latched over the loop and the handle raised as high as possible. The rod end was then positioned into one of the holes below the loop. By pushing down on the handle, the rod end took the strain and the hook pulled the loop downwards, which forced the lower tenter beam downwards and so stretched the felt. Whilst one operator held the handle down a second inserted a rod through the loop and into one of the tension holes in the poss. The handle of the handy was then raised so that the rod that had just been inserted took the strain and the tool was removed so that the operation could be repeated at the next poss. The procedure was continued for each section of the beam so that the felt was secured under tension by the rods on each of the posses. The felt was then left to dry overnight, during which time it became dimensionally stable and relieved the tension on the restraining rods making them easy to pull out. In order to detach the felt it had to be lifted over the tenterhooks and this could only be achieved by raising the lower beam. This was done a section at a time using two operators: the first took the weight of the beam with a lever, whilst the second removed the rod and replaced it in a hole that was this time higher up the poss. The beam was then lowered so that the newly placed rod took the weight of that section of the beam, the lever was removed, and the process continued for the other sections. The lower edge of the felt was then loose, making it an easy task to pull the felt off the hooks. The felt was then lifted off the top hooks, laid flat on the floor, and rolled up ready for dispatch.

In most cases, the felts arriving at the tenter room were milled to the correct length, but there were occasions when the felt came in short and needed to be stretched. To do this a winch and crane were installed at one end of the tenter room capable of servicing up to four double-sided tenters. The winch had to be mobile and it was therefore fixed to an A-frame mounted on pulley-like wheels. The wheels ran on a rail track so that the frame could be positioned at any tenter when required. The apex of the frame rested on a wooden beam fixed to the ceiling and this took the load when the felt was stretched. To stretch a felt, one end was fixed, full width, to a vertical post and the felt unplaited to its full length and an iron bar threaded through the free end of the felt, which was then attached to the winch. Winding the winch pulled the bar making the felt taut and then stretching it to the required length. The felt was then hung on the tenterhooks as before and the winch disconnected[19].

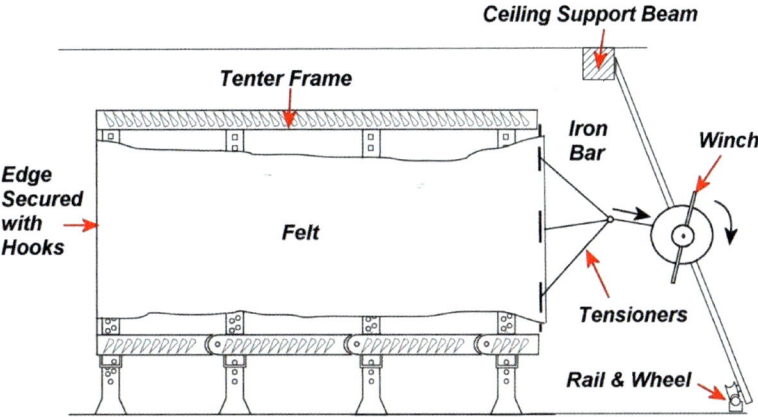

Stretching a felt lengthways on a tenter frame, this is similar to the picture of hand tentering in Vicenza shown on page 224

Although hand tentering may seem on the surface to have been economical, it was an inefficient and slow process that ultimately limited the output of the mill. The invention of the machine tenter around 1880[20] reduced the drying time from hours to minutes and its drying efficiency was such that it needed only two machines to satisfy almost the whole of the drying needs of a mill. It was only the denser, thicker felts, particularly half inch and upwards, that proved to be beyond the capability of the machine tenter. This was because the permeability and heat conductivity of these felts was so low that the water locked in the middle needed time to vaporize and percolate through them. Hand tentering therefore could not be dispensed with altogether and a tenter room with three double tenter seams was still in operation at Baltic Mill in 1982.

MACHINE TENTERING

The machine tenter had to perform the same functions as a hand tenter but had to do it dynamically at high speed and continuously. Therefore, the tenterhooks and the two rails holding them had to move both longitudinally and laterally. The flexibility to do this was solved by mounting tenterhooks on small blocks three inches long and one inch wide and attaching each block to the link of a chain. The links were assembled together to make a continuous chain over fifty yards long with the ends joined to make it into an endless chain.

There were two chains for each tenter machine one equivalent to the top beam of a hand tenter and the other equivalent to the lower beam and they were responsible for dragging the felt into the hot air oven. For ease of operation, the two chains were located horizontally relative to each other rather than vertically as in the hand tenter. In the first part of the machine, the chains ran in two separate guide rails set at an angle to each other and separated by the approximate width of the incoming felt. One edge of the felt was fed onto the tenterhooks of one chain and the other edge fed onto the second chain. On each side, a circular brush with very stiff bristles pushed the felt firmly onto the tenterhooks that mimicked the hammering operation in hand tentering. On later machines for thin felts, clips replaced the tenterhooks. By having the guide rails of the two chains angled, the distance between the chains widened as they went forward, which had the effect of stretching the felt. Sometimes, after dyeing, the felt may have shrunk to sixty inches wide when they should have arrived at the tenter at seventy inches, so the chains had to be significantly angled to stretch the felt to the correct width. The design of the tenter was also governed by the rate of stretching that a felt could tolerate. If the felt were stretched too fast, it would tear at the pins so it was important to have as slow a rate of stretch as possible. To generate a slow stretch the angled lead in to the oven of the tenter therefore had to be as long as possible and this explains the distinctive design of the tenter where the operator is a considerable distance away from the oven.

A machine tenter showing the initial guide rails for the tenter chains holding the tenter clips, which stretched the felt and fed it into the oven, inset is the guiding mechanism locating the felt on the tenter clips.

The oven had to contain the full length of a felt, and therefore had to accommodate a length of around forty yards, which could only be achieved economically if the felt made multiple passes through the oven. This was done by running the tenter chains backwards and forwards in the oven with the chains passing over massive sprockets at each end of the machine. In the straight lengths between the sprockets there was a guide rail that supported each chain so that it did not sag and these also acted as a shield that prevented any of the high temperature grease on the chains from dripping off and contaminating the felt passing below it.

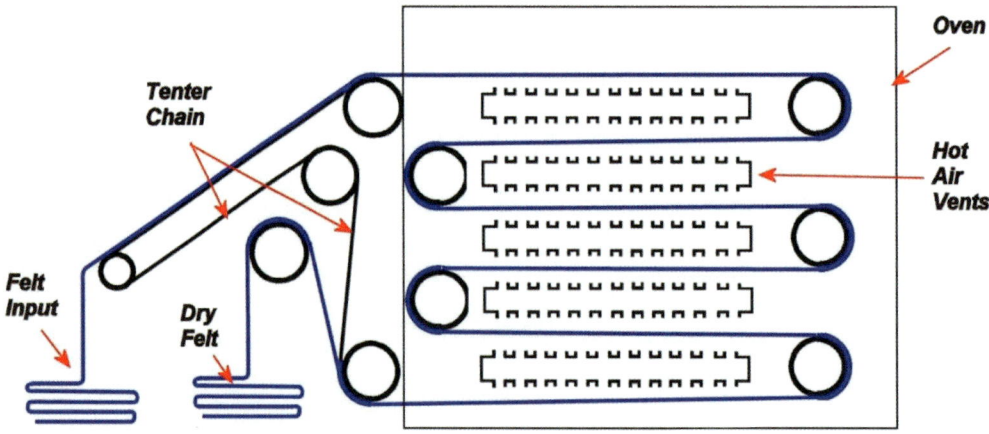

The drying arrangement in a machine tenter for drying thin felt

The distance between the sprockets and guide rails on either side of the machine could be adjusted to accommodate different widths of felts. Some tenters had cylinders fixed between the sprockets to support the felt as it changed direction in the oven, which was particularly beneficial for thin felts where there was a risk of the felt tearing off the tenterhooks. Without these cylinders, the felt bowed in the middle as it changed direction but the forces involved were small and only light pressure on the cylinders was needed to correct this. In order for the tenter to facilitate width changes there needed to be two parts to the cylinders one sliding inside the other similar to opening or closing a telescope. This could only be achieved because the cylinders were acting in a secondary support role to the tenter chains and the pressure exerted by the felt was light. The size of the oven was measured by the number of cylinders counted at the rear of the machine. Most felt tenters were three cylinder machines, though some could be as large as five cylinders. When the chains and felt exited the oven the felt passed over a roller that effectively pulled the felt off the tenterhooks enabling the chains to go one way and the felt the other. The felt was plaited and stacked for further treatment and the chain returned to the starting point to pick up more wet felt. The fact that the dried felt was plaited on the same side of the machine as the input minimised the labour required since the tenterer could monitor both input and output at the same time.

The inside of a Krantz tenter showing the sprockets, chain, and chain guides

The circulation of the hot air within the oven was critical to its efficient operation. This was not just due to the oven dynamics but also to the interaction with the felt and the mechanics of extracting the moisture from within the felt itself. Thick dense felts had low permeability so that that moisture could only be removed at a slow rate whatever happened at the surface. The speed of the tenter therefore had to be matched to the maximum speed of drying that the felt could sustain. Hot air circulation in the oven was not therefore critical and fans were situated at the sides of the oven. Thin felts, however, had high permeability and their natural rate of drying was high, and this enabled ovens to be used that were much more efficient. In these cases, hot air could be directed straight onto the surface of the felt to give accelerated drying.

On some tenters, there was a facility for stretching the felt along its length before it reached the tenter chains where it was stretched across the width. This was particularly important for technical felts because of the need for adherence to strict property specifications. William Whiteley produced a tenter specifically for processing felt that contained a pre-stretching unit that was positioned in front of the oven, before the felt was fed onto the tenterhooks. The stretching unit was achieved using two large diameter drums rotating at different speeds. The drums were connected by gear wheels on the side of the machine that made changing the draft between them a simple task.

THE CHARLESWORTH-WHITELEY PATENT TENTERING MACHINE
Patent No. 408400.

A Whiteley tenter for thick felts c1940 from their machinery catalogue

It was never certain how dry a felt was as it left the oven, nor how uniform the drying was across the width of the felt. The extreme outside edges, known as selvedges, that were held by the tenterhooks, were always thicker than the rest of the felt so ended up with higher moisture content. If these were to be dry, then the rest of the felt was over-dried, which was the common practice. Felts exiting the tenter contained two to five percent of water, which was lower than the natural moisture regain of wool at thirteen percent. A dried felt therefore regained at least a further eight percent of water as it stood after tentering, which swelled the felt causing it to cockle on the surface, and in the case of superfine felts causing it have characteristic dimples. The aim in tentering was therefore to try to achieve a final moisture content of between eight and twelve percent and since there were no reliable methods of measuring moisture in a felt, it depended on the skill of the tenterer to achieve this.

A William Whiteley tenter c 1948 in the Greenbank shed at Bury Felt Manufacturing Company's Hudcar Mill showing a white technical felt being stretched before tentering

Because of the limitations of tentering, sheet felts were dried slowly in conventional ovens without any mechanical stretching or intervention, being laid either flat or as in the case of piano felts, hung vertically. Microwave ovens were experimented with, but the high speed of heating did not match the slow speed of moisture escape of these felts. The consequence was either blown felts, or felts where the middle had charred because the heat build up was greater than the rate at which the water could escape. This form of heating was therefore abandoned.

INSPECTION

Superfine felt inspection frames in the inspection department of Bury Mill in 1980

Once dried, the felts were inspected either on a long table for thick felts or on a special backlit frame for superfine thin felts. The felts were examined for faults or for surface blemishes caused by milling, and for any extraneous debris that might have escaped processing or been included as a result of contamination. Amongst the repairable faults were burr fragments and tar, the tar being an ever-present problem in fleeces. The burrs and any other vegetable debris were picked out carefully with tweezers and the tar dissolved out with a suitable solvent of the time like carbon tetrachloride. Superfine felts were inspected at speed on a frame that ran the felt over a screen through which light was projected to make the faults more visible. When a fault was spotted, the felt was stopped and the fault dealt with. Other more difficult faults were when the felt had not been securely fastened to the tenterhooks and had either missed the pins altogether or had torn off. This resulted in the felt being bowed at the torn end with the felt being thicker there than the rest of the felt. In these cases, there was no remedy and an allowance had to be made in the price equivalent to the length of the fault. Whenever the fault could not be corrected, a tag was inserted into the selvedge of the felt so that when the felt was rolled up the tags projected from the end of the roll. Different faults had different colours to signify the seriousness of the fault so that any allowance given off the price of the felt could be easily assessed without subsequently unrolling the felt. Milling faults were usually surface effects, most often where bits of loose felted wool had been milled into the surface causing a hard lump on the surface. These were rectified by further processing like cropping and sanding.

CROPPING

After milling and drying, most felts had a hairy and often irregular surface. For domestic felts, this was aesthetically displeasing and for technical felts was detrimental to its required properties. All felts therefore, with the exception of superfine felts were cropped. Cropping was performed on a machine equipped with a rapidly rotating roller that had metal blades spiralled around it, similar to the blade in a traditional lawnmower.

The blade of a cropper showing the dial for the height adjustment of the blade, on the right of the machine

For roll felts, the felt was passed under tension over a small diameter roller that sat just below the blade, the curvature of the roller ensuring that the felt surface was presented precisely to the blade. The cutter blade itself could be adjusted to fractions of an inch, and in modern machines, micrometer settings could be used.

The croppers at Baltic Mill c 1980 used for roll felts

The cropping operation was critical for some specialised felts for example for hats and slippers. Hat felts required an extra smooth finish and were therefore cropped five times each side, whereas slipper felts were cropped four times on the face side and only once on the back[21]. Sheet felts were stiff and flat enough to pass directly under a cutter blade without the need for them to be bowed over a roller, so they were therefore fed into the machine on a flat table to pass directly under the cropping blade.

Cropping a sheet felt on a modern cropper at Royal George Mill in 1981

Cropping polishing wheels presented its own problems because of their thickness and limited size, which required a special machine and careful handling, reminiscent of the timber industry.

Cropping a polishing wheel at the Brynmawr Factory of Cooper and Co (Birmingham) Limited. Note the use of the wooden spatula to feed the bob through the cutter.

SANDING

The precise specifications for dense technical felts required a surface smoother than could be achieved by cropping alone and therefore these felts needed to be sanded to give the correct surface characteristics. A sanding machine was similar to a cropping machine except that the rotating blade was replaced by a roller covered in emery or carborundum paper.

Sanding roll felts and sheet felts at Baltic Mill in 1980

CONDITIONING

Since most felts were over-dried, they were susceptible to moisture changes, which affected their properties. Machine dried felts tended to have a harsh handle bordering on stiffness, even after cropping and sanding. Ironically, after expending large amounts of energy drying the felts, the feltmakers found that they needed to add moisture back into the felt in order to produce the quality of finish required commercially. Of all the techniques for doing this, the most important was decatising, also known as blowing, where steam was blown through the felt whilst it was under light pressure. The felt was wound onto a perforated drum together with a fine linen cloth that separated the felt layers, ensuring that none of the felt surfaces touched. This cotton cloth also provided the light pressure needed for the best finish and it was tensioned to provide just the right amount of force on the felt. To ensure that the outer layers of felt received the same pressure the cloth was longer than the felt and was wound outside the felt in several extra layers. Steam under pressure was then blown into the drum, through the perforations and through all the layers of the wrapped felt. Steaming was carried out for around ten minutes after which the cotton wrapper and the felt were unwound. The maximum thickness of a hard felt suitable for steaming was three eighths of an inch[22]. The piano felt makers had their own form of decatising for steaming sheet felts. In this process, a sheet felt was placed over the segment of a drum rather than a complete cylinder. A thick linen cloth was then placed on top of the felt and steam forced through the assembly from the underside.

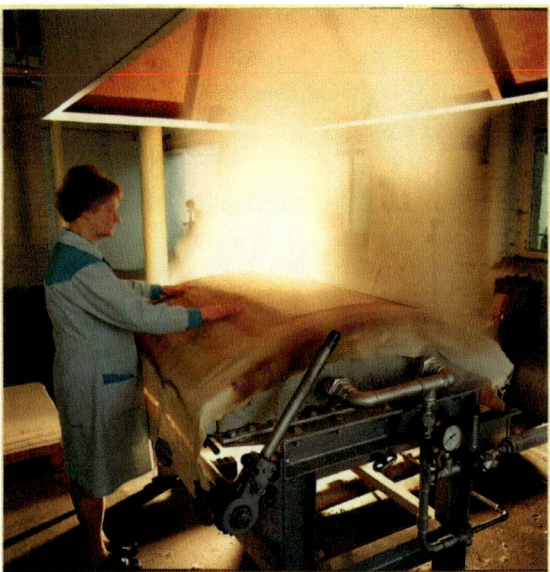

Decatising or blowing a sheet of piano hammer felt

Thick grey felts were treated very differently because they could not easily be steamed around a drum and were too long to be treated as piano felts. Instead of using steam, the felts were conditioned at room temperature by storing them in a wet conditioning room, called a nuzzery, which was suspended over a pool of water.

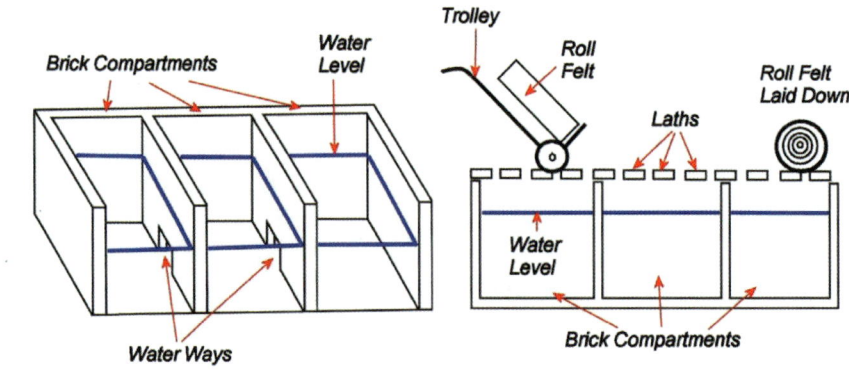

The wet room or nuzzery for conditioning felts in Baltic Mill

The room was fifty feet long and twenty foot wide with a floor that was an open wooden structure made of laths two inches wide and positioned one inch apart. The floor rested on a brick structure divided into walled compartments two feet in depth, and which were flooded with water up to three quarters of the height of the walls. There were gaps in walls to allow free passage of water between the different compartments and the spaces between the laths allowed water vapour to percolate up into the room providing hundred percent relative humidity. Rolls of felt were trucked into the nuzzery and laid horizontally across the laths and left there to take up the moisture from water vapour rising from the reservoir below.

After 1939, machines called dewers became available that made the nuzzery obsolete and most mills installed them to control the moisture in the finished felt. In this process, the felt passed over two driving rollers between which there was the dewing head, which consisted of a large diameter pipe with an arrangement of jets along it. Water was pumped under pressure into the pipe and exited from the jets as a fine mist that sprayed water directly onto the surface of the felt.

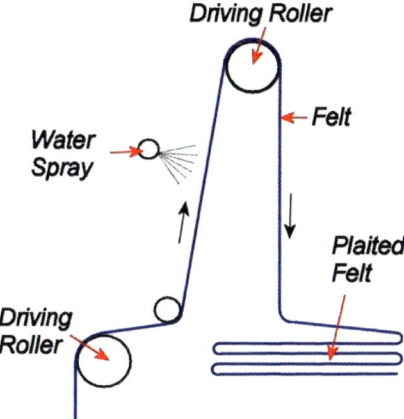

Schematic diagram of a Dewer used to spray water on a felt

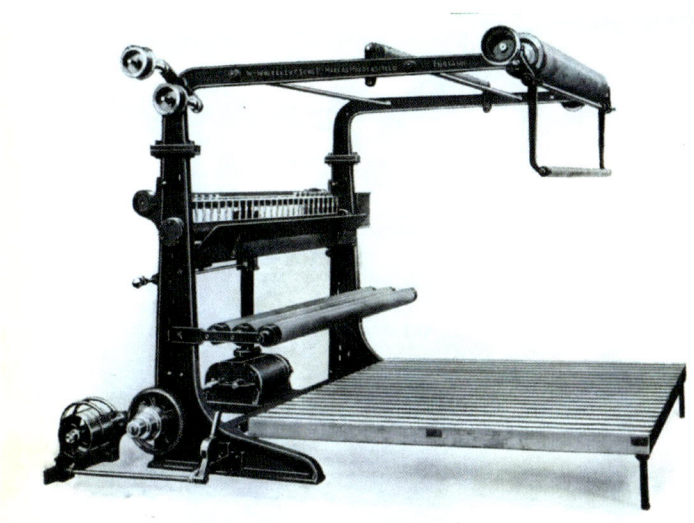

A dewer manufactured by William Whiteley c1940, the spray head is middle left and the plaiting mechanism top right

FELT IN BRITAIN

The sprayer was designed to deliver a constant volume of water so that the amount sprayed onto the felt was controlled by the speed of the machine. By carefully controlling the speed, precise moisture levels in the felt could be achieved to meet exact specifications[23]. Moisture in grey and technical felts was a critical issue since, unlike superfine felts, these were sold by weight and hence their profit margins depended on how much moisture the felt could tolerate[24]. The felt was finally plaited and sent for pressing.

PRESSING

Pressing was the final finishing process for felt. For domestic felt this was very much like ironing clothes with the same object of smoothing out all the creases and giving the surface a pleasing surface texture. For thin technical felts, pressing was necessary to fine-tune the thickness to meet the appropriate specification.

Usually the felt was decatised first, or put through the dewer, before it was processed through a rotary press. This press consisted of a large cylindrical drum three feet in diameter and eighty-four inches wide, and which was steam heated. Underneath the drum was a heated box-like container the same width as the drum and having a surface curved to the same diameter as the drum, but shaped to be a quarter of a cylinder. This box could be raised with an hydraulic ram so that it pressed against the drum and the whole assembly acted like a curved clothes iron.

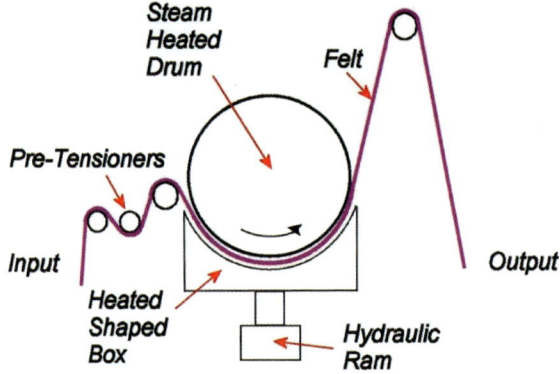

Diagram of a rotary press, the drum rotates with the felt and the shaped box remains stationary, thereby ironing the felt

To operate the machine the box was lowered and the felt fed between it and the drum, after which the box was then raised and the pressure adjusted to suit the type of felt being pressed. The drum was then rotated to pull the felt through the machine and across the stationary box. Because the felt was supported by the drum, there was no drag on it and therefore there was no loss in its width or length. The combination of the moisture from decatising or dewing, the heat of the drum, and the hot friction caused by the surface of the stationary box gave a smooth finish to the felt. Additionally, it served to make the felt dimensionally stable and the resulting decrease in thickness gave it a beneficial handle. After pressing, technical felts were rolled full width, and in the case of domestic or superfine felts they were folded in half, selvedge-to-selvedge, on a special rigging machine and then rolled up on a flat cardboard former.

DYEING AND FINISHING

The rotary press at Hudcar Mill in 1980. the feed bars and rollers are at the front of the machine and top left the output plaiting mechanism

Thick felts, dense felts, sheet felts and polishing wheels could not use a rotary press and had to be pressed in a conventional flat press. These could exert far more pressure than a rotary press and could engineer felts to very precise thickness specifications. Several different types of flat press were used depending on the type of felt to be pressed. The simplest machine was the Leachman press that had just two plates operated by an hydraulic ram, the pressure of which was adjusted to give the exact thickness required. Both top and bottom plates were steam heated, which with the moisture added by the dewer heat-set the thickness into the felt. All the grey felts produced by Bury and Masco Industries Limited passed through this type of press.

A Leachman press in Baltic Mill, note the thickness measuring gauge on the lower left hand side of the machine

For thinner dense white technical felts a double daylight press was used that could process two felts at a time and thereby maintain production efficiency. This sort of press had three plates, the top plate was fixed and the bottom plate was driven by an hydraulic ram, the middle plate was free to move up and down. As the lower plate rose it pushed the first felt up against the middle plate and then all three moved up to the top plate and engaged with the second felt. The four components then compressed against the fixed top plate and pressure was generated equally through the two felts.

A Sellers double daylight press for pressing white technical felts at Bury Mill

Simple single and double daylight presses were uneconomical machines for pressing polishing wheels because these bobs were of relatively small size, high density, and considerable thickness when compared to sheet felt. To be commercially competitive the bob manufacturers had to press as many bobs as possible at the same time, which necessitated the use of multi-daylight presses. These presses were an extension of the double daylight press but instead of one floating pressure plate, there were three or more allowing up to four layers of polishing wheels to be pressed at once. As the lower plate was driven upward it collected all the floating plates and layers of bobs sequentially, until it reached the fixed top plate. Thereafter, further movement by the lower plate generated an equal pressure in all the layers at once.

Loading polishing wheels into a multi-daylight press ready for pressing to thickness, the machine was sited at Cooper and Co (Birmingham) Limited factory at Brynmawr

FABRICATION AND DISPATCH

Market demand for felt was not only for rolls and for sheets but also for specific parts made according to specified engineering drawings. Traditionally, this extra service provided by feltmakers for their customers originated with the supply of gun wads in 1850. For sheet felts, too, there was a demand for different shapes and sizes other than the standard width and length that was produced at the end of the manufacturing process. Piano hammer felt for instance had to be cut into strips that were wide enough to cover a wooden piano hammer, and long enough to accommodate the full set of piano keys.

Cutting a sheet felt with a guillotine at Royal George Mill.

All felt makers, therefore, established fabrication units that took in the finished felt and converted them into whatever a customer demanded, from felt washers to thin strips of dense white felt. Most fabrication units were attached to the main mills but MASCO considered it such an important aspect of their business that they set up a felt fabrication unit in 1956 that had its own premises and operated almost as an independent business. It was responsible for its own profit and had to buy in felt from the other mills in the group as though it was a separate customer. Creating a fabrication operation meant investing in equipment that was very different to felt making, machines such as guillotines, clicker presses and punches. The operation also had to be in a secure dry environment separate from the hot steamy conditions of the felt making mills.

Many orders were small or required special shapes and were therefore manufactured with hand-operated machines such as a clicker press or an engineering fly press. A clicker press consisted of a robust top plate that could be made to hammer down on a cutter that was placed on the felt. It was operated by two handles with buttons on them, which ensured that the operatives could not catch their hands in the machine When the buttons were pressed the plate thumped downwards onto the cutter and returned to the upright position ready for the next cut.

Clicker presses cutting sheet in the Brynmawr factory of Cooper and Co

A fly press was a machine normally used in the engineering industry to stamp out metal parts. It consisted of a cutter fixed to a vertical shaft that could move vertically in a bearing; above this was a second shaft with a coarse screw thread cut into it, which seated into a threaded hole. Attached to the top of the screw was a lever arm with a handle on one side and a heavy counterweight on the other. By swinging the handle rapidly, the screw turned and travelled downward forcing the shaft with the cutter to follow it. This downward movement, aided by the counterweight, gave the momentum and power to the cutter to enable it to cut through the felt. After the cut, the handle was turned slowly in the opposite direction to lift the cutter and the machine was ready to process the next component.

A fabrication line at Coopers and Co. (Birmingham) Limited at their factory in Brynmawr c1980, using hand operated fly presses to cut felt

For large orders automatic punching machines were used and these had to be fed with long lengths of felt. Full width pieces of felt were processed on slitting machines to provide individual narrow width rolls that matched the widths of the punching machines. The end of a roll was fed into the machine and the felt parts were stamped out automatically with minimum maintenance. The machines were organised in banks of six, each bank being managed by a single operative, who made sure that the machines were constantly being fed and operating correctly. The establishment of such fabrication units was the perfect way to add value to felt and increase profitability with minimal extra cost. Not only could they offer customers a wide range of products but they could also reclaim felt that might otherwise have to be downgraded or scrapped. Because of their versatility and diverse product range these units were the most energetic and optimistic departments within a felt company, and significantly, only the felt fabrication operation of E. V. Naish remains as the last vestige of the felt industry in Britain.

The fabrication unit of Cooper and Co. (Birmingham) Limited, typical of the industry

DISPATCH

Dispatch was a vital part of the whole felt manufacturing operation because sales depended on the speed and efficiency with which the felt could be delivered to customers. Products from the fabrication units were dispatched by a different system than the way roll felts were sent out from the mill. Felt fabrication units had to be flexible, deal with small components, and dispatch small orders, whilst the mills were inflexible, handled large packages, and had to cope with large orders.

The dispatch and warehouse of Cooper and Co., which were typical of the felt industry

Typically, orders from the fabrication department were dispatched by independent carriers in cardboard boxes addressed to a variety of destinations However, dispatch from the mill had to be loaded onto lorries destined for just a few major customers.

FELT IN BRITAIN

TRANSPORT

To handle the large volumes from the mills, felt makers had their own transport departments that began in the earliest days when the road and railway networks were still underdeveloped.

A Bury and Masco Industries Limited lorry leaving Longholme Mill loaded with felts for delivery

Even in 1908, MASCO had a large transport fleet, which in those days consisted of horses and carts. They employed so many animals that the accumulated horse dung was a major problem and they had to resort to paying local school children to clear it[25]. By 1938, powered wagons were being used manufactured by Jensen and P&N and for long distances, much of the felt was transported by rail. However, transport by rail was slow taking four to five days for felt to travel from Rossendale to St. Helens. At its height MASCO owned thirteen lorries mostly purchased from the British Motor Company (BMC) and Guys.

The transport department was arranged so that every package and route was costed and charged out to the dispatching mill. There was a handling charge of 2s/6d per hundredweight and a charge was made for the length of the journey, usually of the order of fourteen shillings to £1.

By the 1970s, the haulage industry had become a sophisticated logistics operation and owning a dedicated lorry fleet was by comparison inefficient and prone to high capital and running costs. It made sense therefore, to contract the transport out to a professional haulage company and realising this Bury and Masco Industries disbanded its lorry fleet and transport department.

11 BLOCK PRINTING

BLOCK PRINTING AND FELT

The importance of block printing to the felt industry cannot be overestimated. In the early days, block printing was inextricably linked with felt and without this connection it is doubtful whether felt making would have developed into such a vibrant industry in Rossendale. Block printing was one of the earliest forms of textile printing, The process consisted of coating dye paste onto a carved wooden former and then transferring the incised design onto a fabric in order to pattern it. All the major felt makers had block printing works attached to them and it was a thriving industry with over a thousand block printers employed. Even the pioneer of felt making, John Wilkinson, had his own block printing works in his mill, and this included his own first-class designers, block cutters, colour mixing department, and an extensive block store[1].

The block printers of Mitchell Brothers felt works at Albert Mill c 1889 [2]

There were printing works at Myrtle Grove, Siss Clough, Todd Carr, Whitewell Vale, Albert Works, and Longholme Mill. Each printing works was divided up into different departments, known as sheds, each dealing with a different aspect of the block printing process. This ensured an efficient operation that controlled each part of the process separately and minimised contamination of the felt.

Paradoxically, as the felt industry expanded the block printing operation declined and one by one the printing works were shut until the last operation at Albert Mill was moved to Whitewell Vale Mill where only Masonic carpets were printed. By 1918, there were only a few block printers left, since most had been replaced by machine printing using copper rollers, which was well in progress by then[3]. Some time in the late 1950s, block printing ceased altogether, except for the printing of Masonic carpets, and at that time a huge bonfire, ten feet high, was made of the stored wooden printing blocks at Albert Works[4]. In 1957, Harry Clark became the principal printer of Masonic carpets, situated at Longholme Mill, and the printing had become so sporadic that it was a part time occupation for him, a role that he shared with warehousing duties. He had the distinction of making the last block printed Masonic carpet in July 1971 just before Longholme Mill shut, and as such he was the last block printer of felt in Britain and probably the world[5]. In fact, there were no new blocks made since 1957 and most were kept operational by the joiners.

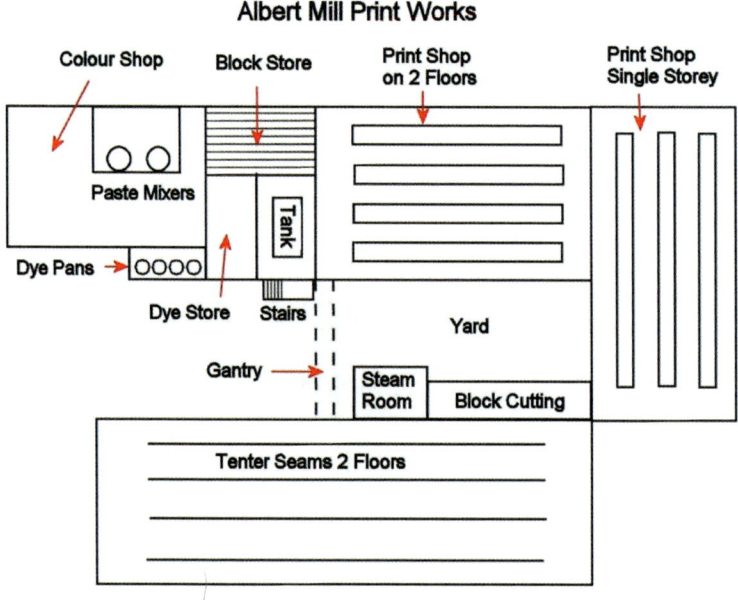

How the block printing works at MASCO's Albert Works Mill was arranged into sheds

Mitchell brothers tried to continue the printing tradition at Albert Works using two rotary printing machines, one with a three-colour facility, and another with a six-colour capability. Unfortunately for the feltmakers, the printing trade developed faster than they could, and it became less attractive for them to print on their own premises. Eventually it became expedient to outsource the printing of their felt altogether.

PRINTING BLOCK CONSTRUCTION

Originally, the blocks were cut by craftsmen in Albert Works from designs made "in house". In the latter days of printing in Albert Works, there was only one cutter and one designer (Alan Hanson), whilst at the very end of the block printing days, the blocks were sent away for cutting because there was no longer any expertise within the company to make the blocks. The wooden blocks used in the felt industry were sophisticated constructions made by craftsmen and were very different from the original blocks, which were simple wooden forms with a pattern carved on one face. Each block was made up of four sections: the printing face, a middle section, a back section, and a removable top. The printing face was usually made from hardwood such as ash or sycamore while the middle and back sections were made from softwood such as pine, and the removable top was a hardwood such as ash or oak.

BLOCK PRINTING

The author in 1982 with a block rescued from scrap, showing the printing face inset with hat felt

Apart from the removable top, each section was made up of boards six inches wide by one inch thick, which were stacked like layers of ply wood with the grains of one layer being orientated at ninety degrees to the adjacent layer.

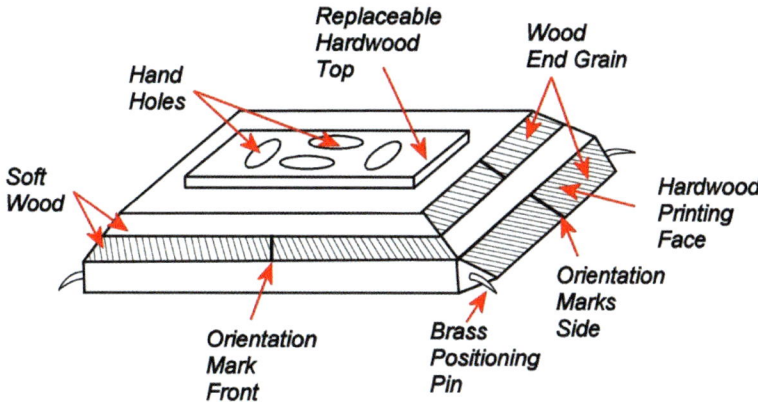

The construction of a printer's block

The laminated boards were bought from the timber yard in sheets approximately eighteen inches square and then cut to size by the block makers. The removable top was a single piece of hardwood in which the holes had been cut to take the thumb and fingers of the block printer's hand. Each top was tailor made on site to accommodate the individual printer's hand span. For a large block (about eighteen inches square), there were four span holes, and a smaller block had two, though four span holes were also used when it was necessary for the block to be turned when completing a pattern. The printer carved marks on the back of the block so that he could tell without looking at the pattern which way round his block was. The top was joined to the block with special iron nails that had a square shank with a flat circular head. In later times, these nails were replaced by screws; a practice frowned on by the traditional block printers. These tops were made within the mill and replaced at regular intervals since they were often damaged by the impact of the printer's hammer, or mawl.

The blocks were carved by a team of five block makers working on high stools at a high bench. The pattern was transferred onto the block by tracing over the design through carbon paper onto the block face and the pattern then carved out to leave a wooden relief, usually a depth of about a quarter to a half of an inch. The block was first chiselled out with a flat chisel by cutting V-shaped grooves on either side of the relief, making successive cuts until the grooves were wide enough and deep enough. Then with a special crank-shaped chisel the area between the grooves was chiselled out to a depth of a quarter to a half of an inch, making sure that the base of the cut was completely flat. For some extreme designs, the carving could be so deep as to expose the soft wood middle layer. During the carving, it was vital that the printing surface of the block was kept flat; therefore, the carver rubbed the surface over a completely flat sandstone plate, when he felt it necessary.

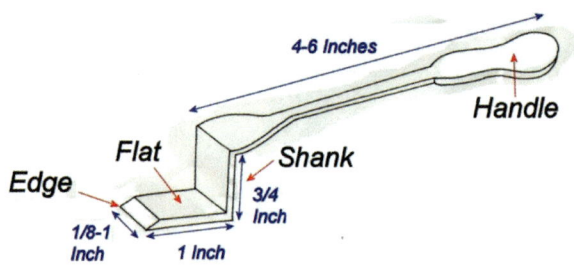

The special chisel for carving out the design in a printing block

Often a hat felt insert had to be used to improve dye transfer, and it was important that the base and surface were very level so that the insert gave an even surface. A felt insert was used when a large area of printing was required. For this, the area requiring the insert was chiselled out of the block except for a small retaining shoulder an eighth of an inch thick, which contained the felt. The material for the insert was a hard felt made from rabbit hair sourced from hat manufacturers based in Stockport. This felt helped to pick up the colour and gave good cover during printing.

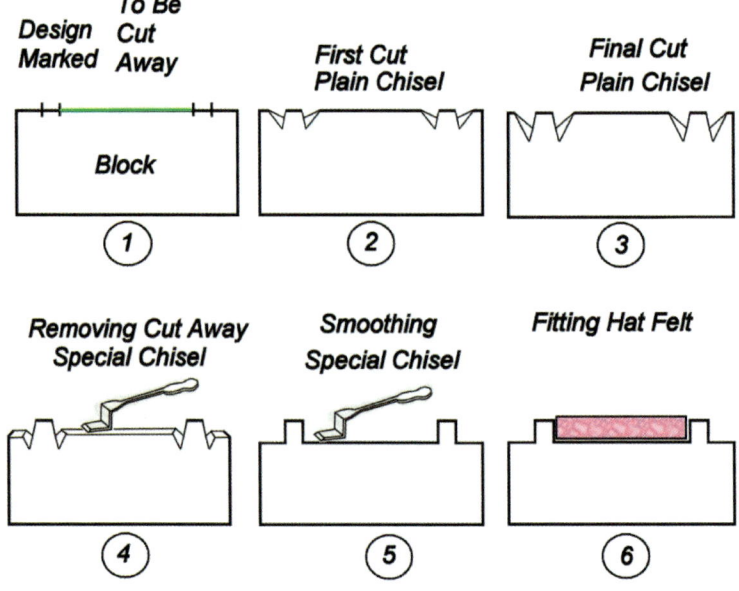

The sequence of carving out a printing block

To fit the hat felt, it was boiled in water and then knocked into the block for a tight fit, though sometimes glue was used to attach it to the wood. This ensured a good even cover over a wide print area, but the wooden outer edges of the retaining shoulder gave a crisp outline to the pattern. Where there were large areas that did not require to be printed, a large cavity had to be left in the block, and these cavities tended to trap air, as the block made contact with the felt to be printed. This air escaped sideward across the face of the block and carried with it some of the colouring, which spattered onto the felt and spoilt the pattern. Air holes were therefore drilled through the block into these cavities, which allowed the air to escape through the hole rather than across the face of the block.

The edges of the block were slanted so that the printer could clearly see the edge of the face section so that he could position the block accurately when printing. As a further adaptation, the four corners of the block were chamfered away and brass pointed claws, called pitch pins, were attached to them in such a way that they were visible to the printer from above. The objective of these pins was to precisely position the block to give an accurate register of the pattern, though to do this the pins had to be exactly square to prevent misalignment of the pattern. Before printing, the printer had to square the pins so that the design could be repeated accurately and in register. Using a set rule, the diagonals were measured and the pins adjusted until the diagonals measured the same. The squareness was crosschecked by setting the rule to be the same as the block width and then measuring the four sides.

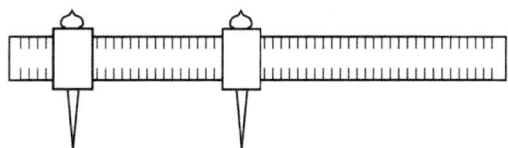

The set rule for aligning a block and marking out the pattern; the ruler was made of hardwood, and the two sliders made of brass

For simple prints or filling-in plain areas of a design, the printing blocks did not require pitch pins on them, but for complicated designs it was essential to have pins fitted to the blocks. When printing detailed designs, the very first block applied to the felt the pitch pins left four tiny holes in the felt where the pins had been and these were used to guide the positioning of the next part of the design. In the next application of the pattern, the block was positioned so that two of the pins on one side of the block were positioned into two of the holes that were furthest from the starting edge of the felt. When the block was removed after printing, there were two new holes made in the felt, which were now further along the felt. These holes were then used to locate the block for the next print application. This whole process was repeated for the full length of the felt. When one row had been completed, the pitch pins had left a complete row of pinholes running the length of the felt, and these separated the printed part from that awaiting printing. These pin marks also served as a guide for locating the block for printing the second row of the pattern.

Each block was a standard size, though the printer would also use a half-size block, for completing a pattern at the ends or borders[6]. Some of the patterns were simple and used only one or two blocks to complete the design, but some, such as Masonic carpets were extremely complex. The average Masonic carpet required twenty blocks to complete the design, whilst a typical carpet would require twenty-five blocks by eighteen blocks[7].

FELT IN BRITAIN

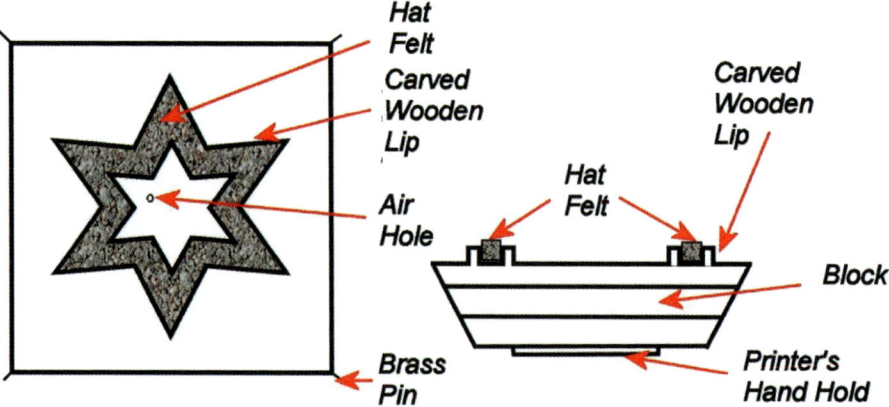

Showing the face of a printers' block for producing a star pattern, and a side view showing the carved lips containing the hat felt made from rabbit hair

The printers took great care of their blocks, which were scrubbed diligently after printing. They were stored overnight immersed in water in order to close any cracks in the wood that had developed and to keep the blocks receptive to the water-based printing paste. The hat felt inserts also had to be serviced. Where they were glued into the block, the adhesion had to be checked, and where they were fixed with panel pins, the pinheads had to be carefully covered with paste before printing.

THE PRINTING TABLE

The printing table was made out of four-inch thick stone slabs six feet by four feet mounted on six inch by six-inch wooden legs. Tables were around ten yards long and of two widths: one seventy-two inches wide for printing felts measuring seventy-eight inches, and one fifty-four inches wide for sixty-inch wide felts. The joints between the slabs had to be made with great care to ensure that the table was completely flat. This was done by chamfering the underside of the edges of the joining slabs and filling the joint with clay filled felt.

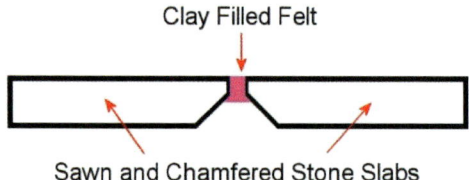

How the slabs in the block printer's table were joined

The surface of the table was covered with a special permanent dense felt, a quarter of an inch thick, to provide a cushioned support for the felt that was to be printed, and to absorb the impact from the printer's hammer as he struck the block. This protective felt was held in place by folding it over the edge of the table and bolting wooden battens over it along the full length of the table. Attached to these wooden battens was a metal rail or gill, divided into six-foot lengths on which tenter pins were mounted with the points facing downwards. These pins were for anchoring the edges of the felt so that it could not move whilst it was being printed. The edge of one side of the felt was first pulled over the pins and pressed into them so that they pierced the felt and held it firm. The same procedure was carried out for the other edge of the felt, on the opposite side of the table, though in this case the felt was pulled to stretch it to remove any creases and make it taut before it was engaged with the pins. To protect the printer during printing there was a hinged flap, which covered the points of the pins that had protruded through the felt.

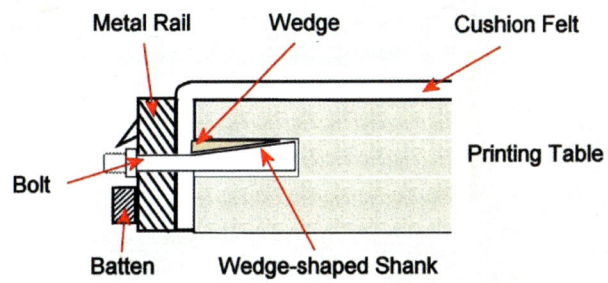

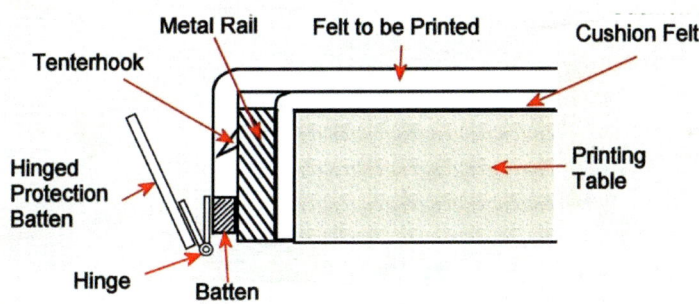

Fixture of the metal rail and tenterhooks on the edge of the printer's table, and the positioning of the felt and the protective flap about to be closed

THE PRINTER'S ACCESSORIES

THE TEAR TROLLEY

The heart of block printing was the tear trolley that contained the dye paste and all the accessories needed to prepare the printer's block for transferring the design evenly onto the felt. The trolley was a wooden tray two feet six inches square by six inches deep fixed to four wooden legs mounted on two axles which had cast iron wheels fitted to each end. This enabled the paste tray to always be on hand and follow the printer as he printed along the length of the carpet.

The tray was first filled with cow dung mixed with water to a depth of around two inches to act as a resilient layer followed by a fine mesh screen stretched over a two-inch deep frame, which contained the dung and prevented contamination. A third frame supporting a tightly woven hessian cloth was then placed on top of the screen, to contain the paste and allow smooth transfer of the paste to the block, later this was replaced by oilcloth when it became readily available. The importance of the cow dung was that it was cheap, gave good buoyancy to the upper frames, had the right resilience, and most importantly it did not dry up or change consistency. Once installed, the dung required changing perhaps once a year or every other year. Bull's dung was prized by the printers as it was reputed to give the best transfer of paste to the block[8].

FELT IN BRITAIN

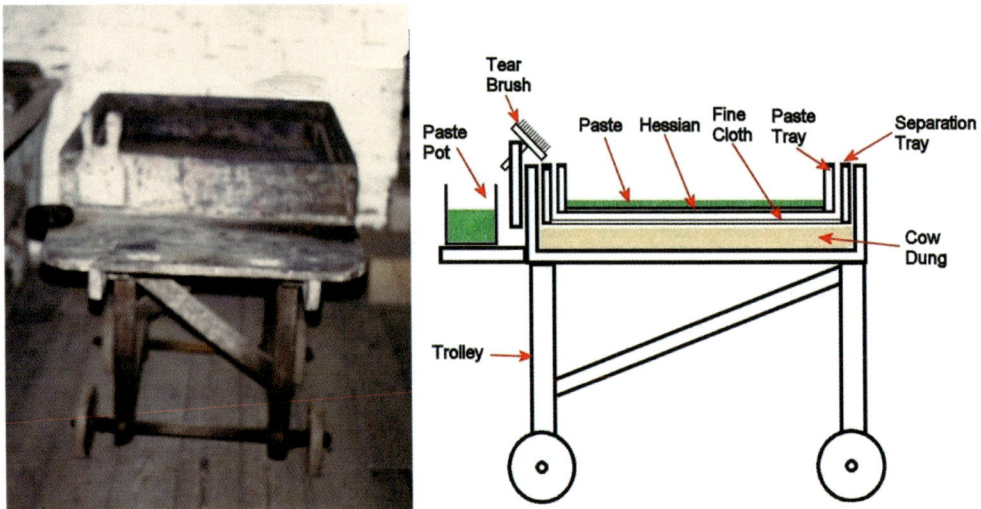

The tear trolley for applying printing paste to a block.

A fifth small wheel was mounted horizontally on the side of the trolley that ran along the edge of the printing table to guide the trolley and keep it at a constant distance from the table. Attached to one end of the trolley frame was a vertical U-shaped piece of wood that was used as a rest for the paste brush, which was used to spread the printer's paste.

THE PRINTER'S MAWL

Apart from the block itself, the mawl was the most important tool that the printer possessed. It had the appearance of a stubby hammer with a short squat handle; it was never used as a hammer. It was used by holding the mawl upright and striking the block with the base of the handle. The top hammer-like top was merely a heavy weight to give the necessary impact strength to ensure a good transfer of printing paste from the block to the felt.

The printer's mawl shown relative to a block used to make Masonic carpets.

The printer held the mawl close to the hammerhead, supporting its weight with his thumb in order to control it and have his hand furthest away from the block. After long sessions of printing, his thumb could become quite sore, so to protect it, the printer wore a leather pouch over it.

The mawls came in three basic sizes corresponding to the size of block that was being printed. The smallest had a cast iron head four and a half inches long and weighing five pounds and two were six inches long, one weighing six pounds the other seven pounds. The hafts were usually of oak but ash was also sometimes used.

TEAR BOY

Although not a material accessory, tear boys were essential to the block printer to provide him with all the material he needed at the correct time. In particular, the tear boy had to do all the messy jobs of dealing with the dye paste so that the printer could stay free of paste and therefore minimise the risk of contamination of the felt being printed.

One of the last block printers, Henry Suart on the right, printing a Masonic carpet with his tear boy, Ken Ritson (aged 15) who is brushing the paste onto the frame in the tear trolley, 1948.

The worst job that the tear boy had to perform was the preparation of the cow dung, which he also had to collect from the local farm. The main activity was during the printing process when the tear boy had the responsibility of keeping the paste pot filled and the tear trolley fed with the right amount of paste. The paste was applied by brushing the paste onto the hessian cloth in the top tray of the trolley, and making sure that the layer applied was spread evenly. The application of the paste was critical and the canvas had to be brushed both across and down the tray to get a good even coating. If

FELT IN BRITAIN

there was too much on the canvas it would cause blurring of the printed pattern, too little and the print would be patchy. The printer worked at considerable speed and the tear boy had to both move the trolley to keep up with him and apply the paste after each print of the block. The operation also had to be synchronised with the printer otherwise the tear boy, if he was too slow, would receive a painful reminder of a knock on his hand from the printers block. After each print run and after a day's printing, the tray had to be cleaned out or "teared" for the next printing, which was yet another messy job to be completed by the apprentice. Tearing consisted of scraping off the excess colour from the second tray and throwing the old dye paste away. The trays were washed in a large water tank three to four feet deep that was surrounded by draining boards specially constructed to facilitate cleaning the print blocks. The draining boards were of wood with wooden battens spaced at intervals to hold the block, so it could not move. The height of the battens was just less than the block so that the surface of the block was exposed to facilitate cleaning. The blocks were placed on the draining board and then scrubbed with a scrubbing brush and boiling water until none of the dye paste remained.

Although printing was essentially a male dominated activity, girls were also employed as tear "boys". Being a tear boy was the starting point for a career in the felt industry and many employees, later went on to command senior positions in the industry.

PREPARATION FOR PRINTING

The felt used was usually a coarse white that was one quarter to three eighths of an inch thick, and had been cropped and sanded to give a very smooth surface. Sometimes blue or red felt was used, particularly for church seating, which in these cases the printing was usually black. In some cases the felt presented to the printers had flaws in them and had to be corrected before printing. Repairs to carpets were done by cutting out a square, sewing in another piece of felt and printing over it. The most common repairs were from candle burns, rotting holes and moths, even though the felt was mothproofed before printing.

The felt was presented to the printer, either on the roll or plaited on a trestle, so that it was either unrolled on the table or pulled along the table from the pallet. One edge of the felt was then hooked over the pins on one side table and secured using a rubber hammer. The printer then pulled the other edge of the felt, fixed it to the pins on the other side of the table so that it was taut, and crease free on the surface. When the felt was especially narrow at a particular part, a special tool was used to hold the felt in place.

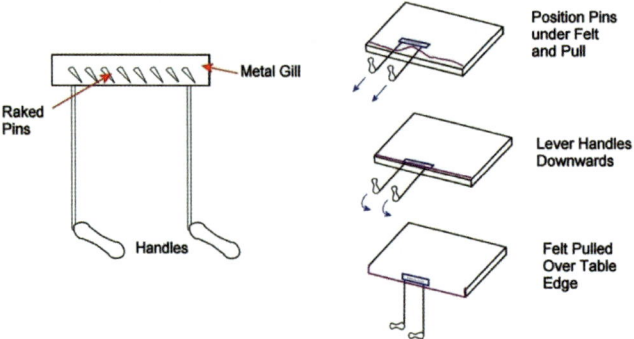

The printer's tool for stretching areas of felt where the width was narrower than it should have been.

The tool consisted of a set of raked pins fixed to an iron frame. The frame was attached to two handles, which were fixed at right angles to the frame and were gripped so that they pointed upwards. The pins were hooked into the felt and by pulling on the handles; the felt was stretched until the frame of the tool reached the edge of the table. The handles were then pushed down to increase the leverage until the felt was positioned over the edge of the printing table and the handles dangled downwards. The weight of the handles was sufficient to keep the felt in place and allow the printer to leave them positioned there until he printed over it.

The printer planned out on paper just how he would tackle the printing, knowing that his blocks were a standard size he was able to use this as his unit of measurement for the plan, which for a carpet design would be, typically, twenty five blocks by eighteen blocks. Using a wooden rule with sliding pointers, the printer measured and marked the centre of the felt at each end with a piece of chalk. A chalked piece of string was then stretched taut across these two marks, and plucked so that the impact of the string on the felt surface left a straight chalk line right down the middle of it. The line was kept stretched on two nails fixed to the walls and was refreshed regularly by the tear boy who walked up and down the line rubbing it with a block of chalk. This centre line was fundamental to the symmetry of design. The printer had to avoid leaning over freshly painted felt and therefore had to work from the centre of the felt outwards and so depended very heavily on the chalked centre line. The chalk was washed out at a later stage in the processing[9].

PREPARING THE DYE RECIPES

The two main ingredients of the printers paste were: china clay, (known as pipe clay), wool dye, starch and water. The china clay was first mixed with water in a wooden drum that was four feet high and thirty inches in diameter fitted with an agitator, and a tap at the base for emptying it. To make the mixture, the drum was filled with water until it was three quarters full, and two hundredweight of pipe clay added. The mixture was then agitated for thirty minutes until it was the consistency of cream.

The dye was mixed in a separate steam-jacketed copper cauldron, or kettle, which was three feet in diameter and two feet six inches deep. Ten pints of water were poured into the jacketed pan and raised to the boil, after which the dye powder was added and the mixture stirred well until the dye dissolved. To facilitate the measuring, special copper jugs and ladles were used that were designed to hold appropriate amounts of the dye ingredients.

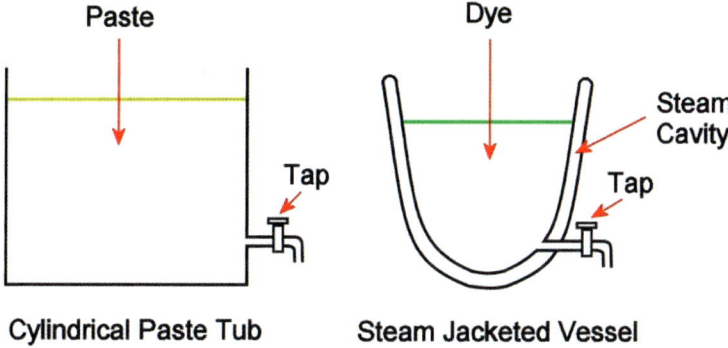

The two main vessels for producing the dye paste for block printing, the first is a cylindrical tub with a mechanical stirrer, the second is a steam jacketed vessel for boiling the dye.

A pound of starch was measured into a ladle and two pints of water added slowly without stirring in order to make a smooth "cream". The starch was then added to the boiling dye liquor stirring well all the time to make sure no lumps formed. When the starch had thickened one and a half gallons of pipe clay were decanted from the drum and added to the dye, stirring constantly to give an even distribution of colour. For some recipes, acetic acid was added and stirred in, to improve the dispersion of colour, whilst for some other recipes glaubers salt was also added to the boiling liquor. A typical recipe for bright orange was: two ounces acid yellow R, eleven and a half ounces of acid orange, and two gallons of paste. Whilst the mix was still hot and fluid, it was drained out through a tap into a bucket under the vessel and left to stand overnight. In the morning, it was just like jelly[10].

When cool, the paste was transported from the colour mixing area to the printing area by means of colour tubs. Each tub had hooks on the side in which poles were located so that it could be lifted and transported to the print room, with one worker at the front of the tub and one at the rear.

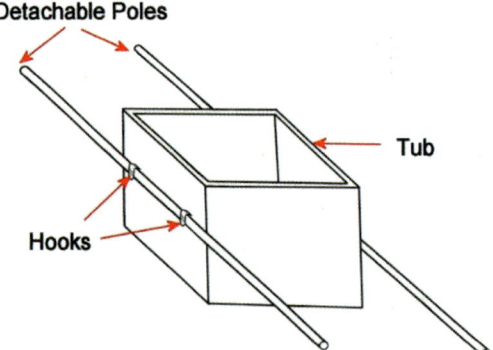

The paste tub used to transport paste to the printing shed

Once in the print room the tub was put into position and the poles removed to enable the dye-paste to be transferred to the container on the tear trolley using a special scoop. Everything was then ready for the printer to start work. When the tub was empty, the poles were reinserted and it was then carried back to the colour mixing room to be filled with more paste.

Occasionally during printing there would be areas missed by the block and so a special paste was required to fill in the gaps and correct the design. This was a mixture made up of methylated spirits, shellac, and the matching dye.

PRINTING THE CARPET

Planning how to execute the printing of the carpet was essential, because of the number of different blocks that were employed in building up a design, particularly for Masonic carpets. Transferring this plan onto the felt was also an important stage involving careful measurements using the printer's measuring rule. The measuring rule was set to the width of the block and the pointed tips of the rule were dipped in the printing colour and then pressed into the felt on the centre chalk line, which acted as a reference. The rule was used like a pair of dividers to make locating marks along the full length of this centre line. These marks were consequently spaced apart at a distance exactly equivalent to the width of the block. The first marks to be made were the most critical since the register of the design for the whole carpet depended on them. Great care was therefore taken over measuring these first marks from the leading end of the felt.

For every print pattern, there were two sets of blocks. The first set provided only the outline of the pattern and were carved so that the pattern stood in relief on the blocks to give the complete pattern in outline. The second set of blocks contained the pattern detail and this always involved large areas of in-fill, and for these, the hat felt inserts provided an even spread of the paste. To ensure a good even print layer the tear boy painted the canvas in the trolley with exactly the right amount of paste and the printer thumped the block hard down onto the painted canvas. The combination of the two actions gave just the right distribution of paste on the surface of the block ready for printing.

When printing, the printer relied heavily on the use of the pitch pins at the corners of the block to reproduce the design accurately. To start the printing he first located the two pins on the leading edge of the block onto the first two marks made by the rule when the design was planned. Once this block transferred the design and was lifted, it left two new marks in the felt from the pitch pins on the trailing edge of the block. These new pinholes served as markers for re-locating the block and the printer made sure that the pitch pins of the next block fitted neatly into these holes. This guaranteed that the register of the pattern was maintained. Once the block was in place on the felt, it was struck with the haft of the printer's mawl twice, once at each corner of a diagonal. The block was then carefully lifted vertically and the whole process repeated. This was a repetitive process and the printer and tear boy established a rhythm of applying paste, pasting the block, and printing, as they steadily worked along the full length of the felt.

Once the outline pattern had been completely printed using the first set of blocks, a second printing had to take place immediately to fill in the detail. If this was not done quickly, the outline would dry and harden, which would create a noticeable edge when the second set of design blocks were printed. If the outline dried by mistake, it had to be scraped off and a fresh colour outline printed

For Masonic carpets there were two main block sizes, twelve inch square and six inch square; though on occasions a sixteen inch block was used for high-speed printing.

The standard designs available for Masonic carpets produced by MASCO

Because of the design complexity only twelve feet of Masonic carpet was printed at a time, otherwise the outline would have dried before the second printing could occur. A Masonic carpet was also difficult to print because it needed two full-width felts sewn together to make one carpet. One felt on the table ready for printing represented only half a carpet and therefore the printer was working with an asymmetric design and this made it difficult to keep the pattern register exact. Each carpet had a centre pattern, a border pattern, and an extra border surrounding the whole carpet. For a Masonic carpet, the border was usually twelve inches wide with a two inch black surround. In the case of the outlines for these carpets, the printing had to be done twice to give a clear outline edge. The outline was then filled in with a six-inch square or in some cases a block with a pattern of two squares. Each masonic carpet had its own description and designation and for the benefit of the printer, it was given a number specifying the centre and border designs. Therefore, a carpet could be assigned the number C2 B11 meaning centre pattern 2 with border pattern 11. The most impressive Masonic carpet, not shown on the brochure was the Eastern Star, which had many feature designs such as a lamb, star, lily, and lion.

For all printed felts, once the printing was complete the surface of the felt was sprinkled with sawdust and released from the tenterhooks on the table. The sawdust prevented the printed surface from sticking to anything it touched so that the integrity of the design was maintained. The felt was dragged off the table by attaching a rope to one end and hauling it over a roller suspended from the ceiling in order to plait it onto a trestle. The felt was then transferred to a specially designed trolley made from a rectangular frame, measuring six feet long by four feet wide and six feet deep, which had hooks along its top edge on which to hang the felt.

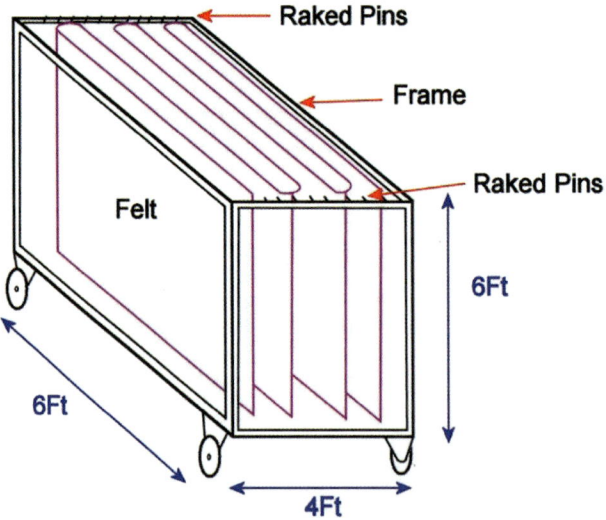

The trolley used for steaming the finished printed felt in the steam chamber

One edge of the felt was first hung from a pin on one side of the frame then fed to the other side of the frame, to fit on a separate hook. By repeating this backwards and forwards across the frame, the whole felt length could be accommodated within the small space. The edge that was hooked was the selvedge that contained the tenterhook marks and so was not printed, and was later cut off. The trolley containing the felt was then transported to the steaming room.

STEAMING WASHING AND DRYING

The frame was designed so that it could be wheeled directly into a special steam chamber, where three trolleys at a time could be steamed. The chamber had a door that slid closed and was secured with a closing wheel, similar to a submarine hatch. The locking mechanism had a hook welded onto it so that a long bar could be attached to it to increase the leverage in order to seal the chamber securely. Live steam was fed from a Lancashire boiler into the chamber and through the perforated floor, allowing the pressure to build up to a level of between five and ten pounds per square inch. At that pressure, the door clicked into place. The felt was left steaming at that pressure for thirty minutes to one hour in order to set the dye into the wool, after which the pressure was released and the chamber allowed to cool down.

When the felt was removed from the steamer, it was lifted off the hooks, put onto a trolley, and wheeled to a washing betty where the paste and excess dye was washed off. After a thirty-minute wash, the felt was mangled one last time before loading it via an overhead winch into an hydro-extractor, where it was spun until no water came out of the outlet. The felt was then removed for drying in the hand tenter seams.

The drying of the printed felt had to be done by hand on tenters to ensure that the integrity of the design could be maintained by suitable adjustments of the tenter rails whilst tensioning the felt. Special care had to be taken over the Masonic carpets because they were mostly of a checker board design which had to be maintained square as any distortion was immediately obvious. Also to make a finished Masonic carpet two felts had to be sewn together and the pattern had to match exactly along the full length. For this reason, machine drying could not be used because it always distorted a felt during the process and matching the design of two felts exactly was therefore impossible[11].

The felts were left in place overnight on the tenter seams whilst the felt dried, after which they were ready for final finishing.

FINISHING

The carpet was trimmed by hand with scissors and the border was cut off, just in front of the tenterhook holes, to leave a clean edge. The felt then had the MASCO phoenix trademark stamped on the back together with the design number, and it was finally packed ready for dispatch. This trademark was also block printed and the phoenix block for this was special in that it consisted of a wooden base with metal strip inserts that were raised a quarter of an inch above the wood to give the high definition required.

For a Masonic carpet, the two felts involved were laid face to face and the middle edges joined with over-locked stitches using white cotton. The carpet was then opened out and because of the over-locked stitching, there was a ridge down the middle of the carpet. A wooden bobbin was then run along the length of the joint, which pushed the two edges together and stretched the stitching to give a flat joint. Where the white cotton cut across a black square it was touched up with black ink and when it crossed other colours it had to be painted with the appropriate ink.

MISCELLANEOUS BLOCK PRINTING FACTS

It took one man three days to complete the printing of a twelve feet by eight feet carpet, whilst a twenty-four feet by twelve feet carpet took fourteen days to complete.

FELT IN BRITAIN

Church seating was printed four at a time on a single felt fifty-four inches wide using a table that was sixty inches wide. There was a black border separating the designs with an allowance to give half an inch border to each. The felt was printed with twelve-inch blocks and every yard of carpet required two outliners, and one filler-in, which meant twelve printings for each foot; or forty-eight blocks per yard.

One printed felt carpet went to Buckingham Palace with a leopard skin design around the time that Harold Macmillan resigned as Prime Minister. There were one dozen pieces fifty-seven inches wide and thirty yards long and the design required its own special rack for holding all of the blocks required for the different colours. It was around this time that printed mats and oval rugs were very popular

MECHANISED PRINTING

Machine printing eventually replaced block printing and when this happened the felt makers lost their major added-value advantage as machines could produce good commercial products without the skill necessary in block printing. The felt makers tried to maintain its printing capability by investing in machines but soon lost out to dedicated printers.

Each of the two rotary printing machines installed in Mitchell Brothers' Albert Works had a huge main cylinder with large copper rollers mounted on it. Each copper roller was engraved with the pattern to be printed. The roller dipped into a bath of printing paste, so that the paste filled the engraving and the excess was scraped with a steel wiper so that the paste only lay in the recesses of the rollers.

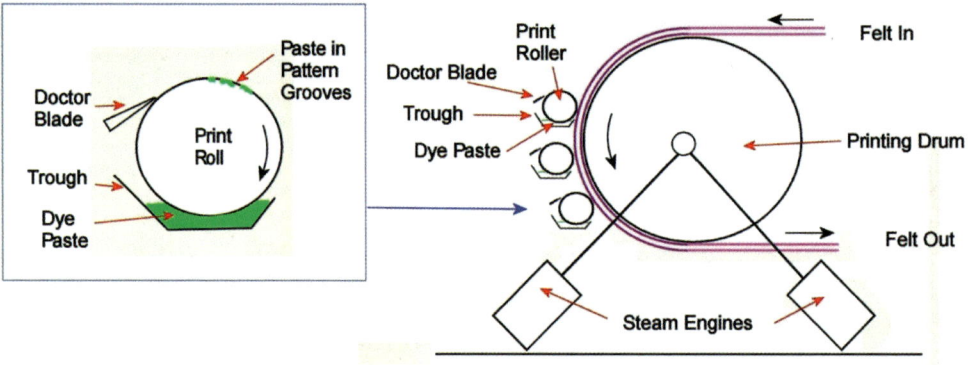

The three colour-printing machine installed in MASCO's Albert Works.

As the felt moved round with the main cylinder it passed under the roller and the paste was transferred onto the felt. Each roller had a key attached to the bearings on one side of the machine to alter the register of all the rollers before the machine was activated. This ensured that each of the different colours applied by the different rollers matched the printing design so that there was no blurring, and the pattern was crisp and sharply defined. The machines were driven by two inclined opposed steam engines with twelve-inch diameter bore and twenty-four inch long stroke[12]. After exiting these machines, the printed felt was treated the same way as that produced by block printing.

12 THE PROPERTIES OF FELT

OVERVIEW

The properties of a felt are derived from four fundamental characteristics: dimensions, weight, density, and fibre composition, though these can be modified by the finishing treatments used. The effects of dimensions, thickness, width and length, are tangible and self-evident but they are critical to the application for which the felt is used. For example a felt seal will be of little use if it is undersize, and there would be little point in having a wick that is too short to deliver a lubricant. The measurement of these dimensions, together with the weight, enables the density of the felt to be clearly defined, and this in turn determines virtually all of the physical properties. How the fibres are laid in the carding process can also affect the physical properties of a felt depending on whether they were laid straight or cross-laid or whether the felt was made in layers that contained different fibres.

The chemical properties of a felt are controlled by its constituent fibres. For an all-wool felt the properties would be those of wool fibres and since these are composed of mainly keratin, the chemistry of such a felt will be that of keratin. Fibre blends containing other fibres such as viscose rayon or casein alter the chemical properties of the felt away from keratin and more towards their individual chemistry. For example, an all-wool superfine will not burn but decompose into a char, but a superfine with seventy-five percent rayon in the blend will burn happily because viscose is a flammable material. The choice of fibres also has an effect on the aesthetic and subjective character of the felt, such as colour, texture and handle. Finishing treatments can add properties to a felt to enhance felt's natural characteristics. These treatments can be chemical, such as mothproofing and flameproofing, or they can be physical such as, cropping, and pressing.

MEASURING FELT

Measuring the width, length and weight of a felt are simple operations because they are done on a macro scale and the act of measurement does not interfere with the result. However, measuring the thickness of a felt is fraught with difficulties because the thickness is on a micro scale and the thickness changes with the least pressure applied. Different people measuring with the same calliper or micrometer will therefore record completely different thicknesses. Even an optical method would not work satisfactorily because of the diffuse or hairy surface of the felt. A universally accepted standard for measuring the thickness was therefore devised and adopted by the various standards organisations such as the Society of Automotive Engineers (SAE), American Society for Testing and Materials (ASTM), British Standard BS 4060, and British Defence Standard 83/19/1. This method involved measuring the felt with a dial gauge micrometer under a standard pressure. The pressure was set at 0.62 pounds per square inch for all felts with a density of over 0.14 grammes per cubic centimetre, which covered the majority of felts produced. However, felts below this density, such as waddings, are ultra-sensitive to pressure so a much lower level of 0.13 pounds per square inch was set as the standard for measuring their thickness. A special instrument was devised to make measurements to these standards, which consisted of a circular steel disk welded to a spring loaded micrometer, that was mounted vertically, on a frame with a solid base. The surface area of the disk was one square inch and weighed ten ounces so that the instrument could exert the necessary pressure. The whole assembly resembled a miniature press.

The felt was placed on the base plate and the disk of the micrometer gently lowered onto the felt and then left to settle under its own weight, before the value was read off the dial. This reading gave the standard thickness of the felt.

Measuring the thickness of a piano felt at Royal George Mill showing the dial micrometer calibrated in millimetres and the disk resting on the felt and generating the right pressure for a standard measurement

This technique was perfect for testing in a laboratory or for small pieces of felt that could easily be transported, but was too cumbersome for use in the mills. Under production conditions, the thickness of a felt had to be measured at intervals across its width, which could be up to seventy-two inches across, therefore the standard testing instrument was impractical. Because it was necessary to measure the thickness in the middle of the felt, a portable gauge had to be developed that was at least thirty-six inches long. The resultant instrument was an extended C-shaped frame with a jaw thirty-six inches long and a micrometer fixed to one side of the jaw at the opening. A disk was welded to one end of the micrometer and another of the same diameter was welded to the opposing jaw. The micrometer was spring loaded so that it could generate the standard pressure between the two. The whole assembly had to be extremely stiff so that the arms did not bend and cause a false or variable reading.

At the same time, the gauge had to be light in weight so that the operative could handle it easily with one hand without being fatigued. The instrument was therefore made from aluminium and the structure braced with strategically spaced ribs to give it the necessary stiffness.

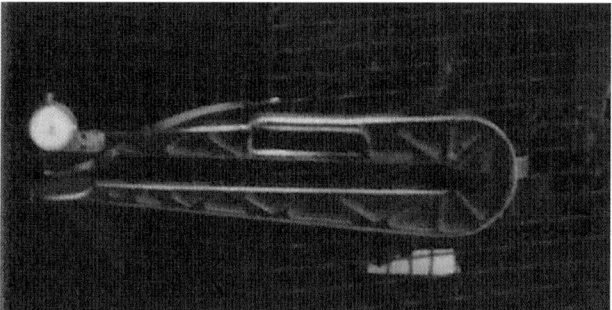

A portable thickness gauge for measuring felt thickness across a felt.

To make a measurement, the plates were opened by a trigger that was positioned on the handle, and the felt was slipped between the jaws. The trigger was released, the plates were closed over the felt, and the thickness recorded on the dial of the micrometer. To ensure consistency, the gauges had to be regularly calibrated against the laboratory standard gauge. These gauges were the indispensible mainstay of the industry and were to be found throughout the mill ensuring that felts were made to the correct quality specification.

Measuring the felt thickness accurately was vital, because the density of the felt and all other physical characteristics of the felt were derived from this measurement. To calculate the density, both the volume and the weight of a piece of felt had to be measured. Firstly, the volume was determined by measuring the area of a selected piece of felt and multiplying it by its thickness. The piece of felt was then weighed using a sensitive balance, and the density calculated by dividing this weight by the volume. If the area was measured in square centimetres, the thickness in centimetres, and the weight in grammes, then the density was recorded in grammes per cubic centimetre (gm/cc). The convenience of this unit of measurement was the fact that water has a density of 1 gm/cc, making it easy to compare the felt density to that of water. For example a felt of density 0.5 gm/cc was 0.5 times that of water, i.e. a half. The measurement of felt density when compared to that of water is therefore known as specific gravity, so a felt of density 0.5 gm/cc is a felt of specific gravity 0.5. In other words to convert density expressed as gm/cc to specific gravity, just miss off the units gm/cc. Other units of density were also used such as pounds per cubic yard but these do not have the simplicity or versatility of gm/cc. As an extension to specific gravity, felt density was also referred to as "percentage specific gravity", which was calculated by multiplying the specific gravity by one hundred. The only reason for doing this was for the convenience of dealing with a whole number rather than a decimal.

Felt is the only textile that can be produced at any specific gravity from 0.1 to 0.7, which means it can be made as fluffy as goose down or as compact as oak. To add to this uniqueness it can also be produced at virtually any practical thickness up to six inches. To cope with such an infinite number of variations the felt industry and its customers organised standards based on a defined range of felt densities. For technical felts, the most commonly used standard was that devised by the Society of Automobile Engineers (SAE), which accorded a simple identification symbol for each of the densities, though other organisations such as the UK Ministry of Defence, and ASTM had their own standards.

The fact that some densities had more than one identification label indicates the complexities of classifying felts by their density. For a given density, there could be significant differences in the fibre type, blend, and even the fineness of the wool that could alter the nature of the felt. The importance of this was recognised by the ASTM by indicating felt differences in its nomenclature. The first part of the identification was a number that described the density, which was designated as half the value of its percentage specific gravity, giving a number ranging from nine to thirty two. The second part was a letter defining whether the felt was manufactured in the form of a roll (R) or a sheet (S). The last part was another number from one to four to show whether the felt was white or grey, and whether it was made from fine or coarse wool.

THE DESIGNATIONS OF FELTS OF DIFFERENT DENSITIES BY DIFFERENT STANDARDS

Density gm/cc	0.12	0.14	0.154	0.18	0.26	0.34	0.35	0.4	0.45	0.56	0.68
SAE Specification			F-26	F-10 F-11 F-12 F-13	F-5 F-6 F-7 F-55	F-1 F-2 F-3 F-50 F-51					
Ministry of Defence Def 1138A Specification	T1407	T1404	T1120 T1406	T1115 T1121 T1282 T1119	T1114 T1118	T1116 T1117	T1403	T1113 T1281	T1402		
ASTM Specification CF 206				9R1 9R2 9R3 9R4 9R5	12R1 12R2 12R3 12R3X 12S1	16R1 16R2 16R3 16S1 16S3 16S4	18R1		20S1 20S3 20S4	26S1 26S3 26S4	32S1 32S3 32S4

THERMAL CONDUCTIVITY

Felt is an excellent insulator of heat. The heat resistant properties of a felt are determined partly by the wool, which is a good insulator, but mostly by the air that is trapped in the voids of the felt. This is because air trapped in small spaces is almost a perfect insulator. The more spaces that there are in a felt the better insulator it becomes. Because the free space in a felt is related to the density, there is a direct relationship between the thermal conductivity of a felt and its density.

The thermal conductivity of felt is linearly related to its density. The values show that felt was able to compete with the very best of insulators: low-density felts gave the same thermal insulation as kapok and at higher densities performed like cork or wood. With this sort of versatility, felt outperformed the majority of existing thermal insulators.

The relationship between density and the voids in a felt also has implications for other felt properties. Knowing the free space in a felt can give a useful insight into how a felt will perform in other situations, particularly if the space can be quantified The free space can be calculated by dividing the density of the felt by the density of pure wool, which is 1.314 gm/cc, and then subtracting the result from one. This gives the volume of the space as a fraction of the volume of the felt. For example, a felt of 0.44gm/cc will have free space of (1- 0.33) = 0.67, or two thirds, of the volume of the felt, which means this felt has more spaces than fibre.

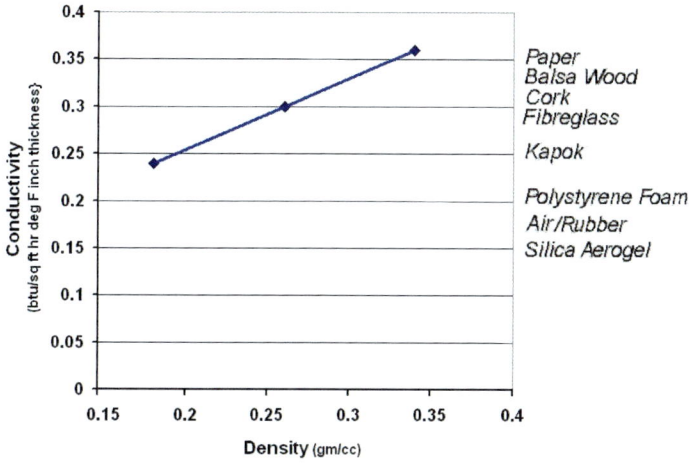

The thermal conductivity of felt at different densities compared to other materials

AIR PERMEABILITY

The air permeability of a felt is a measure of how much air can pass through it at low pressure. The airflow was usually measured in cubic feet per minute when a pressure difference of half an inch of water can be sustained across a felt one millimetre thick This low-pressure drop was set at this level to simulate the conditions of breathing, because permeability is the most important property used for assessing facemask filters. The airflow through a felt also depends on the area over which the air blows, thus, for comparison purposes, the permeability is calculated for the flow over an area of one square foot. The units for air permeability are therefore cubic feet of air per square foot per millimetre of felt.

Air permeability depends upon how many holes there are in the felt for the air to pass through, the more spaces the greater the permeability. Low-density felts have a large proportion of free space and give little resistance to air flow so that they have a high permeability. Dense felts are more compact and resist air flow so they have low permeability. The relationship between permeability and density is hyperbolic, which means that if a felt could be produced at zero density the flow would be infinite and if it could be compacted to have no spaces the flow would be zero.

For low densities, below 0.2 gm/cc the felt was used extensively for facemasks because it was easy to breathe through and at the same time it was capable of trapping particles that were thirty to forty-five microns in diameter. These felts were therefore capable of filtering a wide range of unwanted particulates such as pollen, hair, and coal dust. Felts at the higher densities such as 0.5 gm/cc the felt could remove particles as low as one micron but at low permeability, therefore they needed more pressure to force air or fluid. These were therefore used to great effect for filtering compressed air in sub-aqua gear and anaesthetic equipment.

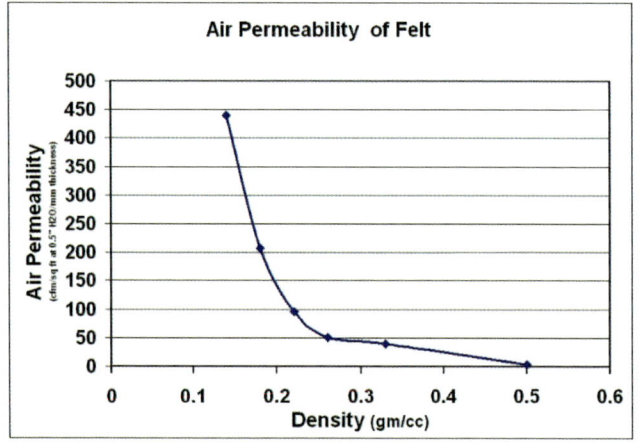

The air permeability of felt related to density[1]

TENSILE STRENGTH

The other physical properties of tensile strength, split resistance, hardness and compressibility, are also related to density but are more dependent on the degree of entanglement of the fibres than directly on the voids as is the case with permeability and thermal conductivity. Tensile strength is determined by measuring the force needed to pull a dumbbell shaped piece of felt at constant speed and measuring the force at which the felt breaks. Unlike most homogeneous materials like metals or plastics, felt does not break with a clear snap but the force gradually reaches a maximum and then tails away. This is because the fibres gradually disentangle rather than break under the stress. Tensile strength, therefore, gives a measure of the degree of felting that has taken place.

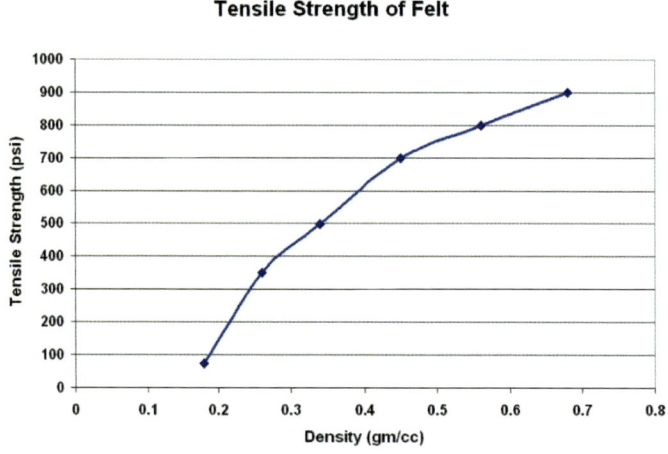

The maximum tensile strength of a felt when compared to its density

Typically, the strongest felt breaks at around one thousand pounds per square inch whilst the breaking strength of a wool fibre is around twenty thousand pounds per square inch. Another consequence of the unravelling of a felt under load is the extension of the felt to its breaking point, which can be in excess of thirty percent of its original length.

The strength of a felt also depends on how the fibres are laid down during the carding process. The strength of a felt when tested in the direction of the fibre can be twenty-five percent higher than when tested perpendicularly to the fibres, though this difference is much smaller in the case of a cross-laid felt. Dense felts tend to be homogeneous because they are heavily milled and the high degree of fibre entanglement minimises any directional strength difference.

SPLITTING STRENGTH

Closely allied to tensile strength is the splitting strength, which is a measure of the force required to split the layers of a felt apart. The test consists of making a cut through the thickness of a felt to form two wings that can be gripped and pulled apart.

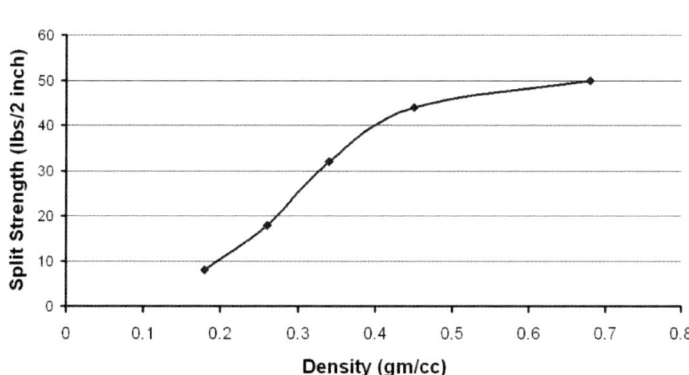

For low density, felts the wool fibres are only lightly interlaced and so pull out easily without any individual fibres breaking, and so gives a low split strength. As the density increases, the split strength also increases because to achieve these higher densities the felt has to be milled more heavily, a process that achieves greater entanglement of the fibres. Consequently, greater force is needed to disentangle the fibres and in some instances, there may even be fibre breakages. At very high densities the fibres are even more locked together and many more wool fibres are broken than are disentangled as the layers are split apart, leading to the highest split strength. This is shown by the way that the graph flattens out at high densities.

The splitting strength is a direct measure of the degree of felting that has taken place in a felt. Pulling on the wings of the felt during the test has the effect of straining the fibres between the adjacent layers of the felt. Before felting, there are no fibre linkages between the layers, and split strength is zero. Hardening and milling, migrates fibres across the layers to bind them together, and as the felting increases so does the number of fibre linkages. The force splitting the layers apart therefore measures the number of these linkages and the total felting that has taken place.

HARDNESS

For some engineering and technical uses of felt, its hardness was an important property. For example, felt became a rubber substitute during the two World Wars, because it was as hard and resilient as rubber, and rubber was in short supply. The match was so good that felt was even considered for use as vehicle tyres. Examining the hardness of felts at different densities shows just how realistic a proposition this was, in spite of the seemingly improbable concept.

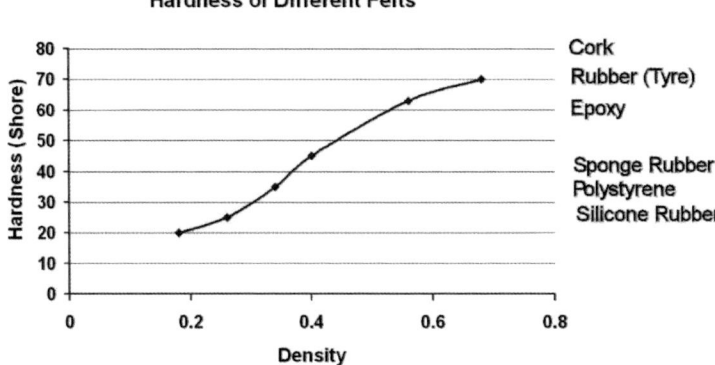

The hardness of a felt at different densities compared to other materials

In terms of hardness, felt could match a whole range of different soft materials from silicone rubber to cork. In particular, the hardness at a density of 0.68 gm/cc matches that of the rubber used in motorcars

COMPRESSIBILITY

Compressibility is not commonly used but it has relevance where a felt is put under a load, such as in civil engineering applications where there are load-bearing applications.

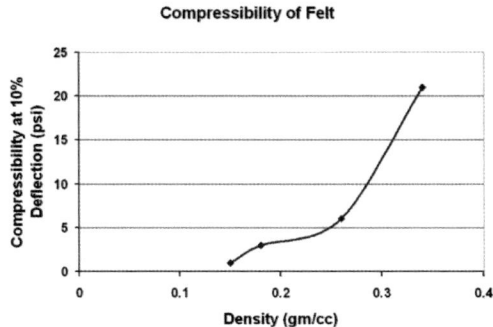

The compressibility of felts at different densities.

More important is the degree to which a felt can recover from being compressed. Virtually all felts have a remarkable ability to recover to ninety-seven percent of the original dimensions after a load is removed. This made felt ideal for anti-vibration applications and as seals, where the felt could maintain a constant contact with a rotating surface even when the shaft was grossly distorted,

ANTI-VIBRATION

Because felt can be made with an infinite variety of properties, it has the ability to dampen any vibration, whether it is sound or mechanical vibration in solid objects.

In the case of sound two situations arise where deadening is required. The first is where sound needs to be prevented from rebounding from a surface, for example to restrict echoing in a room or for creating a sound proof booth. This is known as reflection. The second is where sound needs to be prevented from travelling between two separate areas, for example two rooms separated by a wall, and this is known as transmission. These two forms require two very different materials to be effective. In the case of reflected sound, the material needs to be soft, pliable and open to absorb the sound waves. To prevent transmission of vibration, a very heavy dense layer of material is needed to dissipate the energy as the vibration travels through it. Significantly, a material that absorbs sound allows a high transmission through it, whilst a material that does not allow sound to pass through it reflects most of the sound falling on it. It is remarkable that felt can satisfy both of these criteria. A low density felt is very effective at absorbing sound, whilst high-density felts are very efficient at preventing the transmission of sound.

In many applications, mechanical vibration is caused by machinery with rotating parts, which produce vibrations at frequencies linked to the rotation. These need to be isolated from the surroundings in order to limit the noise and discomfort that they produce. Any anti-vibration mounting must therefore have the ability to oppose the frequency of vibration and this involves an understanding of the principles of resonance. Every object when struck will vibrate at its own natural frequency and unless it is struck again the vibration will rapidly die away. However, if the object is repeatedly struck at the same frequency as the natural frequency of the object, the vibration will amplify and build up sufficiently to destroy the object. This is known as resonance. If a material has the same natural frequency of vibration as that of a machine they will vibrate together and there will be total transmission of the vibration through the material. Therefore, to stop the transmission of the vibration an anti-vibration material needs to have a natural frequency that is as far as possible from that of the machine. Most machine vibrations are above twenty cycles per second (Hertz) and the resonant frequency of felt is between one and eight cycles per second (Hertz), which makes felt an excellent anti-vibration material. However, if felt is to be a useful anti-vibration material it must be able to support the weight of any machinery placed on it. If low density felt were used for heavy machinery, the weight would compress it and, though it would act as a high density felt in its compressed state, it would not be a stable mounting. Therefore, it is important that the density of felt matches the weight of the machinery. When a machine vibrates, it effectively jumps up and down, varying its force on the mounting, which therefore needs to be made from a material that can recover quickly from compression. The excellent resistance and recovery from compression of a felt makes it one of the most efficient anti-vibration materials available and because it can be manufactured to any density, it can be specifically engineered to give the maximum effect for any installation.

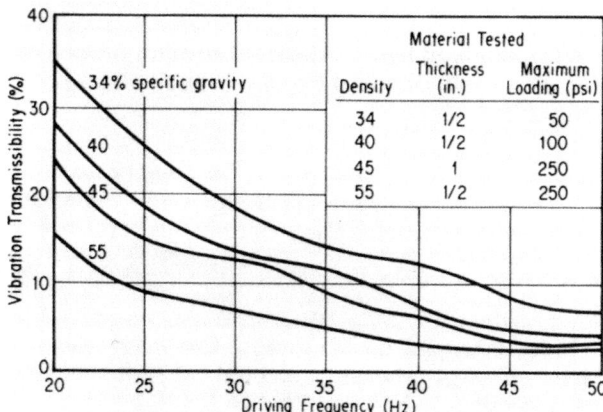

The effect of density on the anti-vibration properties[2] of felt. The density is measured here as % specific gravity which is the same as density multiplied by one hundred

The design of anti-vibration materials is a complex calculation that is often unique to the circumstances involved and designing with felt is no exception. The advantage that felt gives to designers is the way that the resonant frequency of a felt depends on its density, the lower the density the lower the resonance. Meanwhile, the higher density felts can withstand considerable loading in terms of pressure that can be precisely engineered for each unique situation. A designer could, therefore, select a suitable anti-vibration felt by specifying its density.

When a machine is vibrating at twenty cycles per second, a high density felt of density 0.55gm/cc (specific gravity 55%) it will only allow fifteen percent of the vibration to be transmitted through it, which is referred to as a transmissibility of fifteen percent. By contrast, a felt of density 0.34 gm/cc will allow thirty-five percent of the vibration to pass through it. At higher frequencies, all the felts give transmissibility far less than ten percent. Lower densities, however, could not support commercial loads and are therefore not included in the graph overleaf. Where these low-density felts excelled was in floor coverings where floor vibration or the action of walking produced low frequency vibrations of around eight cycles per second and the pressures in these situations were very low.

WATER SWELL

To achieve the optimum felt properties, the felt must be milled to the correct density. In practice, the density often fell short of the specification by milling alone, particularly for the denser felts and in order to meet the requirements the felt was pressed in a steam heated press. Of course, by doing this, the tensile properties were lower than they should have been in a fully milled felt, along with other properties. Fortunately for the feltmakers, the allowed tolerances (usually plus or minus ten percent) ensured that, providing there was not too little milling, the adjusted felt could meet the lower end of the specification. Pressing rather than milling properly was a tempting option since this was a lower cost operation. At first sight it was difficult to spot whether a felt had been pressed rather than milled, though felts that had been pressed tended to give a more wrinkled surface than a properly milled felt. The clearest method of establishing the degree of pressing that had taken place was by immersing the felt in water. A felt that had been pressed would swell in thickness whilst a fully milled felt would hardly swell at all. By measuring the thickness change, the degree of pressing could be determined.

The water swell test consists of first measuring the original thickness of the felt when dry and fully conditioned. The felt is then immersed in water and thoroughly wetted out, after which it is dried and then allowed to be conditioned to the same moisture content as the original. The final thickness is then measured and compared to the original thickness. Water swell is then the difference between the two measurements when expressed as a percentage of the original thickness. Water swell therefore measures the degree to which a felt has been pressed.

OTHER PROPERTIES

Most of the chemical properties of felt are dictated by the properties of wool and to a lesser extent by other fibres that are constituents of the blend. Wool is a natural protein fibre that is similar to human hair and made up of keratin, which is a combination of around nineteen different amino acids joined together into a long polymer chain. This chain is difficult to break down by chemical treatment and because of this wool felt too is resistant to most chemical treatments. Therefore, felt is resistant to most acids, such as nitric, hydrochloric and sulphuric acids, even at raised temperatures. In fact, sulphuric acid is commonly used in many felt processes such as milling, dyeing, and in the carbonising process to remove vegetable matter. However wool, and hence felt, is particularly vulnerable to alkaline substances at high concentrations and will actually dissolve in caustic soda. When the alkali concentration is weak there is little effect on the wool or felt, and this makes it possible to mill felt in soap solutions that are in themselves alkaline. In addition, because of the stability of the keratin molecule, wool felt is unaffected by the use of organic solvents.

Felt is unaffected by heat and does not melt at higher temperatures nor does it decompose at temperatures less than two hundred and fifty degrees Celsius. Because wool has a low heat of combustion and a low rate of heat release, it provides felt with a degree of flame resistance when exposed to a naked flame. Furthermore, if wool comes into direct contact with another burning surface, it will not melt or stick, and is self extinguishing once the initial ignition source is removed. When exposed to a flame the surface of a felt bubbles as the wool decomposes and then turns to carbon forming a flame resistant layer that inhibits further burning. In this state, any flame present on the felt is just the burning of the gases that are released from the high temperature decomposition of the wool. The flame is therefore not easily propagated along a felt. Wool felt is harder to ignite than most equivalent synthetic felts because it has a higher ignition temperature,

A greater degree of flameproofing can be achieved by the application of flame proofing agents derived from the borate and phosphate salts such as Flamcide™. These treatments are usually applied as a solution and dried to deposit a flame retardant salt on the surface of the felt and, because this is not permanent and can be easily washed off, they are termed non-substantive. The International Wool Secretariat developed a flame retardant system whereby the chemicals were bonded onto the wool molecules and were therefore permanent and resistant to washing. This is known as a substantive system and used complex zirconium chemicals such as zirconium hexafluoride and was trademarked under the name Zirpro™

Wool felt is an efficient absorber of potentially harmful indoor air pollutants such as formaldehyde, nitrogen dioxide and sulphur dioxide, and because of the porous nature of the felt it presents a high surface area to volume ratio that can be very effective in removing these unwanted chemicals from the local environment[3].

Although wool is an efficient absorber of potentially harmful ultra violet, UV-A and UV-B, radiation in sunlight[4] wool can decompose by the action of sunlight where the sulphide links in the keratin are broken down to form sulphuric acid, giving the surface of the felt a discoloured harsh feel. Dyed felts, too, suffer from UV exposure and the surface discolouration is enhanced by the deterioration of the dye colour.

Felt also has an abundance of other less explored, property advantages that have been instrumental in ensuring its use in a myriad of technical applications. Felt is amazingly durable since it resists ageing and remains dimensionally stable for decades, as witnessed by the recent ancient discoveries in Russia[5]. The durability arises from the extreme flexibility of the wool fibre as well as the structure of the felt. A wool fibre can be bent back on itself more than twenty thousand times without breaking, compared to about three thousand times for cotton and two thousand times for silk. This effect is enhanced in a felt because its structure allows the wool fibres to move over each other during the flexure of the felt. This enables more fibres to share the flexing action and diluting the flexing forces on each individual fibre. Wool fibres are inherently abrasion resistant because of the presence of the scales and the hard outer structure of each fibre. However, the fibres in a felt are mechanically interlocked and can be pulled out during any abrasion action to give a fluffy surface or produce a pilling effect. The abrasion resistance of felt is therefore dependent on its density. The low-density felts do not really abrade, but fibres are pulled out. In medium and high density felts the wool fibres are so tightly interlocked that they cannot be pulled out during abrasion and therefore the resistance becomes that of pure wool. At these densities, the abrasion resistance is high, making it eminently suitable to be used as seals for rotating shafts.

Wool fibres are hydrophobic, because the surface oils tend to repel water, which gives felt a degree of water resistance. However, water vapour can penetrate the structure of a wool fibre most readily and to a surprisingly high degree. Wool can absorb up to thirty-five percent of its own dry weight of water, which is far superior to synthetics that take up less than four percent and cotton less than twenty-four percent. This is known as moisture regain. Because of this, felt is anti-static since the presence of this trapped water is sufficient to prevent the build up of any charge on the surface of the wool. Because of the oil on the surface, wool fibres can attract other oils ensuring that a high surface tension exists between them. Because of the porous nature of felt, there are a large number of effective capillaries within its structure. These coupled to the high surface tension makes the felt highly oleophilic ensuring that any oil in contact with a felt will be rapidly sucked up. These properties can be readily appreciated by dipping a piece of felt into an oil/water suspension; the oil is immediately removed by the felt leaving all the water untouched.

Among its other features, felt can be machined, cut, ground, formed and die-cut into intricate, high-precision shapes, and will keep these shapes because, unlike other fabrics, it is non-fray. It remains flexible and dimensionally stable from temperatures as low as minus fifty to plus eighty degrees Celsius. It can also be moulded, heat formed and bonded to virtually any surface. Felt is truly an amazing material.

13 PRODUCTS

BACKGROUND

Innovative uses for felt were pioneered by the makers of hat felt and they set a trend that was continued by the feltmakers who followed them. It all started when they combined felt with asphalt, which led to a host of new applications that were far removed from the modern concept of felt as a decorative material. George and William Borradaile (also known as Borrodaile) were the first to promote asphalted hat felt for use as a building material, which they sold for use in the construction of bridges and railway lines. They also encouraged the use of their material in the cladding of ships during the process of copper bottoming. From this sprang the roofing felt industry where asphalted felt was used as a low cost alternative to thatch in farm buildings. The move to continuous processes to satisfy these demands created a ready availability of product in long lengths, which led to the establishment of very new markets undreamt of by the Borradailes. Although the industry split into two forms of manufacturing, namely hair felts and wool felts, there was always an overlap between the two, with hair felt producers having a small capacity for making woollen felts and the wool felt makers maintaining a limited production of hair felt. However, both industries often pursued the same product end uses such as insulation and carpet underlay. For those markets where asphalt impregnation of hair was necessary, a third separate industry developed, which also adopted the name "felt" even though it evolved in a completely different direction.

It was only when sufficient quantities of woollen felt became available that its range of properties and versatility were fully appreciated, and from this felt was able to penetrate almost every aspect of life. In many cases felt became so inextricably linked with the end use that the product became identified with the name "felt" even when the product no longer contained any woollen felt. Hence the use of terms such as "roofing felt", "felt tip pen", and "fuzzy-felt", which are household names and yet do not contain a single fibre of wool.

In the early days of felt production, the outlet for most of the capacity was for floor coverings in a variety of forms, from rugs and mats to twelve feet wide carpets. By the turn of the nineteenth century, technical products were in the ascendant as the carpet production declined, so that the market profile of the industry was split equally between domestic and engineering products. This continued to be the pattern up to the 1980s, but as the synthetic felt industry started to gather pace many of the products previously supplied by woollen felt were gradually replaced. Although the market profile remained little changed, the total output of the woollen felt mills declined dramatically, and without the investment and new product development, the felt industry's demise was inevitable.

Alarmed by the decline, all the British felt manufacturers met together to form the Pressed Felt Manufacturers Association with the objective of trying to reverse the trend. They pooled resources to promote pressed felt through technical brochures, magazine articles and public relations events. They also met regularly to share data, to monitor trends and to decide on future actions such as research into felting, but this was to no avail. Then as felt companies merged, the association itself fell into terminal decline, and by the twenty-first century, it was defunct.

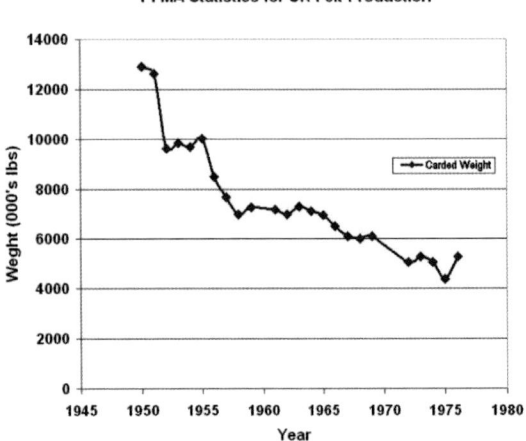

The decline in the woollen felt industry measured by the weight of carded wool produced, as recorded by the Pressed Felt Manufacturers Association.

Despite this decline, felt still penetrated a huge range of markets and in some cases dominated them. By 1980, the majority of felt was being used in the engineering sector, where its properties were highly valued, though the craft and exhibition industries were still dominant markets.

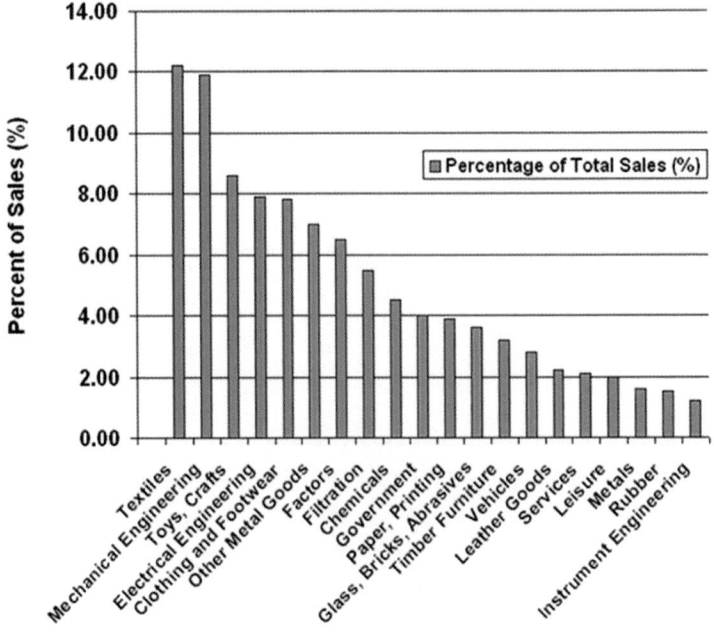

The relative importance of markets penetrated by felt products in 1982

CARPETS AND FURNISHING

Before the invention of the pressed felt process, a carpet as floor covering was a luxury only affordable by the rich. Before 1840, carpets were made by hand in a tapestry weave, with one weaver capable of producing only five yards in twelve hours. These carpets were also severely limited in width, being nine inches wide, and it took one weaver a week to make a thirty-six yard length[1]. In contrast to these statistics, a thousand yards of felt carpet fifty-two inches wide could be made using one carding engine[2]. This gave the early feltmakers a distinct economic and commercial advantage. The resultant low cost of felt carpets made them affordable to the middle and even lower classes. As production machinery and power looms became available for making tapestry, Brussels, Kidderminster, and Wilton carpets, prices of woven carpets dropped significantly. By the 1860s Kidderminster carpet was selling at 2s/6d per yard, tapestry at 2s/6d per yard, and Brussels at 4s/1d at a width of thirty-six inches[3], whilst felt carpet was selling at 1s/7d per yard fifty-two inches wide. At less than half the price of woven carpet, felt remained highly competitive, so it is hardly surprising that the output of felt carpet in 1856 was still substantial at around 3.6 million yards per year[4].

Until 1850, there were only two manufacturers making felt carpets: The Patent Woollen Cloth Company who trademarked their felt under the name of Royal Victoria, and John Wilkinson Son and Co. These companies' products were highly regarded in their time and both of them won gold medals when they exhibited at the Paris Universal Exhibitions of 1851, 1862 and 1867. Wilkinson was also a prizewinner when he exhibited his felt products in the Yorkshire Industrial Exhibition of 1862. At that time, his carpets were made and sold in a large assortment of designs, in various qualities, and prices ranging from 10d per yard, for a thirty-inch width, to 3s/6d. per yard for fifty-two inch width[5].

After 1854, carpets were increasingly manufactured in Rossendale and by 1867, there were two hundred people making one million yards of felt per year there, most of which was for carpets. In 1893 there were four manufacturers of felt and tapestry carpet in Rossendale, employing four hundred people paying them £400 per week to produce 3.7 million yards/week with a capital of £160,000[6].

By the 1930s, the mechanisation of the manufacture of woven carpets had expanded to such a degree that the speed of production and the economies of scale made them the preferred floor covering. Even so, the width limitations of woven carpets and their cost restricted them to squares positioned in the middle of the room, leaving a surrounding border of floorboards. In 1888, the costs were: 5s/9d a yard for the carpet and 6d for making and laying[7]. The border round the carpet was decorated either by staining the boards, or more aesthetically by laying down a layer of plain felt carpeting around the edges. This plain woollen surround felt was made fifty inches wide in up to eighty different colours, and because felt was non-fray, it could be cut to any width to fit the carpet border. The felt itself was of medium weight, a sixty-seven-yard piece weighed a hundred and thirty to a hundred and forty pounds, and though mostly plain, it was printed with various designs to supplement the main carpet. This gave the production of felt carpeting an extended lease of life, even though it was at a significantly reduced volume. The central woven carpets had a much harder tread than felt and customers preferred the soft luxurious feel of a felt carpet. By putting a coarse felt underneath a woven carpet, it provided the carpet with a resilience and feeling of comfort that the market demanded. This was the birth of the modern underlay market. Underlay felt was very different than the traditional woollen felt, because it had to be much cheaper and was therefore made from mostly cow or horsehair, and waste fibres. Although this market was developed by the feltmakers, it rapidly diverged from the industry and was taken over by specialist hair felt manufacturers who used needle-punching manufacturing processes.

An exhibition of Mitchells, Ashworth, Stansfield, and Co in the early 1900s, rugs and carpets were major markets, a small number of industrial items are on the right just below the red saddle felt

As well as making carpets, the majority of feltmakers manufactured smaller pieces such as felt druggets and rugs, which included animal rugs, hearthrugs, decorative rugs and even bath mats. For example, Richard Rostron was manufacturing white, green and crimson druggets[8] in 1891, as advertised in the local directory. The bath mats were printed in bulk and later cut to the standard size of fifty inches by twenty-five inches, though for large orders they could be cut to any specified dimensions. Druggets were a special kind of low cost floor covering that could be cut to size and used in several ways. They were mostly used to cover and protect an expensive woven carpet, particularly in dining rooms, or they could be used as a cheap square or a rug to cover the floor, and occasionally they were used underneath good quality rugs. The market for these products proved to be particularly enduring, more so than mainstream carpets, with production being continuous from the inception of the first felt making machines in 1840 until the late 1950s.

Printed felt was also produced for stair carpet and, as woven carpet replaced it, a low cost felt was produced, which was used as a stair tread underlay in the form of stair pads. The felts that were used as stair pads were made of jute and cow hair, manufactured in continuous lengths, and then cut to size. The pads were then finished off by stitching around the edges with braiding. After this, they were impregnated with a stiffening solution and dried around hot pipes in such a way that they had a lip at one edge. This was designed to fit over the riser of the stair to improve the wear that usually occurred at the edge of the step.

Gem stair pads made by the Bury Felt Manufacturing Company Ltd. from a print of a copper litho block

With all this activity on floor coverings, it made sense for Mitchells, Ashworth, Stansfield, and Company to take over the Boulinikon Felt Company that made an impregnated floor covering. This would have fitted their flooring distribution network and be an addition to their range particularly since they had production facilities that could manufacture it. Invented by John B. Wood in 1865, Boulinikon was the forerunner of linoleum and consisted of animal fibres such as hair and wool, as well as vegetable fibre such as jute, impregnated with a solution of vegetable oxide with colouring matter. It seemed to offer the durability of "oil cloth" in its resistance to dust and damp but at the same time had the elasticity that gave the feel and warmth of a carpet. Apparently, it was highly regarded by Bolton Town Hall Committee in 1874 because they installed it in their town hall to general approval[9]. However, in general Boulinikon received only limited acceptance and was soon eclipsed by the versatility of linoleum[10].

Mattress pads were also made with a similar process to making stair pads, though they were manufactured without stiffening and were made in lengths of six feet three inches and widths of two feet six inches, three feet and four feet six inches. They were made of coarse grey felt three quarters of an inch thick, which was cut to size and then fitted with eyelets at each corner The mattress pads were used in the days before spring interior spring mattresses when the springs were fixed to the base of the bed. The pads were placed directly over the springs and secured to the bed with string through eyelets inserted in each corner, and then a feather bolster, similar to a modern duvet, was placed on top of the bed for added comfort. Eventually the pads were sold in significant volumes to overseas markets as bed mats, affectionately called saddles. As a supplement to this market, blankets were manufactured for the native tribes of South Africa, with each tribe having its own stripe pattern.

When interior sprung mattresses were introduced felt found an alternative market in soft white felt washers that were shaped like a flower and used for reinforcing the stitching that held the two sides of the mattress together. At each end of these stitches and on the surface of the mattress, was a small metal pin that supported the tension needed to secure the internal springs. On its own, this pin would have worn through the mattress cover very easily by the constant movement of someone sleeping on it. To cushion the pin against the cover the felt washer was threaded on to the stitching string so that it was positioned underneath the pin. The pin was pulled down tightly on the felt, which because of its softness enveloped it almost completely, so that anyone sleeping on the cover could not feel it. The softness of the felt enabled the pin to move around and dissipated any frictional forces within the felt layers without damaging the cover. This market was one of the most durable for felt and these washers were being manufactured right up to the closure of the British felt mills in 1994.

There were many attempts to move felt into other furnishing areas such as upholstery but the tendency of felt to bagginess precluded it for this application and felt never penetrated this market. Nevertheless, it did find a most surprising use for church seating, where it was used as a covering for the wooden pews of most churches.

Poster advertising block printed MASCO church seating, it was the same quality as carpet felt

Felt gave some level of comfort from the unforgiving hard wooden seats and was particularly warm on a cold winter's day. They were made eleven to thirteen inches wide to fit exactly the pew dimensions and were sold in lengths of forty-two yards, which was enough to cover several rows of pews. The seating was sold in a range of printed patterns as well as being sold in plain colours, mostly crimson, green and blue. There were three grades: best quality designated CS, Medium quality designated MCS, and a cheap quality labelled LCS. It is a mark of the durability of these felts that examples can still be seen in some churches in the twenty-first century over sixty years after their manufacture.

Even though felt was generally unsuitable as an upholstery fabric it was used extensively as seat padding, particularly in the growing transport market. When orders were received for seat padding they were usually for very large quantities that could fully occupy a felt mill. It was such a large order from the Metropolitan Carriage and Wagon Company of Birmingham for the London General Omnibus Company that was the saviour of Siss Clough felt works.

Allied to the furnishing market were products that used felt for its display qualities rather than its other physical attributes. The first of these uses was as a table cloth, described as a significant market for The Patent Woollen Cloth Company in 1851, in both printed and embossed forms. Tablecloths and table mats made from superfine felt were still in use by the 1950s and even by the twenty-first century it was still being used as the backing material for Unique Table Pads, which was a table protector that folded up into a compact shape for ease of storage. In the early days, felt was also used as a curtain material but this was not popular for very long.

The display characteristics of felt came into their own in a relatively recent new market as an exhibition covering. Felt had long been known as a covering on a small scale for products like notice boards and shop window displays, and there was even a felt wallpaper made from felt laminated to a paper backing. From these beginnings felt became popular as a covering in major exhibitions where it was used on an altogether different and massive scale. In setting up a major exhibition, shell stands were erected to an overall design and the spaces rented to exhibitors. Originally these stands were painted by an army of painters working to a strictly short deadline. Over time, the cost of painting escalated with the cost of raw materials, and exhibition deadlines were often compromised by the contract painters going on strike for more pay. The use of felt became an attractive lower cost alternative to paint, particularly when using a superfine felt made with seventy-five percent of cheap viscose rayon fibre. Also, large areas of exhibition space could be covered faster with felt than by painting. As an added advantage, covering exhibition stands with felt could use unskilled labour because only stapling was needed to fix it to the boards. In 1982, virtually every major exhibition used felt for its covering and Bury and Masco Industries Ltd. had a Krupp cross-laying machine working continuously with ninety percent of its output producing display felt. By 1984, the cost difference between the two methods was marginal and other materials such as synthetic non-wovens and loop pile material were beginning to compete in the market, heralding the end of felt as a mass display material. An interesting but minor market for felt in the display market was in the exhibition of bricks by a prominent brick manufacturer who used felt in a totally different way. This company used strips of off-white felt three-eighths of an inch thick to simulate mortar at their showroom, and at exhibitions where they built temporary dry walls to show off their bricks to best effect.

In spite of the dominance of woven carpets, felt was still popular as a floor covering well into the twentieth century and was still highly valued as witnessed by the fact that Bury and Masco Industries Limited was granted the Royal Warrant as felt and carpet makers to Queen Elizabeth II. This honour was accorded for the felt carpet that was supplied to cover the royal ballroom. The Masons too valued the aesthetic and spiritual quality of felt that transcended from ancient times and they adopted felt as the material of choice for their ceremonial carpets. So important was this, that Masonic carpets were in continuous production right up to the late 1950s, and were the very last felt carpets to be manufactured and block printed. In modern times, the expertise for making carpet felts was fortunately retained and used to develop a new and unexpected outlet as an indoor bowling green surface known as "Cambria". This felt had the ideal characteristics to simulate the playing surface of grass and it was laid down in specially built indoor rinks that enabled flat green bowlers to continue playing indoors during the winter months when the outdoor season was over. The surface was judged to be so good that the world indoor bowling championships were held on it. Indoor greens used significant quantities of felt, since one rink used twenty one rolls forty two yards long, sixty nine inches wide, and four millimetres thick. A single bowling club had up to six rinks.

A promotional leaflet published by Bury Cooper Whitehead Limited explaining the rules of the short mat bowling game, and two Regalgrene short mat carpets laid out in a village hall

Even as late as 1980 bowling green carpet was being manufactured and the market was extended by the introduction of a new foam-backed carpet designed exclusively for the growing sport of short mat bowling. This new sport consisted of a mat up to forty-five feet long and six feet wide with an obstacle placed at its centre around which bowlers had to negotiate their bowls to a jack at the opposite end. The great advantage of the sport was that every hall or club could accommodate one and however uneven the floor the foam backing could guarantee an even playing surface. This brought indoor bowling within reach of anyone without the need for expensive maintenance fees. By 1984, the newly formed Bury Cooper Whitehead Limited Company had become the leading supplier of short mats with their trademark "Regalgrene"

PIANOS

From the earliest days of piano making by Christofori and Silbermann the piano action has seen a continuous evolution into the complex mechanism of modern times. Throughout this time felt has played a prominent role in its development and found increasing usage in different parts of the mechanism.

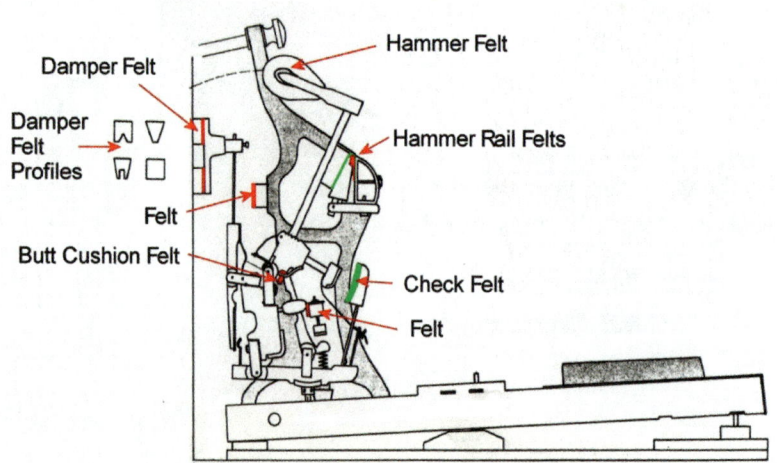

A piano action designed for an upright piano showing all the areas where pressed felt is used

The first, and by far the largest, usage for felt was as a covering for the hammer that strikes the wire strings. The properties demanded of a piano hammer are extremely exacting because it had to be capable of producing a mild soft tone for pianissimo playing and yet have sufficient resilience to deliver and survive fortissimo playing[11]. Felt is ideal for this purpose since the more it is struck the denser it becomes. It is therefore hardwearing and resistant to constant striking against the wire strings. Furthermore, its homogeneous nature means that the surface can easily be re-softened by pricking it with a needle when the felt becomes too hard and the piano needs re-tuning.

Felt was first used as a hammer felt in America via a patent by Alpheus Babcock in 1833, who used hat felt for the purpose. At that time, three felts of different densities had to be used for the bass hammers in order to produce the correct tone and resilience. It was only in 1887 that Alfred Dolge developed hammer-forming machines that could handle felt as thick as one and a half inches thick, which made it possible to produce a hammer with a single felt rather than with three different types. Although single felt hammers were commonly used from this time, high quality pianos used two felts in the hammer to produce the best tone: a dense felt as an inner layer known as under-hammer felt, and a somewhat softer felt on the outside. A further complication to making a hammer was that the different notes required the felt to have differing properties, the higher the note the denser and thinner the felt needed to be. Henri Pape, in 1839, improved on Babcock's invention by making a complete sheet of felt for all the hammers from bass to treble, the sheet being thick on one side at one and three quarters of an inch, and thin on the other at one sixteenth of an inch.

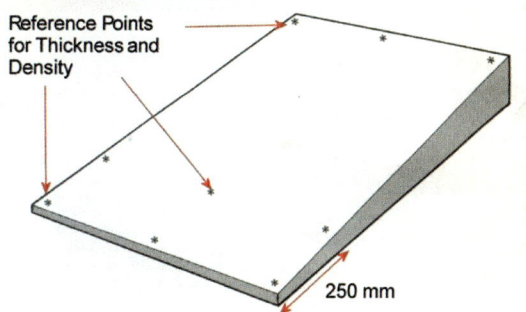

A tapered hammer felt sheet showing the points necessary to define the characteristics of the piano hammer set. The thicker part of the felt is for the lower notes and the thinner part for the higher notes

Henri Pape could therefore be said to be the inventor of tapered hammer felts, which were universally used right up to the twenty-first century. This made it possible to cover all the hammers in a piano at once using a special forming machine, Once the hammers were covered and glued in place, the felt was then easily cut between the hammers to release them individually.

Three types of piano felt were made: top hammer felt for the outer covering of the hammer in a natural white colour, under hammer felt for the layer nearest the shank that was dyed in a range of shades, and celeste moderator felt also natural white in colour. The celeste felt was a thin felt that was hung on a rail in the piano so that when the middle pedal of the piano was depressed the rail dropped the sheet between the hammers and the strings in order to mute the sound. The reduction in loudness achieved by this made it ideal for practicing, hence the name "practice pedal".

Because each piano manufacturer had their own preferences for the performance of their pianos, the felts had to be individually made to their exact specifications. To do this the felt makers required the length and width of the overall sheet and the properties of the felt at nine crucial points on the sheet, three at the bass end, three at the treble end and three two hundred and fifty millimetres from the treble edge. The most important properties required were the thickness in millimetres and the hardness, usually measured in SHORE units. An alternative to hardness was a measure of the density because there was a direct relationship between hardness of a felt and density; information on one gave the value for the other. However, this was a destructive test since samples had to be cut out to measure the density at specific points. Most of the major piano makers were continental or from the Far East, therefore measurements were made in metric units rather than the traditional imperial units, which were preferred by British feltmakers.

Common dimensions for top hammer felts were widths and lengths between nine hundred and eighty and one thousand and seventy millimetres, a thickness between three and a half, and fifteen millimetres for high-pitched notes, and a length of twenty-one millimetres and a thickness between, five and thirty-eight millimetres for low notes[13]. Under-hammer felts were usually dyed red and of a standard size, seven hundred and fifty millimetres long by nine hundred and eighty millimetres wide, and two millimetres thick for the treble and eight millimetres for the bass. The total weight of the sheet was two kilogrammes[13]. On average, a single taper hammer felt sheet provided the felt for fifteen pianos.

The inside of an upright piano showing the piano hammers. The hammers are resting on the back rail cushion, which is a green baize, the red felt at the top, damps any vibration outside the string bridge.

The celeste or moderator felt was made in standard sizes in a range of different weights and thicknesses. The sheet was nine hundred and ten millimetres wide and one thousand two hundred and fifty millimetres long. The lowest weight sheet was two hundred and twenty-five grammes and was two millimetres at the bass end and one millimetre at the treble. The medium weight was three hundred and forty grammes measuring three millimetres thick at the bass and one and a half millimetres at the treble; the heaviest weight was four hundred and fifty grammes, four millimetres thick at the bass and two millimetres at the treble[14]. To fit the celeste rail the sheets were cut into strips one thousand two hundred and fifty millimetres long by forty millimetres wide and attached by one edge to the wooden celeste rail so that it hung down like a curtain in the piano.

The damper felts were also made in sheets four hundred and forty millimetres square but of a constant thickness and there were two types, one for the treble dampers, and one for the bass dampers. The treble dampers were produced in two densities, 0.13 gm/cc and 0.15 gm/cc, and two thicknesses, eight millimetres and nine and a half millimetres. The bass dampers were made in 0.23 gm/cc and 0.27 gm/cc densities with the same thickness as the treble dampers. The damper felts were available in sheets measuring four hundred and eighty millimetres by five hundred and seven millimetres. The piano felt makers also offered a service to produce the dampers cut to shape so that they were ready for assembly during the manufacture of the piano. E. V. Naish for example offered cut bass damper felt and quoted the number of pieces that could be obtained per kilogramme of felt: a 0.23 gm/cc density felt gave one hundred and twenty-five pieces of wedge and seventy seven of clips whilst the 0.27 gm/cc density felt gave one hundred and four pieces of wedge and sixty pieces of clip. There were four types of damper shapes, wedge, clip, split and square. The wedge was cut as a V-shaped strip, the clip was a square strip with a V-shape cut into it, and the split was similar to the wedge but with a cut down the middle, and the square was self-descriptive. The dimensions of each of these types could vary between piano manufacturers as they sought their unique tones and performance from their pianos. The wedge damper felt was used to mute two strings at a time by fitting between them, and the clip damper was used to stop a single string from vibrating.

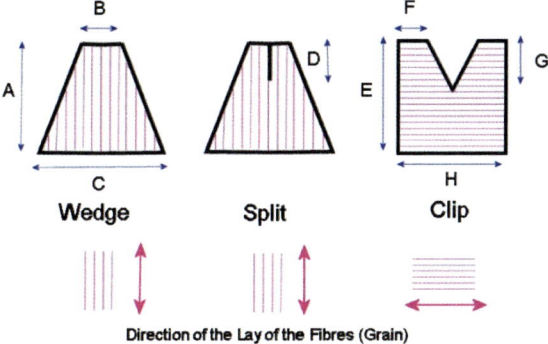

The main shapes of damper felts showing the measurements needed to specify them, the fibres of a felt were mostly in one direction or lay

The need for the different types of dampers was dependent on the construction of the piano. A piano has around eighty-eight keys, black and white, but two hundred and thirty strings. The ten lowest notes were produced using a single wire-wound string, the next eighteen pitches have two, and the last sixty have three strings each. The clip-type damper felt was used to mute both the single string and the three-string arrangements, and the wedge-type was used for the double stringed notes. For the ten low notes, the single string was positioned in the centre of the V of the clip and for the three strings one string, one string was positioned in the V and the shoulders of the clip muted the others as it passed between the gaps. The wedge felt silenced the two string note by moving between them, one side of the wedge muting one string and the other side muting second one. Square damper felts were also used to stop three string notes from sounding. Since the strings for the very high pitches did not sustain the note for long, they did not need to be damped and hence a piano had only seventy dampers in total.

Elsewhere within the piano, felt was used to cushion the moving parts, in order to absorb the energy of movement, so that parts like the hammer did not rebound, and the piano action itself made no sound. For the feltmaker, the most important of these was the back check felt that caught the hammer after it had struck the string and prevented it from rebounding. This was made in two densities, 0.34 gm/cc and 0.40 gm/cc, from two to eight millimetres thick, and sold in one and a half metre widths. To distinguish them, the lower density was a light green colour and the higher density a dark green. Other felts such as cushion felts for the butt of the wippen, hammer rail felt, and the damper spring rail felt, were of limited economic value to the felt maker because they required very little felt, but they were vital for piano construction. The cushion felt was usually red or green, made from felt having a density of 0.18 gm/cc, and was also supplied in one and a half metre widths with thickness in the range two to eight millimetres.

The full range of piano felts manufactured by R. R. Whitehead including piano parts containing their felt.

Strangely, the fortunes of the felt industry appear to have mirrored those of piano manufacturing. Between 1840 and 1870, the number of manufacturers of pianos doubled in both Britain and the world, thereafter the number of new manufactures steadily declined up to 1900.

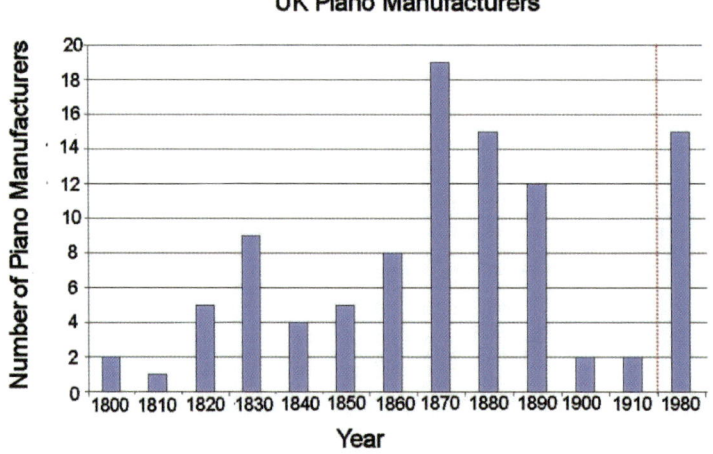

The number of new UK piano manufacturers established for the years 1800 to 1910[15], for comparison is the number of piano makers operational in 1980

For felt manufacture, the same thing occurred with The Patent Woollen Cloth Company and Wilkinson dominating until 1850 and then a surge in the number of new felt makers in Leeds and Rosssendale. It is interesting to note that The Patent Woollen Cloth Company was advertising piano felt in 1848 and yet it was not until Naish and others like the Wandle Felt Company, started manufacturing piano felt around 1859. By 1886, there were thirty-five thousand pianos made in England, seventy-three in Germany, twenty-five thousand in France and twenty-five thousand in America, each country having its own piano felt manufacturers.

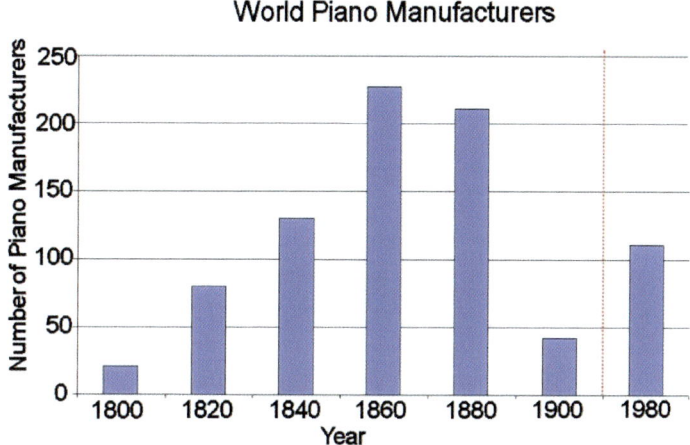

The number of new world piano manufacturers established for the years 1800-1900[16], for comparison are the number of piano makers that were operational in 1980

By 1886, both E. V. Naish and R. R. Whitehead and Brothers had established a high reputation for the quality of their felts and were consequently exporting worldwide to the best piano makers, a situation that remained right up to the time they discontinued production. In 1990, R. R. Whitehead was given the Queen's Award for export achievement, as ninety-five percent of piano felt production was exported. When they were at their peak, the hammer felt produced at Royal George was enough for over one hundred and sixty thousand pianos in one year[17]. In 1982, this would have represented eighteen percent of the world supply, since at that time around nine hundred thousand pianos were being manufactured. In 1998, the manufacture of the world famous Royal George piano felt was taken over by AMBIC Ltd. in China.

FOOTWEAR

The invention of slippers was a major milestone for the felt industry, creating a very new and a surprising market for felt. From its humble beginning in 1875, when off-cuts of felts were hand-stitched and sold for four pence a pair, it rapidly built up into a shoe industry that eclipsed that of felt making. By 1893 there were ten slipper factories employing one thousand three hundred people producing seventy thousand slippers and canvas shoes per week[18]. At its peak in 1900, there were thirteen firms in Rossendale employing three thousand employees, but after 1914, the industry concentrated on making shoes and boots with leather uppers[19]. Thereafter in Rossendale, the shoe industry fell into decline and by 1980, there were no manufacturers left there. However, there was still significant business in felt for slippers even up to the 1950s and around this time, the Bury Felt Manufacturing Company engaged in a promotion campaign to stimulate the market.

Proof copy of an advertisement for men's slipper felt and ladies' slippers by the Bury Felt Manufacturing Company Limited c 1950s.

Originally, the whole slipper was made of felt with a thin felt upper, which was sewn onto a thick dense felt that was the sole. As the industry progressed the construction of the slipper became more complex with a thin white felt stitched to a thin, dense white or grey felt, known as a socking, and then stitched to a leather sole. These felts were referred to as FT20, FT22, and FT24, which corresponded to the weights of twenty ounces, twenty-two ounces, and twenty-four ounces per yard.

As competition from other materials increased the high cost of all-wool felt came under increasing pressure and the feltmakers had to cheapen the product and yet keep the overall aesthetics and properties of an all-wool felt. This was done by making the felt in three layers. The slipper felts (designated SF) were carded as a three-layer structure, the first layer being fine wool, the second usually cheaper wool containing cotton waste, then a final face-layer containing good quality noil. Slipper felts were also custom-made for individual companies such as NHLG 18, an eighteen ounce felt for Northampton Legging Company, and NSF in twenty-four, twenty six and thirty ounces for Newmans Slipper Company. These felts were dyed before milling to provide a felt with little or no shrinkage. Most upper felts were dyed, but printed felt was also used to give a great range of design possibilities. Slipper felts were initially patterned by block printing and later by mechanical printing processes.

Apart from slippers, felt was also used in specialist outlets such as climbing boots, ski boots and Russian Valenki boots. Kletterschuhe were continental climbing boots which had a felt sole attached to uppers made of felt or canvas, and which had the toecaps and sides reinforced with leather.

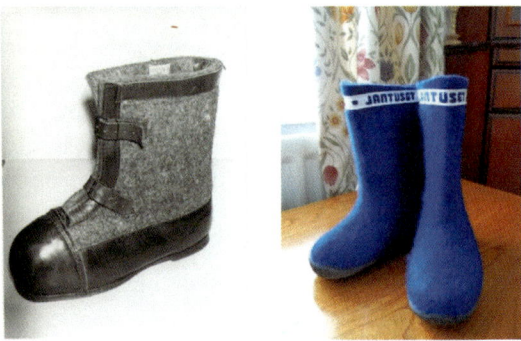

A Kletterschuh for climbing and felt boots for children made in Finland in 1980

The felt was a dense felt up to three quarters of an inch thick and used because it facilitated difficult climbs particularly on wet and greasy rock where it gave excellent grip[20]. It was for this reason that felt soles were also used during the Second World War on the boots of commandos[21].

In 1942, there was worldwide attention in manufacturing boots for use in arctic conditions and in particular for supplying the Russian army with Valenki boots. The reason felt was so useful in intensely cold conditions was because of its superb insulation properties and because it remained flexible at sub-zero temperatures. In fact the colder the conditions the better felt performed since at extreme temperatures the snow was so dry and powdery that it did not penetrate the felt. It must have been an important potential market because the Bury Felt Manufacturing Company went to the expense of establishing two patents on their manufacture[22]. Felt boots with rubber soles are still used in the twenty-first century in Arctic Circle Scandinavian countries of Norway and Finland.

CLOTHING

Despite many attempts felt never became a mainstream fashion material because it could not compete with the stability of woven materials or the flexibility of knitted fabrics.

Felt flared skirts from 1955, Brenda Lees is on the left, her skirt was red with grey flecks

In the 1930s, it had a brief popularity as ladies underskirts, though this was by no means universal across the country. A line could be drawn across the country below Birmingham where all the sales were north of this line and south of it there were none. Then again briefly in the 1950s there was a renewed interest in felt when flared outer skirts became the fashion. They were made from cutting a complete circle out of one width of felt and cutting a hole in the middle for the waistband. Therefore, the skirt had no seams in it, which was something no other material could do at the time. The skirts had good drape, were warm and by twirling round they could be made to spin outwards so they were good for dancing. Because they were loose fitting garments, they did not suffer from the bagging problem associated with felt when it recovered from stretching.

In the early days of felt making, felt was popular for making pilot jackets, which were also known as reefer jackets, p-jackets, and affectionately referred to as pea coats. John Wilkinson was showing felt pilot fabric at the Great Exhibition of 1851 in indigo, blue, and brown. As the name suggests these were jackets first worn by the British Navy, particularly the pilots where a warm woollen overcoat was a necessity. They had a distinctive style being double breasted and sporting distinctive large buttons and made out of thirty two-ounce woollen felt. Although dense, all-wool felt fabrics had the necessary warmth and durability they were largely superseded by woven woollen cloth. Associated with the military and other formal organisations and clubs was the use of badges sewn onto the jacket, usually on the top left hand pocket. For this, felt proved to be the ideal medium to act as a base material that could support the heavy embroidery involved in badge manufacture. This proved to be a significantly durable market that survived well into the 1980s, after which it was superseded by stiffened synthetic non-woven materials.

A typical double-breasted pilot jacket with characteristic large buttons.

The most enduring of all the uses for felt was as a padding material for the lining of suits and shoulder pads. The earliest record of felt used for this market was when John Wilkinson patented padding for clothing before 1851, though in 1848 The Patent Woollen Cloth Company was selling felt for "waistcoatings". Later the Rossendale felt makers were selling felt for padding to specialist clothing firms such as Agar and the Featherweight Clothing and Pad Company. This must have been in significant quantities since the three major manufacturers Mitchells, Ashworth, and Stansfield merged with them when the MASCO combine was formed. The Featherweight Clothing Pad continued trading as a sales branch of the merged company and supplied the clothing industry with white and grey soft felts, to such companies as Montague Burton, then known as the "Fifty Shilling Tailor". Volumes could be huge at times with as many as one hundred and twenty pieces forty yards long being sent out each week filling the mill capacity, with the carding engines, hardeners and other machinery working flat out to meet the demand. In 1947, the Featherweight Clothing and Pad

Company was closed and the premises at Newton Street used as a sales distribution centre for all MASCO products. With the onset of synthetic needled products, the woollen felt padding market declined rapidly but lingered on at low volume with some was still being sold as late as 1980.

Allied to the suiting industry was the use of felt underneath the collar of a suit jacket, Once an all-wool superfine felt, it was never a significant market for British felt makers but other European felt manufacturers had significant volumes of business in this market. In 1982, Bury Cooper Whitehead Ltd. collaborated with another continental manufacturer to re-engage with the collar felt market to produce a special, sophisticated three-layer felt. This was made with outer layers of wool/viscose blends and an inner layer that contained fibres that could melt and fuse with other fibres. The outer layers were blended differently so that one side was dark in colour and the other side light. During the drying process the fibres in the inner layer were glued together so that it created a thin smooth felt that stabilised it so that it acquired a crisp handle and was shrink proof.

Early in the 1980s, Bury and Masco Industries and later the newly formed Bury Cooper Whitehead Ltd. tried to re-awaken the clothing market and explore whether felt, including industrial felt, had the potential to find a niche in fashion. They commissioned an innovative designer at Goldsmith College, Rozanne Hawksley, to explore the fashion potential of industrial felt, and though this was a seemingly impossible task, she produced some remarkable clothing that demonstrated a possible way forward in generating a new clothing market.

Felt clothing designed by Rozanne Hawksley commissioned by Bury Cooper Whitehead Ltd. in 1982[23]

Following the success of her proof of concept, a Fibre Art Exhibition was organised jointly by Bury Cooper Whitehead Limited and Bury Museum and Art Gallery in 1984, in order to harness the latent design talent of other designers known to be working with felt. This resulted in a flood of ideas that demonstrated clearly the enormous potential still to be unlocked using felt. Unfortunately shortly after the exhibition Bury Cooper Whitehead Limited, was reorganised and the approach was never followed through commercially

The Fibre Art Exhibition in 1984 at Bury Museum and Art gallery

MILLINERY

In the early days of felt making, the industry developed independently of the hat trade and there appears to have been no penetration into this market until well after 1904. None of the publicity material describes the use of pressed felt for hats and this is supported by the fact that there is no mention of millinery in the formal documents of the amalgamation of Mitchells, Ashworth, Stansfield, William Blaikie, and the Featherweight Clothing and Pad Company in 1904. If there were a significant interest in millinery at the time, such a company would have certainly been involved in the merger. The first sign of pressed felt used for hat making is shown in a MASCO exhibition where the hat on display can be dated to around 1927. It was always difficult for woollen sheet felt to compete with the fineness of rabbit and beaver fur that was the norm for the hat industry. Also, it was more difficult to mould a sheet of felt into a hat shape than it was to block the hood shape of the traditional hat maker, and because woollen felt produced more waste. The extended shape of the hat in the MASCO exhibition means that the hat must have required a very deep draw to mould it, which is very difficult to achieve with sheet felt. Therefore, MASCO must have developed special millinery felt to secure this market. Bury Felt Manufacturing also decided to penetrate this market as part of their fashion approach and they had good contacts through the Chesham Hat Company, as they were close neighbours, and they eventually took over their premises when that company failed.

Tailored hats were also promoted as an alternative to berets that were fashionable in the 1930s and 1940s, but despite all this activity pressed felt made only minor inroads into the millinery trade. One company, Bermona Limited, mastered a method that enabled them to compete against traditional hoods by using a specially manufactured hat felt code named SIS, and they were still highly active in the 1980s, even as the hat trade suffered a significant decline.

A promotional leaflet by Bury Felt Manufacturing Company extolling the virtues of felt for millinery and fashion, probably dated in the late 1930s and a felt beret produced circa 1940

One area where felt did make an impression was in the production of bowler hats, which used a felt with the finest wool and which was given a fine finish by cropping. The market ceased after the Second World War, though there was a brief revival in the 1970s and 1980s when they were exported to Nigeria for tribal chiefs and their entourage. The agent buying the hats arrived at the factory, collected the consignment, paid by cash and left, only appearing again when the next consignment was due.

By a strange set of circumstances the demise of the hat industry provoked a new market for pressed felt in the novelty hat trade with volumes far in excess of any felt used for millinery. The novelty hat trade came to prominence due to the popularity of the "British seaside holiday" when it was customary to wear fancy hats with slogans written on them, variously known as cowboy hats and kiss-me-quick hats. The trade was centred largely around Southend-on-Sea and was pioneered by a number of companies notably: Burgess, Bantin, Durrant, W. R. Davies, and McBell. Most of this business depended on old hats, known as ash cans, which were de-loused, reprocessed and remoulded, mostly into a cowboy hat shape. With the decline of the millinery industry, ash cans were harder to acquire and Bury Felt Manufacturing Company began trials with Bantin in the early 1960s with a special cheap mouldable felt designated 51517 which was starch stiffened at Bury, while at the same time, MASCO was also trying to secure this market. It was not until 1966 that a mouldable felt, 4483, was produced that was commercially acceptable, though the hat makers had to impregnate it themselves with gelatine. By 1970, there were only three producers left: Burgess, W. R. Davies, and Durrant. In 1980, Bury and Masco Industries developed a thermoplastic stiffening agent based on polyvinyl alcohol (PVA) that replaced the need for gelatine and the felt just needed steaming before moulding. Not only did this give added value to the company but also made the hats cheaper to produce, as well as relieving the people of Southend of the smell of boiling gelatine. At its height, the business was worth £100,000 in 1982.

CRAFT AND TOYS

There appears to have been no feltcraft or felt toys before 1900 at the least, and feltcraft books only started being published from 1927 onwards, pioneered by Elsie Mochrie[24]. She went on to publish books on making felt toys with Penelope Roseaman in the mid thirties, sparking a new market and industry that became the height of popularity in the 1950s[25].

The display by Bury Felt Manufacturing Company limited at the International Homcraft and Hobbies Exhibition 1954, on the left are felt skirts and dresses that were popular at the time.

It was then that the felt industry took this new market seriously and manufactured superfine felts specifically for making toys and for general craftwork. Initially, the superfine felt was an all-wool felt pressed and cropped, trademarked "Fleur", which was then supplemented by a wool/viscose felt called "Floret" and then by a cross-laid blended felt called Florina. The increase in the number of products for this outlet was an indication of the market expansion that took place and there was hardly a soft toy that did not contain felt in some form or another right up until the early 1980s.

A Christmas selection of soft toys using felt in 1980. Note Paddington bear with felt hat and coat, also the purple dinosaur Posh Paws that was the mascot on Swap Shop a television programme for children aired in the 1970s

However, this success also brought with it competition from other materials such as brushed warp-knitted nylon fabric that eroded the profit margin for felt and forced the felt industry to maintain the market by diluting the fibre blend with increasing quantities of low cost synthetics such as viscose rayon. By the 1990s, the market was taken over completely by all-synthetic felts made by a needle-punching process far removed from felting.

As the activity in soft toys and crafts gathered pace, one event completely transformed the image of superfine felt. That was the launch in 1950 of "fuzzy-felt™" by Lois Allan. This was a creative toy which became so popular that superfine felt was forever identified in the public imagination as fuzzy felt, despite all the effort and expense undertaken by the felt makers to change this image.

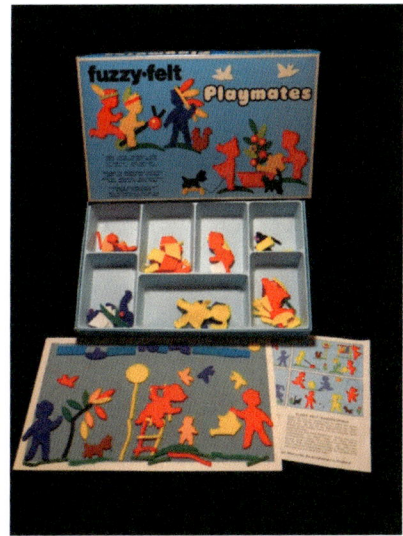
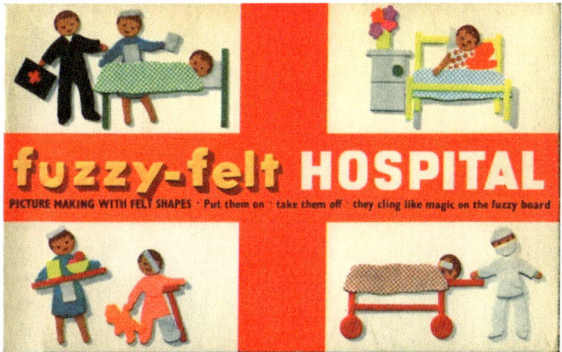

Two examples of fuzzy-felt™ by Allan Industries one showing the contents and the other showing an example of another one of the annual themes

"Fuzzy-felt" as conceived, was a box containing different felt shapes and a board covered with fibre flock. The felt pieces when placed on the board stuck to the flock, which enabled pictures to be made out of the shapes. The idea appealed to youngsters because their imaginations were stimulated by a theme contained in each box, which included ideas and suggestions printed on a sheet inside the box From this time onwards the importance of felt as a key universal craft material was eclipsed by fuzzy-felt's success, labelling it as a fun product and only suitable for soft toys.

Despite this, felt was still used in reasonable quantities for more serious handicrafts. It was not until the late 1970s that felt shed its fuzzy-felt image to become a serious medium again. This was the beginning of the new age of craft felt makers who were individuals returning to the ancient traditional ways of hand felt making. In Britain the movement seems to have developed at West Surrey College of Art & Design, though individuals were already following the inspirational book by Mary Burkett entitled the "Art of the Feltmaker". At the same time Bury and Masco Industries attempted to raise the market profile for its superfine felt through a series of exhibitions and the commissioning of more adult craft designs.

An Exhibition in 1980 by Bury and Masco Industries aimed at raising the image of craft felt

In 1981, to further stimulate the market, the company promoted a competition to design the most inventive use of felt, which was surprisingly won by a hand made felt piece. Although the winner was not quite what was expected, it alerted the company to the high level of activity in hand felting and the potential impact this could have on the image of felt. As a result, Bury and Masco Industries encouraged hand felters by making available production felt machines to explore design capabilities, notably Annie Sherburne, who supplied her felt to Jean Muir, the eminent fashion designer, and Jenny Cowern a revered fine artist famous for her landscape images.

Bury Cooper Whitehead Ltd. continued its support for the craft felters by hosting the inauguration of the Feltmakers Association pioneered by Mary Burkett. In 2012, it is now known as the International Feltmakers Association and is a major international focus for felt makers around the world, who are achieving success with stunning innovative designs in felt.

PRODUCTS

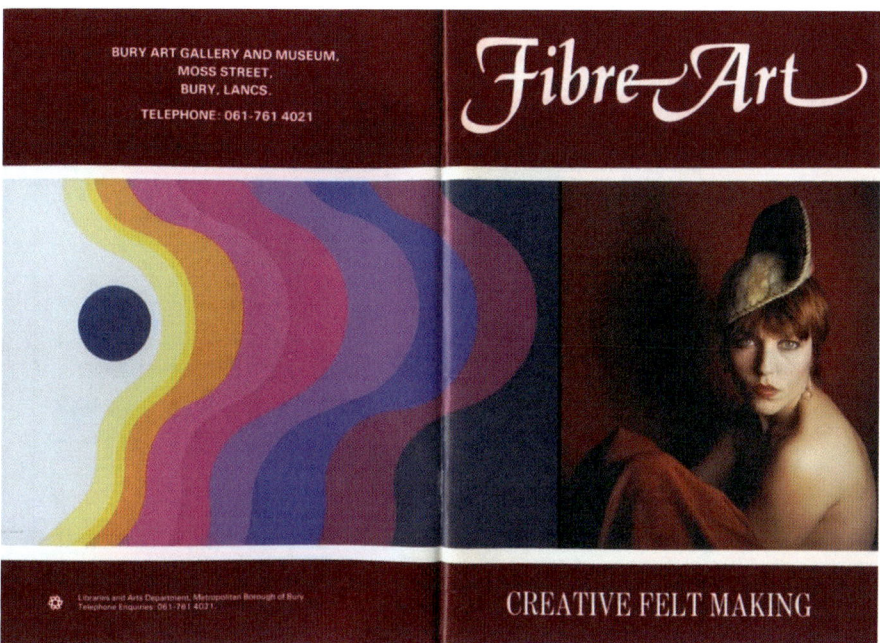

The cover of the catalogue for the Fibre Art Exhibition at Bury Museum and Art Gallery, March 1984. The photograph shows Annie Sherburne modelling one of her felt hat creations

Unfortunately for both the pressed felt industry and the craft felters there was a significant change in the management structure within Bury Cooper Whitehead, and the potential of the approach was misunderstood and support terminated. Prophetically, craft felting has gone from strength to strength whilst Bury Cooper Whitehead Limited and the British felt making industry no longer exists.

MEDICAL

Although the story of St. Clement and the magical healing of his feet by wool and felt there is an element of truth in it, for even in the twenty first century felt finds a variety of uses in chiropody. It is still used for protecting sore feet, where it is ideal for relieving pressure and friction, whether for bunions, heels or the balls of the feet. The unique properties of the felt enable it to mould around the foot and absorb any sliding forces without slipping, whilst at the same time the natural resilience of the wool fibres provides cushioning. These low-density felts were made of best quality wool, dyed to a skin colour, and the very nature of its production through the variety of steaming processes it was virtually sterile and hypoallergenic. This felt was sold on a roll or was cut into pads or washers, to be used as corn pads.

Even as early as the mid 1800s soft lightweight white felts were being used in surgical applications such as padding for splints or impregnated with oils or other medical mixtures to be used as poultices. In 1862, the Wandle Felt Company considered the market so important that it bought out Markwick's Patent for a product called Spongio Piline that was a replacement for poultices. It was described as economical, comfortable, quick in its action, and admirable for retaining warmth and moisture[26]. As needled synthetic materials and paddings became readily available, they replaced wool as the material of choice for surgical and medical applications and woollen felt usage was limited to all but the most specialised areas.

A more mundane use for grey felt was in deodorisers in urinals. The felt was placed in an oval chromium plated box with slits in it and dipped in an antiseptic aromatic solution. These were flushed at regular intervals to disinfect the urinal and emit a fragrant smell. There was significant business in this market as they were used in virtually every public toilet and there was a ready replacement market since the pads had to be changed at regular intervals. As more modern materials became available, and as labour costs rose, it became uneconomic to maintain this system and the market disappeared after the early 1980s.

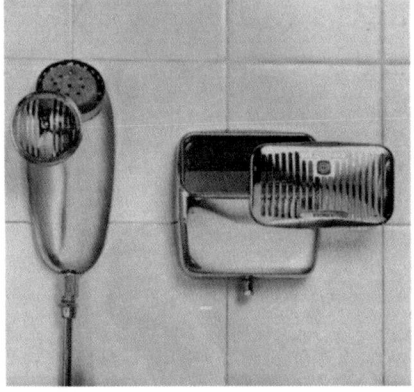

Deodorisers used in British public toilets, the lids are removed to show the grey felt pads

Dense felts were also used in the allied medical field of dentistry, where they were used for polishing teeth. The felt was so hard and dense that it could be precisely turned to produce tiny bobs that could be drilled and mounted onto metal spindles that could fit into a dentist's drill. They were made in a variety of shapes from spherical to cylindrical to suit all the conditions that a dentist might face in polishing teeth. A typical spherical bob was five millimetre in diameter with a shank that was forty millimetres long and two millimetres in diameter. They were used either on their own for buffing or for polishing with a suitable abrasive paste. Because of their small size these bobs were equally ideal for polishing jewellery and even in 2012 there was a flourishing market for them. On a much grander scale the same technique for making the spherical bobs with shanks was used in the manufacture of bass drumsticks and snare drum hammers.

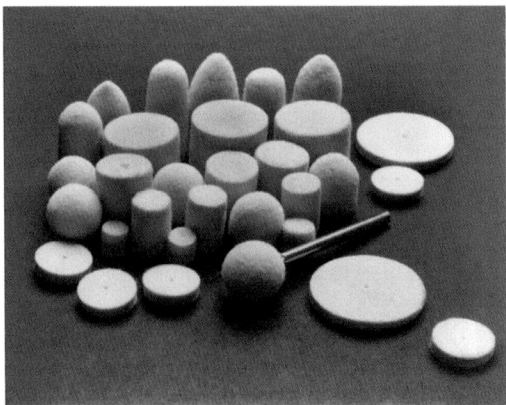

Small felt bobs for dentistry and polishing jewellery

SADDLERY AND LEATHER

John Wilkinson pioneered the use of felt in saddlery by patenting a felt numnah some time before 1850. The definition of a numnah derives from an Indian word referring to a blanket placed beneath a saddle to protect the horse's back from an ill-fitting saddle. Blankets have been used for centuries to cushion the saddle, often folded many times to protect the horse's back, particularly after a long campaign when the horse would have lost considerable weight. The felt numnah was saddle shaped in outline and just slightly larger than the saddle itself, usually white or coloured brown and weighing five pounds six ounces[27]. The resilient quality and permeability of felt protected the horse from shocks, minimised muscle fatigue, and allowed its skin to breathe without sweat penetrating the leather of the saddle.

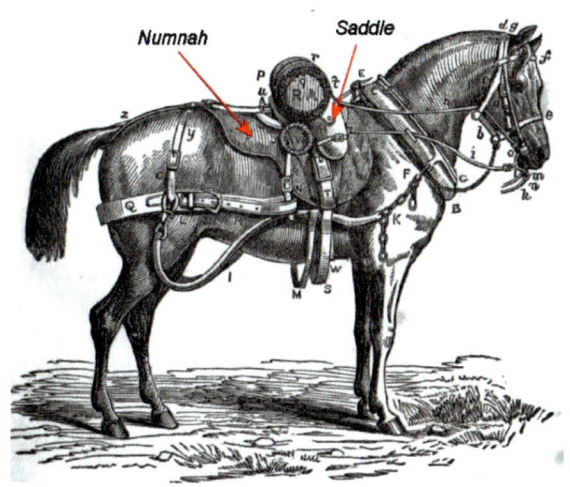

A felt numnah placed under the saddle of an artillery horse[28]

From a commercial point of view, the timing of the invention was ideal since the Crimean War was fought in 1853-56, and involved large-scale cavalry battles that must have required significant numbers of numnahs as materiel. This was followed soon after by the American Civil War from 1861-65, when many saddle pads were exported to America, particularly for the Confederacy[29]. During this time, other feltmakers realised the potential of this market and developed numnah designs of their own; for example, James Heywood Whitehead patented a numnah by felting wool onto a woven fabric in 1868[30]. Then came the First Boer War from 1880 to 1881 where the felt numnah came into its own and its outstanding performance there projected it into the international spotlight that opened up a worldwide market. Thereafter, there were no shortage of wars to keep the saddle market buoyant: the Second Boer War in 1879-1915, the First World War 1914-18, and the Second World War 1939-44. Therefore, R. R. Whitehead and Brothers' felting company, the Wandle Felt Company, was openly advertising numnahs for sale in 1891[31]. By this time, John Wilkinson's company had disappeared and other felt companies had taken up the production of saddle felts. Even in 1939, there was a significant volume of saddle felt sold with large quantities being exported as far afield as New Zealand, where shipments were sent to Wellington, Timarn, and Oamaru by the Bury Felt Manufacturing Company. This proved to be the turning point in numnah sales as horsepower rapidly gave way to mechanised warfare and after the Second World War sales declined rapidly as the market shifted from military use to recreational use. Although not generating spectacular sales, the business in saddle felts continued to be steady throughout the time from 1945 to 1990.

Allied to saddlery was the trade in straps and bridles that afforded an extension to the equestrian felt market. Here felt was used as a backing material for leather straps, to which it was glued or stitched in order to provide a backing surface that did not chafe or irritate the animal's skin. Such straps and belts were used in a variety of other markets, both for ceremonial occasions and for utilitarian uses such as leather bonnet straps for Morgan Cars or for guitar straps. In modern times, felt backed straps were used either as reins for small children in high chairs or whilst walking. They were also used as collars for pets since the felt could be impregnated with chemicals to protect them from fleas, a market that was still strong in the 1980s and persists even in 2012.

ANTI-VIBRATION

Felt was a remarkable material for controlling unwanted vibration because it could be made with such a wide variety of properties and engineered to eliminate any form of vibration. For airborne sound, a soft felt at a density of around 0.12 gm/cc, or less, was used. At this level of felting the fibres were loosely held together and were able to move when the sound waves struck them, which absorbed the energy of the sound and prevented it from rebounding. Increasing the thickness of the felt could increase the sound deadening effect, because a thicker felt had more intricate pathways that could absorb more of the sound energy. A coarse grey felt was most effective for soundproofing because its thicker fibres could absorb more energy and its low cost enabled it to compete against other materials. A common use for this felt was in telephone booths in public places like hotels. A typical booth was mounted on a wall and was like a small porch with an arched roof, just large enough to cover the head of the caller. The booth also had a thick back plate to absorb the sound. The inside of the booth was clad in a perforated metal sheet to let the sound through and behind this was the thick layer of grey felt that absorbed it.

Because of its excellent vibration control, low density felt was used in the very best loudspeakers to prevent internal reverberation in the enclosure and provide the highest fidelity. It was also marketed and used for sound insulation in the 1950s and 60s under the bonnets and boot lids of cars, though in this case it was laminated with a thick rubber sheet. The felt stopped the airborne sound and the rubber stopped any vibration in the bonnet or boot. Mitchells, Ashworth, and Stansfield, and Co marketed a product under the name "Murmuride".

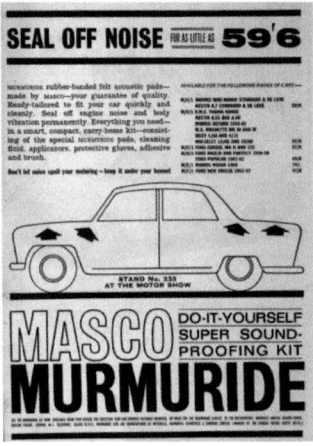

Advertisement for the Birmingham Motor Show in 1962 by MASCO's Murmuride sound proofing

As an extension to this approach felt bonded to rubber mats was used under typewriters to reduce the clattering noise in busy offices. The felt used was a half-inch thick "grey" felt that was dyed dark blue, and the rubber was black with a corrugated surface and the mat used with the rubber side uppermost. This market lasted until typewriters were replaced by computers and word processors towards the end of the 1980s. Fortunately as the typewriter disappeared it was replaced by dot matrix printers which were also noisy and in a busy office they had to be sound proofed by fixing felt to the inside of metal enclosures placed around the printers to deaden the sound.

As synthetic needle felts and polyurethane foams became readily available and were significantly cheaper than wool, felt was replaced as a sound deadening material. However, felts were still used in specialist markets where moving parts had to be protected from rattling. One example was window channelling for cars that consisted of a metal or plastic moulding lined with felt, which guided the window and allowed it to slide smoothly as it was wound up and down.

Window channelling for cars

It also acted as a draught excluder by making an airtight seal between the window and the car body. Even as late as 1980, these channels were being used in Rolls Royce cars to provide a luxury feel to opening and closing the windows. Black felt was used traditionally and this had to be completely dye-fast or colour would bleed from it into the paintwork of the car.

Another notable use for felt was as a bush bearing for the steering columns of cars in the 1950s, consisting of a strip of dense felt that fitted around the steering column axle to separate it from the housing. This enabled the steering wheel to be turned smoothly without rattling. Even when this market virtually disappeared by the 1970s, there was still significant profitable business in exporting felt strips to India. This was because many Morris Oxford cars, which used these bushes, were exported to India and the car remained a cult form of transport right up to the 1990s. This was a lucrative continuing market, because felt bushes in the steering gear had to be changed at regular intervals.

Controlling the transmission of sound and vibration through materials is a much more complicated problem, particularly controlling vibration or shock loading by heavy machinery. For this the feltmakers designed a series of products that could be engineered to eliminate vibration in virtually every situation.

It was the use of Borradaile felt that opened up the market for felt in civil engineering in the 1830s by using asphalt impregnated hat felt in bridge building and the laying of railway tracks as a means of absorbing shocks and vibration. The confidence and experience gained over the years enabled Mitchells, Ashworth, Stansfield, and Co. to introduce "Mascolite", their own version of bitumen impregnated woollen felt to be used as a shock absorber and anti-vibration mounting for bridges and other load bearing structures. It had such a good reputation that it was used in the building of the Waterloo Bridge in London 1942 to 1945[32]. The company also developed a range of what they termed Mascolite Vibrosonic Isolators that had other treatments than bitumen. There were three types of felt anti-vibration products on the market from 1945 onwards: grey felts of densities 0.30 gm/cc to 0.6 gm/cc, a composite product consisting of alternate layers of felt and cork, and for heavy loads a further layered composite of felt and rubber. R. R. Whitehead and Brothers Limited also had a product called Regalpak as well as a product called Regalmount, similar to Mascolite

Regalpak anti-vibration leaflet by R. R. Whitehead and Engineered Mascolite anti-vibration pads by Bury and Masco Industries

Most layered products had three layers with the felt on the outside, and cork or rubber on the inside, though there could be up to nine layers with five felt and four cork or rubber layers, depending on the nature of the vibration. It was well known in engineering circles that having two different materials layered together was much more effective in damping vibrations than each material on its own. The felt was mothproofed and waterproofed and if required could also be stiffened with a thermosetting resin. If the mounting was in a waterlogged or oil environment the edges had to be sealed with bitumen or wrapped in a waterproof material to prevent these liquids gradually seeping into the structure. For less demanding environments the felt was treated with tallow to give a degree of waterproofing, as when it was used by the Royal Navy as stern gland stuffing, or in boxes for sealing propeller shafts.

Anti-vibration felts and felt composites were mostly available in sheet form, each usually measuring forty-eight inches long and either forty-eight or sixty six inches wide, though they could also be fabricated into different sizes and shapes. The felt could even be produced in three-dimensional constructions, which could be as complicated as I-section girders or as a sleeve to completely isolate the anchor bolt for machinery.

Natural wool felt was the first choice for most machinery since it could support moderate loadings and the vibration frequencies were generally in the range twenty to forty Hertz. This was mainly because motors powering such machines ran at around one thousand five hundred revolutions per minute, which equates to twenty-five Hertz. The choice of which felt to use depended on how heavy the machine was, and it was important that the felt did not distort appreciably under the weight of the machine or the anti-vibration characteristics of the felt would change. In general, the heavier the machine was, the denser the felt needed to be; the maximum loading for a felt of density 0.3 gm/cc was ten pounds per square inch compared to a felt of density 0.5 gm/cc at two hundred and fifty pounds per square inch. For small machines the felt was usually used a quarter of an inch thick but for heavy machines a thickness of one or two inches was recommended.

For civil engineering applications, an anti-vibration mounting was required to have longevity with a working life lasting tens of years. A properly treated felt or Mascolite was virtually indestructible and could outlast any civil construction. For buildings and bridges, felt had excellent resilience so that, after a transient load had passed, the felt always came back to its original shape, just like rubber. Furthermore, felt retained its vibration characteristics throughout its life, and unlike rubber, it worked effectively at both very high and sub zero temperatures. This springiness also made it ideal for absorbing shock loads such as those from a punch press. It was even used to silence pneumatic hammers using a specially constructed anti-vibration enclosure, which consisted of a layer of felt isolator like Mascolite that completely surrounded the machine base and then the whole structure surrounded by concrete. In this way, the whole machine mounting was completely separated from the floor by anti-vibration felt. For larger structures such as bridges and other civil constructions, layered isolators were used and these were used for floating floors where floor supports rested on sheets of layered Mascolite.

An exhibition of Mascolite and its uses, sometime after 1960, the square frame on the left demonstrated a floor support on a Mascolite pad for a "floating floor"

The use of Mascolite peaked in the 1970s and Bury and Masco Industries went to considerable effort to publicise it in order to maintain momentum in sales; but by 1980 sales had declined to a level at which they only manufactured it sporadically.

WICKING AND LUBRICATION

The structure of felt with its network of interlocking fibres provides an infinite variety of capillaries that are capable of absorbing and transmitting liquids of all kinds, particularly oils. The combination of this structure and the liquid surface tension can pull a liquid into the felt or even upwards when it is held vertically; the denser the felt the finer the capillaries and the higher the liquid can climb. Also important is the rate at which a liquid can wick along a felt because this determines how much fluid a felt can deliver in any situation where lubrication is involved. In most applications fluid delivery only needed to be low, therefore denser felts were used since wicking rates are less for denser felts than for those of lower density.

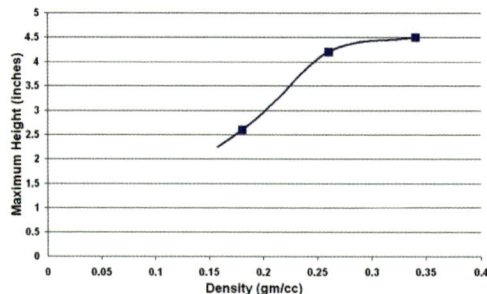

The maximum wicking height for oil of viscosity 940SSU for different felt densities

This wicking ability made felt ideally suited for a myriad of lubrication applications that led it to become an essential element in engineering design. Because wool has a natural affinity for oil, felt has a preference for absorbing and transmitting it, and felt will even take up oil in preference to water when presented with an oil/water emulsion. It is not surprising, therefore, that before the introduction of synthetic materials virtually every machine or device that contained a moving part also contained a felt component.

There were four methods by which a moving part could be lubricated: by a bottom feed wick, a top feed wick, a syphon feed wick, or by being surrounded by felt totally saturated in oil. Design of the wick's performance in practice depended on the rate at which oil could be delivered for a particular viscosity, and on where the oil reservoir was located because of design limitations. A top feed wick delivered the most oil and was used where copious quantities were needed for the bearing, though the excess oil had to be collected and returned to the reservoir. The syphon wick delivered the least lubricant but because the wicking was aided by gravity, the reservoir could be sited a considerable distance from the rotating shaft. The bottom feed wick gave the greatest control because changing the length of the wick changed the rate of delivery of the oil in a simple relationship. In designing a felt wick there were simple rules that governed performance: (a) delivery rate was proportional to cross-sectional area, (b) wicking delivery rate increased with density up to 0.34 gm/cc, (c) the practical maximum wick length for a bottom feed wick was four and a half inches, (d) the height to which an oil could be raised was inversely proportional to the viscosity[33].

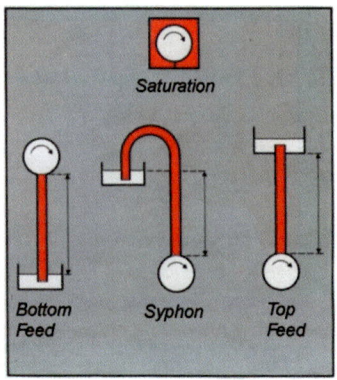

Configurations of a felt wick for lubricating a rotating shaft

In many cases, different felts were used in the same application to control the lubricant in different parts of the bearing. Typically a low density felt was used as a reservoir feeding a dense felt that transferred the lubricant to the bearing, the fast wicking rate of the low density felt made the fluid readily available to the high density felt that controlled the final flow.

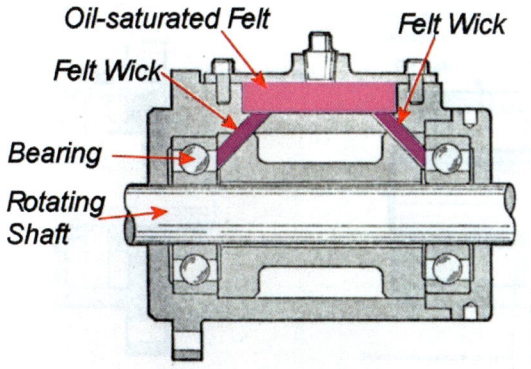

Felts of two different densities used to lubricate the bearing on a rotating shaft. the high-density wicks are fed by a low-density felt oil reservoir

This was because the high density felt, though good at controlling the flow, could not hold enough oil within its structure to maintain the delivery, whereas the low density felt could hold large amounts of fluid but would flood a bearing rather than control the delivery. By having the felt acting as a reservoir, the bearing could still be lubricated no matter what inclination the bearing had, which was most beneficial for automotive use.

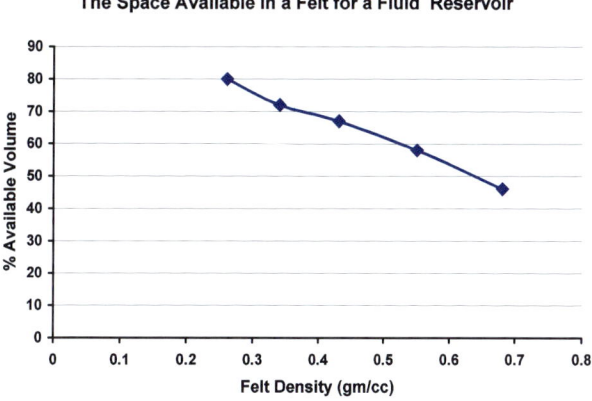

Felt's wicking ability was used to great effect in the 1950s in a deodoriser trademarked "Airwick". This consisted of a bottle of deodorising fluid in a dark glass bottle that had a small plastic frame that fitted through the neck of the bottle and into the fluid in such a way that it could be pulled up or down. Around this was stretched a piece of grey felt that dipped into the liquid and which could be raised or lowered into the bottle with the frame. When the felt was totally immersed the top of the bottle could be screwed on to seal it. When the deodoriser was activated, the top was taken off and the frame pulled upwards to expose the saturated felt, the more the felt that was raised, the greater the surface area that was exposed and the greater the evaporation. As the fluid evaporated, more liquid wicked up the felt to replace it, a process that continued until the bottle was empty. This simple device was revolutionary in its day, creating a new mass market. This was the pioneer of the modern deodoriser industry, which became increasingly prolific and sophisticated in the new millennium.

The Airwick deodoriser using a grey felt on a plastic frame dipping into a bottle of deodorising liquid.

The technology gained in supplying and designing wicks was applied successfully to the creation of the felt tip pen and felt marker that was invented by Lee Newman in 1910. The principle of wicking for oil lubrication was exactly the same mechanism used in making a marker pen. The pen had a built-in reservoir and a felt nib that acted as a wick to deliver the ink at the rate needed for writing or drawing. Generally, the nib was a dense felt of density 0.3-0.5 gm/cc and was fabricated to fit the penholder, while the end was specially shaped for optimum writing. The ink was solvent based rather than oil, to overcome the natural oleophilic nature of the wool fibres. By 1958, the use of felt-tipped markers was commonplace, though for fine pens with narrow nibs, felt was gradually replaced by stiffened synthetic materials. In an effort to protect the market, Bury Cooper Whitehead Limited created a synthetic felt, impregnated with urea formaldehyde, designed specifically for use as nibs, which they trademarked as "Juxtafelt". The only pens that still do not use synthetic materials are broad-nibbed markers, which maintain the use of genuine woollen felt.

WIPERS AND SEALS

The surface of a felt is not solid, but consists of a network of fibres crossing each other at different angles, creating significant gaps and voids. When felt makes contact with a moving surface, the woollen fibres sweep away any dust, abrasive particles, or debris, into the voids. If the particles are much smaller than the gaps between the fibres local turbulence at the surface propels them into the body of the felt and away from the moving surface. Larger particles become trapped by the wool fibres, which then bend around them to effectively lift them off the surface so that they cannot generate sufficient pressure to cause any damage. Both these phenomena can be enhanced by the use of lubricants such as oil or water that create hydrodynamic effects that can push debris deeper into the felt. Furthermore, the felt can be engineered to cope with particular conditions to deal with a range of particle sizes through the manipulation of its density.

Felt has a natural resilience that enables it to ride any high spots on a moving surface or to accommodate any eccentricities in a rotating shaft, and can therefore provide a low dynamic friction. Felt itself is also a low friction material since only the surface network of fibres touches a moving surface and microscopically it is only the tips of the scales on the outer layers of each wool fibre that actually touch the surface. Because wool is oleophilic, there is always a very thin layer of oil surrounding each fibre and this helps to keep the friction low. Even if friction did cause a build up of heat it would have little effect on the felt because of the wide range of temperatures that wool fibres can tolerate. All these properties make felt an ideal material for use in wipers and dust seals in engineering applications.

There were significant sales for felt as wipers in the manufacture of steel and aluminium strip where they were employed to clean, lubricate, tension, and protect the newly formed metal strip. In the steel industry, the rolled steel strip left the furnace at temperature of up to one thousand four hundred degrees Celsius at a speed of a hundred feet per minute before being cooled to one hundred degrees in a water bath. After this, the strip passed between two sets of rollers that stretched and rolled the sheet. Positioned on the entry side of the first set of rollers was a two-inch thick white dense felt of density 0.6 gm/cc which was pivoted so that the edge touched the sheet and prevented the cooling water from settling on the metal strip. After these rollers was a second felt strip that swept away any other harmful particles in preparation for the next processing stage.

In both cold rolling steel and aluminium strip production, felt was used to both clean and provide tension during manufacture. A half-inch thick grey felt of density 0.4 gm/cc was mounted on battens and was made to contact the metal strip at a pressure of forty-five pounds per square inch so that it acted as a brake and prevented "whip" as the strip was being rolled. Despite the surface temperature rising to one hundred degrees Celsius, the felt performed happily without melting or degrading and maintained its efficiency in wiping away any contaminants that could score the surface.

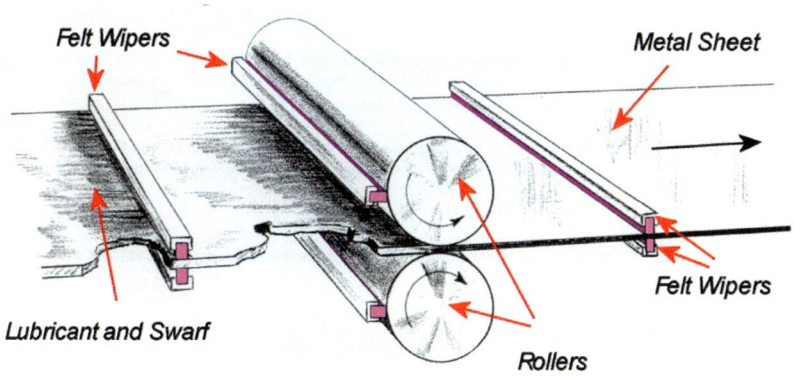

The positions of felt wipers in a metal rolling mill to protect the metal strip, note the wooden battens holding the felt

A further grey felt three eighths of an inch thick was also used to clean the outer surface of the metal as it was coiled up. A special version of these wipers was known as a black streak wiper and consisted of a felt laminated between two textured nitrile rubber strips. The rubber layer removed any excess lubricant used in the rolling process and the felt removed any unwanted particles by maintaining good contact with the metal. These wipers were available in lengths from nine inches to thirty-six inches with a depth of half an inch and a width varying from a half an inch to three inches.

In 1980, the motor industry needed the steel strip to be supplied with a protective film of oil and this had to be closely controlled during manufacture of the strip. This was done with a roller that was fitted with a sleeve of grey felt. The felt roller was rotated at three thousand revolutions per minute and positioned to make contact with the metal strip that passed underneath it travelling at five thousand feet per minute. Oil was fed onto the fast moving metal strip in front of the roller and the felt on the roller dispersed the oil at an even rate across the width of the metal, and because of felt's low friction there was no heat build up and hence no risk of the oil burning.

In 1980, a coil of steel strip was worth £1000 and therefore had to be handled with care so half-inch thick felt was fixed to all the handling equipment to ensure that there was no damage in transit. Felt was also used on the shoes of the conveyor belt that carried the coils from the rolling mills to the cut-up lines. The conveyors to the dispatch area were also protected by felt, and, where coils were lifted by cranes, the lifting gear was covered with a sleeve of half-inch thick felt.

On a much smaller scale, felt was used in the construction of tape cassettes. These devices recorded sounds on a polymer tape impregnated with a magnetic iron oxide material in a particularly compact format. To replay them, the tape had to pass across a magnetic head that decoded the magnetic data into sounds, but over time, some of the oxide particles rubbed off and these could accumulate on the head and muffle the sound reproduction. A small piece of white high-density felt, approximately one quarter of an inch square was placed behind the tape at a position opposite the magnetic receiver head to remove any stray oxide particles before the tape was rewound.

The felt also tensioned the tape to stabilise it as it passed over the magnetic head and at the same time acted as a resilient "frictionless" spring to ensure good contact with the head to give the highest possible fidelity. Even though millions of cassettes were made it was a relatively small but profitable business that had more promotional impact than financial. Fortunately the tape recording industry also required felt in somewhat larger quantities in the form of specialist filters for the manufacturing process of iron oxide and these were made from five eighths of an inch thick felt sewn into eight inch long sleeves that were four inches in diameter.

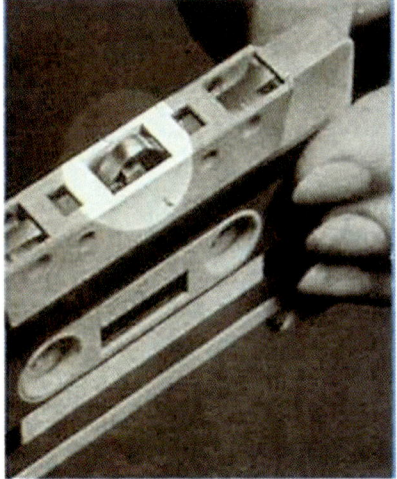

A tape cassette showing the small piece of felt protecting the recording tape

SEALS

At the beginning of the twentieth century, the growth of the car and electrical industries established felt as an important engineering material, and as a result, the felt industry began the commercial large-scale production of washers and strip felt. Until around 1928, moving parts were protected by lashings of oil and grease, which was applied manually into built-in lubrication channels using oilcans and grease guns. The nearest mechanism to provide automatic lubrication was an up-turned bottle with a small tube fitted to the neck that dripped oil onto the shaft at a very slow rate. The advent of cars, electric motors, and dynamos, meant that installations were much more mobile and prolific, so that constant manual servicing was impractical. The engineering solution was the development of seals designed in such a way that any lubrication could remain surrounding the shaft and prevent any external debris from outside contaminating it. The importance of felt in these applications was acknowledged by the Society of Automotive Engineers (SAE), which devised a comprehensive set of quality standards for the use of felt in cars. Two types of seals developed: a dry seal to protect against dust, and a "wet" seal to retain the lubricant.

Dry seals were mainly used in electrical goods wherever there was an electric motor. These seals were usually an annular washer made from soft grey felt that fitted over the shaft and was held in place by a holding plate or fitted into in a recess in the machine housing. There could be many such felt washers in an appliance such as a vacuum cleaner, which because of the large volume of machines produced, provided a significant lucrative business for the feltmakers. Felts of 0.18 gm/cc were recommended for shaft speeds up to seven hundred and fifty feet per minute surface speed, 0.26 gm/cc for speeds up to one thousand feet per minute, and 0.34gm/cc for speeds over one thousand feet per minute[34]. Virtually every electrical appliance up to at least 1980 had felt washers of this type in them, protecting all the moving parts. Later, PTFE (poly tetra fluoro ethylene) washers became popular as they had the same low friction characteristics of felt and could be made with very tight tolerances, the washers were able to fit tightly on a rotating shaft. However, unlike felt, if dust did succeed in penetrating the PTFE washer, particles would embed in the plastic and then, over time, would score the shaft. With felt, dust particles just buried themselves into the body of the felt and hence caused no damage.

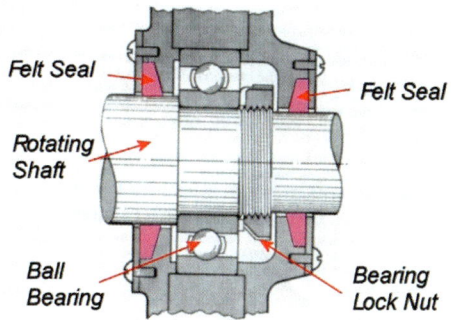

A roller bearing assembly with integrated lubricating felts

Lubricating seals were much more complex in design and depended on whether they were used on a plain shaft, a ball bearing or a roller bearing. The basic design was a felt ring made from a high-density white felt soaked in lubricant and which had the inner diameter marginally greater than that of the shaft. The felt therefore barely touched the shaft but allowed a thin film of lubricant to be transferred to it. Usually the felt was saturated with oil, grease, or micronised graphite, and performed as a reservoir, a dust trap, and a barrier to moisture. To increase the efficiency, the felt was laminated to an oil resistant rubber such as nitrile rubber that prevented the lubricant from leaking out of the sides and concentrating it onto the shaft. The rubber laminate could be bonded to the outsides of the felt or have different felts bonded to each side, forming a sandwich, and the exact construction depended on the precise application. For ball bearing or roller bearing applications, the felt became part of the engineering assembly.

The felts were fitted to the bearing in specially machined enclosures and locked into place with plate covers completely sealing the bearing and ensuring that the lubricant did not leak out. The construction of these seals was so efficient that the lubrication lasted the lifetime of the bearing and needed no maintenance.

ROLLER SLEEVES

At the beginning of the nineteenth century, papermaking developed as a major industry due to the invention of a continuous process developed by the British inventors Henry and Sealy Fourdrinier. This generated a new market for felt sleeves to cover the various rollers of the process.

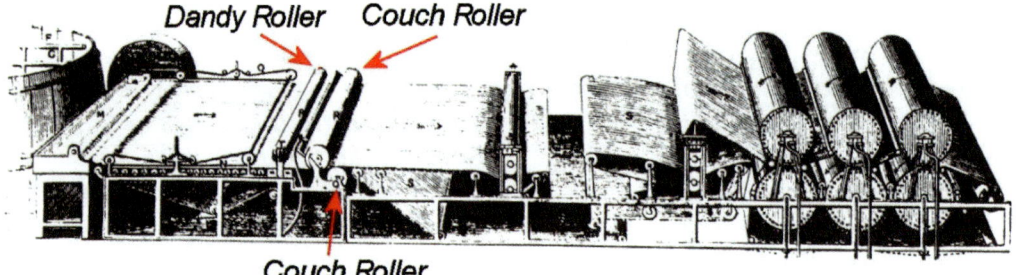

Fourdrinier paper making machine c1915 showing where the couch rollers were positioned[35]

The Fourdriniers' production machine was in four main parts: forming, pressing, drying and calendering. Of these individual operations, forming was the most critical, and it was here that woollen felts were used. In this section, the wet pulp was laid down and the mass of water was evacuated before it passed between two rollers, called couch rollers, which squeezed out the excess water and formed the paper web. The rollers then delivered the web to the press rollers that consolidated the paper ready for drying and calendering.

Each couch roller was constructed from a wooden cylinder that was covered with an endless felt sleeve that had been shrunk onto it with boiling water to ensure a tight fit. Although most machines used standard felt sleeves, special grades were made for machines that produced special papers, such as bank notes. As the paper industry expanded, so did the market for felt sleeves and MASCO had significant profitable business that enabled their production lines at Higher Lumb and Whitewell Vale Mills to prosper.

There was also a flourishing export market for their sleeves, which were shipped to worldwide markets, particularly Finland, Russia, France and India. From this strong base, the company was able to capitalise on the technology of making sleeves by penetrating other markets that required soft covered rollers, such as the confectionary, and leather industries. Amongst the speciality sleeves made for steel rollers there was one notable application for thick felt sleeves which were made into tyres for a company called Slingsby Ltd. who needed to make wheels without the use of rubber. These dense felts were fitted over flanged wheels and were then shrunk on to them with boiling water, after which they were turned on a lathe for trueness. This application was probably the only known use of felt as an alternative to rubber in tyres, despite the well-established similarity in their technical characteristics. Of course, the move from solid tyres to pneumatic ones ensured that felt could never compete in this market.

Advertisement for MASCO trademarked couch felts

Some of the sleeves could be very small with an internal diameter of one inch and an external diameter of two inches. These were commonly used in the printing industry as inking rollers, where the wicking and retention properties of felt gave the best performance.

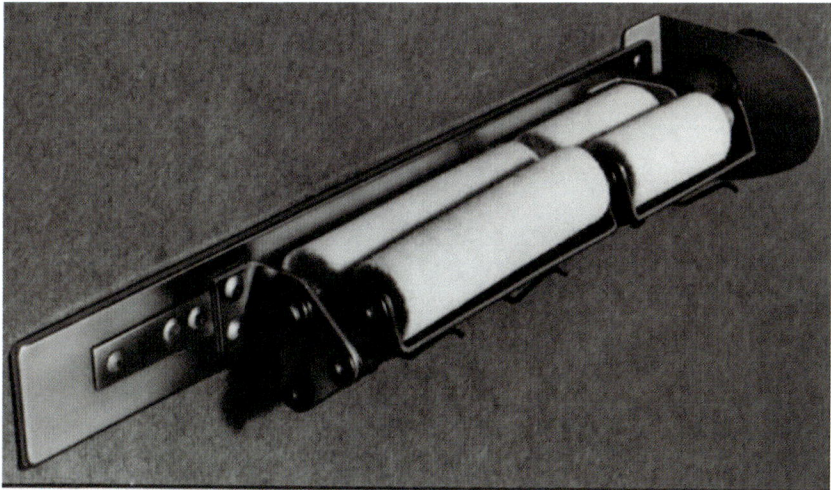

Inking rollers used in Roneo Vickers equipment

ARMAMENTS AND DEFENCE

The Ministry of Defence was always a major customer for felt with a host of uses throughout the armed forces. Principal amongst these was the protection of armaments of all kinds, particularly for lining ammunition boxes for grenades, mortars, artillery shells, and flares. It was also used for lining bomb transports and in arsenal trucks that transported the armaments and explosives. Felt was ideal for these purposes because of its cushioning properties and the fact that it was naturally anti-static so that there was no risk of any metallic contaminants that could accidentally cause the ignition of the explosives. Felt was used in box linings to protect delicate equipment such as radio equipment, gun carriage batteries, and other electronic parts. As the ultimate in protection, felt was also used in helmet linings. For all these end uses the felt was supplied either in rolls or sheets, with most packaging materials being made of grey felt to tight tolerances. Amongst other uses was the complete lining of aircraft cabins with felt, to give both acoustic and thermal insulation[36]. Felt was even used in relatively mundane applications such as the covers for soldiers' water bottles, the felt being supplied to a company called A C Shoppee.

At the start of the Second World War, there was also a large demand for washers and strips for the many maintenance duties required for logistical supply. Much of this was used as seals, grommets, and bumpers, used for servicing the various cars, trucks and tanks of the army, as well as parts for marine equipment and aircraft. Other parts were used for instrument mounting, general anti-vibration, and lining for harnesses and straps, notable in the manufacture of parachutes. The volume of cut parts was so great that whole departments were set up at feltmakers mills just to produce cut parts and gaskets for the Ministry of Defence.

A more direct use of felt in armaments was as a constituent of rifle and small arms cartridges. It was usual in the manufacture of cartridges to interpose wadding between the bullet and the explosive powder so that the maximum amount of energy from the explosion of the charge was transferred to the bullet. This was even more important in shotgun cartridges where the wadding prevented the gases from the explosion dissipating between the individual pellets of the shot. Up to about 1830, these wads were made of cardboard, which was not particularly efficient. From 1835 onward, disk-shaped felt wadding was used up to a half an inch thick, which proved to be far superior to the use of cardboard, particularly those wads patented and made by John Wilkinson[37].

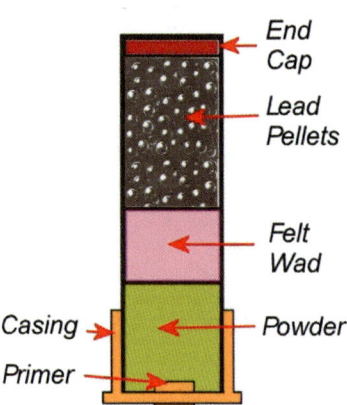

A simple shotgun cartridge showing the positioning of the felt gun wad.

The benefit of felt was its elasticity, which ensured that the wad made a tight seal, not only with the cartridge case but also with the gun barrel. Therefore, the bullet was propelled down the barrel as though it were a tight fit, because the elasticity of the felt prevented any gases from escaping through the sides. For even greater efficiency, the Wilkinson Patent Wad was shaped like a concave lens with the thicker parts nearest the barrel walls. Design of cartridges remained virtually the same from this time and into the twenty first century.

POLISHING AND BUFFING

From 1900 to around 1990, polishing was a major stage in most glass and metal finishing processes. This industry was so large that every felt maker had large departments working exclusively on polishing felts and the market was sufficiently robust to support one company, Cooper and Co. to devote all its production to the manufacture of polishing products.

Before the days of Pilkington's float glass process all sheet glass had to be polished, as did all the mirrors and lenses for scientific and domestic use. The glass industry was a particularly large market for very dense white felt in the form of disks that could be as large as twenty inches in diameter and three inches thick. They were used with the disk face down on the glass sheet on which there was a slurry of polishing grit. The grit and water filled the interstices in the felt, and the circular motion of the disk gave a unique local turbulent action between the felt and the glass. This action ground away minute particles of glass, to leave a smooth flat surface. To replenish the grit the slurry was fed through holes drilled through the felt, and in some cases, the disk was cut into quarters and the slurry fed into the gaps. For polishing lenses a thin dense felt was used that was cut to the shape of the polishing former and moulded around it to give a perfect shape. Again, grinding was done with a wet grinding paste. In handling the glass workers needed protection from the sharp edges and special "hand hats" were made out of felt for this purpose. They were effectively gloves without fingers similar to oven mitts, which were made by hardening the felts once and putting the hand through the soft middle of the felt to separate the layers, then hardening them once more. Further protection for the glass operatives was made in the form of sleeves that were tapered to accommodate the forearm. Once the float glass production was firmly established the market for glass polishing bobs virtually disappeared though in 1980 there were still some specialised glass processes that still used them. At the same time, the need for operator protection was obviated by the use of suction devices and the automatic transportation of the glass sheets. However, some grey felt was still used as pads to separate the sheets when they were stacked for warehousing.

Felt polishing wheels were of great importance to the metal finishing industry, particularly for the automotive industry for taking burrs off moulded parts and imparting a smooth finish. Wheels of different diameters and thickness were used depending on the type of metal parts to be polished and they had to be capable of being used at surface speeds between four thousand and eight thousand feet per minute. For polishing, an adhesive was applied to the circumference of the wheel and then impregnated with carborundum grit of size between sixty and one hundred, depending on the level of polishing required. The grit penetrated the outer layers of the felt wheel giving a uniform abrasive surface even when the surface wore down with use.

The resilience of the felt also ensured that it could accommodate any high spots in the metal, maintaining contact with the entire surface, to give a uniform polish. This was in contrast to the alternative of a rigid wheel covered with emery cloth or paper, where the performance declined with wear and polishing action was unforgiving of irregularities in the metal surface. By using felts of different densities and different grit sizes, the polishing action could be adjusted from coarse to fine and could be designed to match any type of metal to be polished. For rough polishing aluminium, brass, cast iron and steel, a felt of density 0.6 gm/cc was used with a grit size of sixty and for fine polishing a density of 0.45 gm/cc one hundred and twenty grit was employed. For stainless steel a hard felt at a density of 0.6 gm/cc was used for all polishing, the rough to smooth operations being made by grit size alone. Buffing was done using wheels or mops without any abrasive grit.

A Cooper and Co's polishing wheel being used to polish a metal casting

The market for felt polishing wheels and cloth was at its height during the 1950s and 1960s with the automotive industry and the Sheffield cutlery industries at their peak. At that time, many car parts were chromium plated and required polishing. Similarly, cutlery needed polishing operations to finish them to a commercial standard even as the industry was transitioning from plated metal to stainless steel. Later plastic for car parts and stainless steel cutlery completely replaced chromium and both the automotive and cutlery industries declined dramatically in Britain as imported products undercut them. The manufacture of felt polishing wheels declined in parallel with these industries. By 1980, production of felt wheels became more of a speciality item than a mainstream product, and output was a small fraction of the past.

FILTRATION

Because of its fibrous nature, felt has a vast surface area compared to its volume, which makes it eminently suitable for filtering both liquids and gases. Its homogeneous structure is efficient at particle retention and can hold large quantities of solids without affecting the flow of fluid through it. Furthermore, felt does not easily block up with solids and consequently has a low plugging rate.

The surface characteristics of woollen fibres are such that particles cling to wool by a contact force known as Van der Waals forces, so that particles much less in size than the spaces between the fibres can be trapped. This gives a high filtration capability with a high porosity, making it ideal for facemasks where comfortable breathing is essential. Many felts were therefore used in miners' respirators. Wool felt is also resistant to many chemicals and because it can be made completely sterile, it was ideal for use as a filter in much surgical and anaesthetic equipment. Wool's natural affinity for oil also made felt suitable for filtering lubrication oils from air compressors and deep-sea diving gear, which were required to deliver uncontaminated air. These felts were usually thick dense white felts and fabricated into complicated shapes to fit the equipment and the required pipe work. The non-clogging property of felt found good use in large-scale industrial dust filters, particularly in chemical plants where fine particles had to be eliminated[38]. These dust filters were sewn into a variety of shapes from conical to cylindrical or even hemispherical depending on the type of filtration unit. The non-fray characteristic of felt made this a simple operation.

Because wool felt is immune to oils, greases, and solvents, and a host of other chemicals, it was employed as a filter for all kinds of fluids such as petrol, paints, latex, and engine oil, particularly as it could be fabricated into a wide variety of forms. As a plug filter, it was used to filter an hydraulic oil or petrol line where it could remove particles as small as one micron across. To increase the effectiveness of a filter, the surface area of the felt was increased by pleating it onto a wire screen and assembling it into a compact cartridge. These cartridges were used to filter oil in automobiles, diesel engines and domestic oil supplies.

The manufacture of a cartridge oil filter

Cartridges could also be constructed by fabricating thick felt into a particular shape such as a triangle, square or cross and stacking them one on top of the other. Each component had a hole in the middle so that when stacked together it constituted a pipe through which a liquid like oil was pumped. The liquid therefore flowed edgewise through the felt rather than from the top face of the felt to the bottom face as conventionally. This used the homogeneity of the structure of felt to advantage in producing a filter with a lower construction cost. Felt was also sewn into bags and fitted to the end of a gravity fed pipe in order to strain used automotive paint so that it could be re-used. Using the same principle conical bags were manufactured as jelly bags for straining fruit in the preparation of jam, though later these were replaced by woven bags using synthetic yarn.

Perhaps the simplest of all filtering techniques was drumhead straining, where a felt was stretched over a drum and the liquid to be filtered, such as latex, was poured on top. The fluid passed through the felt and was collected into the drum, while the unwanted debris was left on the surface of the felt. Eventually the accumulation of solids on top of the felt would prevent any further liquid from passing through it, and when it reached this stage, the felt had to be replaced.

A much more complex filtering application for felt was its use in rotary vacuum filters, which were designed to extract solids that were suspended in a slurry. In this respect, its operation was the reverse of the simple drum strainer. The rotary filtering machine consisted of a large perforated metal drum covered with a thick dense felt, a reservoir to hold the slurry, and a knife to remove the solids from the surface of the felt. The felt was manufactured as an endless sleeve that was stretched over the drum to give a tight fit over the drum.

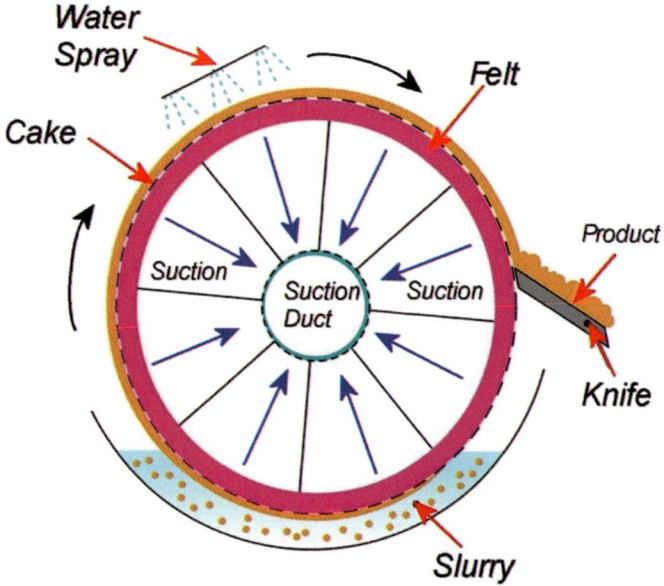

A rotary vacuum filter using a felt sleeve over a perforated metal drum extracting solids from a slurry

A powerful fan extracted air from inside the drum through a central duct, which caused suction at the surface of the drum. Where the drum dipped into the slurry, it pulled solid particles onto the felt but without penetrating it. As the drum rotated further, the vacuum drew out all the water through the felt, making the solids form a cake-like layer on it, which was then scraped off with a knife blade. The performance of the felt in this use was exceptional since it could handle slurry with up to two hundred parts per million and was capable of delivering seven pounds of dry solids per square foot per hour with an operating life of six hundred hours[39]. Without doubt, this end use epitomises the versatility, durability and performance of felt in industrial applications.

APPENDIX

SOME USES FOR WOOLLEN PRESSED FELT

INDUSTRY AREA	APPLICATION
Aero Engine Components	Washers, wicks,
Agricultural Machines	Fabricated parts, tractor parts
Aircraft	Instrumentation parts, hydraulics, switchgear, metal finishing
Aluminium Rolling	Wiping during processing, protective pads on polished plate
Asbestos Building Board	Used on thickness planer as a backing pad
Atomic Energy	Canister transit protection of cores prior to insertion at reactor
Audio-Visual Aids	Sound absorption, acoustical correction, anti-vibration mounting
Automobile	Sound vibration insulation, eyeball vents, washers for dynamos, trim
Brake Lining Manufacture	Fabricated parts for use on moulding machines.
Business Machines	Typewriter mats
Cable, Wire Manufacturers	Wiping, de-greasing, and insulation applicators
Chemical Filters	Dry cleaning fluids, pharmaceuticals
Clothing Trade and Uniforms	Collar felts, padding, embroidery support, interlinings, shoulder pads
Compressors	Air filtration, oil separators
Computers	Tape spindle washers, print out lubricators
Confectionery	Felt rollers on process machinery, machine cloths
Conveyor Belts	Seal at each joint
Cutlery	Drawer lining
Dentistry	Polishing bobs
Diesel Engines and Generators	Fabricated parts, oil seals, gaskets
Domestic Appliances	Fabricated parts for washing machines, dryers, vacuum cleaners
Drilling Rigs	Rings for mountings of seismographic, oceanographic instruments
Education	Blackboard cleaners as strips of felt bonded to a block of wood
Electric Motors	Dry seals for all types from fractional horsepower to traction units
Engine Manufacturers	Lubricating seals for automobile and marine engines, gaskets
Entertainment	Gaming tables, printed playing mats, bowling mats
Explosives and Fireworks	Packing, case linings, hopper seals, chemical fuses, powder ramming
Exhibitions	Display felts
Fancy Goods	Bases for Clocks, table lamps, woodcraft
Filtration	All types, face masks, fluid, air, and dust filters
Flags	Pennants
Flour Milling	Door seals
Fork Lift Trucks	Fabricated parts
Furniture and Upholstery	Padding, polishing, mattress stitch protectors, table pad backing
Gardening	Lawnmower washers, seals, lubrication wicks
Glass Manufacturers	Bench felt, polishing, beveling, storage, carrier racks, optical grinding
Industrial Clothing	Safety helmets, headbands, glove lining, miners' knee pads
Industrial Lighting	Light cover gaskets
Jewellery Manufacture	Polishing wheels
Joinery	Sanding pads, discs, drawer linings
Leather Processing	Roller covering, leather polishing, dyeing, vacuum drying equipment
Livestock	Cat and dog collar linings, canary nest linings
Machine Tools	Fabricated parts, tool polishing, anti-vibration mounts
Metal Boxes	Printing canisters, machine ejectors
Metal Finishing	Polishing bobs and cones

Millinery	Ladies hats, novelty hats, gents fashion hats
Mining Equipment	Fabricated parts, sound absorption, instrumentation
Monumental Masons	Polishing
Motor Car Batteries	Protective pads
Mountaineering	Haversack, harness lining, glove lining puttees, kletterschuhe
Musical Instruments	Piano felts, seals in woodwind, drum beaters, case linings
North Sea Gas	Isolating valves (used under rim of diaphragm)
Ozonisers and Deodorants	Wicks for dispersion of chemicals
Orthopaedic Appliances	Padding, artificial limbs
Printing Machinery	Fabricated parts for type-setting machines, mould cleaning
Paper-making and Conversion	Fabricated parts
Petro-Chemicals	Filtration, seals, insulation, paint filtration, hopper seals
Piano	Under keyboard, hammer felts, damper felts
Pneumatic Carriers	Carrier buffer
Pumps	Seals, gaskets, filters
Radio, TV Manufacturers	Transformer mountings, scanner coil mountings, knob washers
Rubber Moulding, Fabrication	Fabricated parts
Rugs	Backing
Saddlery	Horse blankets, backing for leather straps
Shipbuilding	Cable trunking, vent mountings
Shoes and Slippers	Linings, uppers, heel blocks
Soap Powders	Hopper seals
Soil Pipes	Impregnated seals
Sports Equipment	Boxing rings, bowling greens
Stationery	Marker pens, nibs, pen reservoirs, reservoir in ink pads
Steel Rolling Mills	Wiping
Surgical Applications	Padding
Telecommunication	Keyboard buffers, seals, contact wipers, packing
Textile Machinery	Rollers, shuttle guides, yarn tensioners
Ticket Machines	Inking rollers
Traction Engines	Fabricated parts
Toys	Soft toy components, craft shapes, craft squares
Typesetting Machines	Lubrication, mould cleaning
Vacuum Flasks	Vacuum bulb protector
Warehousing	Anti-vibration on automated systems

According to The Pressed Felt Manufacturers Association,
P0 Box 9, Ramsbottom, Bury, Lancashire, 1980

14 PEOPLE

EARLY PERSONALITIES

Throughout the history of commercial felt making, there have been only a limited number of pioneers with the entrepreneurial ability to take felt making to new levels of enterprise. Although little is known about the lives, of the earliest pioneers of commercial felt making, their contributions were paramount in laying the foundations of felt making and their names at least have survived as a matter of record. Amongst these early names, John Wilkinson, T. R. Williams, and William Abbott stand out as the prime movers of the industry. So far, only snippets of information about them have become known and more research is needed to uncover their stories. Both John Wilkinson and William Abbott were established textile manufacturers and astute businessmen whilst T. R. Williams appears to have been an entrepreneur and inventor of independent means. Amongst his inventions were improvements to the manufacture of hats[1], a machine for separating burrs, or other substances, from wool, hair and fur[2], the invention of a lancet for removing cataracts[3], a means of making artificial skins[4], and then manufacturing of felt for covering the bottoms of vessels[5]. All of this was done whilst he was living at 17 Norfolk Street, the Strand, London, though he appears to have moved addresses during 1833.

The early days of The Patent Woollen Cloth Company were fraught with difficulty and insolvency but stability was achieved under the leadership of one Roy Stewart[6] ably assisted by his financial secretary Thomas Lawson who clearly recognised the importance of the contribution of the company by eventually lodging key documents in the Leeds Library archives. Once there was universal recognition of the importance of the felt industry, it was somewhat easier to trace the key entrepreneurs through the local newspapers because of the impact most of them had on their local communities.

ROSTRONS

There were two Rostrons engaged in feltmaking in Rossendale: Edward Rostron and Jordon Rostron, Jordon being the son of Edward's brother James. Edward and James were the sons of James Rostron and Ann Butterworth who married at Newchurch on 3 January 1809. James and Ann had nine children: John born about 1809, William 1811-31, James 1815-90, Edward 1816-82, Richard around 1819, Ann born in 1821, George 1823-47, Thomas 1827-32, and Jordon 1829-36[7].

Edward Rostron can justifiably be described as the father of feltmaking in Rossendale since he was not only the first to make felt there but also the first to demonstrate that it was a route to profits unheard of in the district. He undoubtedly acted as a catalyst for the other entrepreneurs to follow.

His path to riches was hard, with success coming from his long experience in the woollen industry coupled with his aptitude for business, and his determination to finish things that he started. He was born on 23 December 1816 at Hugh Hill, Waterfoot, the home of his father, and he was educated at Newchurch National School.

James Rostron born 1785 died 1863
the patriarch of the Rostron family

When he was 18 years old, he went to Manchester to work for one of his uncles in a woollen warehouse in Turner Street. He later started his own business as a commission agent in Friday Street. In 1851, when he was thirty-five he returned to Rossendale and continued his business there as a woollen merchant[8], whilst living in Glenbottom. This must have enabled him to build up sufficient capital to invest in plant and machinery for making felt from 1854 onwards.

Edward Rostron, pioneer of feltmaking
in the Rossendale Valley

By 1855, he was able to build his own house called Glen House to accommodate his growing family. He had married Maria sometime before 1851, and is said to have had ten children, four boys and six girls[9] but there are only seven recorded at St Nicholas Church, where he worshipped. These were:

James born in 1853, Sarah Ann born in 1855, Maria born in 1856, Dora Isabel born 1860, William Henry born 1861, Butterworth born 1863 and Francis Maude born 1868. By the time of his last child, Edward had built Myrtle Grove Mill and Myrtle Grove House opposite the Mill. His success in business was truly meteoric as he continued expanding by building mills at Cloughfold and Tunstead and even ran a sawmill at Myrtle Grove.

He was a deeply religious man and took a keen interest in St Nicholas Church, Newchurch, also known as the felters church because so many from the felt industry worshipped there. All his children were baptized there and on his death after a severe and painful illness on 30 January 1882, he was buried in the family vault in the churchyard, as was his wife on her death. He was appointed a warden of the church in 1876 and he therefore took a great deal of interest in its fabric and structure.

St Nicholas Church where Edward Rostron worshipped.

During his tenure as warden, the grounds were enlarged, the churchyard walled in, the tower and walls cemented, and a new organ installed. In particular, he paid for a new peal of eight bells to be cast and hung at a cost of more than £1000[10]. The parishioners were so appreciative of his efforts that they organised a special festival of thanks at which he was presented with oil portraits of himself and his wife. With a turnout of two hundred and fifty people, he must have been well respected in church circles. As further evidence of his standing, in June 1890, an altar was consecrated to Edward Rostron of Myrtle Grove. The altar was made from a grey granite slab on a granite pedestal and with a brass plate with IHS inscribed in the centre and the words "Do all to the Glory of God" around the rim.

When Edward died, his sons took over the business but some had a penchant for horse racing that jeopardised the operation. There was "some unpleasantness" that caused the company to be wound up, and the remaining funds were distributed amongst the family. This enabled Maude to go to Australia around 1888 and then on to California, USA. Butterworth too went to Australia, settled down, and had five children: Constance, Ann, Bert, Jack, and Nell, of these Ann was the mother of T. G, Ames who provided the photograph of Edward Rostron. Mr. Ames believed that the other brothers also settled in America.

James Rostron (1815 -1890) was as astute a businessman as was his brother Edward and like him developed his acumen the hard way. When a young man and starting his own business, he carried bales of hair fibre on his back, going from Bacup to Haslingdon and every week he used to travel to Bradford to buy wool[11].

James Rostron the brother of Edward Rostron photograph from Jane Rostron

He steadily built up his business until he owned three mills: Hardsough, Branwood, and Stacksteads where he built thirty-six houses for his people and from whom he collected rent. He lived at Newson House Stacksteads and then lived in Mayfield. It was at Hardsough mill that felt was made as well as woven cloth prior to 1888 when he let his son, Jordon Rostron, manage it together with his other sons. Collectively the brothers were uncoordinated and their father became so annoyed with them he wanted to teach them a lesson in co-operation. To do this he cut up a £100 note and sent each a piece telling them they could only redeem it by them getting together and visiting him. It was no surprise therefore in 1888 that the partnership between the brothers was dissolved and Jordon Rostron continued the business on his own[12]. His father James bequeathed Hardsough to him on his death in 1890 and Jordon ran the business successfully until 1904 when he sold it to the newly formed MASCO combine.

James had three wives the first was an Ashworth, the second was named Laidlaw and who had two children of her own, and the third was called Elizabeth. By his first wife he had a son Jordon and by his second he had a daughter called Ada, a son James, and two other daughters, Hilda and Mary (Mrs. Lord). In total, he had twelve children and sixty-nine grandchildren. He was a member of the Church of England and attended a church in Spotland, though he was buried in Newchurch, but his third wife, Elizabeth, who outlived him, was buried at Edgeworth.

Jordon Rostron was the most able of James' Rostron brothers but although he maintained the business for some years was not able to make it grow like his father. However, he was prosperous and built the Rostron buildings. There was also some connection to the Rostron Arms in Edenfield. He married and had six children: Annie, Maggie, Ada, Edward, Susanna, and Jordon Rostron (II) (born 1860). This Jordon married a Maria Rawston and their daughter Jane Rostron (1899 -1982) provided photographs of the family as well as James Rostron's will.

Jordon Rostron the feltmaker of Hardsough Mill with his wife Maria Rawston

ROWLAND RAWLINSON

Roland Rawlinson came from Cumberland and arrived in Rossendale with all his equipment on the back of a lorry and with half a crown (12½ p) in his pocket. He started at Higher Lumb Mill dyeing woollen fabric. At that time, the Whitewell Vale was stocked with fish, and the river became the subject of a preservation order, which forced Roland Rawlinson to build dye pits to catch the dye or close down. With no available finance, he discussed the problem with his workers and they agreed to give up some of their wages to help finance him. Having built the pits and established his business he prospered sufficiently to be able to move to Myrtle Grove Mill, previously owned by Edward Rostron. He never forgot what his employees did for him and most of them were promoted to senior or management positions as his business expanded.

Roland Rawlinson had two brothers, Frank and Harold, and three sisters. After marrying he had four sons: Herman, Neville, Ernald, and Irwin; and two daughters: Ada and Useta, the choice of mostly German names was strangely out of place in Rossendale. The eldest son Herman eventually took over the business while both Neville and Ernald joined the army during the Second World War, with Neville fighting in the North African desert campaign. Roland could speak fluent Spanish and Portuguese, which he used to great effect in gaining lucrative markets in South America. He was an astute businessman and had considerable interests in many industries, such as gas and railways, and it was reputed that he was a part owner in the Lancashire/Yorkshire railway. He was such an important shareholder that trains used to stop specially to let him alight between stations. Roland Rawlinson was a man of considerable ingenuity and he applied this wherever possible to reduce costs and improve efficiency. For example, he recognised the importance of electricity as a future power source for his mill and built his own electric plant to generate his own electricity on-site. He was equally ingenious in minimising the costs of the local government rates when he rebuilt his wool store. The rateable value was calculated on the area of the ground floor and on the number of storeys. The old wool store was a single storey building with a small floor area and Roland decided to add several new floors. He built the store so that each storey had a larger area than the floor below it, but since his rates only took account of the ground floor area, he made significant savings on the amount he had to pay the local council.

Both Roland and his brothers were experts on wool and they could tell a quality of wool by drawing fibres across their lips to assess the scaly nature of the fibres. They also used to oil felt before storage in order to give the felt a good lustre. No wool was wasted, all was segregated and put into different bags and used for different felts. They even encouraged children to bring in wool waste from the hedgerows where sheep were grazed on local farmland by paying so much a handful. Most collected them in sugar bags for which they were paid pennies.

At first, Roland Rawlinson lived at Myrtle Grove House built by Edward Rostron. Then he moved to Horncliffe House, which he had built on the Burnley Road. It was said that no mortar was used, being all dressed stone and white lead. He was by then a millionaire[13].

For Roland, felt making was not an exclusive operation and, like R. R. Whitehead and Brothers, he was equally comfortable managing a woollen weaving operation. In terms of felt manufacture, he produced many of the products made by other manufacturers though in the later stages of his business he concentrated on hair felts. He was very friendly with Richard Ashworth and there seemed to be a mutual respect between them, which led to an agreement whereby they agreed not to compete in each other's market. His weaving operation was dependent on one major market, which was for the supply of the woven cloths for serapes (ponchos) for the South American Indians of Paraguay and Uruguay. Of all the felt manufacturing companies, Roland Rawlinson remained independent the longest, but when the South American market collapsed, his successors sold the business to Bury and Masco Industries in 1966.

THE MITCHELL BROTHERS

All commentators on the Mitchell brothers report that there were three of them born to John Mitchell of Fearnes, a local Rossendale businessman who was associated with the woollen textile trade. The eldest was William, the second born was Thomas and the youngest Robert John Chadwick, known as RJC and born on 14 July 1847. However, a fourth brother called George was recorded as competing with them in the Liverpool Olympics of 1865[14]. However, he does not seem to have been involved in the business.

William, who was born in 1839, had a keen interest in politics and in later life stood for Parliament, contesting the Accrington Division in 1895 as a Conservative candidate, but without success. He tried again in 1897 standing for the Middleton Division. He eventually became a member of parliament for Burnley in 1900 when he wrested the seat from the Liberals, no mean feat considering that this had always been a Liberal stronghold. At the next General Election he retired and the seat returned to the Liberal fold. Although clearly a charismatic politician he was not without his critics particularly in his home district, where he was publicly criticised for his ultra Conservative views. One journalist, commentating in the Rossendale Free Press, mocked him sarcastically with a quote from Shakespeare's play Julius Caesar recording: "but Mr. Mitchell is an honourable man", but meaning precisely the opposite. However, William Mitchell was revered by his local Conservative Association and his initials are inscribed on a foundation stone in the Conservative Club at Waterfoot. As a renowned athlete, he achieved an outstanding feat at Liverpool "Olympic Festival" of 1863 by winning the two hundred yards hurdles in twenty-six seconds and the long jump with "19½ft". The first authenticated two hundred and twenty yard hurdles time was thirty seconds by J. Brindley, and in Liverpool the following year, the best long jump until then had been 20ft 11 inches by Charles Buller earlier in 1863[15].

All of the Mitchell brothers were accomplished athletes. Some idea of the athleticism can be gleaned from their performances at the Liverpool Olympics where from 1863 to 1870, the four brothers dominated the national amateur athletics scene. After William's successes in 1863, both William and Thomas competed in 1864, both being described as the epitome of English athleticism with "arms banded with muscle and bound with tendons of steel" and "prepared to bear either victory or defeat without presumption or despondence".

The first Liverpool Olympics in 1862 showing how the Mitchell brothers would have competed

At that meeting, William broke the International Association of Athletics Federations (IAAF) record for one hundred yards in nine and three-quarter seconds, whilst Thomas won the high jump with a leap of five feet seven and a quarter inches, despite an ungainly style. George managed to make the hundred yards final with William but was unplaced. In 1865, all the brothers dominated the event with William winning the two hundred yards, two-hundred-yard hurdles, and the standing wide jump, with a leap of over sixteen feet, which was a record. Thomas won the running wide jump with William coming second. Meanwhile Robert made his first appearance at the age of eighteen but he was beaten into second place in the eight-eighty yards, and pole vault. George, however, won the broadsword fencing. Robert went on to exceed his brothers in athletic achievement by winning the pole vault at the AAC Championships of 1868 with a leap of ten feet six and a half inches as well as the high jumps at the AAC Championships of 1870 and 1871, with jumps of five feet nine inches and five feet nine and a half inches. These were all amateur best performance. In total, Robert won eleven national titles at four different events.

Of the four brothers, Thomas Mitchell probably received the most public acclaim through his military association. He was born at Fearnes Hall in 1839 and educated privately at Preston Grammar School. During his youth he developed a keen interest in military matters and soldiery and in 1859 when the Secretary of War, General Jonathan Peel (fifth son of Sir Robert Peel), called for the enlistment of a Voluntary Corps, Thomas was one of the first to enlist. He joined the East Lancashires on June 26 1859 as a private and rose rapidly through the ranks: making Corporal in 1860, Sergeant in 1861, ensign in 1863, Lieutenant in 1864 and Captain in 1866. It was then twelve years before his promotion to Major and then ten years to make Lieutenant Colonel in 1888, becoming an honorary Colonel, one year later. This gave him a continuous period of service of just over forty-five years, which at that time was a record. He was clearly a charismatic leader and when he was a Captain, he was presented in

1866 with a silver sword and scabbard with the inscription: "To Captain Mitchell as a mark of regard and esteem by members of the 4th Lancashire Volunteer Rifles." No doubt, he led from the front, as he was a fine rifle shot winning the Silver Challenge Cup at Altcar. As a mark of his leadership when he was a Colonel, he mustered one thousand two hundred men in readiness for the South African War, with only three of the whole battalion absent due to health. In 1902, he was created a Commander of the Bath. He retired from the army on 6 November 1904, and was awarded the Volunteer Decoration in the same year that the Mitchell Brothers business joined the formation of the MASCO combine[16].

In his private life, he married Miss Margaret Ann Lord, a daughter of John Lord a Justice of the Peace of Bacup, the marriage being blessed with a son, John Lord Geoffrey Mitchell, and a daughter. When he was a Colonel, he became a Justice of the Peace for the County of Surrey. Just like his brothers, Thomas Mitchell was a staunch Conservative and was a member of the Junior Carlton and Constitutional Clubs.

Col. Thomas Mitchell, C.B., V.D., J.P.

The Colonel, as a renowned athlete, always kept himself in shape with regular exercise. To maintain his skill at jumping he always elected to jump over the river Whitewell to the mill rather than walk across the bridge by Albert Works. He exercised regularly with two Indian clubs and a set of hand weights that he kept in his office. The clubs were legendary each being about four foot high, and could only just be lifted by an average man with two hands, and yet Colonel Mitchell often swung both of these clubs together, one in each hand. He also exercised each morning with hand weights of cast iron. Being a devout Christian, Colonel Mitchell laid the foundation stone for the chapel (called "The Mission") by Woodleigh Cottages and there is an inscription there dedicated to him[17].

The sons of the Mitchell Brothers all entered the business in various capacities. Thomas's son, John Lord Geoffrey Mitchell, learned the manufacturing side of the business by working at Albert works, living in the cottage known as the Cott by the side of the factory. He then joined his father in London at the sales warehouse, Newgate Street, and afterwards at 23/24 Old Bailey. When he retired, his son

T. D. Mitchell (Derek) took charge of sales in Manchester, London, and Rossendale. He was the last of the Mitchells to be involved with the business, which had then become Bury and Masco Industries Limited.

T. Derek Mitchell, in 1954, the last Mitchell involved in the felt business

Robert J. C. Mitchell's son, Robert John Howarth Mitchell, became concerned with, and subsequently in charge of, the manufacturing side of the company. When he married his cousin Gladys (daughter of William) he became remote from the factory by living first at Spring Hill, Higher Cloughfold and then moving to Gisburn. He retired early sometime after 1918 to a farm at Great Rissington Hill, near Bourton-on-the-Water where he died in his middle 50's, leaving no issue. R. J. H. Mitchell was known affectionately as Mr. Bertie and was the last Master of the now defunct Rossendale Hunt[18].

THE ASHWORTHS

Richard Ashworth was another of the outstanding feltmakers of Rossendale. He was a skilled businessman who built up his business by expansion rather than acquisition, growing it from nothing to eventually rivalling that of the Mitchell Brothers. No doubt, he learned his skills from his mother Deborah Ashworth, who was the daughter of John Tattersall who owned a woollen manufacturing company at Shawclough, and she was a well-known popular local figure. As Deborah Tattersall, she married George Ashworth, a weaver from Newchurch in 1847 and a year later Richard was born. Her husband George died young and Deborah was left to fend for herself by running a small shop in Newchurch[19].

The bond between mother and son must have been very strong because Richard was always known in the area as "Dick O' Debs" or even more fondly "Dicky Debs", and it was she who funded his first venture into felt making[20]. Deborah was a renowned raconteur and was endeared for her fondness for chatting to people, which is probably where Richard developed his interest in the local dialect. He was in fact an acknowledged expert and was invited to lecture the Bacup Natural History Society on the Rossendale dialect in 1896[21]. He was also a keen orchid grower, collector of works of art, and an ardent cyclist.

Richard Ashworth's rise in business was remarkable since he had a scant education, having to work at the age of nine as an office boy at Captain Law Schofield's felt works at Baltic mill. He was clearly very bright as he rose to become chief clerk there[22]. This must have been where he learnt the felt trade. This expertise enabled him to start up production at Bridge End Mill with twenty employees, eventually expanding into the huge Longholme Mill. In 1877, he married Jane Worswick and they produced five offspring, three boys and two girls. The three boys, James, Oliver, and George all entered the business in prominent positions and had a major impact on the running of the Mitchells, Ashworth, Stansfield Combine. Their father Richard built houses for them close together in Rawtenstall, each, as was the custom, had a name bestowed on them: James had Ashville, Oliver had Dunram and George had Waverly. Meanwhile Richard himself lived at Ashlands, Waterfoot, but his mother remained at Old Street Newchurch where she had always lived and where she also died in 1904 at the age of 84.

Richard Ashworth founder of the Ashworth branch of Mitchells, Ashworth, Stansfield and Co., Limited

George and Oliver were keen on horse racing and between them owned three racehorses: Mascolet, Masco, Pegomas. They must have been top class horses as two of their stable once won on the same day at the same race meeting. They were so enthusiastic about horse racing that they allowed their employees the afternoon off to go to the Grand National; the employees worked until noon and were then transported to Aintree in thirteen coaches[23]. James was also keen on cars and was a shareholder in Armstrong Siddley. Despite their expensive pastimes, the brothers did not let them interfere in the business and they were diligent at minding the factory, making it a routine to tour the mill every day at nine o'clock.

James managed Albert works and was noted for his sternness, which frightened some of the staff, though at the same time he commanded respect through his fairness and appreciation of staff efforts. His marriage to Sir Henry Whittaker Trickett's daughter in 1903 was the society wedding of the year. Sir Henry Trickett was the mastermind behind the slipper and shoe trade in Britain and was a philanthropist of considerable standing. At the same time, James' father Richard was equally renowned as the leading felt manufacturer and employer in the district. Unprecedented, it led to the publication of a supplement in the Rossendale Free Press announcing the wedding to the world and after the wedding, the celebrations went on for two days.

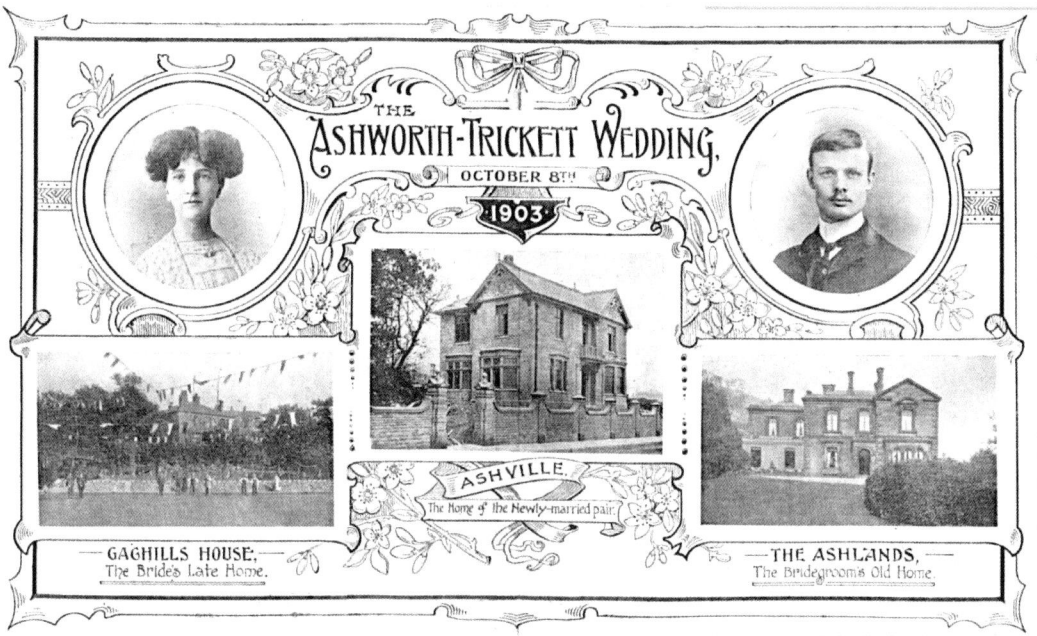

The marriage of James Ashworth announced as a supplement to the Rossendale Free Press

Their union was blessed with three children: Henry Richard Trickett Ashworth, Joan Elizabeth, and James Whittaker (who died in 1940 at the age of 29). Henry Richard Trickett, known as Harry, was the last Ashworth to be involved with the business, and though his son John worked for a short while in the business he never became involved and eventually went to work in London.

Harry was an intelligent sensitive man who was well liked by his employees and his progressive thinking was responsible for setting up a research unit in order to apply a scientific approach to felt making, which had been for decades an empirical art. As well as his duties in the company, he took an active interest in the local community. Every year he sponsored a competition for the local children of the local church, with the prize being a weekend in London. He maintained the family support of St Nicholas's Church, Newchurch, and was a member of the parochial church council as well as representing the church on the diocesan committee for finance and education. He was a keen Conservative and was treasurer of the Rossendale Conservative Association from 1939 to 1959, eventually becoming president four years before his death in 1971. He was also president of the Lumb Valley Conservative Club from 1937 to beyond 1967, and encouraged youngsters to be involved with the Conservatives through the Junior Imperial league, for which he was chairman from 1932 to 1939. He was also a Freemason.

Henry Richard Trickett Ashworth, the last Ashworth involved in felt making

There was a long standing friendship between the Rawlisons and the Ashworths that started with Richard Ashworth's friendship with Roland Rawlinson and later H. R. T. Ashworth was very friendly with Ernald Rawlinson, one of Roland's sons. When MASCO took over Rawlinson's felt works it was rationalised in a way that upset Harry and this was compounded by the decision to close Albert Works against his wishes. Although he had become a major shareholder and millionaire on the death of his father and uncles, he was unable to prevent the closure. This was especially difficult for him as his father, James, had been manager there for many years.

Harry's sister Joan Elizabeth married Douglas Garnham who became chairman of Bury and Masco Industries Limited in 1969. The merger of MASCO with Bury Felt in 1962 took place after the death of Mrs. James Ashworth (H.R.T.'s mother). Although the merger had been discussed ten years earlier, Mrs. Ashworth would not agree, because she regarded Bury Felt as a breakaway company and there was possibly some personal history behind the early beginnings of the Bury firm.

Of Richard Ashworth's two daughters, Beatrice Alice married Mr. Henry Heys Ratcliffe of Holly Mount, Rawtenstall and they had two sons the eldest, John Ashworth, and Geoffrey. John Ashworth Radcliffe (1902-1987) who after gaining a first class honours.at Cambridge became the famous radio physicist and later the Director of the Radio Research Organisation. Geoffrey became a director in the Mitchells Ashworth and Stansfield combine at Longholme but left to form his own company and died in 1979. His son Michael did not become involved with felt.

Geoffrey Ratcliffe

Richard Ashworth's youngest daughter Marjorie, married Dr. James Helm who was the Medical Officer of Health for Rawtenstall and who lived it Newchurch. All the Ashworths were members of "the feltmakers church" of St Nicholas's and there is a family vault there, on the left of the entrance to the church.

STANSFIELDS

William Stansfield, the founder of the Stansfield branch of the felt industry, was a very different character than all the other feltmakers in Rossendale. He was a very reserved man who shunned the public limelight and actively avoided public service, declining many times to be nominated to stand for the town council. However, he was always supportive of local activities and gave generously to help the poor in the community. He was both liberal in attitude and in his politics and was vice-president of the Waterfoot Liberal Club, though he took no part in the public side of politics. In line with his involvement with the community, he was a governor of Newchurch Grammar School and president of the Rawtenstall Cricket Club; he was also a Freemason. It was only towards the end of his life that he allowed himself to be appointed as county magistrate.

William Stansfield (1850 – 1908, and his grandson George Alfred Stansfield (1917-1980) the last Stansfield involved in the felt industry

As a self-made man, William rose in business the hard way, working himself up in the woollen trade to eventually become a manager in his brother Joseph Stansfield's company. Joseph was also making felt for carpets at Higher Hollin Bank Mill at Scout Bottom, Newchurch until the mill burnt down in

1881[24]. The same fate befell William when he started his own business at Lumb Holes Mill and he nearly abandoned hope of re-establishing it. It was his wife who encouraged him not to give up and urged him to rent Baltic Mill, which had just ceased felt production, she even gave him her savings for the rent. From renting just a small portion of the mill, he gradually worked up the business in stages until he occupied the whole mill and eventually he was able to buy it[25] and even restore Lumb Holes Mill. He maintained his competitive position in the industry through his acute foresight, being one of the first to replace the open gas lighting with electric lights run by his own generator, since at the time there was no public electricity supply. He even managed to light his own house, Mytholme, with electricity by stringing wires from the Mill to the house. He was conscious that he needed to future-proof his business through his son, George, and sent him to learn felt making in Germany, which was flourishing at the time. It also provided a completely different perspective on the business. Significantly, his two daughters did not enter the business, as was the custom of the time.

William was well liked and respected by his employees and instilled loyalty in all those that worked for him. In the community at large, too, he was highly esteemed and it was noteworthy that the success in his business did not alter or spoil his disposition. When he died early at the age of fifty-eight it was considered he was a great loss to the community. Clearly, through his life he was sustained by his religion, which unlike the other Rossendale feltmakers was Baptist, and in which he took a deep interest. During his life, he fully supported the Bethel Baptist Chapel, Waterfoot, as well as its school and all its other functions. He was buried in the Sion Baptist churchyard, Cloughfold in the family vault.

At the formation of the MASCO combine, William's son George took over the running of Baltic and Lumb Holes Mills and continued in his father's footsteps maintaining both his care for his employees and the competitive edge of his production through investment in innovation. He later introduced his son George Alfred Stansfield into the business.

The young George was the last Stansfield to be involved in the felt industry and became one of the most powerful influences in the Bury and Masco company right up to the time of his death in 1980. This was remarkable since the Stansfield side of the MASCO empire was the smallest division, both in terms of size and share allocation, which indicates the considerable political skill that he undoubtedly had.

When he was twenty-three, he should have gone into the business but the Second World War intervened and he joined the armoured Corp fighting in the North African Campaign and later in the invasion of Europe. He served with distinction from 1940 to 1945 with the Derbyshire Yeomenry and the 51st Highland Division, achieving rank[26]. Like his grandfather, George was highly single minded and fought for and protected Baltic Mill at Board level; so much so that it was the Mitchells' Albert works, and Ashworth's Longholme Mill that were closed whilst the most unlikely Baltic Mill remained open right up to the final demise of the industry. In fact, the mill was restructured at a cost of £250,000 in 1978 and was renamed Stansfield Mill in his honour. His independent spirit sometimes led to disagreements with his fellow board members, for example when the company's transport system was centralised he did not allow Baltic's lorries to be included. There was also an instance where he restructured part of Baltic Mill without the other directors knowing about it[27]. By 1969, he was joint managing director of Bury and Masco Industries Limited with Geoffrey Beetson[28]. By that time there were no longer any Mitchells or Ashworths in executive positions and from here on his influence in the company was absolute.

Geoffrey Harley Beetson, Joint Managing Director of Bury and Masco Industries Ltd in 1969

George Stansfield was also an influential force in the felt industry as a whole. For nine years, he was chairman of the Pressed Felt Manufacturers Association and represented the industry on the Council of Wool Industries Research Association. He was also a member of the Worshipful Company of Feltmakers and a Freeman and Liveryman of London.

He was a keen yachtsman and member of the Royal Windsor Yacht Club. On his retirement, he moved from his house on Newchurch Road, Cloughfold to Tree Tops, Post Knott, Bowness, Cumbria, to be able to pursue his interest. In his private life, he was married to Kathleen and had three children. When he died at the age of sixty-three, he was buried in St Nicholas's churchyard rather than the family Baptist vault at Cloughfold.

WILLIAM OPENSHAW STREET

William Openshaw Street was one of the most enlightened leaders in the felt industry who rescued the Bury Manufacturing Company from certain liquidation and transformed it into the most prosperous felt operation in the country, rivalling and surpassing the once mighty MASCO combine.

W. O. Street in his younger days

Bill Street, as he was known, came from a humble background in Bury where his father worked as a butcher. Born in 1907 in Bury, he lived with his family on Walmersley Road, and was educated at Bury Municipal Secondary School. Later he studied accountancy and it was as an articled clerk that he first encountered the Bury Manufacturing Company in 1928, when he undertook its year-end financial audit. During that time he uncovered serious financial mismanagement that could have liquidated the company[29] and managed to pull it back from the brink. As a result of this he was invited to become their Company Secretary first on a temporary basis and then permanently. In 1930, the Managing Director retired and Bill Street was appointed in his place in order to continue revitalising the company's fortunes. His position became secure in the business when his Mother, Mrs. Street, married Mr. John Hill when his father died in 1938. Mr. Hill was one of the founders of Bury Manufacturing Company Limited along with a Mr. Laurence Clegg and Mr. J. Turner who was a builder who lived on the Manchester Road and did all the new building and repairs for the company[30]. Laurence Clegg was a senior Manufacturing Manager who at the formation of MASCO, left after a disagreement and set up the company supported by a consortium of some twelve local businessmen[31]. He became the first Managing Director of Bury Felt Manufacturing Company Limited in 1904, and lived in a house by Sedgeley Park in Prestwich. Mrs. Street outlived John Hill and inherited his shares, and being an astute woman, knowing that her husband had been the major shareholder, she bought out all the smaller shareholders' holdings, which she bequeathed to her son on her death. Bill Street then controlled the company as well as being the Managing Director.

He knew the needs of his employees and did everything to make working life as pleasant as possible. He organised a nursery in a separate building to look after employees children and in the works canteen he installed a piano that enabled employees to conduct their own entertainment[32]. He also bought the workers a sports club for football, tennis, bowling, cricket, and a lovely pavilion to go with it off Walmersly Rd called "Burrs and Rose". It was well used until the army commandeered it for the troops about 1939. Despite this, in 1947, he bought another premises on the Jericho Road, which was fondly referred to as the "Gentleman's Club"[33]. On the twenty-first anniversary of him taking up a position with the company, in 1948, he gave a bonus to each of his employees of £5, £10, £15, and £21 depending on the length of service. He recognised the conditions in the mills and led by example, in that for most of the time he and his directors worked from a spartan makeshift office that was boiling hot in summer and freezing in winter[34]. It was only in the 1950s that a new boardroom and sales office was built. The Boardroom was resplendent in its oak panelled walls and its three frosted glass windows, which had scenes of feltmaking etched into them. The first had a representation of St. Clement, the second was of a fuller beating a batt with a hammer and the third was of a stock mill, all of which were meant to show the progress of felt making.

Bill Street seems to have considerable judgement of character and surrounded himself with very able and forward thinking people that helped him drive the company forward both technically and financially. He himself was not technically qualified but his co-directors were, and even as an accountant, he encouraged the spending on new buildings and machinery. However, by 1945, he must have been a recognised authority on felt making because the British Government, in the form of British Intelligence Objectives Sub-committee commissioned him to review the scope of the felt industry in Germany at the end of the Second World War[35].

Even as MASCO was stagnating, he was taking over mills such as Chesham, and Springfield to fuel the expansion of his company. He was so proud of his achievements that in the late 1940s he undertook the photography of every aspect of his business, even including a picture of the nursery. He also had scale models of his mills made which indicates a supreme business confidence. In a shrewd move he invited Colonel Buckley to become Chairman after the previous Chairman, Mr. Holt, died in 1949. The Colonel was the Wool Controller of Great Britain and his three brothers had a wool merchanting business in Liverpool and the Bury Felt Company bought a large proportion of their wool from the Buckleys, particularly East India Wool. At the same time, Geoffrey Beetson was appointed Managing Director and was allocated some of W. O. Street's shares[36]. During this time, Bill Street controlled the finances as effective Company Secretary until the appointment of Clifford Snape in 1949. Mr. Graham Buckley was his nephew and became Technical Director. Colonel Buckley retired as Chairman in 1959[37] and D. S. Robinson succeeded him.

Although he was completely dedicated to the company and at times virtually slept there, Bill Street still found time to participate in the wider aspects of commerce. He was president of the Bury Chamber of Commerce in 1951/2 and was a one-time president of the Pressed Felt Manufacturers Association. He was also a member of the City of London Livery Company of Feltmakers. In his remaining spare time he enjoyed horse riding, and was keen on hunting with hounds. Both he and his right hand man Geoffrey Harley Beetson rode with the Holcombe Hounds, and he won the Hunt Cup at Bally Boogal, so he must have been an accomplished rider.

Being an accountant he was very careful with money but never stinted with charity if he felt it was for a good cause. His first known donation was to Bury Royal Infirmary in 1938 when he donated £1000 in honour of his stepfather John Hill. He ever forgot those institutions that had helped him and on his death in 1981 he bequeathed Bury General Hospital £20,000 from his estate, and to Bury Grammar School £40,000 as a bursary to underprivileged or sick boys and girls to receive a good education[38]. The bequest to children is an interesting action, not for its undoubted generosity, but because Bill Street never married and spent most of his life living with his mother at Oaklands, Walmersley, near Bury, and therefore had little experience of children. His economy with money stretched to his private life, when he objected to the cost of removal of an old ceramic bath that he had replaced. He decided to break it up himself with a sledgehammer, and unfortunately, he did not wear protective goggles, as at that time health and safety concerns were non-existent. On striking the bath, a chip flew up and lodged in his eye blinding it. After that, he always wore a black eye patch that gave him a somewhat distinguished cavalier appearance.

Bill Street, with eye-patch, as Chairman of Bury and Masco Industries in 1962, Geoff Beetson is on the far left, and George Stansfield is next to him. The Mayor of Bury on the right is Fred Spurr, the chief dyer at the company

At the peak of the company in 1959, Bill Street went into semi-retirement and to everyone's surprise, he sold a large portion of his shareholding. Without him, the company struggled because of internal difficulties between the Chairman D. S. Robinson and the Managing Director Geoffrey Beetson. The relationships within the company deteriorated and Bill Street was banned by the Chairman from entering any of the mills, causing the situation to come to a head, ultimately leading to the resignation of the Chairman in 1960. Bill Street then returned as non-executive chairman in 1961[39]. He then steered the company into an amalgamation with Mitchells, Ashworth, Stansfield and Co. in 1962 to form Bury and Masco Industries Limited with him as Chairman. He remained Chairman of the new company until 1968 when he finally retired to Jersey where he died in February 1981.

PEOPLE IN THE LAST DAYS OF BURY AND MASCO

In 1973, Geoff Beetson retired from Bury and Masco Industries and the old board disintegrated. A new Managing Director, Richard Newton, was appointed, with George Crainer as Financial Secretary.

Richard Newton, Managing Director of Bury and Masco Industries responsible for rationalisation and George Crainer, Chairman of Bury and Masco Industries at the takeover by the Scapa Group.

Richard Newton had the unenviable task of rationalising the company, which involved making uncomfortable personnel decisions at all levels of the company, and many well-established managers and staff left the company. Eventually he was replaced by Alexander F. D. Ferguson, known as Sandy, with a remit to re-energise the felt operation. George Crainer was elevated to the position of Managing Director of the holding company that was formed to manage the complex diversity of the organisation. In this role, he also became the Chairman of Bury and Masco Industries Limited. He was a qualified accountant, had a good grasp of business, and was not afraid of taking risks, favouring expansion rather than financially managing a company into paralysis. In addition, he was gifted with exceptional man management skills.

Sandy Ferguson was also an exceptional character who possessed a phenomenal intellect and, being over six feet tall, he had a commanding presence. He ran the company with a modern management style that was at times also autocratic, which was a necessity when dealing with a company steeped in traditional ways. At the time he took over, there was a pervading belief by the staff that the company was dying and he set about demonstrating that by innovation, felt sales could be increased and profit margins increased. He invested in a new, state-of-the-art, chemical laboratory as well as establishing a development facility for creating new products. He also encouraged a greater downstream marketing approach by opening a mill shop and developing a series of craft kits for sale to wholesalers. The social aspects of the company and its impact on local communities mattered a great deal to him, and in 1978 when the structure of Baltic Mill was in danger of collapse he had to make the difficult decision to either rebuild it or close it. He was aware that the mill was a significant employer in the area and its closure was likely to have a major impact on the livelihoods of many people in the district. In an act of faith in the future, he therefore took the courageous decision to renovate the mill at a cost of £250,000 rather than shutting it down.

Alexander F. D. Ferguson, Managing Director Bury and Masco Industries Limited, and Peter S. James, the last Managing Director of the merged company Bury Cooper Whitehead Limited

When the Scapa Group took over the company, it merged Bury and Masco Industries with Cooper and Co. (Birmingham) Limited and R. R. Whitehead and Brothers Limited to form Bury Cooper Whitehead Limited. Then, it had to decide on which of the three Managing Directors of these companies should become the Managing Director of the new company. In the event, they chose Peter Stoyle James, the Managing Director of Cooper and Co., and Sandy Ferguson left the company, as did Laurence Notley, the Managing Director of R. R. Whitehead. Unfortunately, the Scapa Group Board had no affinity for pressed felt and they believed that there was no future for it. Members even derided the new developments that were being pioneered and considered them to be a waste of time. After this, there was little in the way of new products, and Peter James had the distinction of being the last Managing Director of a once powerful company.

HERBERT SMITH

Herbert Smith (22 June 1872 – 14 July 1943)
founder of Longmeadow Felt Company

Sir Herbert Smith was a giant of the textile industry whose contributions have largely been forgotten outside his hometown of Kidderminster. His particular expertise was in carpets where he virtually single-handedly rescued the British carpet industry from collapse in the early years of the twentieth century. He restructured it to form the major carpet conglomerate Carpet Trades Limited that ultimately became known as Carpets International. He was a man of considerable business acumen and foresight with an ability to make a success of any venture he set his mind on. Just before the First World War, he foresaw the need for army blankets and anticipated the possibilities of a large potential demand. In fact, the British, French and Russian governments demanded quantities that all other textile companies believed were so impossibly large they could not supply. However, this did not faze Herbert smith who set about meeting this demand. To this end, he acquired Longmeadow Mill, which had the capacity to manufacture woven woollen cloth and mill it to the appropriate density and physical properties. He also saw the potential of making felt blankets without the expensive process of weaving. The established Lancashire felt makers of the time ridiculed his aspirations to become a felt manufacturer since they believed it was impossible for any one outside the industry to manufacture commercially acceptable felt. They sorely underestimated Herbert Smith's ability, energy, and sheer determination. Within a very short time he had installed hardeners in Longmeadow Mill and using the milling experience gained from the woven cloth enterprise, he was soon manufacturing felt at a level that challenged the rest of the industry in both volume and quality.

Not only was he a man of incredible energy but also had exceptional social skills that endeared his workers to him and also enabled him to establish strong relationships with his customers and with the upper echelons of society. Amongst his many friendships, he valued that of T. E. Lawrence whom he entertained many times at his home and ranked him as one of his "intimate friends". He developed particularly strong links with the Ministry of Defence that eventually guaranteed him large volumes of business for his new felt production unit. His phenomenal organising abilities came to the fore during the Great War of 1914 to 1918 when his skills were recognised by the Government and he was appointed to the Manpower and Protection Committee as well as becoming the Chairman of the Carpet Trades Rationing Committee. Later he became a leading member of the Board of Control of the Wool and Textile Industries, which effectively rationed the available wool to the various textile operations including felt. Records show that in spite of a probable vested interest, he ensured an evenhanded distribution to the other felt makers of the industry as well as other carpet manufacturers. It is worthy of note that of all the feltmakers in the country he was the only one prepared to actively contribute personal effort in favour of the national effort, rather than for parochial interests. His amazing energy, willpower, and capacity for physical exertion, enabled him to work night and day to both satisfy Government demands and keep his businesses running at the same time. At the end of the war, his efforts were recognised by his being awarded a baronetcy, which was by all accounts well deserved.

He had a way of instilling great loyalty from his staff and always managed to encourage the best performance out of them. Whether out of affection, derision, or a sense of informality he was popularly known as Piggy Smith. This no doubt referred to his small stature, demeanour or perhaps his facial features. Some idea of the loyalty of his staff can be gauged from the tributes that they gave him on his award of baronetcy. To mark the occasion of the award he threw a party for all his employees numbering some one thousand four hundred and sixty guests. No expense was spared and everyone was conveyed by tram to Stourport and then by steamer to Tewkesbury where the actual party was held. At the party, his employees presented him with a self-portrait in oils with the following dedication:

"On behalf of your employees we beg to offer you our hearty congratulations upon the honour so well deserved, recently conferred upon you by His Majesty the King, during the trying times of the last few years and surrounded by the many and great difficulties caused by the war. Your business ability which has done so much to retain and improve the staple industry of your native town in addition to successfully introducing new industries has been admired by us all and in asking your acceptance of the accompanying token of esteem we sincerely trust that you will long be spared to enjoy the distinction bestowed on you".

However, he was also capable of complete ruthlessness when the occasion demanded it. He demonstrated this clearly when he took command of the carpet company of James Humphries and Sons Limited that was making heavy losses and in serious financial trouble. In this case, he had no compunction about decimating the numbers of staff in order to return the company to profit. He was clearly successful in turning the company around as he eventually came to own it. Possessed of a considerable intellect himself, he did not suffer fools gladly and was particularly brutal in dealing with what he considered inept or inefficient.

Rolls Royce Phantom III originally owned by Sir Herbert Smith

His talents stretched well beyond superb business acumen into many other fields. Like his father, Horatio, he was a designer by trade and had a genius for design and colour, anticipating well what the market wanted. Many of his designs became best sellers that fuelled the carpet revival in Kidderminster. His love of the arts extended to music and he was an accomplished violinist and at one stage conducted a small orchestra. As a keen advocate of music, he encouraged his employees to appreciate it by forming a workers choir led by a professional choirmaster. As if this were not enough Herbert Smith had a fascination with cars: so much so that he bought the Castle Motor Company in New Road, Kidderminster and was instrumental in putting many famous cars onto the road.

His outdoor pursuits also extended into sailing. He was a keen yachtsman, though unfortunately, late in life it was also the cause of him becoming incapacitated. When on a sailing trip along the South Coast he missed his footing, slipped from a jetty ladder and injured his legs so that thereafter he had restricted mobility. It was typical of the man that, faced with limited movement, he threw himself into more mental pursuits becoming a great reader, philosopher, raconteur, and philanthropist. It could be said that he had always been a philanthropist as he was always generous with the money he had built up. He served on the Prince of Wales Relief Fund as well as giving donations. He gave generously to many charities but it is not possible to gauge this as he always donated anonymously. The only time he allowed his name to be revealed, after much cajoling, was when he donated one hundred guineas to the Spitfire Fund organised by local newspapers during the Second World War.

No doubt, he had a great ego to go with his exceptional talents and this manifested itself in his acquisition of property. His first major purchase was Blakebrook House from James Humphries, the owner of the firm that once employed him and his father. This may well have been his way of demonstrating publicly how far he had risen in status, from employee to owner.

Blakebrooke House in April 1921 when it was put up for sale by Sir Herbert Smith[40]

However, he did not stop there, for as his wealth grew he was able to purchase Witley Court from the Second Earl of Dudley who had built it up to become renowned as the byword for luxury and extravagance attracting the epithet "Palladian Palace" by High Society[41].

He tried to maintain the opulence of the house by lavishing great sums of money in fitting it out with all the luxuries of life, in order to make it the ideal place of retirement. He even built his own cinema within the building. On taking possession of Witley Court a different side to his character came to the fore when he alienated the local population by closing all recognised public footpaths through his estate. However for once in his life, by buying Witley Court, he had overstepped his resources and he did not have sufficient finances to maintain it in proper order.

Witley Court showing the magnificent fountain

He let the magnificent fountain and fire hydrants fall into disrepair and he could only maintain a very much-reduced number of staff, which limited him to living in just the southwest corner of the house[42]. The net result of the eventual neglect was that the main hall and east wing caught fire in September 1937 and the resultant damage was beyond repair. Later the property was sold to demolition contractors and Herbert Smith moved to Park House where he eventually died.

The fire at Witley Park House in September 1927

Unlike most pioneering feltmakers, Hebert Smith saw felt as a business and when the time came for retirement he left it completely. To all the other major feltmakers felt was not just a business but also a way of life that consumed them entirely and most of them ran their businesses right up until the time they died. By contrast, Herbert Smith had been retired for over twenty years before he died, enjoying the fruits of his labours.

Most of this information on Herbert Smith has been taken from his obituary written in the Kidderminster Shuttle for July 1943

THE WHITEHEADS

The Whitehead family had a long traditional involvement in the Yorkshire woollen industry with an ancestry that could be traced back to the sixteenth century, and which exerted a powerful influence over the community in the Saddleworth district. The patriarch of the Whitehead family was William Whitehead whose profession was recorded as "stapler", which at the time meant merchant of wool and woollen goods. He was clearly successful and was able to take on the lease of the Lydgate Estate from the Lords of the Manor of Saddleworth, which he passed onto his sons. He is remembered by a stone tablet set in the wall of Saddleworth Church, proudly recording that he was father to fourteen, grandfather to fifty-one and great grandfather to eighty. He was born in 1637 and died in 1715. Not all of the fourteen children that his wife Catherine bore survived, and the names of those known to have lived were: Thomas, Mary, John, and James. Of these, it was John's line that eventually produced the Whitehead Brothers who conducted business at Royal George Mill. John married Anne Radcliffe and it was in honour of her that "Radcliffe" passed through the family dynasty. The other inheritance from Anne's father was Shaw Hall. Between them, the couple had five siblings: Radcliffe, Sarah, John, Mary, and Patience. Of these, Radcliffe is important in tracing the origins of the feltmakers. He married Mary Corbishley and they had just one son, also called Radcliffe, The second Radcliffe married Anne Kenoway and they had three siblings, Ralph, John, and Anne. Radcliffe too must have been successful for he had Critchley Cottage specially built for the couple. They had also inherited Shaw Hall, which they later sold and moved to Oak View Mill. Ralph married Betty Taylor and they had three boys: William, John Dicken, and Edward. This William sired the Whitehead Brothers. William married Sarah Heywood in 1806 but the marriage was short lived as Sarah died in 1817 aged thirty-four, and William himself died young at forty-eight in 1832. Nevertheless, William and Sarah had six children: Ralph Radcliffe, James Heywood, Francis Frederick, John Dicken, Mary Ann, and Anna Maria[43]. The four brothers were the founders of the company to become R. R. Whitehead Brothers.

An engraving of Ralph Radcliffe Whitehead, the founder of R. R. Whitehead Brothers Limited

Although the early family members were merchants, they still maintained a level of manufacturing through the ownership of Oak View Mill, which has been described as a scribbling mill. This indicates that they were at least processing raw wool into a more usable form such as a carded sliver. Ralph Radcliffe concentrated the family's efforts into manufacturing and with his brothers, he formed the firm of R. R. Whitehead and Brothers that became a limited company in 1870.

Together they pooled their business skills and acquired more mills in order to move into more downstream processing. First they invested in yarn spinning, through the acquisition of a throstle mill, and then they started weaving, creating a completely vertically-integrated company. They embraced innovation wherever possible and James Heywood was an inventor with several key patents to his credit. In fact, he eventually ran the business when it was consolidated at Royal George Mill.

Although Ralph Radcliffe was the initiator and head of the company he eventually retired to Amberely Court, near Gloucester, in 1838, having just married Rebecca Hudson on 29 May[44]. This left his brother James running the company with Francis Frederick. In 1847, Francis Frederick assigned his shares in the company to his brothers. John Dicken initially seems to have been a sleeping partner in the business because he was living in Glanwa, Caernarvonshire, Wales and where he married Elizabeth Mary Pritchard in 1848. Whilst there he became a Justice of the Peace and died there in 1886 at the age of seventy-two. By then in 1861, he had already assigned his shares in the company to his brothers, from which it can be assumed that it was James who was running the company, which he did until he died in 1869 after falling off his "velocipede". The first general meeting of the limited company on 21 October 1870 showed that Ralph Radcliffe still had an interest in the business, as he was the Chairman. Also present at that meeting were: William Wyatt Turner, with John F Tanner, Thomas Hoare Tanner, and James William Tanner.

Ralph died at a critical time when the company was taking over the Wandle Felt Company. He must have been ailing when the discussions were being held because the board meeting that decided to purchase it on 29 March 1871 was chaired by John Dicken with W. W. Turner and the Tanners also being present. Ralph died on 12 April 1871[45].

Etching of an unnamed Whitehead brother, possibly John Dicken

After 1871, John Dicken became Chairman, a position that he maintained until his death in 1886. On John Dicken's death his shares were transferred to William Wyatt Turner who must then have owned the largest share holding since he became Chairman, with the three Tanners remaining as directors.

This situation remained up to at least 1892, which is when the archived record of the R. R. Whitehead and Brothers Limited minutes end. However it is known that a Colonel Walker Wyatt Turner took over ownership of the company because he bought out the Cotton Tree public house in Greenfield, close to the mill, which he renamed The Royal George, and integrated it into the ownership of R. R. Whitehead and Brothers Limited in 1908[46]. It is also known from former employees that Colonel Turner at some time became the owner of R. R. Whitehead and Brothers Limited. In 1932, Cyril Philip Porritt became the owner when Porritt and Spencer Limited took the company over in 1932[47].

The Whitehead family had always been wealthy even from the time of John Whitehead in the seventeenth century, not only husbanding their wealth carefully but also continually prospering with each generation. None of their wealth was ever squandered and there is no record of any wastrel or dissolute member of the family. The genealogy of the family indicates a family in complete harmony with itself and with the society within which they lived. This is reflected in the way each generation named its children after other members of the family, which often makes tracing individuals confusing. Every generation had its "John" when they had sons, and "Mary" when they had daughters. Hence, Ralph Radcliffe was christened in honour of his grandfather and great grandfather, and James of his great great grandfather. John Dicken was named after his uncle and the "Dicken" part of his name came from a close friend of his great grandparents. Unlike many families, there does not appear to have been any sibling rivalry between the Whitehead brothers and Francis Frederick even named his son Ralph Radcliffe in honour of his brother. After gaining a master of fine arts degree at Bailiol College, Oxford, this Ralph Radcliffe forsook business and founded the Byrdcliffe arts and crafts colony near Woodstock, New York in 1901.

Ralph Radcliffe Whitehead,
the founder of Byrdcliffe arts
and crafts colony

This younger Ralph Radcliffe used his family wealth to buy a thousand acres of land near Woodstock, and undertook the construction of buildings for studios, workshops, library, and housing for resident artists. When he married Jane Byrd McCall in 1892, they too named their first-born son Ralph, but he died in 1928 at the young age of twenty-nine in a shipwreck[48]. Their second son was Geoffrey Jocelyn, later known as Peter, and he died in 1975.

The Whitehead family members were devout Christians and fully supported the local church, taking a deep interest in the well-being of their community. The patriarch John was baptized at St Chads Church, Saddleworth, and buried at Saddleworth Church.

St Chads Church, Saddleworth, also known as Saddleworth Church, where the early Whiteheads worshipped and Christ Church, Friezeland founded by James Heywood Whitehead

His son John and family also attended St Chads, though in 1809 William Whitehead offered for sale his "three sittings in the front on the west side of a pew situate in the east gallery of Saddleworth Church". In 1849, the Whiteheads bought the Friezland Estate and built a new church, Friezland Church on the land[49], and James Heywood was buried there on his death, when it was then known as Christ Church.

In 1859, Francis Frederick, then living at Beech hill, was elected as a trustee of Lydgate School and later his son Ralph Radcliffe was also appointed in 1877[50]. Lydgate was the estate leased by the Whiteheads. It is no surprise therefore that this Ralph Radcliffe went to study at Oxford university.

The family was noted for the care to its employees, particularly James Heywood at Royal George Mill. On James' death the employees at R. R. Whitehead and Brothers Limited, erected a monument to him in the form of a red granite obelisk in grateful remembrance of a kind-hearted master. This caring streak in the family manifested itself in the Ralph Radcliffe of Byrdcliffe, not only in his utopian dreams of artistic colonies but also in his attitude to the conditions of the workers in mills. In 1907, he visited the family's Royal George Mill and was ashamed of the conditions under which employees whom he knew had to work[51]. At this time, the mill was no longer under Whitehead control.

From the 1930s onwards there were a succession of managers at Royal George, among whom were: Ned Maladaine, Bert Buckley, and Udal Shaw who had to serve during the Second World War. During the war, Bill Stock took over and when the Second World War ended, the operation was split into weaving and felting units, with Bill Stock manager of weaving, and Udal Shaw manager of the felt works. The next manager was a Mr. Steiger and the last Managing Director of R. R. Whitehead was Laurence Henry Notley[52].

Laurence H. Notley, the last Managing Director of R. R. Whitehead

Laurence was of the same mould as the Whitehead brothers, with a natural sympathetic management style, which came from his admirable communication skills. He also had a similar philanthropic attitude to community activity and supported local interests.

He was musically gifted and as well as being able to play the flute, he was an outstanding singer performing with a number of renowned singing groups. As chairman of the Salisbury Cathedral Concert Series, he was instrumental in raising considerable sums to support the cathedral school. When the merger with Bury and Masco took place and Bury Cooper Whitehead Limited was formed, the resultant operation did not suit his style and he left to become Managing Director of E. V. Naish, where he made a considerable beneficial impact.

Unlike many of the major feltmakers the Whitehead brothers did not perceive felt making as a unique textile proposition, to them it was a natural adjunct to their involvement with wool and to their innovative character. For them weaving and felt hardening were just different parts of making a woollen fabric that met market needs, and so they were comfortable operating an integrated production facility at Royal George Mills. They would not have described themselves as feltmakers, more likely woollen textile manufacturers. Herbert Smith and Roland Rawlinson were the only other feltmakers to master both weaving and feltmaking, but they were characters very different to the Whitehead brothers.

NAISH

The first Member of the Naish family to be involved in textiles was William Naish around 1800 at a place called Quidhampton. He moved from there around 1840 to the mill at Crow Lane, Wilton, which he rented and which later became the centre for Naish's felt business. William died in 1852 and it was left to his son, also called William, to continue the business. This William started the felt production at Crow Lane, making piano felt for Joseph Goddard.

In keeping with other feltmakers, he was a true innovator and pioneer of piano felts. In line with his forward thinking, he was quick to adopt steam engines to power his machines rather than waterpower. He was very community-minded, was a town councillor in the 1870s, and was elected mayor of Wilton in 1875. He was married twice, having a son, William John by his first wife and by his second wife; he had a daughter, Rowena Vawdry, and a son, William Vawdry, who became a General Practitioner in Worcestershire and known as Dr. Willie. When William died in 1882 his second wife Elizabeth Vawdry took control of the Company with her stepson William John becoming General Manager and later Managing Director.

Under the control of Elizabeth Vawdry, the company became known as E. V. Naish, the EV being her initials and when she died in 1901, her eldest daughter Rowena Vawdrey Naish controlled the business. She was a highly intelligent woman with a strong independent personality who dominated the company until her death in 1937. She had the distinction of being one of the first women to gain a degree at Cambridge University, which at the time must have required considerable strength of character, in order to succeed in a male dominated society. This same trait led her to adopt an authoritarian style of management by which she had to control every aspect of the company. For example, she insisted on opening all the incoming correspondence at ten o'clock every morning with no regard to whom the mail was addressed to. In another instance, she only signed the weekly wage cheque at her convenience, often on a Saturday morning a day after the normal pay date.

William Naish, the founder of E. V. Naish when he was Mayor of Wilton in 1875 and William John Naish II noted for promoting Naish piano felts

By 1920, William John was seventy years old with failing eyesight and there was no one in the family who could replace him. His son, Harold Walter Naish, had become a successful chartered accountant in London and had no interest in the production side of the business. The company therefore had to recruit a new Managing Director, Clifford Hunter Robinson, from outside the family, and his role was bolstered by the appointment of Leslie G. Miles as the new works manager. However, Rowena's style left them little in the way of authority as she continued to maintain an iron grip in day-to-day activities of the company. The extent of her autocratic style can be judged by the fact that any employee requesting a new ball point pen had to take the old one to the Managing Director who would ceremoniously bend it in half before issuing the new one. However, despite her management approach, Rowena did value her employees and, on her death, she bequeathed a legacy to every single employee based on their years of service.

Control of the company came to Dr. William Naish who held seventy-five percent of the shares when the business became a limited company in 1945. His daughters, Rowena and Betty together with Harold Walter Naish held the remaining twenty-five percent of shares. On Dr. Willie's death in 1953, his shares went to Rowena and Betty who then controlled the company and became Chairman and Vice Chairman until Rowena's death in 1987. Nothing therefore changed in the attitudes in the company and it suffered from a paralysis of technological improvement that stifled the company, and when it did institute change such as a new steam engine the results were far from satisfactory.

It was only around 1965, on the retirement of Clifford Robinson and Leslie Miles, that the fortunes of the company were revitalized. This coincided with the appointment of George Kay as managing Director and with John R. Naish becoming Production and Works Manager. John Naish was the son of Harold Walter Naish and he had joined the company in 1950 and worked his way through all the different production processes. He graduated as an engineer and completed a postgraduate course on textile technology at Leeds University, and was therefore well versed with modern textile management. Around 1980, Vice Chairman Betty died and John R. Naish took her place eventually becoming Chairman in 1987 on Rowena's death.

In the 1980's, Laurence Notley became Managing Director after George Kay and the company prospered and diversified its product range until the recession of the 1990s. Through Laurence Notley, the company established good relations with Bayerische Wollfilzfabriken (BWF) a major German felt maker who provided E. V. Naish with superfine felts that they marketed in Britain in competition to Bury Cooper Whitehead Ltd. Then, ironically, this German company bought out Bury Cooper Whitehead Ltd. when it closed and offered Naish their machinery, but they refused it because it was so dilapidated. Thereafter, Naish consolidated its partnership with BWF and ceased production of felt to take on the marketing of the German company's product range in Britain. Although there is no more felt production at E. V. Naish there is still one member of the Naish family left as a director in the business and he is Geoff Naish, the son of John R. Naish who retired as a director of the company after the year 2000.

George Kay, Managing Director of E. V. Naish
from 1965 to 1980s sitting on a block of felt

E. V. Naish was unique in the felt industry, and possibly in British industry as a whole, in that it was controlled by women for most of its working life, at a time when business was a "male only" occupation.

The information about the Naish family comes from the book of the history of E. V. Naish Limited by John Naish[53] and the pictures reproduced with his kind permission.

WORKING CONDITIONS

In the early days of felt making there was an unwritten social contract between the owners of the business and the employees, where each perceived their place in an almost feudal hierarchy and in Rossendale, at least, it was manifested in a very paternalistic management style. The owners took the role of masters and the employees assumed the positions of servants, in many ways mimicking the social structure of the day. By way of example the employees in the Mitchell branches of the MASCO combine always addressed their superiors by using the title "Mr." followed by the Christian name, so

Oliver Mitchell was known as Mr. Oliver and James as Mr. James. The owners undertook to look after their employees according to the standards of the day and the employees obeyed the instructions of their duties conscientiously, without complaint. As such, the organisations were largely autocratic, but the paternalistic nature of the management led to a loyal and dedicated workforce where unions failed to penetrate to any large degree. Social functions were encouraged, such as lunchtime concerts, sports and music with many mills having their own cricket teams and brass bands, all supported by the company as an example, both MASCO's Albert Works and Whitewell Vale Mills had their own bands supported by Colonel Mitchell[54].

Albert Works brass band, with Colonel Mitchell, on the back row without a uniform

Special occasions, such as the Queen Elizabeth II's coronation, and the fiftieth anniversary of the formation of MASCO, were celebrated in style in a way that all employees benefitted. For the fiftieth celebrations on 29 May 1954, all the employees were taken for a day out in Blackpool with a lunch at twelve o'clock with the return coach leaving at eleven o'clock at night. In fact, no opportunity was missed to have a works outing, such as the time when Richard Ashworth turned eighty in 1920[55] or for long service awards such as in 1952. The camaraderie in the mills spilled over into the local community and the company always supported the employees in entering the local events such as carnivals, like the Bacup and Rawtenstall Pageants where they annually entered a decorated lorry. They often received prizes: first prize in the Bacup pageant for the Festival of Britain celebrations 23 June 1951, first prize in Bacup carnival 26 June 1971, second prize in the Rawtenstall carnival 16 June 1953, third prize in the coronation procession on 30 May 1953.

Despite the hierarchical structure within the felt companies, there was a bond of mutual loyalty between the workers and the directors or owners. During both world wars the companies supported any of the employees that were drafted into the armed forces and each were guaranteed a job on their return from the war. They were also sympathetic to new employees who returned from the war and who had been wounded, men who would otherwise have found it difficult to obtain work[56]. The companies also stood by their employees during the depression and there are no recorded lay-offs, other than as a result of company liquidation. It was only until the late 1950s, when the social structure changed, that redundancies became common. Much of the employee loyalty came from the recruitment policy that the companies had, particularly in Rossendale, whereby new recruits had to be recommended by existing employees. The sponsor therefore stood as surety for the new employee and this ensured that he/she conformed to the company rules and performed diligently. It is not surprising therefore that there were many family members working in the same mill. It was also common for up to three generations to be working in the same mill and many employees having thirty and forty year's service. Consequently it was difficult for someone outside the felt industry to become employed in felt making, and though this made for a very introspective industry it guaranteed a reliable workforce without the need for advertising for prospective employees.

Discipline within the felt companies was rigid, if not harsh, and was rigorously enforced. It started with the morning call from the works whistle that was sounded at 7.00 am, then at 7.15 am, and finally at 7.30am. The whistle was powered by steam from a boiler that was connected to it by a pipe that was one and a half inches in diameter and was controlled through a valve operated by a long handle. The sound was so loud that it could be heard over half a mile away. Using the handle the boiler man could produce different sounds, giving long or short blasts like Morse code to signal the time. In the Rossendale valley, different mills had different whistle sounds for their workers so there was therefore no excuse for the local workers to be late for work. The starting time for each worker was checked through a special manual system that was used until around 1930-40, when time clocks were introduced. Each worker was given a brass disc (about one and a half inches in diameter) with his own number stamped on it.

Roy Giddins brass check for Albert Works, compared to a pound coin

When he arrived at work, he put his disc into a box kept outside the timekeeper's office. At 7.30 am the checks were removed and hung up on a board as a visual record of who was working in the mill. The box was then sealed and anyone arriving late could not put their check in the box and were not allowed to go into work until the box was next unsealed at 7.45 am. All workers putting their checks in then would lose a quarter of an hours pay. The final check for the shift was 8.00am. Before the end of the shift, the checks were returned to the workers to be ready for the next day. On paydays, when the checks were returned, each worker received an extra hexagonal coin with his number on it, which he handed over to the wages clerk in return for his money. Curiously, the money was not put into pay packets but counted out into individual cloth bags made from old cotton cloths previously used on the hardening machines. The following day, when the day's checks were returned to the workers, the cloth bags were collected and delivered to the accounts office ready for the next payday[57]

The rigid time keeping that was enforced at Albert Works even influenced toilet arrangements. To reach the toilets a worker had to pass the timekeeper's office so that he could monitor how long he was taking. The toilets also had no doors on them so that it was possible to see who was inside and who was loitering. It was not until 1950 that doors were put on the workers' cubicles, but even then only half doors, of the saloon type, were installed so the top and lower halves of the occupants could be seen. In Baltic mill there were urinals positioned around the building so that employees did not have to even leave their place of work to relieve themselves. In the days before chemical milling agents, even this urine was collected and used in the felting process. Arrangements for the staff were slightly more civilised since the toilets were more private and had full-sized doors, but they also had to pass the timekeeper's office to reach them. The staff used a clock system for signing in that consisted of a large clock with a handle, which moved round with the time and allowed each person to punch the time on a card[58]. The staff hours were 8.30 am to 5.30 pm, and one hour for lunch, for five days and mornings on Saturdays.

Pay in the felt industry was at least equivalent to the rest of the textile industry, though Bury Felt Manufacturing Company tended to pay above the local pay rates. In 1922 a worker was paid £2/15s (£2.75) for sixty hours and youngsters aged fourteen years old were paid 10 shillings (50p) for a forty eight hour week[59]. By comparison, in 1942 a secretary was paid seventeen shillings and six old pence per week (75p)[60].

By modern standards the working conditions in the mills were brutal, and workers were constantly surrounded by dangers that they needed to take care of, if they were to avoid serious injury. Until the advent of electric motors and a powerful electricity supply, all the machines were driven by belts from overhead line shafting that ran the length of the mill to a water wheel or steam engine. The line shafting rotated all the time but the machines had to be started and stopped at will. To do this, the belt on a machine had to be manually disengaged by moving it to an idler pulley and this could be a dangerous manoeuvre. None of the belts was guarded and it was easy for clothes to become entangled in the belts, which either stripped the worker of his jacket or propelled him bodily up to the ceiling. It was common for these belts to lose their grip and slip so that the operator had to apply paste by hand onto the leather, which had to be done on the moving belt. One employee recalled that, in 1933, a Joe Bradbury, working in the milling room, was applying paste when he was caught up in the belt and was killed[61]. Despite this, workers respected the dangers these belts represented and developed a mock frivolous attitude towards them. The older experienced lags, who often chewed tobacco, would tease a new young employee by waiting till he was opposite a moving belt and then spit on the belt so that the youngster was sprayed by bits of tobacco flung off by the belt as it sped round the drive wheels.

Hardening, milling and dyeing all relied heavily on steam for their processes and since it could not be contained, it pervaded the whole of these working environments, making them very uncomfortable places to work in. In these places, it was like working in a permanent fog, with condensate everywhere, dripping off the ceiling and rafters, saturating the workers' clothes, as well as soaking the floor. In winter and on cold days it was particularly bad because the mills were not heated, with the only heat coming from the processes themselves. Operatives therefore experienced extremes of temperature with conditions bitterly cold away from the machines and boiling hot near them. In the hardening and milling areas, the workers had to tolerate high noise levels from the clatter of the jigging rollers to the thump of the milling stocks. The noise in the hardening area was particularly irksome because of its relatively high frequency and the sheer number of vibrating rollers. In contrast, the thump of the hammer mills, though loud, was hypnotic and the millers were tuned into the noise and could easily recognise a problem by any change in the rhythm.

Conditions were even worse in the milling room and dye house, since not only was there steam and boiling fluids everywhere but the areas dripped with corrosive fluids such as sulphuric acid. The floor was so wet with chemicals that leather shoes barely lasted a week before they disintegrated. Even in 1984, workers in the dye house were given a special shoe allowance to compensate them for wear and tear on their footwear. Most men in the dye house therefore wore wooden clogs.

Typical working conditions in a felt mill around 1948

The dye vats themselves were full of potential danger and it was common for workers to fall into the boiling liquor and drown. Even the chemicals used in production had their effects and one felt worker recollects that his colleague ended up with his grey hair being turned yellow from bending over the steaming vats[62]. The danger was also not just physical but also psychological as there was considerable strain on the chief dyer who was responsible for ensuring the final quality of most of the felt that went through the mill. On more than one occasion, the chief dyer could not stand the strain and committed suicide.

Until the later Factories Act, children were employed in the felt mills to perform a variety of mundane tasks such as running messages, or taking the lant cart around the villages to collect urine for the milling process. Often they worked long hours under the same conditions as the mill workers and open to the same dangers and because they were not always so vigilant, accidents involving youngsters were quite common. For example, in one report, a girl of ten was killed in a lift at Todd Carr Mill in 1881 when it was owned by Messrs Barcroft[63]. Probably the worst job was that of the "tear boy", who worked for the block printer and had the job of maintaining the printing paste and the trolley, which was a messy job that involved preparing the tear trolley to accept the paste. To do this the tear boy had to visit the local farm and collect cow dung in a bucket, bring it back to the mill, and make it up to the correct consistency before assembling the trolley ready for printing. Being a tear boy was almost a rite of passage for a youngster to become a feltmaker and many illustrious personalities in the district and in the felt industry started their careers in this way. Because of the various Factory Acts the employment of children had virtually stopped by 1950 and in Bury Felt Manufacturing at least, children were well cared for in the company nursery.

Despite all the hardships and autocratic regimes most, if not all, employees remained faithful to their companies, there were rarely any disputes of any note, and there had never been a strike in any felt mill. Although there was a union presence, it was hardly militant and by no means universal, at least until the 1970s. In fact, at E. V. Naish when a union movement was started there, it was hardly supported at all and eventually disappeared altogether.

In Rossendale there was a close knit society within the mills with a high degree of community spirit, where everyone knew each other intimately and everyone knew each other's business. As a last reminder of this spirit, it is worth highlighting a few of the ordinary characters that made the industry what it was. Roy Giddins records such colourful characters as: Joe Wilson, foreman of hardening room who was also a part time hair dresser, and George Harker who pulled out rats' teeth with pliers to enable young dogs to practice ratting and who was so strong he could carry a full wet roll of felt on his back. Then there was Tony Kyme who was the boiler man and mechanics labourer who in his spare time was an Irish Folk singer and a solid Conservative, and J. T. Howard who was once a thatcher and worked as a blacksmith striker. One of the few union men was Fred Rushton who was known as "Awd Lump Yed" which was the Rossendale dialect for "he had a lump on his head. Lastly, he recalled Charlie Lord who was the foreman of first floor card room, who chewed tobacco. As a postscript, all the workers, employed or retired, who were interviewed in the course of making this book, had nothing but praise for the companies they worked for and there is no doubt that working in the felt industry was a special experience unmatched by any other textile operation.

15 GLOSSARY OF FELT INDUSTRY TERMS

Acid-Free Felt
This is a felt that contains no acid. Felt is usually milled in acid, which leaves a residue of acid. In most applications, this does not matter, but in certain circumstances, for example a felt seal in a bearing, the acid in the felt may corrode the metal touching it. This acid is neutralised in an alkaline bath.

Air Permeability
This is a measure of the ability of air to pass through a felt. A water gauge is used to measure this resistance through a specified area of felt. Thus automotive products for example specify the "Air resistance when flowing 1.5 cubic feet per minute of air through 50 sq. cms. of felt" measured in millimetres of water pressure,

Ash Content
Wool being a natural protein will burn away to nothing. However, there may be other impurities in the wool that have been picked up on its journey from sheep to felt which form ash when they are burnt, particularly inorganic material. Measuring the weight of ash produced when a felt is burnt indicates the level of impurities in it. The ratio of the weight of the ash when compared to the original weight and expressed as a percentage is known as the ash content.

A.S.T.M.
The American Society for Testing Materials, which sets down standard methods of testing felt.

Baize
A woven material made from wool, usually green. Baize is used on billiard tables, and is thus sometimes referred to as billiard felt, though it is not a felt. Being woven it can be more tightly stretched than can felt,

Barr
Two tenter frames or rails connected in a back-to-back configuration.

Bat, batt
Also known as a batt, and lap. These refer to the substantial thickness of loose fibres, prior to felting that are built up from webs of wool from a carding machine. The loose fibres in this form is usually referred to as a batt and when in length and rolled up as a lap.

Batt Frame
A frame containing sets of endless conveyor belts on which the web from a carding engine is accumulated to make a long thick layer of wool fibres suitable for making into felt.

Bench Felt
A black felt used to cover glass-cutting tables.

Benzene Test
See under Tetrachloride Test

Betty or Dolly
A washing or scouring machine for washing pieces of felt or other-fabric, consisting of a mangle mounted over a large tank.

Billiard Felt
A green woollen woven fabric baize, with a felted surface for use on billiard and snooker tables.

Blending
The first process in making felt where various qualities of wool and/or waste are mixed evenly together.

Blending Bin
The storage container for a woollen blend for feeding into a carding engine.

Blocking
The moulding process in hat making where a felt is pressed between two halves of a hat shaped mould, known as a block, to form the finished hat shape.

Block Printing
The method of patterning felt by spreading dye on a wooden block with an incised pattern and pressing it onto a felt.

Blowing
The process for passing steam through a felt when it is under light pressure. It imparts a "permanent set" finish that improves handle, and gives a very smooth surface. The felt is wrapped tightly round a cylinder in several layers, steam is forced through it for a given time, then cold air is drawn through it.

Bob
A hard felt wheel used, with an abrasive compound for polishing, wheels eight inches in diameter were made individually and small bobs were cut from a sheet of felt.

Bocking
A coarse woven woollen fabric usually used for floor covering, to cover carpets. Bockings were made from worsted warp and woollen weft, principally for exportation. It was a rough kind of material, and was named after the village of Bocking in Essex, where the manufacture of it was first introduced from Belgium in the time of Edward III. Most felt mills were at one time made bockings

Bonded Felt and Bonded Fibre Fabric
A simple type of non-woven material made from fibre, usually synthetic, which after carding is sprayed with a bonding solution or adhesive, and then cured in an oven.

Bowing
An early method of separating wool fibres prior to felting. Using a stringed bow, the bowstring was hit with a hammer and the vibrating string put into contact with the fibres to separate them.

Botany Wool
Originally wool from Botany Bay, Australia, today it refers to any wool of 60's quality or upward.

Box Milling
A form of milling where an endless length of felt is pulled through a narrow aperture formed from two sets of rollers set at ninety degrees to each other.

B.S.I
British Standards Institute, the organisation responsible for determining standards for felt in the United Kingdom.

Bratt Cloth
The thick woven cotton cloths used to support the wool fibres during the hardening process.

Burrs
Vegetable matter, plant particles, seeds, etc. frequently found in wool.

Butt Joint
The joining of felt pieces or strips by aligning the ends together and joining them by stitching or other means so that there is no overlap of the pieces being connected.

Bywater
William Bywater, manufacturer of roller and flat hardening machines, later known as Garnett-Bywater

Capillary Action
The process by which a felt absorbs liquids. The surface tension and angle of contact between a liquid and the wool fibres creates a force that drags the liquid into and along a piece of felt. Felt is particularly good at absorbing oil and alcohol.

Carbonising
A process of cleaning wool, using dilute sulphuric acid. It removes burrs and other foreign matter from the raw wool by turning them into carbon and crushing tem to dust.

Carboniser
A machine for immersing a felt in dilute acid to remove burrs and seeds in the felt

Carding
The process of opening or teasing out the wool and separating the fibres after blending and willeying. The machine used is the carding engine, which may be fitted with varying grades of "comb" or card clothing. Fine quality felts are made on fine cards, coarse felts on coarse cards.

Carding Engine
The machine used to card wool and other fibres. A carding engine consists of a large central drum, known as a swift, which is covered with fine wires protruding from the surface like a brush. The swift is surrounded by pairs of rollers which also have protruding wires and which are called workers and strippers (or clearers). The drum and these rollers rotate in such a way as to shear the fibres that pass between them, so that they are effectively combed. At the end of the machine, there is a comb that oscillates up and down and peels a fibre web away from the carding engine.

Card Clothing
A strip of material about two inches wide that has wires stapled through it to form a continuous wire brush. The wires can be of different coarseness and stapled at different intervals of pitch. This strip is then wound over the surface of rollers or the swift to cover the whole surface. Fine wire is used for carding fine wools and coarse wires for coarse wool.

Carpet
Floor covering that gave rise to the felt industry as an alternative to the narrower woven Brussels, Axminster, and Tapestry coverings. The first felt carpets were made by The Patent Woollen Cloth Company of Leeds and sold under the Trademark Royal Victoria Carpets

Camel Balls
Balls of felt that have been regurgitated by camels.

C.F.M.
Cubic feet per minute,

Chamfering
Putting a tapered face on to a strip of dense felt, sheet or washer.

Check Felt
A thin felt used in a piano to absorb the force of a piano hammer after it strikes a string

Cotty Wool
Matted, entangled or felted wool in a fleece.

Count
The measure of the fineness of a wool yarn, measured by the length in relation to weight.
A yarn of 60s count has yields 60 hanks, each of 560 yards, from a pound of wool. 70s count is thus a thinner yarn.

Craft Felt
A thin lightweight felt made in many different colours, suitable for handcraft and making soft toys.

Crimp
Waviness of a wool fibre. The number of crimps to the inch, and their regularity, increases with the quality of wool.

Crossbred
Any "mongrel" crossbred sheep, and hence qualities of wool below 60's quality. There are fine, medium, and coarse crossbred qualities

Cross Lay
The configuration of fibres in a batt when a carded web is laid down by a side-to-side motion so that the fibres are perpendicular to the length of the batt. A carding machine that cross lays the fibres does not have a batt frame and batts can therefore be made of any length.

Cuprammonium
A method of proofing a felt against rotting

Comeback
A sheep that is a cross between a merino and a fine crossbred.

Cones
Small felt bobs, mounted on a mandrel, and turned to a variety of different shapes. They are used mainly in precision work, making jewellery, dentistry.

Contact Wheel
A wheel of cloth, leather, felt or rubber that is used in polishing using abrasive belts. The belt passes over the contact wheel, which supports the polishing area. Contact wheels can be plain or serrated.

Copper Napthanate
A chemical used for moth proofing

Damper Felt
A soft thick felt that is used in pianos to deaden the vibration of the strings when the damper pedal of the piano is depressed. The edge of the felt is shaped into a wedge or fork to fit around the string.

Dead Wool
Wool pulled from sheep that have died, but have not been slaughtered.

GLOSSARY

Decatiser
A machine for steaming a felt to stabilise it. Fine felt is rolled and wrapped in a cotton liner and steam is blown through it.

Decatising
Blowing steam through a felt to stabilise it, also known as blowing.

Density
The density of a felt is its weight per unit volume, this can be: pounds (weight) per cubic foot, pounds (weight) per linear yard at fixed thickness, ounces per square yard at fixed thickness, or grammes per cubic centimetre.

Devil
A machine for tearing apart matted fibres, consisting of a drum covered with metal teeth and surrounded by rollers also covered with teeth.

Dielmoth
A chemical for moth proofing.

Differential Frictional Effect (DFE)
Description of the fact that wool and animal fibres are rough when stroked one way and smooth when stroked in the opposite direction, the greater this difference in friction, the greater the differential frictional effect.

Display Felt
A thin coloured felt used for window dressing or covering exhibition boards

Doffing
The term used to describe the removing of a batt, lap, felt, or fabric from a process or machine.

Dolly
Also called a washing betty. A washing or scouring machine for washing pieces of felt or other-fabric consisting of a mangle mounted over a tank.

Drum Carding
Accumulating a web of fibres from a carding machine on a drum instead of a batt frame. This technique is used for making sheets and polishing bobs by a batch process.

Fabrication
The general term to describe the conversion of sheet and roll felts into shaped products such as washers, discs, squares, and strips. It is also used for operations such as drilling, lathe turning, and laminating felts to create engineering products.

Felt
Generic name to describe any fabric where the fibres are randomly interlocked, three-dimensionally
Pressed felt – woollen felt made by the natural felting of wool and animal fibres
Needle felt – a non-woven product made by intermingling fibres using barbed needles
Hat Felt – Felt made from rabbit and beaver fibres using special chemical treatments
Woven Felt – A woven woollen cloth that is heavily milled to lock the structure
Roofing Felt – A paper or hair felt impregnated with bitumen or asphalt
Bonded Felt – Synthetic fibres locked together by an adhesive

Fettling
Cleaning the card cylinders.

F. & R.
Folded and Rolled. Tailoring and other lightweight felts are usually folded in half width, and rolled.

Flat Hardening
The carded laps are first steamed over a steaming chest, and then felted between two heavy steam-heated plates one or both of which vibrates.

Fleece
The complete covering of a sheep, usually when sheared, but also refers to the wool when still attached to the skin of a slaughtered sheep

Fulling
Increasing the density and strength of a felt by hammering it, synonymous with milling.

Garnett
A coarse type of carding engine that has metal teeth rather than wire in order to tear coarse material.

Garside Hardener
A small flat hardener usually used in making hats consisting of a lower steam heated steel platen and an upper wooden plate that oscillates.

Gatterwalker
A milling machine that mills felt continuously with sets of wooden planks.

Gauge
An instrument for measuring the thickness of a felt at a predetermined pressure, to give consistent readings. Most felt gauges have a two-inch diameter foot fitted to contact with the felt and prevent compressing the felt and give a false reading. Various gauges can be used for measuring the thickness a piece of felt (a) Caliper Gauge, Micrometer Gauge, Vernier Gauge are insensitive to pressure. (b) Baty Dial Gauge, Mercer Dial Gauge are preferred gauges.

Grey Felt
An industrial grade of felt that has any colour other than white, shades may vary from light grey to dark brown.

Goit
Stream or small waterway

Hair Felt
A felt made mainly or entirely of hair. Cows' or goats' hair is most commonly used, and the felt is of a coarse cheap quality. A proportion of hair is used in the cheaper UK Government specified felts.

Handy
A special tool for pulling down the lower beam of a hand tenter frame in order to stretch a felt

Hardening
The process in felt manufacture that comes between carding and milling. Its effect is to lock together fibres in the carded lap, by means of pressure heat and friction, There are two methods: roller hardening for thin felts and flat hardening for thick felts

Hard Pressed Felt
This is a felt that has its density increased by the application of heat and pressure. This increased density is not permanent, and may be lost if the pressed felt comes into contact with moisture,

Hydro-extraction
The process in felt manufacture that follows milling and scouring. Excess moisture is removed by centrifugal force in a machine similar to a domestic spin dryer.

Hydro-extractor
A machine similar to a horizontal domestic spin dryer that removes water from a felt by centrifugal force. Known colloquially as a Wuzzer.

Jigging
The side-to-side movement of a top roller in a roller hardener.

Kambola
A felted blanket made in India

Kemp
Coarse, fairly short, straight, wool fibres that are shed periodically by the fleece. They are white, and do not take dye, so that in a dyed felt or fabric they remain easily visible.

Kepenek
A traditional sleeveless felt coat or mantle worn by shepherds in Iran, Afghanistan, and Turkey.

Khozai
A thick felt made in Afghanistan

Kletterschuh
A climbing boot having a felt sole for providing grip a on wet or icy rocky surfaces

Knife-edged Bob
A bob with the face tapered to a sharp edge, used for polishing V-shaped grooves.

Lant
Urine used as a milling liquor to aid fulling in the early days of felt making and right up to the 1930's. The urine was collected from door to door in a barrel on wheels known as a lant cart.

Lap
The lap is the sliver of wool that is built up on the batt frame or cylinder of the carding engine, and consists of a series of layers of carded wool. Laps are made to weights according to the density of felt.

Lap Joint
The ends of a felt strip, to be joined by a lap joint are each cut in the form of steps, which fit into each other and overlap.

Lodge
A reservoir that was situated next to the mill and which supplied it with water for washing, steam generation, and for powering the waterwheel.

L.P.C.P.
Laurate pentachlorophenyl, a chemical used to rot proof felt.

Masonic Carpet
Special block printed carpet made for Freemasons up to 1970

Mawl
A hammer used principally for facilitating block printing, also the hammer used to fasten felt to the tenter pins in a hand tenter.

Merino
A breed of sheep providing fine wool (60's quality and upwards).

Milling
Also known as fulling or felting. Milling is the process in felt manufacture that comes after hardening. The hardened felt is shrunk to the necessary length and width to give the density required by turning in the liquid (Rotary Milling), pummelled by stocks (Stock Milling), or kneaded in a milling machine.

Mixture Felt
A felt made from a mixture of wool and synthetic fibre.

Mitin
A chemical for moth proofing felt

Mother felt
In traditional hand felting this is a milled felt used as a carrier cloth to felt another batt of wool fibres.

Mungo
Fibres recovered from re-processing fabrics, and which have become shortened during the operation.

Mystolene Treatment
A water repellant treatment

Namad
An Iranian felt carpet that is one metre wide and up to six metres long

Needleloom Felt
A coarse type of "felt" where the fibres, mainly jute, are "needled" onto a woven hessian or paper framework, without felting. It is used as a carpet underlay, for lagging, packing and sound deadening.

Neps
Small clusters of curled wool fibres.

Noil
Short wool fibres extracted during the process of making carded slivers for worsted yarn production

Nominal
Reference to the expected value of a measured property, which can have a tolerance either side of this value, for example nominal thickness or nominal density.

Numdah
A felt rug, often highly embroidered

Numnah
A medium density felt, about three quarters of an inch thick, usually dyed in a khaki shade, used in saddlery, originally as a saddle blanket.

Nuzzery
A colloquial term for the room where felt is conditioned prior to pressing, consisting of a platform raised above a water reservoir.

Oil Retention
A measure of how much oil a felt can hold. A felt weighing 1 gramme, that absorbs, and retains 1 gramme of oil, is said to have an oil retention of 100%. Soft felts absorb oil best, but may not retain it well. Very hard felts will not absorb much oil, but retain well what they do absorb.

Packing Felt
Coarse felts used for packing applications to cushion sensitive goods in transit.

Padding Felt
Soft thick low density felt used in the clothing industry for shoulder pads or jacket padding

Patent Woollen Cloth
The name given to felt when the mechanical method of felting wool was introduced in 1840

pH
The acidity or alkalinity of a substance can be measured, and the measurement is expressed on a pH scale. pH 7 is neutral. Larger numbers indicate increasing alkalinity, smaller numbers acidity. Hard felts may be as acid as pH 2.5, although Government Specifications usually require pH 5 to pH 8.

Piano Felt
Any felt that is used in a piano

Piano Hammer Felt
Felt that is used to cover the wooden hammers that strike the strings of a piano. The felt is made in a single sheet suitable for making a full set of hammers. The bass hammers require softer felt than the treble hammers, which also need thin dense felt. These requirements are met in one sheet that is thick on one side and thin on the other and is known as taper hammer felt.

Picking
Plucking, by hand, bits of seed, pitch, or other small contaminants out of a finished felt.

Pilling
Small balls of fibre that gather on the surface of a felt caused by rubbing during wear. This usually occurs when synthetic fibres are used as part of the fibre blend.

Pilgrim Step
A continuous milling machine consisting of two sets of oscillating rollers that knead the felt and inch it gradually through the machine.

Pitch
Traces of tar and bituminous materials embedded in wool and which survives processing into the finished felt

Planking
The process of milling a hat body in the hat felt trade.

Plaiting
A method of stacking felt between processes by laying the felt backwards and forwards onto a temporary platform or trolley.

Polo Felt
Felt used to protect the legs of polo ponies.

Poss
The vertical support beam of a hand tenter frame

Pressed Felt
Pressed felt is held together entirely by the natural felting of the wool, and is not woven nor bonded with an adhesive solution. Pressed felt must therefore contain a proportion of pure wool.

Proofing
Processes that prevent the felt from deteriorating either by rotting, by vermin, by fire, or water. Those commonly used are: L.P.C.P. (Laurate pentachlorophenyl.), Cuprammonium, Dielmoth, Copper Napthanate, D.A.N, (Dinitro-1-Napthol.)

Pulled Wool
Wool taken from slaughtered sheep

Quality
Wools are given quality numbers, which are a measure of the fineness or diameter of the fibre. "60's quality" describes wool of which one pound weight will yield 60 hanks of yarn, 560 yards in length. Quality numbers range from 20's to 100's, and the higher the number the better the quality, 60's quality and above is classed as "Botany" or "Merino", those below as Crossbred.

Rail
Also known as a Barr. One length of a tenter frame on which a felt is dried. Most tenter frames are constructed in pairs of rails called seams.

Roll Felt
Felt manufactured in long lengths and flexible enough to be rolled.

Roller Hardening
The process where a lap of carded wool, supported between two cotton cloth, is passed through a series of vibrating rollers, in order to felt it.

Roofing Felt
Originally a coarse hair felt or needled jute felt that was impregnated with asphalt and used in roofing, now any class of reinforced asphalt or bitumen used in roofing.

Saddle Felt
A padding felt used in saddle making or as saddle blankets

S.A.E.
The Society of Automotive Engineers, in the United States, which has drawn up a series of specifications for felts.

Sandwich Felt
A sandwich felt is made with a layer of cheaper felt in the middle between two faces of better quality.

Scales
The plates covering the surface of animal fibres that make the fibres rougher in one direction than the other

Scarf Joint
The ends of a felt strip that are joined by a scarf joint are tapered to an angle usually 45 or 60 degrees and then overlapped.

Scotch Feed
A conveyor arrangement that transports the fibres from one carding machine to another, in the form of a sliver of fibres. When feeding the second carding machine, the sliver is cross-laid across the width of the second card, to improve the subsequent processing.

Scoured Wool
Wool that has been washed either with hot water or a solvent to remove suint, dirt, dust, and yellowness from the wool in order to produce a clean product ready for processing

Scray
A wooden platform slightly raised off the ground on which a felt is stored between processes

Scribbler
A coarse carding machine which pre-separates wool before carding

Shearing
The process by which surplus fibres are removed from the surface of a felt to improve its finish. The machine that does this has a spiral blade that operates like a rotary lawn mower

Sheathing Felt
A bitumastic felt used for sound deadening and insulation in the building and motor industries.

Sheet Felt
Hard felts, manufactured in sheet form, and too hard to roll.

S.F.P.M.
Surface feet per minute. A measure of the speed of a polishing surface, obtained by multiplying the circumference of the mop or wheel by the revolutions per minute.

Shive
Small plant fragments found in wool.

Shoddy
Material recovered from re-processed or re-used fabrics.

Shuffle
The circular movement of the top plate of a flat hardener.

Skin Wool
Wool removed from slaughtered sheep, also known as pulled wool. It has poor felting properties.

Skirtings
Inferior or stained wool extracted from around the edges of a fleece.

Slipe
Skin wool removed from a fleece with the aid of lime

Slippers
Soft indoor footwear responsible for a revival of felt manufacture and the cause of the growth of the shoe industry in Rossendale.

Sliver
The web of wool as it comes off the card, when collected together in loose rope form.

Specific Gravity
Specific Gravity (S.G.) is a measure of density and expressed as a ratio of felt density to the density of water. One cubic centimetre of pure water weighs one gramme, and water has a Specific Gravity of 1. A felt with a S.G. of 0.5 weighs half a gramme per cubic centimetre, and it is half as dense as water.

Splitting Resistance
The load required to split a piece of felt in two across its thickness.

Staple
An alternative descriptive name for a fibre, indicating that it has a definite length.

Stocks
Machines for milling felt by hammering it in a specially shaped vessel.

Stiffened felt
Felt which has been stiffened to a required hardness, using a stiffening agent such as animal glue, lacquer, starch, or poly vinyl alcohol (PVA)

Striker
The assistant who helped a blacksmith by holding the ironwork whilst the blacksmith manipulated the work. Most often, the striker was needed when the line shafting was being repaired.

Strings
Pieces of string that are threaded to the edge of a roll of felt to denote faults and for which an allowance in price was made.

Suint
Sheep's sweat, which stains wool, so that it can only be used in dyed blends.

Surgical Felt
The purest felt made using the finest, cleanest wool for chiropody applications and surgical paddings

Tailoring Felt
A soft grade of felt used in padding the fronts, lapels and shoulders of men's jackets and overcoats.

Tallowing
Impregnating felt parts with melted tallow to render the felt waterproof and oil resistant. The process made the felt more pliable than when it was waxed.

Taper Hammer Felt
Sheet felt varying in thickness and density and used for making piano hammers

Tear
A term used in block printing referring to the help and assistance given to the block printer

Tear Boy
The boy who helps a block printer with the block printing routine.

Tear trolley
The trolley containing the printing dye and cow dung base used for coating the block when printing

Tensile Strength
The measure of how strong a felt is when it is pulled under tension, measured in pounds per square inch or Newtons per square metre

Tenter
A tentering machine stretches a piece of felt to an even width as it dries. The felt is drawn between two endless travelling chains on which tenterhooks are mounted.

Tentering
The process of simultaneously drying and stretching felt

Tenter Fields
A field close to the mill where the static tenter frame was sited for drying outdoors

Tenter Hooks
The raked pins on a tenter frame that pierce and grip the felt when it is stretched and during drying.

Tenter Pins
The pins attached to the chains on a tenter machine that are similar to tenterhooks on a tenter frame

Tenter Seam
A frame that can hold a full length of felt up to 40 yards that allows it to be stretched and dried. A seam can hold two such frames built back to back.

Tetrachloride Test
A test used to determine the percentage of residual greases in a felt by washing the felt in carbon tetrachloride to remove the grease and then evaporating the carbon tetrachloride to leave the grease, which was then be weighed. Benzene or methyl alcohol could also be used.

Tolerance
It is not possible to manufacture felt to a precise thickness or density over its whole width, although hard felts can be sanded down to a required thickness very exactly. Tolerance is the amount of variation that is acceptable, usually quoted as percentage above and below a mean figure, usually 10%.

Top
A sliver of wool that has been combed by the worsted process, which leaves the long fibres lying parallel and well separated. Broken top is when the this sliver is deliberately pulled so as to give discrete bundles, which are useful in feltmaking for producing lightweight felt of good quality.

Tummer
A colloquial name for a scribbler or scribbling machine, which pre-separates wool before carding.

Underfelt
A coarse felt that was originally an animal fibre such as cow hair and which was put underneath a woven carpet to improve the feel and durability of the carpet. Later underfelts were made from animal and vegetable fibres such as jute by needling them together rather than felting them.

Valenki Boot
Felt boot used largely in Siberia and Scandinavian countries where sub zero temperatures occur

Virgin Wool
New, unused, raw wool.

Washed Wool
Wool that has been cleaned by a washing process.

Water Gauge
An instrument consisting of a U-tube part filled with water used to measure pressure differences when measuring air permeability.

Water Thickness Swell
The increase in thickness in a felt obtained after wetting it in water or ethanol solution. The increase is expressed as a percentage of the original thickness.

Waxing
Impregnating felt parts with melted paraffin wax to render the felt waterproof and oil resistant.

Wicking Action
The way in which a liquid travels through a felt when one end is immersed in the liquid.

Winch Dyeing
Dyeing a felt by putting the felt into a vessel containing the dye and then hauling it vertically out of the vessel and over a winch and then returning it to the vat. By stitching the ends together, it is made into a continuous process so the felt is constantly being moved in and out of the dye liquor.

Willey
A machine for breaking up clumps of wool to enable them to be carded into a fine web by a subsequent process

Willeying
A machinery process to open or loosen hard and tangled bunches in wool, before carding.

Wool Content
The proportion of wool to other fibres in a felt expressed as a percentage

Worshipful Company of Feltmakers
The London Guild of Feltmakers

Woven Felt
This is a woven woollen cloth that is heavily milled so that the surface is felted to mask the warp and weft, which makes it superficially resemble a woollen felt. Woven felt has greater strength than pressed felt, particularly when wet. It is used as a filter, in the papermaking and brewing industries.

Wuzzer
A hydro-extractor, a machine similar to a horizontal domestic spin dryer that removes water from a felt by centrifugal force.

Yield of Wool
The percentage of clean wool remaining after raw wool has been washed free from impurities,

Yield of Felt
The percentage weight of felt manufactured from a given "floor weight" of wool.

Yolk
Grease or natural fat contained in raw wool.

REFERENCES

CHAPTER 1

1. Mau, Auguste, Professor, Pompeii, its Life and Art, translated by F.W. Kelsey, 1899)
2. Frozen Tombs, The Culture and Art of the Ancient Tribes of Siberia, British Museum Publications Ltd., ISBN 0 7141 0097 8
3. Photograph of the etched window in the board room of Bury Felt Manufacturing Co, Hudcar Mill
4. History of the Worshipful company of the Art or Mistery of Feltmakers of London J.H. Hawkins 1917
5. Burkett, Mary, Art of the Feltmaker, Abbott Hall Art Gallery, 1979, ISBN 0 9503335 1 4
6. Monge, Annales de Chimie 6, 300-311 1790
7. Shorter, S.A., Journal of the Society of Dyers and Colourists, 39,1923, pp270-276.
8. Martin, A. J. P., Journal of the Society of Dyers and Colourists, 61, 1945,pp173-174
9. Speakman, J.B., Stott, E., Chang, H., A Contribution to the Theory of Milling – Part 2, The Journal of the Textile Institute Transactions, July 1933
10. Rhodes, W. K., Textile Research Journal, 37 pp814 – 815, 1967.
11. Makinson, K., Rachel, Shrinkproofing of Wool, pp 206 – 211, Marcel Dekker, 1979
12. Makinson, K., Rachel, Shrinkproofing of Wool, pp 171 - 175, Marcel Dekker, 1979.
13. Sherman, J. B.,Balasubramaniam, Whiteley,K. J., Textile Research Journal, Volume 40. No. 4, pp297 – 302, 1970
14. Bohm, L., The Frictional Properties of Wool Fibres in Relation to Felting, Journal of Society of Dyers and Colourists, Volume 61, Issue 11, pages 278–283, November 1945
15. Ibid
16. Makinson, K., Rachel, Shrinkproofing of Wool, pp 191 - 192, Marcel Dekker, 1979
17. Mrozewska, H., The influence of the Length and Grading of Wools on different End Uses of Felts, British Hat and Allied Feltmakers Research Association, Technical Publication L.T.84, 25th March 1964
18. Mrozewska, H., The influence of the Length and Grading of Wools on different End Uses of Felts, British Hat and Allied Feltmakers Research Association, Technical Publication L.T.84, 25th March 1964
19. Dietrich, H., Melliand Textilberichter, English Edition No. 1), pp 3-6, 1961
20. Speakman, J. B., Stott, Emma, A Contribution to the Theory of Milling, Part I, Journal of the Textile Institute, pp 339 – 348, July 1931
21. Rae, A, Bruce, R., The WIRA Textile Data book, WIRA 1973
22. Blankenburg, G., Zahn, H. , Textil – Praxis, 16, pp 228 – 232, 1961
23. Chaudri, M. A.,Whiteley, K. J., The Influence of Natural Variations in Fibre Properties on the Felting Characteristics of Loose Wool, Textile research Journal, Volume 40 Number 4, April 1970
24. Offermann, H., The Appraisal of wool in the Light of its Treatment in the Felt Industry, British Hat and Allied Feltmakers Research Association, Publication L.T. 69, 29th January 1962
25. Spencer, Joseph, The Manufacture of Felt, Central Library, Rawtenstall, 1948
26. Makinson, K., Rachel, Shrinkproofing of Wool, pp200-201, Marcel Dekker, 1979
27. Whewell, C.S.,Journal of the Textile Institute, July1950,I, p593
28. Foulds, K. L., Wool and Woollen Pressed Felt, The Textile Manufacturer, August 1952, p401
29. Spencer, Joseph, The Manufacture of Felt, Joseph Spencer (1968) typescript in Rawtenstall Library

CHAPTER 2

1. British Patent Number GB3892, 1815
2. Return to an Order of the Honourable The House of Commons dated 16 July 1860. A copy" of all correspondence with the Board of Inland Revenue or the Treasury, on the subject of the exemption of felt and scaleboard from paper duty.
3. A Practical Treatise on the Construction and Formation of Railways by James Day - Railroads – 1839
4. Catalogue of the Library of the Institution of Civil Engineers - Page 370 by Institution of Civil Engineers (Great Britain) Library, Institution of Electrical Engineers Library, Henry Storks Eaton, Benjamin Lewis Vulliamy, Library, Institution of Electrical Engineers - Engineering – 1866
5. British patent GB5791, 1839

[6] The register of Arts and Journal of Patent Inventions edited by Luke Herbert 1827 p240
[7] London Journal of Arts and Sciences and Repertory of Patent Inventions by W.Newton Vol X 1837
[8] British Farmer's Magazine, New Series Vol xxii, London, Henry Wright, 51 Haymarket, 1852 - Page 148
[9] Law Reports of Cases by William Carpmael, A Macintosh, 20 New Street, 1851
[10] Australian Building a cultural investigation, Roofing Felt History: d. Tarred Felts 10.07.7, by Professor Miles Lewis
[11] "A Series of Letters on the Improved Mode in the Cultivation and Management" - James Hill Dickson - Flax industry - 1846 – pages 3-5
[12] British Patent GB9122
[13] English Heritage publication of 1994 Survey of London volumes 43 and 44 pp 113-117
[14] William Bywater Day books held in Leeds library archives
[15] National archive 104607 Liverpool filed by BICC
[16] The Merchant's Magazine, Statist, And Commercial Review New Series.— Vol. I. London : Richardson Brothers, 23, Cornhill. 1855
[17] Crystal Palace and Park - Page 45 by Samuel Phillips, Philip Henry Delamotte - 1854
[18] Australian Building a cultural investigation, Roofing Felt History: d. Tarred Felts 10.07.7, by Professor Miles Lewis
[19] Transcription of the Minutes of the Pressed Felt association 1972
[20] The Register of Arts and Journal of Patent Inventions Fourth New Series edited by L Herbert Published in London by B. Stiell 1830
[21] Mechanics Magazine, Museum Register, Journal and Gazette Volume Twelfth, London, published by M. Salmon 115 Fleet Street 1830 p334
[22] The Mechanics Magazine, The Museum Of Foreign Literature Science And Art , April,—September, 1839. Vol. xxi. London: Published For The Proprietor By W. A. Robertson, Mechanics' Magazine Office, Fleet Street 1839
[23] British Patent BP 8926 dated 17 April 1841)
[24] The Official Illustrated Guide To The Great Northern, Manchester, Sheffield, and Lincolnshire, and Midland Railways By George Measom London Griffin Bohn 1861
[25] British Patent BP 8387 dated 14 February 1840
[26] Fire insurance policies including policy number19529, Acc1715 Leeds Library Elmwood Mills papers
[27] Acc1715 Leeds Library, Elmwood Mills papers
[28] National and Commercial Directory by Pigot and Co. 1841
[29] British Patents GB8642, 9109, 13862, 2053
[30] Court case Allen v Rawson 1845 Common Bench Reports vol.1 Philadelphia, T & J.W.Johnson, Law Booksellers
[31] Reports Of Cases In Chancery, Argued And Determined In The Rolls Court During The Time Of The Right Honorable Sir John Romilly, Knight, Master Of The Rolls. By Charles Beavan, Esq., M.A. BarristerAt Law. Vol. Xvi. 1852, 1853. 15 & 16 Victoria.London: W. G.Benning And Co., Law Booksellers, 43, Fleet Street. 1854, Anderson V. Kemshead page 329.
[32] Acc1715 Leeds Library, Elmwood Mills papers
[33] Acc 1715 Leeds library, Elmwood Mills papers note 13)
[34] Notes by T.Lawson, Acc 1715 Leeds Library
[35] Common Bench Reports cases argued and determined, the Court of Common Pleas, Philadelphia, 1846, p 551
[36] Cases Argued And Determined Relating To the Poor Laws, To Points In Criminal Law, And Other Subjects Chiefly Connected With Duties and Offices of Magistrates : Commencing With Michaelmas Term, 8 Victoria. Reported Principally By Philip Bockett Barlow, Esq., Henry Selfe Selfe, Esq., George Morley Dowdeswell, Esq. And Henry John Hodgson, Esq. Barristers-At-Law. Forming Part Of Vol. Xiv. Of The New Series, And Vol. Xxiii. Of The Old Series, Of The Law Journal Reports. London : Printed Bv James Holmes, 4, Took's Court, Chancery Lane. Published By E. B. Ince, 5, Quality Court, Chancery Lane. 1845 Page 4
[37] Exposition Universale de 1851 Liste générale des récompenses décernées par le jury international, Exposition Universelle de 1851, published 1854
[38] Advertisement in the puppet Show 9 December 1848 and MASCO letter heading 1917, New Monthly Magazine And Humourist Edited By W. Harrison Ainsworth, Esq. Vol. 84. Being The Third Part For1848. London, Chapman And Hall The Strand
[39] Exposition Universale de 1867 a Paris- Liste générale des récompenses décernées par le jury international
[40] Reports Of Cases In Chancery, Argued And Determined In The Rolls Court During The Time Of The Right Honorable Sir John Romilly, Knight, Master Of The Rolls. By Charles Beavan, Esq., M.A. Barrister At Law. Vol. Xvi. 1852, 1853.— 15 & 16 Victoria. London: W. G. Benning And Co., Law Booksellers, 43, Fleet Street.1854, Anderson v Kemshead page 329
[41] Acc 1715 Leeds University, Elmwood Mills papers

REFERENCES

[42] Acc 1715 Leeds University, Elmwood Mills papers
[43] The Mechanics' Magazine. January 2nd— June 26th, 1858. Edited By K. A. Brooman & E. J. Reed. Vol LXVIII, Page 199
[44] Acc 1715 Leeds Library, under "Sundrie information"
[45] Post Office Directory of the West Riding of Yorkshire part 2 page 63
[46] Acc1715 Leeds library, Elmwood Mills papers
[47] As recorded in the MASCO letterhead of 1904 after they took over the Patent Woollen Cloth Company
[48] Dolge, Alfred, Pianos and their Makers: A Comprehensive History of the Development of the Piano, Covina, 1911
[49] Carpeting the millions, The Growth of Britain's Carpet Industry, by J. Neville Bartlett, John Donald Publishers Ltd pages 40 - 43
[50] Acc 1715 Leeds University, Elmwood Mill papers
[51] Measom, George S. The Official Illustrated Guide to the Great Northern Railway: Including the Manchester, Sheffield, Lincolnshire and Midland Railways, London, 1861 - Page 469
[52] Leeds and Clothing Districts Directory William White 1847
[53] Official Descriptive and Illustrated Catalogue: Great Exhibition of the works of industry of all nations, volume II, 1851, Robert Ellis, Great Britain Commissioners for the Exhibition of 1851, under Woollens and Worsteds - Page 570
[54] Greener, William, The Science of Gunnery as applied to the Use and Construction of Firearms, Asso. Ins. C. E, London, Published by Longman and Co. Whittaker.& Co., Simkin & Marshall, C. Tilt ,W. Smith, Ackerman & Co And T. Mclean, and by F. Loiraine , Newcastle on Tyne, 1841
[55] Official Descriptive and Illustrated Catalogue: Great Exhibition of the works of industry of all nations, volume II, 1851, Robert Ellis, Great Britain Commissioners for the Exhibition of 1851, under Woollens and Worsteds - Page 570
[56] Personal Narrative of the Origin and Progress of the Caoutchouc or India-Rubber Manufacture in England, by Thomas Hancock, 1st Published 1857
[57] Measom, George S. The Official Illustrated Guide to the Great Northern Railway: Including the Manchester, Sheffield, Lincolnshire and Midland Railways, London, 1861 - Page 469
[58] Leeds Directory, Jones 1863
[59] Leeds Directory, William White 1857
[60] Leeds and Neighbourhood Directory, Porter 1872
[61] Leeds Directory, McCorquodale 1878
[62] Directory of the West Riding of Yorkshire, Slater 1887 part 1, and 1891
[63] Kelly's Directory of Leeds 1899
[64] Directory of Leeds and Bradford Kelly 1900 vol 1
[65] Kelly's Directory of Leeds 1881
[66] Directory of the West Riding of Yorkshire, Slater 1887 part I
[67] Kelly's Directory of Leeds 1905
[68] Kelly's Directory of Leeds 1906
[69] Leeds Directory, William White 1845
[70] British Patent BP 8642 dated 24 September 1840, also BP 9109 with co-inventor Joseph Weight dated 7 October 1841
[71] British Patent BP 13651 dated 19 December 1851
[72] British Patent BP 2053 dated 20 July 1857
[73] Post Office Directory of West Riding of Yorkshire Part 2 1861
[74] The Post Office Directory of the West Riding of Yorkshire part 2 1861
[75] Clothing District Directory, White 1875
[76] British patent BP 466 dated 5 February 1874
[77] Acc1715 Leeds Library, Elmwood Mills Papers
[78] Directory of Leeds and Woollen Districts, White 1866
[79] Clothing District Directory, William White 1870
[80] Leeds Directory, Jones 1863
[81] Clothing District Directory, William White 1870
[82] Leeds Directory, McCorquodale 1878
[83] Kellys Directory of Leeds 1881
[84] Directory of the West Riding of Yorkshire part 1, Slater 1887
[85] Directory of Leeds and Bradford, Kelly 1900 volume 2
[86] British Patent BP 21304 dated 6 November 1894) British Patent BP 10851 dated 1May 1894)
[87] Acc 1715 Elmwood Mills papers, Leeds Library
[88] The Textile Colourist - Textile industry – 1876, Page 406

[89] Wm. Bywater day books in Leeds Library
[90] Monumental/Memorial Inscriptions St. John's Church, Roundhay, South Section.E33 Large Celtic cross, decorated
[91] Inda Journal of Nonwovens Research, INDA, Winter 1992 issue, the Association of the Nonwoven Fabrics Industry; 1001 Winstead Dr., Suite 460; Cary, N.C. 27513).

CHAPTER 3

The Development of the Textile Industry in Rossendale Anonymous thesis in Rawtenstall Library
[2] History and Directory of Mid Lancashire 1854
[3] Directory of Lancashire by Slater 1865
[4] Richard Ashworth J.P., Richard, The Felt Trade in Rossendale, Rossendale Free Press 21 May 1921
[5] Macdonalds Directories for Rochdale, Bacup, Rossendale 1879
[6] Bacup Times 27 May 1882 p8 col 2, and Eastaugh, Oliver, Oliver Eastaugh Tells Rossendale Free Press 12 August 1933
[7] Rossendale Free Press 10 May 1902
[8] Rossendale Free Press 30 November 1907
[9] Bacup Times 24. September1881
[10] Royal National Commercial Directory of Lancashire and the Manufacturing District around Manchester 1879 vol 11 p623
[11] Worral's Cotton and Spinners and Manufacturers for Newchurch 1891
[12] Rossendale Daily Gazette 4/1/1896)
[13] The Felt Trade in Rossendale, Rossendale Free Press 21 May 1921
[14] Davies, John, Typescript, Mills of Rawtenstall
[15] Directory of Lancashire 1865 by Slater
[16] Bacup and Rossendale News 14 October 1871
[17] Bacup and Rossendale News 5 July 1879 recorded by John Davies
[18] The Felt Trade in Rossendale, Rossendale Free Press 21 May 1921
[19] Bacup and Rossendale News 27 July 1878
[20] Cronkshaw M.A., Phyllis, An Industrial Romance of the Rossendale Valley: The Development of the Shoe and Slipper Industries, Rawtenstall Library RC 6853
[21] Davies, John, The Mills of Rossendale, Auction at Bridge End Mill 28 November 1878
[22] Davies, John, Mills of Rawtenstall Typescript in Rawtenstall Library
[23] Bacup and Rossendale News November 1879
[24] Rossendale Free Press 21 August 1886
[25] Bacup and Rossendale News 24 June 1871
[26] Bacup and Rossendale News 1872
[27] Bacup and Rossendale News 28 May 1887
[28] Bacup and Rossendale News 31 July 1880
[29] North East Lancashire Directory, Volume 2, Mannex
[30] Bacup Times 4/2/1881
[31] Bacup Times 23/7/1881
[32] Bacup Times 4/2/1881
[33] Simpson, J.A., A History of Edenfield and District, Edenfield Local History Society (16 Jun 2003) ISBN-10: 0951666916
[34] Bacup Times 17 December 1870 p4, recorded by Joseph Spencer
[35] Leeds Clothing Districts Directory, William White 1853
[36] Leeds and Neighbourhood Directory and Gazetteer by Gillbanks 1856, and, Leeds Directory by William White 1857
[37] Lancashire Leaders, Social and Political by Ernest Gaskell 1907
[38] Reference Rossendale Free Press July 6th 1895
[39] Leeds and Neighbourhood Directory and Gazetteer by Gillbanks 1856
[40] Directory of Lancashire by Slater 1865
[41] British Patent GB3722
[42] Bacup and Rossendale News 20/1/1868
[43] Davies, John, Mills of Rawtenstall Typescript in Rawtenstall Library
[44] Bacup and Rossendale News 23 December 1865
[45] Bacup and Rossendale News 16 June 1866
[46] Rossendale Free Press July 6 1895
[47] Bacup and Rossendale News 18 June 1870

REFERENCES

[48] Agreement re Ground Rents by John Sutcliffe August 16 1886 and the original map of 1876 held with the documents of Bury and Masco Holdings Limited and agreement between Mitchell Brothers of Waterfoot Limited and Mitchells Ashworth and Stansfield
[49] Rossendale Daily Gazette 25 February 1893
[50] North East Lancashire Directory Volume 2 by Mannex 1876, and Royal Commercial Directory of Lancashire and the Manufacturing District around Manchester 1879 Volume II p623
[51] Davies, John, List of auction goods at Baltic Mill 1878, Mills of Rawtenstall Typescript in Rawtenstall Library
[52] Hardman, W., The History of Waterfoot 1922, Free Press Office, Rawtenstall p34-39
[53] Cronkshaw M.A., Phyllis, An Industrial Romance of the Rossendale Valley: The Development of the Shoe and Slipper Industries Rawtenstall Library RC 6853)
[54] Rossendale Free Press 29 March 1890
[55] Cronkshaw M.A., Phyllis, An Industrial Romance of the Rossendale Valley: The Development of the Shoe and Slipper Industries Rawtenstall Library RC 6853).
[56] Bacup and Rossendale News 25 May 1889
[57] Bacup and Rossendale News 13 June 1890
[58] Rossendale Daily Gazette for 14 and 25 February 1893
[59] Correspondence between Richard Brutton & Co and Colonel Mitchell, Bury and Masco file archive
[60] Recollection of H.R.T.Ashworth
[61] Agreement for sale of Business between Mitchells of Waterfoot Limited and Mitchells, Ashworth, Stansfied Company Limited dated 28th October 1904
[62] Agreement for sale of business between Mitchells of Waterfoot Limited and Mitchells, Ashworth, Stansfied Company Limited dated 28th October 1904
[63] Rossendale Free Press 6th July 1895
[64] Advertisement by Bovard, Rose of Fifth Avenue, Pittsburgh Post, Wednesday April 24 1889 page 5
[65] Bartlett, Neville, Carpeting the Millions, The Growth of Britain's Carpet Industry, John Donald Publishers Ltd. ISBN0 85976 025 1), page 82
[66] Rossendale Daily gazette 3 June 1893
[67] Private phone call from Mr. Deely
[68] Rossendale Free Press 6 July 1895
[69] Encyclopaedia Britannica 1911
[70] British Patents GB6118 1901, GB8390 of 1903
[71] Agreement between Mitchell Brothers of Waterfoot Limited and Messers. Richard Ashworth and William Stansfield
[72] Rossendale Free Press July 1928
[73] Bacup and Rossendale News 21 November 1874
[74] Bacup and Rossendale News 28 February 1880
[75] Rossendale Daily Gazette 14 December 1894
[76] Contract between Richard Ashworth and Mitchells, Ashworth, and Stansfield & Company Limited Bury and Masco Holdings Limited 28 October 1904
[77] Contract between Richard Ashworth and Mitchells, Ashworth, and Stansfield & Company Limited Bury and Masco Holdings Limited 28 October 1904
[78] Memorandum of Agreement 1905 Between M.A.S.& Company Limited and Letitia Jane Bridge, Bury and Masco Holdings Limited archive
[79] Bacup Times 17 December 1881
[80] North East Lancashire Directory Volume 2 by Mannex
[81] Bacup Times 17 December 1881
[82] Bacup Times 23 July 1881 page 5 col 3
[83] Bacup Times 17 December 1881
[84] Rossendale Free Press 24 July 1908
[85] Davies, John, Mills of Rawtenstall Typescript in Rawtenstall Library
[86] Rossendale Daily Gazette 15 July 1893
[87] Recollections of the Felt Industry Number 30 Mr. Barker
[88] Davies, John, Mills of Rawtenstall Typescript in Rawtenstall Library pages 12 & 25
[89] Bacup and Rossendale News for 10 March 1888 and 9 September 1888
[90] Bacup Rossendale News 8 July and 1889
[91] Rossendale Free Press 7 May 1902
[92] Davies, John, Mills of Rawtenstall typescript in Rawtenstall Library
[93] Cronkshaw M.A., Phyllis, An Industrial Romance of the Rossendale Valley: The Development of the Shoe and Slipper Industries Rawtenstall Library RC 6853)
[94] Worral's Cotton Spinners and Manufacturer's Directory, Newchurch, 1891

[95] Ashworth, Richard, The Felt Trade in Rossendale, Rossendale Free Press 21 May 1921
[96] Bywater Day Books 1917 –1934 held at the Leeds Library
[97] Recollections of the Felt Industry Number 30 Mr. Barker
[98] Agreement between Mitchell Brothers of Waterfoot Limited and Messrs. Richard Ashworth and William Stansfield, 18 August 1904, in the Bury and Masco Holdings Limited archive
[99] Agreement between Mitchell Brothers of Waterfoot Limited and Messrs. Richard Ashworth and William Stansfield, 18 August 1904, in the Bury and Masco Holdings Limited archive
[100] Agreement of 28 October 1904 between Thomas Mitchell, esq. and others and Mitchells Ashworth and Stansfield and Company Limited, Bury and Masco Holdings Limited archives
[101] Agreement for Sale, G. Walter Knox, Esq. As receiver for the Debenture Holders of the Patent Woollen Cloth Company Limited (in Liquidation) and Thomas Mitchell, Esq. and Others 14 September 1904 Bury and Masco Holdings Limited Archives
[102] Agreement Messrs. Thomas Mitchell, Richard Ashworth, and William Stansfield and Mitchells, Ashworth and Stansfield and Company Limited dated 28 October 1904
[103] Lewis, Professor Miles, Australian Building a cultural investigation, Roofing Felt History: d. Tarred Felts 10.07.7
[104] Agreement for Sale of the Bouinikon Felt Company Limited 28 October 1904 Bury and Masco Holdings Limited Archives
[105] Agreement for sale of Business Mr. William V. Blaikie and Mitchells, Ashworth, Stansfield and Company Limited 28 October1904 in Bury and Masco Holdings Limited Archives
[106] Agreement for sale of Business Mr. William V. Blaikie and Mitchells, Ashworth, Stansfield and Company Limited 28 October1904 in Bury and Masco Holdings Limited Archives
[107] Agreement for sale of Business Mr. William Stansfield and Mitchells, Ashworth, Stansfield and Company Limited, Bury and Masco Holdings Limited Archive
[108] Agreement for sale of Business Mr. Richard Ashworth and Mitchells, Ashworth, Stansfield and Company Limited Bury and Masco Holdings Limited Archives
[109] Who's Who in Business c 1905 p 125
[110] Bury Times 7/4/62
[111] Cooper and Co., Company Minutes held in Bury and Masco Holdings Limited Archive
[112] Coopers Private Letter Book held by Bury and Masco Holdings Limited archive
[113] British Patent GB10851 May 1 1897
[114] Cooper and Co. (Birmingham) Limited Felt Polishing Bob Brochure
[115] Cooper and Co (Birmingham) Limited Board Minutes
[116] Oldham Local Studies and Archives R.R.Whitehead and Brothers Limited files D-AAJ/4
[117] Provisional British Patent GB2235 10 September 1863
[118] R.R.Whiteheads Minutes held by Bury Cooper Whitehead Limited
[119] R.R.Whiteheads Minutes held by Bury Cooper Whitehead Limited
[120] Dolge, Alfred, Pianos and Their Makers: A Comprehensive History of the Development of the Piano - Page 120
[121] Recollections of the Felt industry Number 22 Mr. Haig
[122] Advertisment in Year-book of Pharmacy 1875 - Page 700
[123] McGow, Peter, Notes On The Wandle Mills, held by The Wandle Industrial Museum, March 2005; and Recollections of the Felt Industry Number 22 Mr.F. Haig
[124] Recollections of the Felt Industry Number 22 Mr. F. Haig
[125] Pressed Felt Manufacturers Association statistics
[126] Walter, Peter Estimate from a market survey undertaken for Bury Cooper Whitehead 1980
[127] History of E. V. Naish web site, http://www.naishfelts.co.uk
[128] The Quidhampton Story, In memory of Stan Cousins the Author of this work 1919 - 2002.First printed in 1994. Second print in 2006
[129] Naish, John, R., E.V. Naish Ltd, The First 200 years 1800 – 2000, Wilton Graphics, 2000
[130] Dolge, Alfred, Pianos and Their Makers: A Comprehensive History of the Development of the Piano - Page 120)
[131] Wiltshire Cuttings xxi and information from Messrs. E. V. Naish Ltd.
[132] Pressed Felt Manufacturers Association statistics
[133] Naish, John, R., E.V. Naish Ltd, The First 200 years 1800 – 2000, Wilton Graphics, 2000
[134] McGow, Peter, Wandle Mills, paper held by Wandle Industrial Museum, Mitcham
[135] Official Catalogue of the New York Exhibition of the Industry of All Nations 1853 page 105
[136] Hillier, J., Old Surrey Water Mills (1951) p178
[137] Advertisement in the Medical Times and Gazette 1859 p622
[138] Cassell's Illustrated Exhibitor International Exhibition, 1862 - P xiii by Cassell Ltd

REFERENCES

[139] McGow, Peter Notes, On The Wandle Mills, March 2005 held by The Wandle, Industrial Museum; also Recollections of the Felt Industry Number 22 Mr.F. Haig
[140] Lewis' 1820 Directory "Worcestershire General and Commercial Directory, for 1820, Part First. Containing the City & Suburbs Of Worcester, The Borough Of Droitwich, And the Towns of Bromsgrove and Stourbridge"
[141] Pigot's 1829 directory for "Stourbridge, Swinford, Brierley Hill, Cradley and Neighbourhoods"
[142] The 1845 "Post Office Directory for Birmingham, Warwickshire and part of Staffordshire"
[143] Post Office Directory 1854
[144] The entry for Cradley in Kelly's 1860
[145] Kelly's 1868 Directory
[146] "Littlebury's Directory and Gazetteer of the County of Worcestershire", 1873
[147] Communication from the personal secretary, Joan Roberts, secretary to the Company Secretary of Bury and Masco (Holdings) Limited
[148] Ponting, M. G., The Decline of the Woollen Industry in the Trowbridge and Bradford on Avon Area in 19th Century M Sc Thesis 1974
[149] Bartlett, Neville J., Carpeting the Millions – the Growth of the Carpet Industry, John Donald Publishers Ltd. Edinburgh also Kelly's Directory of Kent 1870
[150] Jurist vol. xv part II . Sweet, Chancery Lane, London, 1852 P34
[151] Law Reports Of Patent Cases.Vice Chancellor's Court. April 4, 1837, Abbott v. Williams* And Others
[152] The Civil engineer and architect's journal, Volume 31, January 1868
[153] Board of Trade journal, Volume 19 By Great Britain. Board of Trade 1895
[154] Belfast And Its Environs; Or Strangers Guide With A Map Of The City, John Henderson Booksellers To The Queen, Castle Place, Belfast 13 1855
[155] The Commercial Directory and Shippers Guide, Fourth Edition, Published By R. E. Fulton, Leicester Buildings, King Street.Liverpool 1872
[156] Records of C. Davidson and Sons Ltd., Paper Manufacturers, Mugiemoss Mills, Bucksburn, Aberdeen, 1852 – 1977, held at: University of Aberdeen
[157] Papworth], W., The Dictionary of Architecture, 1853–92
[158] Bolton Evening News, Wednesday 3rd Nov 1874
[159] Recollection of the Felt Industry Number 1, Peter Fuller

CHAPTER 4

[1] GB2688, 1803
[2] GB5412, 1826
[3] GB3892, 1815
[4] Minutes of Proceedings of the Institution of Civil Engineers, p48, Institution of Civil Engineers (Great Britain)
[5] Wright, G. N., Scenes In North Wales. With Historical Illustrations, Legends, and Biographical Notices, London: Printed for T. T. and J. Tegg, Cheapside; B. Griffin and Co. Glasgow; J. Cumming and W. F. Wakeman, Dublin. 1833
[6] GB5791, 1829
[7] GB8176, 31 January 1839
[8] Carpmael's Reports of Patent Cases 1837
[9] Return to an Order of the Honourable The House of Commons dated 16 July 1860. A copy of all Correspondence with the Board of Inland Revenue or the Treasury, on the subject of the Exemption of Felt and Scaleboard from Paper Duty
[10] GB8230, 1839
[11] The Jurist - Great Britain Courts – 1852, Bankruptcy in 1849 Bankrupt and dividend register. p34; also The Law Journal for the Years 1832-1949: p23
[12] Measom, George, The Official Illustrated Guide To The Great Northern,Manchester, Sheffield, And Lincolnshire, And Midland Railways, London, Griffin Bohn 1861
[13] Patent number 8646
[14] Common Bench Reports cases argued and determined, the Court of Common Pleas, Philadelphia, 1846, p 551
[15] Acc 1715 Elmwood Mills papers, Leeds Library
[16] Acc 1715 Elmwood Mills papers, Leeds Library
[17] Leeds Directory - William White 1845
[18] British patents GB4986 July 7 2824 – Raising Cloth, Gb55 1825 – Cleaning, milling, fulling cloth, GB5268 Addition to patent number GB5118, 6586 March 31 1834 – raising pile of woolen fabric, and 8642 September 24 1834 – Fulling and milling – felting
[19] BP9109
[20] British Patent BP13862 in 1851

[21] British Patent GB2053 July 28 1857 – Novel felting
[22] Hirst 24 September 1840 BP 8642 and 19 December 1851 BP 13651, Henry Augustus Wells 17 April 1841 BP 8926, Junius Smith 20 October 1841 BP 9122
[23] BP 3722 of 31 December 1862
[24] BP 2460 22 August 1872
[25] BP 1686 1 June 1869
[26] BP 16702 14 July 1897
[27] BP 3808 in 1868 and BP 5934 in 1891
[28] BP 2507 1869
[29] BP 2680 of 1803
[30] BP 9772
[31] BP 8642, BP 9109, BP 13862
[32] BP 9772
[33] BP 8642, 1840
[34] BP 8951, 1841
[35] BP 1123, 1846
[36] BP 2053, 1857
[37] BP 2654, 1856
[38] BP 408, 1862, BP 215, 1863.
[39] BP 2811, 1856
[40] BP 2917, 1868
[41] BP 3560, 1868
[42] BP 1686, 1869
[43] BP 2147, 1868
[44] BP 7889, 1868
[45] BP 4109, 1841
[46] BP 466 1874
[47] BP 5804 1892
[48] BP 1545
[49] BP 2553, 1855
[50] BP 4791, 1885
[51] BP 332, 1854, BP 1648, 1860, BP 382, 1864, BP 661, 1868
[52] BP 8387, 1840
[53] BP 5029, 1881
[54] BP 2625, 23 July 1875
[55] US patent 123136
[56] BP3959 26 February 1884
[57] Letter dated 29th June 1892 to Colonel Mitchell "as to Messrs Firth account, Needle Loom Patents from Richard Brutton & Co. and Report on Firth's Accounts in Respect to Needle Loom Patents", MASCO files
[58] BP 12386, 1895,
[59] BP 3523, 1900, BP 1916, 1900, BP 18167, 1905),
[60] BP 6118, 1902, BP 8390, 1904, BP 2523, 1905)
[61] Agreement for Amalgamation Mitchell Brothers of Waterfoot Limited and Messrs. Richard Ashworth and Stansfield dated August 18th 1904, MASCO files

CHAPTER 5

Measom, George S. The Official Illustrated Guide to the Great Northern Railway: Including the Manchester, Sheffield, Lincolnshire and Midland Railways, London, 1861 - Page 469
[2] Acc1715 Leeds Library Elmwood Mills papers
[3] *LEODIS*
[4] Recollections of the Felt Industry, Number 15, Mr. D. Rodgers, Mr. D. Fearnley
[5] Map held in the Bury and Masco Holdings Limited archive
[6] Bacup and Rossendale News 16/6/1866
[7] Bacup and Rossendale News 23/6/1866
[8] Bacup and Rossendale News 25/5/1889
[9] Rossendale Division Gazette 6/5/1893
[10] Davies, John, The Mills of Rawtenstall, manuscript in Rawtenstall Library
[11] Newbiggin, Thomas, The History of the Forest of Rossendale, 2nd edition, J J Riley 1893 p297
[12] Lancashire General Directory 1818

REFERENCES

[13] Rossendale Free Press 21/5/1921
[14] Bacup and Rossendale news 29/3/1873
[15] Davies, John, The Mills of Rawtenstall, manuscript in Rawtenstall Library
[16] Bacup and Rossendale News 27/7/1878
[17] Recollections of George Stansfield, Souvenir brochure of the re-opening of Baltic Mill
[18] Davies, John, The Mills of Rawtenstall, manuscript in Rawtenstall Library
[19] Bacup and Rossendale News 14/10/71
[20] North East Lancashire Directory Volume 2 Mannex
[21] Spencer, Joseph, The Manufacture of Felt, manuscript in Rawtenstall Library, 1948
[22] Rossendle Free Press 20/8/1887
[23] Memorandum of Agreement 1905 Between M.A.S.& Company Limited and Letitia Jane Bridge, Bury and Masco Holdings Limited archive
[24] Rossendale Free Press 14/11/1911
[25] Davies, John, The Mills of Rawtenstall, manuscript in Rawtenstall Library
[26] Rossendale Free Press 7/11/1953
[27] Davies, John, The Mills of Rawtenstall, manuscript in Rawtenstall Library
[28] Bacup and Rossendale News 4/1/1879
[29] Agreement for sale of Business between Mitchells of Waterfoot Limited and Mitchells, Ashworth, Stansfied Company Limited dated 28th October 1904
[30] Simpson, John, A History of Edenfield and District, Edenfield Local History society 2003
[31] The will of James Rostron
[32] Rossendale Free Press 21/5/1921
[33] Simpson, John, A History of Edenfield and District, Edenfield Local History society 2003
[34] The Agreement between Thomas Mitchell Esq. 7 others and Mitchells Stansfield and Company Limited dated 28 October 1904
[35] Newbigging, Thomas, History of the Forest of Rossendale, 2nd edition , J J Riley 1893 p196/7
[36] Slaters Northern Directory 1848
[37] History and Directory of Mid Lancashire 1854
[38] Rossendale Free Press 21/5/1921
[39] Davies, John, The Mills of Rawtenstall, manuscript in Rawtenstall Library
[40] Bacup and Rossendale News 14/10/1871
[41] Directory of Lancashire, Slater, 1865
[42] Bacup and Rossendale News 14/10/1871
[43] Bacup and Rossendale News 19/9/1874, 10/10/1874
[44] North East Lancashire Directory, Mannex vol 2, 1876
[45] Royal National and Commercial Directory of Lancashire and the Manufacturing District around Manchester 1879 Vol II p623
[46] Bacup and Rossendale News 6/9/1879
[47] Bacup and Rossendale News 10/10/1885
[48] Bacup Times December 17 1881, also Rossendale Free Press 5/8/1933
[49] Davies, John, The Mills of Rawtenstall, manuscript in Rawtenstall Library
[50] Burnley Evening Star 13/7/1979
[51] Davies, John, The Mills of Rawtenstall, manuscript in Rawtenstall Library
[52] Bacup and Rossendale News 11/3/1865, 27/4/1867, 29/1/1870, 24/9/1870
[53] Bacup and Rossendale News 5/8/1876
[54] Bacup and Rossendale News 26/9/1888
[55] Agreement between Mitchell Brothers of Waterfoot Limited and Mitchell Ashworth, Stansfield and Company Limited dated 28 October 1904
[56] Rawtenstall Daily Gazette 18/1/1896
[57] Rawtenstall Daily Gazette 18/1/1896
[58] Rossendale Free Press 23/7/1977
[59] The History of James Moorhouse, Preston Guardian 31/8/1918
[60] Roberts, E. M., An Economic and Social History of Rossendale, unpublished thesis 1967 held by Hereford College
[61] Slaters Royal National Commercial directory and Topography of the Counties of Chester and Cumberland 1848
[62] Bacup and Rossendale News 22/11/1879
[63] Bacup and Rawtenstall News 18/2/1882
[64] Bacup Times 3/1/1885, 13/6/85 and 24/7/1886
[65] Bacup and Rossendale News 11/9/1886

[66] Recollections of the Felt Industry Number 6, Tommy Crook
[67] Rawtenstall Daily Gazette 14/12/1895
[68] Memories of the Ashworth family, Rossendale Free Press 3/7/76
[69] Bacup Times 17/8/1935
[70] Rossendale Free Press 7/12/1971
[71] Nuttall, Jennie, History of Lumb-in-Rossendale, manuscript in Rawtenstall Library, 1965
[72] Bacup and Rossendale News 24/10/1863
[73] Davies, John, The Mills of Rawtenstall, manuscript in Rawtenstall Library
[74] Bacup and Rossendale News 3/9/1870
[75] Bacup and Rossendale News 18/5/1872
[76] Bacup and Rossendale News 31/7/1880
[77] Bacup Times 12/1/1929
[78] Davies, John, The Mills of Rawtenstall, manuscript in Rawtenstall Library
[79] Bacup Times 27 May 1882 p8, also Oliver Eastaugh Tells, Rossendale Free Press 12 August 1933,
[80] Rossendale Free Press 10 May 1902
[81] Rossendale Free press 18/2/1888
[82] Bacup and Rossendale News 10/3/1888
[83] Bacup and Rossendale News 30/3/1889
[84] Rossendale Free Press 7/5/1902
[85] Davies, John, The Mills of Rawtenstall, manuscript in Rawtenstall Library
[86] Rossendale Free press 18/2/1888
[87] Recollections of the Felt industry Number 30 Mr. Barker
[88] Davies, John, The Mills of Rawtenstall, manuscript in Rawtenstall Library
[89] Simpson, John, A History of Edenfield and District, Edenfield Local History society 2003
[90] Newbigging, Thomas, History of the Forest of Rossendale, 2nd edition , J J Riley 1893
[91] Bacup and Rossendale News 21/11/74
[92] Rossendale Free Press 19/10/1974
[93] Davies, John, The Mills of Rawtenstall, manuscript in Rawtenstall Library
[94] History and Directory of Mid Lancashire 1854 p492
[95] North East Lancashire Directory Vol 2 Mannex 1876
[96] Rossendale Free Press 30 November 1907
[97] Bacup Times 24. September1881
[98] Royal National Commercial Directory of Lancashire and the Manufacturing District around Manchester 1879 vol 11 p623
[99] Worral's Cotton and Spinners and Manufacturers for Newchurch 1891
[100] Rossendale Daily Gazette 11/2/1893
[101] Rossendale Daily Gazette 4/1/1896
[102] Bacup Times 23/8/1952
[103] Bacup Times 23/8/1952
[104] Holdens National Directory 1816
[105] Taylor, W. G., Bacupian Mills, vol I A-I, Rawtenstall Library
[106] Bacup and Rossendale News 15/8/1863
[107] Pigot's Directory for 1838
[108] Taylor, W. G., Bacupian Mills, vol I A-I, Rawtenstall Library
[109] Bacup and Rossendale News 20/1/1868
[110] Bacup and Rossendale News 13/2/1886
[111] Slaters Directory 1895
[112] Bacup Times 1/3/1924
[113] Davies, John, The Mills of Rawtenstall, manuscript in Rawtenstall Library
[114] Bacup and Rossendale News 10/6/1865
[115] Rossendale Free press 26/6/1920
[116] Bacup and Rossendale News 14/3/1868
[117] Bacup and Rossendale News 1/7/1871
[118] Davies, John, The Mills of Rawtenstall, manuscript in Rawtenstall Library
[119] Bacup and Rossendale News 28/5/1887
[120] Bacup and Rossendale 8/6/1889
[121] Bacup and Rossendale News 21/3/1890
[122] Agreement between Mitchell Brothers and Mitchells, Ashworth, Stansfield and Company Limited dated 28 October 1904
[123] Recollections of the Felt Industry, Number 13, Bill Davis

REFERENCES

[124] Pigot and Deans Directory for Manchester and Salford 124/5
[125] The Gregs of Styal, Mary Rose, Quarry bank Development Trust, 1978, p11/12
[126] Encyclopedia Britannica 1911 Volume V12, Page 555
[127] Pigot and Sons General Classified and Street Directory of Manchester and Salford 1838
[128] The Bury Directory including all the Townships in the Bury Union, printed by John Heap ,1850
[129] Rose, Mary, The Gregs of Styal, Quarry Bank Development Trust, 1978, p11/12
[130] Recollections of the Felt Industry Number 6 Tommy Crook
[131] Worralls Directory of Bury and Bolton with the Parishes and Townships of Heywood, Radcliffe, Ramsbottom, Farnworth, and Neighbourhood 1871
[132] Recollections of the Felt Industry Number 5, A Coupe
[133] Conveyance of Hudcar Mill to the Bury Felt Manufacturing Company In the Bury and Masco (Holdings) Limited archive
[134] Bury and Masco (Holdings) Limited Archive
[135] Pigot and Dean's Directory for Manchester and Salford 1824/5
[136] The Bury Directory including all the townships in the Bury Union, John Heap, 1850
[137] Worralls Directory of Bury and Bolton with the Parishes and Townships of Heywood, Radcliffe, Farnworth and Neighbourhood
[138] Directory and Topography of Bury, Ramsbottom, Radcliffe, Pilkington and adjoining villages and townships, P.Barrett and co, 1880; also Bury Times Street Guide Business Directory for Bury 1889
[139] Conveyance of properties from Bury Felt Manufacturing Company Limited to Bury and Masco Industries Limited 21 December 1962
[140] Worralls Directory of Bury and Bolton with the parishes and Townships of Heywood, Radcliffe, Ramsbottom, Farnworth, and Neighbourhood 1871
[141] Conveyance from Bury Manufacturing Company Limited to Bury and Masco Industries Limited 31 December 1965
[142] The West Riding Wool Textile Industry 1770 – 1835 D. T. Jenkins, University of York, Pasold Fund Limited, 1975
[143] Dolge, Alfred, Pianos and Their Makers: A Comprehensive History of the Development of the Piano, Covina, 1911 - Page 120
[144] McGow, Peter, Notes On The Wandle Mills, March 2005 held by The Wandle Industrial Museum; also Recollections of the Felt Industry Number 22 Mr. F. Haig)
[145] Naish, J. R., E. V. Naish The First 200 Years 1800-2000, Wilton Graphics, Salisbury
[146] Curtesy of Wandle Industrial MuseumMap
[147] The story of British Carpets, Bertram Jacobs, British Continental Trade Press Limited, 1968, p96
[148] Goad Insurance Map for 1897
[149] Kidderminster Shuttle, July 17 1943
[150] 100 years of progress, undated leaflet published by Cooper and Co (Birmingham) Limited
[151] Census of Felt Machine for the Committee for Wool Rationing 1917
[152] Airdale Costing Elmwood Mills Lawson Papers Leeds Archive Acc 1715
[153] Patent licencing to J. Wilkinson Elmwood Mills Lawson Papers Leeds Archive Acc 1715
[154] Valuation for insurance purposes Elmwood Mills Lawson Papers Leeds Archive Acc 1715
[155] Census of Felt Machine for the Committee for Wool Rationing 1917
[156] Bury Felt, Inventory, Valuation and Apportionments of fire Insurance, W.Salisbury Hamer 1913
[157] Census of Felt Machine for the Committee for Wool Rationing 1917
[158] Bury Felt, Inventory, Valuation and Apportionments of fire Insurance, 1944
[159] Figures reproduced in 1980 from Bury and Masco Holdings Limited archives, with permission from the Company Secretary

CHAPTER 6

[1] Holden, Roger N., Supplies For Steam-Powered Textile Mills, Industrial Archaeology Review, Volume 21, Number 1, June 1999, pp. 41-51(11), Maney Publishing
[2] Acc 4715, Elmwood Mill, Leeds Library
[3] Acc 4715, Elmwood Mill, Leeds Library
[4] Bury and Masco Document on the review of Water Supplies Abstraction and Distribution May 1974
[5] An application by Bury and Masco Industries Limited for an increase in abstraction rate to the Mersey and Weaver River Authority in the London Gazette, Friday 11 May 1973
[6] Pressed Felt Manufacturers Association Minutes, and Bury and Masco Industries archive
[7] Bury and Masco Archive Document on the Review of Water Supplies, 1974
[8] Recollections of the Felt Industry Number 15, D. Rodgers/D. Fearnley

[9] Rossendale Free Press 21/5/1921
[10] Recollections of the Felt Industry, Number 3, C. Dyson
[11] Recollections of the Felt Industry, Number 6, T. Crook
[12] Water extraction licence Mersey and weaver River Authority 1974 for Bury and Masco Industries Limited
[13] Recollections of the Felt Industry, Number 6, T. Crook
[14] Naish, John R., E V Naish The First 200 Years, Wilton Graphics
[15] Recollections of the Felt Industry, Number 3, Mr. Barker).
[16] Hills, Richard Leslie, Power from Steam: A History of the Stationary Steam Engine, Cambridge University Press, 1987, ISBN 052145834X, 9780521458344).
[17] Ibid
[18] Acc 4715, Elmwood Mill, Leeds Library
[19] Note by J R Clarke Lawson Papers Leeds
[20] Recollections of the Felt Industry, Number 5, C Dyson
[21] History of Royal George Public House web site

CHAPTER 7

Beaumont, Roberts. Woolen and Worsted: The Theory and Technology of the Manufacture of Woolen, Worsted, and Union Yarns and Fabrics, Vol. 1, The Library Press Limited, 1916
[2] Foulds, K. L., Pressed Felt Carding Manufacture II – Carding, The Textile Manufacturer, May 1955, p245).
[3] The Wira Textile Data Book, 1973, ISBN 0 900820 07 1
[4] Spencer, Joseph, The Manufacture of Felt, Manuscript in Rossendale Library, 1948
[5] Foulds, K. L., Wool and Woollen Pressed felt, The Textile manufacturer, August 1952
[6] Ibid
[7] Ibid
[8] Spencer, Joseph, The Manufacture of Felt, Manuscript in Rossendale Library, 1948
[9] ICS 65-3
[10] Spencer, Joseph, The Manufacture of Felt, Manuscript in Rossendale Library, 1948
[11] Cyclopaedia of Textile Work, American technical Society, Chicago 1907

CHAPTER 8

Frohndsorff, R. S. M., and Whewell, C. S., Some Observations on the Hardening Process used in Felt Manufacture, Journal of the Society of Dyers and Colourists 1951,Vol. 67, pp 142-8,
[2] Speakman, J. B., Menkart, J., Liu, W. T., On the Existence of a Critical Temperature for Milling, The Journal of the Textit. Institute, Transactions, April 1944, p 141
[3] Schofield, J., Transactions of the Journal of the Textile Institute, Researches in Wool Felting Part III, November 1942, p 181
[4] Frohensdorff, R.M.S., Whewell C.S., Some observations on the Hardening Process Used in Felt Manufacture, I "Factors influencing Hardening, Journal of the Society of Dyers and Colourists, 1951. vol. 671 pp 142.8
[5] Makinson, K. Rachel, Shrinkproofing of Wool, Marcel Decker Inc. 1979 ISBN 0-8247-6776-4, pp. 214.215
[6] Recollections of the Felt Industry 23 J Roberts, E Townsend
[7] Recollections of the Felt Industry, Number 23, J Roberts E Townsend).
[8] Frohlich, H.G., Survey of the manufacture of true felts from animal fibres, British Hat and allied Feltmakers association Technical Publication Lt 42, May 1958
[9] Cyclopaedia of Textile Work, American Technical Society, Chicago 1907
[10] Ibid
[11] British Patent 2247 dated 2 June 1868
[12] British Patent 9772 to W. G. Bywater and T. B. Beanland 5 July 1884
[13] The Manufacture of Pressed felts, Wool Science Review No 26, 1965, p15
[14] Enhanced picture from a brochure by E.V. Naish circa 1980
[15] Textile Recorder, October, 1952, p79
[16] Recollections of the Felt Industry, Number 9, H Nuttall
[17] Richard Ashworth J.P., Richard, The Felt Trade in Rossendale, Rossendale Free Press 21 May 1921

CHAPTER 9

Beaumont, Roberts, Finishing of Textile Fabrics, Scott Greenwood and Sons, 1926
[2] Technical information from the Tuchmacher Museum, Bramsche, Lower Saxony, Germany
[3] The Young Millers guide 1829

REFERENCES

[4] Acc1715 Leeds Library, Elmwood Mills papers
[5] Benson Anna, Textile Machines, Shire Publications Limited, 2002
[6] Beaumont, Roberts, Finishing of Textile Fabrics, Scott Greenwood and Sons, 1926 p122
[7] Acc1715 Leeds Library, Elmwood Mills papers
[8] Beaumont, Roberts, Finishing of Textile Fabrics, Scott Greenwood and Sons, 1926
[9] Foulds, K. L., Wool and Woollen Pressed felt, The Textile manufacturer, August 1952
[10] Recollections of the Felt Industry, Number 16 Davis, Knight, Livesey; also Recollections of the Felt Industry, Number 23 J Roberts, E. Stott)
[11] Ibid
[12] William Whiteley Textile Machinery Catalogue undated
[13] Ham, A. F., A Study of the Multi-roller Felting machine Part I, The British hat and Allied Feltmakers Research Association, TR12, June 1955
[14] Marcel Casse US Patent Number US2093709
[15] Holme, I., Wool Science review, Number 61, March 1985 p40
[16] Louis R Mizell, The properties, Functions and Uses of Pressed Wool Felts, Wool Science Review Number 61, March 1985
[17] Ibid
[18] Recollections of the Felt Industry, Number 24, Mr Sagar

CHAPTER 10

Foulds, K. L., Wool and Woollen Pressed Felt, The Textile Manufacturer, August, 1952)..
[2] Ibid
[3] Knecht, Edmund, A Manual of Dyeing: for the use of practical dyers, manufacturers, students, and all interested in the art of dyeing, London, C. Griffin and Co Limited 1893
[4] Unnamed and undated review of Bury Felt Manufacturing Limited technical issues, from Bury and Masco Industries archive, before 1962
[5] Acc1715 Leeds Library, Elmwood Mills papers
[6] Knecht, E., Rawson, C., A Manual of Dyeing Volume 1, 1920
[7] Spencer, Joseph, The Manufacture of Felt, Manuscript in Rossendale Library, 1948
[8] (Ref Unnamed report on process in Bury Felt Manufacturing Company before 1962)
[9] Pratt, H. T., Lant: Gone and best forgotten, WTA Vol 19. Number 6 , June 1987
[10] Spencer, Joseph, The Manufacture of Felt, Manuscript in Rossendale Library, 1948
[11] Recollections of the Felt Industry, Number 13, Davis
[12] Ibid
[13] Spencer, Joseph, The Manufacture of Felt, Manuscript in Rossendale Library, 1948
[14] Shaw, T., Allanach, D., Mothproofing and the Environment, International Wool Secretariat Development Centre 1990
[15] Hindson, W. R.; May, F. G. J.; Moore, B. T.; Southwell, G. Mothproofing Treatment for Ammunition Felt, Materials Research Labs Ascot Vale (Australia), Feb 1978
[16] OSPAR Commission, The Convention for the Protection of the Marine Environment of the North East Atlantic, Report on Pentachlorophenol, 2001
[17] Unnamed and undated review of Bury Felt Manufacturing Limited technical issues, from Bury and Masco Industries archive, before 1962
[18] An Episode and a History: The Centenary of a Woollen Mill -- Marzotto 1836/1936, 1936
[19] Recollections of the Felt Industry, Number 12, Tommy Simpson the last UK hand tenterer
[20] Spencer, Joseph, The Manufacture of Felt, Manuscript in Rossendale Library, 1948
[21] Foulds, K., Textile Manufacturer August 1955
[22] Ibid
[23] Ibid
[24] Recollections of the Felt Industry, Number 9, Lovell
[25] Recollection of the Felt Industry, Number 19, W Law

CHAPTER 11

Measom, George, The Official Illustrated Guide to the Great Northern, Manchester, Sheffield, and Lincolnshire, and Midland Railways, Griffin and Bohn, London, 1861
[2] Photograph in the Rossendale Free Press 5 October 1929, from a photograph supplied by Mr. E Bann of Waterfoot.
[3] Recollections of the Felt Industry, Number 1, W. Suart

[4] Recollections of the felt Industry, Number 3, C. Dyson
[5] Recollections of the Felt Industry, Number 28, H. Clark).
[6] Recollections of the Felt Industry, Number 4, R. Giddins
[7] Recollections of the Felt Industry, Number 18, K. Ritson
[8] Recollections of the Felt Industry, Number 18, K. Ritson
[9] Ibid
[10] Ibid
[11] Recollections of the Felt Industry, Number 4, R. Giddins
[12] Ibid

CHAPTER 12

The American Felt Company Data Sheet Number 17 Wool Felt – Liquid Filtration, 1956.
[2] Becker, William E., Felt Manufacturers Council Northern Textile Association Publication, The Penton Publishing Co. Cleveland Ohio, 1969
[3] Causer, S. M.; McMillan, R. C.; Bryson, W. G., The Role of Wool Carpets in Controlling indoor Air Pollution. In: Proceedings of the 9th International Wool Textile Research Conference, Biella (Italy), 28th June to 5th July 1995
[4] Gambichler Dr Thilo, Consultant Dermatologist, BMC Dermatology 2001, 1:6 doi:10.1186/1471-5945-1-6,
[5] Frozen Tombs, The Culture and Art of the Ancient Tribes of Siberia, British Museum Publications Ltd., ISBN 0 7141 0097 8

CHAPTER 13

Bartlett, Neville, Carpeting the Millions: the growth of Britain's Carpet Industry, Donald, 1978, the University of Virginia, ISBN 0859760251, p16
[2] Acc 1715 Elmwood Mills, Leeds Library
[3] Bartlett, Neville, Carpeting the Millions: the growth of Britain's Carpet Industry, Donald, 1978, the University of Virginia, ISBN 0859760251, p16
[4] Measom, George The Official Illustrated Guide to the Great Northern Manchester Sheffield and Lincolnshire and Midlands railways, Griffin Bohn 1861
[5] Entry in Paris Universal Exhibition of 1867: Catalogue of the British Section
[6] Newbiggin, Thomas History of the Forest of Rossendale, 2nd edition printed 1893, by J.J.Riley at Rossendale Free Press Offices
[7] Great Exhibition, 1851, Catalogue, I, advertisements p 583; II, p 572
[8] Worral's Cotton Spinners and Manufacturer's Directory published in 1891,Newchurch
[9] Bolton Evening News, Article headed 125 Years Ago,3rd Nov 1999
[10] Lewis, Professor Miles, Melbourne University, Faculty of Architecture, Building and Planning, Australian-building/pdfs/finishes/finishes-floor-coverings.pdf
[11] Dolge, Alfred, Pianos and Their Makers: A Comprehensive History of the Development of the Piano, Covina Publishing Company, 1911
[12] Royal George felt specification from AMBIC Co Ltd.
[13] Naish Piano Felt Brochure 1980
[14] Ibid
[15] Sourced from Alfred Dolge's book "Pianos and their Makers", A Comprehensive History of the Development of the Piano, Covina Publishing Company, 1911.
[16] Ibid
[17] Association of Blind Piano Tuners (ABPT)
[18] Newbiggin, Thoms, History of the Forest of Rossendale, 2nd edition, J. J. Riley,Rossendale Free Press Office, 1893
[19] Cronkshaw, Phyllis, An Industrial Romance of the Rossendale Valley: The Development of the Shoe and Slipper Industries, Rossendale Library 1973
[20] The Mountaineering Handbook. Association of British Members of the Swiss Alpine Club 1950
[21] The Argus (Melbourne), Saturday 1 September 1945
[22] British Patents BP563211, and BP600831
[23] Embroidery Magazine, Winter 1982
[24] Mochrie, Elsie, Coloured Felt Work, Dryad Handicrafts, 1927 63 pages
[25] Elsie Mochrie, Ivy Penelope Roseaman, Felt Toys Illustrated, 1935
[26] The Medical times and gazette - Volume 2 - Page 548 1860

[27] Knopp, Ken R., British Saddlery and Horse Equipments Imported by the Confederacy, North South Trader's Civil War,Vol XXIV, Christmas 1997
[28] Illustration taken from Short Notes on Field Batteries by Capt. C. Orde Brown, 1871.
[29] Ibid
[30] British Patent Application 2147, 1868
[31] Board of Trade Journal volume 9 1891
[32] The Argus, Melbourne, Saturday 1 September 1945
[33] Becker, William E., Designing with Felt, Machine Design, June 26 1969, p 113, also American Felt Company Data Sheet No 11 May 1951
[34] Becker, William E., Designing with Felt, Machine Design, June 26 1969, p 113, also American Felt Company Data Sheet No 11 May 1951
[35] Picture adapted from Papermaking Ancient and Modern by Richard Herring, Longman Green.
[36] Felt –Wool, The Felt Association Inc., undated
[37] Greene, William, The Gun; or, A Treatise on the various descriptions of Small Fire-arms, Longmann, Orme, Brown, Green, and Longman 1835. p173)
[38] F&T Industries Limited, technical brochure, With a little help from a Felt
[39] American felt Company Leaflet, Wool Felt –Liquid Filtration

CHAPTER 14

[1] Philosophical magazine: A Journal of Theoretical, Experimental and Applied Science, 1828, page 316
[2] The Register of Arts, and Journal of Patent Inventions, edited by Luke Herbert, 1827, page 240
[3] Mechanics Magazine - Page 448, Industrial Arts, July 16 1825
[4] The New Monthly Magazine, edited by Thomas Campbell et al, 1833, page 243
[5] Annual Register, 1830, page 549
[6] Acc1715 Elmwood Mill Papers, Leeds Library
[7] Genealogy by Christopher Rostron Pickup
[8] T G Ames private letter 16 April 1980
[9] Ibid
[10] Rossendale Free Press, November 3rd 1877
[11] Recollections of the Felt Industry, Number 32, Mrs. Lord
[12] The London Gazette 12 June 1888
[13] Recollection Number 30 Barker
[14] Liverpool "Olympic Festivals" of the 1860's by Bob Phillips for Northern Athletics association
[15] Phillips, Bob, Records of Liverpool "Olympic Festivals" of the 1860s, article in Northern Athletics
[16] Gaskell, Ernest, Lancashire Leaders Social and Political, 1907
[17] Recollections of the Felt Industry, Number 19 W Law
[18] Recollection of the Felt Industry, Number 7, H. R. T. Ashworth
[19] Rossendale Free Press 7th July 1928
[20] Memories of the Ashworth Family, Rossendale Free Press, 3rd July 1976
[21] Ashworth, Richard, The Rossendale Dialect and its Derivations, Reprint from The Bacup Times, Isaac Leach, undated
[22] The Death of Richard Ashworth, Rossendale Free Press, July 1928
[23] Recollections of the Felt Industry, Number 9, W Law
[24] Rossendale Free Press, Dec 17 1881
[25] Recollections of George Stansfield, publicity brochure for the re-opening of Baltic Mill
[26] Obituary, Rossendale Free Press, 14th June 1980
[27] Recollections of the Felt Industry, Number 9, W Law
[28] Organisation Chart of Bury and Masco Industries limited for 1969
[29] Bury TimesMarch 26th 1982
[30] Recollecions of the Felt Industry, Number 16, Livesey
[31] Recollections of the Felt Industry, Number 25, Mr. S
[32] Recollections of the Felt Industry, Number 20, Kath Entwistle
[33] Recollecions of the Felt Industry, Number 16, Livesey
[34] Recollections of the Felt Industry, Number 25, Mr. S
[35] Manufacture of Compressed Woollen Felt and Hair Felt in Germany, BIOS Final Report No. 1450, Item No. 22, 1946
[36] Bury Felt Manufacturing Company Minutes 1939 to 1959
[37] Recollections of the Felt Industry, Number 25, Mr. S
[38] Bury Times March 26th 1982

[39] Bury Felt manufacturing Company Minutes of Board Meetings 1959 to 1966
[40] Gilbert, Nigel, Building RecordingBlakebrook House, Mason Road, Kidderminster Historic Kidderminster Project Ref: 282,5th August 2007
[41] Open internet letter from David Chaudry to Ashley James quoting recollections of his Grandmother
[42] Daily Telegraph 26 August 2000
[43] Unnamed genealogy of the Whitehead family from the R R Whitehead Brothers Limited archives
[44] Business Archives Council, Survey of the Records of R R Whitehead and Brothers Limited, 1983
[45] Minutes of R R Whitehead and Brothers Limited Board Meeting Minutes
[46] History of the Royal George, recorded by the Royal George public house
[47] Recollections of the Felt Industry, Number 18, Haig
[48] McKinstry, Rich, Devoted to the Betterment of Man: Byrdcliffe: An American Arts & Crafts Colony, Winterthur Museum archives; also Parry, Anne, From the Saddleworth-America Connection, Saddleworth Festival of Arts 1979, British Vita: also Green, Nancy E., Edwards, Robert, Wolf, Tom, Paul, Ellen, Byrdcliffe: An American Arts and Crafts Colony, Denker
[49] Business Archives Council, Survey of the Records of R R Whitehead and Brothers Limited, 1983
[50] A lecture delivered to the Saddleworth Historical Society, Tuesday 6th April 1976)
[51] Parry, Anne, From the Saddleworth-America Connection, Saddleworth Festival of Arts 1979, British Vita
[52] Recollections of the Felt Industry, Number 18, Haig
[53] Naish, J. R., E. V. Naish The First 200 Years 1800-2000, Wilton Graphics, Salisbury
[54] Recollections of the Felt Industry, Number 19, W. Law
[55] Recollections of the Felt Industry, Number 29,Mr M
[56] Recollections of the Felt Industry, Number 24, Sagar
[57] Recollections of the Felt Industry, Number 4, Roy Giddins
[58] Recollections of the Felt Industry, Number 21, Mrs Hamer
[59] Recollections of the Felt Industry, Number 16, Livesey
[60] Recollections of the Felt Industry, Number 21, K Entwistle
[61] Recollections of the Felt Industry, Number 22, Haig
[62] Recollections of the Felt Industry, Number 4, Roy Giddins
[63] Rossendale Free Press, September 24 1881 page 8 column 3

INDEX

A.V. Humphries, 50, 54
Aachen Felting Test, 20
Abbot hardener, 62, 66
Abbott, William, 29, 63, 67
Acid milling, 208
Acid trough, carbonising, 217
Acids, effect on felt, 16
After-milling, 197
Agar Limited, 52, 53
Agar, William Henry, 53
Air laying, 66, 75
Air permeability, 265
Aire, river, 125
Airedale Mill, 35, 38, 39, 124, 191
Albert Works, 45, 55, 90, 126, 134, 224, 245, 260, 347
Alkalis, effect on felt, 16
American Society for Testing and Materials, 261, 264
American stock mill, 194
Anderson, roofing felt, 31
Anglo Felt Company, 31
Anthrax, 23
Anti-vibration, 221, 268, 298
Apperley web layer, 149, 151
Ardil, 25
Ashworth, Deborah, 49, 325
Ashworth, Henry, Richard, Trickett, 327
Ashworth, James, 327
Ashworth, Oliver, 327
Ashworth, Richard, 49, 51, 53, 54, 95, 97, 98, 102, 105, 120, 126, 322, 325, 326, 328, 347
Asphalt felt, 29, 36, 52, 65, 67

Badge, 288
Bales, 137
Baltic Mill, 23, 44, 50, 54, 56, 93, 125, 127, 134, 208, 229, 236, 330, 335, 349
Banana Roller, 182
Barcroft, James, 44, 105, 135, 350
Barcroft, John Thomas, 44, 98

Barley lodge, 127
Batt frame, 153-156, 184
Batt frame, cylinder, 156
Batt frame, horizontal, 68
Batt frame, vertical, 68, 69, 155
Bayerische Wollfilzfabriken, 61, 346
Beam dyeing, 214
Bearing felt, 303
Beetson, Geoffrey, Harley, 330, 333
Befama, 151
Bensly, Eric Frank, 58
Bensly, Francis George, 57
Bermona, 290
Betty, 45, 108, 199, 216, 221
Birtill and Blaikie, 52, 53
Birtill, F.M., 76
Black streak wiper, 305
Blaikie, William Veitch, 53
Blamire web layer, 149
Bleaching, 220
Blend bin, 143
Blending, 18, 24, 137, 143
Blends, 21, 22, 23, 24, 43, 137
Blends, synthetic, 24
Block construction, 246
Block Printing, 245
Block printing facts, 259
Blowing, 236
Bob, 167, 197, 240, 296, 311
Bob, dentistry, 296
Boreholes, 127
Borradaile, 299
Borradaile, George, 29, 65, 273
Boulinikon, 277
Boulinikon Felt Company, 52, 53. 64, 277
Box miller, 200
Bratt cloth, 68, 179, 185
Breaker, 138, 144, 218
Breast, carding, 146, 147
Breast, fulling, 190
Bridge End Mill, 4, 49, 50, 54, 94, 125, 132

Bright Street Mill, 56, 112, 125
British Defence Standard, 261
British Standard, 261
Broadhead, James, 46, 76
Brynmawr Works, 58, 119
Buckley, Colonel, 332
Buckley, Graham, 333
Bump, 194
Bumper stock mill, 194
Burr, 23, 128, 139, 146, 152, 216, 218
Bury and Masco, 25, 42, 56, 60, 94, 103, 111, 118, 119, 124, 127, 129, 159, 186, 215, 244, 279, 289, 301, 322, 325, 328, 334, 338, 344
Bury Cooper Whitehead Limited, 22, 58, 60, 94, 115, 119, 280, 282, 289, 294, 304, 335, 346
Bury Felt Industry, 56
Bury Felt Manufacturing Company Limited, 22, 101, 103, 109, 127, 140, 150, 193, 217, 285, 287, 290, 332, 349, 350
Bury Felt Mills, 109
Butterworth, George, 38
Byrdcliffe, 342
Bywater hardener, 166
Bywater-Beanland hardener, 42, 73, 167
Bywater, William, 30, 40, 41, 51, 74, 75, 166, 168, 176, 185, 186, 187, 188
Bywater, William Gaines, 41

C. Davidson and Sons, 53, 64
Cambria bowling green, 279
Camelback feed, 150
Carbon, residue, 23, 216, 218
Carboniser, 217
Carboniser measurements, 219
Carboniser, general, 219
Carbonising, 23, 215, 216
Carding, 22, 33, 44, 68, 120, 138-158, 184
Carding action, 34, 144
Carding engine, 23, 34, 68, 120, 144-152
Carding set, 144
Carding wire, 152
Carpet, 33, 36, 38, 43, 44, 48, 56, 105, 118, 246, 259, 275-277, 336

Carpet and furnishing, 275
Carpet felt, 39, 182, 212, 217, 279
Carpet printing, 256
Carpet Trades International, 58, 118, 336
Carpet underlay, 273
Carr and Butterworth, 38, 85, 89
Carr Mill, 50, 54, 102
Carrier Cloth, 67, 69, 169, 170, 171, 173, 179, 182, 183, 185,
Casse Roller miller, 42, 185, 201
Celeste felt, 281, 282
Channelling felt, 61, 299
Check system, 348
Chesham Hat Works, 56, 290
Chesham Felt Works, 112, 113, 135
Chesham Fields Mill, 111, 112
Chesham Hat Company, 290
Chimneys, 136
Chiropody felt, 295
Chisel, block printing, 248
Christ Church, Friezland, 343
Church seating, 254, 260, 278
Clarence Lido, 129
Clarendon reservoir, 130
Clegg, L. H., 56, 332
Clicker press, 241
Clip felt, 60, 283
Clothing, 287
Cockcroft and Marsden, 40
Cockcroft, J.M., 57
Cockcroft, Thomas, 40
Collar felt, 25, 289
Collecting Fibres, 153
Compressibility, 266, 268
Conditioning, 235
Conditioning room, 236
Configuring cards, 148
Configuring the scribbler, 146
Contamination, 23, 137
Conveyor, fibre, 149, 151, 153, 158
Cooper and Co., 120, 311
Cooper and Co (Birmingham) Limited, 58, 119,
Cooper, Josiah, 57

Copper bottoming ships, 29, 65
Couch felt, 309
Couch roller, 308
Couch roller sleeve, 308, 310
Coupe, Henry, 50
Cow dung, 25, 253, 350
Cowboy hats, 291
Craft and toys, 292
Crainer, George, 334
Crimp, 15-17, 21
Crimp amplitude, 17
Crimp form, 17,
Crimp frequency, 17
Croggon, roofing felt, 30
Cropper, 234
Cropping, 233
Cross laid webs, 75
Cross laying, 148, 150, 152, 157, 158, 184
Crow Lane Mill, 62, 115, 133
Crown Mill, 62, 117, 133, 344
Cushion felt, 284
Cutting, 61, 241
Cylinder batt frame, 156
Cylinder, carding, 143, 145

Damper felt, 283
DAN, 219
Decatising, 235, 236, 238
Density, 18, 21, 263, 267, 303
Density designations, 263
Dentistry, 296
Deodoriser, 296, 304
Deodoriser felt, 296
Devil, 140
Devilling, 140
Dewer, 236
Dewing, 236
Dicky Debs, 325
Directional Frictional Effect, 14, 16, 19, 21
Dispatch, 242, 243
Displacement, 160, 175, 283
Display felt, 279
Doffer, 146, 148, 149, 153

Dolge, Alfred, 59
Dolly, 216
Double daylight press, 74, 240
Drugget, 276
Dry felt seal, 306
Drying, 215, 218, 221-232
Dye vat, 211
Dye vessel, 211, 220
Dyed felt, 23, 24, 214, 271
Dyeing, 24, 210-215
Dyeing and finishing, 211
Dyeing techniques, 211
Dyer, John, 190, 198
Dyes, 25, 96, 211, 212, 213,

E. V. Naish, 52, 59, 61, 115, 116, 128, 133, 176, 285, 344-346
Early Personalities, 317
Early Years and Leeds Feltmakers, 29
East India Wool, 22, 132
Eccentric, 70, 162, 163, 167, 168, 174, 178, 192
Edmunds of Berryfield, 62
Edward Rostron, 43, 102, 108, 133, 317-319
Effect of Acids and Alkalis, 161
Effect of soap and detergent, 162
Effluent, 61, 125, 126, 129, 134, 218, 220
Effluent treatment, 129
Electricity, 50, 94, 95, 116, 133, 136, 321, 330,
Elmwood Mill, 32, 36, 85, 123-125, 191, 321, 349
Eulan, 219

Fabrication, 61, 103, 241
Fabrication and dispatch, 241
Fancy, 146, 149
Fearnought, 140-143
Featherweight Clothing and Pad Company, 52, 76, 288, 290
Felt Association, 13
Felt blankets, 26, 118, 277, 336
Felt Mills, 85
Felt Mills of Rossendale, 90
Felt Mills, other, 114

Felt Patent, 68
Felt Patents 1803 -1908, 78
Felt Product Profile, 274
Felt production statistics, 274
Felt tip pen, 304
Felt types, 11, 25
Feltability, 16, 18, 20
Feltmakers Association, 294
Feltmakers, lesser known, 62
Ferguson, Alexander, F. D., 334, 335
Fettling, 152
Fibre Art Exhibition, 289, 290, 295
Fibre Fineness, effect on felt, 19
Fibre Length, effect on felt, 17
Fillighan, Samuel, 40
Filter felt, 312
Filtration, 312
Final carding, 148
Fineness count, 19
Finishing block prints, 259
Fixing block printing, 259
Flameproofing, 271
Flat hardener, 165-177
Flat hardener configurations, 169
Flat hardener specification, 187
Flat Hardeners for Batch Production, 162
Flat Hardeners in Practice, 162
Flexure, milling, 208, 271
Fly press, 241
Fly-comb, 148, 152
Footwear, 285
Fountain Mill, 47, 96, 134
Friezland, 343
Fulling, 189, 190
Fulling polishing wheels, 197
Fulling rate, 192, 194
Fuzzy-felt, 293

Garnett wire, 147
Garnham, Douglas, 328
Garside hardener, 73, 162, 163
Garside, Thomas, 162
Gatterwalke, 71, 204

Glossary of Felt Terms, 353
Grate planker, 204
Great flood, Rossendale, 43, 50, 102, 105
Green Brook, 110, 130
Greg, William, 56, 109
Grey felt, 23
Grey wool, 28
Grinding, card, 152
Grueber, roofing felt, 31
Guides, batt frame, 69
Guillotine, 241
Gun wads, 37, 241, 310
Gypsy Brook, 131

Hair felt, 26, 30, 31, 47, 63, 272
Hammer, fulling, 189-194, 197
Hammer, piano, 60, 61, 176, 177, 281, 282, 284
Hand hats, 311
Handy, 227, 228
Hardening pressure, 160
Hardener speed, 181, 182
Hardener, flat, 73, 162, 165-177
Hardener, roller, 69, 178-186
Hardener, table, 73, 75, 164, 166-168
Hardening, 69, 70, 71, 74, 159
Hardening frequency, 161
Hardening piano felts, 177
Hardening temperature, 161
Hardening, wet, 159
Hardness, water, 128
Hardness, felt, 267, 282
Hardsough Manufacturing Company, 97
Hardsough Mill, 50, 52, 96, 132, 125, 132
Harrop and Mason, 39
Hat felt, 65, 174, 234, 248, 290, 291
HEH, 186
Higher Hollin Bank Mill, 45, 97
Higher Lumb Mill, 47, 97, 108, 127, 209, 308, 321
Highfield Mill, 39, 88, 125, 132
Highfield Mill documents, 122
Hill, John, 56, 332, 333
Hirst, William, 32, 39, 73, 74
Hodgetts Felt Company, 48, 62

Hodgetts, Charles, 62
Hollin Bank Mill, 50, 97, 98, 135, 329
Hollin Mill45, 97
Hollin Print Works, 97
Hopper, 138, 143, 148, 149, 155
Horseshoe restrainers, 154
Hudcar lodge, 130
Hudcar Mill, 56, 109-112, 124, 128, 129, 136, 215
Hudson, James, 40
Hydro-extractor, 222, 223

Ingham Taylor, 97
Inspection, 233
International Feltmakers Association, 294
Iron Felt, 64
Irwell river, 55, 90, 127, 134
Isle of Man Mill, 55, 90, 98, 133

Jackson and Whittaker, 44, 108
James Humphries and Sons Limited, 338
James, Peter S., 325
Jigger, 179
Jigging, 59, 69, 70, 71, 74, 201, 202, 206
John Mitchell and Sons, 45
John Wilkinson, 32, 33, 35, 36, 85, 87, 120, 132, 275, 288, 297, 310
John Wilkinson Son and Co., 32, 36
Jones, Richard, 61, 117
Juxtafelt, 304

Karakul, wool, 23, 140
Kay, George, 345
Kemps, 16
Kilburn, William, 191
Kletterschuh, 286
Knock, milling, 191-194
Krafft Goebbel, 71, 185, 204, 205
Krantz tenter, 231
Krupp cross-laying card, 158, 279

Lancashire Felt Company, 64
Land Drainage Act, 123
Lant, 196, 216

Lant cart, 196
Lap, 153, 171, 174, 182, 185
Lap weight, 160
Lashing, 184
Lattice conveyor, 205
Lattice feed, 148, 150
Law Schofield, Captain G.W., 44, 49, 50, 54, 91
Lawrence, T. E., 341
Lawson, Thomas, 41, 74, 321
Layered felt, 25, 156
Leachman press, 74, 241
Leaks Water, 130
Leeds hardener, 165
Leeds Felt Industry, 31
Leeds Felt Mills, 85
Licker-in, 146, 148
Limy Water, 90
Line shafting, 35, 116, 134
Lodge, 124, 130
London Patent Felt Company, 63
Longholme Mill, 49, 54, 56, 99, 100, 101, 125, 128, 133
Longmeadow Felt Company Limited, 26, 118, 216, 336
Lord Salisbury, 51, 103
Lower Lumb Mill, 47, 107
Lumb Holes Mill, 44, 50, 54, 101, 102, 125, 135,
Lumb Mill, 43, 51, 107, 133

Machine Manufacturers, Leeds, 41
Mangle, 210, 215, 221, 222
Mangling, carbonising, 218, 221
Marker pen, 304
MASCO, 49, 50, 56, 94, 96, 97, 102, 103, 106, 212, 221, 224, 241, 244, 259, 288, 290, 328, 330,
MASCO Stockholdings, 54
MASCO combine formation, 52
MASCO output, 121
MASCO phoenix, 259
Mascolite, 221, 300, 301
Masonic carpet, 245, 246, 249, 253, 256, 257, 258, 279
Mather Road reservoir, 129

Matheson and Tavernier, 40
Mattress pads, 277
Mawl, 247, 252
McCall, Jane Byrd, 342
McKibbin, roofing felt, 30
McNeill, Forbes, 29, 63, 67
McTear and Co., 63
Measuring Felt, 261
Mechanised printing, 260
Medical felt, 37, 62, 295
Merino, Australian, 22
Merino, South African Cape, 22
Mersey and Weaver River Authority, 123, 124,
Microwave oven, 232
Midland Mill, 39, 89
Mill Capacities, 120
Millinery, 290
Milling, 189-210
Milling dynamics, 189
Milling machines, 198-210
Milling solution, 196, 207
Mitcham, 59
Mitchell brothers, 38, 41, 43-49, 52, 55, 73, 75, 94, 96, 98, 106, 120, 134, 186, 260, 322-324
Mitchell Brothers of Waterfoot Limited, 48, 55
Mitchell, Colonel Thomas, 324
Mitchell, George, 323
Mitchell, John, 45, 92, 106, 322
Mitchell, Robert John Chadwick, 45, 77, 92, 322
Mitchell, Robert, John, Howard, 325
Mitchell, T. Derek, 325
Mitchell, Thomas, 45, 327
Mitchell, William, 45, 49, 92, 322
Mitchells, Ashworth, Stansfield and Co. Limited, 86, 108, 208, 276, 300, 326, 334
Mitin FF, 219, 220
Moderator felt, 281, 282
Monge, 14
Mothproofing, 220, 261
Multi-daylight press, 240
Multi-felt manufacture, 174
Multi-roller milling machines, 201
Murmuride, 298

Myrtle Grove Mill, 43, 51, 102-104, 124, 135, 319, 321, 322

Naish, Betty, 345
Naish, Dr William (Willie), 345
Naish, Elizabeth, Vawdry, 61, 344
Naish, John R., 345
Naish, Rowena, Vaudry, 344
Naish, William, 61, 116, 346
Naish, William, John, 345
Needle felt, 11, 24, 104, 299
Needle loom, 26, 46, 51, 76, 104
Needle punching, 41, 46, 76, 104, 158, 186, 293
Needles, 76
Newton, Richard, 334
Noils, 18, 23, 28
Notley, Laurence, 58, 335, 343, 345
Novelty hat felt, 291
Numnah, 37, 297
Nuzzery, 236

Old fulling mill, 92
Old Mill, 46
Ollerant, H. A., 57
Operation of a Fulling Stock, 195
Ormerod, John, 106
Ormerod, Lawrence, 44, 93
Oven, carboniser, 218
Oven, tenter, 230-232

Padding, 278, 288, 295
Paste dye preparation, 255
Paste, block printing, 255
Patent Challenge, 73
Patent Effects, 73
Patent Felting Company, 86
Patents and Innovation, 65
Pattern register, 249, 258
PCPL, 220
Pea jacket, felt, 288
Pendulum stock, 192-194, 197
Pentachlorophenol, 220
People, 317

Peralta roller, 147, 217, 218
Percentage specific gravity, 263, 264
pH, 161, 210, 220
Piano, 282
Piano felt, 35, 52, 59-62, 115, 116, 117, 176, 209, 232, 236, 281, 285, 344
Piano hammer felt, 60, 61, 176, 177, 281, 282,
Pigs Lea Brook, 129
Pilgrim step miller, 205-207
Pitch pins, 249
Plaiting, 184, 189, 202, 218, 219
Plunge Mill, 184, 189, 202, 218, 219
Pocock, roofing felt, 30
Polishing and buffing, 311, 312
Polishing bob, 311
Polishing disk, 311
Polishing felt, 56
Polishing wheel, 156, 162, 169, 197, 198, 235, 311
Porritt and Spencer, 60
Porritt, Cyril, Phillip, 60
Poss, tenter, 225-228
Power, 131
Preparing the Fibre, 137
Pressing, 238-240
Pressed Felt Manufacturers Association, 12, 31, 331, 333, 337
Pressure, hardening, 160
Pressure, milling, 202
Printer's Accessories, 251
Printing preparation, 254
Printing shed, 246,
Printing table, 250, 251
Products, 273
Properties of Felt, 261
Properties, Felt, other, 270-272
Protein Fibres, 25
Punching, fabrication, 242

R. R. Whitehead and Brothers, 52, 58-61, 114, 120, 223, 285, 300, 335, 341, 345
Rack, hardener, 168
Radcliffe, Geoffrey, 329

Radcliffe, Richard Ashworth, 329
Ratchet effect, 14
Rawlinson, Ernald, 103, 321, 328
Rawlinson, Herman, 103, 321
Rawlinson, Irwin, 103
Rawlinson, Neville, 103, 321. 322
Rawlinson, Roland, 43, 51, 103, 108, 120, 129, 322
Rawlinson, Useta, 103, 321
Rayon, 25, 158
Regalgrene, 280
Regalpak, 60, 221, 300
Register, printing, 249, 258
Reinits hardener, 164
Reservoir, 45, 54, 85, 110, 123-131
Resonance, 269
Restrainer, 154
Rider and Mallet, 40
Rigby, Agar and Company, 53
Robinson, Clifford, Hunter, 345
Robinson, D. S., 333
Rodgers, Alfred, 59
Roller conditioner, 203
Roller hardener, 69, 178-186
Roller Hardener Machine Manufacture, 185
Roller Hardener Operation, 182
Roller hardener specification, 188
Roller hardeners for sleeves, 184
Roller Hardening, 178
Roller milling, 71
Roller milling superfine felt, 203, 204
Roller set, 185
Roller sleeves, 308, 309
Rollering machine, 197
Roofing felt, 30
Root, wool fibre, 13
Roslington, William, 40
Rossendale, 35, 43, 46, 48, 90, 275, 285, 348
Rossendale Printing and Dyeing Company, 45, 90
Rossendale Feltmakers, 43
Rostron, Edward, 43, 102, 108, 133, 317-319
Rostron, James, 317
Rostron, Jordon, 317

Rostrons, 317
Rot proofing, 220
Rotary milling machine, 194, 200
Rotary press, 238, 239
Rotary Printing, 246, 260
Rothwell, Henry, 44, 46, 93, 94, 102
Rothwell, John William, 44
Rothwell, William, 102
Royal George felt, 60, 285
Royal George Mill, 58-60, 114, 115, 133, 136, 340, 343, 348
Royal Victoria Carpet, 33, 275
Rug, 273, 276

S. S. Stott and Co., 44, 98, 103, 135
Saddle felt, 35, 75, 297
Saddlery, 297
Saddleworth Church, 340, 343
Sanding, 235
Scapa Group, 60, 104, 335
Schuko, 168
Scotch feed, 149
Scouring, 216
Scray, 195, 203, 212, 214, 221
Scribbler, 144, 146, 147
Seals, 304, 307
Seam, tenter, 224-226
Seed, 23, 138, 140, 147, 218
Serapes, 51, 322
Shackle hardener, 70
Shake, 200
Shawclough Mill, 44, 49, 105, 106
Shear, milling, 202
Sheet felt, 205, 207, 234, 236, 243, 281, 282
Short mat bowling, 279, 280
Shrinkage, 14, 159, 194, 196, 199, 205
Siss Clough Mill, 35, 43, 48, 105-106, 135, 224
Skirts, felt. 44, 287
Sleeve, 200, 209, 184
Sleeve, milling, 200
Sleeve production, 173, 184
Sleeves, rollers, 308
Slipper felt, 21, 23, 25, 105, 234, 284-286

Slipper industry, 44, 46, 152, 212
Slipper manufacture, 98
Slippers, 21, 23, 26, 96, 212, 234, 254-256
Smith, Herbert, 118, 336-339
Smith, Piggy, 336
Society of Automobile Engineers, 261, 263, 307
Soundproofing, 298
Specific gravity, 210, 263, 270
Spin drying, 215, 222, 223
Split felt, piano, 283
Splitting strength, 266-267
Springfield Mill, 56, 111-112, 119, 124
Springfield Mill lodge, 124, 130
Sprinkler system, 124
St. Chads Church, 342
St. Clement, 11, 295, 332
St. Helens Mill, 35, 86, 125, 132
St. Nicholas Church, 318, 319, 329
Stair pads, 226, 278
Stanchions, 157, 172
Stang, 208
Stang, tenter, 225
Stanging, 198
Stansfields, 50
Stansfied, John, 97
Stansfield, George, 329
Stansfield, George, Alfred, 330
Stansfield, John, 50, 52
Stansfield, Joseph, 45, 50, 98
Stansfield. William, 49, 50, 52, 54, 97, 102, 329
Staple length, 17, 18, 49, 50, 52
Steam engine, 34, 35, 51, 95, 98, 102, 107, 108, 123, 125, 131, 132, 135
Steamer, print, 123, 134, 259
Stepped hammer, 192, 193
Stewart, Roy, John, 33, 72, 317
Stiffening, 216, 221, 291
Stock Mill, 194, 195, 196, 210
Stock Milling, 190
Strap felt, 298, 310
Street, William Openshaw, 56, 331-334
Stripper, carding, 142-145, 147, 149
Stepped hammer, 192, 193

Superfine felt, 24, 25, 60, 61, 113, 140, 147, 158, 174, 203, 214, 216, 232, 238, 261, 289, 292-294,
Swift, carding engine, 145-147, 149, 152
Synthetic felt, 47, 75, 158, 273, 279, 288, 289, 295, 299, 304
Synthetic fibres, 11, 22, 24-25, 76, 137, 158

T. H. Firth, 47, 76
Table hardener, 73, 164, 166-168
Tanner, James William, 59, 341
Tanner, John F., 59, 341
Tanner, Thomas Hoare, 59, 341
Taper hammer felt, 281, 282
Tapestry carpet, 46, 48, 92, 275
Tappet, 67, 71, 190
Tatham, William, 152
Tattersall, John, 64, 97, 108, 325
Tavernier, 39, 75
Taylor Wordsworth, 35, 40-41, 64, 89, 97, 185
Taylor, James, 64, 98
Taylor, Ingham, 97
Tear boy, 253, 254, 255, 257, 350
Tear Strength, 175, 176
Tear trolley, 251, 256, 350
Teazer, 97, 138-140
Teazing, 138-140
Technical felt, 24, 25, 26, 61, 73, 156, 194, 196, 221, 224, 231, 233, 235, 238, 263
Tensile Strength, 266
Tenter, 85, 91, 224-229
Tenter chain, 214, 229-231
Tenter frame, 224
Tenterhook, 226-229, 231, 232, 233, 258, 259
Tenterhook Willey, 140, 141
Tentering, 224-229
Tentering machine, 229-232
Tests, Feltability, 20
The Patent Woollen Cloth Company, 32, 33-38, 43, 52, 53, 55, 73-75, 85, 86, 119, 120, 191, 213, 275, 279, 285, 288, 317
Theory of Felting, 13, 14, 16
Thermal Conductivity, 264, 265
Thickness, 261-263

Thickness gauge, 263
Thomas and Mark Hutchinson, 62
Tip, wool fibre, 13
Todd Carr Mill, 35, 42, 48, 105, 135, 245, 350
Transport, 244
Trickett, Sir Henry, Whittaker, 327
Tunstead Mill, 43
Turner, Colonel William, Wyatt, 59, 341, 342
Turner, Cornelius, 35, 38, 40, 75, 119, 132
Turner, N. W., 59
Twaddell, 210, 219
Typewriter felt, 299

Underlay felt, 273, 275
Underskirts, felt, 287
Unions, 347, 351
Urine, 196, 210, 216, 350
Uses for felt, listing, 315-316

Valenki boot, 163, 286
Vertical batt frame, 68, 69. 155
Vibration amplitude, 160, 161, 168, 183
Vibration displacement, 160
Vibration frequency, 183, 269
Vibration reflection, 268
Vibration transmission, 268
Vibration, hardening, 160, 177, 178, 183
Viscose Rayon, 24, 158, 279, 293
Voids, 264, 266, 304

Wadsworth, John, 45, 104
Wahl, Nik, 168, 194, 197
Waite, Benjamin, 40
Wallgate Limited , 61, 114
Wandle Felt Company, 59, 62, 115, 117, 285, 295
Washing, 215
Washing, Scouring, Proofing, 215
Water and Power, 123
Water Capacity, 123, 131
Water flow, 127, 130
Water Management, 129
Water Quality, 128
Water Sources, 125

Water swell, 272
Water tower, 108, 124, 127
Water usage, 124, 125, 131
Water-powered mills, 132
Water, effect on felt, 15
Water, hard, 128
Water, soft, 128
Waterbarn Mill, 45, 106, 132
Waterwheel, 98. 107, 108, 115, 123, 132, 133, 191
Web, 147, 153
Webron Limited, 47, 104
Wedge felt, piano, 283
Welker, roller miller, 203
Wells, Henry Augustus, 32, 36, 74
Wet felt seal, 307
Whams farm, 47, 55
Whipple, Hyman, Welcome, 46, 76
Whitehead, Francis Frederick, 58, 340
Whitehead, James Heywood, 58, 340
Whitehead, John Dicken, 58, 340
Whitehead, Ralph Radcliffe, 58, 340
Whitehead, Ralph, Radcliffe Jr, 343
Whitehead, William, 340
Whiteheads, 340
Whiteley tenter, 231
Whiteley, William, 35, 231
Whitewell river, 45, 51, 55, 90, 98, 107, 126, 127, 134
Whitewell Vale Mill, 47, 107, 108, 127, 245, 308,
Whitham, J., 132
Wick, 301-304
Wick, bottom feed, 302
Wick, syphon feed, 302
Wick, top feed, 302
Wicking and Lubrication, 301
Wilkinson patent wad, 275
Wilkinson, John, 32-38, 58, 62, 68, 75, 85, 120, 245, 275, 285, 288, 297, 310
Wilkinson, John Company, 36-38
Willey, 138-140
William Bywater, 30, 40, 41, 166-168, 176, 185,

Williams, Thomas Robinson, 29, 32, 33, 36, 63, 69, 71-73
Willowing, 138
Winch, dyeing, 195, 211-212
Windsor Loom, 41
Wiper felt, 304, 305
Wipers and Seals, 304
Wipolan, 25
Witley Court, 338
Wood, William, 29
Wool characteristics, 20
Wool, English 23
Wool quality, 19
Wool Selection, 21
Wool store, 49, 90, 98, 137
Wool type, 137
Wool, New Zealand, 23
Wools of the Felt Industry, 27
Wordsworth, Joshua, 41
Worker, carding, 139, 142, 145, 147, 149
Working Conditions, 346
Worshipful Company of Feltmakers, 12
Worsted count, 19
Wright, Joseph, 73
Wuzzer, 91, 215, 222

Zahl, felting machine maker, 168
Zirpro, flameproofing. 271

PERSONAL PROFILE

With over twenty-five years of working in the textile industry, Peter has had personal experience of nearly all the textile processes from synthetic yarn production to woven and non-woven fabrics. Of all these industries, it was felt making that made the most impression on him. It was also a turning point in his career when he changed from being a textile technologist to becoming a marketing man. He was ideally suited to this new discipline and he eventually became a Marketing Director. In his later working life, he became a business consultant, sharing his accumulated knowledge to help other companies to expand. Peter is now retired and lives with his wife Liz in Cambridgeshire.

Printed in Great Britain
by Amazon.co.uk, Ltd.,
Marston Gate.